Toward A New Legal Common Sense

Law, Globalization, And Emancipation

Law in Context

Below is a listing of the more recent publications in the Law in Context Series

Editors: William Twining (University College, London) and Christopher McCrudden (Lincoln College, Oxford)

Toward A New Legal Common Sense

Law, Globalization, And Emancipation

Second edition

Boaventura de Sousa Santos

Members of the LexisNexis Group worldwide

United Kingdom	LexisNexis Butterworths Tolley, a Division of Reed Elsevier (UK) Ltd, Halsbury House, 35 Chancery Lane, LONDON, WC2A 1EL, and 4 Hill Street, EDINBURGH EH2 3JZ
Argentina	LexisNexis Argentina, BUENOS AIRES
Australia	LexisNexis Butterworths, CHATSWOOD, New South Wales
Austria	LexisNexis Verlag ARD Orac GmbH & Co KG, VIENNA
Canada	LexisNexis Butterworths, MARKHAM, Ontario
Chile	LexisNexis Chile Ltda, SANTIAGO DE CHILE
Czech Republic	Nakladatelství Orac sro, PRAGUE
France	Editions du Juris-Classeur SA, PARIS
Hong Kong	LexisNexis Butterworths, HONG KONG
Hungary	HVG-Orac, BUDAPEST
India	LexisNexis Butterworths, NEW DELHI
Ireland	Butterworths (Ireland) Ltd, DUBLIN
Italy	Giuffrè Editore, MILAN
Malaysia	Malayan Law Journal Sdn Bhd, KUALA LUMPUR
New Zealand	LexisNexis Butterworths, WELLINGTON
Poland	Wydawnictwo Prawnicze LexisNexis, WARSAW
Singapore	LexisNexis Butterworths, SINGAPORE
South Africa	Butterworths SA, DURBAN
Switzerland	Stämpfli Verlag AG, BERNE
USA	LexisNexis, DAYTON, Ohio

© Reed Elsevier (UK) Ltd 2002

A CIP Catalogue record for this book is available from the British Library.

ISBN   0 406 94997 2

Printed and bound in Great Britain by Thomson Litho Ltd, East Kilbride, Scotland

Visit Butterworths LexisNexis *direct* at www.butterworths.com

For M.I.R.

Contents

Chapter 3

Legal Plurality and the Time-Spaces of Law: the Local, the National and the Global   85

Chapter 4

The Law of the Oppressed: the Construction and Reproduction of Legality in Pasargada   99

Chapter 5

Globalization, Nation-States and the Legal Field: From Legal Diaspora to Legal Ecumenism?   163

Chapter 8

Law: A Map of Misreading   417

Chapter 9

Can Law Be Emancipatory?   439

Preface

Perhaps no book has ever been so deeply revised for its second edition as this one. Suffice it to say that four chapters were eliminated and four others added. The changes in the title indicate the extent and orientation of the revisions.

Most readers, commentators, and critics agreed almost unanimously that the book was too long, dealt with too wide a range of topics, and was difficult to grasp as a whole. Only the most persistent and resilient of my readers succeeded in handling the book in its entirety. In this second edition I did not manage to come up with a much shorter book, but I did force myself to focus on some of the topics and to subject them to the development they require and had not received in the first edition.

My broad definition of the book's problematic in the first edition is kept intact. What is changed in the second edition is the fact that now I only pursue one of the two large topics into which the problematic unfolds. Let's first consider the problematic. The subject of this book is the paradigmatic transition, the idea that our time is a time of transition between the paradigm of modernity, which seems to have exhausted its regenerating capacities, and another, emergent time, of which so far we have only signs. The signs are unmistakable, and yet so ambiguous that we don't know if the paradigm of modernity will give rise to one or, rather, to more paradigms, or indeed if, in lieu of new paradigms, we are approaching an age whose novelty consists in not being paradigmatic at all.

The idea that we live between historical inertia, on the one hand, and the 'ascending vibrations' (*vibrations ascendants*) of the new, as Fourier called the signs of emergent realities, on the other, is therefore central to this book, both in its previous edition and the present one. From the sixteenth and seventeenth centuries onward, modernity emerged as an ambitious and revolutionary sociocultural paradigm based on a new dynamic tension between social regulation and social emancipation. By the mid-nineteenth century, this tension began to tilt gradually in favour of regulation, to the detriment of emancipation, until the latter was totally absorbed by the former. This is the situation we find ourselves in at the beginning of the twenty-first century.

The collapse of emancipation into regulation, and hence the impossibility of thinking social emancipation consistently, symbolizes the exhaustion of the paradigm of modernity. At the same time, it signals the emergence of a new paradigm or new paradigms. Times of transition are difficult to characterize and even to name. Such times are half blind and half invisible, inasmuch as they represent a transition between what is old and familiar, on the one hand, and what is new and strange, on the other. To bring them under one sole designation, such as postmodernity, for example, is thus necessarily inadequate. But precisely because the inadequacy is necessary, the designation itself has a grain of truth, and hence its use is legitimate, provided it is duly specified.

According to my definition, the paradigmatic transition has two main dimensions: an epistemological and a sociopolitical dimension. The epistemological transition occurs between the dominant paradigm of modern science and an emergent paradigm that I call the paradigm of a prudent knowledge for a decent life. The sociopolitical transition occurs between the paradigm of global capitalism – broadly conceived of as a mode of production, a system of norms and institutions, a model of consumption and lifestyles, a cultural universe, a regime of subjectivities – and the signs of a different future contained in the alternatives to this paradigm, which are emerging variously in various fields of social activity.

These two transitions abide by distinct logics and rhythms but they share the fact that they start from the same paradigm. For this reason, they share something else as well. They both question the two factors that, although having been responsible for modernity's extraordinary development, are likewise responsible for this paradigm's final crisis: modern science and modern law. This is where the second edition swerves from the first. Whereas in the first edition I dealt with science and law together, in the second edition I focus entirely and elaborate further on law. The relevance of modern law in our time and the specifity of the crisis it undergoes, convinced me of the need to devote myself exclusively to law for the time being, and leave further analysis of modern science for later studies.

Before I proceed to present this book's different chapters and their arguments, I must clarify my stance vis-à-vis the two central issues that provide the book with its global coherence: the theoretical-political issue and the theoretical-methodological issue. The theoretical-political issue concerns the construction of the theory that best accounts for our time and is capable of identifying in it both the risks and the opportunities it contains. For the past decades, this issue has been formulated in terms of the binary opposition between modernity and postmodernity or modernism and postmodernism. According to the modernist stance, our time is not a time of transition toward something that is beyond modernity (or, by antonomasia, beyond Western modernity). Our time is problematic because many of modernity's promises of social emancipation are still unfulfilled, therein residing the modern problems of our time. According to this theoretical stance, however, the paradigm of modernity has plenty of resources available to fulfill the promises of modernity and solve the modern problems. In other words, there are modern solutions for the modern problems. Modernity is but an incomplete project, as Habermas says, and it is susceptible of being radicalized in such a way as to render possible the total fulfillment of its objectives, as Roberto Unger argues.

According to the postmodernist stance, our time is probably not even one of transition, since we are already in a new condition, the postmodern condition. This condition is characterized by the deconstruction of all the modern promises and hence of all the modern problems that resulted from the idea that the promises remained unfulfilled. Together, they are accountable for our incapacity to live in good terms with the contingency, fragmentation, irony, de-essentialization, pragmatism, and even irrationality of our time. We can only celebrate our time, the only one we have after all, if we are not constantly measuring it by the criterion of other exhilarating, utopian, and emancipatory times that only exist in our arrogant imagination. According to this theoretical-political stance, the modern problems are as illusory as the promises whose unfulfillment gives rise to them.

My theoretical stance, which I develop in this book as far as law is concerned, does not recognize itself in either of the theoretical fields described above. I am not a modernist; nor am I a postmodernist in the sense stated above (I call it celebratory postmodernism), although I do argue that we are undergoing a period of postmodern transition. Between modernism and celebratory postmodernism, I propose a third stance: oppositional postmodernism. According to this stance, it is as important to acknowledge the historical and political actuality of the modern problems, as the impossibility of finding answers for them in the paradigm of modernity. According to oppositional postmodernism, there are modern problems with no modern solutions. Herein lies the transitional nature of our time. The paradigm of modernity may contribute to the solutions we look for, but it can never produce them. Indeed, its contribution consists merely in retrieving the fragments of alternative forms of modernity that were marginalized, disqualified or suppressed, as modernity's dominant version went on consolidating itself.

Throughout this book, the contribution of the paradigm of modernity toward the solutions we look for concerning law, will become clear; but so will the reasons why such solutions can only be reached outside and beyond this paradigm. As a strong critique of the dominant paradigm, this book situates itself in the critical tradition, but it swerves from it in two fundamental ways. First, modern critical theory is subparadigmatic, that is to say, it tries to develop the potential for social emancipation within the dominant paradigm itself. On the contrary, the assumption of this book's argument is that the dominant paradigm has long exhausted all its potentialities for emancipation, as is quite manifest in the voracity with which it transforms them into as many forms of social regulation. Critical thought must therefore assume a paradigmatic stance for a radical critique of the dominant paradigm from the standpoint of an imagination sound enough to bring forth a new paradigm with new emancipatory horizons. The critique's radicalism is justified only inasmuch as it allows for the formulation of radical alternatives to the mere repetition of 'realistic' possibilities. Otherwise, the critique will lose all efficacy and tend towards Phyrronism, closing all alternative gateways and choking itself to death in the confined space thus created by itself. This has been the tragic (or farcical) destiny of the critical legal studies movement in the USA. So, the paradigmatic critique must be critical of the critical tradition itself. Secondly, the paradigmatic critique distinguishes itself from the subparadigmatic critique in that, unlike the latter, it does not wish to stop at the oppositional, centrifugal, and vanguardist moment. To be sure, all critical thought defamiliarizes. But the mistake of modernist vanguardism was to indulge in the belief that defamiliarization is a goal in itself, whereas, on the contrary, defamiliarization is but the moment of suspension necessary to create a new familiarity. To live is to become familiar with life. The true vanguard is transvanguardist. The goal of postmodern critical theory is, therefore, to turn into a new common sense, in this particular case, into a new legal common sense.

The second central issue is the theoretical-methodological issue. In this domain as well, this book does not recognize itself in either of the two conventional fields: theoreticism and empiricism. In this book, I engage in deep theoretical work that, however, is not based on deductive reasoning, nor is it exclusively articulated in dialogue with the theoretical tradition. Its underlying theoretical energy is based on empirical, often minutely empirical, research. Furthermore, as I have just said, although this book takes into account a lot of empirical research, it does not conceive of empirical research as the proper site of scientific 'truth', nor does it think that empirical research alone defines the range and merit of the theory that it is possible to construct. Between theoreticism and empiricism, I argue in this book for a grounded theory, a theory that has its feet on the ground while refusing to be tied down and prevented from flying. I know that my stance runs the risk of displeasing theoretical Greeks – who will get impatient with the empirical details to which they ascribe no relevance at all – and practical Trojans – who see no reason to 'complete' the richness of the analyses with theoretical exercises considered to be hermetic and even arbitrary. Although I am fully aware of these risks, I present this kind of work in this book because it clearly reflects my life as an intellectual and as a citizen. I have conducted research projects in various countries and continents, and exchanged ideas with people of many different cultures, professions, and lifestyes, be they intellectuals, activists of social movements, or simply ordinary people. I never aimed to transform this wide experience into a 'controlled experiment' that might give me access to privileged knowledge. But my experience was always by my side when, in the solitude of my office, I developed the theories I present in this book. In a word, I hereby offer a kind of knowledge that is made of experience, though not entirely based on experience alone.

The plan of this book is not very conventional, and as such it requires an explanation. Theoretical 'moments' and empirical 'moments' alternate in this book. The first three chapters are theoretical chapters in which the need for a new sociological and political theorization of law is grounded. Chapters Four, Five, and Six are empirical chapters; they aim to unveil a vast legal landscape that does not find itself reflected in the available conventional theory, and thus underscores and justifies the theoretical lacks identified in the first three chapters. The next two chapters (Seven and Eight) present the prolegomena of a theory – an oppositional postmodern theory of law. Finally, in Chapter Nine I return to an empirical register, although distinct from the previous one. In this chapter, the theoretical and empirical analyses conducted in the previous chapters converge to define a new politics of law.

My subtitle – *Law, Globalization and Emancipation* – clearly reflects the analytical trajectory of this book. The title, in its turn – *Toward a New Legal Common Sense* – suggests the political orientation that sustains and gives coherence to the theoretical and empirical analyses. The aim is to contribute to a new legal common sense capable of devolving to law its emancipatory potential. Here is, chapter by chapter, how this analytical and political path is trodden.

In Chapter One I trace the general profile of the paradigmatic transition and try to characterize my stance in some detail. My objective is to avoid the misundertandings that resulted from readings of the first edition, particularly as regards the attention given to some key words (such as modernity and postmodernity) without a careful consideration of their context. Chapter One is new, particularly as concerns the characterization of oppositional postmodernism and how it is distinguished both from modernist stances and the stances of celebratory postmodernism.

In Chapter Two I engage in a theoretical-historical analysis of law in modernity, a modernity that in the case of law is long lasting and can actually be traced back to the twelfth century. My aim is to show how law kept alive, for a long historical period, the tension between social regulation and social emancipation, from the reception of Roman law to the theories of the social contract. I then proceed to analyze the way in which such tension kept decreasing from the nineteenth century onward with the consolidation of the liberal state. The present situation is that modern law does not respond adequately either to the demands of social regulation or the demands of social emancipation. This paradoxical situation symbolizes the theoretical and analytical lacks of our present legal time. With these lacks in mind, I propose a vast process of law unthinking. The second chapter is a revised version of the correspondent chapter in the first edition.

In Chapter Three I start from a conventional conception of anthropology and sociology of law – legal pluralism – to construct a new legal landscape capable of encompassing different scales of law, be they local, national, or global. This is a new chapter, even though it draws somewhat from scattered analyses in several chapters of the first edition.

In Chapter Four I engage in a detailed empirical analysis of a non-official legal system – Pasargada law. My objective is to reveal many legal experiences that, because they do not fit the legal modernist canon, are ignored, marginalized, silenced, in a word, wasted. This chapter is a shortened version of Chapter Three of the first edition. A detailed analysis of legal rhetoric has been eliminated and the theoretical framework reduced to what is strictly necessary for the development of the chapter's argument.

In the long Chapter Five, I broaden the legal landscape by means of a global scale – the globalization of law. As I understand it, however, the globalization of law includes the translocal networks of local laws as well as the complex interaction between the national state and its law, on the one hand, and the imperatives of globalization, on the other. In this chapter also, I swerve from conventional conceptions, in the case in point, the conventional conceptions of globalization. I submit that there is not one kind of globalization alone, but rather two, and I draw a crucial distinction between hegemonic globalization and counter-hegemonic globalization.

In Chapter Six the tension between the global and the national scale of law is further studied through an analysis of the court reforms that are occurring everywhere. I inquire into the recent protagonism of courts in handling political conflicts and restructuring economies according to the Washington Consensus (the judicialization of politics), and analyze the impact this transformation has had on the judicial system itself (the politicization of courts). The globalization of the reform of the judicial system is thus understood as a form of globalization of law, particular attention being given to the contribution that the reformed courts may bring to democracy. This is a new chapter, partly based on articles written after the book's first edition came out and published in quite a different form.

In Chapter Seven I return to theory. My aim is no longer to criticize conventional theory, a task undertaken in Chapters one and two, but to present a new theoretical proposal based on the distinction among several modes of production of law that operate in society in articulation with as many modes of production of power and knowledge. This chapter is a revised version of the correspondent chapter in the first edition.

In Chapter Eight I continue my theoretical endeavours, this time drawing on a conception of law as a map and offering an analysis of law from the point of view of cartography and its procedures (scale, projection, and symbolization). This chapter is but a slightly revised version of the correspondent chapter in the first edition.

Finally, in Chapter Nine – a new chapter – I attempt to answer the following question: Can Law Be Emancipatory? The answer takes into account the previous analyses, and aims to give political-juridical content to the oppositional postmodern conception of law. Drawing on examples of concrete political-juridical practices occuring in various parts of the world, I formulate the conditions for an emancipatory use of law. The set of these conditions and the practices into which they translate themselves, I designate as subaltern legal cosmopolitanism.

This second edition would not have been possible without the enthusiasm and obstinacy of two young men – a young man more or less my own age, and a young man more or less of my sons' age: William Twining and César A Rodríguez. William Twining is one of the most distinguished and best-known legal theorists in the Anglo-Saxon world. A widely acclaimed comparatist, unquestionably among all theoreticians of Western law, William Twining is most aware of the global vastness of the experiences of law, and hence of the limits of conventional Western legal theory to grasp such vastness. The idea of this second edition was his; he outlined its profile and encouraged Butterworths to undertake its publication. He did everything with great intellectual generosity, subtlety, and complicity, even though he is quite critical of some aspects of my work, as witness his excellent book *Globalisation and Legal Theory* (2000, Butterworths). While insisting that the book was mine and the options should be mine as well, William Twining managed to be persuasive enough to make me attempt a better book in this second edition. If the book happens to fall short of the desired outcome, the fault is certainly not his.

The other young man without whom this edition would not have been possible is César A Rodríguez, a young Colombian legal scholar who is now completing his PhD in sociology at the University of Wisconsin-Madison. In my many travels around the world I have encountered many brilliant young people full of promise. None of them, however, comes close to the extraordinary gifts of César Rodríguez. Endowed with exceptional intelligence, he combines a most stringent intellectual and professional discipline with a gentle character, woven of deep feelings and strong political solidarity with all those who fight for a better world. The scholarly world will hear of him in due time. William Twining's proposal was demanding. By myself, I could never accomplish it in so short a period of time. César made it all possible by helping me to revise and update the several chapters of the book. To work with him for the past few months was a privilege and a high-level scientific experience.

Nonetheless, there is no question but that this book is the second edition of a previously published book. The writing of this book took shape in the course of many years, and benefited immensely from the generous support of so many institutions and individuals that it would be impossible for me to name them all here. But even running the risk of omissions, I would like to express my gratitude to a few. Two universities, one Portuguese, the other American, are my greatest institutional creditors. I am first of all deeply indebted to the University of Coimbra, the School of Economics and the Center for Social Studies in particular, for their enduring support for a project that lasted many years and required prolonged stays abroad. I am likewise grateful to the University of Wisconsin-Madison, particularly the Law School and the Institute for Legal Studies, but also to the Sociology Department. A very warm word of thanks to the Deans of the

Law School, first Daniel Bernstine and then Kenneth Davis, and the Directors of the Institute for Legal Studies, first David Trubek, then Marc Galanter, and lately Howard Erlanger. Howard Erlanger took the initiative to have the title of Distinguished Legal Scholar conferred on me, for which I am greatly honored. My very special gratitude to him and to the Assistant Director of the Institute for Legal Studies, Pam Hollenhorst, who beautifully combines affection and solicitude with efficiency and professionalism.

A large portion of this book was written in Madison, where I have always found a most congenial intellectual climate, an atmosphere built on a human scale, demanding yet free from arrogance, cosmopolitan yet with a strong sense of place. Besides the enabling milieu that this scholarly community provided me with, I must thank the Law School for its precious logistic support. In the course of my research I benefited greatly from the generous availability of the excellent facilities of the University of Wisconsin-Madison libraries. Mike Morgalla and Telle Zoller, of the Law Library, were indefatigable in their efforts to procure books that were sometimes quite out of the ordinary and hard to come by; as this book was reaching its completion, Telle Zoller, the foreign law librarian, provided precious aid with citations and bibliographical references. I am once again indebted to Mike and Telle for their precious assistance in the preparation of this second edition. Theresa Dougherty took great pains with the word processing of the manuscript of the first edition in its various versions along the years with unsurpassable professionalism, graciousness, and good cheer. In the final stages of preparation of the manuscript, Lynda Hicks provided her invaluable computer skills to solve all the technical problems resulting from the length of the entire document. I am also pleased to acknowledge the kind support I received from Joy Roberts, of the Institute for Legal Studies. Several other institutions are my creditors as well. On more than one occasion the London School of Economics and the Institute for Advanced Studies of the University of São Paulo provided me with the right kind of stimulation for the development of my ideas. Though all the above-mentioned institutions have also assisted me financially at one time or another, this project could not have been completed without the substantial support of the Gulbenkian Foundation, the British Council, Luso-American Foundation for Development, Luso-American Educational Commission (Fulbright), and Foundation for Science and Technology, the Portuguese institution for financing scientific research.

Parts of this book were debated with many colleagues and friends in Europe, the United States, and Latin America. Although I could not possibly acknowledge them all individually without becoming tedious, I must name a few, hoping that some others will also recognize themselves in the finished product. First of all, I would like to thank collectively all my colleagues at the Center for Social Studies (CES). Then, for intellectual encouragement, stimulus and aid of many different sorts, I am grateful to Richard Abel, Sérgio Adorno, André-Jean Arnaud, Richard Bilder, John Brigham, Kristin Bumiller, Ascension Cambron, Celso Campilongo, Juan Ramon Capella, Wanda Capeller, Bill Clune, Amelia Cohn, Gabriel Cohn, Jacques Commaille, Murray Edelman, Eliaz Díaz, Joaquim Falcão, José Eduardo Faria, Peter Fitzpatrick, Marc Galanter, Yash Ghai, Linda

Gordon, Armando Guevara-Gil, Christine Harrington, Allen Hunter, José Geraldo Sousa Junior, Leonard Kaplan, Maivan Lam, Andrew Levine, Stewart Macaulay, Sally Merry, Carlos Guilherme da Mota, Alexandrina Moura, Nikos Mouzelis, Tim Murphy, Laura Nader, Germán Palacio, Maria Célia Paoli, Sol Picciotto, Paulo Sérgio Pinheiro, Simon Roberts, Fernando Rojas, Albie Sachs, Austin Sarat, Richard Schwartz, Gay Seidman, Susan Silbey, Francis Snyder, Aldaiza Sposati, Betty Sussekind, Göran Therborn, Philip Thomas, Joe Thome, David Trubek, Vincent Tucker, Immanuel Wallerstein, Bill Whitford, Patricia Williams, Erik Wright, and Barbara Yngvesson. A final word of thanks to David Delaney, on whose generous time and competence I counted during the last phases of preparation of the manuscript of the first edition.

Besides William Twining and César A Rodríguez, many other people contributed toward the preparation of the second edition. Among them, I would like to single out two fine research assistants: Luis Carlos Arenas helped me to unravel the intricate complexities of indigenous law; Maria Paula Meneses supplied invaluable assistance to Chapters Five and Nine and thoroughly revised the bibliography. Maurício García-Villegas read and commented on Chapters One and Three; Maria Manuel Leitão Marques, José Manuel Pureza, João Paulo Simões and Eduarda Goncalves read and commented on parts of Chapter Five. A very special thanks to all of them. Chapter Nine was first presented and discussed in two meetings of the Collaborative Research Network on Law and Counter-Hegemonic Globalization that I organized with César A Rodríguez in 2001. The first meeting, held at Oxford University, was sponsored by the *Modern Law Review,* and the second was held at the Central European University in Budapest under the auspices of the Law and Society Association. I am grateful to the members of the CRN who participated in both meetings – Fran Ansley, Leonardo Avritzer, Raquel Yrigoyen, Bronwen Morgan, Ruth Buchanan, Sundhya Pahuha, Paula Meneses – for their comments.

At Butterworths I could always count on the understanding, professionalism, and solidarity of the Editor. He made sure I was granted the best conditions to prepare this second edition, and never failed to acknowledge, with great kindness and patience, the difficulties involved in such an exacting process of revision.

Were I to add up all my other debts, however great, the amount would not even come near what I owe my wife, Maria Irene Ramalho. To thank her would be trivial. *De nobis sibi silemus.*

Boaventura de Sousa Santos

September 2002

Acknowledgments

The parts of this book that were published before have been extensively revised, in some cases beyond recognition. For permission to use previously printed material I would like to thank the following periodicals: *Journal of Law and Society* ('Law: A Map of Misreading. Toward a Postmodern Conception of Law,' 14, 3:279-302); *Law and Society Review* ('Law of the Oppressed: The Construction and Reproduction of Legality in Pasargada Law,' 12:5-125); *Oñati Papers,* ('The Gatt of Law and Democracy: (Mis)Trusting the Global Reform of Courts', 7 (1999), pp 49–86)

Chapter 1

The Tension Between Regulation and Emancipation in Western Modernity and its Demise

1 MODERN REGULATION AND EMANCIPATION

Western modernity and capitalism are two different and autonomous historical processes. The sociocultural paradigm of modernity emerged between the sixteenth and the end of the eighteenth century, before industrial capitalism became dominant in today's core countries. From then on, the two historical processes converged and interpenetrated each other. However, the conditions and the dynamics of their development remained separate and relatively autonomous.[1] Modernity did not presuppose capitalism as its own mode of production. Indeed, conceived as a mode of production, Marxist socialism is as much a part of modernity as capitalism. Conversely, the latter has coexisted with, and indeed thrived in conditions that, viewed from the perspective of the paradigm of modernity, would definitely be considered premodern or even antimodern.

It is my contention that we are living in a period of paradigmatic transition and, consequently, that the sociocultural paradigm of modernity, which was formulated before capitalism became dominant as a mode of production, will eventually disappear before capitalism ceases to be dominant. Such disappearance is complex because it stems partly from a process of supersession and partly from a process of obsolescence. It entails supersession to the extent that modernity has fulfilled some of its promises, in some cases even in excess. It results from obsolescence to the extent that modernity

---

[1] The modernity I am concerned with in this book is Western modernity. Therefore, I do not delve into the existence and characteristics of other, non-Western modernities. The relationship between Western modernity and capitalism is itself an historical process that is far from linear, and in which it is possible to distinguish different moments, temporalities or 'phases'. Elsewhere I have tried to trace this historical process along three periods: liberal capitalism, organized capitalism, and disorganized capitalism. Santos, 1995, pp 79–118. See also Chapter Two.

is no longer capable of fulfilling some of its other promises. Both the excess and the deficit in the fulfillment of historical promises account for our present predicament – which appears to be on the surface a period of crisis but which at a deeper level is a period of paradigmatic transition. Since all transitions are both half invisible and half blind, it is impossible to name our current situation accurately. This is probably why the inadequate designation 'postmodern' has become so popular. But for the same reason, this term is authentic in its inadequacy. This paradigmatic transformation will be of consequence for the development of capitalism, but its specific impact cannot be predetermined. The efficacy of the postmodern transition consists in constructing a new broad horizon of alternative possible futures, an horizon at least as new and as broad as the one that modernity once constructed and then destroyed or allowed to be destroyed.

The paradigm of modernity is very rich and complex, as capable of immense variability as it is prone to contradictory developments. This capacity for variation and contradiction is grounded on the discrepancy between social experience and social expectation. In modernity, for the first time in Western history the current social experience of vast social groups – and not just of the elites as before – no longer coincides with their expectations concerning their future experience. She who is born poor may end up dying rich. She who is born illiterate may end up dying educated or the parent of an educated child. Expectations exceed experiences, an excess that is measured by the dimension of the promises of modernity rendered credible by the idea of progress.

The discrepancy between experiences and expectations is thus part and parcel of Western modernity. This potentially destabilizing discrepancy rests on the two pillars underlying the paradigm of modernity: the pillar of regulation and the pillar of emancipation. Modern regulation is the set of norms, institutions, and practices that guarantee the stability of expectations. They do so by establishing a politically tolerable relation between present experiences, on the one hand, and expectations about the future, on the other. Modern emancipation is the set of oppositional aspirations and practices that aim to increase the discrepancy between experiences and expectations, by calling into question the status quo, ie, the institutions that constitute the extant political nexus between experiences and expectations. They do so by confronting and delegitimizing the norms, institutions, and practices that guarantee the stability of expectations – ie, by confronting modern regulation. Modernity is thus grounded on a dynamic tension between the pillar of regulation and the pillar of emancipation. This tension is well expressed in the dialectics of order and good order, or of society and good society. While regulation guarantees order in society as it exists in a given moment and place, emancipation is the aspiration for a good order in a good society in the future. The success of emancipatory struggles is measured by their capacity to constitute a new political relationship between experiences and expectations, a relationship capable of stabilizing the expectations on a new and more demanding and inclusive level. Put differently, the success of emancipatory struggles resides in their capacity to transform themselves into a new form of regulation, whereby good order becomes order. It is, however, typical of the paradigm of modernity that such success should be always fleeting: once the new form of regulation becomes stable, new aspirations and oppositional practices will try to destabilize it on behalf of more demanding and inclusive expectations. Thus, order ceases to coincide with good order. The tension between regulation and emancipation is therefore unsolvable; there is no possible final reconciliation between the two of them.

The pillar of regulation and the pillar of emancipation are each constituted by three principles or logics, that is to say, by three criteria that provide meaning and direction to social action, be it regulatory or emancipatory. The pillar of regulation is constituted by the principle of the state, formulated most prominently by Hobbes, the principle of the market, developed by Locke and Adam Smith in particular, and the principle of the community, which presides over Rousseau's social and political theory. The principle of the state embodies the vertical political obligation between citizens and the state, an obligation that is variously insured, according to time and space, by coercion and legitimacy. The principle of the state stabilizes expectations by establishing the horizon of possible (and hence the only legitimate) expectations. The principle of the market consists of the horizontal, mutually self-interested obligation among the agents of the market. It stabilizes expectations by guaranteeing that, within the politically established horizon of expectations, the fulfillment of expectations is obtained with a minimum of imposition, through universal promotion of self-interest in the market place. Finally, the principle of community entails the horizontal obligation that connects individuals according to criteria of non-state and non-market belongingness. It stabilizes expectations by defining what a particular group collectively may expect or attain within the political boundaries set by the state and outside or beyond any market obligation.

The pillar of emancipation is constituted by three logics of rationality as identified by Weber: the aesthetic-expressive rationality of the arts and literature, the cognitive-instrumental rationality of science and technology, and the moral-practical rationality of ethics and the rule of law. These three logics – each in its own way – destabilize the horizon of possible expectations by expanding the possibilities of social transformation beyond a given regulatory boundary. In other words, they create possible futures that do not fit the political relationship in force between experiences and expectations. They have therefore a Utopian dimension. Using the power of the imagination, they explore new modes of human possibility and new forms of deployment of the human will, and contest the necessity of whatever exists – just because it exists – on behalf of something radically better that is worth fighting for, and to which humanity is fully entitled. For instance, the aesthetic-expressive rationality creates possible futures through what, towards the end of the eighteenth century, the German poet Friedrich Schiller designated as aesthetic appearance (*das aesthetische Schein*). Here are Schiller's words:

> 'In the midst of the fearful kingdom of forces, and in the midst of the sacred kingdom of laws, the aesthetic impulse to form is at work, unnoticed, on the building of a third joyous kingdom of play and of semblance, in which man is relieved of the shackles of

circumstance, and released from all that might be called constraint, alike in the physical and in the moral sense'.[2]

Just as the aesthetic-expressive rationality, the cognitive-instrumental rationality creates possible futures by freeing human beings from the chains of circumstance and established limits, but it does so through the potentially infinite succession of technological revolutions. Finally, the moral-practical rationality creates possible futures by transforming new ethical demands of liberty, equality, and fraternity into political imperatives and juridical demands.

The paradigm of modernity is an ambitious and revolutionary project, but it is also internally contradictory. On the one hand, the breadth of its claims opens up a wide horizon for social and cultural innovation; on the other, the complexity of its constituent elements make the overfulfillment of some promises and the underfulfillment of some others hardly avoidable. Such excesses and deficits are both at the heart of the paradigm. The paradigm of modernity aims at a reciprocal development of both the pillar of regulation and the pillar of emancipation, as well as at the undistorted translation of such development into the full rationalization of collective and personal life. This double binding – of one pillar to the other and of both to social practice – is supposed to ensure the harmonization of potentially incompatible social values, such as justice and autonomy, solidarity and identity, equality and freedom.

With the privilege of hindsight, it is easy to predict that the hubris of such an overreaching aim carries in itself the seeds of frustration: unfulfilled promises and irredeemable deficits. Each pillar, based as it is on abstract principles, tends to maximize its potential – be it the maximization of regulation or the maximization of emancipation – thereby blocking the potentially infinite unfolding of the tension between them. Similarly, each pillar consists of independent and functionally differentiated principles, each of which tends to develop a maximalist vocation. On the side of regulation it tends either to the maximization of the state, or the maximization of the market, or still the maximization of the community. On the side of emancipation, it tends to the aestheticization, the scientificization, or the juridification of social practice.

2   THE ROLE OF SCIENCE AND LAW IN THE MANAGEMENT OF EXCESSES AND DEFICITS OF MODERNITY

Given the inner tensions and breadth of the paradigm, excesses and deficits were to be expected. What is crucial, however, is that both excesses and deficits were conceived of in a reconstructive manner. The excesses were viewed as contingent deviations, the deficits as temporary shortcomings, and both as problems to be solved through a better

---

[2]   Schiller, 1967, p 215.

and broader use of the ever-expanding material, intellectual, and institutional resources of modernity. This reconstructive management of excesses and deficits was gradually entrusted to science and, in a subordinate but equally central position, to law. Boosted by the fast conversion of science into a force of production, the scientific criteria of efficacy and efficiency soon became hegemonic, and gradually colonized the rational criteria of the other emancipatory logics.

At the beginning of the nineteenth century, modern science had already been converted into a supreme moral instance, itself beyond good and evil. According to Saint-Simon, the moral crisis that had plagued Europe since the Reformation, and the consequent separation between secular and religious power, could only be solved by a new religion; that religion was science. In a similar vein, politics was converted into a provisional social field of less-than-optimal solutions for problems that could only be adequately solved once transformed into scientific, technical problems: the well-known Saint-Simonian transformation of the administration of people into an administration of things. On the other hand, both liberal microethics – a principle of moral responsibility concerning exclusively the individual – and legal formalism – a broad intellectual legal constellation that extends from the German pandect to the codification movement (whose most outstanding landmark is the Napoleonic Code of 1804), and to Kelsen's pure theory of law[3] – were valued for usefulness to a scientific management of society. As to the aesthetic-expressive rationality, the avant-garde movements of the turn of the century – Futurism, Surrealism, Dadaism, Russian constructivism, proletcult, and so forth are eloquent expressions of the colonization of art by the idea of the scientific and technological emancipation of society.

The reconstructive management of the excesses and deficits of modernity could not, however, be achieved by science alone. It required the subordinate but central participation of modern law. Such participation was subordinate because, as I have just mentioned, the moral-practical rationality of the law, in order to be effective, had to surrender to the cognitive-instrumental rationality of science. But the role of law was fundamental because, in the short run at least, the scientific management of society had to be guaranteed against eventual opposition by means of normative integration and coercion provided by law. In other words, the depoliticization of social life through science would be achieved through the depoliticization of social conflict and social rebellion through law.

This co-operative relationship and circulation of meaning between science and law, under the aegis of science, is one of the basic features of modernity. In my view, therefore, Foucault overstates the mutual incompatibility of juridical power and disciplinary power, and overlooks the deep interpenetrations between them. Foucault's major thesis is that since the eighteenth century the power of the state – what he calls the juridical or legal power – has been confronted with and gradually displaced by another form of power

[3]   Kelsen, 1967.

– what he calls disciplinary power. The latter is the dominant form of power in our time and is generated by the scientific knowledge produced in the human sciences as it is applied by professions in institutions such as schools, hospitals, barracks, prisons, families and factories.[4] Foucault characterizes the two forms of social power in the following way. Juridical (or state) power is based on the theory of sovereignty. It is power as a right possessed or exchanged, a zero-sum power that is centrally organized and exercised from the top down. Juridical power distinguishes between legitimate and illegitimate exercise of power, applies to autonomous preconstituted recipients or targets and is based on a discourse of right, obedience and norm. In contrast, disciplinary power has no centre. It is exercised throughout society. It is fragmented and capillary. It is exercised from the bottom up, constituting its own targets as vehicles of its exercise. It is based on a scientific discourse of normalization and standardization. Although Foucault is rather confusing on the relationship between these two forms of power, it is clear that, according to him, they are incompatible, and that the scientific, normalizing power of the disciplines has become the most pervasive form of power in our society.[5]

This conception has a long tradition in Western thought, and indeed can be traced back to Aristotle's distinction between law as a normative command and law as a scientific description of regularities among phenomena. But in my view this distinction undergoes qualitative changes within the paradigm of modernity, and the changes occur in an opposite direction to the one indicated by Foucault. Foucault is right in stressing the predominance of disciplinary power, which, in my analytical framework, corresponds to the centrality of science in the reconstructive management of the excesses and deficits of modernity. But he is wrong in assuming that disciplinary power and juridical power are incompatible. On the contrary, the autonomy of law and science vis-à-vis each other has been achieved through the transformation of the former into an alter ego of the latter. This explains why it becomes so easy to move from science to law and vice versa within the same institutions. The defendant, depending on the 'legal-scientific' verdict on his or her mental health, can be referred by the very same institution (the court) either to the medical field or to the penitentiary-juridical field. Actually, women have often been 'located' in either or both fields at once – as mad women in the attic or as prostitutes – under the same sexist and classist presuppositions of both science and law. Such affinity between science and law and the circulation of meaning it allows give rise to social processes that function as symbolic melting pots, configurations of meaning in which elements of both science and law are present in complex combinations.

---

[4]   Foucault, 1976, 1977, 1980.
[5]   The following are some of the relations between juridical power and disciplinary power most commonly found in Foucault's work: juridical power is the wrong conception of power, while disciplinary power is the right one; juridical power is the agent of disciplinary power; disciplinary power goes beyond juridical power; disciplinary power is less legal, or exists where juridical power itself is less legal ('at the extremities'); disciplinary power is colonized by juridical power; juridical power and disciplinary power are the two sides of the same general mechanism of power; they coexist though they are incompatible; juridical power conceals and legitimates the domination generated by disciplinary power.

One such symbolic melting pot is the social process by which doctors have been able to decide questions of life and death of their patients. More generally, sociologists of the professions have shown how professional privileges derived from scientific knowledge legitimate decisions in which scientific judgments glide into normative judgments. For instance, in his analysis of discretionary decisions, Joel Handler has shown how the 'domination arising out of the exigencies of the bureaucratic task finds a comfortable home in the ideologies of the working professions'.[6]

To my mind, both the presentation of normative claims as scientific claims and the presentation of scientific claims as normative claims are endemic in the paradigm of modernity. And indeed the idea that law as norm should also be law as science has a strong tradition in modern social thought, a tradition that goes back at least to Giambattista Vico. In 1725, Vico wrote in *Scienza Nuova,* contrasting philosophy and law: 'Philosophy considers man as he should be and so can be of service to but very few, those who wish to live in the Republic of Plato and do not wish to fall back into the dregs of Romulus. Legislation considers man as he is in order to turn him to good uses in human society'.[7] The same ideal of creating a social order based on science, that is, a social order in which the commands of law are emanations of scientific findings on social behavior, is paramount in the eighteenth and nineteenth-century social thought, from Montesquieu to Saint-Simon, from Bentham to Comte, from Beccaria to Lombroso. In the twentieth century this ideal was most notably present in Roscoe Pound's theory of law. Against legal formalism, Pound called for a type of law grounded in the social sciences. According to him, it was up to sociology to identify the social interests to be secured by law.[8]

3   A PARADIGMATIC TRANSITION?

In my view, the reconstructive management of the excesses and deficits of modernity through modern science and modern law is undergoing a final crisis and not surprisingly such crisis is most evident in science and law. In my view, what most strongly characterizes the sociocultural condition at the beginning of century is the collapse of the pillar of emancipation into the pillar of regulation, as a result of the reconstructive management of the excesses and deficits of modernity which have been entrusted to modern science and, as a second best, to modern law. The gradual colonization of the different rationalities of modern emancipation by the cognitive-instrumental rationality of science led to the concentration of the emancipatory energies and capabilities of modernity in science and technology. Not surprisingly, the social and political theory that explored the emancipatory potential of modernity in the most systematic way – that is, Marxism – saw such potential in the technological development of productive

---

6   Handler, 1983, p 62.
7   Vico, 1961, p 20.
8   Pound, 1937, 1950, 1959.

forces, and used the cognitive, instrumental rationality to legitimate both itself (Marxism as a science), and the model of society envisaged by it (scientific socialism). Curiously enough, this is equally true of Utopian socialism. Its most sweeping and consequent version, Fourierism, relied heavily on the scientific rationality and ethos, as is tellingly illustrated in Fourier's mathematical calculations of the exact size of the phalansteries and of their constitutive elements.[9] The hyperscientificization of the pillar of emancipation allowed for brilliant and ambitious promises. However, as time went by, it became clear not only that many such promises remained unfulfilled but also that modern science, far from eliminating the excesses and deficits, contributed to recreate them in ever new moulds and, indeed, to aggravate at least some of them. Let's examine in turn some of the central promises of modern emancipation.

Regarding the promise of equality, that is, the promise of a more just and freer society made possible by the plenty resulting from the conversion of science into a productive force, according to the latest figures available from the UN Food and Agriculture Organization (FAO), in 1997–99 there were 815 million undernourished people in the world: 777 million in developing countries, 27 million in countries transitioning to market economies and 11 million in industrialized countries.[10] In the twentieth century, more people died of hunger than in any of the preceding centuries, and even in the developed countries the percentage of the socially excluded, those living below the poverty line (the 'interior Third World'), continues to rise. Based on UNDP data, the Global Policy Forum has estimated that 'three decades ago, the people in rich countries were 30 times better off than those in countries where the poorest 20 percent of the world's people live. By 1998, this gap had widened to 82 times (up from 61 times since 1966)'.[11] A World Bank economist concluded in a 'wide ranging study covering 85 per cent of the world's population from 91 countries' that 'the richest 1 per cent of the world have income equivalent to the poorest 57%. Four fifths of the world's population live below what countries in North America and Europe consider the poverty line. The poorest 10% of Americans are still better off than two-thirds of the world population'.[12]

Concerning the promise of liberty: violations of human rights in countries living formally in peace and democracy reach overwhelming proportions. According to a conservative estimate by Human Rights Watch, out of the 60 to 115 million working children in India, at least 15 million are working as virtual slaves (as bonded child labourers).[13] The prison population continues to rise around the world – reaching 2 million in the US alone in 2000 – while police and prison violence are inordinate in such countries as Brazil and Venezuela. Racial conflicts in the UK increased almost threefold between 1989 and 1996.

---

9   Fourier, 1967, p 162.
10   FAO, 2001.
11   http://www.globalpolicy.org/socecon/inequal/gates99.htm. As visited on 6 June 2002.
12   Figures estimated by Branko Milanovic, World Bank economist, as reported by *The Guardian* (http://www.guardian.co.uk) on 18 January 2002.
13   Human Rights Watch, 1996.

Sexual violence against women, child prostitution, street kids, thousands of victims of anti-personal land mines, discrimination against drug addicts, HIV positives and homosexuals, trials of citizens by faceless judges in Colombia and Peru, ethnic cleansing and religious chauvinism – such are some of the manifestations of the diaspora of liberty.

With respect to the promise of perpetual peace that Kant formulated so eloquently: according to the figures quoted by Giddens, in the eighteenth century, 4.4 million people died in 68 wars; in the nineteenth century, 8.3 million people died in 205 wars; in the twentieth century, 98.8 million people had died in 237 wars by 1990. Between the eighteenth and the twentieth centuries, the world population increased 3.6 times while the number of war casualties increased 22.4 times.[14]

Lastly, the promise of the domination of nature and its use for the common benefit of humankind led to an excessive and reckless exploitation of natural resources, the ecological catastrophe, the nuclear threat, the destruction of the ozone layer, and the emergence of biotechnology, genetic engineering and the consequent conversion of the human body into the ultimate commodity. During the past 50 years the world lost about a third of its forests. According to FAO estimates, more than 150,000 square kilometers of tropical forests are lost annually.[15] Nowadays, multinational corporations hold the right to fell trees in 12 million acres of the Amazon forest. Desertification and water scarcity are the problems that will most affect Third World countries in the next decade. A fifth of humankind no longer has access to drinking water.

In order to grasp the full impact of the unbalanced, hyperscientificized development of the pillar of emancipation conveyed by these figures, it is necessary to bear in mind the concomitant and equally unbalanced development of the pillar of regulation in the last two hundred years. Rather than a harmonious development of the three principles of regulation – the state, the market and the community – we have, in general, witnessed the overdevelopment of the principle of the market to the detriment of both the principle of the state and the principle of the community. From the first wave of industrialization, with the expansion of commercial cities and the rise of new industrial cities in the period of liberal capitalism, to the dramatic growth of the world markets with the emergence of worldwide systems of production, the industrialization of the Third World and the rise of a world ideology of consumerism in the current period of 'disorganized capitalism', the pillar of regulation has undergone an unbalanced, market-oriented development.

The reduction of modern emancipation to the cognitive-instrumental rationality of science and the reduction of modern regulation to the principle of the market, fueled by the conversion of science into the primordial productive force, are the key conditions of the historical process by which modern emancipation has collapsed into modern

---

[14]   Giddens, 1990, p 34.
[15]   FAO, 2001. As visited on 6 June 2002.

regulation. Rather than being dissolved in the pillar of regulation, the pillar of emancipation has continued to glow, but with a light that no longer comes from the original dialectical tension between regulation and emancipation – still present in the nineteenth-century positivist motto of 'order and progress' – but rather from the different mirrors in which regulation gets reflected. In this process, emancipation has ceased to be the other of regulation to become the double of regulation.

Hence, the syndrome of exhaustion and of global blockage. The proliferation of the mirrors of regulation allows for ever-more contingent and conventional social practices, but such contingency and conventionality coexist with an ever higher degree of rigidity and inflexibility at the global level. Everything seems possible in art and science, religion and ethics, but, on the other hand, nothing new seems to be possible at the level of the society as a whole.[16] The collapse of emancipation into regulation brought about by the hyperscientificization of emancipation combined with the hypermarketization of regulation, while effectively neutralizing the fears that were once associated with the prospect of fundamental social transformation and alternative futures, has produced a new sense of insecurity stemming from the fear of uncontrollable developments likely to occur here and now, precisely as a result of the generalized contingency and conventionality of specific social practices. Regulation itself becomes ideologically discredited as a pillar of modernity, not, as in the past, because of its contradiction with emancipation, but rather because of its internal contradictions. In other words, global contingency and conventionality undermine regulation without promoting emancipation. The former becomes impossible as the latter becomes unthinkable. At a deeper level, this sense of insecurity lies in the growing asymmetry between the capacity to act and the capacity to predict. Science and technology have expanded our capacity to act without precedent, and with it the spatial-temporal dimension of our actions. While in the past social actions and their consequences shared the same spatial-temporal dimension, today the technological action may prolong its consequences, both in time and in space, far beyond the dimension of the action itself and through causality chains that are increasingly complex and opaque.

The collapse of emancipation into regulation signals, above all, that we are witnessing a paradigmatic crisis of science. Given the role played by law for the past two hundred years, however, I believe we are also witnessing a paradigmatic crisis of law. As I said, law became a second-rate rationalizer of social life. It embodies a kind of surrogate scientificization of society. Law represents thus the closest we get – at least for the time being – to the full scientificization of society that could only be brought about by modern science itself. But in order to perform this function, modern law had to surrender to the cognitive-instrumental rationality of modern science and become scientific itself. Therefore, the paradigmatic crisis of modern science carries with itself the paradigmatic

---

[16]   A powerful analysis of the sense of exhaustion and global blockage in the core countries can be found in Offe, 1987.

crisis of modern law. To conceive of the present crisis of modern science and modern law as a paradigmatic crisis implies the belief that the solution of the crisis as defined by modernity – ie, as a dialectical tension between regulation and emancipation – is no longer viable and that we are, therefore, entering a social, cultural, and epistemological transition toward a new paradigm.

Periods of paradigmatic transition are doubly ambiguous for several reasons. First, because, given the dominance of the old paradigm, it is possible to argue persuasively that the crisis can indeed be solved within the current paradigm and that there is no transition after all. Secondly, because even those that believe that we are in a period of transition rarely agree either on the nature of the paradigm where we come from or, even more rarely, on the nature of the paradigm that we are heading to. For example, as regards modern science, it is today almost consensual that the enormous capacity for action that it made possible did not go on a par with a similar capacity for prediction. As a result, the consequences of scientific action are necessarily less scientific than the action itself, this asymmetry harboring the deepest crisis of science. The asymmetry, however, may be read in two different ways, as either excess or deficit. The capacity to act is excessive in relation to the capacity to predict the consequences of the action, or, inversely, the capacity to predict consequences is deficient in relation to the capacity to produce them. The two readings are not interchangeable because they focus on different processes and emphasize different concerns. The first reading leads to questioning the concept of scientific progress, while the latter limits itself to asking for more scientific progress. The second reading – deficit of science – has indeed so far prevailed, and is anchored in what Hans Jonas has called the automatic Utopianism of technology: the future as 'clonic' repetition of the present.[17] The first reading (science as excess) is still a marginal reading, but the concern it leads to is gaining more and more credibility: how is it that modern science, rather than eradicating the risks, the opacities, the violence and the ignorance which were once associated with premodernity, is indeed recreating them in a hypermodern form? The risk is now the risk of mass destruction through war or ecological disaster; the opacity is now the opacity of the chains of causality between actions and their consequences; the violence continues to be the old violence of war, hunger and injustice, now coupled with the neo-violence of industrial hubris over the ecological systems and the symbolic violence of globally networked mass communications over captive audiences. Finally, the ignorance is now the ignorance about a necessity – the automatic Utopia of technology – that manifests itself as the culmination of free will voluntarism – the opportunity to create potentially infinite choices.

To opt between these two readings of the current condition of modern science is no easy task. The symptoms are fundamentally ambiguous and lead to discrepant diagnoses. If some seem to argue convincingly that modern science is the solution for our problems, others seem to argue with equal persuasion that modern science is itself

---

17   Jonas, 1985.

part of our problems. If we think of the synergy theory of Herman Haken,[18] we may say that ours is a most unstable visual system, the least fluctuation of our visual perception causing ruptures into the symmetries of what we see. Looking at one and the same figure, we now see a white Grecian urn upon a black background, now two black profiles facing each other upon a white background. Which one is the true image? Both and neither. Such is the ambiguity and complexity of our time.

The same duplicity and ambiguity may be observed regarding law. Elsewhere I tried to show that as far as modern science is concerned we are facing a final crisis and a paradigmatic transition, and I identified its main features.[19] In this book, I shall attempt the same in relation to modern law. Before I proceed, however, because of the ambiguities mentioned above, I must explain the way in which I conceive of the paradigmatic transition in general and the transition from modern law in particular.

3.1   *On oppositional postmodernism*

The characterization of a given historical situation does not determine the nature and content of the characterization of the theory that accounts for it. Thus, it is one thing to define the current historical situation as one of postmodern transition, and quite another to put forward a postmodern theory to characterize it. For instance, Fredric Jameson elaborates a modern theory to account for postmodernism, which he conceives of as a cultural form adequate to the demands of late capitalism. Contrariwise, it is possible to advance a postmodern theory to characterize the current situation without ascribing to the latter any transitional character, and rather denying the very idea of a transition toward something different. This is the dominant position in the postmodern thought, which I critique as celebratory postmodernism.

My argument is that we find ourselves in a paradigmatic transition which, lacking a better name, we may designate as a postmodern transition, and that to account for its emancipatory potential adequately we need an appropriate postmodern theory. The latter is what I call the theory of oppositional postmodernism. According to this theory, it is possible and necessary to think of social regulation and emancipation beyond the limits imposed by the paradigm of modernity. To accomplish this much, an oppositional postmodern theory of science and an oppositional postmodern theory of law are called for.

This stance takes the promises of modernity very seriously, be they liberty, equality, peace, or the domination of nature. It submits them to a radical critique that allows us to do two things. First, to understand the perversities concerning the fulfillment of some of the promises and the impossibility of fulfilling others. Secondly, it allows us to

---

[18]   Haken, 1977.
[19]   Santos, 1995, Chapter One.

identify the emancipatory potential that the promises keep intact but that can only be fulfilled within postmodern social, cultural, political, epistemological, and theoretical boundaries.

Either because they remain irredeemably unfulfilled within the boundaries of modernity or because they evolved on to perverse results, the promises of modernity have become problems for which there seems to be no solution at all. In the meantime, the conditions that brought about the crisis of modernity have not yet become the conditions to overcome the crisis beyond modernity. Hence the complexity of our transitional period as portrayed by oppositional postmodern theory: we are facing modern problems for which there are no modern solutions. The search for a postmodern solution is what I call oppositional postmodernism.

This stance is clearly different both from modernist conceptions and theories and from the best-known postmodern conceptions and theories – ie, celebratory posmodernism. According to the former, modern problems have modern solutions, and hence no talk of paradigmatic transition is justified. There is a lot of variation within the modernist stance. On the one hand, there are those who think that Western modernity encompasses many kinds of modernities and that the problem resides in the version of modernity that ended up dominating; thus, the new modern solutions for the new modern problems must be sought for in the other versions of modernity. There are, on the other hand, those who think that the solution has nothing to do with the different forms of modernity but rather with the intensity with which the paradigm of modernity was fulfilled. This is the position of Habermas, for whom modernity is an incomplete project that must be fulfilled. A variation of this stance – albeit one with a more experimentalist and pragmatic tone to it – is that of social scientists like Roberto Unger, who propose a triumphant radicalization of modernity as a means to solve all the problems that modernity has so far left unsolved and fulfill all the promises that modernity has so far left unfulfilled. Indeed, for Unger the way to overcome the tension between what he sees as the twin goals of modernity – 'practical progress' understood as economic growth and innovation, on the one hand, and individual emancipation, on the other – is precisely to exploit the potential of other varieties of the classical institutional repertoire of Western modernity – ie, market economies, free civil societies and representative democracies.[20]

My stance is, however, to be distinguished as well from prevailing postmodern conceptions and theories. For the latter, the absence of modern solutions for the modern problems is not in itself a problem: it is rather a solution. The exhilarating promises formulated by modernity – therein resides the problem. It is therefore healthy, according to this view, to realize today that those promises were a sham and an illusion. This is the condition for us finally to reconcile ourselves with the society in which we live and

---

[20] Unger, 1998.

celebrate what exists merely as it exists. Herein resides the celebratory character of the dominant version of postmodernism – *à la* Derrida or *à la* Braudillard.

My view on the postmodern transition is thus clearly distinguished from all the other ones mentioned above. It alone confers relevance to the idea of a paradigmatic transition while considering it a true transition, that is to say, a provisional stage. On the contrary, modernist stances maintain that there is no question of speaking of transition because all ongoing or merely imagined transformations occur inside a paradigm – the paradigm of modernity – that is ample and multifaceted enough to encompass them all. Celebratory postmodernists believe too that there is no transition to speak of. Modernity is over and with it the idea of both paradigm and transition. According to the stance I hold, there is no postmodern condition; there is rather a postmodern moment. The postmodern designation of this moment, however, only aims to signal our incapacity to characterize this transitional moment adequately, a moment between a paradigm that is still dominant – even in the way it goes about denouncing its irremediable contradictions – and another emergent paradigm, or paradigms, of which there are only intimations or signs. Under these circumstances, the issue of the direction of the transformations becomes crucial. As a result, it is not so important to distinguish between modernism and postmodernism; what is really important is to distinguish between oppositional and celebratory postmodernism. In a nutshell, for the oppositional postmodernism I argue for, what is necessary is to start from the disjunction between the modernity of the problems and the postmodernity of the possible solutions, and turn such disjunction into the urge to ground theories and practices capable of reinventing social emancipation out of the wrecked emancipatory promises of modernity.

3.2   Oppositional postmodernism and law

The third way I propose between a modernist and a postmodernist celebratory stance is admittedly complex. Given the academic predominance of the two rival stances, mine is particularly prone to being misinterpreted. Because it is so difficult to conceive of the social, cultural, epistemological, and theoretical situation independently of either of the two dominant stances, my own view has been considered by some as modernist, by others as postmodernist. Frankly, I am not sure whether, under the current circumstances, the diverging assessments of my work are a sign of the weakness or of the strength of my stance. Be it as it may, in what follows I shall try to further elaborate on the oppositional postmodern view of law. In doing so, I seek to prepare the theoretical ground for the arguments that I will make in the subsequent chapters and to respond to some of the invitations for greater elaboration of my position that have been made by the readers of my previous work.[21]

---

[21]   See, for instance, Twining, 2000; Darian-Smith, 1998. See my reply to the latter in Santos, 1998a.

As stated above, the way I conceive of the postmodern transition implies a postmodern conception of science and law – the two core conduits of the rise, consolidation and decline of Western modernity. The postmodern conception of science and the postmodern conception of law are distinctive epistemological, theoretical, and analytical processes. They do have in common, however, the demanding task of facing up to the same challenge, namely that of conceiving the unfulfilled emancipatory promises of modernity beyond modernity itself, so that they can be redeemed from the collapse of emancipation into regulation that marks the end of modernity. Since science and law were the principal agents of this collapse, the role I attribute to them in the paradigmatic transition presupposes a wide process of unthinking the dominant conceptions of science and law. Unthinking is similarly demanding, both as regards tasks of deconstruction and tasks of reconstruction. Since the seventeenth century in particular, science has colonized our notions of reason and rationality in such a way that the process of unthinking may very well be labelled irrational.[22] I invoke Stephen Toulmin to reply that what is truly irrational, or at least strange, is the drastic separation that has occurred since the seventeenth century between the related concepts of rationality and reasonableness, theory and practice, logic and rhetoric, and that total priority was given to rationality, theory, and logic. Against the grain of all previous Western history, reason was then charged with the only task of producing absolute necessities and certainties by means of abstract concepts, universal laws, and general, timeless, decontextualized and neutral formal arguments.[23] As I conceive our transitional moment, the core epistemological and cultural task consists precisely in retrieving reasonableness, practice, and rhetoric. Rather than irrationalism, what is at stake is to give back to reason a broader rationality. The North-American poet Wallace Stevens speaks eloquently of a 'later reason'.

As far as science is concerned, I took up this task elsewhere.[24] As regards law, the following chapters will show to what extent my conception of law is grounded on the

---

[22] This is indeed the label that Twining, drawing on Susan Haack's work on epistemology, gives to some of my views. Responding to this critique as it relates to science is beyond the scope of this book. I will reply to it below, however, insofar as it pertains to my view on law.

[23] Toulmin, 2000, p 24.

[24] Santos, 1995, Chapter One. Because there is no direct, immediate relation between subject and object, scientific knowledge cannot but be a social construction. There are mediations between subject and object that go beyond their relation: theories, concepts, methods, protocols, and tools that both make knowledge possible and define its limits. This is not to say that scientific knowledge is arbitrary. It is not, for two main reasons. First, because mediations are the result of broad consensuses within the scientific community. These consensuses make possible the conflicts through which knowledge progresses. What counts as truth is the provisional absence of a meaningful conflict. Scientific knowledge is a socially organized practice. Far from being external to the rationality of science, the social is part and parcel of it. For instance, the proceedings of proof do not do away with the intervention of trust and authority mechanisms in force in scientific communities; they are therefore irreducible to the scientists' procedures taken individually. Secondly, although all knowledge intervenes in the real, that does not mean that the real can be changed arbitrarily. On the contrary, the real resists, therein residing its

demands of reasonableness, practice, and rhetoric. From them I cull inspiration and energy to give back to law its potential for opposition and emancipation. Here I limit myself to presenting the main features of my conception of law.

I start from a critique of the modern conception of law. To my mind, the modern conception of law is grounded on three pillars: the law as state monopoly and scientific construction; the depoliticization of law under the distinction between state and civil society; and the law as principle and universal instrument of politically legitimated social transformation. My starting point is, thus, the critique of and the formulation of alternatives to each of these pillars. Against the first pillar – the state-centred and scientific nature of law – I propose a strong conception of legal pluralism and a rhetorical conception of law. My purpose is to show that the modernist conception of law led to a great loss of legal experience and practice, and indeed legitimated a massive *juricide*, that is to say, the destruction of legal practices and conceptions that did not fit the modernist legal canon. The recuperation of rhetoric aims to offer an alternative to the positivist theory of law, which, one way or another, has become the 'natural consciousness/conscience' of modern state law.

Refering to Anglo-American jurisprudence, William Twining criticizes precisely, on the one hand, its 'parochialism', which treats 'societies, national-states and legal systems as largely self-contained units',[25] and, on the other, its expository tradition, which tends to be ahistorical, decontextualized and uncritical'.[26] The same could easily be said of continental jurisprudence.

I entirely agree with Twining's diagnosis. My only contention is with his proposal: 'We need a jurisprudence', he argues, 'that can transcend jurisdiction and cultures, so far as that is feasible and appropriate, and which can address issues about law from a global and transnational perspective'.[27] Behind a transcultural jurisprudence lurks the modernist hubris of a general theory of law that, although claiming to be universally valid, cannot but be a globalized localism.[28] Inside the bounds of modernity, Twining is perhaps the Anglo-Saxon legal theorist that goes furthest in taking into account the

---

active character. What we know of the real is our intervention in it and its resistance. Resistance causes the certification of the consequences of knowledge to remain ever short of its total foreseeability. That is why scientific actions tend to be more scientific than their consequences. That is also why new knowledge always produces new ignorance, therein residing its unavoidable uncertainty.

The existence of the real does not presuppose the transparency of the real. Even the most transparent image – the mirror image – is an inverted image, and knowing the rules of inversion, however accurately, does not eliminate inversion. Critical, pragmatic, and action-bound realism is what allows for the most creative tension between the possibilities and the limits of knowledge.

[25]   Twining, 2000, p 47.
[26]   Twining, 2000, p 48.
[27]   Twining, 2000, p 49.
[28]   For an elaboration of the concept of globalized localism, see Chapter Five.

juridical diversity of the world. I don't think, however, that the pursuit of this objective, correct in itself, may be facilitated by a general theory, and a theory at that in which, in the analytical tradition, conceptual clarification and formal description continue to be the central tasks. In lieu of legal transculturalism, I propose legal multiculturalism. This does not imply cultural relativism in any way. In his excellent analytical critique of my work, Twining suggests that I oscillate between imaginative postmodernism (which he views favourably) and irrational postmodernism (which he feels very strongly against). One of the issues on which he sees me as tending toward irrational postmodernism is exactly cultural relativism. Now, in Chapter Five I argue that, on the contrary, all cultures are relative but cultural relativism as a philosophical stance is wrong. In fact, rejection of cultural relativism is perhaps what best distinguishes the oppositional postmodernism I maintain from celebratory postmodernism.

Concerning the second pillar of modern law – depoliticization of law through the distinction between the state and civil society – as shown in detail in Chapter Seven, I propose that this distinction be overcome and replaced by a set of structural time-spaces – the householdplace, the workplace, the marketplace, the communityplace, the citizenplace and the worldplace – that can all be politicized and thus become the conduit for freeing politics from its confinement in the state and political society, a confinement imposed by modern political theory. Such liberation from conventional politics makes possible the repoliticization of law – which, to my mind, is the necessary condition to return to law its emancipatory energies. In this domain as well, the oppositional postmodernism I sustain is clearly distinguished both from modernist conceptions of law and postmodern celebratory conceptions. The former actually produced the depoliticization of law by turning it into a science – the juridical science or sociological jurisprudence – as well as into a monopoly of the state. The eminently political gesture of reducing law to the state is, according to this conception, the condition of depoliticization. This is true of all modernist theories of law, including those that within the modern paradigm are seen as opposite to each other. For instance, Hart's 'soft positivism' and Dworkin's view of 'law as integrity' – which have come to be seen as the two strongest rival candidates for theoretical hegemony within Anglo-Saxon jurisprudence – both aim at isolating law (understood exclusively as state law) from politics, either by formulating a positivist rule of recognition (Hart) or by resorting to the moral principles constituting the consensus that allegedly underpins social practices in well-ordered societies (Dworkin).[29] Even those conceptions of law that seek to radicalize modern law fail to live up to their task. For instance, Unger's legal theory – which explicitly aims at re-orienting legal analysis in the direction of institutional imagination and rightly criticizes the reconstructive and depoliticizing aim of mainstream legal theory – remains trapped in the reductionist conception of law as state law, and of politics as state politics. Indeed, Unger's invitation to institutional tinkering and experimentation amounts to an exercise in top-down transformative social policy whose privileged actors are enlightened intellectuals, government officials and social elites

---

[29]   Hart, 1961; Dworkin, 1986.

and whose privileged time-spaces are electoral politics and technocratic policy making.[30] Thus, by radicalizing the modern legal canon, Unger's work belies the dilemma the latter is enmeshed in.

Celebratory postmodernism, in turn, relishes and furthers depoliticization by turning law into a cultural object that concerns individual 'legal consciousness' rather than social transformation. As Munger has shown in his assessment of recent law and society scholarship, sociolegal studies in the US have increasingly become concerned with the study of legal consciousness and rather skeptical about narratives of social emancipation.[31] From a different epistemological perspective – that of a modernist scholar who has made the 'interpretive turn' – Kahn has made a similar claim recently. In his view, the problem of legal theory is having become too politicized rather than depoliticized as I have been arguing, and has called for a decisive turn in the study of law towards the study of legal culture and consciousness.[32]

And thus I reach the third pillar – law as principle and universal instrument of politically legitimated social transformation. If the modern conception of law reduces the transformative capacity of law to what is legitimated by the state, the postmodern celebratory conception eliminates altogether the idea of social transformation carried out through law. It is here that the cynical reason of celebratory postmodernism becomes most apparent. Disenchantment with any political project going beyond the workplace – and the ivory tower in particular – is evident, for instance, in the Derridian postmodern turn of former CLS scholars such as David Kennedy[33] and Duncan Kennedy.[34] Aestheticization of law or law as irony are the leitmotifs of celebratory postmodernism. If it has a politics at all it is the politics of deconstruction, the climactic

---

[30]   Unger, 1996; 1998. Unger's proposal for the re-orientation of modern legal analysis is as intellectually bold as it is politically empty. Any treatment of the social base or political supporters of the institutional reforms he proposes is strikingly missing from his recent legal and political works, apparently out of the belief that ideas come first and coalitions come later. See, for instance, Unger, 1996, p 137: '[I]f social alliances need institutional innovations to be sustained, institutional innovations do not require preexisting social alliances. All they may demand are party-political agents and institutional programmes, having those class or group alliances as a project – as a project rather than as a premise'.

[31]   Munger, 1998.

[32]   Kahn, 2000, p 27: 'We cannot study law if we are already committed to law [...] A new discipline of law needs to conceive its object of study and its own relationship to that object in a way that does not, at the same moment, commit the scholar to those practices constitutive of the legal order'.

[33]   See David Kennedy, 1988, 1999.

[34]   For instance, see Duncan Kennedy, 1997, deconstructing mainstream legal discourse seeks to shock rather than to transform: 'it aims to *épater les bourgeois* (rather than to nationalize their property), in the modes of aggression and exhibitionism [that deconstruction fosters]' (p 354). Deriving pleasure from deconstruction –'the pleasure of shedding Reason's dead skin' (p 344) – becomes oftentimes in this approach an end in and of itself.

enjoyment in the imagination of a social life without values or alternatives.[35] On the contrary, the position I hold conceives of a broad repoliticization of law as a condition for the dialectical tension between regulation and emancipation to be reconsidered outside the limits of modernity. As far as law is concerned, such limits entailed reducing legitimacy to legality, and this is how emancipation ended up absorbed by regulation. The question about what is legitimacy and what is legality and about the relation between the two of them is central to my theoretical proposal in this book. The intertwining of legality and legitimacy is so deeply inscribed in the dominant modern conception of law that to propose separating them may sound Utopian and be subject to criticism for that very reason. Given the narrow conception of pragmatism and realism that ended up prevailing and that we live with today, retrieving Utopia is, to my mind, one of the conditions of a new realism – a wider realism that may prevent the reduction of reality to what exists.

The positive answer to the question: Can Law be Emancipatory? – to which I devote the final chapter – depends on a series of conditions which, as we shall see, are not the result of any deduction from the postulates of Western modernity, as in Unger. They rather emerge from the practice of oppressed social groups and classes. Struggling against oppression, exclusion, discrimination and the destruction of the environment, these groups resort to law, or rather to different forms of law, as one more instrument of resistance. They do so now within/now without the limits of the modern official law, mobilizing various scales of legality (local, national, and global), and building translocal and even transnational alliances. These struggles and these practices are what nourishes what below I designate as counter-hegemonic globalization. In general, they do not privilege juridical struggles, but to the extent that they resort to the latter they return to law its insurgent and emancipatory character. These practices taken as a whole I designate as subaltern cosmopolitanism, a concept that I will elaborate on in Chapter Nine.

In sum, my oppositional postmodern conception of law is clearly distinguished from modernist stances and the role they ascribe to law in social transformation, be they Twining's moderate modernism or Unger's maximalist modernism. But it is equally different from celebratory postmodern stances, be they Duncan Kennedy's or David Kennedy's liquidating postmodernism, or Peter Fiztpatrick's[36] skeptic (Derridian and Freudian) postmodernism.

Nonetheless, the conception of law I hold has been often criticized by modernists for being postmodern – this is Twining's case, regardless of our otherwise convergent views – and by postmodern authors for being modernist, as in the case of Fiztpatrick's

---

[35]   See for instance Schlag, 1990, 2002; Berman 1999. The internal variety of celebratory postmodernism does not concern me here. For a general view see Minda, 1995. A very lucid critique of celebratory postmodernism is in Handler, 1992.

[36]   Fitzpatrick, 2001.

critique.[37] I am willing to concede that this diversity of readings of my work is grounded on the ambivalence or at best the complexity of my third way between modernism and celebratory postmodernism. What remains to be seen, as I suggested above, is whether this must be interpreted as a sign of weakness or, on the contrary, a sign of strength. I do submit, however, that rather than lingering on disputes on labels – which recall nominalist debates that were better left alone – we should concentrate on the substance of the different positions and their contribution to building a better world.

---

[37]   Fitzpatrick, 2001, p 191. Similarly, Tie, 1999, considers my position to be either moderately realist or neo-realist.

Chapter 2

Toward an Oppositional Postmodern Understanding of Law

In this chapter I will argue that the conversion of modern law into scientific state-centred law went hand in hand with the conversion of modern science into a hegemonic rationality and a central productive force. Given the thematic focus of this book, I will concentrate in this chapter on the gradual process whereby modern law came to be dominated by science and the state. I will claim that in this process law lost sight of the tension between social regulation and social emancipation that was imprinted in its roots in the paradigm of modernity. The loss was so thorough and irreversible that the recovery of the emancipatory energies called for in this book must involve as radical an unthinking of modern law.

In the first section of this chapter, I analyze the original imprint of the tension between regulation and emancipation in modern law, selecting three of its major moments: the reception of the Roman law, the rationalist natural law, and the theories of the social contract. In the second section, I analyze briefly the historical process by which this tension was eliminated by the collapse of emancipation into regulation, distinguishing among three periods of capitalist development: liberal capitalism, organized capitalism, and disorganized capitalism. Finally, in the third section I plead for the unthinking of modern law. I then state the major topics for the unthinking of law in the transition between social paradigms. Some of them are dealt with in greater detail in the following chapters, and for that reason will be here only briefly enumerated.

I THE TENSION BETWEEN REGULATION AND EMANCIPATION

I.I *The reception of Roman law*

The historical unfolding of the tension between regulation and emancipation in the legal field, is even older than the one in the scientific field, and can be traced back to the reception of Roman law in Europe from the twelfth century on. This phenomenon was so decisive for the future development of law that legal historians are almost unanimous in considering it the single most important factor in the birth of the modern or Western legal tradition. However, they may differ as to the interpretation of its sociological insertion in the European history.[1] Harold Berman, for instance, emphasizes in this period (1050 to 1150 AD) what he calls the papal revolution –the struggle to make the Bishop of Rome the sole head of the church and to emancipate the clergy from the control of emperors, kings, and feudal lords – and the 'new canon law' to which it gave rise,[2] while Michael Tigar and Madeleine Levy stress the adequacy of Roman law to the interests of the rising bourgeoisie.[3] Closer to this latter interpretation, and with a much broader analytic scope in mind, Fernand Braudel cites with approval the historians that describe the period between the tenth and the thirteenth centuries as the true Renaissance.[4]

The reception of Roman law was indeed an astounding intellectual movement (the 'learned law'), which started at the University of Bologna at the end of the eleventh century and then swept throughout Europe. It represented a process of law creation – the 'adoption' of Justinian's *Corpus Juris Civilis*, compiled in the sixth century AD – which was independent from the feudal rulers, and indeed at odds with what we could call, without much rigor, the feudal legal system.[5] Indeed, in all its legal, political, social, cultural and economic dimensions, feudal society was very fragmented and pluralistic,[6] 'with several temporal and spiritual overlords jostling and fighting for the right to exploit each piece of arable or livable land – and the people on it'.[7] As regards law, feudal society comprised a situation of radical legal pluralism, which Harold Berman considers to be 'perhaps the most distinctive characteristic of the Western legal tradition'.[8] Besides canon law, there was the feudal or seignorial law, royal law, manorial law, urban law and *lex mercatoria* (merchant law). Since the same person might be subjected to different bodies of law in different types of cases, and there were no clear rules as to the boundaries of the different laws, the 'legal system' was thus complex, cumbersome, chaotic and arbitrary.

This, of course, could also be a source of freedom. As Harold Berman points out, ' [a] serf might run to the town court for protection against his master. A vassal might run to the King's court for protection against his lord. A cleric might run to the ecclesiastical

[1]   One of the best analyses is Wieacker, 1967, pp 45–80. See also Von Mehren and Gordley, 1977, pp 7–93; Merryman, 1985, pp 6–14.
[2]   Berman, 1983, pp 85–119. See also Wieacker, 1967, pp 71–80.
[3]   Tigar and Levy, 1977, pp 8–52.
[4]   Braudel, 1979, p 413.
[5]   Levi Bruhl, 1971, p 12; Wieacker, 1967, pp 97–203; Poggi, 1978, p 73.
[6]   In view of this structural fragmentation, historians have increasingly become 'allergic' to the concept of feudalism, as is the case of Fernand Braudel, 1979, p 413.
[7]   Tigar and Levy, 1977, p 9.
[8]   Berman, 1983, p 10.

court for protection against the King'.[9] This was, however, a chaotic freedom to be exercised only in emergency situations. It was not the kind of freedom that the rising urban commercial classes longed for. Their freedom was to be exercised on a routine basis, as routinely as commercial transactions were carried out, and was to be secured against arbitrary interference: contractual freedom and contractual security had to be combined as the two sides of the same legal constellation. Such a legal constellation was provided by the 'learned law' and by the legal rationalization of social life it propounded.[10] The reception of Roman law suited the emancipatory projects of the emergent class by developing a form of legal regulation that maximized the interests of that class in a society which the latter did not dominate, whether politically or ideologically. Under the prevalent political and social conditions of Europe until the sixteenth century, the *jus commune* – 'a common body of law and of writing about law, a common legal language and common method of teaching and scholarship'[11] – was definitely an 'intellectually superior system', at the service of progressive interests.

When Irnerius started teaching on the *Corpus Juris Civilis* at the University of Bologna, in the late eleventh century, Western Europe was undergoing profound political and economic changes.[12] Once the first Crusade of 1096 had definitely reopened the Mediterranean as a European trade route, a large expansion of commerce and of a monetarized economy along both the Mediterranean and the northern coasts of Europe promptly evolved. Moreover, the Italian cities cultivated a republican spirit of autonomy and freedom socially grounded on a cultivated society, for which the local feudal systems, and their untrained, unpredictable and unfair administration of justice, were becoming culturally anachronistic, rather than simply inadequate.

As Wieacker rightly emphasizes,[13] the reception of Roman law is thus the product of a unique convergence of economic and cultural interests. Such convergence made possible the emergence of an autonomous, humanistic, laic form of legal knowledge and legal reasoning, which put the authority of the *imperium romanum* and the glamour of the Roman cultural ideal (the *Romidee*) at the service of a new legal, political and social project. Contrary to the northwest European universities of the time (Paris and Oxford), the Bolognan *studium civile* is not an ecclesiastic hierarchical corporation but rather a *universitas scolarium*, an association of scholars.[14] In accord with the argument on the interpenetration between disciplinary power and juridical power – which I presented in Chapter One in criticism of Foucault – the 'learned law' started as an academic study, that is to say, as disciplinary knowledge. It became juridical power –

---

[9]   Berman, 1983, p 10.

[10]   Such legal rationalization of social life became most evident after the fourteenth century in the work of the post-glossators, Bartolus (1313–1356) being the most distinguished among them.

[11]   Merryman, 1985, p 11.

[12]   Von Mehren and Gordley, 1977, p 7; Wieacker, 1967, p 47.

[13]   Wieacker, 1967, pp 48, 52, 69.

[14]   Wieacker, 1967, p 53.

that is to say, the form of power that Foucault counterposes to disciplinary power – only later on, when it began to be applied as residual law at the end of the twelfth century. From then on, Roman law combined the two forms of power-knowledge, and that was probably the secret of its remarkable achievements. By the end of the twelfth century, there were at Bologna alone ten thousand students in law, who quickly spread the new learning throughout Europe in their appointments as diplomats, royal counsellors, judges, notaries and so on. Alongside the cleric, there emerged the jurist or legist, who was to monopolize the public administration and the judicial system of Europe in the centuries to come.

For several reasons, the tension between regulation and emancipation is constitutive of the reception of the Roman law. I have already suggested that this new regulatory project is at the service of the progressive interests of the social class that is entrusted at the time with a broad cultural and political project of social emancipation. But probably more decisive is the fact that, in the teachings and exegesis of the Glossators and Commentators, the Roman law is a combination of authority (the *translatio imperii*) and reason (the *ratio scripta*).[15] The pragmatic needs of regulation must be subordinated to the rational experience, and the latter, far from being a mere technical artifact for instrumental purposes, is rather the search for new social and political ethics tuned up to the new times and their call for autonomy and freedom. As Toulmin reminds us,[16] as late as the sixteenth century the model of 'rational enterprise' was, for the scholars, not science but law. The tension between regulation and emancipation lies in the fact that the regulatory power derives its legitimacy from its autonomy vis-à-vis the factic powers involved in conflicts for whose settlement the regulation is called for. In twelfth-century Europe, this amounted to less than a revolutionary leap. Under the specific conditions of the time, the autonomous juridification of dispute settlements and the centrality of legal reasoning allowed for a regulation that did not lose sight of its emancipatory purposes.

I refer to the specific conditions of the time because, as these conditions changed, the features of Roman law that had accounted for the tension between regulation and emancipation also changed and became devices through which emancipation got absorbed into regulation. This occurred along a protracted historical process that cannot be analyzed here. I will merely refer to its unhappy ending in the nineteenth century with the German *Pandektenschule* (*Pandectist School*) (Savigny, Puchta, Windscheid). Saturated with a positivistic epistemology, the Pandektists transformed Roman law into a formal, hierarchical structure of legal rules following a strict logical system. The complex combination of authority, rationality and ethics, which characterized the Roman law of the Glossators, was thereby transformed and reduced to a rational, technical formalism, which was supposedly neutral to ethics and solely concerned with technical perfection, logical coherence, gapless coverage and total predictability. The

---

15   Wieacker, 1967, p 52; Von Mehren and Gordley, 1977, pp 8ff.
16   Toulmin, 1990, p 34.

emancipatory potential of Roman law, which had brought it into the centre of the conversation of European humankind in the twelfth century, was thus lost by converting, in Ihering's words, 'the science of law into mathematics'. And Ihering adds:

> 'Institutions and principles which in Rome were, considering the circumstances and customs of the time there, intelligible, became here, on account of the complete disappearance of their conditions precedent, a real curse; and there never was in this world a mode of administering justice with more power than this to shake a people's confidence in the law and all belief in its existence'.[17]

Under the new sociological context of capitalist domination, nationalism and imperialism,[18] the turn of law toward science allowed for by Roman law in the nineteenth century – the latter's futile erudition and inscrutable, esoteric character – shows how, in a period of positivist hegemony, social regulation was made scientific in order to maximize itself and also in order to maximize the oblivion of the social and political ethics that had kept the emancipatory energies alive since the twelfth century. The specific type of tension between regulation and emancipation, which characterized the reception of Roman law, was part and parcel of the historical project by which the rising European bourgeoisie struggled for economic, cultural and, lastly, political power. Once political power had been conquered, such tension no longer had any historical use; accordingly, Roman law was reduced to the blueprint of a form of social regulation that, because of its scientificity, became, by itself, the only possible emancipation.

1.2 The rationalist natural law

The rationalist natural law of the seventeenth and eighteenth centuries was based on the vision of the foundation of a new 'good order', according to the law of nature, by the exercise of reason and observation. Its most sophisticated version can be found in the work of Grotius (1583–1645).[19] The new rationality of individual and collective life is a secular rationality, and is to prevail both in domestic and in international affairs. It rests on secular social ethics, emancipated from moral theology. In a courageous formulation, Grotius states, in *De Jure Belli ac Pacis*, that 'among the traits characteristic of man is an impelling desire for society, that is, for the social life – not of any and every sort, but peaceful, and organized according to the measure of his intelligence, with

---

[17] Ihering, 1915, pp 121–122.
[18] It is illustrative in this respect to trace the debate in the sixteenth century between the *mos gallicus* and the *mos italicus*, particularly the way French jurists questioned the universalism of Roman law, in light of French customary law, with the objective of urging the independence and even superiority of French monarchy and its traditions. See DR Kelly, 1984 (Chapter on 'The Development and Context of Bodin's Method'), pp 277ff.
[19] The natural law school or movement includes many other social thinkers besides Grotius. Grotius belonged to the first phase of the school, together with late Spanish scholastics and Althusius. Other prominent philosophers in the school were Pufendorf, Christian Wolff, Leibniz, Spinoza, Thomasius and Hobbes (see Wieacker, 1967, p 270).

those who are of his own kind. . . . This maintenance of the social order, which we have roughly sketched and which is consonant with human intelligence, is the source of law properly so called. . . . *What we have been saying would have a degree of validity even if we should concede that which cannot be conceded without the utmost wickedness, that there is no God, or that the affairs of men are of no concern to Him.*'[20] (my italics). Moreover, the new rationality is universal and universally applicable[21] and its unfolding requires a new methodology in which both reason and experience have a part:

> 'Proof *a priori* consists in demonstrating the necessary agreement or disagreement of anything with a rational and social nature; proof *a posteriori*, in concluding, if not with absolute assurance, at least with every probability, that that is according to the law of nature which is believed to be such among all nations, or among all those that are more advanced in civilization. For an effect that is universal demands a universal cause; and the cause of such an opinion can hardly be anything else than the feeling which is called the common sense of mankind'.[22]

As is well known, the rationalist natural law served to legitimate both the 'enlightened despotism' and the liberal and democratic ideas that led to the French Revolution.[23] But the tension between regulation and emancipation as the foundation of a new good order lies precisely in this duplicity. As Tuck rightly notes, Grotius's *De Jure Belli ac Pacis* 'is Janus-faced and its two mouths speak the language of both absolutism and liberty'.[24] Buckle also distinguishes in Grotius's thought between the absolutist strain and the anti-absolutist strain, and sees the latter in Grotius's concern with the right of property and the right of resistance, a concern usually associated with the political

---

[20]   See Grotius, 1964, pp 11–13 (Prolegomena, Sections 6–11). It is worth noting that the epistemological claim of validity is argued by Grotius in a manner strikingly similar to Galileo's, when he says that, 'with regard to those few [propositions] which the human intellect does understand, I believe that its knowledge equals the Divine in objective certainty, for here it succeeds in understanding necessity, beyond which there can be no greater sureness'. Galileo, 1970, p 103. This convergence illustrates the early mutual connection between modern science and modern law that I have alluded to in this and the previous chapters. Cassirer, 1946, p 165, cites a letter written by Grotius in which he expresses the greatest admiration for Galileo's work.

[21]   In Book 1, Prolegomena Section 40, Grotius's Cartesian attitude is shown when he emphasizes that the authority of the past can only be resorted to in a highly selective way if the new universal methodology is to impose itself: 'In order to prove the existence of this law of nature I have, furthermore, availed myself of the testimony of philosophers, historians, poets, finally also of orators. Not that confidence is to be reposed in them without discrimination; for they were accustomed to serve the interests of their sect, their subject or their cause' (1964, p 23). As theory and reality never matches, Grotius served several political agendas during his life. Sixteen years prior to *De Jure* he published anonymously his famous pamphlet on the freedom of the seas (*Mare Liberum*) to refute the Portuguese position on the access to the high seas (*mare clausum*).

[22]   Grotius, Book I, Section XII, 1 (1964, p 42).

[23]   On the relations between the *Vernunftsrecht* and the Enlightenment, see Wieacker, 1967, pp 312–322.

[24]   Tuck, 1979, p 79.

thought of John Locke.[25] In Grotius's theoretical construction of law and politics, the basis of collective life is an impelling desire for society (an *appetitus societatis*), a natural bond disembedded from both the state and the *corpus mysticum*.[26] Thus conceived as *custodia societatis* (*the guardian of society*), law becomes inherent in collective life and in the different social groups in which it is organized. According to the nature of the social group, law can promote hierarchy or equality. Grotius distinguishes three great frameworks of law: the *jus latius patens* (law in a broader sense) of the international society, the *jus civile* (civil law) created by the states, and the *jus arctius* (law in a narrower sense) developed in smaller groups. The third one is differentiated into the *jus rectorium*, which regulates relations of hierarchy between parents and children, masters and servants, administrators and administered; and the *jus equatorium*, which regulates relations among equals, among fraternal and voluntary associations.

This concern with systematization and rationalization, which is typical of seventeenth and eighteenth-century iusnaturalism, has its roots in the legal humanism of the fifteenth and sixteenth centuries. The latter, in turn, was inspired by Cicero's ideal of reducing law to an art or a science (*jus in artem redigendo*) by means of revealing the abstract reason contained in Roman law (the *recta ratio* or *ratio juris*). This concern with *methodus*, with *schemata*, with *ratio* is combined in the seventeenth century with the enthusiasm for the new science of Galileo and Descartes, a combination that is indeed an early manifestation of the complicities between modern science and modern law.[27] One generation after Grotius, Leibniz proposed in 1667 a 'new method' of jurisprudence, ultimately based on mathematics, the *jurisprudentia rationalis*.[28] Some decades later, Giambattista Vico proposed another 'new science', proudly geometrical in nature, which developed the argument presented in a previous treatise on *Diritto Universale* ('universal law').[29]

Vico's theories are particularly important for my argument, because in them the tension between regulation and emancipation is played out with such sophistication that both the similarities and the differences in the ways modern science and modern law experience it become quite clear. Vico sets out to do for the human past what Newton had done for nature, that is, to discover the principles of history (*Historia nondum habet sua principia*, history does not yet have its principles).[30] However, Vico is acutely aware that the science of

[25] See Buckle, 1991, p 3.
[26] See Gurvitch, 1942, p 81.
[27] See Kelly, 1984 (Chapter on 'Gaius Noster: Substructures on Western Social Thought'), p 637; Wieacker, 1967, p 253. See also Toulmin, 1990.
[28] Cited by Zweigert and Kotz, 1987, I, p 49. See also Cassirer, 1946, p 165.
[29] Vico, 1961.
[30] The idea of break with the past in Galileo and Descartes is also present in Vico: 'So, for purposes of this inquiry, we must reckon as if there were no books in the world' (1961, p 52). In formulating his purposes as the 'discovery of the principles of history', Vico anticipates, by a century and a half, Karl Marx, who originally wanted to dedicate the first volume of *Das Kapital* to Charles Darwin because he felt that in his book he was doing for the evolution of society what Darwin

history or of society cannot be developed according to the same principles and methods as the science of nature. Vico criticizes the Cartesian naturalism and rationalism for their incapacity to attain true wisdom and equity in social affairs (*aequitas civilis*), which is the ultimate objective of the study of human culture and history. Vico finds the alternative principles, adequate for such a study, in philology and jurisprudence. Concerning philology, Vico says:

> 'The mental vocabulary of human social institutions, which are the same in substance as felt by all nations but are diversely expressed in language according to their diverse modifications, is exhibited to be such as we conceived it.... These philological proofs enable us to see in fact the institutions we have meditated in idea as touching this world of nations, in accordance with Bacon's method of philosophizing, which is 'think and see' (*cogitare videre*)'.[31]

As regards philology, Kelly rightly emphasizes that, for Vico, 'if mathematics was the language of the book of nature, as Galileo had taught, philology was indispensable for anyone who hoped to penetrate the book of humanity'.[32] Language is a symbolic expression of social reality and social transformation through which we can 'enter' inside a given culture and/or society and reconstruct it imaginatively (what Vico called *fantasia*). And as regards jurisprudence, it was scientific, as jurists had argued for centuries, 'both because it dealt with things in terms of cause and effect and because it was universal, though, unlike natural philosophy, it had as its goal human welfare'.[33] Vico saw himself as discovering a *jus naturale gentium* (natural law of peoples), thereby continuing the work of Grotius, whom he considered the 'jurist of mankind'. Basically, Vico considered that the evolution of law and jurisprudence was the most revealing indicator of the evolution of civilization. In this he was also a pioneer. He anticipated Durkheim's theory on the evolution of social division of labour and its relationship with the evolution of the forms of law by more than a century, when he argued that repressive law prevailed in societies dominated by mechanical solidarity, while restitutive law prevailed in societies built upon organic solidarity.

---

had done for the evolution of nature in the *Origin of the Species*. See also Kelly, 1984 (Chapter XII on 'Vice's Road: From Philology to Jurisprudence and Back'), pp 16–29.

[31] Vico, 1961, pp 64–65. Isaiah Berlin, 1976, considers that one of the major innovations of Vico's thought is the idea 'that those who make or create something can understand as mere observers of it cannot' (p XVI). Here lies the radical distinction between the sciences of nature and the sciences of society: it is possible to have an 'inside' view of language, not of nature; the realm of nature obeys (knowable but not intelligible) laws, while the man-made is subjected to (intelligible) rules (p XXI). In Vico's words: '[W]hoever reflects on this cannot but marvel that the philosophers should have bent all their energies to the study of the world of nature, which, since God made it, he alone knows; and that they should have neglected the study of the world of nations or civil world, which, since men had made it, men could come to know' (1961, p 53).

[32] Kelly, 1984, XII, p 19.

[33] Kelly, 1984, XII, p 27.

The way the tension between regulation and emancipation is played out in the legal field is revealed, in my view, by Vico's most basic distinction between the certain (*certum*) and the true (*verum*). At the beginning of *Scienza Nuova*, Vico sets forth the axioms or *degnitàs* (dignities) that will orient his research. Among them the following two concern us here:

> '*Degnità CXI:* The certain in the laws is an obscurity of judgment backed only by authority, so that we find them harsh in application yet are obliged to apply them just because they are certain. In good Latin *certum* means particularized or, as the schools say, individuated; so that, in over-elegant Latin, *certum* and *commune* are opposed to each other.
>
> *Degnità CXIII:* The truth in the laws is a certain light and splendor with which natural reason illuminates them; so that jurisconsults are often in the habit of saying *verum est* for *aequum est*'.[34]

The *certum* is the authority, the arbitrary, the particularized outcome of human will, while the *verum* is the truth, the emanation of reason, the universality derived from the necessity of nature. Both are facets of the law – the latter being indeed a bridge over the chasm that separates them. But such a bridge is a movable one, which gets dislocated as the human experience unfolds. For Vico, natural law is not a fixed normative entity. It is rather:

> 'the movement of the process of the historical formation of the structures of positive law towards an immanent ideality. . . . The universality of the natural law consists, not in the fact that in all times and in identical places identical positive law should prevail, but that in all the forms of positive law, despite the diversity of material circumstances which dictate the immediate force of the law, the same ideal principle is at work'.[35]

This movement is not a circular one, however. The historical trajectory of human experience shows that the latter proceeds from the *certum* to the *verum*, from authority to reason, from the particular to the universal. This trajectory is best revealed by law. At every moment in history, law is constituted by the tension between regulation (authority) and emancipation (reason); but as the human experience unfolds, emancipation wins over regulation. This process takes place – and this is crucial for my argument – because the *verum* is not a mere cognitive reason. The *verum* (*the true*) is the *aequum* (*the just*). The emancipatory potential of law lies in that its rationality is not distinguishable from universal social welfare, the *aequitas civilis*.

---

[34] Vico, 1961, pp 50-51.
[35] See d'Entreves, 1972, p 160.

1.3   Theories of the social contract

The third prominent manifestation of the tension between regulation and emancipation at the origin of the modern legal field was the rise of the theories of the social contract. Among these theories, Rousseau's is the most important for my argument. The idea of a social contract to justify a political obligation is an old one.[36] Lessnoff traces it back to the work of an Alsatian monk, Manegold of Lautenbach, who in the late eleventh century took up the idea of social contract on behalf of Pope Gregory VII in his struggle with the Emperor.[37] What is new in the theories of the social contract in Hobbes, Locke and Rousseau is that they result from the debate on the rationalist natural law – from which they also depart, of course – and that they see themselves as part of an emerging new social and political order and of a new modern scientific method for analyzing reality.[38] In one way or another, the universality of a new legal and political obligation is connected with the truth claims of modern science. This connection is more problematic in Rousseau than in Hobbes, whose project is to build a 'science of natural justice' fashioned according to the method of geometry, 'the only science that it hath pleased God hitherto to bestow on mankind'.[39]

The way Rousseau conceives of the state of nature makes it of little use to found, much less to dictate, a political structure. As a matter of fact, Rousseau, who always criticized the Enlightenment from the point of view of the Enlightenment, does not see himself bound by any scientific naturalist methodology. On the contrary, in his *Discourse on the Sciences*, Rousseau submits modern science to the harshest criticism for its inability to confront the most serious ethical and political problem of the time – that 'man is born free, and everywhere he is in chains'[40] – in its own terms, that is, in terms of ethics and politics. For this reason, I believe, Rousseau expresses the dialectical tension between regulation and emancipation at the roots of modernity better than anyone else. This tension is presented at the outset, when Rousseau says, in the opening sentence of the *Social Contract*, that his purpose 'is to inquire if, in the civil order, there can be any sure and legitimate rule of administration, men being taken as they are and laws as they might be'.[41] The tension is here between certainty and justice, very much in the same way as Vico formulates it – ie, as the tension between the *certum* and the *verum*, that is, the *aequum*. Justice and certainty are both at the root of a new social project for which human beings bear moral responsibility. Since human beings are both free from the state of nature and free to exercise moral choice, society is a product of human choice. Given the individuality of human choice, how is it possible to build collective life upon it? In other words, how is it possible to create a political obligation on the basis of freedom?

---

[36]   It exists at least since the stoic idea of the *consociatio humana*, expounded by Cicero. This is indeed the myth of the origin, or *fabula docet*, of the European political tradition.

[37]   Lessnoff, 1990, p 5. See also Wieacker 1967, pp 267–269.

[38]   Weinreb, 1987, p 67.

[39]   See Hobbes, 1946, p 21.

[40]   Rousseau, 1973, p 165.

[41]   Rousseau, 1973, p 165.

The idea of social contract is the master narrative through which the Enlightenment tries to respond to these questions.[42] As in many other instances, Rousseau goes beyond his contemporary 'contractarians'. For him, the problem is not so much how to found a social order upon freedom, but rather how to do it in such a way as to maximize the exercise of freedom. According to him, it would be absurd to enter freely in a contractual relationship if the result were to be the loss of freedom (as in the Hobbesian contract). For Rousseau, there is only one possible solution: the general will as a substantive exercise of inalienable, indivisible sovereignty. The general will, as conceived by Rousseau, represents a synthesis between regulation and emancipation. Such synthesis is best expressed in two apparently contradictory ideas: the idea of 'obeying only oneself' and the idea of 'being forced to be free':

> 'To find a form of association which may defend and protect with the whole force of the community the person and property of every associate, and by means of which each, coalescing with all, may nevertheless obey only himself, and remains as free as before.
> . . .
>
> Whoever refuses to obey the general will shall be compelled to do so by the whole body. This means nothing less than that he will be forced to be free'.[43]

Indeed, the two ideas stem from the same basic premise of Rousseau's social contract: through the social contract, the individual will may be good or bad, but the general will cannot be other than good.[44] Individual freedom is always contingent, but it is guaranteed against self-denial by the non-contingent collective freedom it contributes to by association. When people act against the general will they are not morally free; they are rather slaves of their passions and appetites. To be morally free means to act according to self-prescribed laws, the laws that promote the common good as defined by the general will. The general will does not necessarily coincide with the will of all. What generalizes the will is not the number of voices but the common interest uniting them.[45] Given the combination of the ideas of 'obey[ing] only oneself' and ' [being] forced to be free', the foundation of the body politic lies in a horizontal political obligation, from citizen to citizen, in relation to which the vertical political obligation, from citizen to the state, is derivative.

Under these conditions, the highest exercise of regulation is the highest exercise of emancipation. Law and civil education are the key instruments of such synthesis. Concerning law, its complexity lies in the fact that it combines maximum unavailability with maximum instrumentality. As an emanation of the general will, law cannot be used for any purpose that violates the general will. For instance, law cannot particularize the

---

[42] As Cassirer (1946, p 174) rightly points out, '[w]hat we are looking for is an origin in reason, not in time'.
[43] Rousseau, 1973, pp 174, 177.
[44] Cobban, 1964, p 74.
[45] Rousseau, 1973, Book II, Chapter 3, pp 184–186.

subjects of its regulations, because it must be as general as the general will from which it proceeds: 'law considers subjects *en masse* and actions in the abstract, and never a particular person or action'.[46] Conversely, inasmuch as it conforms to the general will, law is necessarily an instrument of infinite capabilities because 'the original act by which the body [politic] is formed and united still in no respect determines what it ought to do for its preservation'.[47] Thus, contrary to Hobbes, Rousseau conceives of law both as an unconditional ethical principle, and as an efficient 'positive' instrument of social ordering and transformation. Such multi-dimensionality of law corresponds to that of the state. On the one hand, the state is all-powerful, because it is empowered by an absolute principle of legitimacy: the general will. On the other hand, the state is indistinguishable from the citizens, in that they have an inalienable right to enact the laws by which they will be ruled. Thus, we have to conclude[48] that Rousseau's political theory leads to the abolition or the withering away of the state.

Rousseau represents the climax of the broad conception of moral-practical rationality originally inscribed in the paradigm of modernity, the conception of a creative tension between regulation and emancipation, which assumes a most distinguished political form in the *Declaration des droits de l'homme et du citoyen* (1789). Rousseau's vision of a new social and political principle, as elaborated in the *Social Contract* and other political writings, illustrates, better than any other produced by the Enlightenment, the dilemmas and complexity of a social regulation aimed at furthering rather than suffocating the emancipatory promises of modernity. Such a social regulation would balance freedom and equality, autonomy and solidarity, reason and ethics, authority and consent, in the name of a full rationalization of both collective and individual life.

In Chapter One, I argued that the complexity of modern social regulation manifests itself in each one of the three principles that support it – the principle of the community, the principle of the state, and the principle of the market – as well as in the relations that develop among them. Like the other two great 'contractarian' political philosophers of modernity, Hobbes and Locke, Rousseau covers all the three principles with his analytical framework, and seeks a dynamic relationship among them. But while Hobbes privileges the principle of the state and Locke the principle of the market, Rousseau privileges the principle of the community.

In light of Rousseau's views on associations and on civil religion, it may seem strange to identify him specifically with the principle of the community, and not with the principle of the state. The debate that Rousseau's views have sparked will not be pursued here. As I interpret Rousseau, the community is for him the whole community to which the sovereignty of the state corresponds. This is the community whose strength Rousseau wants to maximize. Hence his emphasis on the general will and on the inalienability of

<hr>

[46]   Rousseau, 1973, Book II, Chapter 3, p 192.
[47]   Rousseau, 1973, Book II, Chapter 3, p 191.
[48]   See also Colletti, 1974; and Medina, 1990, p 61.

people's sovereignty. Thus his emphasis on the horizontal and solidary political obligation of citizen to citizen, in relation to which the authority of the state is unequivocally derivative. In order to safeguard this community, it is necessary to eliminate all obstacles that might come in the way of the citizen-to-citizen political exchange, and thus hinder the formation of an undistorted general will.[49] Associations and corporations may become privileged and powerful groups, and swerve the general will in favour of their particularistic interests. Because of the inalienability of the sovereignty of the whole community, Rousseau does not need to conceive such associations as barriers to the tyranny of the state, as Montesquieu did in *The Spirit of Laws*. Rousseau is, rather, concerned with the possibility that such associations might become corrupt and tyrannical themselves. Since he is realistically aware that it is impossible to do away with the associations, Rousseau recommends their proliferation: '[B]ut if there are partial societies it is best to have as many as possible and to prevent them from being unequal, as was done by Solon, Numa and Servius'. And he adds: '[T]hese precautions are the only ones that can guarantee that the general will shall be always enlightened, and that the people shall in no way deceive itself'.[50] What Rousseau wants more than anything else is to guarantee the transparency of the general will. Associations can be accepted if they do not endanger such a guarantee; and indeed, in other works, Rousseau allows a wide room for 'those associations ... smaller ... tacit or formal'.[51]

While in Rousseau the *contrat social* makes the sovereignty of the state derivative and precarious, in Hobbes the *Covenant* makes it original and absolute. For this reason I consider Rousseau the archetypical expounder of the modern principle of the community, and Hobbes the archetypical expounder of the modern principle of the state. According to Hobbes, the social contract is the device by which people renounce the state of nature – that is, the absolute freedom and equality that necessarily leads to the war of everyone against everyone – and create a civil society based on the absolute sovereignty of the state which, in exchange for freedom and equality, guarantees peace, effective authority and, in the end, the only possible just society. Because the sovereign is absolute, he cannot obey any law, not even the laws he promulgates. On the contrary, people have a fundamental self-interest in obeying the sovereign, at least as long as the sovereign guarantees the safety of their lives.[52]

As in Rousseau, the social contract is established 'by everyone with everyone'. But while in Rousseau the contract represents an act of empowerment that reproduces itself in the body politic it creates, in Hobbes the commonwealth's empowerment exhausts itself in the act of the contract. From then on, the objective of peace demands absolute subjection to the sovereign. While in Rousseau the sovereign is 'internal' to the contract, in Hobbes

[49]   See also Cobban, 1964, p 46.
[50]   Rousseau, 1973, pp 185–186.
[51]   See Cobban, 1964, p 47.
[52]   See Hobbes, 1946, pp 113–129. According to Cassirer (1946, p 175), this unconditional and absolute transfer of rights to the ruler led the most influential writers on politics in the seventeenth century to reject the conclusions drawn by Hobbes.

the sovereign is 'externalized', since there can be no covenant between subjects and their sovereign. The sovereign is a mortal god, but very little distinguishes him from an immortal one. It is commonly accepted today that, as in Rousseau, in Hobbes, too, the state of nature is a logical device or a theoretical construct to justify the institutionalization of the civil society. Hobbes's 'unrelieved grimness of the state of nature', as Weinreb calls it, is probably better seen as a rhetorical truth or as a premise of the argumentation on the foundations of the civil authority. Weinreb indeed concludes that, 'when the whole argument is exposed, it is plain that the state of nature is made expressly for the leaving of it'.[53]

The process of reductionism that the paradigm of modernity undergoes once its development is conflated with that of capitalism is already present in Hobbes to a much greater degree than in Rousseau or in Locke, as I will show below. Two main reasons account for this. Hobbes is particularly seduced by modern science and values and, above all, by science's potential to achieve incontrovertible order.[54] Though, in general, seventeenth-century rational philosophy is anxious to emulate the method of geometry or mathematics and to produce a systematic knowledge that can progress from natural law to 'experimental philosophy', Hobbes, more than anyone else, assumes the objective of reaching certainty and incontrovertibility (both in knowledge and in politics). Through different paths, such an epistemology leads to reductionism: politics is separated from ethics; morality becomes a function of self-interest; good and evil are reduced to objects for which there is either an appetite or an aversion.

The seeds of reductionism in Hobbes's vision of modernity lie also in the fact that the tension between regulation and emancipation is, in his theory, reduced to a tension between war and peace. Peaceful regulation is the only possible emancipation that is accessible to human beings, whose 'natural passion' is war and anarchy. It is true that for Hobbes the objective is still to build a just society. However – although he believes, in a rather ambiguous formulation, that 'the good of the Sovereign and People cannot be separated' – the fact of the matter is that effective authority in Hobbes is by definition a just authority and that, except in the extreme case of risk to self-preservation, there is in his thought no safeguard against tyranny.[55]

It is clear, then, that Hobbes's thinking already carries in itself the seeds of statization as an impoverished form of modern regulation. The same cannot be said of Locke. On the contrary, Locke strongly argues against the idea of absolute sovereignty and connects the legitimacy of the government with the limits of its purposes: government is legitimate as long as it respects the natural rights, and it exists solely to protect them. Government acts by consent. Since unanimous consent is difficult to obtain, it is allowed to govern by majority rule. There are, in fact, two social contracts. One is established

---

[53]   Weinreb, 1987, p 74. See also Medina, 1990, p 12.
[54]   See also Buckle, 1991, p 55, and Toulmin, 1990.
[55]   For a convergent interpretation of Hobbes, see Medina, 1990, pp 13–26.

among the people, whereby which the people decide to abandon the state of nature and found the civil society. Another contract is established between the people and the sovereign government, in terms of which the government is entrusted with the regulation of civil society according to the majority rule. Government is thus bound by law, the latter being the only guarantee against abuses of power and tyranny. Whenever such guarantee fails, the people have the right to rebel and resist. Anything else would amount 'to think[ing] that men are so foolish that they take care to avoid what mischiefs may be done them by polecats or foxes, but are content, nay, think it safety, to be devoured by lions'.[56]

The features that distinguish the Hobbesian and the Lockean conceptions of the civil society correspond to those that distinguish their conceptions of the state of nature against which civil society is built. Locke's state of nature is far less grim and violent than Hobbes's. Indeed, it is a state of perfect freedom, of equality and independence and, in general, a state of peace and of goodwill and mutual assistance. Under these conditions, the pressure to leave the state of nature is not as compelling as it is for Hobbes: what we leave is not so grim; what we gain is obviously not so much better.[57] What we gain is basically certainty and a way of solving peacefully those disputes that in the state of nature would lead inevitably to war. Such disputes and uncertainty would above all affect the enjoyment of property. In Locke's own words, 'the great and chief end, therefore, of men's uniting into commonwealth and putting themselves under government, is the preservation of their property'.[58]

There is an ongoing debate about the concept of property in Locke, its distinct features in the state of nature and in civil society and the characterization of its evolution throughout history.[59] For the purposes of my argument, only three aspects of Locke's vision of property that seem relatively incontrovertible need to be mentioned. First, following Grotius's concept of *suum*, Locke defends a broad concept of property that includes not only material goods but also one's life, body and freedom. However, the concept tends to narrow down to material property when discussed in the context of money economy. Secondly, Locke grounds property on labour. In his theory of property, labour plays such an important role as a means to acquire property that Locke can be considered one of the precursors of the labour theory of value: 'For it is labour indeed that puts the difference of value on everything. ... I think it will be a very modest computation to say, that of the products of the earth useful to life of man 9/10 are the effects of labour'.[60] The third aspect of Locke's theory I want to emphasize is that, in his view, the emergence of money changes the social relations of property drastically. This

---

[56]   Locke, 1952, p 53.
[57]   Weinreb, 1987, p 80.
[58]   See Locke, 1952, p 71.
[59]   The debate is also over the evolution of Locke's thought on property from the *Essays on the Law of Nature* to the *Two Treatises of Government*. For contrasting views, see Buckle, 1991, p 152, and Macpherson, 1962, p 237. See also Medina, 1990, pp 29–41.
[60]   Locke, 1952, pp 24–25.

is so because such historical event allows for the break of the equation between property and capacity to use: 'and thus came in the use of money – some lasting thing that men might keep without spoiling, and that, by mutual consent, men would take in exchange for the truly useful but perishable supports of life'.[61] Through the use of money, accumulation of property becomes unlimited.[62]

The contrast with Rousseau is striking. Though Rousseau offers a justification of property very similar to that of Locke – property as a product of labour – he modifies it by incorporating the ideal of equality. Property tends to accumulate and become unequal; therefore, because 'liberty cannot subsist without equality', the state must intervene to secure both liberty and equality: 'it is precisely because the force of circumstances tends continually to destroy equality that the force of legislation should always tend to its maintenance'.[63] On the contrary, for Locke, by tacitly agreeing in the use of money, 'men have agreed to a disproportionate and unequal possession of the earth'.[64]

Locke's treatment of modern property has led me to see in it the founding formulation of the principle of the market as one of the regulation pillars of modernity. It is true that this principle is more thoroughly developed later on by Adam Smith, who in fact criticizes Locke for his mercantilistic view of wealth. Wealth, says A Smith, does not consist in money but rather in commodities, the consumption of which is 'the great cause of human industry'.[65] However, in my view, this conception of wealth and the conception of social relations it calls for would not be possible without Locke's groundwork: labour as the source of property; property as potentially unlimited and legitimate, in spite of inequality, if 'acquired according to the laws of nature'; the state legitimated above all by the certainty it can confer to the relations of property.

All these ideas lie at the roots of modern market relations as universalized by capitalism. Moreover, Locke's theory brings to its highest tension the modern contradiction between the universality of civil laws founded on consent and according to the laws of nature, on the one hand, and the legitimacy of a social order upset by tremendous social inequality and class divisions, on the other.[66] Through this tension the dialectics of regulation and emancipation is present in Locke, probably less so than in Rousseau, but certainly more so than in Hobbes. Locke's main goal is to provide a rational vision of a just, free and happy society. That is why government is to be limited and laws based on consent. Similarly, the rationality of property imposes certain limits on its use. Property must be protected as a guarantee against slavery and political oppression; for that reason, it cannot be used in such a way as to endanger the very social prosperity

---

[61]   Locke, 1952, p 28.
[62]   Buckle's critique of Macpherson, for whom Locke defended unlimited accumulation, does not sound, in this respect, very compelling. See Buckle, 1991, p 152.
[63]   Rousseau, 1973, p 204.
[64]   Locke, 1952, p 29.
[65]   For a contrast between Locke and Smith, see Buckle, 1991, p 156.
[66]   As is well observed by MacPherson, 1962. See also Medina, 1990, p 34.

it is aimed at guaranteeing. It cannot, for instance, be abused or destroyed when there is no rational need for it. Locke's rational contextualization of property is so elaborate that some authors have recently defended that property in Locke is a 'right of use only'.[67] Be it as it may, Locke's 'possessive individualism' is limited both by the idea that the productive capacity of labour assures general though unequal prosperity, and by the idea that, when inequality leads to extreme necessity, the needy have a *right* to charity.

The analysis of the theories of the three founders of modern politics undertaken in the previous pages shows the breadth and the complexity of both the regulatory and the emancipatory claims of modernity, as well as the dialectical tensions between them. Hobbes, Locke and Rousseau, each one in his own way, illustrate how the all-encompassing symmetries of their projects – state of nature/civil society, sovereign/citizens, freedom/equality, natural law/civil law, consent/coercion – are bound to collapse once translated into real life. Indeed, each one of these founding fathers anticipates the possibility of this outcome, and their theories taken together can be seen as an attempt at preventing it from occurring. Herein may well reside one of the factors accounting for the widely acknowledged inconsistencies, incoherences, and contradictions in their theories as well as for the discrepant interpretations they warrant. But the breadth and complexity of the legal-political construction of modernity and, in particular, the tension between regulation and emancipation inherent to it are all the more evident when Hobbes, Locke and Rousseau are viewed together as distinct parts of a single intellectual constellation. Indeed, each one of them symbolizes an archetypal dimension to a global revolutionary project. The principle of the state (Hobbes), the principle of the market (Locke), and the principle of the community (Rousseau), are all constitutive of a new, paradigmatic social ordering, which will measure up to the emancipatory claims of this intellectual constellation if and only if the three principles develop in a balanced way.

Hobbes, Rousseau and Locke are best understood as part of a large project for the rationalization of social life, as a look into their conceptions of rationality and of law easily illustrates. As regards their conceptions of rationality, though the three philosophers see themselves as rational thinkers and agents and bear witness to the birth of reason and Enlightenment out of the darkness of religion and tradition, they differ as to the types of rationality they privilege in their rational reconstruction of society, both in the way it is and as it should be. Hobbes's rationality is most prominently the cognitive rationality of science, of geometry and mathematics. Rousseau's rationality is the moral-practical rationality, and, to a certain extent, also the aesthetic-expressive rationality. Locke's rationality is a combination of moral-practical rationality and common sense. This diversity shows the richness and complexity of the emancipatory energies of modernity. But it also shows the tension among possibly conflictual claims. For instance, while Hobbes seeks the positivity and the incontrovertibility of a superior knowledge, Rousseau delights in dramatizing his moral outrage before injustice and

---

[67]   See, above all, Buckle, 1991, pp 169 and 183.

stupidity, and warns against the loss of wisdom that may result from too much reliance on scientific knowledge. Locke, on his part, tries to reconstruct wisdom out of common sense in such a way that he tends to blend positivity with conventionality and accessibility. While Hobbes – and, to a certain extent, Locke also – distinguishes politics from morals, Rousseau refuses to accept such a distinction. While for Rousseau the community is indispensable to secure the individual's moral life, both Hobbes and Locke have an individualistic faith in the individual. These tensions can be fully understood only as struggles among different dimensions of the same intellectual constellation.

The same point can be illustrated through a look into their conceptions of law. For Hobbes, law is a product of the will, of the sovereign's will, and it is therefore utterly positive in nature and instrumental in scope. The end of the political commonwealth is 'peace and defense of them all, and whosoever has the right to the end, has right to the means'.[68] Among those means, Hobbes includes 'the whole power of prescribing rules' and 'the right of judicature; that is to say, of hearing and deciding all controversies, which may arise, concerning law, either civil or natural'. For Locke, law is a product of the consent by which the commonwealth delegates to the state the right to pass and enforce laws. Indeed, what the state of nature lacks is 'an established, settled, known law, received and allowed by common consent to be the standard of right and wrong and the common measure to decide all controversies between them'.[69] Finally, for Rousseau, law, more than consented to, is self-prescribed, since the community does not alienate to the sovereign the right to pass laws. That is why Rousseau's citizen does not obey but himself and cannot be forced to do anything except to be free (whenever his will fails to measure up to the general will).

The complexity of the paradigm of modernity lies, thus, in the fact that law is potentially sovereign's will, consent and self-prescription all at once. It may vary from extreme instrumentality to extreme unavailability, but, in any case, law is the exercise of regulation in the name of emancipation. Particularly in Hobbes and Locke, in the last instance civil laws derive their universality and legitimacy from their correspondence with the natural laws. The weaknesses, the passions, the self-interest of human beings require that the natural laws be sustained by civil laws. Hobbes, Locke and Rousseau anticipate, each one in his own way, the antinomy between the universality of this legal-political paradigm and the particularistic life-world in which it will be implemented, a society increasingly dominated by capitalism, class divisions, and extreme inequalities. The 'solutions' for this antinomy that the three of them offer are very different. Rousseau confronts it directly by refusing to separate freedom and equality, and by delegitimating social differences based on property. Hobbes suppresses or hides the antinomy by reducing all individuals to a position of extreme and equal powerlessness vis-à-vis the sovereign. Finally, Locke accommodates the antinomy, not by exerting himself in trying to be

[68]   Hobbes, 1946, p 116.
[69]   Locke, 1952, p 71.

consistent, but rather by justifying both the universality of the legal-political order and the inequalities of property.

None of the founders' approaches is reductionist in itself, but we can easily identify in each one of them the seeds of possible reductionisms. In the last instance, the tension between regulation and emancipation that runs through this powerful intellectual constellation is experienced by the founders of modern political thought as an anxiety of justification. They see themselves entrusted with the task of justifying the new social and political order that is emerging under their eyes, but they anticipate and indeed witness the fact that the new order has both a bright side of unprecedented promises and a dark side of irreversible excesses and deficits. The anxiety of justification lies, on the one hand, in their not being prepared to justify what they consider morally wrong, and, on the other hand, in their knowing that, in order to be successfully rescued from its reactionary enemies, the new order must be justified as a whole.

2 LEGAL-POLITICAL MODERNITY AND CAPITALISM

In the legal and political field, the 'test of reality' for the paradigm of modernity takes place in the nineteenth century. This is also the period in which capitalism becomes the dominant mode of production in core countries, and the bourgeoisie emerges as the hegemonic class. From then on, the paradigm of modernity is tied up with the development of capitalism. Following the theoretical tradition begun by Hilferding and developed by Offe and others, I distinguish three periods in this development.[70] The first period, that of liberal capitalism, covers the whole nineteenth century, though the last three decades have a transitional character. The second period, that of organized capitalism, begins at the end of the nineteenth century and reaches full development in the interwar period and in the two decades after World War II. Finally, the third period, that of disorganized capitalism, begins at the end of the 1960s and is still with us.

It is not my purpose here to give a full description of each period, but rather to mention those characteristics that will enable me to trace the trajectory of the paradigm of modernity throughout the three periods. My argument is that the first period already showed that the sociocultural project of modernity was too ambitious and internally contradictory. The second period fulfilled some of the promises of modernity, but failed to fulfill others, while trying, through a politics of hegemony, to minimize the extent of its failures and to make them socially and symbolically invisible. The third period represents the consciousness of a threefold predicament. First, whatever modernity has accomplished is not irreversible and, to the extent that it is not excessive, it must be defended, but it can only be successfully defended in postmodern terms. Secondly, the as yet unfulfilled promises will remain unfulfilled as long as the paradigm of

---

[70]   See Offe, 1985; Hilferding, 1981; Lash and Urry, 1987. See also Winckler, 1974.

modernity dominates. And finally, this deficit, besides being irreversible, is much greater than the second period was ready to admit.

As we move from the first to the second and third period, the paradigm of modernity, as if animated by a laser beam effect, narrows the scope of its accomplishments at the same time that it intensifies them. Such a process of concentration/exclusion is also the process by which the tension between regulation and emancipation, which was constitutive of modern legal thinking, is gradually replaced by an automatic Utopia of legal regulation entrusted to the state.

2.1 *The first period: liberal capitalism*

The constitutional state of the nineteenth century is heir to the rich intellectual tradition described in the previous section. As it took possession of its inheritance, however, the state minimized its ethical claims and political promises so as to make them fit the regulatory needs of liberal capitalism. The sovereignty of the people became the sovereignty of the nation-state in an interstate system. The general will became the majority rule (found among ruling elites) and the *raison d'etat*. Law was uncoupled from ethical principles and became a docile instrument of institutional building and market regulation. The good order became order *tout court*.

This complex historical process cannot be fully described here. In general, ignited by the contradictions of capitalist development, the tension between regulation and emancipation exploded. The liberal state then sought in this chaos the justification for the design and implementation of a mode of regulation that would reduce emancipation to either anomie or Utopia, and thus, in either case, to social dangerousness. The social delegitimation of emancipation occurs more or less at the same time in law and politics, on the one hand, and in science and technology, on the other: the socio-political chaos and the epistemic chaos referred to in Chapter One are thus intimately interconnected. Indeed, the parallelism between the legal-political and epistemological transformations is underlined by the common philosophy that gradually permeates them: positivism.[71] The rise of positivism in the epistemology of modern science and the rise of legal positivism in law and jurisprudence belong together as ideological constructs aimed at reducing social progress to capitalist development and at immunizing rationality against contamination by all non-capitalistic irrationalities, be they God, religion or tradition, be they metaphysics or ethics, be they emancipatory ideals or Utopias. Thus trimmed, modern rationality can then be made to coexist with and indeed accommodate the irrationalities of capitalism, provided that they are presented as empirical (legal or scientific) regularities.

---

[71] On the relations between scientific and legal positivism, see Wieacker, 1967, pp 458–468.

Positivism is the philosophical consciousness of knowledge-as-regulation.[72] It is a philosophy of order over chaos both in nature and society. Order is regularity, logically or empirically established through systematic knowledge. Systematic knowledge and systematic regulation are the two sides of order. Systematic knowledge is the knowledge of observed regularities. Systematic regulation is the effective control over the production and reproduction of observed regularities. Together they constitute the positivistic effective order, an order based on certainty, predictability and control. Positivistic order is thus Janus-faced: it is both an observed regularity and a regularized way of producing regularity. This explains why it can be found both in nature and society. Through positivistic order, nature can be made predictable and certain so that it will be controlled, while society will be controlled so that it can be made predictable and certain. This captures the difference but also the symbiosis between scientific laws and positive laws. Modern science and modern law are the two sides of knowledge-as-regulation.

While the science of nature is of nature as it is, the science of society is both of society as it is and as it ought to be. In society, the gap between the *is* and the *ought* can be determined scientifically (the laws of social evolution) but, for the time being at least, it cannot be filled by the sole recourse to science. It requires an act of will which, however, can be scientifically constructed. Modern law is such an act of will, and the agent of such will is the modern state: Max Weber's legal-rational state.

Scientism and statism are the main features of modern rational law as it developed in the West during the nineteenth century. According to Max Weber, only the West knows the state in the modern sense, with a professional administration, specialized officialdom and law based on the concept of citizenship. Only the West knows rational law, made by jurists and rationally interpreted and applied.[73] Unlike other forms of political domination, such as the charismatic and the traditional ones, the formal legal domination is not simply associated with a certain form of law; it is constituted by rational law. 'It is, however, with respect to 'legal domination' that the form of law is not merely a characteristic of a particular type of political order, but is its central and determining feature'.[74] Legal rational domination is legitimated by the rational system of state-enacted universal and abstract laws, presiding over a bureaucratic and professional administration, and applied throughout society through a form of justice based on logical formal rationality.

Weber's *Rechtsstaat* internalizes the Janus-faced positivistic order, and appears both as a person and as a machine. The metaphor of the state as a person, as an artificial person, is used by Hobbes and later on by Hegel.[75] The state conceived as a monumental,

---

[72] For a detailed analysis of knowledge-as-regulation and its contrast with knowledge-as-emancipation, see Santos 1995, pp 25–27.

[73] Weber, 1978, II, pp 865–900.

[74] Hunt, 1978, p 114; Weber, 1978, I, pp 212–226. See also Trubek, 1985.

[75] See also Weinreb, 1987, p 87.

self-originating and self-empowered subject is the agent of supreme political will. On the other hand, the state is conceived, in Poggi's words, 'as a machine whose parts all mesh, a machine propelled by energy and directed by information flowing from a single centre in the service of a plurality of coordinated tasks'.[76] The same mechanical metaphor underlies the constitutional image of 'checks and balances', and is also present in the conception of the state as an artificial contrivance, functionally specific and exercising its power in a depersonalized way. Indeed, the two metaphors, person and machine, are not as far apart as one might think, since, in the nineteenth century, the archetypal mechanicism of modern science converted the human being, the person, into a living machine (an organism). But, though twins, the two metaphors remain autonomous, and this autonomy turns out to be quite expedient for capitalism. The state-as-a-person guarantees both the externality of the state vis-à-vis the relations of production and the credibility of the state's pursuit of common interest, while the state-as-a-machine guarantees the certainty and predictability of its operations, and above all, its regulation of market relations.

Both the will of the state-as-a-person and the energy of the state-as-a-machine were provided by formal rational law. As the law was reduced to the state, the state was reduced to law. The two processes were, however, not symmetrical. On the one hand, the state reserved for itself a certain excess vis-à-vis its own law, as witness the areas dominated by the *raison d'etat* in which the legal boundaries were quite fuzzy. On the other hand, and more importantly, while the reduction of law to the state turned the law into an instrument of state, the reduction of the state to law did not turn the state into an instrument of law: law lost autonomy and power in the same political process in which the state gained them.

As the law became statist it became also scientific. On the continent, the most striking manifestation of the turn of modern law towards science was brought about, in the field of private law, by the German Pandectist school. The scientific legal formalism of the German Civil Code of 1900 is its most accomplished achievement. But the *Pandekten* was simply the extreme manifestation of a much broader process of the colonization of modern law by science, aimed at transforming law into an effective instrument of official social engineering. As law became fully politicized as state law, it became a scientific law as well. At the same time, law contributed through its scientific reconstruction of the state, to the depoliticization of the state itself: political domination was legitimated as techno-legal domination. Put differently, the hyperpoliticization of law was the precondition for the depoliticization of the state. Inside the state, law became autonomous, as part of the same historical process by which, inside capitalism, the state became external to the social relations of production. This play of mirrors is indeed constitutive of the modern legal field. The division between public and private law creates a real difference between the law that binds citizens to the state, and the law

---

[76]   Poggi, 1978, p 98.

that is at the disposal of and is disposable by citizens in the relations among themselves. This real difference is obtained through the illusion that private law is not state law.

Thus conceived, the technical instrumentality of autonomous state law is virtually infinite in its scope. The functional specificity of the modern state does not refer to the number of functions the state may perform, but rather to the mode of performance. The minimal state of liberal constitutionalism contains in itself both the seeds of the benevolent welfare state of civilized capitalism and the seeds of the fascist state of barbarian capitalism, as well as those of the Stalinist state of anti-socialist socialism. None of these state forms could do away with the positivity of law as a potentially inexhaustible instrument of domination, no matter how perverted and caricatured such positivity became in the last two state forms mentioned above. In sum, scientism and statism fashioned law in such a way as to convert it into an automatic Utopia of social regulation, indeed equivalent to the automatic Utopia of technology engendered by modern science. This means that, though modernity conceived of law as a second-best (and probably provisional) principle of social ordering when compared to science, once reduced to the capitalist state, law itself became a scientific artifact of the first order. From then on the automatic utopianism of technology grew together with the automatic Utopianism of legal engineering, and indeed the two processes have been feeding one another ever since.

It should be borne in mind, however, that the nineteenth century was not just the century of positivism in both science and law. It was also the century that furthered the romantic idealism carried over from the eighteenth century, and that gave rise to the great realist novel. It was also the century that saw the emergence of socialism as a political movement, and of a myriad of Utopian projects and practices. In their own very different ways, all these phenomena are powerful denunciations of the narrowing down of the scope of modernity, as well as acts of resistance against the stigmatization of emancipation and against the abandonment of the promise of a radical rationalization of personal and collective life. The socialist and Utopian projects and movements pointed toward a full and harmonious realization of the ideals of equality and freedom, of autonomy and solidarity, of regulation and emancipation (even if the world contemplated is Fourier's phalanstery). On the other hand, romantic idealism represented – though in an elitist form – the Utopian vision of the full achievement of subjectivity developed by the Enlightenment. In yearning for the totality, for the origins and for the vernacular, against the atomism, the alienation and instrumentalism of modern life, and by placing aesthetics and poetry at the centre of social integration, romantic idealism epitomized the denunciation of and the resistance to the tendency toward exclusion and concentration in the social implementation of the paradigm of modernity.[77] On the other

---

[77]   See Hauke Brunkhorst (1987), for whom 'romantic modernism edges bewilderingly close to the conservative or reactionary fundamental opposition to modern culture and its Utopian rationalism' (p 409). Similarly, according to Gouldner (1970), 'the revolutionary potential of Romanticism derived, in part, from the fact that although basically a critique of industrialism, it could as well be used as a critique of capitalism and its culture' (p 115).

hand, the great realist novel bears witness to a class – the bourgeoisie – that fails to seize the historical opportunity of becoming a universal class and bringing about a radical social transformation,[78] the same opportunity that Hegel had envisaged for the bureaucracy and Marx for the working class. All in all, the period of liberal capitalism sets in motion the social process of exclusion and concentration of modernity. However, as the contradictions of the paradigm explode without mediation, it was still possible in this period to formulate and activate, even if in a deviant or marginal form, the radical and globalizing vocation of the paradigm. This, in turn, dissipated the doubts about the capability of the paradigm to fulfill its promises.

Under these circumstances, the statism and scientism of law – which broadly correspond to the prominence of the principles of the state and of the market at the expense of the principle of the community – developed in a social field full of tensions. On the one hand, the reduction of Rousseau's sovereign community to a dualistic structure of abstract entities – state and civil society; civil society and the individual – was a convulsive one. On the other hand, the principle of the state and the principle of the market often collided over the demarcation of areas of complicity/complementarity and areas of exclusive rule, in a kind of game of complicity and antagonism that has lasted to the present day that has been played most prominently in the legal field. If the principle of the market was boosted by the first wave of industrialization, the expansion of commercial cities, the rise of new industrial cities and the expansion of industrial colonialism, the development of the principle of the state was far more ambiguous, mainly because of the contradictory claims of laissez-faire. As Dicey perceptively noted, laissez-faire involved both the idea of the minimal state and the idea of the maximal state.[79] This explains why, above and beyond moments of collision, the two principles belong together and feed one another. Durkheim's prediction that the growth of market relations would involve the growth of state relations was to be confirmed during the two subsequent periods of capitalism.[80]

2.2   The second period: organized capitalism

Concerning the core countries of the world system, it may be said in general that the period of organized capitalism was truly a positive age in the Comtean sense. Just as a reasonable and mature adult should do (according to Comte), it started out by distinguishing, in the paradigm of modernity, between those promises that can be fulfilled in a dynamic capitalist society and those that cannot. It then concentrated on the former and tried, through socialization and cultural inculcation, to eliminate the latter

---

[78]   According to Georg Lukács (1972), 'the central category and criterion of realist literature is the type, a peculiar synthesis which originally binds together the general and the particular both in characters and structures' (p 5). Hence, his definition of realism: 'a correct dialectical conception of the relationship between being and consciousness' (p 119). See also Auerbach, 1968, pp 454ff; and Swingewood, 1975, Chapter 3.

[79]   Dicey, 1948, p 306.

[80]   Durkheim, 1964.

from the symbolic universe of social and cultural praxis. In other words, this period began by acknowledging the idea that the deficit of unfulfilled promises is both inevitable and irreversible, and then went on to eliminate the idea of deficit itself. In the legal field, this period was characterized by an unprecedented exacerbation of the automatic Utopia of social engineering through law, in the name of which the statism and scientism of law were redefined.

In the first period, the period of liberal capitalism, the autonomy and the universality of law were premised upon the unity of the state, and the unity of the state was premised upon the distinction between state and civil society and upon the functional specificity of the state. Civil society and, above all, market relations were conceived of as self-regulated, and it was up to the state to guarantee such autonomy. The most crucial instrument in the process of building an autonomous market society was private law, complemented by fiscal, monetary and financial measures, aimed in most cases at correcting the imbalances resulting from market failures or imperfections. This latter objective included tasks as diverse as granting land to railway companies, servicing the national debt, protectionism, granting of patents, repression or regulation of trade unions, and colonial policies. It also included the laws on the duration of the working day, so brilliantly analyzed by Marx in Chapter Ten of Volume One of *Das Kapital*, and the laws dealing with 'the social question' – that is, with the set of problems seen as resulting from rapid and autonomous industrialization, such as mass poverty, prostitution, criminality, alcoholism, epidemics, illiteracy, strikes, unemployment, socialist subversion and so on.[81]

This apparently exceptional and unobtrusive intervention of the liberal state brought with itself the potential for 'legal absolutism', a potential, however, that operated very unevenly, resulting in an unequal development of the legal field. Private law, the privileged focus of legal scientism and legal positivism, was conceived of as disengaged from any political or social content, and capable of freeing social relations from *ancien regime* bonds and hierarchies. Its objective was to secure the reproduction of a competitive self-balancing market through negative freedoms, expedient but suppletive legal frameworks, and mechanisms for the enforceability of contracts. Administrative law organized the everyday distance of the state apparatuses vis-à-vis the citizenry, and concentrated on the mechanisms that reproduce that distance, mainly through demarcation of clear boundaries for state action. Finally, constitutional law was based on the assumption that individual freedoms had a pre-legal origin, and that the state could only guarantee them through narrowly defined, certain and predictable political and administrative processes, which it was the task of constitutional law to establish.[82]

At the end of the nineteenth century, this legal and political landscape changed dramatically, mainly as a consequence of the increasing hold of the capitalist mode of production,

---

[81]   See Poggi, 1978, p 115. The transitional period between liberal capitalism and organized capitalism is particularly illuminating in this respect. See, on this, Romein, 1978.

[82]   See, on this development, among others, Preuss, 1988.

not only on economic relations, but also on social life in its entirety.[83] The concentration and centralization of industrial, commercial and financial capital, the proliferation of cartels and monopolies, and the separation of legal ownership from economic control bore witness to the dramatic expansion of the principle of the market, at the same time that they put an end to the competitive self-balancing market. Moreover, the extension of suffrage and the organization of sectoral – and often antagonistic – social interests in employers' organizations and trade unions made the classist nature of political domination all the more visible. As class practices became more easily translated into class politics, trade unions and working-class parties entered the political arena, which until then had been exclusively occupied by oligarchic parties and bourgeois organizations.

Under these conditions, the state/civil society distinction was to undergo a gradual process of transformation that started with successive dislocations of the demarcation line and ended with the blurring of the distinction altogether. Two different but convergent developments fueled this process. The first development was the need for public economic management in the face of the growing complexity of capitalist economy. On the one hand, the externalities of economic growth based on the increasing inequality among economic agents (not only between capital and labour but also within capital) led to the need for state intervention, mainly through state regulation of the markets. On the other hand, and apparently in contradiction with this, the growth of large corporations, the control that they were able to exert over the economic processes, and the political leverage they thereby accumulated, resulted in the increasing availability of the capitalist state to further corporate interests – from the construction of infrastructures and the socialization of the costs of industrialization to the production of educational systems designed to meet the big firms' needs for skills and qualifications, full employment policies, and research and development funds.

Although this process eventually contributed to the dislocation of the line demarcating state and civil society, and indeed to the gradual obliteration of the distinction, there were different social forces involved in it (most prominently the bourgeoisie and the working class) that were mobilized for often contradictory objectives. In addition, the state itself developed an autonomous interest in intervention as a way of securing the reproduction of the big bureaucratic agencies that had been created. Finding its justification in exceptional conditions (the devastation of World War II), in the recognition of market failures (insufficient profitability or investment potential) or in a new political principle (social democracy), such autonomous state intervention sometimes included the nationalization of private industries or even the creation of state enterprises. Poggi is right when he says that 'what makes the trend toward the obliteration of the state/civil society line so powerful is precisely the fact that several phenomena, distinctive and even otherwise mutually contradictory, are at one in causing it'.[84]

---

[83]   A vivid account is in Romein, 1978, pp 271ff.
[84]   Poggi, 1978, p 131; see also Romein, 1978, p 276.

The second development was the political recognition of the social externalities of capitalist development – the politicization of some dimensions of the 'social question' – as a result of the expansion of the political process brought about by the enfranchisement of workers and the emergence of strong working-class parties. The politicization of social inequality involved state intervention both in the wage relation and in collective consumption: job security, minimum wages, workers' compensations, pension funds, public education, health and housing, space management, and so on. These measures were so sweeping and emerged from such an unprecedented social pact (between capital and labour under the aegis of the state) that they led to a new political form: the welfare state. The economic management (Keynesianism) and the social management (welfare state) of capitalism in core countries led to an overall mode of social regulation that has been called fordism. This mode of regulation is based on the convergence of the development of the principle of the state and the principle of the market, so that conflicts between the two principles are seen as provisional, selective and indeed institutionalized. As a result, the emergence of conflict or reciprocal distancing in one social field is easily combined with a new complicity and reciprocal approximation in another social field.

It can be argued that, in the period of organized capitalism, not only the principles of the market and of the state, but also the principle of the community, were strengthened. The argument here is that the distributive nature of the welfare policies are based on an idea of solidarity that resembles the horizontal political obligation, citizen to citizen, which is the nucleus of the principle of the community. However, it must be borne in mind that the principle of the community was not recognized in its own terms. Its recognition was, rather, derivative, for it occurred under the aegis of the principle of the state and as part and parcel of the expansion of the principle of the state. As a matter of fact, under the welfare state, the horizontal political obligation was transformed into a double vertical obligation between taxpayers and the state and between welfare clients and the state. In this way, the exercise of autonomy presupposed by the principle of community was transformed into an exercise of dependence on the state.

Nonetheless, it is unquestionable that, in the period of organized capitalism, the legal-political dimension of the paradigm of modernity was thoroughly redefined to accommodate antagonistic claims and to balance interests that in the previous period were considered unbalanceable. Accommodating and balancing implied also reducing emancipatory ideals to realistic proportions and principled options to contingent compromises. Solidarity, justice and equality could be made compatible with autonomy, identity and freedom, provided that each set of apparently incompatible values were brought down to what was realistically accomplishable in a capitalist society. By this process, two 'realistic' promises could be fulfilled to a greater or smaller extent in the core countries in this period: the promise of a fairer distribution of material resources and the promise of a greater democratization of the political system. The fulfillment of the first promise was made compatible with the continuation of a class society, while the fulfillment of the second promise was made compatible with the continuation of a bourgeois liberal politics. Through a politics of hegemony it was then possible to convert this particular form of compatibility, which was, in fact, one among many others, into the only legitimate one, even, perhaps, the only imaginable one. Such conversion meant the triumph of reform over revolution, and surfaced both in the gradual but steady marginalization of the Communist parties and in the transformation of the socialist parties into social democratic parties.

The impact of the new mode of social regulation on law was tremendous. The intensified monitoring of the economic and social processes by the state led to the development of new realms of law, such as economic law, labour law and social law, which shared the feature of mixing together public law and private law characteristics, thus further blurring the line of demarcation between state and civil society. But the impact of these transformations on the traditional realms of law was also important, most notably on constitutional law and administrative law. Constitutions evolved from being the design of a bureaucratic state and a narrowly defined political system to becoming the arena of intermediation and negotiation among conflicting social interests and social values. The most characteristic outcome of this evolution was the constitutional recognition of socio-economic rights – the third generation of human rights, according to TH Marshall.[85] Similarly, administrative law went from being concerned with the organization of controlled subjection to an authoritarian bureaucratic state to being concerned with the organization of resource allocation and technological regulation undertaken by a facilitating state.

In general, as the state became more and more engaged in the economic and social processes – a transformation that liberal theorists considered to entail the 'loss of the autonomy of the state' – state law became less formalistic and less abstract, the weighing and compromising among conflicting interests became more evident (the 'materialization' of the law), and the social and political integrating function of distributive law became a main focus of political debate (the 'politicization' of the law). Actually, neither the 'materialization' nor the 'politicization' was a new phenomenon. They were so perceived only because they now reached far broader social groups and fields of practice than those affected by law in the period of liberal capitalism. The changes were nonetheless enormous. Once law evolved from setting external boundaries on social practice to tooling social practice from the inside, the instrumentality of law was radically intensified. Only then could state law make credible the automatic Utopia of legal engineering announced in the first period. The increasing complexity of social sub-systems, and the accrued need for social co-ordination and integration among them, called for a potentially infinite legal field whereby the excesses and deficits of economic and social development would be, if not eliminated, at least reduced to manageable proportions.

---

[85]   See TH Marshall, 1950.

This legal Utopia[86] symbolized, above all, a new conception of social chaos and, symmetrical with it, a new conception of order. In the period of liberal capitalism, social relations, and particularly market relations, were conceived as largely self-regulating and hence far from chaotic. As we saw above, chaotic tendencies were observed only at their fringes, and only here was there room for legal boundary setting. In this period, social chaos appeared in the form of the social question. Because the political system was too restrictive to allow for the full politicization of the social question, state law was unable to address it except in a very limited way.

For the reasons mentioned above, the situation changed drastically in the second period. The political, social and economic production of chaos became much more visible, represented in wars and imperialism, global crises and predatory practices, gross social inequalities and ostentatious consumption, social rebellion and anomie, social discrimination and waste of resources and so on. The expansion of democratic rule brought about by the working-class parties allowed for a fuller politicization of the chaotic 'disfunctions' than ever before. Once chaos entered the political field, it was miniaturized to the size at which legal control could operate efficiently. The legal Utopia could then reproduce itself on the condition that the 'miniaturizing effect' itself would be kept out of sight through ideological inculcation.

The profound changes in state interventionism and legal instrumentality that took place in the second period had an equally profound impact on the state itself and on its law. An intervention of the state is always an intervention in the state, and the same is true of law. I will mention briefly some of the reflective changes in the legal field. The most decisive ones can be captured in the transformations that occurred both in the statism and the scientism of state law. The epistemological 'initial condition' for the effective operation of law as state law in capitalist societies is the unity of the state, its functional specificity and its clear separation from the civil society. As I have noted, this initial condition suffered a process of profound erosion in the second period. The juridification of social practice was both a product and an agent of such erosion. The state/law equation was destabilized and, as a consequence, the statism of law became problematic; it became a variable, rather than an inherent feature. In some respects, law became less statist. As the state became a political resource for wider social groups and classes, the trans-classism and autonomy of the state became a credible ideology. However, though the state operated through law, the autonomy of the state did not carry with it the autonomy of law-as-state-law. On the contrary, as law became embedded in the social practices it sought to regulate or to constitute, it distanced itself from the state: alongside the use of law by the state there emerged the possibility of law being used in non-state contexts and even against the state. The strange recoupling of politics

---

[86] This legal Utopia is trapped in a kind of Sisyphean myth: each set of legal interventions, motivated by some 'external' development, calling for a new set of legal interventions, in an endless process.

and ethics that occurred in this period, in however selective a form, allowed for the re-emergence of a social perception of law as natural law, although a natural law *derived from* positive law and emerging at the same time that the preconstituted, prepolitical freedoms and self-regulations of the first period were swept away by an unprecedented juridification of social life.

From a different perspective, however, law became more statist than ever. The juridification of social practice meant the imposition of relatively homogeneous state legal frameworks, categories and interactions upon the most diverse and heterogeneous social fields (family, community life, workplace, public sphere, socialization processes, health, education and so on). The manipulability of state law presupposed the malleability of the social fields to be legally manipulated. When social practice failed to validate this presupposition, the result was what Habermas calls the 'colonization of the life world', ie, the destruction of social relations without adequate legal functional equivalents.[87] Whenever that occurred, the legal benevolence of the welfare state became a qualified human good – qualified, that is, by the fact that it could destroy the eventually benevolent dimensions of the social relations to be regulated without guaranteeing the sustainability of the state-legal benevolence, in view of the latter's dependence on the ever-changing reproduction needs of capital.

The uneven development of the statism of state law took place in a political context characterized by such an intense legal activism that it led to that supreme ideology of modern bureaucratic rule: legal and institutional fetishism. Nevertheless, and in apparent contradiction to this, the overuse of law was coupled with the loss, rather than with the increment, of the centrality of law as the source of legitimation for the state. While the liberal state legitimized itself through the formal-legal rationality of its operation, the welfare state sought its legitimacy in the kind of economic development and form of sociability it saw itself promoting. Law was downgraded from a principle of state legitimacy to an instrument of state legitimacy. The seeds of the trivialization of law were thereby being sown.

The transformations in the statism of state law were coupled with convergent transformations in the scientism of state law. The intitial epistemological condition for the scientistic reproduction of state law is the relative stability of norms and facts, and particularly of the norm/fact dualism. The erosion of this condition was inevitable in light of the dynamism of capitalist societies in this century and of the central role played by the state. As the state gets more and more involved in the economic and social processes, and as the latter become more complex, differentiated and systemic, the universal, abstract formal law yields to contextual, particularistic, ad hoc law. In some areas in which the technological component of legal regulation is paramount, legal rule becomes expertise rule, with norms *and* facts interpenetrating each other to the point of becoming

---

[87] For a complex analysis of this process, see Teubner, 1987; and Preuss, 1988.

indistinguishable.[88] Moreover, in the most dynamic and strategic areas of state intervention, the general conditions of state action, to the extent that they can be provided by abstract laws, are almost irrelevant. The implementing institutions need, above all, wide powers of discretion, ie, of recognized capacity to manipulate both norms and facts as they see fit, given the ever-changing social fields and their regulatory needs. Particularly in the field of economic law, there is much room for negotiable legality, an interstitial and ephemeral legality in which the norm/fact dualism collapses altogether. Finally, the areas in which the dualism holds may become so complex that the conventional legal implementation can only operationalize the dualism after it has drastically reduced the ambit of norms and the ambit of facts to be considered. This is particularly the case when the consequences of technological action are involved (toxic emissions, radiation leeks, Chernobyl, Bophal, deforestation). In such cases, the legally relevant chain of consequences tends to be a ludicrous miniature of the real chain of consequences. As a result, the normative claims of the people affected are accordingly miniaturized.

Throughout the century and in very different ways (*Interessenjurisprudenz*, sociological jurisprudence, neo-jusnaturalism, legal realism, legal responsiveness, legal self-reflexiveness, legal autopoiesis, and so on), legal science has been trying to render a scientific account of such transformations in the legal field. In the third period it has become apparent how all these attempts have failed.

2.3 The third period: disorganized capitalism

Since the early 1970s, the core countries have witnessed a considerable degradation of the fordist mode of regulation coupled with a multifaceted crisis of the welfare state. The changes have been so widely perceived that it is legitimate to speak of a new period, the period of disorganized capitalism. This designation is ambiguous and misleading. It may imply that core capitalism is not organized in the current period. This is far from true. The opposite claim can actually be made that capitalism is today more organized than ever. By disorganized capitalism is meant, first, that the specific forms of organization typical of the second period are gradually being dismantled or reconstituted at a much lower level of coherence; and second, that, precisely because this process is underway, the dismantling of previous organizational forms is much more visible than the profile of the new forms that will eventually replace them. A sign that capitalism is today better organized than ever is the fact that it has gotten hold of social life in its entirety, and has managed to neutralize its traditional enemies (the socialist movement, working-class activism, non-commodified social relations) or benefit from their internal disaggregation. In any case, such organization is still very opaque, and whatever parts of it become visible seem rather provisional, as if merely preparing the way for the institutions, the rules and the processes that will constitute the new mode of regulation.

88   Preuss, 1988, p 371.

In this very specific sense, it is legitimate to designate our time as a time of disorganized capitalism, a period of transition from one regime of capitalist accumulation to another or, as suggested below, as a period of a much broader transition from one social paradigm to another.

Basically, in this period the two 'realistic' promises that to a certain extent were fulfilled in the core countries of the world system in the second period – the promise of a fairer distribution of social benefits and the promise of a stable and relatively democratic political system – have not been sustained, and indeed are being eroded in many ways – increasing social inequalities, alarming growth of poverty, emergence of 'interior Third Worlds', reduction of scope and of resources in the field of social welfare, ideological delegitimation of the facilitative state, new devices of social exclusion and authoritarianism disguised as promoters of autonomy and freedom, 'pathologies' of participation and of representation in the political process, new populism and clientelism in politics, and so on. Furthermore, the two political paradigms of social transformation that were available at the beginning of the second period – revolution and reform – appear to be equally exhausted. The revolutionary paradigm that was rejected in core countries soon after World War I appears to be now undergoing an irreversible final crisis in the peripheral and semi-peripheral countries where it was adopted, in very different ways, particularly after World War II. The reformist paradigm, which originally aimed at a social transformation in the direction of socialism, and gradually settled for the far less ambitious goal of a social democratization of capitalism, was hegemonic in core countries in the second period, but has lost steam in the last two or three decades, and is indeed undergoing as severe a crisis as the social and political forms it promoted (fordism and the welfare state).

The most decisive transformations of the third period seem to be occurring under the aegis of the principle of the market, which appears to be more hegemonic than ever within the pillar of modern regulation, as it generates a surplus of meaning that overflows the principle of the state and the principle of the community, and tends to colonize them to a far greater extent than in the two previous periods. The dramatic growth of the world markets, coupled with the emergence of worldwide systems of production and transnational economic agents, undermines the capacity of the state to regulate the market at the national level. The industrialization of the Third World, the expansion of international subcontracting and franchising, and the ruralization of industry have together contributed to radically altering the geography of production and reproduction in the central countries. While the local endogenous dynamics – often based on complex mixes of agriculture and industry, family production and industrial production – link together, without the intermediation of the national space, the local and the global spaces of the economy, the traditional industrial regions are decharacterized and de-industrialized and, in their place, locality re-emerges as a strategic productive factor. The extensive expansion of the market runs parallel to its intensive expansion, as witness the culture ideology of consumerism, with its increasing differentiation of products and particularization of tastes and consequent increase of number of choices, as well as to the increasing commodification of information and mass communication that allows for virtually infinite opportunities for the expanded reproduction of capital.[89]

The principle of the state is also undergoing sweeping changes. The ideology and practice of neo-liberalism, combined with the transnational operations of corporations and international agencies, have led to a relative decentring of the nation-state as an actor in the world system. As I will try to show in Chapter Five, this is a very complex process full of contradictory developments, but in general it can be said that the state seems to be about to lose its status as a privileged unit of analysis and of social practice. This relative decentring of the state in core countries has had a decisive impact on welfare policies. Deregulation, privatization, cost-sharing, marketization, workfare, and community revival are some of the names of a diversified set of state policies with the convergent goal of reducing the state's involvement in social welfare. Because in most countries the degradation of the social performance of the state has not brought about a significant reduction of the bureaucratic weight of the state, the growing weakness and inefficiency of the state appear combined with the growing authoritarianism of a myriad of often ill-integrated bureaucracies, each one exerting its own microdespotism vis-à-vis increasingly powerless, politically incompetent citizens.

On a world scale, the interstate system is also undergoing important changes. The relative decentring of the state, though a general phenomenon, has very different implications in the core, semi-peripheral and peripheral states. In a context of growing inequality between the North and the South, the peripheral and semi-peripheral states are more and more reduced – both as victims and as partners – to the task of fulfilling the requirements of transnational, industrial and financial capital as these, in turn, are formulated by international organizations controlled by the core states. Such requirements, often packaged in strange mixtures of economic liberalism and human rights protection, erode the already fragile social component of the state to such an extent that the countries in question experience a crisis of the welfare state in discourse and practice, so to speak, without ever having had a welfare state proper. The always-unfinished principle of the community has, as a result of these changes, receded into greater unfinishedness. In the period of organized capitalism, the conversion of the horizontal political obligation (citizen to citizen), which is characteristic of the principle of the community, into a double vertical political obligation (taxpayer to state, welfare client to state) was the product of a complex political process in which class practices and class politics played a decisive role.

In the third period, the combined changes in the principle of the state and the principle of the market have significantly curtailed or transformed the nature of class practices and class politics. The trend towards a more precarious (some say 'flexible') wage relation has been both a cause and an effect of the decline of corporatist mechanisms

---

[89]   On the dramatic intensification of transnational interactions in the last two decades, and its impact on the state, see Chapter Five.

(labour laws, industrial courts, collective bargaining, indirect salaries) and of the organizations that mobilized them, mainly trade unions, whose membership has steadily declined. But class practices and politics have also been affected by significant changes in class structures. The national and transnational segmentation of the labour markets, the increased internal differentiation of the industrial working class, the rise of structural unemployment and underemployment, the expansion of the informal sector both in the core and in the periphery and semi-periphery, the dramatic expansion of the service class, the diffusion of an ideology of consumerism even among classes or countries where such ideology can hardly be translated into some practice of consumption – all these factors combined have contributed to deprive class practices of their intrinsic character or to prevent their translation into class politics. As a result, traditional working-class parties have smoothed out the ideological content of their programmes and turned into catchall parties. The sweeping political transformation of Eastern Europe and the breaking up of the Soviet Union have contributed to 'naturalizing' capitalism and capitalist exploitation, in their most liberal versions to the detriment of their social democratic versions.

Though all these developments have further eroded the conditions upon which the horizontal solidarity called for by the principle of the community might be exercised, it is worth noting that in recent decades this principle has undergone a revival of sorts, not in the state-centred derivative form typical of the second period, but in a new and apparently more autonomous form. This has been a rather ambiguous process covering a wide range of ideological landscapes. On the conservative side, the idea of pushing back the state has basically meant privatization of social welfare, thus creating new fields for capital valorization. But it has also meant a call for the revival of the *Gemeinshaft*, of the traditional, communal networks of mutual help, reciprocity and solidarity as a way of restoring the collective autonomy that has been destroyed or deemed anachronistic by the state provision of individual safety nets in the period of organized capitalism.

On the progressive side, the focus is on the idea that the welfare state, even if it is the most benevolent political form of capitalism, cannot assume the monopoly of welfare provision needed by society. While some currents put the emphasis on the failures of the welfare state[90] – monstrous bureaucracies, market-unchecked inefficiency, rampant

---

[90]   See, in general, Teubner (ed), 1986. Pierson, 1991, has surveyed the most important critiques of the welfare state (or diagnoses of its crisis). First, the exceptionally favourable circumstances for economic growth of the postwar period allowed for a simultaneous expansion of the economy and the welfare state. Such conditions were historically unique, and therefore the welfare state has grown to its limits. The welfare aspirations embodied in the idea of the welfare state can only be met by the transformation of society towards socialism. Secondly, the powers of national governments, national labour movements and nationally based capital – between whom agreements about national welfare states were typically constructed – have been undermined by the greater internationalization and deregulation of the world economy. Thirdly, the postwar welfare state represented a 'historic compromise' between capital and organized labor. Though it served then the interests of both, it is now becoming less and less attractive

corruption, new authoritarianism and social control over dependent citizens, opaque and sometimes unjust solidarity – other currents stress the financial unsustainability of the welfare state, given the paradox that the welfare tasks are most needed in periods (of higher unemployment, for instance) in which the resources are least available (lower tax returns). Both currents, however, coincide in recognizing the limits of the welfare state and hence in calling for a new welfare society.[91] The call is, thus, not backward-looking, to a past that probably never was, but rather forward-looking, to the creation of a third sector, between the state and the market, aimed at organizing socially useful production and reproduction (welfare) through social movements and non-governmental organizations (NGOs) in the name of the new solidarity inspired by the new risks uninsurable by the market or by the postinterventionist state. But even in the most progressive proposals, unacknowledged conservative elements are recurrently smuggled in – for instance, in proposals for a new socialist welfare society it is often forgotten that most of the socially useful work tends to fall on women.

I will now proceed to analyze the impact of these changes on the statism and scientism of law. Since the changes are as much underway as their impact on the legal field, the analysis is necessarily provisional. Indeed, the transitional nature of the current times creates a specific opacity that reflects itself in the analytical debates, for example, by the interference of false debates within real debates.

One of the most sophisticated and consistent debates centres around the critique of the juridification of the social world brought about in the second period of capitalist development. The critique rests on the following general arguments. With the interventionist state (the welfare state) the political instrumentalization of law was promoted to the utmost, thereby reaching its limits, which are also the limits of the welfare state. Such limits signal disfunctions, incongruences, counterproductive results and unintended consequences that surface in the legal field in many different ways.

---

to either. Under these circumstances, the only appropriate strategy for contemporary social democratic movements is to reactivate their traditional commitment to the socialization of the capital investment function, 'bracketed out' in the compromise of the Keynesian welfare state. Fourthly, the welfare state has generated changes in class structures that undermine the class basis of its own continuation. They undermine, for instance, the alliance between the middle classes and the working classes upon which the welfare state was built, thus giving rise to the defection of important sectors of the population from the welfare state. Fifthly, the welfare state was an appropriate institutional means for delivering certain welfare services at a given level of social and economic development. Beyond this level it becomes inappropriate: the expansion of choice/affluence within Western core countries engenders increasing dissatisfaction with state-administered welfare and a greater defection of consumers to market-provided welfare services. Finally, while the welfare state was historically progressive, further progress cannot be generated through conventional welfare policies. This is so because the welfare state is tied to a productivist/economic growth strategy which is no longer consonant with meeting real human needs and securing genuine social welfare. For an excellent feminist critique of the welfare state, see Gordon (ed), 1991. See also Gordon, 1990.

[91]   Rosanvallon, 1981; Ewald, 1986a, 1986b; Lipietz, 1989.

First, they surface as manifestations of the 'colonization' of society. By subjecting contextualized and concrete life histories and ways of life to abstract bureaucratization and monetarization, legal regulation destroys the organic dynamics and the internal patterns of self-production and self-reproduction of the different social spheres – the economy, the family, education and so forth. Though aiming at social integration, it promotes social disintegration. Herein lies, according to Habermas, the dilemmatic structure of the Welfare State.[92] Second, such disfunctions surface as the 'materialization' of law. The other side of the overlegalization of society is the oversocialization of law. While expanding and deepening its regulatory grip on society, law 'is 'captured' by politics or by the regulated subsystems, it is 'politicized', 'economicized', 'pedagogized', etc. with the result that the self-production of its normative elements becomes overstrained'.[93] Finally, the disfunctions result in legal ineffectiveness: to the extent that there is a discrepancy between the internal logic and self-production patterns of law and those of the other spheres of social life to be regulated by law, it is likely or indeed certain that legal regulation will be ineffective or counterproductive.

The specific explanations for these three main limits of legal regulation – what Teubner designates as the 'regulatory trilemma'[94] – vary widely, as do the legal policy recommendations that derive from them. But, in general, the proposed solutions go in the direction of conceiving colonization, materialization and ineffectiveness as outer limits within which new, more strict and more restricted boundaries for legal regulation must be defined, so that law operate effectively and autonomously without losing its character or altering that of the social spheres it regulates. The solutions are variously formulated: proceduralization of law;[95] from regulation to constitution;[96] law as a relational programme or reflexive law;[97] law as critical discussion;[98] from law as medium to law as institution.[99] All of them point to a minimal material orientation as characteristic of a postinstrumental law.

The broadest and most elaborated formulation within this research programme is the conception of law as an autopoietic system.[100] While previous societies were organized according to principles of segmentation or of hierarchy, modern societies are organized according to a principle of functional differentiation. Rather than being structured by

---

[92] Habermas, 1986, p 211; See also Habermas, 1987.
[93] Teubner, 1986, p 311.
[94] Teubner, 1986, p 309.
[95] Wietholter, 1986, p 221. See also Eder, 1986, 1987.
[96] Febbrajo, 1986, p 141.
[97] Teubner, 1986, p 321; Willke, 1986.
[98] Peters, 1986.
[99] Habermas, 1986.
[100] Luhmann, 1984, 1986, 1988a, 1988b; Teubner (ed), 1988, 1988, 1989, 1991, 1992. For differences between Luhmann's and Teubner's conceptions of legal autopoiesis, see Teubner, 1989.

a centre or a functionally dominant system, modern societies are constituted by a variety of sub-systems (law, politics, economy, science, art, religion, and so on), all of them closed, autonomous, self-contained, self-referential and self-modifying, each one with its specific mode of operation and code. Structural correspondence among the sub-systems is basically the chance result of blind co-evolution, while functional interconnections emerging out of the coexistence of such sub-systems in the same society are reduced to forms of 'structural couplings'. Law is one of such sub-systems, a system of legal communications operating with its own binary code: legal/illegal. Law regulates only itself. Law is the environment of other social sub-systems as the latter are the environment of the law. But whatever 'vibrations' or 'perturbations' any system may 'produce' on any other system as a result of their functional interdependence or coexistence, they are irrelevant as long as they are not transformed into autopoietic responses or reactions.

As regards law, this radical Luhmannian version of autopoiesis has been relatively modified by Gunther Teubner.[101] Addressing one of the most controversial aspects of the theory, that of the interdependence among sub-systems, Teubner proposes a modification of the idea of structural coupling.[102] This is not the place to provide a critical analysis of autopoiesis or of autopoietic law as revised by Teubner.[103] But I cannot help pointing out that it is somewhat surprising, after so many decades of extensive and rich research on the sociology of law, to hear Teubner raise an allegedly major and controversial question that in fact, when seen in light of the legal-sociological tradition, is little less than a self-evident state of affairs: 'Is not 'interdiscursivity' in law and society much more dense than mere transitory perturbations could ever produce? And do we not find in the coevolution of law and society significantly more elective affinities than the mere coexistence of structural drift would provide for?'[104]

Only as part of a broader programme of proceduralization and re-autonomization of law will the elaboration on the autopoietic nature of law be object of some critical attention in the following. To my mind, the debate on the proceduralization or reflexiveness of law is to a great extent a false debate. It starts from a conception of the autonomy of law in the liberal state – law as autonomous vis-à-vis the state – that is, in my view, utterly wrong. Indeed, the reduction of law to state law accomplished by the constitutional state in the nineteenth century turned the autonomy of law as autonomy vis-à-vis the state into autonomy inside the state. The autonomy of state law was thereby reduced to its operational specificity as an instrument of state action. The scientism of law as legal positivism was crucial in this process, in that it functioned as a mirror that both reflected and disguised the statism of law. Of course, the changes in state interventionism from the first to the second period had a decisive impact on the operational

---

101   Teubner, 1989, 1991.
102   Teubner, 1992.
103   Among others, Blankenburg, 1984; Jessop, 1990a, pp 320–337.
104   See Teubner, 1992, p 1447.

specificity of law. But, if anything, such changes revealed the adaptability of the legal field to the new conditions of social regulation. This should not be too surprising after all, if we bear in mind that the legal-political paradigm that allowed for legal absolutism and for the global juridification of social life, rather than being an invention of the period of organized capitalism, was indeed laid out in the period of liberal capitalism as the hidden agenda of the constitutional state.

As I tried to show above, the dramatic increase of state interventionism in the welfare state changed the conditions of modern law, both as *state* law and as *scientific* law, but these changes did not signal any general crisis of law in itself. The real crisis occurred in the social fields regulated by law – the family, the workplace, education, health and so on – , when it became clear that the popular classes lacked the political leverage to guarantee the sustainability of the state welfare provisions. The crisis is therefore the crisis of a political form, the welfare state, and not the crisis of a legal form, autonomous law. Indeed, the latter had disappeared much longer ago, with the consolidation of the modern state. As I will try to show below, modern law, as a much broader concept than modern state law, is certainly in crisis, but such a crisis does not derive from the overuse (compared to what?) of modern law by the state, but rather from the historical reduction of its autonomy and efficacy to the autonomy and efficacy of the state. Proceduralization or reflexiveness are therefore being given the Sisyphean task of devolving to modern state law what it never had.

The false debate lies in the assumption that the operational specificity of law is sufficiently 'material' to warrant questioning state law without questioning the state. Of course, such *specificity* raises some *specific* operational problems (for example, justice delays and costs, police brutality, court and prison congestion, underfunded and understaffed legal services, law in books/law in action discrepancy and so on) but beyond the narrow – however important – 'operational' level, such problems are not legal-technical problems. They are, rather, political problems. This is particularly evident in two of the limits of the juridification of social life pointed out by the proceduralists or autopoieticists: ineffectiveness and materialization (overstrain). To be sure, cognitive and organizational resources may be mobilized in alternative institutional strategies that, in view of their different technical quality, may either maximize or minimize the effectiveness of the legal regulation. But the regulatory horizon within which such technical options operate is in no way technically or organizationally determined. It is a political artifact that changes with transformations in the political process. The choice among alternative institutional designs is rarely made solely on technical grounds. Considerations about the amount of resources to be allocated or about the broader or narrower participatory elements in institutional development and in decision making tend to be paramount, and such considerations involve the political process as a whole. Therefore, it is hardly convincing to attribute the ineffectiveness of regulatory law to the fact that the latter 'overreaches the limitations which are built into the regulatory process'.[105] Such limitations do exist,

---

[105]   Teubner, 1986, p 311.

but they are neither structural nor systemic. In other words, in no way are they dictated by the self-referential organization of the regulating or regulated subsystem. They are strategic, and depend, above all, on political agency and on the availability of technical skills. Indeed, one of the major shortcomings of autopoiesis is its exclusive focus on social systems and its total neglect of agency and of the processes and conditions by which agents make a difference.[106]

It is generally recognized that the current wave of deregulation sweeping across the states and the interstate system is highly selective and that, accordingly, deregulation in one area is usually accompanied by reregulation in another area. In such a highly dynamic process the variations in self-referentiality are to be conceived, if at all, as *explananda* rather than as explanations. The political overdetermination of the levels of effectiveness of legal regulation is particularly visible in periods of rapid social and political transformation. As an illustration, I could refer to the wide variation in effectiveness of the new economic, social and labour laws enacted in the aftermath of the Portuguese revolution of 1974.[107] Though the laws remained basically the same in the following years, the pattern of their effectiveness changed in close relation with the changes in the social and political bloc supporting the economic and social reconstruction of post-revolutionary Portugal.

The political overdetermination of the limits of legal regulation applies both in the case of ineffectiveness of the law and in the case of materialization or overstrain of the law. But it applies in a different form. Ineffectiveness is both a legal and an extralegal phenomenon. What it says about law is meant to refer to what law does to the 'world out there'. The 'world out there', be it grounded on a realist or in a constructivist epistemology, is always the other of law. On the contrary, materialization is a legal phenomenon. What it says about law is meant to refer to the internalization by law of the world out there. The symmetry of these two limits is, thus, only apparent. Ineffectiveness has a material extradiscursive existence that can be identified and then variously explained. On the contrary, materialization is an artifact of scientific legal discourse, a mental construction of jurists intended to describe and *at the same time* to explain what, in their view, is the major change of law from the first to the second period of capitalist development. In this case, the limit is a deficit engendered by a postulated excesss – overpoliticization, oversocialization. And as I have been arguing, this excess has been the normal condition of modern law since it was reduced to state law.[108] Why, then, conceive such a normal condition as an excess and not as a deficit? Because the

---

[106] Jessop, 1990a, p 334.

[107] Santos, 1990c, 1993.

[108] Even if social systems are epistemic subjects, as is claimed by autopoieticists, it is hardly conceivable that law be such an epistemic subject as Teubner wants (see, for instance, Teubner, 1989, pp 739–746). The reduction of modern law to state law is but the process by which law relinquishes its subjectivity in favour of the state. The instrumentality of modern state law is thus an original condition, rather than a subsequent adulteration of a previous state of affairs.

subtext of materialization is a conservative or progressive critique of the welfare state as we know (or remember) it. While in the case of ineffectiveness, this critique is made and disguised by interpellating modern law as state law, in the case of materialization, such critique is made and disguised by interpellating modern law as scientific law.

The third limit to the juridification of social life – the colonization of the life-world, as conceptualized by Habermas – is not on an equal footing with the other two limits. While the debate on ineffectiveness and overstrain is for the most part a false debate, the debate on colonization brings forward the real issue raised, though in a mystified form, by the debate on proceduralism and post-interventionism. The real issue is the debate on the welfare state, on its political and social impact, its extent and its form, its development and its sustainability – in sum, its past and its future. The 'colonization of the life-world' is one of the leftist critiques of the welfare state surveyed above.

The critique of the welfare state contained in the ideas of the colonization of the lifeworld is a double one. On the one hand, it says that the welfare state, though appropriate to deliver certain services, is inappropriate to deliver others, particularly those required by highly developed societies. On the other hand, it says that the welfare state, as we know it, is tied up to an economic model based on productivism and economic growth that can no longer meet the real human needs.[109] But neither these nor any of the other critiques can be reconstructed as implying a major role of the legal system in the crisis of the welfare state. It is true that the dominant pattern of welfare provision – bureaucratically organized, based on the dependence-raising clientization of citizens as welfare recipients, geared toward monetarization of social relations and consumerist practices – was brought about by an institutional constellation in which the legal system played a central role. But it is equally true that, under the conditions of the modern capitalist state, had a different pattern been adopted – participatory, self-reliance-maximizing, solidaristic and geared toward mutualistic socially useful production of goods and services – the legal system would have played an equally central role, no matter how dramatically different the operational and organizational legal schemes might have been. The key question is, of course, whether such a pattern of welfare provision could ever be politically or economically viable under capitalism. If so – as an outrageously hypothetical exercise – modern state law would reveal all its regulatory plasticity (which is the other side of its lack of autonomy vis-à-vis the state) and adapt to the alternative project of *Vergesellschaftung* (socialization).

In sum, what is at stake in the overlegalization of social life – or, as I prefer to call it, in the legal Utopia of social engineering through law – is a political evaluation of a specific state form, the welfare state, that emerged in the postwar period in a small minority of countries, ie, the core countries of the world system. Thus, the crisis of the regulatory law says relatively little about the sweeping changes in law, economics and politics that are occurring in the world system as a whole in the current period of transition between

---

[109]   See Pierson, 1991.

regimes of accumulation or, more broadly, as suggested in the following section, between social, political, and cultural paradigms.

What the crisis of the regulatory law says, though in a mystified form, is nonetheless important. It says that, once it is put at the service of the regulatory needs of the constitutional liberal state and of hegemonic capitalism, modern law – which is thereby reduced to scientific, state law – has gradually eliminated the tension between regulation and emancipation that originally lay at its heart. In tracing the long historical process through which such tension was obliterated, I have distinguished three main periods, each one of them representing a different pattern of relations between regulation and emancipation. In the first period, emancipation was sacrificed to the regulatory needs of the states and largely confined to anti-systemic movements. In the second period, state regulation in central countries tried to integrate such anti-systemic emancipatory projects as long as they could be made compatible with capitalist social production and reproduction. Far from being a genuine synthesis between regulation and emancipation, this meant an outright subordination of the emancipatory projects to the regulatory ones. In the third period, this false synthesis has evolved into the reciprocal disintegration of both regulation and emancipation. Far from benefiting from the disintegration of regulation, emancipation – which was transformed in the previous period into the double of regulation – cannot but disintegrate as well. Ultimately, the crisis concerns the reconstructive management of the excesses and deficits of capitalist societies, which, from the nineteenth century on, was entrusted to modern science and, in a subordinate but equally important position, to modern law. The way out of this crisis is the most progressive task of our time. It involves the radical rethinking of both modern science and modern law, a rethinking so radical, indeed, that it may be conceived of as *unthinking*. The unthinking of modern science was hinted at in Chapter One and will not be pursued further here. The unthinking of modern law will be carried out in the next section and in the following chapters.

3   UNTHINKING LAW

3.1   *From the epistemological to the social transition*

The role played by law in the reconstructive management of the excesses and deficits of modern capitalist societies indicates that, although ideally and in the long run the commands of law would be mere emanations of scientific findings on social order and social change, in the short run law's coercive power and potential for normative integration would still be called upon to guarantee that the scientific management of society develop with as little disturbance as possible from social conflict and social rebellion. The paradigmatic crisis of modern science is thus likely to involve also the paradigmatic crisis of modern law.

This does not mean, however, that the conditions of the paradigmatic transition in science are the same – or equally visible, or operate in the same way – as those of the paradigmatic transition in law. This is for two reasons. First, even if it is true that there is a certain epistemological complicity and a circulation of meaning between modern science and modern law as a result of the surrender of the moral-practical rationality of law and ethics to the cognitive-instrumental rationality of science, the symmetry thus produced is limited in its range and derivative in its epistemological content. As a functionally differentiated social field, law has developed a specialized, professionalized self-knowledge that defines itself as scientific (legal science), thus giving rise to the disciplinary ideology I call legal scientism. Legal scientism, I argue, has developed in tandem with legal statism. Legal positivism is the most elaborate version of this ideological development. But the double binding of legal scientism and legal statism also reveals the extent to which the epistemological symmetry with modern science is limited by its efficiency in practice. Legal knowledge was made scientific to maximize the efficacy of law as a non-scientific instrument of social control and social facilitation. This is why Bacon's knowledge/power sequence – the idea that scientific knowledge of nature will bring with it the power to control nature – did not apply in science as it did in law. While in science, knowledge would engender power, in law, from the nineteenth century on, (state) power would engender (professional) knowledge. This explains why legal positivism claimed an operational capability that could not be matched by the knowledge of social order and social change still to be developed by the barely emergent social sciences. This mismatch is indeed endemic to modern state legal culture. From legal positivism to autopoiesis, the ideological assumption has always been that law should ignore as irrelevant the social scientific knowledge of society. Upon such ignorance, according to this view, law should build an epistemological claim of its own ('pure law', 'self-referential law', 'epistemic subjectivity of law').

Here lies the second reason why the theoretical conditions of the paradigmatic transition in modern science do not apply in the same way in the field of law. Since the epistemological claims of law are derivative and, indeed, based on a deficit of scientific knowledge about society, the theoretical conditions of legal knowledge are subordinated to the social conditions of legal power and, in a sense, must be deduced from the latter. The autonomy, universality and generality of the law are premised upon their embeddedness in a concrete state, whose interest – be they conceived as autonomous or as class-bound, as general or particularistic – are served by such features of the law.

But if, for these reasons, law does not unravel the theoretical conditions of the current paradigmatic transition, it may prove to be particularly revealing of the latter's social and political conditions. Moreover, what modern law may reveal about the paradigmatic transition is also likely to reveal the marginality rather than the centrality of law in such a transition. If a paradigmatic transition is, by its very nature, an ample and engaging conversation of humankind, one of its critical aspects may very well be how marginal law has become in such a conversation, both as a voice and as a topic.

One of the major difficulties of the debate on the paradigmatic transition lies in the epistemological status of the knowledge that feeds the debate. This is particularly obvious when the debate is about the epistemological conditions of such transition themselves. Since the formulation of the debate tends to owe more to the outgoing paradigm than to the incoming one, what we say in the debate tends to be less 'transitional' than what we say about the debate. This discrepancy creates obscurity and frustration. A similar though less dilemmatic difficulty tends to develop once the debate is about the social and political conditions of the paradigmatic transition. To begin with, the identification of such conditions is a product of a form of scientific knowledge that is being fundamentally questioned . I am speaking of sociology, economics and political science, the three main social sciences that emerged in the nineteenth century with the aim of uncovering the laws of orderly social change. As Immanuel Wallerstein has recently emphasized, the social construction of these sciences represented the triumph of liberal ideology for which the centrepiece of social process was the careful delimitation of three spheres of activity: those related to the market (economics), those related to the state (political science), and those related to all activities not immediately related either to the state or to the market, that is, personal life, everyday life, family, church, community, crime, and so on (sociology).[110] Since they were developed to consolidate the then-unproblematic hegemony of the paradigm of modernity, these sciences were not likely to provide – either as an epistemological project or as a social project – reliable guidance in the analysis of processes of social transformation that admittedly will transcend the boundaries of modernity. It is thus wise to follow Wallerstein's advice, which urges us to unthink the social sciences.[111] The same must be done in relation to law. But before undertaking such a task, the social and political conditions of the paradigmatic transition must be carefully considered.

I argued in Chapter One that the final crisis of modernity is more visible as an epistemological crisis (a crisis of modern science) than as a social crisis (a crisis of world capitalism). The historically contingent coupling of modernity with capitalism underlies the four main readings of social transformation in our time. According to the first reading, capitalism and liberalism have triumphed and their triumph means the highest possible realization of modernity – the end of history *à la* Fukuyama, ie, the victory of centrist liberal democracy. According to the second reading, modernity is an as yet incomplete project and there is in it the intellectual and political potential to conceive and bring about a non-capitalist future -here I am thinking of Habermas, probably Jameson, conventional Western Marxism, and leftist social democracy. According to the third reading, modernity has collapsed at the feet of capitalism, whose sociocultural reproduction and expansion will assume, from now on, a postmodern form – celebratory postmodernism – *à la* Daniel Bell, Lyotard, Baudrillard, Vatimo, Lipovetski, etc. Finally, according to the fourth reading, modernity is collapsing as an epistemological and cultural project and such a collapse opens up a range of possible futures for society, a non-capitalist, eco-socialist future being one of them – this view

---

[110]   Wallerstein, 1991a, p 19. To these three social sciences, we should add anthropology and orientalism, the two social sciences in charge of the study of the colonial other, whether 'savage' or 'civilized'.

[111]   Wallerstein, 1991a.

is what I have called oppositional postmodernism. My contention is that the last reading captures the perspectives for social transformation at the beginning of the millennium better than any other. The oppositional postmodern knowledge that I have been calling for aims at unveiling, inventing or promoting the progressive alternatives that such a transformation may entail. It is an intellectual Utopia that makes a political Utopia possible.

It is not my purpose to outline here in detail the terms of the possible transition between social paradigms. It is usually believed that paradigmatic transitions last for a long time – several decades, often more than a century. This was the case of the scientific revolution or of the transition from feudalism to capitalism. Such transitions occur when the internal contradictions of the dominant paradigm cannot be managed with recourse to the mechanisms for conflict management and structural adjustment developed by the paradigm in question. In normal times, such internal contradictions manifest themselves as excesses and deficits, and the tensions, the crises and the conflicts ensuing therefrom are resolved by the intellectual, institutional and organizational resources of the paradigm. When this ceases to occur, the cumulative effect of unresolved excesses and deficits engenders a global delegitimation of the adjustment resources, and the internal contradictions become socially visible and are eventually converted into objects of social and political struggle. When the internal contradictions become part of purposive social struggle they lose their structural rigidity, and the type of determinism that the paradigm has generated is drastically attenuated. That is why paradigmatic transitions, once set in motion, are indeterminate, move towards uncertain outcomes and open up to alternative futures. That is why they also expand the 'free will' enormously, that is to say, the capacity for social innovation and transformation.[112] Moreover, such active social consciousness is reinforced by the fact that in periods of paradigmatic transition, similarly to what occurs in Prigogine's states of bifurcation, small changes may produce large systemic fluctuations – contrary to what occurs in normal, sub-paradigmatic times or crisis, in which big changes usually produce very small systemic fluctuations.

The time of paradigmatic transition is a highly contested time, mainly because it comprises multiple temporalities. To begin with, since paradigmatic conflicts – ie, internal contradictions that cannot be dealt with by the dominant paradigm and thus point to its supersession – coexist with sub-paradigmatic conflicts – ie, excesses and deficits that can be solved with the tools of the dominant paradigm – the transition is an inherently contested phenomenon. The temporal framework of those for whom there are only sub-paradigmatic conflicts is by force narrower than that of those for whom such conflicts are surface manifestations of an underlying paradigmatic conflict. Even those who agree that there is a paradigmatic transition may disagree as to the identification of the outgoing paradigm or as to the nature, the duration and the direction of the transition to come. Moreover, because the secular trends, which are the temporality of transition, have to be reduced to the time of the human life-cycle, if the paradigmatic struggles are to

---

[112]   See also Wallerstein, 1991a, p 254.

be efficacious it may be necessary to conceptualize such struggles as paradigmatic (internal contradictions) but to participate in them as if they were sub-paradigmatic (excesses and deficits). The paradigmatic struggle is thus a Utopia whose efficacy may lie in the intellectual and political resources it provides to the sub-paradigmatic struggles. In my view, this accounts for the opacity but also for the vibrancy, for the misunderstandings but also for unexpected convergences, that characterize the paradigmatic transition, both as an intellectual and as a social and political enterprise.

I subscribe to a much broader conception of the paradigmatic transition. According to it, the transition we are undergoing is not only (or not so much) between narrowly defined modes of production but between forms of sociability in the widest sense, including economic, social, political and cultural dimensions. The intertwining of the socio-cultural project of modernity with capitalist development in the nineteenth century conferred on capitalism a social and cultural thickness that reached far beyond the economic relations of production. This fact was somewhat overlooked by Marx and, for that reason, his vision of the paradigmatic transition shares with liberalism more than he would ever be prepared to admit. Marx shared with liberalism:[113] the belief in the liberating potential of modern science; the dualism nature/society that underlies modern science and the epistemological claims grounded therein; the idea of a linear evolutionary process that will finally come to an end (though for Marx the end was still to come), beyond capitalism or industrial society (Spencer), or the positive age (Comte) or organic solidarity (Durkheim); the idea of progress, even though discontinuous (through revolutions); the belief in continuous technological development and infinite growth; and the idea of capitalism as a progressive civilizing factor, no matter how brutal the oppression of the colonies and the destruction of nature might have been.

In the broader perspective I am putting forward, the period of paradigmatic transition we are undergoing started with the epistemological collapse of modern science, and will eventually call into question all the preceding views. For this reason it will entail a civilizational transformation. Though owing much to Marxism, this conception of the paradigmatic transition considers the conventional Marxist transition as sub-paradigmatic in the end, ie, as remaining within the confines of the paradigm of modernity.

I submit, therefore, that a discussion centred around a paradigmatic reading of modern law – ie, one that reads the excesses and deficits of the latter as indicative of the need

---

[113]   Wallerstein (1991a) has recently emphasized the complicities between liberalism and Marxism. In a lecture on 'The Ideas of Natural Law and Humanity in World Politics', delivered in Berlin in 1922, the German theologian Troeltsch commented that whenever the socialists felt compelled to enunciate principles, they generally resorted to the idea of 'a totally unhistorical passion for revolution, to be achieved in the name of Humanity and Equality'. And he added: '[W]hen that happens, socialistic principles become practically indistinguishable, in spite of the Socialist challenge to the bourgeoisie, from the bourgeois philosophy of the west; and the individualistic and utilitarian basis of that philosophy, in particular, is simply adopted wholesale' (1934, p 222).

for a new legal paradigm – together with that of modern science, will highlight the terms and possible directions of the transition toward a new social paradigm. In the following I will enumerate the main topics of such a discussion, which will be elaborated upon in the following chapters.

3.2 The state or the world system?

The confluence of the promises of modernity with the productive capacities of capitalist development – a confluence brought about by liberalism – was made possible by conceiving of social transformation as an *ensemble* of national processes, occurring in national societies, and promoted or controlled by nation-states. The nationalization of social change and the symmetry between society and state were as basic to the social sciences emerging in the nineteenth century as to the changes affecting modern law around the same time.

Today, it begins to be widely accepted that this conception of social transformation misrepresented the dynamics of capitalist development in fundamental ways. The unprecedented intensification of transnational interactions in the last two decades has strengthened the alternative conception put forward by historians and social scientists, such as Fernand Braudel and Immanuel Wallerstein, for whom the national societies had to be understood as parts of a much larger historical system whose internal division of labour and internal dynamics accounted for the social transformation identified at the level of national societies. Wallerstein, in particular, has convincingly argued that we live in a world economy, the modern capitalist world system, which emerged around 1500 and which, by its inner logic, expanded to cover the entire globe, absorbing in the process all existing 'minisystems' and 'world empires'. By the late nineteenth century – at the time of the climax of nationalist visions of society – there existed, for the first time ever, only one historical system on the globe.[114]

Once the world system becomes the privileged unit of analysis, the understanding of its global logic, development and crises is crucial to understanding local manifestations as they occur throughout the interstate system. For instance, the welfare state – as much as its crisis – is one of such manifestations, and one of its most striking features, usually neglected in nation-state centred analysis, is that this political form developed in a tiny portion of the interstate system and within a relatively short time-band (the cyclical rhythm). Assuming that the world system is the privileged unit of modern historical development and, hence, the privileged unit of analysis, the debate on the paradigmatic transition must take place at the level of the world system. This means, on the one hand, that the paradigmatic crisis is unfolding without being much affected by national solutions for its local manifestations; on the other, that any of the possible outcomes of the transition will be generated at the level of the world system. Herein lies the first topic

---

[114]   Wallerstein, 1991a, p 248.

of a paradigmatic debate on law: the absorption of modern law in the modern state was a contingent historical process which, like any other historical process, had a beginning and will have an end.

The constitutional state of the nineteenth century was conceived as the perfect machine of social engineering. Its formal, mechanical and artificial constitution endowed it with levels of strength and plasticity that were not achieved by any previous political entity. Its strength was both external and internal. It was exercised externally by military and economic strength against foreign states and competitors in the worldwide accumulation of capital. And it was exercised internally basically by the law against the internal enemies of normal and orderly social change. Its plasticity derived from virtually unlimited institutional and legal manipulability, and lay in the state's capacity to adjudicate between both normal and abnormal means and normal and abnormal ends of social change. These striking capabilities made the state into the natural unit – homogeneous spaciality and homogeneous temporality – of social change and social intelligibility. This naturalization of the state entailed the naturalization of modern law as state law.

The conception of the world system as the space-time of historical capitalism helps to unveil the ideological and pragmatic strategies underlying these twin processes of naturalization of the state and its law. The constitutional state of the nineteenth century existed in an interstate system in which the effective sovereignty was a function of the position of each particular state in the hierarchically structured interstate system. Thus, both the strength and the plasticity of the state were variables rather than structural features. While core countries tended to be externally and internally strong but externally rigid and internally plastic, peripheral countries tended to be both externally and internally weak but externally plastic and internally rigid. This meant that democracy, which combined internal and external strength with internal plasticity, was unevenly distributed throughout the world system. Between tendentially democratic core countries and tendentially undemocratic peripheral countries, there existed a layer of semi-peripheral states, inherently unstable, bouncing between democracy and dictatorship. As the specific naturalization of the state varied across the world system, so did the naturalization of law. Moreover, they varied not only across space but also across time, as illustrated by the political and legal metamorphoses occurring in core countries in the three periods of capitalist development referred to above.

In practice the state never achieved the monopoly of law. The working of the world system, operating at the suprastate level, developed its own systemic law, which was superimposed on the national law of the individual states across the world system. Moreover, alongside this suprastate law, different forms of infrastate law continued to exist or indeed emerged anew: local legal orders with or without a territorial base, governing specific clusters of social relations and interacting with the state law in different ways, even if denied the quality of law by the state law. This state of affairs had, thus, a double face. On the one hand, different legal orders circulated in society, articulating in different ways with the state law. The latter, however important and even central, was just one of the legal orders integrating the legal constellation of bourgeois societies. The specific constellations varied across the world system, and they were very different in core and in peripheral states, but they always included the combinations of state, suprastate and infrastate legal orders. On the other hand, the existence of such multi-layered legal constellations was denied by a political fiat that attributed the quality of law exclusively to state law.

Both facts (the sociological existence of a constellation of laws and its denial by political fiat) are equally crucial to understanding the relative operational specificity, strength and plasticity of modern state law in different national societies, as I hope to show in the following chapters. For now, the key point to bear in mind is that the unthinking of law in a period of paradigmatic transition must start by uncoupling law from the state. Such an uncoupling will serve a twofold purpose. First, it will show that not only was law never monopolized by the state, but also that the state never let itself be monopolized by its own law. Much beyond the doctrine of *raison d'etat*, the constitutional state operated on a routine basis by both legal and illegal means. The specific mix of legality and illegality (as defined by the state's own legal order) varied across the different areas of state action. It varied, above all, according to the position of the state in the world system. Secondly, the arbitrary denial of the plurality of legal orders eliminated or drastically reduced the emancipatory potential of modern law. All these points will be elaborated upon in the following chapters.

Two cautionary notes are, however, in order at this point. First, the uncoupling of law from the nation-state is a necessary, not a sufficient condition for the recuperation of the emancipatory potential of law. Indeed, as important as the uncoupling as such is the direction that it will take. Secondly, such an uncoupling is relative, that is, it does not collide with the recognition of the centrality of state law in the interstate system. What it questions is the symbolic expansion of such centrality since the nineteenth century: from representing the central role played by state law in a constellation of different legal orders to representing the exclusive role of state law in a monolithic legal order exclusively ruled by the state. This symbolic expansion has been so widely and deeply accepted by legal-political knowledge and by common sense that questioning it amounts to an unthinking of law.

As in the discussion of the other topics or dimensions of the paradigmatic transition of modern law, the unthinking of law will be initially guided by the suppressed or marginalized traditions of modernity. This will require some archeological excavation. In the case of the uncoupling of law from the state I will draw on the transnational legal culture of modernity dealt with in the first sections of this chapter.

3.3   Recoupling law with the polity?

The legal-political uncoupling of the national state from the international society was historically concomitant with the uncoupling of the state, as a separate entity, from the whole of national society. Indeed, as the nation was made symmetrical with the state, the state – turned into a formal power structure separated from both the ruler and the ruled – was uncoupled from the nation. This ideological and political transformation can be traced back to the difference between the Romantic and the Hegelian conception of the nation. While the Romantic conception of the nation as a 'grand historic individuality' ignored the practical imperatives that the attempt to make nation and state coincide would impose on the idea of nation,[115] in Hegel the nation is the 'rational' counterpart of the state, the social basis of its legitimacy and strength. For it to be the basis for the empowerment of the state, the nation must be dispossessed of any power other than the power of the state *over* it. This dialectics of empowerment-disempowerment was congealed in the state/civil society dualism that was analytically reconstructed by the nineteenth-century social sciences.

Of course, the two sides of this dualism were never congealed. For instance, there has been a debate on the precise boundaries of civil society – on whether, for example, the economy was or was not part of civil society.[116] On the other hand, as we have already seen, the state underwent profound changes from the period of liberal capitalism to the period of disorganized capitalism. Moreover, the terms of the distinction between state and civil society also suffered an evolution that has been analyzed by Keane in its four overlapping stages.[117] What was congealed and hidden was the matrix of the dualism, the idea that the two entities, though reciprocally externalized, belonged to each other and could not be thought of as separate entities – civil society was the other of the state, and vice versa. To my mind, this dualism has no substance today beyond the fact that it is a widely accepted illusion. I will offer in Chapter Seven a conceptual alternative, but at this point I will limit myself to summarizing my argument briefly. From the perspective of the world system, this dualism was from the beginning a gross misrepresentation of political reality, particularly so in the postwar period, when most of the colonies became independent states. If in some core countries it could be reasonably argued that civil society had created its state, in the periphery (ie, the former colonies), and even in the semi-periphery, the opposite had actually occurred. In the latter case civil society was thus an even more artificial entity than the state itself. The multiple social processes that were left out of a civil society, so narrowly defined – such as ethnic divisions, local cultures, legal pluralism and so on – were the gauge of the weakness of the peripheral and semi-peripheral states in the world system. A political theory based on such a circumscribed part of the global historical process could not but serve the imperialist hierarchies of the interstate system.

[115]   Smith, 1988, pp 174–208; Guidieri and Pellizzi, 1988, p 10.
[116]   Keane, 1988a, 1988b; Jessop, 1990a, pp 338–369; see also Pierson, 1991, p 205.
[117]   Keane, 1988a.

The state/civil society dichotomy obfuscated the nature of power relations in society, and, indeed, law contributed decisively to that effect. The conception of state power as the exclusive legal-political form of power did not imply that there were no other forms of power circulating in society, but it converted them into factic powers with no autonomous legal base and, in any case, without any political character. If one looks at the actual power relations of early nineteenth-century societies, the reduction of political power to state power is less than obvious. And yet, it allowed for the shifting of the global emancipatory promises of modernity to the promise of state democratization, and, for that reason, it was adopted as the only imaginable solution for the power struggles of the time. From then on, a more or less democratic state power could coexist with more or less despotic forms of social power without the democratic nature of the political system being questioned. Similarly, the more or less democratic law of the state could coexist with more or less despotic forms of non-state law without the democratic nature of the official legal system being questioned.

The state/civil society dichotomy set in motion a dynamic relation between the two concepts that can be characterized, in general, as the relentless reciprocal absorption of one by the other. Marx saw very early on that civil society could reproduce itself in the form of the state – in this lay the capitalist nature of the state – but his reliance on the liberal conception of the state as an artificial contrivance prevented him from seeing that, conversely, the state could also reproduce itself in the form of civil society. Only much later did Gramsci identify this other side of the reciprocal absorption. Gramsci elaborated on this phenomenon through his concept of hegemony and, in particular, through the concept of polity or of the integral state (*lo stato integrate*), the combination of 'civil society' and 'political society', which encompassed for him the global political constellation of capitalist societies.[118]

The reciprocal absorption entails two different processes – the reproduction of the civil society in the form of the state, and the reproduction of the state in the form of civil society. What, to my mind, characterizes the capitalist core state in the period of disorganized capitalism is its expansion in the form of civil society. Therefore, most of the recent proposals to empower the civil society are fundamentally flawed. To empower civil society as a process of disempowering the state amounts to forgetting that state and civil society are two faces of the same political constellation, that the state reaches far beyond its formal apparatuses, and finally that the political relations operating outside those formal apparatuses might indeed be more despotic than those operating inside them.

Once reduced to the legal dimension of the state, law was trapped from the beginning in this play of mirrors. Since the constitutional state was bound by law, the latter could be effectively used against the state, as was assumed by the conception of civil and political rights. To this extent, law represented the empowerment of civil society vis-à-vis the state. But, on the other hand, such exteriority of law vis-à-vis the state was indeed a state effect whose efficacy required that all the other legal orders circulating in society and really exterior to the state be denied

---

[118]   Gramsci, 1971.

existence. Moreover, the fundamental distinction within state law, the one between private law and public law, was both the reflection and the subversion of the state/civil society dualism. Private law, though supposed to regulate social relations in civil society according to the lawful interests of the parties, was as much an expression of state power as public law. In order to address the political dilemmas that thus prevent modern law from being unequivocally anchored in the polity (national, local and transnational polity), it is imperative to abandon the state/civil society framework, to invent new analytical tools that permit us to address the global political constellation of contemporary capitalist societies without subterfuges, and to develop more efficacious political strategies than those generated by the state/civil society dualism. This task will be undertaken in Chapter Seven.

It is worth emphasizing again that the intellectual Utopia of unthinking conceptual orthodoxies, so deeply rooted in our political common sense, may gain from unveiling and re-evaluating some cultural traditions of modernity, which were developed when the tension between regulation and emancipation was lively, and which were suppressed or subverted later on. The semantic history of the concept of the state may be very helpful in this respect.

Skinner has eloquently shown that the concept of the state as an abstract entity, separated both from the ruler and the ruled, is the result of a long conceptual history that goes back to the reception of Roman law in the twelfth and thirteenth centuries.[119] The term state, *status*, meant originally a state of affairs, the condition of a realm or commonwealth. Concepts of classical origin, such as *status reipublicae* or *status civitatum*, were used throughout medieval Europe in advice books for magistrates and in the 'mirrors for princes' literature as referring to the duties of magistrates to maintain their cities in a good or prosperous state (the *optimus status reipublicae*, as in Cicero or Seneca). The state is, then, the community or whole, the well-ordered political life. In the Renaissance republicanism of the Italian city-states, the state comes to be identified with the idea of self-government, Dante's *stato franco*, a state or condition of civil liberty.[120] The republican tradition is particularly relevant for our purposes, since the republican theorists, though they distinguish the state from those who control it, make no distinction between the powers of the state and the powers of its citizens.

3.4 Legal Utopia or Utopian pragmatism?

The transformation of the modern idea of progress into the idea of infinite and ever expanding repetition of bourgeois society in the nineteenth century created what we could call a dilemma of the future: all futures were possible but all of them had to be contained in the same capitalist future. Both the social sciences and the law were called upon to solve this dilemma, and the slogans of 'order and progress' and of 'normal

---

[119] Skinner, 1989, pp 90–131.
[120] Skinner, 1989, p 106.

change' embodied the thrust of the solutions to be found. The social sciences would discover the regularities and the causes of social transformation, and the law would transform them into effective legal regulations. However, because the social sciences were still to be developed, their logical priority had to yield to their pragmatic subordination to the unpostponable imperatives of social regulation. Halfway between regulatory knowledge (order) and regulatory ignorance (chaos), the state law was available both as an *ersatz* of science and as a pre-understanding of the scientific knowledge of society still to be developed. This double availability of the law of the state was at the roots of the latter's conversion into a Utopia of its own. Paraphrasing Jacques Ellul, we could say that state law, as much as technology, ceased to advance towards anything, and it was, rather, pushed from behind, not tolerating any halt, and indeed making possible a large number of solutions for which there were no problems.[121]

This legal Utopia was the engine behind normal change, the idea that social change was a continuous process proceeding by piecemeal and gradual transformations sanctioned by the state law, itself changing continuously, gradually and legally. Concerning its legal dimension, the social credibility of normal change lay in two factors. First, normal change covered a wide variety of legal transformations that were so diversified and fragmented that it was impossible to identify a general trend or a global direction. This opacity was the other side of the plasticity of the state law mentioned above. Secondly, the effectiveness of law could be not only of an instrumental but also of a symbolic nature.[122] This duality enabled state law to be a normal change of its own and relatively independent of the fate of the specific 'normal' change it was intended to produce in social life. Thus, eventual failures of the instrumental effectiveness of law could be compensated for, at least in part, by the symbolic effectiveness of law.

This legal construction of normal change entailed two major political implications. First, due to the opacity of the global direction, the same reformist policies could be reasonably defended by some social groups as anticapitalist policies and, by other groups, as capitalist policies. This had a decisive impact on the patterns of political mobilization, particularly in the core countries of the world system. For decades the labour movement fought for reforms that the hegemonic sectors within the movement considered as socialist, but that the power bloc considered as part of a win-win game whose end result would be the expansion of capitalism. The second implication was that this legal construction would suit the interstate system as a whole. Its global opacity and its operational plasticity equipped it to serve the most diverse accumulation and hegemonic strategies in the core as well as in the periphery and semi-periphery of the world system. Legal rules and institutions or even entire legal systems could be exported from core states to peripheral states. Such legal transplants were in some cases the result of colonial or postcolonial imposition and, in others, the result of voluntary or semi-voluntary

---

[121]   Ellul, 1965, p 89.
[122]   On the distinction between instrumental and symbolic effectiveness, see M Edelman, 1964; L Friedman, 1975.

adoption. In still other cases, modern (Western) law would share the official (state) legal field with other local legal traditions. However, the new state, modern legality tended to become dominant in the regulation of interactions among state bureaucrats and among business people across the world system.

The expansion of this legal model of normal change throughout the world system was in itself an historical process as complex, conflictual and non-linear as any other historical process. While in core countries reformism – the political form of normal change – became hegemonic after World War I, in the periphery and semiperiphery it disputed with social revolution the hegemony over the political field throughout the twentieth century. In the 1960s, the 'Law and Development' or 'Law and Modernization' 'movement'[123] – imposed or 'strongly recommended' to peripheral and semiperipheral states by the core states – highlighted the global scale of this dispute, an historical dispute that only in recent years, with the collapse of the Soviet Union, seems to have been decided – for the time being at least – in favour of reformism.

Curiously enough, this final victory of reformism throughout the world system seems to have occurred simultaneously with its apparently final crisis in core countries, as shown above in my analysis of the third period of capitalist development, the period of disorganized capitalism. This fact alone recommends that we analyze in greater detail this pattern of normal change based on a legal Utopia managed by the national state. Table 1 shows the main features of this pattern. The state is conceived of as an ensemble of three strategies: accumulation, hegemony and trust strategies, which constitute the vertical axis of the table. By virtue of the first strategy, the state guarantees the conditions for private accumulation – through the protection of private property and the rules of the market – that are necessary for it to survive in the context of a capitalist economy. The strategy of hegemony seeks to galvanize popular support for state actions through institutions – eg, forms of political participation – and symbols – eg, the neutrality of the rule of law – that endow such actions with legitimacy. Trust strategies are the set of policies by which the state manages social risks and protects citizens from the potentially destabilizing impact that such risks may have upon their life. Each strategy comprises different dimensions, represented by the horizontal axis of the table. Each of them covers a specific social field, relies for that purpose on a certain form of knowledge, and is targeted at a specific type of subjectivity. Each of the three strategies also mobilizes certain aspects of the legal fields in order to further some social values by activating specific dichotomous codes. Finally, each strategy is supposed to contribute to normal change in its own way. Normal change is viewed here as a mixture of social repetition – the maintenance of the status quo – and social amelioration – the transformation of social conditions. Since this table is, to a great extent, self-explanatory, I will confine myself to a few general comments.

---

[123]   Trubek and Galanter, 1974; Gardner, 1980; Rodríguez, 2001a.

TABLE 1   PATTERN OF NORMAL CHANGE (STATE STRATEGIES IN THE INTERSTATE SYSTEM)

Dimensions	Social Field	Knowledge	Subjectivity	Legal Field	Social Value	Normal Change	
						Repetition	Amelioration
Strategies							
Accumulation	Competitive commodification of labour, products and services	Science as a productive force	Social class, primordial identities (gender, ethnicity)	Contract/property law, economic law, labour law, immigration law, regulatory law	Liberalism; code: market furthering/market hindering	Sustained accumulation	Economic growth
Hegemony I	Political participation and representation	Science as a discourse of truth	Citizenship	Constitutional law; administrative law; political system law	Democracy; code: democratic/undemocratic	Bourgeois rule	Expansion of rights
II	Social consumption		Citizenship, consumership, masses	Welfare law, regulatory law, labour law	Welfarism, consumerism code: fair/unfair	Social peace	Social Equity
III	Cultural consumption, mass information, mass communication and mass education		Citizenship, consumership, masses	Media law, education, and information law	Literacy and loyalty; code: loyal/disloyal	Cultural conformism	Knowledge distribution

Trust	Risk in international relations	Science as a national resource	Nationality	International law	Nationalism; code: war/peace	National security; sovereignty	Improving interstate position
I	Risk in international relations	Science as a national resource			Nationalism; code: war/peace	National security; sovereignty	Improving interstate position
II	Risk in social relations; disputes, crimes, accidents			Criminal law, administration of justice, torts, contract law	Legalism; codes: Legal/illegal; fair/unfair; relevant/irrelevant	Legal security; law and order	Expanding and improving conflict resolution
III	Risk in technological and environmental relations; disputes, crimes, accidents		Citizenship Nationality, citizenship	Environmental law, torts, criminal law	Expertism; codes safe/unsafe; foreseeable/unforeseeable	Expert security	Increasing expertise

Though centred on the activities of the national states, this pattern of normal change is in fact a transnational one that, from the nineteenth century on, provided the logic for state action throughout the interstate system – no matter how 'impurely' or selectively such logic may in practice have operated. State activity is a continuous flux of actions and non-actions, decisions and non-decisions, discourses and silences, and only at an aggregate level is it possible to identify the specific combination of strategies that presides over state activity at a given point in time. The combination varies from state to state and from period to period across the interstate system. Marxist analyses of the state usually focus exclusively on the accumulation and the hegemony strategies. In my view, however, trust strategies are equally important. Indeed, I venture to say that nowadays they tend to be the most stately and autonomous of all state strategies. This is so because they allow the state – which is only a part of society – to act genuinely in the name of society as a whole and to hold the general responsibility for maintaining the integrity of the latter.[124] The centrality of trust strategies lies also in the fact that their competent deployment generates the institutional resources upon which depend the efficacy and credibility of both accumulation and hegemony strategies. Since no attention has been given to trust strategies, a brief comment on them is in order.

Niklas Luhmann[125] and Anthony Giddens[126] have recently drawn our attention to the nature and role of trust in modernity. According to Giddens, the dynamism of modernity derives from having separated time from space thus dramatically changing the conditions under which time and space are organized so as to connect presence and absence. The time-space separation has led to the disembedding of social systems, or, in Giddens's words, to 'the 'lifting out' of social relations from local contexts of interaction and their restructuring across indefinite spans of time-space'.[127] Since the disembedding mechanisms tend to be translated into abstract systems, the consequences of this process for the development of modern institutions are paramount. Among such abstract systems, Giddens sorts out the expert systems – for instance, the environmental impact evaluation system. Expert systems are disembedding mechanisms because they remove social relations from the immediacy of context. Since trust is always related to presence in time and space, modernity has dramatically changed the conditions of trust and trustworthiness. Trust is defined 'as a confidence in the reliability of a person or system, regarding a given set of outcomes or events, where that confidence expresses a faith in the probity or love of another, or in the correctness of abstract principles (technical knowledge)'.[128] Because modernity has replaced the concept of *fortuna* (destiny) with the concept of risk, the context of trust has thereby expanded tremendously: it covers the risks and dangers of human action, from now on freed from divine injunction and endowed with a vastly increased transformative potential. Giddens concludes that 'the

---

[124] On the paradox of the state, though being a part, acting as if it were the society in its entirety, see Jessop, 1990a, p 360.
[125] Luhmann, 1979, 1988a, 1988b.
[126] Giddens, 1991a, 1991b.
[127] Giddens, 1991a, p 21.
[128] Giddens, 1991a, p 34. See also 1991b, 108-143.

nature of modern institutions is deeply bound up with the mechanisms of trust in abstract systems, especially trust in expert systems'.[129]

In my view, through its legal system the modern state has become the central guarantor of the type of massive trust needed in modern society. Moreover, state-produced trust reaches far beyond the expert systems into the immense variety of risk management situations as they develop out of social relations among strangers (individuals, groups, foreign states) or among estranged acquaintances or intimates. The more vast the scope of risk-engendering relations, the greater the dependence on state trust and state risk management. The trust in expert systems is premised upon the availability of the state to monitor their activities and to manage the risks connected with their failures or with the unintended consequences of their operations.

The combined deployment of accumulation, hegemony and trust strategies guarantees the reproduction of normal change. Normal change is a pattern of social transformation based on repetition and amelioration. These two dimensions are inextricably intertwined, as the sustainability of any of them depends on the other: there is no repetition without amelioration and there is no amelioration without repetition. The rhythm of change is determined by the unequal weight of repetition factors and amelioration factors, but, in order to be normal, social change must comprise both types of factors. Thus, normal change is paradoxical: to the extent that the prevailing conditions of any given social field are ameliorated, they do not repeat themselves, and vice versa. This paradox, far from being a paralyzing factor, is indeed the inexhaustible source of energy of normal change itself. To begin with, the fact that normal change is both fragmented and deprived of global direction allows for the same individual social process to be viewed by some social groups as repetition and by others as amelioration. On the other hand, the paradox of normal change allows for different temporalities – ie, the coexistence of different conceptions of time and of social processes unfolding at different rhythms to coexist within the processes of change. Since repetition does not exist without amelioration, and vice versa, the nature of the dominant temporalities is fully indeterminate. In the short run, both repetition trends and amelioration trends can be equally viewed as short-term phenomena or as short-term manifestations of long-term tendencies. Furthermore, only in the long run and retrospectively is it possible to evaluate which of the conflicting views was correct, and to determine whether the long-term trend leaned over to repetition or, inversely, to amelioration. Since the political debate – even when it revolves around long-run trends – always takes place in the short run, the indeterminacy of the different temporalities reinforces the inevitability of normal change, thereby furthering its legitimacy.

This pattern of normal change is based on the following presuppositions. First, no matter how diverse its application from state to state, the pattern of normal change is the transnational political logic of the interstate system. Secondly, the national steering

---

[129]   Giddens, 1991a, p 83.

mechanisms developed and deployed by the state are available and are efficacious throughout the national territory, whose boundaries are also guaranteed by the state. Thirdly, the financial capacity of the state to implement all of its strategies depends above all on the sustainability of economic growth, and hence on the success of the accumulation strategies. Fourthly, human aspirations and the well-being of the people can be fulfilled or guaranteed by mass-produced products and services designed according to a commodity form, even if not distributed by commodity markets. Fifthly, the risks and dangers whose management is the object of trust strategies occur rarely, and are predominantly small-scale or medium-scale.

The analyses in the preceding sections of this chapter and in Chapter One show the extent to which these presuppositions are being fundamentally questioned in the current period of paradigmatic transition. In view of the increasing and seemingly irreversible polarization and inequality between the North and the South, this pattern of normal change has ceased to capture any of the significant transformations the world system is undergoing at the present time. Both in the core and in the periphery of the world system the national steering mechanisms are being eroded in the face of the intensification of transnational transactions and interactions. The unsustainability, on a global scale, of commodified consumerist social welfare, combined with the aggravation of social inequalities, the transformation of cultural values in a post-materialist direction, the intensification of violence and risk both in the core and the semi-periphery and the periphery, and the increased social visibility of forms of oppression up until now kept hidden – oppression of women, children, cultural and ethnic identities, animals and nature – have all contributed to questioning, at a fundamental level, both the quality and the quantity of life engendered by normal change. In fact, normal change is increasingly found to be abnormal. Finally, as a consequence of the growing discrepancy between the capacity to act and the capacity to predict, the risks, particularly those related to high-consequence technological and environmental interventions, have increased dramatically, both in terms of scale and of frequency.

This unprecedented dimension of risk and danger has undermined the credibility of the trust provided by the state. On the one hand, some of the risks and dangers have been globalized. Their control is far beyond the capabilities of individual states, and the interstate system was not, in any case, designed to compensate for the regulatory failures of individual states with enhanced, concerted international action. On the other hand, the increased social awareness of risks and dangers has shown the structural limitations of the legal mechanisms used by the state to manage them – criteria such as standing, liability, relevant evidence, damages; inaccessible or else expensive, selective, disenchanted and slow court systems, and so forth.

The cumulative effect of these adjustment failures on the 'mechanics' of normal change is enormous. They undermine the amelioration side of social change, thereby straining the equation repetition-amelioration to the point of collapse. Since repetition is not sustainable without amelioration, normal change turns into normal stagnation or normal decay. The

3M SelfCheck™ System

Customer name: Watson, Craig

Title: Toward a new legal common sense : law, globalization, and emancipation / Boaventura de Sousa Santos.
ID: 30114013250405
Due: 19-October-13 00:00

Total items: 1
12/10/2013 11:43

Thank you for using the
3M SelfCheck™ System.

already much-diminished tension between regulation (repetition) and emancipation (amelioration) suffers a double collapse: as the last shred of modern emancipation vanishes, modern regulation becomes unsustainable. It is thus by sheer inertia that the pattern of normal change seems to reach full hegemony today across the interstate system. A posthumous hegemony, so to speak.

A new paradigm of social transformation is therefore needed. Since normal change rejected revolution as a credible pattern of social transformation, a good starting point – and only a starting point – may be to re-examine the relations between modern law and revolution. While in the preceding section I called for the uncoupling of law from the state, I now call for the recoupling of law with revolution. The two procedures are, indeed, to be carried out in tandem, if the oppositional postmodern reconstruction of law and politics is to be achieved. As will be argued in the following chapters, the uncoupling of law and state may as likely lead to reactionary outcomes as to progressive ones. To strengthen the probability of the latter, the recoupling of law with revolution must also be done as a starting point. It may seem strange to call for the recoupling of law with revolution at a time in which revolution has been thrown into the dustbin of history. My argument is that revolution has been rejected not because it has ceased to be necessary, but because the dominant forms it has assumed since the nineteenth century have themselves betrayed the necessity of revolution. A glimpse at the injustices and oppressions in the world system suffices to conclude that the emancipatory agenda of revolution is today more necessary than ever. The recoupling of law with revolution that I am calling for has to do with this agenda, not with the specific political forms of revolutionary movements in the twentieth century. As with the preceding topics of a paradigmatic discussion of law, the recoupling of law with revolution also requires some excavation into the suppressed or marginalized traditions of modernity.

We are so used to seeing law and revolution as antipodal and antagonistic concepts that the idea of approximating, let alone recoupling them, may sound little less than preposterous. As a matter of fact, the law-revolution polarity is a remarkably recent phenomenon. Harold Berman has forcefully argued that the mutual embeddedness of law and revolution has been at the roots of the modern Western legal tradition since the twelfth century. Berman sets out to correct what he calls 'the ideological bias in favor of incremental change',[130] which has dominated the study of the origins of the Western legal tradition and which, in his view, has blinded us to the first modern revolution. The first modern revolution, he argues, occurred within the Church of Rome between the eleventh and the twelfth centuries, and out of it emerged the first body of modern law, the canon law. Ever since then, violent revolutions have periodically transformed the historical legal tradition in profound ways, and sent it in new directions. The reason why this phenomenon has eluded us lies in the nature of law itself. Indeed, 'a radical transformation of a legal system is a paradoxical thing since one of the fundamental

---

[130] H Berman, 1983, p 15.

purposes of law is to provide stability and continuity'.[131] Whenever revolutionary legal change happens, something must be done to prevent it from happening again. So that the new law be firmly established, it will be considered to have changed not only in response to new circumstances, but also according to some historical pattern. This explains why 'the myth of a return to an earlier time is, in fact, the hallmark of all the European revolutions'.[132] Once established, the new, revolutionary law must be protected against the danger of another discontinuity; further changes must be confined to incremental changes.

The Western legal tradition has therefore been marked by recurrent revolutions out of which new systems of law have emerged which, once established, negate or minimize the occurrence or the impact of the previous revolution. By this process all the major discontinuities in the Western legal tradition remain within this tradition. According to Berman, the term revolution refers not only to initial violent outbreak by which a new system is introduced, but also to the entire period required for that system to take root, a process that may last for more than one generation. Berman distinguishes six major or 'total' revolutions in the modern tradition: the Russian Revolution, the French Revolution, the American Revolution, the English Revolution (1640–1688), the Protestant Reformation (1517–1555) and the Papal Revolution (1075–1122). In all these revolutions, the fundamental changes in law were interlocked with radical changes in other spheres of social life, but in all cases the new law represented an effort to supersede the failure of the old law in responding adequately to changes that were taking place in society before the revolutionary outbreak. In his view, this failure to anticipate fundamental changes and to incorporate them in time is due to an inherent contradiction within the Western legal tradition, ie, the contradiction between its two basic purposes, that of preserving order and that of pursuing justice.[133]

This reconstruction of the modern law tradition, most elucidating in itself, leads Berman to a gloomy, apocalyptic and rather conservative diagnosis of our time. According to him, in the twentieth century we have been undergoing a revolution of a new kind, which indeed breaks in fundamental ways with the revolutionary tradition of the West. The overwhelming change in all fields of law – in contract and property law as well as in torts and criminal law, in private law as well as in public law – has overturned the complex relation between law and revolution in existence since the eleventh century. While in the past the revolutionary changes in law have always remained within the Western legal tradition and have therefore been transcended by this tradition, today the opposite is occurring as law becomes wholly subordinate to revolution. According to Berman, this amounts to nothing less than the global breakdown of the Western legal tradition. It is not difficult to see here a variation of the recent debates on the autonomy of law and legal autopoiesis. Indeed, the autonomy of law is a key prescriptive text in Berman's

---

[131]   H Berman, 1983, p 16.
[132]   H Berman, 1983, p 15.
[133]   H Berman, 1983, p 21.

historical narrative, and so is the idea of a transcendental justice or natural law, swallowed up by the voracious legal instrumentalism of the twentieth century.

What must be retained from Berman's analysis is his emphasis on the complex, rich, and contradictory relation between law and revolution as the founding characteristic of modern law. To put it in terms of my own conceptual framework, what the historical research undertaken by Berman demonstrates is the existence of a tension between regulation and emancipation as the driving force of modern law that has spanned several centuries. What Berman fails to see is that this tension – which commenced in the twelfth century – collapsed, or was drastically reduced, not in the post-1914 period, as he suggests, but rather after the French Revolution, when the liberal state started the historical process of reducing the proportions of modernity to those of capitalism. The French Revolution was indeed the last revolution jointly accomplished by law and revolution, for it was conducted in the name of a law whose enormous regulatory potential could only come to life in boundary-transcending, emancipatory social practices. In this light, the Russian Revolution is not in continuity with the long modern law tradition, as Berman affirms, but rather symbolizes its breakdown.

The pattern of normal change developed by the post-revolutionary state of the nineteenth century is not, in my view, just another example of the way the new revolutionary law tries to minimize the impact of the previous revolution and to defend itself against a future revolution. It is, rather, the final example. The immense organizational, political and cultural resources concentrated on the state create an unprecedented institutional contrivance capable of extricating law from revolution once and for all. As law became state law, revolution became lawless. Through its hegemonic strategies, the liberal state purports to convert normal change into the exhilarating beginning of the modern legal tradition, whereas, in fact, it accomplishes its final breakdown. From now on we will be living in a postrevolutionary period that – since it declared itself final – becomes also counterrevolutionary. From now on revolution will be totally subordinated to law, and not the opposite, as Berman believes. This explains why the Russian Revolution, rather than standing in continuity with the French Revolution, is 'forced' to try a new beginning, a model of social transformation that completely subordinates law to revolution.

If liberal political and legal theory had expelled revolution from the legal constellation, Marxism, particularly in its Marxist-Leninist version, expelled law from the revolutionary constellation. If it highlights the sharp contrast between liberalism and Marxism, this symmetrical opposition also betrays the underlying complicity between the two. In both liberalism and Marxism, the dialectical relation between law and revolution is lost. At the most, we might say that it stands frozen on one of its legs by political fiat. When Lenin and, later on, Wyschinsky say that 'law is one category of the political', they are in fact doing nothing more than pushing the liberal conception of law to its utmost, since for both of them, as indeed for liberal theory, politics (and hence, law) is the realm of the state. It is not the Russian Revolution but rather the postrevolutionary state of the nineteenth century that brings the modern Western legal tradition to a collapse. The Russian Revolution is a symptom or an effect of that collapse, not its cause.

This preliminary excavation of legal modernity shows how deep we must dig – deeper than Marxism and liberalism – in order to unearth among the rubble the fragments of the modern dialectics of law and revolution we are heirs to.

4   CONCLUSION

In this chapter I have argued that the paradigmatic transition is a broad historical process that is unfolding in multiple social, political and cultural dimensions. Though most visible at the epistemological level – as a final crisis of modern science – it is as an historical process that the paradigmatic transition becomes a topic of utmost sociological relevance. I have also argued that modern law offers a strategic vantage point from which to assess the sociology of the transition, in view of its intimate articulation with modern science in the overall process of rationalization of social life promised by modernity. The task of rationalization, conceived as a dynamic and tense equilibrium between regulation and emancipation, was entrusted to science. The shortcomings of science – such as insufficient knowledge or unintended consequences of knowledge – were to be resolved in the future by a better science, and in the meantime by law. As a second-rate rationalizer of social life, law, in the form of state law, entered a period of infinite growth similar to the one desired for science and for social change in general.

I have also argued that the dramatic intensification and accumulation of the negative consequences of this social paradigm have led us to believe that there is something inherently wrong with the form adopted by law to maximize their efficacy in bringing about the convergence of sociocultural modernity with capitalism. In this process, the matricial tension between regulation and emancipation that was constitutive of both modern science and modern law was made to disappear, in different ways but with the same general outcome: the absorption of emancipation into regulation. In this chapter I tried to show how this came about in the case of modern law. After briefly reviewing the legal transformations that occurred in the three periods of capitalist development (liberal, organized and disorganized capitalism), I analyzed some of the recent debates on the 'crisis of law', only to find them lacking in their ability to identify the real roots of the contemporary discontent with law.

To offer an alternative view, I then argued that the 'crisis of law' is part of a much broader and deeper crisis of the hegemonic pattern of social transformation in course since the early nineteenth century: the pattern of so-called normal change. I briefly characterized this pattern and the central role played in it by state law as a legal Utopia, and set out to show how and why the pattern of normal change is undergoing so deep a crisis that it cannot be solved by the adjustment mechanisms available within the parameters of normal change. I was then led to argue that we are entering a period of paradigmatic transition from modern sociability to a new postmodern sociability, whose profile is hardly visible or even predictable. A paradigmatic transition is a long process characterized by an 'abnormal' suspension of social determinations, which gives rise to new dangers, risks and insecurities, but also enhanced opportunities for innovation, creativity and moral choice.

In a period of paradigmatic transition, old knowledge is a poor guide. We need a new knowledge instead. We need a legal science of turbulence, sensitive to the new intellectual and political demands for more realistic and efficacious Utopias than those we have lived by in the recent past. The new constellation of meaning does not begin from scratch. It has much to gain from excavating into the past in search of suppressed or marginal intellectual and political traditions, whose authenticity emerges in a new light as their suppression and marginalization is 'denaturalized' and even made arbitrary. Above all, the new knowledge is premised upon the unthinking of the old and still-hegemonic legal knowledge, the knowledge that will not admit the existence of the paradigmatic crisis before all progressive or hopeful solutions have been discarded or made impossible. Unthinking is epistemologically complex because it involves both thorough but not nihilistic destruction and discontinuous but not arbitrary reconstruction. Moreover, because undertaken in the wake of modern science and modern law, the destructive side of the unthinking must be disciplinary – that is, it must be carried out within law as a scientific discipline and within each one of the social sciences – , while its constructive side must be non-disciplinary: unthinking amounts to a new cultural synthesis. Finally, not all of the unthinking tasks can be undertaken at a paradigmatic level of inquiry, that is, one that decisively breaks with the dominant paradigm of knowledge in general and of legal knowledge in particular. Some of them may involve detailed empirical analysis to be carried out in genuine but disloyal compliance with the old knowledge, that is to say, at a sub-paradigmatic level. The compliance will be genuine, because the research will be conducted according to the theoretical and technical rules of the old knowledge, but it will also be disloyal, because it will be conducted as if nothing new or intelligible could be thought or imagined beyond the old knowledge.

In this chapter I have selected three areas in which the unthinking of law seems most important and urgent: (1) national state versus world system; (2) state-civil society versus Gramsci's *stato integrale* (the polity); (3) legal Utopia versus Utopian pragmatism. These three topics were presented as dilemmas because they were indeed so perceived at the beginning of the nineteenth century. The constitutional state saw itself endowed with a powerful resource – the exclusive, unified and universal legal system – to confront such dilemmas efficiently, that is, in such a way as to guarantee the self-reproduction of the state itself. The first dilemma was confronted by the dualism national-law/international-law. The second dilemma was confronted by the dualism private-law/public-law. And the third dilemma was confronted by a pattern of normal change premised upon the infinite availability of law. I then analyzed the structural flaws or acts of occultation apparent in these legal constructions. The first one omitted the fact that, in view of the nature of the interstate system, international law would inherently be of low 'legal quality' when compared with national law. The second one neglected the fact that private law was as public as public law, thus making the dualism coincide in its collapse. Finally, the third legal construction was forgetful of the fact that, once isolated from revolution, law could 'normalize' any type of transformation in any conceivable direction, including social stagnation and social decay.

In the effort to unthink law out of these dilemmas and out of the intellectual and political impasses they have led to, I engaged in some digging into modern tradition in search of alternative memories of the future. As far as the first dilemma goes, I found them in the long-lived transnational and local legal culture of modernity. As to the second dilemma, I found them in alternative conceptual traditions of the state, in particular in the Renaissance republican concept of the state as the overall well-being of self-governed society (*optimus status reipublicae*). Finally, concerning the third dilemma, I found the alternative memories of the future in the mutual embeddedness of law and revolution in a long tradition of modernity abruptly interrupted after the French Revolution.

These excavations were no more than the beginning of the process of unthinking law. In the following chapters this process will be continued, both in its destructive and in its reconstructive aspects. And, needless to say, it will be continued after the last chapter by myself and, I hope, by others. The next four chapters will deal mainly with the first dilemma, that is, with the unthinking of the state and of state law as a unit of analysis. The following two chapters (Chapters Seven and Eight) will take on mainly the second dilemma, and will present an alternative to those theoretical constructions based on the state/civil society dualism. Finally, Chapter Nine will concentrate on the third dilemma so as to suggest new constellations of political meaning in which law is allowed to recuperate its emancipatory potential. The general thrust of this analytical trajectory is to regain for law and politics the tension between regulation and emancipation whose origins, unfolding and collapse in modernity I have sketched in this chapter.

Chapter 3

Legal Plurality and the Time-Spaces of Law: the Local, the National and the Global

I INTRODUCTION

The relative uncoupling of law from the state that I called for in Chapter Two means that the nation-state, far from being the exclusive or the natural time-space of law, is only one among others. The nation-state has been the most central time-space of law for the last two hundred years, particularly in the core countries of the world system. However, its centrality only became possible because the other two time-spaces, the local and the global, were formally declared non-existent by the hegemonic liberal political theory. In this chapter I theorize briefly these time-spaces in order to prepare the ground for Chapters Four, Five and Six, where, on the basis of empirical research, I focus on the local and the global time-spaces and on their interrelations with the nation-state time-space. My purpose in this and the following three chapters is threefold. First, to show that the legal field in contemporary societies and in the world system as a whole is a far more complex and richer landscape than has been assumed by liberal political theory. Secondly, I set out to show that such a legal field is a constellation of different legalities (and illegalities) operating in local, national and global time-spaces. Finally, I argue that, thus conceived, law has both a regulatory or even repressive potential and an emancipatory potential, the latter being much greater than the model of normal change has ever postulated. The way law's potential evolves, whether towards regulation or emancipation, has nothing to do with the autonomy or self-reflexivity of the law, but rather with the political mobilization of competing social forces.

This conception of the legal field means that every social-legal action is framed by three time-spaces, one of them being dominant and thereby providing the general profile of the action. Without consideration of other time-spaces, present in however recessive a form, and without consideration of their articulations with the dominant time-space, socio-legal action cannot be fully understood. In this and the following three chapters I present some empirical studies that illustrate this sociological conception of the legal field. In the final chapters of the book a theoretical reconstruction is offered. The legal field analyzed in Chapter Four is predominantly local, but its articulations with the national time-space are central and are analyzed in great detail. In Chapters Five and Six the legal field is predominantly global. In either case, the linkages with the other time-spaces are made clear.

2   THE STRUCTURAL COMPONENTS OF LAW

The sociological conception of the legal field presented here calls for a concept of law that is broad and flexible enough to capture the sociolegal dynamics in such different frameworks of time and space. The concept of law put forward by liberal political theory – the equation between nation, state and law – and elaborated upon by nineteenth-century and twentieth-century legal positivism is too narrow for our purposes, since it recognizes only one of the time-spaces: the national one. Drawing on legal anthropological literature and on the anti-positivistic philosophy of law of the turn of the nineteenth century, I conceive law as a body of regularized procedures and normative standards that is considered justiciable – ie, susceptible of being enforced by a judicial authority – in a given group and contributes to the creation and prevention of disputes, as well as to their settlement through an argumentative discourse coupled with the threat of force. A full explanation of this concept will be given in the next chapter. Here I want to draw attention to what I consider to be the three structural components of law: rhetoric, bureaucracy and violence. Rhetoric is not only a type of knowledge, but also a communication form and a decision-making strategy based on persuasion or conviction through the mobilization of the argumentative potential of accepted verbal and non-verbal sequences and artifacts. Rhetoric as a structural component of law is present, for example, in such legal practices as the amicable settlement of a dispute and retributive (as opposed to repressive) criminal justice. Bureaucracy is here conceived as a communication form and a decision making strategy based on authoritative impositions through the mobilization of the demonstrative potential of regularized procedures and normative standards. Bureaucracy is the dominant component of state law and is present in such legal operations as the adjudication of cases by courts and the passing of laws by legislative authorities. Finally, violence is a communication form and a decision-making strategy based on the threat of physical force. Violence can be used by state actors – eg, the police – to enforce state law or by illegal groups – eg, mafias – to enforce the code that regulates their activities.

These structural components are not fixed entities; they vary internally and in their reciprocal articulations. Legal fields are constellations of rhetoric, bureaucracy and violence. They are distinguished by the distinct articulations of rhetoric, bureaucracy and violence that characterize them. However, a complex legal field, such as modern state law, may comprise different articulations in different sub-fields. For instance, in criminal law the legal constellation may be dominated by violence; in administrative law, by bureaucracy; and in family law, by rhetoric. Indeed, the plasticity of modern state law referred to in Chapter Two is made possible above all by the diversity of structural articulations it may encompass. Comparing legal fields in terms of the different articulations of structural components that constitute each field may allow for enlightening sociological analyses of law. To contribute to this comparative socio-legal analysis, I distinguish three major types of articulation between rhetoric, bureaucracy and violence: co-variation, geopolitical combination and structural interpenetration.

Co-variation refers to the quantitative correlation among structural components in different legal fields. In Chapter Four I describe a legal field – the law of Pasargada, a Brazilian shanty town – in which rhetoric is the dominant component, while bureaucracy and violence are both recessive. This stands in stark contrast with state law, where bureaucracy and violence predominate to the detriment of rhetoric. Indeed, the secular trend (of the last two hundred years) has been toward a gradual retraction of rhetoric and a gradual expansion of bureaucracy and violence. The fact that violence has grown in tandem with bureaucracy has contributed to the obfuscation of the violent character of the state legal field. However complex and internally differentiated, the global legal fields analyzed in Chapters Five and Six – from *lex mercatoria* to the international law of indigenous peoples – seem to point to new structural configurations. Though they are, in general, characterized by low levels of bureaucracy, they combine them in some cases with high levels of rhetoric and low levels of violence and, in other cases, with high levels of violence and low levels of rhetoric. The low levels of bureaucracy in global legal fields are explained by the fact that the mass of institutions developed by the nation-state has no counterpart at the global or interstate level. The twin growth of bureaucracy and violence, which up until recently characterized the national time-space of the legal field, seems thus to be a process taking place primarily in this time-space. However, as Baxi has pointed out,[1] the 'global war on terrorism' launched by the US after the attacks of 11 September 2002, dramatically increased the use of unilateral violence as a means for global conflict resolution. The concomitant refusal of the US to join the International Criminal Court – ie, precisely the institution embodying an international criminal justice system based on bureaucracy and rhetoric rather than unilateral violence – further stresses the rise of violence as a structural component of the global legal field.

Expanding on these findings and on those of Chapters Four and Six, I suggest as a general hypothesis the following relationships: the higher the level of bureaucratic institutionalization of juridical production, the smaller the rhetorical space of the legal discourse, and vice versa; and the more powerful the instruments of violence in the service of juridical production, the smaller the rhetorical space of the legal discourse, and vice versa. Concerning the first correlation, violence may operate as an intervening variable in the relationships between bureaucracy and rhetoric, in which case low levels of bureaucracy may combine with low levels of rhetoric if the levels of violence are high.

[1]   Baxi, 2002a.

Geopolitical combination is a form of articulation centred on the internal distribution of rhetoric, bureaucracy and violence in a given legal field. While co-variation refers to patterns of articulation among structural components in general, geo-political combination focuses on the articulation among different patterns within a given legal field. Different articulations generate different forms of political domination. According to the dominant component of a specific articulation, we may have political domination based on voluntary adherence by persuasion or conviction, on demonstrative strategies leading to authoritative impositions, or, finally, on violent exercise of power. In complex legal fields, different forms of domination may be found in different areas of legal-political action. Elsewhere I have analyzed the 'movement' toward 'informalization of the administration of justice' in the late 1970s and 1980s along these lines, arguing that the increase in rhetoric – and the reciprocal decrease in bureaucracy and violence – in the legal areas selected for informalization signaled a change of political domination, which, however, should be geopolitically evaluated in relation to other legal areas – such as criminal law, labour law and welfare law – in which an increase of violence or of violence together with bureaucracy to the detriment of rhetoric could be identified.[2]

The third major form of articulation among rhetoric, bureaucracy and violence is *structural interpenetration.* This is the most complex form of articulation, because it consists of the presence and reproduction of a given dominant component inside a dominated one. Its complexity lies not only in that it involves the analysis of multiple qualitative processes, but also in that it is only unequivocally debatable in long historical periods. The relations between oral and written culture provide an illustration. It has been established that these two forms of cultural production have different structural characteristics.[3] For instance, oral culture is centred on the conservation (stocking) of knowledge, while written culture is centred on innovation. Oral culture is fully collectivized, while written culture allows for individualization. Oral culture's basic unit is the formula, while written culture's basic unit is the word. If we look at modern cultural history in the light of these distinctions, it becomes clear that until the fifteenth century European culture, and hence European legal culture, was predominantly oral in nature. From then on, written culture gradually expanded and oral culture retracted. But from the fifteenth century to the eighteenth century, it is apparent that the structure of written culture had still to be consolidated, and that in its operation it was permeated by the internal logic of oral culture. In other words, people then wrote as they spoke, and I think this can be detected in the legal writing of the time. In the second phase, from the eighteenth century until the first decades of the twentieth, the written word dominated our culture. But then radio and audio-visual mass media rediscovered the word's sound and we entered a third period: a period of secondary orality. However, this revival of oral culture is different from the previous period of oral culture, in that the structures of the written culture permeate, penetrate and contaminate the new oral culture. In other words, we speak as we write. If we think of modern state law in this context, my argument is that

---

[2]   Santos, 1980a, pp 379–397.
[3]   Ong, 1971, 1977.

rhetoric is not only quantitatively reduced but also internally and qualitatively 'contaminated' or 'infiltrated' by the dominant bureaucracy and violence. In my above-mentioned analysis of the informal justice movement and with reference to bureaucracy, I analyzed the types of arguments that tended to be more persuasive in the informal settings in order to see if, for instance, arguments and modes of reasoning that depended on bureaucratic logic and discourse were being advanced in a non-bureaucratic setting. The aim was to find out to what extent bureaucracy (and possibly also violence) was expanding within the form of rhetoric in reforms that aimed at the informalization of justice.[4]

3   LEGAL PLURALITY

The broad concept of law adopted here, together with the idea that law operates in three different time-spaces, implies that modern societies are, in socio-legal terms, legal formations or legal constellations. Rather than being ordered by a single legal system, modern societies are regulated by a plurality of legal orders, interrelated and socially distributed in the social field in different ways. This raises the issue of legal pluralism. Legal pluralism concerns the idea that more than one legal system operate in a single political unit. The discussion of this issue has been one of the core debates in the sociology and anthropology of law as well as, though in a different way, in the philosophy of law. The existence of a core debate about legal pluralism is significant in and of itself – particularly for the purposes of the rethinking of law put forth in this book – and deserves to be analyzed. Before attempting that, however, I would like to state at the outset that this debate, probably no less than other core debates in other disciplines, is partially a false debate or at least an inadequately formulated one. To begin with, the designation 'legal pluralism' has a definite normative connotation, in that whatever is designated by it must be good because it is pluralistic or, in any case, better than whatever is its non pluralistic counterpart. This connotation may be a source of error and should therefore be avoided. To my mind, there is nothing inherently good, progressive, or emancipatory about 'legal pluralism'. Indeed, there are instances of legal pluralism that are quite reactionary. Suffice it to mention here the highly repressive and violent legal orders established by armed groups – eg, paramilitary forces in connivance with repressive states – in the territories under their control. For this reason I prefer to speak of a plurality of legal orders, instead of legal pluralism, whenever I want to address the issues that have been traditionally associated with the latter expression.

The inadequacy of 'legal pluralism' can be traced back to its origin as a scientific concept. It originated at the end of the nineteenth century in the European anti-positivistic legal philosophy as a reaction against the reduction of law to state law carried out by the codification movement and elaborated upon by legal positivism.[5] It was a reaction

---

4   Santos, 1980a, p 387.
5   Ehrlich, 1936; Bobbio, 1942; Del Vecchio, 1957; Carbonnier, 1979.

against state legal centralism or exclusivism, based on the claim that, in reality, state law was far from exclusive, and in some instances was not even central in the normative ordering of social life. Looking at socio-legal life in European societies at the time of the codification movement, it becomes clear that the reduction of law to state law was, more than anything else, the result of a political fiat, and that empirical reality was on the side of the 'legal pluralists'. However, with the consolidation and expansion of the liberal constitutional state, and with the conversion of the legal positivist hypothesis into a hegemonic (ie, commonsensical) thesis about law, state legal centralism or exclusivism disappeared as such and became law *tout court*. From then on the legal pluralists were to carry the burden of proof of defining law other than as state law. As legal positivism added some analytical thickness to its original political orientation, legal pluralism saw its analytical claims entangled in a politics of definition of law.

This mixture of analytical and political considerations was carried over, though often unnoticed, when legal pluralism became a core debate in the sociology and anthropology of law, from the 1960s onwards.[6] Because of the scientific positivism that dominated these disciplines, the analytical claims of legal pluralism were given absolute predominance, while its political claims were swept under the rug. In other words, legal pluralism became an analytical device that allowed for thicker descriptions of law in action, while the political challenge it mounted against a state whose legitimacy is based on the monopoly of the law was sidelined. In a curious twist, scientific positivism confronted legal pluralism by neutralizing the latter's political claims in the name of alternative claims that, though equally political in nature, could be convincingly argued as analytical, particularly so in a political context in which legal positivism was at its weakest, that is, in the context of the colonial and post-colonial societies. The fact that this complex intertwining of analytical and political claims was rarely acknowledged has obscured the debate till today.[7] The paradigmatic debate of modern law requires that such an acknowledgment be fully made and indeed conceived as one of the premises of the debate. Moreover, in a paradigmatic debate, the political nature of many claims that seem to be purely analytical must be brought to the foreground.

In my view, a broad conception of law and the idea of a plurality of legal orders coexisting in different ways in contemporary societies serve the analytical needs of a cultural political strategy aimed at revealing the full range of social regulation made possible by modern law (once reduced to state law) as well as the emancipatory potential of law, once it is reconceptualized in oppositional postmodern terms. This means, in the abstract, that there is nothing progressive about the idea of legal plurality. The same applies to the different structural components of law. In particular it applies to rhetoric. The progressive

---

[6]   See, among others, Nader, 1969; Hooker, 1975; Moore, 1978; Galanter, 1981; Macaulay, 1983; Fitzpatrick, 1983; Griffiths, 1986; Merry, 1988; Starr and Collier, 1989; Chiba, 1989; Benda-Beckmann, 1988, 1991; Tamanaha, 1993, 2001.

[7]   Starr and Collier, 1989; Benda-Beckmann, 1991; Tamanaha, 1993. A similar critique of legal positivism has been raised in recent studies on legal pluralism and post-colonialism. See Darian-Smith and Fitzpatrick, 1999; Randeria, 2002.

content of rhetoric depends on the nature of the rhetorical audience, on the types of *topoi,* on the social distribution of reasonable arguments, on the relation between persuasion and conviction, on the extent to which the arguments are infiltrated by bureaucracy or violence, and so on. Furthermore, the conception of a plurality of legal orders advanced here tries to counteract the romantic bias of much legal pluralistic thinking by reconstructing the legal field theoretically in such a way as to avoid equating simplistically all legal orders coexisting in a given geopolitical unit, and particularly to avoid denying the centrality of state law in modern sociolegal fields. I therefore strongly reject as careless misrepresentation of my position Teubner's reference to my research of Pasargada law (see Chapter Four) to illustrate his assertion that '[p]ostmodern jurists love legal pluralism. They do not care about the law of the centralized state with its universalist aspirations'.[8] On the contrary, Twining interprets my position correctly when he says that I 'poin[t] out that there is a tendency to romanticise pluralism, especially in the context of reactions against codification, centralisation and claims to monopoly of state power. I agree with [Santos] that 'there is nothing inherently good, progressive, or emancipatory about 'legal pluralism'. Indeed, there are instances of legal pluralism that are quite reactionary'.[9]

It may be asked: Why should these competing or complementary forms of social ordering – from informal dispute-processing mechanisms implemented by neighbourhood associations to commercial practices, codes enforced by non-state armed groups, and so on – be designated as law and not rather as 'rule systems', 'private governments', and so on? Posed in these terms, this question can only be answered by another question: Why not? Why should the case of law be different from the case of religion, art or medicine? To take the last example, it is generally accepted that, side by side with the official, professionalized, pharmochemical, allopathic medicine, other forms of medicine circulate in society: traditional, herbal, community-based, magical, non-Western medicines. Why should the designation of medicine be restricted to the first type of medicine, the only one recognized as such by the national health system? Clearly, a politics of definition is at work here, and its working should be fully unveiled and dealt with in its own terms.

For all its inadequacies and obscurities, legal pluralism has been, no doubt, one of the core debates in the sociology of law and in the anthropology of law. In my view, there are four metatheoretical conditions for a given issue to become a core debate, and they are all met by the debate on legal pluralism. First, the issue must be broad enough and with an inherent plasticity that enables it to include new dimensions as the debate develops. Secondly, the issue must have vague boundaries so that what belongs and what does not belong to the debate is never very clear. Indeed, to know what is being debated is part of the debate. Thirdly, in the field of sociology, such an issue must allow for a macro-micro link; more specifically, it must allow for an easy articulation between

---

8 Teubner, 1992, p 1443.
9 Twining, 2000, pp 86–87.

empirical work and theoretical development. Fourthly, through such an issue it must be possible to open a debate with core debates of other disciplines, so that each discipline in question can keep its identity in interdisciplinary and even transdisciplinary debates.

It is not my purpose here to analyze in detail the extent to which the debate on legal pluralism has fulfilled these metatheoretical conditions. I will limit myself to some interpretative notes as required by the argument expounded in the following chapters. As to the first condition, the debate on legal pluralism is a broad one, and has broadened further with time. In her overview of the literature on the topic, Sally Merry distinguishes two periods in this debate: legal pluralism within the colonial and post-colonial context, and legal pluralism in modern capitalist societies. The second period is clearly an expansion of the debate in the first period.[10] I argue in Chapters Five and Six that we are now entering a third period, the period of postmodern legal plurality. What distinguishes this period from the two previous ones is that, whereas before the debate was on local, infrastate legal orders coexisting within the same national time-space, now it is on suprastate, global legal orders coexisting in the world system with both state and infrastate legal orders. Chapter Five is dedicated to an overview of this new context of legal plurality, and Chapter Six analyzes in detail a concrete case of interface between global and national legal fields – ie, judicial activism and current programmes of court reform both as global trends and as national processes.

But defining the debate according to periods does not mean that any new period cancels out the previous ones. Actually, the three periods are nothing more than the three main contexts or traditions within which the debate continues to be pursued today by different or even by the same social scientists. The following chapters provide a good illustration. If the analysis of Pasargada law in Chapter Four can be said to belong to the second period of the debate, the analysis of the globalization of the legal field in Chapters Five and Six pertains to the third period, while in Chapter Eight some references are made to a study I conducted in the Cape Verde Islands whose political context concerns the first period of the debate. Elsewhere I have dealt with at length with plural legal orders operating in conditions of extreme violence and social and territorial fragmentation, where evidence of legal plurality of the three periods or contexts abounds. In particular, based on wide-ranging research projects on legal plurality and justice in Colombia[11] and Mozambique[12] in the late 1990s, I have shown that in such countries legal plurality exists in complex articulations of infrastate and suprastate legal systems. In Colombia legal plurality outside and within the state combines to produce both highly repressive forms of regulation – as those enforced by illegal armed groups in the territories

---

[10]   Sally Merry, 1988. The author confines her periodization to the debate in the sociology and anthropology of law as we know them today. As I mentioned above, the first context of the debate was European legal philosophy (and also legal sociology) at the turn of the century.

[11]   Santos and García-Villegas, 2001.

[12]   Santos and Trindade, 2002.

they control or by the army through dirty-war tactics – and opportunities for social emancipation – as the legal struggle of the U'wa indigenous people against oil drilling in their sacred territory bears witness.[13] In Mozambique, the global law of structural adjustment imposed by the multilateral financial agencies has weakened the state thereby opening the space for the re-emergence and strengthening of the local legal systems controlled by the traditional authorities.The superposition of the different contexts of the debate on the plurality of legal orders bears witness to the breadth of the debate that thus unequivocally fulfills the first metatheoretical condition of a core debate.

As to the second condition for an issue to become the object of a core debate – the vagueness of boundaries – what I said above about the ambiguity and inadequacy of the expression 'legal pluralism' already fulfills this condition. From the very beginning, in the European legal philosophy of the turn of the century, the debate on the plurality of legal orders has been entangled with the Sisyphean task of defining law. And while in the first (social scientific) period of the debate it was relatively easy – though not as easy as for some time was believed – to distinguish between the main legal orders in place – colonial law, on the one hand, and the indigenous law, on the other – in the second period such a distinction became much more problematic, and it is even more so in the third period we are going through, as the heated and endless debates on the legal nature of *lex mercatoria* show.[14] In this last period the vagueness of the boundaries of the debate has, however, less to do with the question of an adequate definition of law – increasingly perceived as sterile – than with the identification of the three time-spaces of the legal field – the local, the national and the global – and of the complex interrelations among them.[15] Some of the complex analytical demands involved here are explained in Chapter Five.

The last two metatheoretical conditions – the potential for macro-micro links and the potential for interdisciplinary work – are closely related, and have been only very partially fulfilled in the debate on the plurality of legal orders up to now. The following chapters are intended to raise the debate to the level at which both its macro-micro potential and its interdisciplinary potential may be explored. The fact that this debate challenges liberal political theory – though how radically is open to question – has not been given due recognition so far. As a result, its 'almost obvious' interconnection with issues such as state legitimation, forms of social power, legal subjectivities, socio-economic, racial, gender and cultural inequalities, models of democracy, politics of rights and so on has not been elaborated. On the contrary, a narrow intellectual scholarship on legal pluralism has crystallized that has contributed to reproducing the disciplinary isolationism (and even marginality) of both the sociology of law and the anthropology of law. At the roots

---

[13]   Sánchez, 2001; Arenas, 2001.
[14]   See, lastly, Muchlinski, 1997.
[15]   This is particularly visible in the literature on the legal plurality associated with the development of European law. See, for instance, Delmas-Marty, 2002; Bercusson, 1997.

of such an isolationism is the fact that both disciplines have tended, in general, to take the state as a given – that is to say, as a non-problematic entity thus studying law as a social rather than as a political phenomenon. Indeed, the so-called autonomy of law, so dear to legal theory, was made possible only by the conversion of the state into an 'absent structure'. This kind of conceptualization has often been complemented by an active anti-statist stance that is quite visible in much of the legal pluralist scholarship. In Chapter Five I show the extent to which the nation-state has been challenged in recent times as a privileged and unified unit of political initiative, and decentered by the emergence of both powerful infrastate political processes and powerful suprastate processes. However, the analysis of this challenge of state centrism will not benefit from any romantic or pseudoradical anti-state stance. The nation-state and the interstate system are the central political forms of the capitalist world system, and they will probably remain so for the foreseeable future. What has happened, however, is that they have become an inherently contested terrain, and this is the central new fact on which the analysis must focus: the state and the interstate system as complex social fields in which state and non-state, local and global social relations interact, merge and conflict in dynamic and even volatile combinations. These issues are discussed in great detail in the next chapter.

The state and the interstate system thus provide some of the broader contexts within which the debate on the plurality of legal orders may be fruitfully pursued. Specifically concerning the state, the analytical strategy means 'bringing the state back in' but, in a sense, the state is brought back in to a 'place' where it has never been before. As I argued in Chapter Two, under current conditions the centrality of the state lies to a significant extent in the way the state organizes its own decentring, as is well illustrated by the state-sponsored back-to-the-community or community-revival policies. The distinction between the state and the non-state is thereby called into question. This, of course, renders the debate on the plurality of legal orders yet more complex.

My analytical strategy, thus, differs markedly from the one followed by some authors who have theorized this third period of legal plurality as 'global law without a state', notably Gunther Teubner.[16] According to Teubner, '[g]lobal economic law is law with an underdeveloped 'centre''[17] in which legal orders do not stand in a relation of hierarchy but rather one of 'heterarchy'. Moreover, in his view, legal orders coexisting at different scales (local, national and global) are not characterized by sanctions, rules, or a given set of functions, but by the fact that they entail (or, put more accurately, they are) discourses that resort to the binary legal/illegal code. On the contrary, I have emphasized throughout this chapter (and will come back to this point in Chapter Five) that the state is a central player even in producing its own downsizing; that legal plurality in times of globalization is a highly hierarchical phenomenon with quite different manifestations in core, semi-peripheral and peripheral countries; and that what

[16]   Teubner, 1997.
[17]   Teubner, 1997, p 12.

constitutes legal plurality is not discourses tautologically defined in terms of the use of the legal/illegal code but discourses coupled with practices in which sanctions, rules and functions such as social control and dispute resolution play a key role.

Apart from the decentring of the state in social life is the concurrent trend toward an ever-greater internal heterogeneity of state action. Not only are different sectors of state activity developing at different paces and sometimes in opposite directions, but there are also disjunctures and inconsistencies in state action, and so much so that sometimes no coherent pattern of state action can be discerned anymore. This is particularly visible in peripheral and semi-peripheral states, as the above-mentioned cases of legal plurality documented in Mozambique and Colombia clearly show, but can also be observed in central states. The decentring in certain areas may thus coexist with the recentring of state action in others. For instance, the degradation of state-provided material services – housing, health, social security – may coexist with the expansion of state-provided symbolic services – state nationalism; politics as show business; the state as the imagined coherent and cohesive centre of sociability in societies increasingly fragmented by social inequalities and racial, ethnic, gender and generational hate ideologies and practices. Similarly, the demise of state welfare and safety nets vis-à-vis citizens may coexist with the expansion of state welfare and safety nets vis-à-vis corporations and global capital. As much as a decentring of state action, we are witnessing the explosion of the unity of state action and its law, and the consequent emergence of different modes of legal regulation, each one politically anchored in a microstate. As a result, the state itself becomes a configuration of microstates, raising a whole range of new questions that are yet to be answered by political sociology. What is the logic behind the heterogeneization of state action? Is the state a field of political inertia? What holds together the configuration of microstates? Is there an invisible hand, similar to the one that allegedly used to hold together the market, or is such a hand all too visible?

As a result of such multiple and cross-cutting heterogeneities of state action, the debate on the plurality of legal orders may extend to novel and unsuspected contexts. For instance, as the heterogeneity of state action translates itself into the growing particularism of state legality, and as the unity and universality of the official legal system break down, new forms of legal pluralism within state legality may arise which we could call *internal legal pluralism*. Of course, not every form of state heterogeneity will comprise a situation of internal legal pluralism. The latter requires the coexistence of different logics of regulation carried out by different state institutions with very little communication among them. Moreover, such logics of regulation may vary from country to country, even when they are carried out through the same type of legislation, and they also vary across time and space. Just to give an example, in central countries, particularly in those with a strong welfare component, labour law, together with social legislation, has been 'located' – particularly in the period of 'organized capitalism' – on the promotional or facilitative side of state action, while criminal law and restrictive legislation – from immigration and refugee laws to *Berufsverbot* (ie, the interdiction of certain professional activities to members of extreme-left organizations) of different kinds – have been located on the repressive side of state action. However, in colonial legislation, labour law and criminal law almost overlapped, and indeed labour law was in some cases the privileged form of criminalization of colonized people.[18]

Similar 'dislocations', calling for innovative theorizing, may take place within the three major time-spaces that have provided the framework for the debate on the plurality of legal orders. In situations of regional interstate integration in which the pooling of sovereignty occurs, such as in the EU, the national time-space that was before the time-space of state action may be gradually recodified as local or infrastate and, when viewed from the hegemonic global time-space – from Brussels, Strasbourg or Luxembourg – may actually assume characteristics that are generally associated with the local time-space, such as particularism, regionalism, closeness to people's practices and discourses.

In the following chapters I demonstrate that the state is in fact one of the components of the wider context in which the plurality of legal orders must be debated. But, as I said, modern states exist in an interstate system that is the hegemonic political configuration of the capitalist world system and world economy. At the beginning of the twenty-first century, the interstate system is undergoing sweeping changes – most notably in the European region of the world system as a consequence of the demise of the Communist regimes in Central and Eastern Europe. But, more generally, the dramatic intensification of global practices in the last three decades has produced transformations in state structures and practices which, though they may differ according to the location of the state in the world system – core, semi-periphery, or periphery – are nonetheless decisive. Contrary to what happened before, the main driving force behind the transformation of the state and its legality is the intensification of global practices and global interactions. Under such pressures the regulatory functions of the nation-state become derivative, a kind of political franchising or subcontracting.

Even assuming that this is a universal phenomenon, it takes very different forms in the core, the periphery or the semi-periphery of the world system. The world system position of the state affects its role in social regulation, as well as its relationship with the market and with civil society – phenomena that world system theory has discussed in terms of the relative strength of the state, both internal and external. The consequences of this for the production of law inside each state territory are not automatic, but they are certainly decisive. The question to be answered is not only about the degree to which the legal monopoly hypothesis is falsified but also about the degree of isomorphism or symmetry between state-produced law and non state-produced law. As I argue in Chapter Two, we are going through a period in which the state reproduces itself in the form of the civil society. Thus, we may expect in many areas a high degree of affinity or parallelism between state law and non-state law. But, on the other hand, the recent protagonism of powerful private actors in social regulation is due to their ability to

---

[18]   Van Onselen, 1976.

generate forms of legal private government that would be politically unacceptable or even unconstitutional if generated by the state.

The diversity of the phenomenon observed calls for a comparative effort on a global scale. Moreover, the world system perspective does not limit itself to emphasizing structural location. It also emphasizes historicity and temporality. In Chapter Five, I present a multidimensional comparative framework designed to account for the historical differentiation among various forms of legal globalization occurring simultaneously throughout the world system.

Besides the state and the world system, another wider context for the debate on the plurality of legal orders should be mentioned: the political meaning of legal plurality in the specific historical conditions in which it occurs. After the collapse of the Communist regimes in Central and Eastern Europe; after the democratic transitions throughout Latin America in the last decade; after the cases of revolutionary regimes voted out of office through democratic elections, as in Nicaragua and the Cape Verde Islands; after the end of apartheid in South Africa; after the conversion of powerful guerrilla movements into parliamentary parties in El Salvador, Guatemala, Mozambique and partially (M19) in Colombia – after all these developments at the beginning of the century democracy assumes a seemingly uncontested legitimacy, a fact that strikingly contrasts with other concepts of political transformation nurtured by modernity, such as revolution, reform and socialism. However, in apparent contradiction with all this, the less contested the political value of democracy, the more problematic its identity. Is there a unitary concept of democracy? Is it possible to explain through a general theory all the different political processes across the world system that can be identified as processes of democratization? Is democracy a Western device of social regulation, or a potentially universal instrument of social emancipation? Is there any relation between the seemingly universal trend toward democracy and the globalization of the creed of economic liberalism? To what extent is the democratic trend articulated with some other trends of an opposite sign – growing social inequality both between the North and the South and within countries of the North and South; growing authoritarianism over private life? How can democracy be so uncontested when almost all of its satellite concepts are increasingly problematic, be they representation, participation, citizenship, political obligation or the rule of law?

These questions are indicative of the great theoretical effort that lies ahead. Many more can be asked. For instance, a whole set of questions refers to the impact of legal plurality on the legal experiences, perceptions and consciousness of the individuals and social groups living under conditions of legal plurality, above all the fact that their everyday life crosses or is interpenetrated by different and often contrasting legal orders and legal cultures. This intersubjective or phenomenological dimension of legal pluralism I call *interlegality*, a concept which will be elaborated in Chapter Eight.

In my view, the clarification of the relationship between law and democracy is particularly crucial, and here the discussion on legal plurality may be very illuminating.

A conception of socio-legal fields operating in multilayered time-spaces is likely to expand the concept of law and, consequently, the concept of politics. It will be thus suited to uncover social relations of power beyond the limits drawn by conventional liberal theory and, accordingly, to uncover unsuspected sources of oppression or of emancipation through law, thereby enlarging the field and radicalizing the content of the democratization process. As is explained in detail in the following chapters, democratization is every social process entailing the transformation of power relations into relations of shared authority. In light of this definition, the idea of legal plurality has no fixed political content. It may serve a progressive or a reactionary politics. The same situation of legal plurality may 'evolve' from one type of politics to the other without much change in the structural or institutional arrangements that support it. It comprises, as much as the state itself, social relations that change over time. The despotic or democratic value of specific legal orders varies widely across the legal configuration of any given society. Such variation may be related in different ways to the world system position of the country and also to the specific historicity of the construction or transformation of the state. In light of this, there is no intrinsic reason why state law should be less despotic or, for that matter, less democratic than non-state law. There are, of course, many non-state legal orders that are more despotic than the state legal order of the country in which they operate (for instance mafia law). Indeed, I would submit that in core states, particularly in those with a strong welfare state, the state legal order is probably less despotic than many non-state legal orders existing in those societies. The extreme variety of situations in peripheral and semi-peripheral societies should caution us against the formulation of a general inverse hypothesis concerning these societies. In situations in which state law can be considered more democratic than non-state law, the importance of the conception of legal plurality lies in its relativization of democratic content within a broader legal configuration. In other words, the democratic content of state law may be premised upon its coexistence with despotic non-state legal orders with which it interacts and interpenetrates in different ways. As already indicated in Chapter Two, though part of the legal configuration, such non-state legal orders are denied the quality of law by the hegemonic liberal theory of the state and law. For that reason, their despotism is prevented from overshadowing and relativizing the democratic nature of the only officially recognized legality – the state law. By denouncing this ideological occultation, legal plurality may reveal some hidden faces of oppression; but by the same token it may open new fields of emancipatory practice.

The state, the world and the politics of legality are the signposts of the broad context in which the multiplicity of legal time-spaces is discussed in Chapters Four, Five, and Six. In Chapters Seven, Eight and Nine a theoretical reconstruction is proposed that is aimed at putting the politics of legality on a new footing and on a new and hopefully emancipatory course.

Chapter 4

The Law of the Oppressed: the Construction and Reproduction of Legality in Pasargada

I INTRODUCTION

Pasargada is the fictitious name of a squatter settlement (or *favela*) in Rio de Janeiro. Because of the structural inaccessibility of the state legal system, and especially because of the illegal character of the *favelas* as urban settlements, the popular classes living in them devise adaptive strategies aimed at securing the minimal social ordering of community relations. One such strategy involves the creation of an internal legality, parallel to – and sometimes conflicting with – state official legality. From the perspective of legal plurality outlined in the previous chapter, this chapter describes Pasargada legality from the inside – through the sociological analysis of legal rhetoric in dispute prevention and dispute settlement and in its (unequal) relations with the Brazilian official legal system.

The study of Pasargada law arose out of my interest in unveiling the operation of the legal system as a whole in a class society, namely Brazil. At the time of the field research (1970) there were in Rio de Janeiro more than two hundred squatter settlements (*favelas*), where approximately one million people lived. Then, as now, not all the poor of the city lived in the *favelas*, nor were those in the *favelas* all poor. There were many lower-class people living outside the *favelas* (including some of the poorest), and lower-middle-class people living in the *favelas*. It is undeniable, however, that the large majority of people in the *favelas* belonged to the lowest strata. I chose for my study one of the oldest and biggest *favelas* in Rio. I called it Pasargada, from the title of a poem by the Brazilian poet Manuel Bandeira. The field research was conducted according to the method of participant observation. I lived in Pasargada from July to October of 1970, participating in the community life as much as I could. Although the period of fieldwork was short, I could engage in participant observation from the start, since Portuguese is my native language.

The dispute settlement studies in legal anthropology provided the main analytical framework for the research. In the course of my work, however, I came to pay as much attention to dispute prevention as to dispute settlement, since – as it became apparent in the early stages of the field research – the ways in which people prevent disputes are related to the ways in which disputes are settled when they occur. As I concentrated my research on the dispute prevention and dispute settlement mechanisms associated with the Pasargada Residents' Association, I came to conceive of these mechanisms and their institutional setting as forming an unofficial legal system, which I called Pasargada law. I then analyzed this law in its dialectical relations with the Brazilian official system, as an instance of legal plurality. I used a class analysis framework, examining that particular instance of legal pluralism as the relation between a dominant legal system – the official legal system controlled by the Brazilian dominant classes – and a dominated system – Pasargada law controlled by the oppressed classes.

Except for the work of Gluckman,[1] Fallers[2] and Bohannan,[3] the research in legal anthropology and legal sociology had given until then only scant attention to the structures of legal reasoning and argumentation in socio-legal processes. The analysis of legal rhetoric had been left to legal philosophers, who had characteristically ignored the sociological context in which legal discourses operated. The study of Pasargada law was thus conceived as an attempt to develop an empirical sociology of legal rhetoric. I begin the presentation of such study by sketching the theory of dispute processing and of legal rhetoric that underpin it.[4] I then analyze in depth the legal rhetoric underlying dispute prevention and settlement by the Residents' Association in Pasargada.

2   JUSTICIABILITY, DISPUTE PROCESSING AND LEGAL RHETORIC

According to the conception of law put forward in Chapter Three, the regularized procedures and the normative standards must be 'considered justiciable in a given group or community'. Justiciability is defined by H Kantorowicz as the characteristic of those rules 'which are considered fit to be applied by a judicial organ in some definite procedure'.[5] By 'judicial organ' Kantorowicz means 'a definite authority concerned with a kind of 'casuistry', to wit, the application of principles to individual cases of conflict between parties'.[6] As we can see, Kantorowicz uses the concept of judicial organ in a very broad sense or, as he puts it, in a very 'modest and untechnical sense',[7] since it includes state judges, jurors, headmen, chieftains, magicians, priests, sages, doomsmen, councils of tribal elders, kinship tribunals, military societies, parliaments, international institutions, areopagi, sports umpires, arbitrators, church courts, *censores*, courts of

---

[1]   Gluckman, 1955.
[2]   Fallers, 1969.
[3]   Bohannan, 1957.
[4]   For a full version of this theoretical framework, see Santos , 1995, Chapter Three, section I.
[5]   Kantorowicz, 1958, p 79.
[6]   Kantorowicz, 1958, p 69.
[7]   Kantorowicz, 1958, p 80.

love, courts of honour, *Bierrichter* and eventually gang leaders. It is precisely this breadth and flexibility that makes the concept useful here. Justiciability means that the normative standards I will be discussing are applicable by a third party – to use a concept with a wide currency in legal-anthropological literature[8] – within a dispute context and according to certain regularized procedures. According to Gulliver:

> 'A dispute arises out of disagreement between persons (individuals or subgroups) in which the alleged rights of one party are claimed to be infringed, interfered with, or denied by the other party. The second party may deny the infringement, or justify it by reference to some alternative or overriding right, or acknowledge the accusation; but he does not meet the claim. The right-claimant may, for whatever reason, accede to this, in which case no dispute arises. If he is unwilling to accede, he then takes to attempt to rectify the situation by some regularized procedure in the public arena'.[9]

Law can be mobilized in the dispute context in three basic ways: dispute creation, dispute prevention, and dispute settlement. These phenomena are structurally related; consequently, the full understanding of one requires the analysis of the others. For instance, if we take the dyad dispute creation/dispute settlement, the use of the case as the unit of analysis necessarily leads us to conceive of the creation of a dispute as logically and chronologically antecedent to its settlement. This remains true even if we extend the analysis to the prehistory and long-range consequences of the case. But if, instead of analyzing isolated cases of dispute, we examine the constant flow of disputing behaviour in a given society, the logical and chronological relationship just mentioned breaks down. The basic premises upon which disputes are created, framed and prevented are structurally related to settlement in two opposing ways: (1) by anticipating and accepting the established settlement norms, procedures and structures; (2) by consciously refusing such norms, procedures and structures, and proposing others. Creation, settlement and prevention of disputes are stones in a fast creek coming down from the mountains in early summer: they stay together in the current but they change their relative positions all the time.[10] Therefore, the fact that settlement of disputes in

---

8   Abel, 1974, p 247, uses the term 'intervener' because, although 'an ugly neologism', it is 'free of the connotations which attach to such alternatives as judge, mediator, or dispute settler'. 'Third party' is at least as ugly.

9   Gulliver, 1969, p 14.

10   A similar point is made by Epstein, 1967, p 205; van Velsen, 1967, p 129; and Gluckman, 1955, p XI in their discussion of the extended case method, or of the situational analysis, as van Velsen prefers to call it. But while these authors want to emphasize the existence of conflicting norms which, by imposing normative choice upon the parties, become a source of dispute whose social meaning can only be captured by a close diachronic analysis, I am mainly concerned with the fact that a given norm, or a set of non-conflicting norms, may also, over time, be a source of conflict within specific social relations, determining both the creation and the settlement of disputes. Our point of agreement is a common concern with social processes, with the dynamic dimension of the social structure or, as Gluckman says, '[with] an ongoing process of social relations between specific persons and groups in a social system and culture' (1955, p xv).

one society is dominated by adjudication ('win or lose') and in another by mediation ('give a little, get a little') will not be fully explained until we analyze the different structures and processes of dispute creation and prevention in those societies.[11]

Dispute prevention occupies a peculiar structural position halfway between the absence of a dispute and its creation. This may seem misleading, not only because dispute prevention appears to imply, by definition, the absence of disputes, but also because, whenever the movement away from this situation begins, we are already in a field of dispute creation. Nevertheless, it is as absurd to speak of dispute prevention after the dispute has been created as it is before the conditions for the creation of the dispute are present. A dispute may be prevented when the conditions for its creation are present in an inchoate, latent or potential form. From another perspective, a dispute may be prevented when, through a kind of short circuit, it is settled before it has actually taken place. For instance, dispute prevention, thus conceived, is what people do when they have decided to enter a contractual relationship and work together to make their agreement explicit, following certain established procedures.

One or more individualized third parties may be identified as dispute preventers, and all of them (or only one) may be the third party that would intervene as dispute settler were the dispute not effectively prevented. The relevance of this fact will become clear when we analyze, in the empirical part of this study, the feedback mechanisms between the dispute settlement and the dispute prevention functions of the third party. The norms that govern co-operative behaviour between parties in a given relationship (the dispute prevention context) relate in significant (but not always obvious) ways to the norms that govern settlement when a dispute arises between those parties.

The general working hypothesis of this research is that argumentative discourse (rhetoric) is the main structural component of Pasargada law, and that, accordingly, it dominates the procedures and mechanisms of dispute prevention and dispute settlement

---

On the other hand, my interest in the role of law in creating disputes seems to be at odds with the view, common among sociologists of social conflict, that law is created and modified by conflicts. Coser, referring both to Simmel, 1955, and Weber, 1954, concludes: 'We need hardly document in detail the fact that legislative enactment of new statutory laws tends to occur in areas in which conflict has pointed out the need for the creation of new rules. . . . Conflicts may be said to be "productive" in two related ways: (1) they lead to the modification and the creation of laws; (2) the application of new rules leads to the growth of new institutional structures centring on the enforcement of these new rules and laws' (1956, p 126). Indeed, the two perspectives are complementary: law is both a product and a producer of social conflict.

[11]   Richard Abel has convincingly argued that, in any given society, we may find different styles or types of dispute settlement, or 'outcomes', as he prefers to call them (1973, p 228). Criticizing Nader, he asserts that either/or decisions are extremely rare in any legal system. Abel has also helped to elucidate, both at the microsocial and at the macrosocial level, possible correlations between dispute structure and dispute process, by means of an elaborate set of variables. My point in the text is merely that, in order to account for the actualization of law in the dispute context, both dispute structure and dispute process must be analyzed in terms of the creation and prevention of disputes, as well as their settlement.

existing in Pasargada. In fleshing out this hypothesis, I draw on Chaim Perelman's theory of rhetoric. Elsewhere I have dealt with rhetoric in detail both as a form of knowledge and as a conduit for the resolution of legal disputes.[12] This is not the place to dwell on these topics, which go well beyond legal rhetoric and pertain key epistemological issues. For the purposes of explaining the operation of rhetoric in a non-state legal order – ie, Pasargada law – I will limit myself here to sketching the notion of rhetoric and its key concepts.

Perelman starts from Aristotle, who deals with argumentative discourse in a systematic way in the *Topic* and, with reference to contexts of application, in the *Rhetoric*. Rhetoric is a form of knowledge that proceeds from probable premises to probable conclusions through various types of arguments, some of which may be presented in syllogistic form, though they are not syllogisms (they are *enthymemes*, 'quasi-logical arguments presented in syllogistic form').[13] Arguments are of an immense variety, but in order for them to be activated in a concrete process of argumentation, two conditions must be fulfilled: there must be some premises that are generally accepted and function as starting points of the argumentation, and there must be a relevant audience to be persuaded or convinced.[14] Among the premises, two types are of utmost importance: facts and truths, on the one hand, and *topoi*, on the other.

From a rhetorical point of view, facts and truths are objects of sufficiently intense agreement as not to necessitate further intensification through argumentation. No statement enjoys this status indefinitely, and when the level of intensity of agreement decreases, facts and truths cease to be so and become arguments themselves. On the other hand, *topoi*, or *loci*, are 'common places', widely accepted points of view with very open, unfinished or flexible content easily adaptable to the different contexts of argumentation. As Walter Ong writes, 'in all its senses, the term (*topos*) has to do, in one way or another, with exploitation of what is already known, and indeed often of what is exceedingly well known'.[15] For Perelman, *topoi* 'form an indispensable arsenal on which a person wishing to persuade another will have to draw, whether he likes it or not'.[16]

Aristotle makes the distinction between *topoi* that belong to a particular realm of knowledge – such as the *topos* of the just and the unjust, which can be used in politics, ethics and law, but not in physics – and *topoi* that can be used indiscriminately in any realm of knowledge – such as the *topoi* of quantity, which can be used in politics, in physics and so on. Though this distinction was abandoned in subsequent treatises of rhetoric,[17] Perelman recuperates and articulates it with the other necessary condition of argumentation: the relevant audience.

---

12   See Santos, 1995, Chapters 1 and 3.
13   Perelman, 1969, p 230.
14   On the distinction between persuasion and conviction, see Perelman, 1969, p 26.
15   Ong, 1977, p 149.
16   Perelman, 1969, p 84.
17   See Ong, 1977, p 149.

For an argumentation to take place, 'an effective community of minds must be realized at a given moment', there must be a 'contact of minds' – in other words, an audience, which Perelman defines as 'the ensemble of those whom the speaker wishes to influence by his argumentation'.[18] In rhetorical terms, the community at any given moment is the relevant audience of those engaged in argumentation, that is, the ensemble of those they want to influence through persuasion or conviction. In order to be successful in influencing the audience, the 'speakers' must adapt to the audience; and in order to be successful in their adaptation, they must know the audience.[19]

The following are the issues of rhetorical analysis which will be most pertinent in dealing with the empirical analysis carried out in this chapter.

2.1   *Explicit and implicit issues: the object of the dispute as the result of a bargaining process*

To fix the object of a dispute is to narrow it down. That is exactly what the legal process does in defining what is to be decided. This selection is determined by the needs and purposes of the legal process. A dialectical relationship exists between the totality and the selected parts, as well as between the relevant and the irrelevant issues. This is best illustrated in the operations of *topoi* and, particularly, in their interaction with legal rules. The narrowing of issues is the result of the gradual exclusion of alternatives, and not vice versa. Besides, this move from breadth to narrowness is not irreversible; during the processing of disputes, shifts of direction are frequent, which expand the inquiry into new areas. And the key to a deep understanding of the legal process lies in the explanation of this dialectic. Such an explanation can most profitably be attempted by analyzing structural interactions between the participants in the dispute process, and between them and the relevant audience.

At any given point, the selection of issues is a product of the needs and purposes of the dispute process mechanism, and of the ways in which participants and audiences accommodate or react to these needs. The object of the dispute is the result of a complex bargaining process between the parties, the third party, and the relevant audience. This perspective can be helpful in clarifying points obscured in previous studies on dispute processing. In the analysis of Pasargada law two issues will be highlighted: the breadth or narrowness of the dispute, and the discrepancy or coincidence between the object of the dispute as presented by the parties and the *real* dispute between them.

---

[18]   Perelman, 1969, p 19.

[19]   *Topoi* must be distinguished from judicial protopolicies: the latter are not an integral part of the argumentative discourse, though they condition it. Judicial protopolicies are organizational principles, principles of action or rules of thumb, on the basis of which strategic decisions are made about how to proceed. These policies are derived from the interests, needs, limitations and potential of the dispute processing mechanism itself, as these are perceived by the social groups that control it or by the dispute settler.

2.1.1 THE BREADTH OR NARROWNESS OF THE DISPUTE

The criterion for measuring the breadth or narrowness of a dispute is very elusive. The object of a given dispute consists both of explicit and implicit issues. What is not discussed, or even mentioned, because it is self-evident to the participants, is crucial to an understanding of the internal dynamics of the dispute process.

The implicit discourse is the fluid from which the explicit discourse emerges and becomes meaningful. The two discourses interact in two ways. In the early stages of the process, when the *topoi* and the valuations work together to achieve a gradual approximation of facts and norms, implicit discourse progressively excludes implausible solutions. As the dispute proceeds, and facts and norms are clarified, implicit discourse is redirected to making the selected solutions appear self-evident.

Between explicitness and implicitness there is a whole range of intermediate communication processes, because statements that explicitly express one thing may implicitly symbolize another. The third party may not express his hostility to the introduction of an issue, but may transmit signals of his feelings. A party who fails to recognize such signals may be adversely affected. Any participant can evoke symbolic meanings favourable to her claim. But when the role of the third party becomes significantly professionalized, it may be more difficult for the disputing parties to perceive and interpret the symbolic meanings of the third party. This is probably one of the reasons why the professionalization of the dispute settler tends to lead to professional representation of the parties.

Two intermediate communication processes studied by rhetoric are particularly important in dispute processing: *signs* and *indices*. Both have a double meaning: the factual meaning and the evoked meaning. But while signs are intentionally used to evoke a certain meaning, indices evoke a meaning regardless of intent. Signs have a closed texture in two senses: the meanings they evoke are specific, and those meanings may be comprehensible only to certain interpreters. Indices, by contrast, have an open texture. We have a sign when, for instance, the dispute settler, lacking formal power to summon someone to 'court', sends him an invitation through a policeman on duty in the community with the intention of evoking the meaning that adverse consequences might be expected if the 'invitation' is not accepted. We also have a sign when, during the proceedings in court, the representatives of the parties make a gesture or utter a word which, by prearrangement, signifies that their constituents have allowed them to pursue a given path toward settlement. We have an index when a gesture or word is interpreted by any of the participants as evoking a certain meaning without prearrangement, even though the party who gestured or spoke did not want to communicate that meaning. I suggest that as the professional, social or cultural gap between the parties and the third party increases, the use of indices tends to decrease and the use of signs to increase.

2.1.2 THE PROCESSED DISPUTE AND THE REAL DISPUTE

The degree of discrepancy or coincidence between the dispute as it is processed and the real dispute between the parties is obviously related to the preceding variable of breadth, but it must be analyzed separately. Whenever a discrepancy exists between the processed and the real dispute, the topic-rhetorical reasoning cannot be fully understood without understanding the reasons or the purposes of the discrepancy. Among people bound by multiplex relationships, or by simplex relationships persisting over time, it is likely that numerous disputes will arise. Many of these disputes will not come to the attention of a third party, either because the parties feel that they can handle them or because the third party offers no remedy, or still because the remedy is too costly or otherwise dysfunctional. If one or both parties do choose to submit the dispute to a third party, it may not be possible to tell from the processed dispute, by itself, why this has happened. Such an explanation has to be found in the overall history of disputes between the parties. One or both parties may want the third party to consider all past disputes, or they may prefer to restrict the intervention of the third party to the immediate issues. Unless all participants agree, the processing strategy will depend upon their relative bargaining power.

It is necessary to determine the social factors that account for both the emergence of the discrepancy between the real and the processed dispute, and the permanence or elimination of such discrepancy during the process. I suggest that the more formalized and bureaucratized the dispute process, the greater the probability that the discrepancy between real and processed dispute will be maintained. When it is, there is a lower probability that the outcome of the dispute process will also be the final settlement of the dispute.

2. 2 Topoi, *forms and procedures: forms as arguments*

Forms are gestures made, words uttered, formulae written, ceremonies performed, when these must occur in specific ways and at specific times so that their objective in the dispute process is achieved. Procedures are sets of forms. Forms and procedures determine, in an automatic way, decisions about the processing of the dispute. In the legal systems of modern capitalist societies, forms and procedures are not supposed to raise questions of substance. The latter are to be answered in terms of the rights and wrongs (the merits) of the situation, whereas questions of form turn upon the presentation of the situation and its conformity or non-conformity to a preformulated model.

These categories have been used to distinguish formal from informal dispute processing contexts and to measure formalism. Since *topoi* involve points of view that relate to questions of substance, it can be hypothesized that, as formalism increases, topic-rhetorical legal argumentation decreases. In a highly formalized legal system, large portions of the dispute process will be insulated from such legal argumentation, and thus rhetoric will appear in a recessive form. On the contrary, I would expect to find in Pasargada extensive use of topic-rhetorical argumentation.

Just as *topoi* interact with substantive norms, so they interact with forms and procedures to produce the gradual approximation of facts and norms. Forms and procedures may be used as arguments for the exclusion of implausible solutions. This is why informal legal systems do not decide cases on the basis of technicalities, but construe forms and procedures as arguments that touch upon the merits of the cases. In connection with this, two issues must be raised: the relationship between formalism and ethics in the state law of capitalist societies, and the emergence of folk systems of formalism. The official legal system under modern capitalism tends to be strict on formalism and loose on ethics. The forms and procedures governing each stage of the creation, development and extinction of legal relationships are described in detail, but very little is said about the ethical content of such relationships. Thus, though any violation of forms and procedures prompts the intervention of the legal system, the unjust or unethical character of the relationship must reach extreme proportions before legal intervention will occur, and then only reluctantly. On the contrary, in societies only selectively penetrated by the official legal system, folk systems of legal formalism may emerge that are strict on ethics and loose on formalism. The degree of legal formalism that people require will vary with the type of relationship in which they are involved. As a consequence, different groups and classes in society may develop different folk legal systems of formalism which they superimpose upon the official legal system of formalism. In Pasargada I would expect a folk system that would be relatively loose on formalism and strict on ethics.

The forms used in the folk system are often derived from the official legal system and then modified in order to fit the needs of the group. Thus, folk and official systems may share cultural postulates but differ in the way they specify them, and in the use to which forms and procedures are put. This may be illustrated by the meanings that Western culture attributes to *writing* as a ceremony and to the *written product* as expression of commitment. When people express themselves orally, their words are never fully divorced from them. This is true even when these words are heard by witnesses, who later confront the speaker, because of the plastic and transitory character of the medium. Written words, on the other hand, create a gap between the author and her expression, between a personal affirmation of will and an impersonal fetish living its own life. This gap, which closely follows the myth of the sorcerer's apprentice, has two dialectically related sides. On the one side, there is the autonomy of the written commitment, and the possibility of its use against the committed self. On the other, there is the sense of alienation experienced by the self before her own creation, the sense of dispossession and thus of powerlessness to confront and control the commitment as her own.

It appears, then, that the writing and the written are a rhetorical *topos* in our socio-legal culture. Antithetical *topoi* frequently exist. We know that in our culture the *topos* of the obligatory character of the written promise is opposed by the *topos* expressed in the old saying: 'My word is as good as my bond'. It is difficult to elucidate the hierarchical relations between the two, for we lack much of the necessary sociological information. My suspicion is that the *topos* of the written word has a predominantly legal outlook, while the *topos* of the spoken word is predominantly moral.

2.3   *Language and silence in dispute processing*

The rhetorical analysis of legal reasoning makes language the nuclear reality of dispute processing. However, non-language arguments must also be important: gestures, postures, flags, furniture, Bibles, crucifixes, pictures of political or religious leaders, files, written papers, gavels, typewriters, dress, division and allocation of space in the courtroom, rituals of initiation and termination of proceedings, stratification of floor levels and of visibility, and so on. In general, these artifactual arguments provide the framing for the use of verbal language which remains thereby central to the topic-rhetorical circle. Two issues must be mentioned at this juncture: the common language, and the relations between language and silence.

2.3.1   COMMON LANGUAGE, TECHNICAL LANGUAGE, FOLK TECHNICAL LANGUAGE

At first sight, common language does not appear to be an issue: either the participants in the process speak the same language or interpreters must be used. Such an assumption cannot go unquestioned. Articulation, communication and understanding depend, indeed, on common language; without them legal reasoning becomes an absurdity. Closer analysis reveals, however, a myriad of intermediate situations between 'the same language' and languages perceived as so different by the groups dominating the dispute processing context as to require the intervention of interpreters. Except in the context of magic and ritual, words are not exchanged as words but rather as meanings. Thus people with different cultural backgrounds may speak different languages with the same words. Furthermore, each language has both a potential and an actual vocabulary. Different social and cultural groups carve out different actual vocabularies from the same potential vocabulary.

When the dispute process is only partly professionalized, the distinction between technical and everyday language is also blurred. In Pasargada, where there is an even lower degree of professionalization, I would expect legal argumentation to be based on everyday language. But I must refine this hypothesis by specifying further the relations between technical and everyday language. In the preceding analysis it has been assumed that technical language derives its basic meanings from the common sense expressed in everyday language. But the reverse may also be true: technical languages develop verbal formulas and technical meanings that are then popularized and infused with commonsensical connotations. Thus what happens with formalism may also happen with technical language: parallel to the official technical language, a folk technical language may develop. Everyday language must then be conceived to include the folk technical language.

2.3.2 LANGUAGE AND SILENCE

The relationship between language and silence deals with the internal rhythm of communication and the alternation of communicative strategies in dispute processing. Although some may dismiss this issue as trivial, I regard it as crucial. It may be said that silence is merely the chaotic vacuum between spoken words, and therefore cannot be analyzed by itself but only in terms of the words whose absence creates it. On the contrary, I want to argue that silence is as significant a communicative reality as language itself, and that, without the recognition of a dialectical relationship between silence and language, it is impossible to reach a deep understanding of the internal dynamics of dispute processing from a rhetorical point of view.

Silence is not equally distributed across cultures, nations or even groups and classes in the same society. Silence is a scarce resource, and the ruling classes in every society tend to allocate it according to their convenience and their cultural postulates. When language is important, the ruling classes tend to appropriate it, imposing silence upon the people. Thus, in a totalitarian society, the ruling classes will distribute silence to the people, keeping language for themselves. Conversely, when silence is important, the ruling classes tend to appropriate it, relegating language to the people. In a formally democratic society, people may be freely endowed with language, while a few silent actors make all the crucial decisions pertaining to the nation. But societies cannot be evaluated only in terms of the amount and distribution of silence, for there are different kinds of silence, and these differences may be even more important.

Silence is not an amorphous infinite, but a reality delimited by language, as much as language is delimited by silence. Silence is not an indiscriminate absence of language, but rather, the self-denial of specific words at specific moments of the discourse so that the communication process may be fulfilled. What is silenced, therefore, is a positive expression of meaning.[20]

It seems to me that the analysis of the relationship between language and silence may contribute significantly to our understanding of features of the dispute process that have thus far been neglected. For instance, one measure of the dispute settler's control over the processing of the dispute is the number of questions he asks and the number of times he interrupts the parties and the witnesses. But such control can also be expressed by the absence of questions and interruptions, that is, by silence. To take one example from Hinduism, it is instructive to observe the contrast between two of the officiants in

---

[20] Arjuna, the warrior, in the *Bhagavad Gita*, is in possession of such knowledge when he asks Krishna: 'How is the man of tranquil wisdom, who abides in divine contemplation? What are his words? *What is his silence?* What is his work?' (2, 54, my italics). Arjuna recognizes that words alone will not tell him the full meaning of an attitude or behaviour. That is why he asks about silence and about works. Words, silence and works are thus conceived as a necessary triad of communication and knowledge. Arjuna also shows that he is not interested in knowing just any kind of silence, but rather the silence of the man of wisdom, that is, a positive and delimited reality.

the ancient Vedic rituals, which are, after all, dispute settlement processes between people and gods. The *hotr*, though he recites extensively and loudly, has little control over the ritual, while the *brahman*, though he remains silent, exercises full control.[21]

The structure of language and silence in dispute processing is very complex because, at any given stage, different kinds and amounts of silence may be expressed by different participants (judge, parties, witnesses, audience), each having different meanings. Various classifications of silence are thus possible. The first one distinguishes between procedural silence (for instance, when I am silent in order to let someone else speak) and substantive silence (for instance, when I am silent in order to express my assent). The third party may exert more or less control over the distribution of procedural silence among the parties and audience. In the formal processes of complex societies, he exerts an almost absolute control. In any event, he tends to have little or no control over the substantive silences of the other participants.

Within the category of substantive silence, further classifications are possible: acceptance, rejection, assent, reprobation, intimidation, total disagreement, unenthusiastic acceptance, emotional approval, revolt, powerlessness and resignation, respect or disrespect, explosive tension or need for calm and further deliberation. From the perspective of the other participants and the relevant audience, it is important to distinguish between deviant silence and normal silence. Deviant behaviour in court can be explained in part by the tension between contradictory definitions of deviant and normal silence. The relative bargaining positions of the participants will dictate which definitions will prevail. The sanctions for deviant silence may be formal or informal, and may be applied in the same process in which the deviance occurred or in a separate process.

From the point of view of its weight in the communication process, there is also the distinction between heavy silence and light silence. Heavy silence takes place in moments of particular tension in the dispute process, when important decisions are made and dramatic turning points are reached. The more formalized the dispute process, the greater the tendency for a specific meaning to be assigned *a priori* to the silence of a particular party at a particular stage. If the party remains silent at a given moment or after being asked a given question, her silence will have legal significance (assent or admission, for instance). If, after the decision, the losing party remains silent for a specific period of time, this will constitute legal acceptance of the decision and preclude the possibility of

---

[21]   Louis Renou contrasts them in the following way. The *hotr*, who was originally the libation pourer (as the etymology of the word suggests), later becomes primarily a reciter; but his invocations, though impressive, play only a small part in the liturgy, rather like the music of the chanters. The *brahman* is the repository of the unexpressed power of the formula, a silent spectator who is responsible for seeing that the ritual is carried out with accuracy; he is a professional expert, like the Roman Catholic priest. *His silence is just as valuable as the speech and melodies of his colleagues*. Renou, 1968, p 32.

appeal. It is in this sense that I speak of the formalization of silence in formal dispute processing. It seems to me, however, that the language/silence structure of the audience remains informal (in this sense) even in formal dispute processing. To be sure, the judge can distribute procedural silence and can even sanction violations (clearing the courtroom). But she cannot force the audience into substantive silence. In this respect, the judge is herself an object of judgment by the audience.

The meaning of a specific instance of silence has to be inferred from the logical connections of the discourse, from the structural position of the silent participant and from the language of the participant that precedes and follows the silence. In general the language/silence structure of the third party can be divided into two phases. In the first, the third party has begun the process of excluding implausible decisions, but the range of those that remain is still very broad. Either the third party has not yet reached a decision, or else her preferences are still shaky and inarticulate. In the second phase, either the range of plausible decisions has narrowed to the point where the third party concentrates on weighing the relative merits of a few alternatives, or she already has a definite preference and has begun to clarify the reasons for it.

In the first phase, the third party uses silence in order to obtain all the information that his initial understanding of the case suggests he may need to reach a decision. He shows no preference for either specific pieces of knowledge or specific pieces of ignorance. At this stage the parties retain the right to knowledge and ignorance, to decide the ratio of knowledge and ignorance upon which they want to base their claims. But since the third party's silence is only rarely punctuated by language, it becomes very difficult for the parties to control the meaning of that silence. Furthermore, what little the third party does say is also ambiguous. The questions asked tend to be open and multidirectional, less questions than invitations to speak freely. The third party is aware of the fact that the less she asks, the more she knows. Consequently, the parties are induced to produce information that they might otherwise suppress or withhold until a later stage.

In the second phase, the language/silence structure of the third party undergoes profound changes. To decide is to specify and to intensify both knowledge and ignorance. To achieve this, however, it is necessary to control the direction of the inquiry. For this purpose the third party is likely to alternate between specific silences and specific questions. In this way, the third party reaches two objectives. On the one hand, he assures himself that he will know more of what he already knows and ignore more of what he already ignores, thus supporting his preferences for a particular decision. On the other hand, he communicates these preferences to the parties, inviting them either to share or to oppose them (particularly when a few alternatives are still open). Thus in this phase, the questions and silences, though they appear to be factually related to knowledge and ignorance, are in essence normative. They point to what *should* be known and ignored. They also indicate that the right to knowledge and ignorance now belongs to the third party.

The objectives of the third party are different in mediation, and so the language/silence structure also differs. In mediation the parties never fully relinquish the right to knowledge and ignorance. They may even retain full control until the end of the dispute process, as is the case when the third party is merely a go-between or errand boy. But when the third party has the power to participate in decisions about what is to be mediated and how it is to be mediated, then the right to knowledge and ignorance is shared by the parties and the judge. In mediation – as Pasargada legal process will illustrate – the third party is mainly concerned with participating in the creation of a horizon of concessions. He does this through the elaboration of *ad hoc* criteria of reasonableness and of legitimate expectations. By making the horizon visible he transforms it.

Assuming that the parties belong to the species of *homo juridicus*, they advance their proposed concessions according to a plan of minimum risk. It is up to the third party to transform them into maximum risks. That is why the parties in mediation are often confronted with proposals that appear to be their own but are somehow alien to their intentions and even to their interests. When they try to pull back from the mediator's proposal they may, depending on his skills, go not to their original positions but to some different position. Thus a step back may, in fact, be a step forward. It seems to me (other factors remaining constant) that control of adjudication may be achieved (at certain stages) through prolonged and ambiguous silences, but that control of mediation requires prolonged instances of language coupled with short and unambiguous silences.

In what follows, the central concepts and issues of legal rhetoric sketched above are used to characterize the type of legal reasoning that pervades the mechanisms of dispute processing developed by the popular classes in a Brazilian *favela* – Pasargada. As the presentation of the case study below will make clear, Pasargada law illustrates both the existence of local legal orders – and thus of the locality as one of the time-spaces of legal plurality – and the domination of rhetoric as a structural component of law, which stands in stark contrast with the domination of violence and bureaucracy in modern state law.

3   DISPUTE PREVENTION AND DISPUTE SETTLEMENT IN PASARGADA LAW

3.1   The Setting[22]

Pasargada is one of the largest and oldest squatter settlements in Rio de Janeiro. In 1950 its population was 18,000; by 1957 it had doubled; in 1970 it was more than 50,000. The settlement began in about 1932. According to the oldest residents, there were then

---

[22]   For a detailed analysis of the ecological, socioeconomic, political, religious, associational and cultural characteristics of the favelas of Rio, and of Pasargada in particular, see Santos, 1974, Chapters I and II.

only a few shacks at the top of the hill; the rest was farmland. The land was then privately owned, but to whom it belonged and how it subsequently became government land remains uncertain.

Physically, Pasargada is divided into two main parts:[23] the hill (*morro*), and the flat section on the two sides of the river that flows at its foot. The latter is very small, muddy and subject to flooding. Many of the shacks are built upon stilts. It is here that the most precarious dwellings are to be found. The streets – whenever they are more than mere gaps between shacks – are narrow and muddy. Sewage sometimes runs through them freely, underneath the miserable wooden huts, into the heavily polluted river. There are a few shaky wooden bridges connecting the two sides of the river. Most of Pasargada lies on the hill, which is neither very high nor, with a few exceptions, steep, and is therefore well suited for construction. Brick and cement are the most common building materials, though the quality of construction varies widely. Most houses have electricity and running water. There are several water networks in Pasargada, drawing from the city main, whose functioning varies greatly. The irregularities are due either to financial mismanagement or technical problems, such as pipe repairs or lack of pumping power. Residents in houses and shacks without running water get it from public taps or neighbours. About 80 per cent of the households belong to the electricity network administered by the 'electricity commission'; the rest are served by other small networks.

Today Pasargada is practically in the middle of the city, so that access to the surrounding areas is easy. But at its inception, Pasargada was located at the periphery of Rio, on land that at the time had no speculative value. Thus Pasargada was able to develop more or less freely for three decades. And when land prices began to inflate as the city grew around Pasargada – its land presently is highly desirable for both housing and industry – the *favela* was already so big and so developed that outright removal would have involved high social and political costs.

Pasargada's internal economic life is very intense. It includes traditional commercial houses and modern grocery stores and bars. Many factories surround it, a dozen (or more) of which can be reached in a five-minute walk. The bulk of the economically active population is made up of industrial workers labouring in nearby factories. The remainder work as entrepreneurs inside Pasargada, low-level public officials, municipal workers, and odd-jobbers. Most industrial workers earn the legal minimum wage, but per capita income within Pasargada is about one quarter of the minimum salary.

Associational life in Pasargada is very intense. There are recreational clubs, soccer teams, churches (whose members often organize themselves in social clubs and charitable

---

[23] In what follows, I will use the anthropological present to refer to the period of the fieldwork (1970). Since then, social and political life in Pasargada has changed dramatically, in great part due to the control of drug dealers over community action, occurring mainly in the 1980s, but due also to the process of democratization of the Brazilian state in the same decade. See, for instance, Junqueira and Rodrigues, 1992.

associations under the aegis of the catholic priest and other religious leaders), the electricity commission and the Residents' Association (hereafter RA). Because of its relevance for the analysis of Pasargada law, the RA will be described more fully. The RA was the first community-wide, community-controlled, agency in Pasargada. It was created in order to organize and promote the collective participation of the inhabitants of Pasargada in infrastructure and community-building projects in the neighbourhood. The RA's statutes emphasize the following objectives:

I   To plead before the competent state or federal authorities measures intended to ameliorate the public services concerning its associates.

II   To act as a linking element between the local population, assisting the latter in the resolution of all the problems concerning the community.

III   To act legally and with great zeal for the maintenance of order and for the security and tranquility of the families.[24]

The RA rapidly became known in the community. Though many people may not know about its organizational details or who its directors are, few today are ignorant of its existence. Despite its statutory functions, the RA is identified in the community with 'improvements and as a place to go when one has a house or shack problem'. The folk meaning of this very broad expression is actually much narrower. Nobody would think of seeking the association's help in solving a technical construction problem. But residents may turn to the association when they want to organize communal work to build or repair their house or shack, when they think they should obtain authorization to repair or expand it or want to make (or renounce) a contract concerning it, and when they have a dispute with neighbours over construction rights, demarcation of boundaries, passage rights or occupancy rights. This enumeration suggests that residents bring to the association only those housing problems that involve their public legal relationships to the community as a whole, or their private legal relationships to each other.

Although the RA had done little in the way of public works, because the state has not come up with the material assistance promised, its original commitment to the community development was strong. This connection with construction, both public and private, was reinforced by the power it then held to authorize and supervise any house repairs, and to demolish any house built without its authority. The RA soon became known as having jurisdiction over questions involving land and housing throughout Pasargada. The genesis of this, as of any informal social function, is obscure. The official power to authorize repairs and to promote public works was certainly a factor. On the other hand, the directors of the RA spoke of the 'official character' of the association, implying that all actions were backed by state authority, which was not the case. Finally, there

[24]   A detailed analysis of the RA's statutory objectives can be found in Santos, 1974, pp 98ff.

was the belief that the association not only reflected the stability of the settlement, but would also enhance the security of social relations by giving the settlement legal status. All these factors may have contributed to the emergence of the idea of jurisdiction, by way of analogy with the official legal system.

As the RA conceives of its role in the community, it claims no jurisdiction over criminal matters. When confronted with a situation that appears to involve a crime, the association neither handles the matter nor reports it to the police. All it will say to the alleged victim is: 'This is not a question for us to solve. This is a question for the police'. The RA abstains from criminal matters for several reasons. First, although maintenance of order was one of the statutory objectives of the RA, its directors consider that the primary goal of the RA is community development, not social control. Secondly, were it to assert criminal jurisdiction, the RA would inevitably devote more of its energies to the 'bad neighbourhood' of Pasargada, where drug dealers, career criminals and prostitutes are concentrated and crime is more frequent . This would not only divert the RA from tasks that it and the community deem more important, but would also damage its image in the more respectable neighbourhoods of Pasargada. Thirdly, the authority of the RA has been progressively undermined by an increasingly authoritarian state that abandoned the community development policies of the early 1960s, thereby denying the association the material resources necessary for it to provide the services and public works it had promised the residents.[25] Because criminals, in particular, would deny the legitimacy of this weakened RA, any attempt by its leaders to exercise power over them would be (even physically) dangerous. Finally, state officials and the 'official' society in general view *favelas* and crime as nearly synonymous. Repressive action against the *favelas*, from the almost daily police raids to the removal of entire populations and the razing of shacks, is often justified in the name of the fight against crime. By getting involved in criminal matters, the RA would expose itself to the arbitrary actions of an authoritarian state, and might be outlawed. It is true, as will be seen later, that the RA handles many disputes involving some kind of criminal conduct. But in such cases the association proceeds as if the matter were exclusively of a civil nature. On the other hand, the RA conceives its civil jurisdiction as limited to cases involving land and housing rights, although disputes will be processed in which other issues are raised.

The relations between the RA and the state agencies operating in Pasargada are deeply ambiguous. In the early 1960s the populist state seemed to be committed to a policy of more or less autonomous community development in the *favelas*. This policy was abandoned when the military dictatorship came into power in 1964, and since 1967 the state has emphasized control *of favela* organizations and leadership, and the elimination of any 'dangerous' autonomy. Community organizations are presently offered 'assistance' by various state agencies, but sanctions are imposed should they fail to

---

[25] In 1964 a military coup put an end to the democratic government of Joao Goulart. The military dictatorship lasted until the 1980s.

accept the offer. Under these circumstances, Pasargada's RA has been using different strategies to neutralize state control: refraining from refusing assistance explicitly, yet continuing to ignore the orders that accompany it, while seeking to evade the formal sanctions that are threatened.

The relations between the RA and the police, who are stationed near the association in the central part of the *favela*, are very complex. Police and community are reciprocally hostile. The community avoids the police, who are aware of this fact and of its negative consequences for social control. In order to increase its penetration within the community, the police have tried to maintain good relations with representative associations, particularly with the RA. Thus they have offered their 'good services' to the RA, which the RA has accepted, while conscious of the purpose behind it. In extreme cases, the RA may resort to the police in order to implement a decision, as will be seen below. But most of the time the RA will only threaten the recalcitrant resident with police intervention, without taking further action to punish non-compliance. For the RA knows the risk of becoming too closely identified with an institution ostracized by the community. As a consequence, the association and the police engage in ritualistic interaction, in the course of which they exchange signals of mutual recognition and goodwill that are not followed by substantial co-operation.

The RA's office is located in the central part of Pasargada and occupies a brick and cement two-story house. On the ground floor there are two rooms: a very spacious front room with a large door opening to the street and a small back room that gives access to the first floor, which is still under construction and almost unfurnished. Most of the activities take place in the front room. The back room and the first floor are occasionally used by the *presidente* to hold closed meetings – with the parties in a dispute, for instance. The front room is modestly furnished: a long bench against the wall and three desks with chairs – one for the *presidente*, another for the secretary and a third for the treasurer. Behind the desks are the files. Though the statutory functions of the *presidente* are limited to co-ordination and representation, he is currently the central figure of the RA. When incumbent directors resign, the *presidente* may temporarily assume their jobs. He and the treasurer are the only members of the board of directors who work daily in the RA's office. The *presidente* arrives about 9:00 or 10:00 AM, leaves for lunch from 2 PM until 5 PM, and stays until 8:00 PM. The evening is usually the busiest part of the office day. Whenever he presides over meetings of the board of directors he does not leave the building before 10:00 or 11:00 PM.

Membership in the RA is restricted to Pasargada residents (or people otherwise integrated in the community) who pay a monthly fee. The RA has about fifteen hundred members but not all pay their fees regularly. Although only members can participate in the general assembly, the association does not restrict its benefits to them. Occasionally, however, non-members who solicit services from the RA may be induced to join it. In what follows, I first look into the activities of RA in relation to dispute prevention and then analyze those related to dispute settlement.

3.2   Dispute prevention in Pasargada

3.2.1 THE RATIFICATION OF LEGAL RELATIONS BY THE RESIDENTS' ASSOCIATION

When residents want to draft a contract or enter any other type of legal relationship, they may come to the RA to see the *presidente*. Usually they are accompanied by relatives, friends or neighbours, some of whom will serve as witnesses. The parties explain their intentions to the *presidente*, who may question them about the legitimacy of the contract. For instance, if the contract involves the sale of a shack or house, the *presidente* will request the prospective seller to prove ownership. He will also ask both parties whether they are firmly committed to the contract and willing to comply with the conditions agreed upon, and may seek more detailed information about those conditions.

The secretary or treasurer then writes the contract. The parties may bring with them a draft, which they dictate to the typist, or they may ask the *presidente*, the treasurer or the secretary to draft the text in accordance with the agreed terms. In the latter instance the official will read the draft to the parties, who must agree to it before it is typed. In certain types of contracts – leases, for instance – the official may also resort to routine formulas. After the contract has been typed the *presidente* will read the text to the parties, who will then sign it in his presence. Two witnesses will also sign it. The *presidente* will imprint one or more of the stamps of the association on the document. One copy is given to the parties; the other will remain in the association's files. This intervention of the RA in the mutually agreed creation and termination of a legal relationship – similar to the function performed by a notary – is called *ratification*. In this way the RA contributes to the prevention of disputes in Pasargada. The ratification not only invokes the norms that will govern the relationship while the agreement between the parties is in force, but also anticipates the consequences of a dispute.

The ratification is a constitutive act in two senses. First, the RA not only ratifies the agreement proposed by the parties, but may also suggest changes – for instance, additional clauses. This happens when the *presidente* foresees a possibility of future conflict not anticipated by the parties, and brings it to their attention in order to prevent it. Secondly, the ratification is constitutive in that it is perceived by the parties as an autonomous source of security for their relationship. This is so, I believe, because it is produced by an act of institutional rhetoric, a persuasive institutionalization of forms and procedures conceived as rhetorical arguments. This is indeed a process of reinstitutionalization in the sense that some of the forms and procedures are already settled as customary, but are integrated through the process of ratification with new ones in a totality that invests its constituent parts with new meanings and orientations. This (re)institutionalization is intimately related to the atmosphere of officialdom. Since the RA is an organization in which the state has vested some administrative functions, these forms and procedures derive their persuasive power not only from themselves but also from the institutional setting in which they take place. The forms and procedures that constitute the ratification process are conceived here as rhetorical arguments not only because they contribute to the discussion of the merits of the case, but also because their role in dispute processing can only be fully understood when we take into account how and by whom they are introduced into the process. Let us look briefly into each of the main forms and procedures that constitute the process through which the RA ratifies a contract.

3.2.1.1   *Objects as arguments*

I will begin by considering the non-linguistic arguments that precede the ratification process and operate throughout it, for they are at the core of the institutional rhetoric and are some of the new forms and procedures through which the RA accomplishes the above-mentioned reinstitutionalization of the relationship between the parties. Elements of this institutional setting include the building where the RA is located, which is one of the more substantial structures in Pasargada; the furniture of the front room – the desks, the typewriter, the flag, the rubber stamps and the documents upon the desks, the files where documents are kept, the posters on the wall advertising the latest state programmes seeking popular participation (for instance, the campaign against illiteracy, the vaccination campaign); and finally the officials standing or sitting at their desks. The integration of all these arguments within a spatial and temporal unit helps to imbue the interactions of parties with a sense of normative commitment. Such commitment is aimed predominantly to the creation of order – which stands in contrast with the normative commitment typical of state institutional discourse, based upon compulsory participation and sanctions. For although the RA invokes the threat of sanctions, its rhetoric focuses more on the desirability of compliance to achieve shared objectives, as will be seen later.

3.2.1.2   *Questioning*

The questions asked by the *presidente* about the nature, legitimacy and conditions of the contract perform different functions. First, they provide the information with which he will decide whether the relationship should be ratified. Ratification is most commonly denied when the RA does not have jurisdiction over the matter or the territory involved. But the *presidente* may also refuse to ratify when, through questioning the parties or from personal private knowledge, he comes to suspect fraud – for instance, when the would-be seller does not own the property. In any case, ratification was never denied in the sessions I attended.

I submit, however, that the main function of questioning is not to obtain information, but rather to assert the right of the RA to ask such questions. By doing so, the RA reasserts its jurisdiction, reinforces the official atmosphere of the proceeding, and claims to represent the concerns of the community about the eventual consequences of the relationship. The rhetorical aspect of such questions lies in the fact that they have an impact independent of the answers obtained. Moreover, the act of questioning seems more important than the questions asked. This does not mean that the questions are framed arbitrarily. To question the parties on the nature and conditions of the contract is to assert that the freedom of contract is not an absolute principle in Pasargada, but can be restricted to protect overriding interests of the community. The answers also contribute to the ratification process. By answering, the parties not only clarify their commitments for themselves but also make such commitments public, which intensifies the motivation of the parties to honour them.

3.2.1.3   *Drafting*

From a rhetorical perspective, the drafting of the contract, like the object of a dispute, is a process of bargaining between the parties, and between each of them and the officials. The RA is oriented toward championing community interests and protecting the weaker party. Whenever the parties bring a draft of the agreement that they have prepared in advance, the bargaining process between them has already taken place, and there is little room for the RA to intervene. Whenever a routine contractual formula is used, as in the case of leases, the influence of the RA is embodied in the formula, and is effective when the parties accept it. But the formula has substantive value and creates a sense of normative order that goes beyond its content, since the parties, in subscribing to phrases that have been used routinely by many other residents, come to perceive themselves as involved in an ongoing legal structure that precedes and survives their relationship. Furthermore, even though the terms of the formula become part of the contract only after they have been accepted, the parties perceive the formula as manifesting a normative order that transcends their will. The routinization and standardization of legal formulas are a constitutive part of their normative content. Nevertheless, formulas are not mechanically applied. Beyond the obvious need to fill in the blanks – prices, dates, and so on – some clauses may be eliminated and other clauses may be added.

Through drafting, the RA helps to clarify the content of the relationship. It stimulates a dialogue between the parties about unanticipated possibilities for conflict, thus forcing a reopening of the bargaining process. It diffuses legal knowledge by advising the parties about the consequences of their line of conduct, such as failure to pay or to sign a promissory note. It intervenes in the relationship, for instance, when – upon learning that the poorer, less articulate party is accepting a particularly onerous commitment – suggests different conditions, such as a longer time to pay the balance of the purchase price.

3.2.1.4   *Writing*

Once the terms of the contract have been settled, the contract must be reduced to writing. Here we must distinguish between the act of writing and the written product. Though I did not systematically collect information on this point, it seems to me that, in

Pasargada, the *topos* of the written word dominates that of the spoken word, suggesting that such relations are permeated by a legal rather than a moral discourse.

With respect to the activity of writing, its substantive value is not limited to progressively separating the promise from the person making it. Writing is a ritual with its own dynamic, oriented to the creation of a legal fetish that it is superimposed upon the material base – the elements of the contract, the paper, the writer. The RA performs this superimposition by substituting typing for handwriting. The keyboard of the typewriter extracts from the white paper a legal fetish in much the same way that the chisel extracts a statue from stone. The fact that a technological medium stands between the writer and the writing only enhances the myth of impersonality and transcendence, particularly in a community like Pasargada, where typing is not a generalized skill, and a typewriter is a rare object. On the other hand, the persuasive power of the *topos* of the written word increases to the extent that the writing apparatus is perceived as less destructible – closer to printing than to handwriting.

3.2.1.5   *Reading*

After being typed, the document is read to the parties. This is probably the first moment when the parties to the contract experience fully the dialectics of autonomy and alienation that their relation goes through during the process of ratification. Through the reading, the written agreement appears to stand on its own feet, reflecting, as in a distorted mirror, a strange travesty of the personal affirmation of will. The fact that the document is read aloud by a third party only increases the independence of what is read from the parties who conceived it. Thus, the reading is an important moment in the process of dispute prevention through ratification. The RA presents the agreement to the parties, thus increasing the sense of externality and of alienation that is at the core of any normative structure.

3.2.1.6   *Signing*

The reading is followed by the signing. Superficially this may appear to be the dialectical synthesis, the moment at which the parties overcome their alienation and reappropriate their commitment for themselves. On further reflection, however, it can be seen that this is a false overcoming. The moment of signing represents the greatest polarization between the promise and the person making it. In the presence of others, the parties have to certify as their own something that has just been handed to them, thereby denying their role as creators. True synthesis will come later when there is actual compliance with the terms of the contract. Indeed, the recognition of polarization rather than synthesis at the moment of signing is what justifies the complementary signing by two witnesses. Indeed, the witnesses testify to the autonomy of the written agreement, thereby intensifying the gap between the parties and the agreement before them.

3.2.1.7 *Witnessing*

So far we have lumped the parties together in our analysis, but it must be recognized that the agreement establishes a division of labour in which the parties assume different and sometimes antagonistic positions, which the witnesses may help to secure. For instance, each may regain some sense that the agreement belongs to her through her perception that the agreement is autonomous in relation to the other party. The presence of the witnesses corroborates and reinforces such perception. On the other hand, the witnesses make a grassroots contribution, collectivizing the relationship between the parties, imbuing it with a sense of popular normative order. They represent not only social consensus and social control, but also an ongoing legal process with its aura of continuity and tradition within which the individual agreement must be integrated.

The RA is also interested in the collective and popular construction of a normative order. Thus, it works in tandem with the witnesses, albeit from a different perspective. For whereas the RA belongs to the institutional superstructure, witnesses are an unmediated part of the community. This is why one witness is not enough. A single person is an individual, an expression of freedom, while two persons are a community, an expression of social control. By negating each other's individuality, the two witnesses create an autonomous entity which can function as a source of normative order, an efficient community that symbolizes the actual community.

3.2.1.8 *Stamping*

After the document is signed, the *presidente* will stamp it. Here again it is useful to distinguish between the stamps as end products and stamping as an activity. Stamps are signs through which the RA symbolically manifests its prerogative to participate in the creation of the normative order embodied in the relationship. Structurally, they resemble the questioning at the beginning of the ratification process. In both, the RA asserts its right to extricate the relationship from the intimacy of the parties. The difference is that this assertion is hypothetical in the questioning, whereas in the stamps it is definitive. In a sense, the stamps are the answer that the RA gives to its own questions. The normative order symbolized by the stamps is reinforced by the fact that they are also used in administrative documents of the RA. Thus the atmosphere of officialdom is communicated to the ratification process.

Stamping as an activity has its own meaning. It is an up-down movement in which the stamp hits the paper firmly and strongly. The activity is structurally similar to the irate patriarch banging his fist upon the table to command obedience from his children, the priest banging his hand upon the edge of the pulpit to stress an important point, or the angry child hurling his toy or stamping his foot against the floor. All of these activities symbolize command, stress points, reinforce a normative order. Just as a writer puts in italics what he wants to emphasize, so these activities are the italics of social relations.

Indeed, the stamping is more important than the stamps. It symbolizes the exercise of control over the finally and the irrevocable character of the transaction.

3.2.1.9   *Filing*

Finally, one copy of the document is given to the parties, and another is kept in the RA's files. Just as funerals are ceremonies that adjust the relationships among the survivors – and between them and the deceased – by re-enacting the death, so the act of filing re-enacts the ratification process. The parties do not take home the document, which is buried in the files, but a copy of it, much as relatives keep at home a photograph of the deceased. Filing symbolizes security for the relationship, and thus affirmation of collective normative order, because from now on the behaviour of the parties will be supervised by the document, which is out of their control. For the document can reveal discrepancies between the terms of the agreement and the actual behaviour of the parties.

In the preceding discussion I have argued that the ratification process is a constitutive act, both because it imbues the relationship between the residents with a normative order, and because it may influence the future of the relationship. Earlier I predicted that forms and procedures in Pasargada will lack the mechanical character of those in formalized legal systems. This prediction seems to be substantiated by the ratification process: agreements may be drafted by the parties, by the *presidente*, or by all in co-operation; the number of stamps is not fixed; and even the number of copies of the document may vary. In particular, the extent to which the *presidente* questions the parties is highly variable. The length of the questioning is inversely correlated with the *presidente's* knowledge of the parties – their honesty and reputation for fulfilling their commitments – and directly correlated with the value of property that is the object of the contract. Since the ratification process is aimed at investing transactions with a sense of normative order that will increase the security of contractual relationships in Pasargada, the *presidente* perceives those threats as greater when he does not know the parties, and when the value of the property is high. Thus, the ratification process is structured to give greater security to those relationships that need it more. In this way, the instrumental character of forms and procedures is maintained.

3.2.2 Substantive norms defining the type and range of the relationships

There are striking differences between the types and range of legal relationships handled by the RA in Pasargada and those handled in the city by the legal aid offices. At the time of my empirical research, roughly 85 per cent of the caseload of the legal aid offices was alimony and child support cases. Brazilian legal officials tend to conclude from this that such cases are the most typical legal problems of the poor. On the contrary, the pattern of relationships processed by the Pasargada legal system shows that even though most Pasargadians are poor, they are involved in a wide variety of relationships, many of which are structurally – though not substantively – similar to relationships that Brazilian legal officials would consider typical of the middle classes. I will demonstrate this here in the context of dispute prevention, and later in the context of dispute settlement. In both contexts, I will proceed by analyzing actual cases that were handled by the RA during my fieldwork. I begin by studying contracts of sale.

Case 1

I, EL [full identification], declare that I sold to Mr OM [full identification] a *benfeitoria* of my property located at [location]. He paid [amount] as down payment and the balance of the price will be paid in eight promissory notes beginning [date]. In case Mr OM defaults in making the payment for three months, this document will be declared invalid. This agreement is free and legal and the property is free of charge and encumbrances. The land does not enter in the transaction because it belongs to the State.

This contract will be signed by the parties and by two witnesses in two copies, one of which will be kept by the Association for any contingencies that may arise.

Date:
Signature:
Witnesses:

The normative structure of Case 1 is complex, as can be seen through an analysis of the object of the transaction. Even though that object is a house, it is called a *benfeitoria* in the document. *Benfeitoria* is a technical expression used in the official legal system to refer to improvements upon material things. These improvements may or may not be transferred separately from the things to which they are attached. It is important to explain the borrowing of this technical expression, both because I predicted that legal language in Pasargada would be very close to ordinary language, and because the expression is extensively used in Pasargada.

In Pasargada law, the term *benfeitoria* does not refer to any kind of improvement, as it does in the official legal system, but mainly to houses and shacks, revealing the selective character of the linguistic borrowing. Moreover, the term is used in Pasargada to certify that the parties do not intend to transfer the land upon which the house or shack is built, for this belongs to the state. To include the land in such a transaction would be a crime, if done intentionally; the use of the term *benfeitoria* precludes that possibility. In order to understand the use of this term it is necessary to conceive Pasargada law not as a closed system that, despite borrowings, remains independent, but rather as one partial legal system coexisting, in a situation of legal plurality, with another partial but dominant legal system. The term *benfeitoria* is addressed not to the Pasargadians themselves but, rather, to the Brazilian official legal system and legal officials. For this latter audience, what matters is the certification of a specific legal intention. Once this intention is ritually certified, the internal audience asserts itself: from the point of view of Pasargada law, the actual transaction involves both the house or shack and the land upon which it is built.

It may appear that, with reference to houses and shacks, Pasargada law has borrowed the official norms concerning *benfeitorias*. But according to the official legal system, permanent buildings are the outstanding example of *benfeitorias* that cannot be transferred without the land upon which they are built – except in strictly specified and regulated situations – which is precisely the opposite of what is done in Pasargada. Pasargada has borrowed not the norm but simply the idea of separating things that are physically attached. This idea has then been adapted to the needs of Pasargada, and in such a way that the resulting norm is the antithesis of the official rule. To be sure, this contradiction is not based on any profound cleavage in the cultural postulates underlying Pasargada law and the state law, but derives from the dependence of Pasargada law upon the state law in the determination of the legal status of land. The autonomy of Pasargada norms on *benfeitorias* is thus adaptive and instrumental, aimed at minimizing conflict with the official legal system. The basic conflict over the legal status of land is transformed into a superficial conflict between norms on *benfeitorias*.

Because the minimization of conflict in situations of change has often been achieved through legal fictions, I suspect that Pasargada norms on *benfeitorias* embody the fiction that the land is not included in the transaction. This fiction recurs in different forms, for it expresses a conflict between the basic norms of Pasargada law and official law.[26] In terms of the basic norm of the state law – the 'law of the asphalt',[27] as Pasargadians call it – land tenure in Pasargada is illegal and the land belongs to the state. This basic norm and its consequences is known in Pasargada not only through repeated experience – for instance, the state uses the illegality of land tenure to justify its failure to provide public services – but also through the contacts of Pasargada with legal officials. Indeed, it underlies their behaviour toward state agencies in general, and toward those in charge of the 'squatter settlements problem' in particular. Even the movement in the early 1960s toward progressive legalization of *favela* land tenure started from the acceptance of the same basic norm.

---

[26]   I borrow the term basic norm (*Grundnorm*) from H Kelsen (1962, pp 2ff), though I use it in the broader sense of the norm or set of norms that establish the general legal foundation for the regulation of specific areas of social life, rather than in Kelsen's sense of the constitutional norm, conceived as the logico-transcendental presupposition of the legal pyramid.

[27]   Legal documents in Pasargada contain references to the 'laws in force', a technical expression meaning the 'official laws'. In more informal oral discourse, Pasargadians refer to the official laws and to the official legal systems in general as the 'law of the asphalt' because it is the law that governs social relations in the urbanized areas which, unlike Pasargada, have paved (asphalt) roads and streets. Depending on the circumstances, this folk category is used to connote either that the law of the asphalt is also applicable to Pasargada or that, because it is the law that governs social relations in the urbanized areas which, unlike Pasargada, have paved (asphalt) roads and streets. Depending on the circumstances, this folk category is used to connote either that the law of the asphalt is also applicable to Pasargada or that, because Pasargada is not in the asphalt, official law does not apply. I use the expressions 'law of the asphalt' and 'official legal system' interchangeably.

Within Pasargada, however, this basic norm is inverted by means of the fiction mentioned above, rendering land tenure legal. The Pasargada basic norm provides the foundation of legitimacy for transactions among Pasargadians involving houses and shacks viewed as real objects, and not as *benfeitorias* in any technical sense. Although these transactions are officially invalid, because a house cannot legally be transferred without the land on which it stands, and *favela* land cannot be privately owned, this official label of invalidity remains inoperative among Pasargadians as long as these transactions and the social relations they create are kept within Pasargada and under the jurisdiction of Pasargada's legal institutions and mechanisms. Thus, the basic legal fiction permits two mutually contradictory ideas of legality to coexist without interference so long as their jurisdictions are kept separated.

These normative dynamics, to which I shall return, elucidate the structure of borrowing in Pasargada law. Borrowing is innovative and selective in order to achieve two goals. First, to guarantee the normative survival of Pasargada law in a situation of legal pluralism in which the official law has the power to define normative problems, but cannot solve them. And second, it is innovative and selective to respond to social conditions and institutional resources of the community that differ from those in the larger society that gave rise to the official law. While the first process may require clear-cut innovation, as I tried to show in the preceding paragraph, the second tends to preserve the general outline of the borrowed norm, innovating at the level of substantive or procedural technicalities. Case 1 involves a contract of sale without conditions other than payment of the balance of the purchase price. But sales in Pasargada often include additional conditions, as the following cases illustrate.

Case 2

I, UL [full identification], declare that I sold to Mrs AM one room of my house located at [location] for the price of [amount]. We agreed that in case Mrs AM intends to sell the room I would have the right of first refusal.[28] Made in the presence of two witnesses.

Date:
Signature:
Witnesses:

Case 3

I, ED [full identification], declare that I received [amount of money] from Mr JM as the first installment of the total price [total amount] of the *benfeitoria* I sold him. Mr JM has the

---

[28] The right of first refusal appears in Pasargada documents in much the same form as it does in legal documents in the official system, because Pasargadians have been socialized in the official legal culture, and neither conditions in Pasargada nor relations between Pasargada law and the official legal system require in this case the normative autonomy of Pasargada. More on this in the following.

obligation to move the second wall backwards to the level of the third wall. The house has three rooms with the following measurements [width and length].

Date:
Signature:
Witnesses:

In Case 2 the object of sale is a room in a house. Although such a sale would not be possible under official law, in the sale of individual rooms is not only frequent, but does not create any legal problems. Given the unavailability of land for new construction and the rise in housing prices, there are people in need of shelter who can afford to buy a room but not a house. In addition, there are homeowners in urgent need of cash who find that selling a room is an ideal solution, because they retain their own shelter and yet raise an amount of money that mere rental would not produce. Since these transactions do not endanger the overriding interests of the community, there is no reason for Pasargada law not to legitimize them.

In Case 3, Mr ED requires Mr JM to reconstruct one of the walls, because he owns the contiguous house and wants to guarantee access to the street. Since demolition and reconstruction are involved, Mr ED gives a full description of the house, with complete measurements. In the law of the asphalt – ie, official, state law – it is always necessary to include a full description of the house. Pasargada law does not rigorously insist on this, and many documents merely indicate the location of the house. In general, transactions within Pasargada are confined to houses and gardens, which have unambiguous limits. In case 3, however, the obligations created by the contract justified and demanded a description of the house, which is another revealing instance of the instrumental character of formalities in Pasargada law.

In the preceding cases, contracts of sale created social relationships. Other contracts terminate relationships, exchange houses or shacks for others located in Pasargada or a different squatter settlement or for cars or plots of rural land, and create or terminate a landlord-tenant relationship. Gifts and wills are also among the legal agreements, as illustrated by Case 4.

Case 4

I, SE [full identification], live in a '*benfeitoria*' of my property [detailed description of the *benfeitoria*]. For ten years, Mr and Mrs XO have lived in my company and have helped me and treated me with respect, love, and tenderness. For one year I have been paralyzed on my left side and have lain in bed all the time and moved only with the help of this couple. Having received from this couple so many attentions and assistance and not having any other resources with which to compensate them for so much [again the same expression about care and help], I decided in full lucidity and consciousness, that after my death my '*benfeitoria*' will become their property. This is my way of showing my gratitude for so much [again the same expressions]. Since I am illiterate I put my fingerprints in the presence of two witnesses.

Date:
Fingerprint:
Signature of the couple and witnesses:

Case 4 involves an action that expresses attitudes at the same time as it produces legal consequences. Moral discourse tends to dominate legal discourse, and its rhetorical orientation aims at creating a persuasive argument in favour of the legality of the action undertaken, thereby enhancing the security of the relationships that result from it. The need for intense rhetoric stems from the fact that the legality of the action may be doubtful, and there is a significant probability that others will challenge it. All the cases previously analyzed are governed by materialist motives. Here, however, the donor suffers a clear material loss. His only gain is emotional, and also personal in the sense that it cannot be transferred to other people who may later assert rights to his property. Therefore the parties in this case are anxious to neutralize subsequent legal claims by the wife or heirs, by emphasizing the close connection between the ethical imperatives and the legal consequences of the gift in order to prevent a conflicting norm from later overturning that result.

This rhetorical strategy is visible at different levels. In the first place, the *topos* of repetition is widely used. The same expression of gratitude for love, care, tenderness and respect appears over and over. Far from being a product of clumsy legal drafting, this is intended to stress the norms that create the intended legal consequence. At the same time, this moral argument suggests a parallel legal argument, thus undercutting the attempt to isolate the transaction from legal discourse. The rhetoric of the moral argument employs the *topos* of retribution and restitution, through which future and past are connected. It emphasizes the need to compensate the beneficiaries for the services they have provided to the donor by presenting a detailed and dramatic description of his illness, thereby implying the magnitude of their services. Performance of these services has created a legal right to compensation. Thus the moral discourse is aimed at transforming the gift into a bilateral contract in which the services are paid for in property.

Contracts in Pasargada are remarkably well adapted to the needs and interests of the parties. They clearly display the intentions of the parties to obtain the mutual advantage that they anticipate. These contracts also reveal the dialectical relation between dispute prevention and dispute creation. By expanding the areas of anticipated conflict and by drafting clauses to handle them, the parties enhance the dispute prevention function of the contract. At the same time, by multiplying the terms of the agreement, the parties increase the probability of contract violation, and thus of dispute creation. From the perspective of the law of the asphalt, these contracts are very 'complex'; were they to conform to all the requirements of that law, they would require cumbersome legal preparation. In Pasargada law, however, they remain extremely flexible, and yet do not demand much time or great skill to draft.

In this section I have dealt with the substantive norms of Pasargada law with regards to contracts and dispute prevention. I now turn to the study of its forms and procedures. This distinction, however, is made here for clarity of presentation. In practice, as will be seen below, form and substance are intertwined in Pasargada law.

3.2.3 FORMS AND PROCEDURES FOR LEGALIZING RELATIONSHIPS

Legal forms may be non-verbal or verbal; the latter are couched in legal-technical language. I will argue in this section that Pasargada legal forms are consistently instrumental, oriented to the substantive goals that they are supposed to serve. Pasargada law is loose on formalism and strict on ethics. Whenever it borrows legal forms from the law of the asphalt, the pattern of borrowing is similar to that observed for substantive norms. The relative autonomy of Pasargada formalism in this situation of legal plurality suggests that a folk system of formalism and a folk technical language have evolved.

The ratification process previously mentioned – which has shown how forms can be used to create or reinforce a normative order – centres around the written document that certifies the legal transaction. In the law of the asphalt, two major types of legal documents can be identified: private and public. The latter are written by a notary public according to special procedures, and are mainly used to certify the transfer of legal title to immovable property. They are attached to the official files of property in the appropriate registry of titles. Both private and public documents are usually signed by the parties and by witnesses. Pasargada documents are structurally similar to the private documents of the asphalt, and are signed by the parties and two witnesses. But Pasargada law uses these documents to certify legal transactions (transfer of title to immovable property) that would require a public document in the law of the asphalt.[29] Therefore, Pasargada law borrows from the state law the general outline of the legal form. A written document is considered necessary to certify contractual intentions and deeds, but the security thus obtained is not dependent upon compliance with the technical distinctions and procedures prescribed by the law of the asphalt. Witnesses are used because they are important symbols, are inexpensive, and do not create delays.

---

[29]   Pasargadians could not possibly have their legal transactions certified by the public documents of the asphalt, not only because their land tenure is illegal, but also because their houses violate the housing code (they have not been granted the *habite-se*). From the point of view of the law of the asphalt, the private documents used in Pasargada might be viewed as valid transfers of rights to possession, not property. But Pasargadians only make this distinction when referring to the official legal system. Under Pasargada law, these transactions transfer property, and indeed the rights transferred exceed mere rights of possession as these are conceived by the law of the asphalt.

Forms are flexible and are adapted to the circumstances. A good example is the signing of the document by the parties. Since they may be illiterate, both Pasargada law and the law of the asphalt accept the fingerprint of illiterate parties. But while in the law of the asphalt the fingerprint has to be printed in the presence of a state official according to formal procedures that establish its authenticity, in Pasargada law nothing more is required than its printing on the paper in just the way that a name is signed. These are not mere differences in form, but in functional conception. While in the law of the asphalt the fingerprint can *substitute* for the signature, in Pasargada law one *signs* by fingerprint, and accordingly the same expression is used for signature and fingerprint. What has been borrowed is the logical structure of the fingerprint, the possibility of an alternative material sign to express a legal commitment.

Other contingencies may affect the form of the contract. In the following case the seller's son had publicly expressed misgivings about the sale, and the buyer was concerned that he would use his mother's illiteracy as a pretext to try to upset the sale. The buyer, therefore, refused to buy the shack unless the seller convinced her son to sign as a witness.

Case 5

I, CE [full identification], declare that I received [amount] as the just value of a *benfeitoria* I sold to Mr LP [full identification]. The *benfeitoria* is [measurements of the shack, a very small one]. It is made of wood and French tiles; with water and light. The buyer has full rights over the *benfeitoria* from now on and he can do with it whatever he pleases.

Since I am illiterate I present my oldest son to answer for this sale, signing as an eye witness (*testemunha de vista*) of the contract. Date:

Signature of the buyer: Witnesses (one of whom is Mrs CE's son):

Mrs CE's son signs as more than a simple witness to the contract, for he is her legitimate heir, and thus a party whose consent is relevant in Pasargada law to the security of the legal transaction. Indeed, this concern with security is also evident in the full description of the measurements of the shack and of the rights that the buyer acquires. This case indicates that the parties to an agreement under Pasargada law are not limited to those who buy and sell, but may include persons whose consent is considered particularly relevant. These persons are not agents of the parties because their consent is autonomous, and this consent may substitute for, reinforce or even counteract the consent of the person with whom they have a relevant relationship. The cases that follow illustrate this.

Case 6

Mr NT enters the Association and explains his case to the *presidente*. The following is their dialogue.

MR NT: I bought my shack from Mr SD He promised to give me a receipt six months later, after I completed the payment. But he never did and in the meantime four years went by. Now I sold my shack to Mrs CA but first she wants to see the document showing that I in fact bought the shack from Mr SD. But I don't have it.

PRESIDENTE: I understand your problem. You don't have any evidence to show that you are the owner of the shack. In that case you have to ask Mr SD to come to us. He will sign the document concerning the selling of the shack to you and after that you can sell it to Mrs CA.

MR NT: But the problem is that Mr SD does not live in Pasargada anymore. He lives very far away and I don't have money for the transportation. But his sons live in Pasargada and they know of everything. They saw me buying the shack from their father.

PRESIDENTE: In that case what you have to do is to try to bring Mr SD to us. If you can't, then bring his sons and they will testify concerning the contract between you and Mr SD.

Case 6 illustrates the importance of the written document in certifying legal transactions in Pasargada in two different ways. When Mr NT bought the shack from Mr SD, they agreed that the payment would be made in installments. Mr SD did not trust Mr NT and promised to sign a document of sale only after the payment was completed, for without this Mr NT would not be able to prove the sale and thus assert his rights over the shack. But Mr NT never needed the document, and thus did not press Mr SD to sign one. Now he wants to sell the shack, and the buyer wants to see the document first. Mr NT comes to the RA because he knows that the RA is in charge of solving this kind of problem. The *presidente* recognizes the problem, and rephrases it in a way that, though more precise and technical, is readily understood by Mr NT: 'You don't have any evidence to show that you are the owner of the shack'. The legal skills of the *presidente*, though greater than those of Mr NT, are not expressed in esoteric language. The problem is not the existence of Mr NT's right but its proof. It is therefore morally and legally imperative that he be helped, because problems of form must be subordinated to the normative substance.

The solution is approached by logical steps. The best solution would be to have Mr SD sign a document, but Mr NT tries to convince the *presidente* that this would be very onerous. Instead, he proposes an alternative. If the adult sons of Mr SD testify to the sale, their consent substitutes for his. They are not just witnesses but surrogate parties, because their material interests are presumed to be identical to those of their father. This legal reasoning is shared by the *presidente*, but there are some subtle differences. The *presidente* wants to stress the logical order of the solutions. First, Mr NT should try to bring Mr SD; only if he cannot do so (not an absolute impossibility, but perhaps an impossibility for Mr NT) will the second alternative be accepted. The solution ultimately adopted is the most feasible among several that achieve the same substantive goal.

This case shows that there may be bargaining over forms, just as I predicted there would be over the object of the dispute. Mr NT actively participates in the creation of the form that will be followed in his case. This is possible because forms are not applied automatically in Pasargada. There is a basic structure – the need for a signed document – from which different paths can be followed. That one is the most logical is not sufficient, since this must be weighed against the burdens it imposes. It would not be just to force Mr NT, who clearly owns the shack, to spend part of the cash that he will get from the sale in trying to bring Mr SD to the RA. This is another example of how Pasargada law is strict on ethics and loose on formalism.

Case 6 illustrates surrogate parties reinforcing the presumed consent of a missing party. But surrogate parties can also be used to substitute for and counteract the will of a person who might refuse to consent, as shown by the following case.

Case 7

Mr GM comes to the RA with Mr MT and explains his problem to the *presidente*.

MR GM: You know I own that *benfeitoria* on [location]. I want to sell it to Mr MT but the problem is that I cannot obtain the consent of my wife. She left home nine months ago and never came back.

PRESIDENTE: Where is she now?

MR GM: I don't know. Actually I don't think that her consent is very important in this case because, after all, the whole house was built by my efforts. Besides, there is no document of purchase of construction materials signed by her.

PRESIDENTE (silence, then): Well, I know you are an honest person and your wife has behaved very badly. (Silence) How long has she been away?

MR GM: Nine months.

PRESIDENTE: That is really not very long. (Silence.) I think that your oldest son should agree to the sale of the benfeitoria and sign the document as a third witness.

MR GM AND MR BT: We agree.

MR GM TO MR BT: We could draft the document right now....

The document is then drafted in the following way:

I, Mr GM [full identification], being separated from my wife, who disappeared without notice, and living as a good father with my six children, declare that I sold a *benfeitoria* of my property located on [location] to Mr BT [full identification]. He will pay immediately [amount] and the balance will be paid on a basis of [amount] per month. We declare that since there are no documents in my wife's name or in mine, I sell this *benfeitoria* without charges or encumbrances. Indeed it was built through my own efforts. I sign this declaration in the presence of two witnesses and in two copies, one of which will be kept in the Residents' Association in case any contingency arises.

Date:
Signatures:
Signatures of three witnesses:
(one of whom is Mr GM's oldest son)

It is known in Pasargada that the law of the asphalt requires the consent of the legal spouse for the validity of contracts transferring immovable household property. In Pasargada, however, many couples are not legally married, and in any case the consent of the wife is presumed if she is living with her husband at the time of the transaction. But Mr GM and Mr BT are troubled because Mr GM is legally married, and yet his wife is not living with him, so her consent cannot be presumed. They are concerned that the wife may try to upset the sale, especially since the house is a reasonably good one and Mr BT is paying a substantial amount of money. They resort to the RA for two reasons. They want to make sure that, if Mrs GM elects to use the RA to upset the transaction, her endeavors will be frustrated. But they also want to make sure that if she resorts to the legal institutions of the asphalt, those institutions will respect the solution given by the RA.[30]

The *presidente's* question concerning the whereabouts of Mrs GM suggests that the best solution would be to try to obtain her consent. Mr GM promptly answers that he does not know where she is, though he probably does. But the *presidente* does not press the matter, for it is common knowledge that she left with another man and had been unfaithful to Mr GM before leaving him. Under the sexist premises of the male-dominated RA, it would be humiliating for Mr GM to contact her now, a course of action that should not be expected from a 'reasonable cuckold'.

In any case, Mr GM seeks to eliminate this possibility by convincing the *presidente* that compliance with this formality is not very important in his case 'because, after all, the whole house was built by my efforts'. This argument embodies the *topos* of fairness, through which the formal norm requiring the wife's consent is re-interpreted in light of the concrete circumstances of the case. This is a convincing argument because, in Pasargada law, forms are not applied mechanically. The consent of the wife is recognized as a form that must be respected, but the substantive justification underlying that form is what gives it content. It is usually just to require the consent of the wife because she has actively participated in the creation of the wealth of the household. But, if it is possible to demonstrate that such participation has not occurred, the form becomes empty.

There are signs in Case 7 that the *topos* of fairness as a moral justification may not be sufficient by itself to determine whether the formal norm has been satisfied. This is because

[30]   One may wonder why the parties should be concerned about an appeal by Mrs GM to the law of the asphalt, since the latter does not recognize rights and transactions established by Pasargada law. However, one should not forget that in this situation of legal pluralism the informal legal system is dominated by the official legal system, and represents the legal behaviour of dominated classes within a capitalist society. Pasargadians experience this discrimination every day, and thus know that the autonomous legality tolerated in Pasargada may easily be destroyed whenever the state is interested in doing so, under the guise of any one of those slogans through which it reproduces class domination, eg, 'urban development', 'the fight against crime', 'law and order', 'down with unhealthy slums'. (John Steinbeck describes, in *The Grapes of Wrath*, how Hoovervilles were burned in the Depression in the US in the name of law, order and human decency.)

the participants are conscious that they are operating in a situation of legal plurality, and that the law of the asphalt grants considerable weight to the formality of consent – that is, it is more legalistic or formalistic. Therefore, Mr GM feels the need to reinforce his moral discourse with a legal argument: his wife has no legal proof that she has contributed to the construction of the house because there are no receipts for the purchase of building materials signed by her. Unlike Case 4, legal and moral discourses are kept separate, and though they feed back upon one another, the legal discourse remains subsidiary. The *presidente* recognizes the legal argument but does not consider it conclusive; after all, Mrs GM might find other ways to prove her participation in the construction of the house.

The *presidente* considers the case a very complicated one, and his silences are not only indications of his perplexity but also a rhetorical device to communicate those complexities to the parties and convince them that they should not expect the contract to be perfectly secure. The *presidente* tries the only path left open: to dispense with consent. And so he asks for how long Mrs GM has been away. Structurally, the legal reasoning implied here is very similar to that underlying the statute of limitations. If Mrs GM had been away long enough, any subsequent claim against the contract would have little credibility. Had he been living without his wife for a long time, Mr GM could probably contract as if he were not married. But they have been separated for only nine months and this is too short a period. The *presidente* feels that Mr GM deserves, and needs, to make the transaction as secure as possible. In the first place, the *presidente's* male common sense lets him know that, while Mr GM has always been an honest man, respected in the community, his wife had acquired a bad reputation long before she left him. She has no moral grounds for insisting upon the formalities of consent. Secondly, the *presidente* knows that the main reason Mr GM is so anxious to sell the house is that he is ashamed of all that has happened and wants to move out of Pasargada as soon as possible. In light of this, the *presidente* devises a solution that enables the parties to contract without Mrs GM's consent and yet with some assurance that the transaction will not be upset. If the couple's oldest son (an adult) consents to the sale, this will present an additional obstacle to interference by Mrs GM Should she attempt to do so, she will be acting against her children as well as against her husband. Thus her son's participation may discourage her from proceeding, and may contribute to a decision against her claim. Consequently, the oldest son is not a mere witness. Indeed, in the document, Mr GM declares that he signs in the presence of two witnesses; the son is actually a surrogate party. Yet his consent does not really substitute for that of Mrs GM, which is why the document emphasizes the immateriality of the latter rather than the presence of the former. An interesting inversion may be seen in this: while in the dialogue with the *presidente*, the moral argument was dominant and the legal one subsidiary, in the document the inverse occurs. The *benfeitoria* is sold without charges and encumbrances because there are no documents signed in the wife's name. The moral argument ('it was constructed through my efforts') is merely a reinforcer. The document, as a legal instrument, transforms the normative message and induces the legal argument to take the lead.

In this first section of the study of Pasargada law I have tried to discern the internal structure of legal reasoning in Pasargada, focusing the discussion on the context of dispute prevention. Now I will turn to dispute settlement, which constitutes the object of the second part of my analysis of Pasargada law.

3.3   Dispute settlement in Pasargada

3.3.1 PROCESS

Whenever the RA is called upon to settle disputes, the typical procedure is as follows: the plaintiff comes to the Association and explains his grievances to the *presidente* or, in the *presidente's* absence, to one of the directors. If he is not yet a member of the RA, it is highly probable that he will become one on this occasion, and will pay the membership fee and the first month's dues. The official will conduct a kind of preliminary hearing of the case. First, he will ask about the exact location of the *benfeitoria*, to make sure that it belongs to Pasargada and is therefore within the territorial jurisdiction of the RA. His questions will be then oriented toward establishing whether the dispute falls within the subject matter jurisdiction of the RA (property and housing rights). Finally, depending on how well he knows the disputants and how much private knowledge of the dispute he already has, the official will engage in further questioning about the content of the dispute and the *prima facie* reasonableness of the claim. He may conclude that the plaintiff is acting out of spite, or that he is not serious about the dispute or willing to pursue it, or even that he is not involved in a dispute at all.[31]

When the Association accepts the case, the official registers the name and address of the resident against whom the claim has been brought, and sends a written invitation asking him to come to the RA at the date and hour indicated 'to treat matters of his interest'. The plaintiff is also told to return then. In the meantime, the *presidente* or a director may inspect the locale. If the defendant replies that he cannot come on the specified date, another time will be arranged. If he says nothing and fails to show up, and the claimant reaffirms his dissatisfaction with the situation, a second invitation will be issued. If this, too, elicits no response, then other devices may be used, such as personal intervention by the *presidente*, by a friend of the defendant or even by the

---

31   One day I was chatting with the *presidente*, when a sixteen-year-old girl entered the association, carrying her four-month-old daughter in her arms. She explained that she had been living with her mother in her stepfather's shack, her stepfather had just forcibly raped her, she had fled, and now she had no place to live. The *presidente* then said: 'Look, I don't know in what way I can be helpful. Do you want me to invite your mother and your stepfather for a discussion of the case? In fact, I think that your case with your stepfather is of a criminal nature. It cannot be resolved by the Residents' Association. It is a question for the police'. The girl replied: 'No. I don't want to denounce them. I don't even want to talk to them. I just thought that the Association might know of any shack or room for rent'. Trapped between an inaccessible criminal justice and an impotent and insensitive RA, the woman was left without any way of redressing her grievance.

police. Sometimes the defendant will contact the *presidente* before the hearing in order to explain his version of the case and present his own grievances. The parties may be accompanied to the hearing by friends, relatives or neighbours, even though the latter may not intervene in the actual discussion. The *presidente* invites the parties to the back room or to one of the rooms upstairs, where the case will be heard behind closed doors. Usually the plaintiff presents his case first, followed by the defendant. Then, the *presidente* questions them, and the parties may engage in a lively exchange. Finally, the *presidente* will decide.

The procedural steps prior to the hearing create an ambience of interaction and an atmosphere of evaluation which will feed back upon the final stage of the process and contribute to its outcome. The process not only reflects the jurisdiction of the RA, but also recreates and reinforces that jurisdiction. In so doing, it strengthens the authority of the decision ultimately reached, that is to say, the probability that the parties will accept it. Since the RA neither looks for cases nor possesses any official jurisdiction, a resident who invokes its help publicly acknowledges that jurisdiction. An exchange takes place between the resident who wants his problem solved and the RA that wants its jurisdiction recognized.

Sometimes, when either the plaintiff or the defendant contacts the *presidente* about the case for the first time, the *presidente* asks if each knows that the RA has 'legal status' ('*qualidade jurídica*'). The answer is usually affirmative. The purpose of the question, however, is not to obtain information about how well the legal status of the RA is known, but to establish the unquestioned prerogative of the RA to solve cases that fall within its jurisdiction. Since the law of the asphalt has given the RA no official jurisdiction, there is no other way to create it but by affirming it, in a ritualistic fashion, in contexts in which the assertion is persuasive and meaningful. This affirmation of 'legal quality', which takes place so early in the processing of the dispute, is intimately related to the problem of implementing the ultimate decision. Given the weakness of the RA's sanctioning powers, implementation of the decision depends upon its acceptance by the parties without external coercion. But though power can develop suddenly and dramatically, the kind of authority that induces voluntary compliance is always created piecemeal and without drama. The *presidente* wants to point to it early in the dispute process so that its efficacy may unfold at the end.

The determination of territorial jurisdiction also reinforces the RA's authority. The message is not so much that if the shack is located outside Pasargada the RA has no jurisdiction, but rather that, if it is located within it, jurisdiction is indisputable. The same analysis applies to the inquiry into subject matter jurisdiction. By emphasizing the limits of its authority, the RA allays doubts about its authority within those limits. The initial questions concerning the substance of the claim enable the *presidente* to get a preliminary understanding of the case before the processing of the dispute reaches its final stage. This preliminary understanding is also influenced by whatever private knowledge the *presidente* may possess about the dispute, by the defendant's appearance to explain his version of the case and express his grievances, and also by the inspection on the spot of the material basis of the dispute. The *topoi* of dispute settlement are applied in a very vague and inarticulate manner at this stage, but this is sufficient to give the *presidente* a first impression of the relevant features of the case and the norms that may apply to it.

When the *presidente* happens to meet the defendant while inspecting the locale, he will invite him to the hearing orally; otherwise, he will do so in writing. The choice of this latter medium announces the seriousness of the situation and the commitment of the RA to assert its jurisdiction over the case. The message contains an invitation to come to the association 'to treat matters of his interest'. This epitomizes the ambiguity of the invitation process. Because the command emanates from a weak centre of power, it can only be asserted through self-denial, and thus is framed as an invitation. The unity of the explicit message is split into two implied ones: the veiled promise that the resident's interests will be promoted or defended if he accepts the invitation, and the veiled threat that they will be sacrificed if he refuses it.[32] If this strategy fails, the RA will intensify its pressure upon the defendant only when the plaintiff reaffirms her interest in the case by renewing her claim. Persuasive messengers – such as a friend of the defendant, the *presidente* or a director – may hint that the police will intervene, either to bring him to the RA or to enforce whatever decision the RA takes in his absence. I have not personally observed such police action, though I have seen them deliver invitations in cases in which the RA wants to embargo the construction of a house or shack. The *presidente* recognizes that absolute non co-operation would constitute a very serious problem, but he also says that such a situation hardly ever occurs. How true this is I could not ascertain.

In most cases observed, the final stage of the dispute settlement process took place behind closed doors, which ensured an atmosphere of privacy and intimacy that serves several functions. First, the parties may vent their anxieties without being disturbed by the presence of strangers. Secondly, since it is much more difficult for other residents to gain access to the *presidente* while he is in the back room, the legal-rhetorical discourse in which he participates will not be interrupted. If this discourse is to be persuasive, the parties must engage in a continuous exchange of views, through which a normative orientation gradually and precariously unfolds. Since the accumulation of persuasion in legal rhetoric is never irreversible, a break may mean a return to zero.

---

[32]   The use of the invitation as an *ersatz* summons is not limited to Pasargada law. It is used in general by lawyers operating within the framework of the state legal system. The lawyers at Rio's offices of the legal aid, for instance, who also lack the power to summon, invite the defendant to meet with them to try to reach an out-of-court settlement. They believe that, because the invitation is printed on the official paper of the state prosecutor and sometimes served by a court clerk, it will be interpreted by the addressee as a summons. I have no evidence that the Pasargada law has borrowed this strategy from the law of the asphalt. It seems more likely that these are independent responses to similar conditions.

Finally, the movement of the parties from the open front room to the closed back room is accompanied by the removal of the dispute from the natural setting in which it occurred into the legal setting in which it is going to be discussed and eventually settled. The myriad circumstances and implications that comprise the former setting are transformed into the relevant issues of the latter. The dispute does not lose all contact with the natural setting because, like the parties in the back room, it continues to be located in Pasargada and socialized in Pasargada ways. But much as the closed room offers the participants a privileged forum in which to discuss the dispute, so the legal setting gives the dispute a foreshortened perspective.

Once the parties appear at the RA and the hearing begins, we are in the final stage of dispute processing.

3.3.2 TOPOI OF DISPUTE SETTLEMENT

3.3.2.1 *The* topos *of fairness*

In disputes arising out of the conflict of individual interests, this *topos* urges a real or fictitious balance of rights and duties, an outcome that approximates the model of mediation. I have suggested elsewhere that we never find either pure adjudication or pure mediation in practice, and that it may be better to work with the categories of mixed adjudication and mixed mediation.[33] I will argue here that a third category should also be considered: false mediation. It applies to cases in which the rhetorical needs of the argument lead the person who settles the dispute to present a decision as a compromise when it actually grants the claims of only one party.

I will initiate the discussion of this issue with the analysis of Case 8.

Case 8

Mr SB sold his shack to Mr JQ for Cr$l,000.[34] The purchaser paid half of the price immediately and promised to pay the rest in installments. On the date agreed upon he paid the first installment (Cr$50). The second installment of Cr$200 was also paid on time. However, instead of giving the money to the seller himself, Mr JQ gave it to the seller's wife. She kept the money for herself and spent it. Besides, she was unfaithful to her husband and had gone to bed with the purchaser's brother. Having learned this, Mr SB, the seller, killed his wife and demanded repossession of the shack. The purchaser complained that he had duly paid the installments and intended to pay the balance. He had given the second installment to the woman in the belief that she would take it to her husband. The seller's sister was called to the Association to represent her brother who

---

[33]   Santos, 1995, Chapter 3.

[34]   All amounts are given in Brazilian *cruzeiros*, which, at the time, were worth approximately 26 US cents.

could not come since the police was seeking him. The *presidente* said that it would not be fair to revoke the sale since the purchaser had acted in good faith throughout. On the other hand, the seller should not be injured by the purchaser's failure to tender the money directly to him: therefore the installment in question should not be credited to the balance of the price. The *presidente* finally decided, and the parties agreed, that the purchaser would pay the balance in six installments, three of Cr$100 and three of Cr$50.

Because the *presidente* knew the dramatic circumstances of this case before Mr JQ brought his complaint to the RA, he had a preliminary understanding of the facts and norms involved in the dispute. In demanding repossession of the shack, Mr SB was using Mr JQ as a scapegoat for his anger at Mr JQ's brother. But it was clear that Mr JQ had not been involved in his brother's affairs, and had always acted in good faith. After the parties presented their cases, the *presidente* invoked the norm that demands good faith in contractual relations. He also used the *topos* of fairness to eliminate some extreme solutions, thus creating the normative ground upon which a middle-of-the-road decision could gradually be shaped.

Mr JQ had always conducted himself as a reasonable purchaser. He paid all the installments on time. The fact that he made one of the payments to Mrs SB could not be considered as a violation of the contract. Since Mr and Mrs SB were legally married the shack was property of both. Therefore, Mr JQ made the payment to one of the sellers, reasonably assuming that Mrs SB would give the money to her husband. After all, the use of surrogate parties is well recognized in Pasargada law and, indeed, it is being used in this case, as Mr SB's sister is allowed to represent her brother in the hearing to avoid delay. Consequently, it would be unfair to give no consideration to the legitimate interests of Mr JQ by revoking the sale. On the other hand, Mr SB contracted with Mr JQ on the assumption that the installments would always be paid to him, since he did not trust his wife. He got none of the installments to which he was legitimately entitled, and can no longer get it from Mrs SB. It would be unfair to give no consideration to Mr SB's legitimate interest in obtaining full payment for the shack – under the male ethics of the RA, Mr SB's moral standing had not been affected by the killing of his unfaithful wife. By excluding two alternatives that sacrifice completely the interests of one party, the *presidente* legitimated, indeed necessitated, a decision that would 'strike the balance': Mr JQ could retain the shack, but the payment of the second installment should be repeated. Mr SB could not repossess the shack but would receive the money from the installment originally paid to his wife.

It is interesting to notice that the *presidente* avoids any involvement in the criminal issues that gave rise to the dispute. The object of the dispute is strictly maintained within the boundaries of the law of contracts, even though the *presidente* knew that Mr SB was using Mr JQ as a scapegoat for his brother. Indeed, the conciliatory decision that, on the surface of the legal discourse, appeared as the normative result of the exclusion of extreme alternatives, was motivated by the *presidente's* policy of avoiding any involvement with the criminal behaviour. The *presidente* may have been particularly anxious to persuade the parties to accept the mediation as a fair settlement of the processed dispute because this might settle the real dispute without explicit argumentation. The processed and the real dispute were kept separate in order to allow an 'economical' settlement of both.[35]

In Case 9 the problem of the limits of the object of the dispute is raised again, but the *topos* of fairness is used in a somewhat different fashion.

Case 9

The plaintiff, Mrs BW; came to the RA with her sister and the latter's three children. The defendant, Miss AM, came with her oldest daughter (about five years of age). All of them went to the room upstairs where the case was heard by the *presidente*.

Mrs BW: The land belongs to Mrs OL She gave me permission to build my shack there. I did it myself, I furnished it and I lived there for a while. In the meantime I got another shack close to the first one and I moved into it. At the same time, Miss AM (the defendant) came to me with two of her children saying she had no place to live and that she was sleeping on the street with her children. She knew that the first shack was vacant and asked me to let her move in there. Compassionately, I agreed and I even lent her all the furniture in the shack. I never requested any rent from her. Now I want the shack for this sister of mine and her children who just arrived from the hinterland and have no place to live. But Miss AM refuses to leave.

Presidente: Now Miss AM, what do you have to say?

Miss AM: I do know that the shack belongs to Mrs BW But I know that I cannot leave the shack because I don't have any place else to go. I don't have money to pay any rent. And besides I have three children. Nobody will rent a room to me.

Mrs BW (interrupting): She can pay the rent. The truth of the matter is that she is a prostitute and is full of cachaça (alcoholic drink) and of maconha (marijuana) all the time. And the shack is always full of marginais (criminals).

Miss AM: This is not true. And what about you? You lived for eleven years with a guy who was crazy and beat you all the time. He committed all kinds of larcenies and finally was caught by the police. Now he is in the mental hospital. But you said that you would receive him when he comes.

---

[35] One night, some time after the decision of this case, I managed to talk to Mr SB He always carried a loaded gun, wrapped in an old newspaper, and intended to use it, not to resist arrest, but rather to kill Mr JQ's brother. (The latter had fled from Pasargada and gone into hiding in the interior of Rio State. His wife, who had always been mistreated by him, was hesitant about telling Mr SB the whereabouts of her husband, but she never did.) We talked about the case. He manifested his agreement with the decision 'because, after all, Mr JQ should not pay for what his brother did'. He was only annoyed that he could not sell the shack again, because he needed money desperately. This shows clearly the discrepancy between the processed and the real dispute and how, in fact, the settlement of the former might have reached the latter.

Mrs BW: That's nonsense. I am very happy with the man I am living with now. I work in a lawyer's home and he said that I had the right to repossess the shack.

Miss AM: I don't care. More important than all is that you . . .

Presidente (interrupting): No. All this argument is not relevant to our problem. If the shack is not Mrs BW's, neither is it yours, Miss AM And, after all, Mrs BW was very kind to have let you move into the shack and even use her furniture.

Miss AM (in conciliatory mood): I don't deny that. And as a matter of fact she was very nice when I first met her. But the problem is that I can't find a place to live. I would leave the shack willingly if I found a room. But even if I find it I cannot pay the rent.

Presidente: Look. I don't think that it is impossible to find a room at a very low rent. After all you have not tried yet. You have to. Your lack of co-operation is not fair. Mrs BW's sister is here with her children. They also have no place to live. They just came from the Northeast. They don't have money. It is reasonable that Mrs BW wants to help her sister and her children. She has a greater duty to help them than to help you.

Miss AM: I know. I know. But how can I find a room?

Presidente: Look, you have not tried yet. I will give you 30 days to find a room and to leave Mrs BW's shack. Do you agree, Mrs BW?

Mrs BW: Yes, I agree. I wouldn't like to see her on the street.

Presidente: Do you agree, Miss AM?

Miss AM: I agree. But I don't know if I will be able to find a room. I will try.

Presidente: You will try. You will find something.

This case is characterized by normative consensus between the parties concerning the application of the laws of property. Mrs BW was allowed to build on Mrs OL's land, and thus became the legitimate owner of the shack. She then granted Miss AM a precarious tenancy. Mrs BW has the legal right to repossess the shack. None of these legal conditions is questioned by Miss AM This explains why the argumentation lacks the legal tone that can be detected in other cases. The discourse is predominantly moral: the parties accept the same normative principle – the need for shelter – but use it to support contradictory claims. The supporters that each disputant brings to the hearing – Mrs BW's sister and her children, Miss AM's daughter – are used as non-verbal arguments, as symbolic elements that reinforce the parties' claims.

Each disputant tries to describe the facts in such a way that her claim appears morally superior to her opponent's. Mrs BW emphasizes the moral uprightness of her conduct: how *compassionate* she was in lending the shack to Miss AM with *all* its furniture and without asking for *any* rent; only compelling circumstances force her to ask for it back;

she would not like 'to see Miss AM on the street', but her sister and the latter's three children, who fled from the hopelessness and hunger of the hinterland, have no place to live and need her help. On her part, Miss AM tries to demonstrate that she does not refuse to leave out of a selfish motive, but solely because her situation is desperate: she has *no* place else to go; she cannot pay *any* rent, and because she has three children, *nobody* would rent her a room. She pushes the argument of necessity to the extreme, so much so that Mrs BW, afraid of its persuasiveness, interrupts abruptly and tries to neutralize it. She does so by presenting facts that are so loaded with moral opprobrium that they not only eliminate the factual basis of Miss AM's claim, but also cast serious doubt on her motives and her general moral character. If Miss AM is a prostitute, she has money and can pay the rent. She is also a deviant, a characterization reinforced by her alcoholism, drug abuse and contacts with criminals. Mrs BW's argument, in sum, is that the claim of an unworthy person is an unworthy claim.

Miss AM responds by trying to knock Mrs BW off her moral pedestal. Although she denies Mrs BW's accusations, she does not press this point, probably because she recognizes that the facts are so well known that to deny them will further damage her credibility. Actually her rhetorical question – 'And what about you?' – is a confession: 'Yes I am bad, but you aren't any good either'. Miss AM tries to stigmatize Mrs BW as deeply as she has been stigmatized herself: even if Miss AM does have contacts with criminals, Mrs BW had lived eleven years with a man who is not only a criminal but also crazy. Therefore, she cannot be the moral person she alleges to be, and her claim is not worthier than Miss AM's. Mrs BW tries to defend herself, but perceives that she cannot win on moral grounds, and swiftly moves from a moral to a legal argument. She invokes the official law and the lawyer of the asphalt in order to intimidate both Miss AM and the *presidente*. It is at this point that the *presidente* breaks his silence and takes control of the discussion. The emotional dialogue between Mrs BW and Miss AM has shown the *presidente* that the dispute over the shack is only part of the conflict between them. For reasons that I will analyze below, he does not want to extend the settlement context beyond the issue of the shack, and therefore organizes his argumentative strategy around this issue. At the level of moral argument, the claims of the disputants seem to lead to a tie: the principle of need of shelter applies equally to both. At the level of legal argument, Mrs BW has an edge, since Miss AM recognizes that Mrs BW owns the shack.

It is clear that the *presidente* decides this case for himself on legal grounds. But he cannot present his decision in those terms, because the fact that the parties have chosen a moral argumentation makes such a presentation unpersuasive. Accordingly, the *presidente* inverts his legal reasoning. He converts the legal advantage into a tie score – 'If the shack is not Mrs BW's, neither is it yours' – and then proceeds to create a moral advantage for Mrs BW. He begins by emphasizing Mrs BW's kindness in having let Miss AM move into the shack 'and even use her furniture'. The purpose of this moral rhetoric is to induce Miss AM to relinquish her inflexible position by making her feel grateful toward Mrs BW and conciliatory. He is only partially successful, because although she admits that Mrs BW 'was very nice when I first met her', she repeats the argument of necessity. It is here that the *presidente* invokes the *topoi* of fairness to exclude an obviously unfair alternative solution. But while in Case 8 the predominant feature of the *topos* is the balance of interests, in this case it is the conflict of moral duties. The *presidente* argues that, though Mrs BW was performing her moral duty to help the needy when she let Miss AM live in the shack, she had an even greater moral duty to help her own family. It would be unfair for her to leave her sister and nieces on the street to help Miss AM. Miss AM is touched by the argument, and shows some change in her position when she converts her previous assertion into a rhetorical question: 'But how can I find a room?' Promptly, the *presidente* undercuts the rhetorical value of the question by answering that she will find a room if she really tries, and gives her a month to do so. Even though he knows that Mrs BW will agree with this, he asks her consent in order to intensify the conciliation of the parties, since Miss AM is still reluctant.

In the first part of the discussion, the *presidente* kept silent. He wanted to know as much about the case as possible. The parties were free to expand the object of the dispute and to raise any issues they deemed relevant. They could also vent their anxieties and release emotional tensions that would stand in the way of an agreement. But this does not mean that the parties exercised absolute control over the object of the dispute. On the contrary, the *presidente* interrupted Miss AM when she was about to say something that she considered 'very important'. At this point, he had a sufficient understanding of the case and felt that no new issues should be raised. In his argumentation he was careful to concentrate on the issue of the shack, omitting the other facts that the parties had asserted. Why did he proceed in this way? In the first place, he sensed that the dispute over the shack was secondary, and had been triggered by another real dispute between Mrs BW and Miss AM. They were probably fighting over a man. He did not know what the real dispute was, because the parties never disclosed it, but the emotional character of the discussion between the two women and their use of stigma and counterstigma could not otherwise be understood. However, the *presidente* did not show any interest in reaching the real dispute. This case had a 'bad smell'. He knew that both parties were prostitutes deeply involved with career criminals and policemen. The role of the RA in such a case should be kept at a minimum. Besides, he was not sure that the plot of land upon which the shack was built was still under the territorial jurisdiction of the RA. And his male common sense also told him that the feelings of the prostitutes were 'highly changeable': 'they are enemies today, but could be friends tomorrow'. The fate of the agreement was less dependent on what happened in the RA than on what would happen outside, where the real dispute was being fought. The *presidente* was aware of the limits upon his functions in a case like this.[36]

[36]   The accuracy of his doubts was confirmed in a conversation I had, later the same day, with the defendant. She was completely drunk, but she could still articulate her ideas fairly well: 'I won't leave the shack. I just talked to a friend of mine who is a sergeant in the military police and he told me that nobody can force me out. Besides, the Residents' Association of Pasargada has nothing to do with my case because the land where the shack is located does not belong to Pasargada'.

In Case 8, the *topos* of fairness was used to reach a mediated outcome. In Case 9, there was no mediation: Miss AM lost her case, even though she was allowed to stay in the shack for another month. In Case 10, we will see how the *topos* of fairness can be used to reach an outcome of false mediation, that is, a decision that, though presented as a mediation, is really a form of adjudication.

Case 10

Mrs CT, the plaintiff, and Mrs SN, the defendant, were invited to come to the Association to settle the dispute in which they are involved. Mrs SN is very old and sick. Her son, Mr CN, came in her place. The parties were taken to the back room and the case was heard by the *presidente*.

> MRS CT: My sister came from the hinterland and she had no place to live. I bought for her the back room of Mrs SN's shack. I paid Cr$100. My sister lived there for nineteen months. She left a while ago but the man who lived with her is still living there. Now Mrs SN wants to sell the whole shack but she cannot because the back room belongs to me and I am going to sell it myself.
>
> MR CN: This is not true. There was no sale. No Cr$100 were paid. My mother accepted Mrs CT's sister in our house because her sister had no place to live.
>
> MRS CT: But I have witnesses of the sale of the back room.
>
> PRESIDENTE: Let's see. Mrs CT, do you have a document of sale?
>
> MRS CT: No, I don't because she refused to give me the receipt. But I bought the room and I have witnesses.
>
> PRESIDENTE: I'm afraid that is not enough. The Association only recognizes sales for which there are written documents with the Association's rubber stamp printed on them. Witnesses are not enough. The Association is a juridical institution.
>
> MRS CT: But I have witnesses.
>
> PRESIDENTE: It is not enough, Mrs CT We need a document. But let's discuss the case according to logic. I am not saying that you, Mrs CT, are not right in your contention. I know neither you nor Mrs SN I only want to find a fair solution. Let's suppose that you paid Cr$100. Let's further suppose that Mrs SN gives you the money back. In that case you have to pay the rent for the period in which your sister occupied the room. Let's suppose that the rent is Cr$10 per month. Nineteen months of tenancy amounts to Cr$190. You paid only Cr$100. This means that you still owe Mrs SN the amount of Cr$90. Wouldn't it be better if you forget the Cr$100 you paid? In that case, Mrs SN will also forget the Cr$90 that you owe her. As a matter of fact, you may have paid the Cr$100 but your sister also occupied the room for 19 months. I would suggest that you forget the whole thing.
>
> MRS CT: I don't agree. The room is mine. I bought it. I am going to sell it.

PRESIDENTE: Look, in your case I would be cautious. Your case is a lost case. If you want to fight then you should consult a lawyer. I may even refer you to the legal aid agency.

MR CN: I don't care if she wants to go to a lawyer. We will go too.

PRESIDENTE: That's the problem. You may go to the lawyer. But your case, Mrs CT, is a lost one. You don't have a document of purchase. In my opinion you should give the key of the back room to the owner of the house.

MRS CT: All right, I agree.

The legal norms involved in this case are the formal rule requiring a written document to certify the sale of the shack and the substantive rules of property. The basic dispute is about legal title to the shack. Mr CN contends that his mother owns the whole shack, and has the right to sell it because Mrs CT's sister and her lover have been occupying the back room as precarious possessors. Mrs CT contends that she bought the back room from Mrs SN. Both parties use the same moral argument – the principle of need of shelter – to substantiate their legal contentions. Mrs CT's sister came from the hinterland and had no place to live and no way to support herself. Since Mrs CT could not accommodate her in her own house, the only reasonable and morally commendable way of helping her sister was to find her a room. On the other hand, Mr CN contends that his mother was so deeply moved by the helpless plight of Mrs CT's sister that she compassionately allowed her to stay in the back room of the shack, and in these circumstances she would not possibly accept money.

Mrs CT tries to strengthen her position through a formal argument: she has witnesses who will testify that the sale took place. It is at this point that the *presidente* decides to intervene. He responds to Mrs CT's argument by raising the question of formalism. Mrs CT has said that she does not have a document of sale because Mrs SN refused to give it to her, but she does have witnesses, implying that they are just as good evidence as a written document. The *presidente* perceives the implication and disagrees with it as strongly as possible. The RA is a juridical institution and therefore has to maintain a high standard of formalism: witnesses are not enough, nor is just any kind of document – only a document with the association's stamp. The rhetorical device used by the *presidente* to render this formal norm persuasive consists in elevating the standards of formalism by elevating the legal status of the RA. But Mrs CT does not seem persuaded, and the *presidente* recognizes that the formalistic argument is indeed rhetorically weak. He thus turns to argue the substantive issues; he will discuss the case 'according to logic', which is the logic of fairness. However, before doing so, he has to solve two threshold problems. While arguing on formal legal grounds, the *presidente* had indicated to Mrs CT that the case would be decided against her. Now he has to retreat from this conclusion or suspend it rhetorically, because otherwise his argumentation on fairness grounds will lack credibility and persuasive power. Mrs CT will not even listen to him if she knows that the case has already been decided against her. Her resistance has to be overcome and an atmosphere of open-minded evaluation and co-operation has to be created. The *presidente* feels that his formalistic argument may have caused so much damage that he almost implies that Mrs CT may win the case after all: 'I am not saying that you, Mrs CT, are not right in your contention'.

The second threshold problem is the following. The argumentative needs of the formal-legal discourse required an institutional rhetoric that emphasized the legal authority of the RA, but this tone is highly inappropriate to an argumentation based on fairness and co-operation rather than intimidation. Here it is essential to stress the moral authority of someone who stands above the dispute and thus can evaluate impartially the rights and wrongs of the situation: 'I know neither you nor Mrs SN. I only want to find a fair solution'.

Having solved the threshold questions, the *presidente* embarks upon an ingenious argument in which he wants to present a decision against one of the parties as a compromise between them. To achieve this, the *presidente* begins by changing the object of the dispute through imaginary manipulations of reality ('Let's suppose ...'). He transmutes a dispute over the transfer of property (sale) into a dispute over the amount of rent (tenancy). Diagram 1 represents the structure of the argument.

DIAGRAM 1

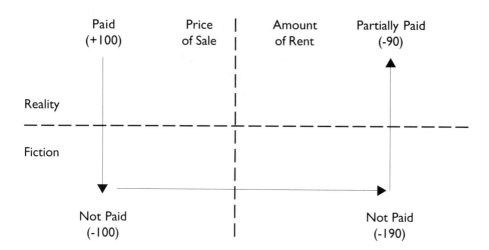

Paid (+100)	Price of Sale	Amount of Rent	Partially Paid (-90)
Reality / Fiction			
Not Paid (-100)			Not Paid (-190)

Through this argument, the *presidente* transforms the plaintiff (Mrs CT) into the defendant. Reality is reconstructed so as to make it appear that her best legal position is to owe Mrs SN Cr$90, and even this is possible only because he is willing to grant, without further evidence, that Mrs CT actually made the payment of Cr$100. The *presidente's* reasoning employs an ingenious device: in the course of the argument he manages to separate the payment of Cr$100 from the legal transaction that required it. He transforms it from a total payment of the purchase price into a partial payment of rent, and on this basis concludes: 'You may have paid the 100 *cruzeiros* but your sister also occupied the room for 19 months'. This would not make sense if the 100 *cruzeiros* had been paid as the sale price. But after the manipulation performed by the *presidente*, the stage is set for his proposed compromise: Mrs CT will forget the payment she made and Mrs SN will forget the rest of the rent.

The overall purpose of the *presidente's* strategy is to show Mrs CT that the amount of money she claims to have paid is so small that it could not reasonably be considered the sale price for the back room: 19 months of a low rent would be almost double that sum. This strategy allows the *presidente* to propose a decision that he considers fair without having to ascertain the facts of the case.

The argumentation is probably too artificial to convince Mrs CT, and she reaffirms her view of the case: 'The room is mine. I bought it'. At this point the *presidente* concludes that it is not possible to obtain spontaneous co-operation, and abandons the *topos* of fairness to return to a formal-legal argument. He seeks to intimidate Mrs CT by warning that if she does not accept the decision of the RA she will have no alternative but to hire a lawyer and try to fight the case in the asphalt. But he admonishes: 'In your case I would be cautious'. And, though he offers to refer her to the offices of the legal aid, this is less an offer of services than a threat. The folk image of the official legal system is immediately reconstructed in the implicit discourse of the participants: financial costs – even if state legal aid is provided, delays and inefficiency. Moreover, the *presidente* predicts the decision of the law of the asphalt: 'Your case is a lost case' (*'seu caso não da pé'*). The formal legal argument, which he recognized as weak within Pasargada law, acquires new strength through its direct connection with the official law: since Mrs CT has no document of purchase, her claim will be rejected by the official law.

DIAGRAM 2

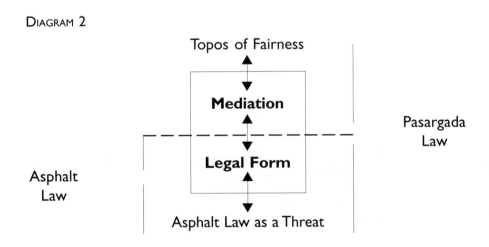

It is interesting to notice that the written document, as a legal form, constitutes the common ground of Pasargada law and the law of the asphalt. In contrast, the argument of fairness is kept within Pasargada law (see Diagram 2).

The official legal system is presented not as a forum to which a litigant may appeal from an adverse decision under Pasargada law, but as a threat aimed at reinforcing the decision of the RA under that law. The dominance of official law explains only partially the recurrent reference to the legal form of the written document in this case, for it fails to account for its invocation in the initial stage, when the discussion is kept within the boundaries of the Pasargada law. Throughout the section on dispute prevention above, I demonstrated the flexibility of Pasargada law in matters of formalism. Indeed, in Case 6, witnesses were allowed to certify the existence of the contract. The present case thus seems to contradict my theoretical prediction that, because Pasargada law is loose on formalism and strict on ethics, nobody would lose a dispute because of a technicality. I want to argue that these inconsistencies are superficial and disappear once the structure of the legal reasoning in this case is analyzed in depth. After the parties presented their claims, the *presidente* realized that it would be very difficult to learn what actually had happened. It was the word of one against that of another: if Mrs CT brought her witnesses, Mr CN would bring his. He therefore sought a solution on the basis of the data spontaneously offered by the parties. In the first place, it looked highly suspicious that Mrs SN had refused to give a receipt of payment. Since the whole purchase price had been paid at the time of the sale, there was no reasonable motive for Mrs SN's refusal. Besides, it did not seem plausible that Mrs CT, who seemed so articulate and so zealous in defence of her interests, would accept this refusal without doing anything about it. Then, too, the *presidente* questioned whether Mrs SN would have sold the back room for the Cr$100 that Mrs CT claimed to have paid. This was a very low price, considering the location of the shack and the fact that its value would diminish as a result of the sale of one of its rooms. Mrs SN would only have agreed to such a sale out of ignorance or because of fraud, and since the evidence of the sale was not unequivocal, her interests should prevail. Finally, Mrs CT does not really need the room, either for herself or her sister. She wants to sell it and make a profit at the expense of Mrs SN Accordingly she must lose the case.

All of this shows that the *presidente* decides against Mrs CT on substantive grounds, with the help of assumptions about reasonable behaviour and reasonable prices. The presentation of his arguments reflects, in an inverted form, the process through which he reached his decision. He uses the legal form of a written document – rhetorically buttressed by such details as the requirement of an official stamp – as persuasion for a decision ultimately grounded on principles of fairness.

3.3.2.2   *The* Topos *of the reasonable resident*

This *topos* is invoked when a resident has asserted his individual interest in opposition to the primacy of community (or neighbourhood) interests. It is far more difficult to apply than norms regulating conflicts among individual interests (as in landlord-tenant controversies), and its currency in Pasargada is open to question. In all the cases collected under the *topos* of the reasonable resident, there are two or more residents who present the same grievance against the same person. In some, the RA represents the interests of the community or the neighbourhood in a kind of administrative proceeding. Let us examine the usage of this *topos* in Case 11.

Case 11

When repairing his house, Mr KS extended one of the walls so much that the street, already very narrow, was almost completely obstructed. Some neighbours complained before the Residents' Association. The *presidente* and one director inspected the locale and concluded that the street had been virtually closed by the construction. They went to see Mr KS and explained the situation to him. He was reluctant to do anything about it but the officials pushed the matter very hard. The argument was: 'Look, if someone dies, the coffin cannot pass down the street. Not even the street cleaner's wheelbarrow'.

Faced with the refusal of Mr KS to co-operate, the *presidente* said: 'Look, I think that's unreasonable. But in any event you know that the Association has powers to demolish unlawful buildings in Pasargada. I have the laws here and I can show them to you. And the police are anxious to help the Association enforce its powers'.

The *presidente* and the director left without Mr KS making any commitment. Shortly after the discussion, Mr KS decided to demolish the wall himself and to rebuild it according to its original dimensions.

Leaders of Pasargada, the *presidente* and directors included, share the view that Pasargadians are individualist. As one leader puts it: 'They may watch someone doing something harmful to the interests of the community, but if they are not directly affected they won't move a straw'. Whether or not this is true it constitutes an assumption for evaluating behaviour. When some residents came to the Association to complain about Mr KS's construction, the *presidente* immediately concluded that they must have been significantly affected, because otherwise they would not have acted. The stereotype of individualism helped to build the *presidente's* expectations about the facts and issues involved.

Suspecting that construction was already under way, if not yet completed, the *presidente* anticipated that the defendant might be obstructive, since Pasargadians are very serious about protecting their interests and property values. He asked a director to accompany him in the inspection of the locale, because he was concerned about Mr KS's reaction and thought that the presence of two officials would have greater impact and deter any violence. Once in the locale, the *presidente* and the director quickly concluded that they faced a flagrant violation of the Pasargada norm that forbids private construction to the detriment of collective interests. The street was virtually closed by Mr KS's construction, and its residents thereby denied access to the main street. The normative needs of the factual situation were so evident that the *presidente* thought that a discussion between the plaintiffs and the defendant in the RA would be unnecessary. The RA took upon itself the task of representing the interests of the neighbourhood against an unreasonable resident.

Mr KS offered a defence at each of the two levels of discourse: the street had always been narrow and he had not exceeded the original dimensions of the house – legal discourse – ; he had invested money in the construction of the wall and had neither money nor time to demolish it and construct it again – moral discourse or discourse of necessity. Since Mr KS showed no respect for the Pasargada norm he had violated, the *presidente* turned to the *topos* of the reasonable resident. By disregarding the interests of his neighbours he was behaving unreasonably because, if all residents behaved like him, Pasargada would very soon be impossible to live in. His co-operation was requested, and in these circumstances the emphasis on co-operation was transformed into a rhetorical *topos* put at the service of (and reinforcing) the *topos* of the reasonable resident: a reasonable resident not only does not violate collective interests, but co-operates to restore them when they have been violated. In the course of the argumentation, the *presidente* managed to magnify the unreasonableness of Mr KS's behaviour by rhetorically expanding the object of the dispute. Mr KS's conflict was not only with those who live on his street, but also with those who die in Pasargada, and whose coffins have to pass through the street on their way to the cemetery. Mr KS was violating the interests of the living and the dead, and to be disrespectful to the dead is an especially heinous moral offense in Pasargada. His transgression extended beyond the neighbourhood in another sense: it damaged the community interest in cleanliness because it prevented the street cleaner, hired by the RA, from carrying the rubbish in a wheelbarrow to the entrance of Pasargada.

Mr KS had invested too much in his wall to be persuaded by the *topos* of co-operation. When this became clear, the *presidente* shifted to the *topos* of intimidation. Pasargada law has developed a characteristic dialectic between these two *topoi*. Intimidation by the *presidente* becomes reasonable only after the unreasonable refusal of the resident to co-operate has been established – even if not explicitly admitted. Once this *topos* was introduced, the legal discourse changed direction. Mr KS's conduct violated both the Pasargada norm about the community interest and the law of the asphalt that forbids (and orders the demolition of) unauthorized construction in squatter settlements. As long as the *topos* of co-operation dominated the legal argumentation, the *presidente* emphasized the Pasargada norm. But when he turned to the *topos* of intimidation he also invoked the laws of the asphalt. Because these are produced by the state, they are more effective in evoking the sanctioning powers, which the *topos* of intimidation manipulates in order to elicit what I would call imperfect co-operation, that is, compliance in which the act of co-operation is denied by the resident who is persuaded to conform through intimidation.

But the laws of the asphalt do not completely dominate this second phase of the legal argumentation. The *presidente* asserts the power of the association to demolish unlawful buildings. Since this power is given by the official law, it may appear that the criteria that determine which buildings are unlawful are also contained in that law. Yet this is not so, as evidenced by the many buildings in Pasargada which are not lawful from the point of view of the official law – because their construction was never authorized – but which the RA has no intention of ordering demolished. Mr KS's construction is unlawful not because it violates the interest of the state in stopping or controlling the growth of squatter settlements, but because it violates the community interest in free passage through the streets. Thus, as mentioned in the previous section, the official laws are selectively invoked to protect a recognized interest of the community. The threat of state sanctions and of the police is put at the service of substantive norms of Pasargada law. This case also illustrates how the threat of police intervention is invoked in tandem with the official laws. Let us now look at another case that uses the *topos* of the reasonable resident.

Case 12

In this neighbourhood, as in every other in Pasargada, there is a water supply network with pipes and pumps installed by the residents. Mr TH, one of the residents living in this neighbourhood, constructed a device to pump the water into his house. However, he installed it on the street and over the pipes of the water network. Some neighbours complained to the Residents' Association, arguing that this would ruin the pipes and would make repairs very difficult and costly. The *presidente* inspected the locale on the next day. He came to the conclusion that the neighbours' complaint was reasonable. The defendant was not at home at that moment, so the Association sent him an 'invitation'. He came before the date set for the joint discussion, and was given a hearing in the back room.

> PRESIDENTE: You know why the Residents' Association invited you to come here, don't you?
>
> MR TH: Yes, I know but I don't see why the Residents' Association has anything to do with my case.
>
> PRESIDENTE: Well, one moment, please. [The presidente went to the desk in the front room and brought back with him the folder with copies of the state laws on construction in squatter settlements.] I am going to read to you the laws that give power to the Residents' Association to order the demolition of unauthorized constructions.
>
> [He read the specific provision.]
>
> MR TH: My problem is that the pumping machine cost me a lot of money and I don't have any other place to install it. Besides, the way I installed it I don't think that any damage can be done to the network.
>
> PRESIDENTE: I have already inspected the place (*a obra*, 'the work') and the situation is not so clear to me. I will set a date for you and your neighbours to come to the Residents' Association to discuss the case.

After Mr TH left, the *presidente* commented to me: 'I am sure that he will be forced to remove the construction. The neighbours will exert too much pressure'. This case illustrates several things: the circumstances under which a defendant comes to the Association prior to the hearing in order to present his own version of the case; the flexibility of Pasargada procedures (the *presidente* first inspected the locale and attempted to meet the defendant on the spot, and only subsequently invited him to a hearing); and the extent of legal argumentation before the dispute even reaches its final stage. In this case – as in the preceding one – the crucial phase of the process is the inspection of the locale. Since the factual basis of the dispute is visible, the *presidente* becomes an eyewitness; the knowledge and authority he acquires in that capacity are a resource in the subsequent processing. Moreover, the issues and the governing norms sometimes appear so unequivocal in this phase that the *presidente* not only acquires a preliminary understanding of the case, but in fact reaches a decision about it. The requirements of legal argumentation, however, may lead the *presidente* to suspend his decision in order to create the rhetorical space within which the legal discourse can be persuasively articulated. This is why the *presidente* ambiguously says to the defendant, 'I have already inspected the work and the situation is not so clear to me', even though he is convinced that the neighbours have a reasonable claim and that Mr TH, by his lack of co-operation, has revealed himself to be an unreasonable resident. The ambiguity is generated by the tension between the contradictory elements in the *presidente's* utterance. The first – 'I have already inspected the work' – informs Mr TH that the *presidente* possesses firsthand, precise knowledge of the case. The linguistic signs of this phrase reflect and create certainty and precision in each semantic element: the agent ('I'), the temporal dimension ('already'), the activity ('have inspected'), and the object ('work'). In the second phrase, by contrast, the *presidente* confesses his doubts, and accordingly adopts the passive voice, employs a vague referent ('the situation'), and describes it only by its lack of a quality ('not so clear').

Water networks are a recurrent source of disputes among neighbours in Pasargada. They involve an initial investment of money, and demand daily management and constant maintenance, both of which may require technical skills that are not always available. The situation is even more complex in the neighbourhoods on the top of the hill, where the lack of co-operation by one resident may create significant hardships for the others, because of the increased difficulty of pumping the water up and into the houses. Mr TH's neighbours were alarmed about the potentially adverse effects of his construction upon their network. By acquiring a pumping machine, Mr TH was becoming independent from the network. Moreover, he showed his lack of concern about their welfare by failing to build a base of reinforced concrete that would have protected their network from possible damage. Because the neighbours' complaint was expressed in strong terms, the *presidente* inspected the locale the next day. When Mr TH heard this, he became concerned about the security of his investment in a water supply, and decided to come to the association in order to forestall further proceedings without his participation. He began by making a legal challenge to the RA's jurisdiction. But by raising this procedural objection,

Mr TH became doubly unreasonable in the eyes of the *presidente:* at the substantive level – by constructing on top of the water network – and at the procedural level – by refusing to recognize the RA's jurisdiction in construction cases.

The *presidente's* first step, therefore, was to assert his jurisdiction, which could only be done through the *topos* of intimidation. The use of that *topos* in this case is very complex, and requires detailed analysis. It is generally characterized by strict legality, precision and impersonality. When the *presidente* left the back room to get the documents, he suspended the action, freezing Mr TH in his own argument, uncertain whether his arrow had struck its target or was ricocheting and would strike him instead. By leaving the room to get the folder, the *presidente* showed Mr TH that he not only had the power to control time and impose silence, but also had access to resources unavailable to Mr TH. Thus the *presidente* created distance between himself and Mr TH. This ritualistic creation of distance was prolonged when the *presidente* returned. The folder and the copies of the laws were used as non-verbal clichés or legal fetishes, whose infrequent appearance among the paraphernalia of everyday life communicated a distinct note of impersonality. The silent opening of the folder was like the unveiling of a secret treasure. Then the *presidente* announced that he was going to read the laws, in much the same way as the trumpets of the King's heralds aroused the burghers to the news that royal decrees were going to be proclaimed. Instead of explaining the law in his own words, the *presidente* preferred to read the official text, another rhetorical device aimed at intensifying the impersonality of the legal argumentation. The state was speaking through the *presidente's* mouth. Thus, the reading, as a ritual, evoked the myth of the all-powerful state. As with an oracle, it was unimportant whether Mr TH really understood the meaning of the law – the official formula was an incantation against Mr TH by an impersonal state.

Mr TH did not accept or reject the argument. Indeed, it was not a question of either/or, but of whether he was sufficiently overwhelmed. This lack of reaction was interpreted by the *presidente* as indicating the success of the *topos* of intimidation. And he might be right, in view of the fact that Mr TH did not interrupt the legal discourse and rather adopted a different line of argumentation that presupposed his recognition of the RA's jurisdiction over the case: the moral argument and the defense of necessity. The *presidente* concluded that the *topos* of the reasonable resident and the *topos* of co-operation could now work in tandem, which is why he decided to create the space for argumentative manoeuvering I mentioned earlier. Even then, he was not convinced that the *topos* of co-operation would be persuasive by itself, and was relying on informal sanctions imposed by the neighbours, who had shown their deep concern by raising the matter in the first place. Given the weakness of the RA's own authority and its reluctance to call for police assistance, such self-performance of law jobs is an accepted practice in Pasargada.

From the point of view of the law of the asphalt, legal title to all houses and shacks in Pasargada is precarious: land tenure is illegal, construction does not comply with the housing code, titles are not officially registered, and many buildings violate special official laws on construction in squatter settlements. These sources of legal precariousness are irrelevant to the status of titles under Pasargada law. Yet there are situations in which the law refuses to recognize a given legal title because the collective interest is at stake. In such cases, the neighbours' complaint may not even be necessary; the RA takes upon itself the task of representing the collective interest, and proceeds like an administrative agency. The distinction between judicial and administrative proceedings is extremely elusive in Pasargada, since in both the RA assumes the support of the neighbourhood, and follows the same dialectical relationship between the *topoi* of co-operation and intimidation.

Case 13 illustrates the collective interest overriding a claim of individual title.

Case 13

I, Mr ZA, [full identification] declare: The area, which is occupied with pipes, in the address where I live, will be delivered to the Residents' Association, spontaneously and free of expenses, at any time that the Residents' Association needs the said area. The board of directors of the Residents' Association declares: The shack in the address [location] cannot be sold without the receipt being made in the Residents' Association. If the shack is disrespectfully sold without this receipt, the buyer will lose all its rights to the shack or area. Mr ZA is in agreement with all these declarations and signs.

Date:
Signature:

Mr ZA built a shack in an area that the RA had reserved for storing pipes before they were used for the improvement of the community. Mr ZA did not damage the pipes, but simply moved them to create a small space where he could build his shelter. The RA found this an infringement of its rights, but since the pipes had not been injured, the principle of the need of shelter prevailed, and Mr ZA was allowed to stay. In the future, however, this principle may collide with the collective interest – for instance, the need to store more pipes – and the RA wants to avoid possible conflict. The solution does not balance the interests of the community and Mr ZA's interests but is based on the illegality of his initial occupation. Accordingly, the legal status of Mr ZA's title over the shack is declared precarious: he will leave when asked, and cannot sell the shack without permission of the RA.

These restrictions reveal some interesting aspects of Pasargada law-ways. The RA recognizes that, in general, people may transfer their property without consulting it. But because Mr ZA has constructed illegally upon an area dedicated to community purposes, he is a squatter under Pasargada law. Mr ZA's right is dependent upon his need for shelter; if he decides to sell the shack he must no longer have such a need, and the RA determines the fate of the shack. The Association may decide that it needs the area, in which case the shack will be demolished. Or, it may allow the sale because it has no immediate use for the land, but in this case the precariousness of the legal title will pass to the next occupant. That is why the RA not only forbids a sale without its approval, but also declares that any such contract will be void, so that even a good-faith purchaser will obtain no rights. Pasargada law deals with squatter settlements inside the *favela* in much the same way as the official law deals with Pasargada itself. This similarity occurs through the inversion of the basic norm concerning rights to land, which I discussed earlier. Once this inversion takes place, it is possible to apply the same legal categories and remedies inside and outside the *favela*. This contrast between Pasargada law and official state law – or 'asphalt law' as it is called in Pasargada – is represented in Diagram 3.

DIAGRAM 3: THE RELATIONSHIP BETWEEN THE NORMATIVE STRUCTURES OF PASARGADA
LAW AND ASPHALT LAW

Asphalt Law		Pasargada Law	
With land tenure	Without land tenure	With land tenure	Without land tenure

A   *The two laws reviewed in isolation*

Asphalt Law		
With land tenure	Without land tenure	
	Pasargada Law	
	With land tenure	Without land tenure

B   *The two laws viewed in a relationship of legal pluralism (inverted basic norm)*

Since it is the inversion of basic norm that allows Pasargada law and the asphalt law to provide similar normative solutions to similar problems, a reasonable Pasargadian accepts both this inversion and its consequences. This is why the Pasargada law 'is like the law of the asphalt'. In the course of a chat with some residents, the *presidente* said: 'If residents rent their shacks to someone and their tenants fail to pay the rent, then the landlords shall have the right to repossess their shacks. Either the tenants leave or they will be forcibly evicted. It is like the law of the asphalt'. I have been arguing that this similarity does not reach into technical details, but remains at the level of the broad regulation. Moreover, even at this level, Pasargada law may have some normative autonomy. For instance, I have discussed how the basic norm governing landlord-tenant relationships is modified by the principle of the need of shelter. In his relations with other residents, the reasonable resident is expected to disregard whatever the law of the asphalt or its officials say about the legal status of such relations because they take place in squatter settlements, and to accept the normative solutions proposed by Pasargada law, which are structurally similar to those proposed by asphalt law for asphalt cases, ie, those taking place outside the *favela*. If a resident tries to take advantage of official law, and, as a consequence, tries to live in Pasargada according to the normative judgments that asphalt law makes about squatter settlements and social relations within them, he is an unreasonable, even a deviant resident, because he places his individual interest above the community interest, under the pretext of the coincidence of his own interest with the state interest. His deviance lies in his being forgetful that it is the community that makes peaceful social life possible in the face of a state that labels it illegal.

4 CONCLUSION

4.1 *The structure of legal plurality*

Pasargada law is an example of an informal and unofficial legal system developed by urban oppressed classes living in ghettos and squatter settlements to achieve the survival of the community and minimal social stability in a capitalist society based on speculation in land and housing. I have argued that this situation of legal plurality is structured by an unequal exchange, in which Pasargada law is the subordinated part. We are thus in the presence of interclass legal plurality, one of the several forms through which the class struggle is fought in Brazil. In this instance, class conflict is characterized by mutual avoidance (latent confrontation) and adaptation. Pasargada law does not claim to regulate social life outside Pasargada, nor does it question the criteria of legality prevailing in the larger society. Both legal systems are based on the respect for the principle of private property. Pasargada law achieves its informality and flexibility through selective borrowing from the official legal system. Thus, although they occupy different positions along a continuum of formality-informality, they can be said to share the same basic legal ideology. Using the concept loosely, Pasargada may be thought of as a microcapitalist society whose legal system is to a great extent ideologically congruent with the state legal system. Although Pasargada is not riven by antagonistic classes, the existence of social stratification is undeniable – there are good and bad neighbourhoods, as shown earlier. The RA has been controlled by the middle or upper strata, who are most familiar with the official society and most eager for integration in it. The RA does defend the interests of the lower strata of Pasargada, but does it in a paternalistic fashion.

The state strategy of mutual avoidance and adaptation may be illustrated by its relative passivity toward Pasargada. Despite its repressive policy of community control, the Brazilian state has tolerated a settlement it defines as illegal, and, by that continuing tolerance, it has allowed the settlement to acquire a status we may call alegal or extralegal. This may be explained by the fact that Pasargada and its law, as they presently exist, are probably functional to the interests of the power structure in Brazilian society. By disposing of secondary conflicts among the oppressed classes, Pasargada law not only relieves the official courts and the offices of legal aid of the burden of hearing *favela* cases, but also reinforces the socialization of Pasargadians in a legal ideology that – through the protection of private property and the promotion of social order – legitimates and consolidates class domination. By providing Pasargadians with peaceful means of dispute prevention and settlement, Pasargada law neutralizes potential violence, enhances the possibility of orderly life, and thus instills a respect for law and order that may carry over when Pasargadians go into town and interact with official society. The state co-opts the RA through both carrot and stick: it starts by granting the RA a privileged position as representative of the *favela* in its relations with all state agencies, and it responds with threats to any attempt by the RA to assert its autonomy. Finally, the preservation of law and order in the *favela* facilitates vote collection and with it the reproduction of patron/client relationships that have always characterized bourgeois rule in Brazil.

In light of the above, it is easy to draw a conclusion from the study of Pasargada law that overestimates the extent to which the two legal systems are integrated and have adapted to each other. The risk of reaching such a misleading conclusion is particularly high for those analyses that view these phenomena in isolation from the social conditions of their production and reproduction. Integration and adaptation are both strategies followed by the antagonistic classes at a given historical moment in a capitalist society. But this situation of legal plurality remains a reflection of class conflict, and thus of a structure of domination and unequal exchange. That the state has tolerated Pasargada thus far is no guarantee against future intervention. There are many examples of large *favelas* in the centre of Rio being totally removed, often with only a few hours notice. This harsh fact is never forgotten by Pasargadians or any other *favelados* (*favela*-dwellers), and accounts for the fundamental insecurity that characterizes the squatter settlements.

Unofficial legality is one of the few instruments that can be used by the urban oppressed classes to organize community life, enhance the stability of the settlement, and thus maximize the possibility of resistance against intervention by the dominant classes, thereby increasing the political cost of any such action. The political evaluation of unofficial legality depends upon the class in whose name it operates, and the social goals at which it aims. In a capitalist society, any attempt to offer a normative alternative to the existing system of land tenure in squatter settlements must be a progressive task. What appears on the surface to be ideological conformism is probably nothing more than a realistic assessment of the constellation of forces and the concrete conditions for social conflict in contemporary urban Brazil.

That this unofficial legality may, under the conditions described above, be considered a strategy of class struggle is illustrated by the ways in which Pasargada law 'deviates' from the official legal system. Although the two systems share the same basic legal ideology, they put it to very different uses. On the substantive level, I have discussed what I call the inversion of the basic norm of immovable property by means of which Pasargada law establishes the legality of land tenure, using the very norm through which the official legal system makes that tenure illegal. This is reminiscent of Renner's historical analysis of the law of property, which retained its verbal content unchanged, while its social function was transformed from a guarantee of personal autonomy in pre-capitalist European societies to the legitimation of class domination and exploitation in capitalist societies.[37] What Renner observed diachronically I have observed synchronically in a situation of interclass legal plurality. However, in order to sharpen the parallel, it would be necessary to analyze in depth the dominant social relations in Pasargada. Pasargada is fully integrated in Brazilian society. The bulk of its active population works outside Pasargada. It has a flourishing commercial sector as well as some industry.[38] The latter – mainly shoe shops, bakeries and ice cream shops – are small, family enterprises producing for the market which sometimes extends outside Pasargada. One of the striking features of this micro-capitalist society is a persistent and even increasing social stratification.

By providing housing for the poor working classes, Pasargada contributes to the conditions of reproduction of labour power, and it is here that Pasargada law plays its role. While its official (external) legal quality as a *squatter* settlement is a reflection of capitalist social relations, its internal legal quality as a *settlement* is an attempt to ameliorate the living conditions of the popular classes and to obtain some room for autonomous collective action – indeed a progressive endeavor in a situation in which widespread unemployment and the consequent availability of an immense reserve army of labour relieves capital of the task of ensuring the reproduction of labour. Though Pasargada law reflects the basic capitalist legal ideology, it actually operates to organize autonomous social action by the popular classes against the conditions of reproduction imposed by capitalism. This is, then, the inverse of the situation found by Renner, where the liberating content of the legal ideology served as a disguise for the oppressive functioning of the state legal system.

The inversion of the basic norm of property is not the only 'deviation' of Pasargada law vis-à-vis the state legal system. Another is what I have called the *selective borrowing of legal formalism*, through which a folk system of formalism evolves. Though informality in general is a function of the absence of professionalization and low levels of role differentiation and specialization, the specific operation of those informal rules – the ways in which they are created, affirmed, refused, changed, adulterated, neglected or forgotten – is a function of social objectives, cultural predispositions and ideas of justice and legality. In Pasargada law, the main function of formalism is to guarantee the security and certainty of legal relationships without violating the overriding interest in creating a form of justice that is accessible, cheap, quick, intelligible and reasonable – in sum, a type of justice that is the obverse of the official justice. Finally, it is important to bear in mind that the structure of deviation of Pasargada law is not rigid. Within limits, it is open to manipulation. Among others, Cases 11, 12 and 13 showed how the official legal system is excluded from or incorporated within Pasargada law through rhetorical argumentation according to the strategies for the settlement of specific disputes.

[37]   Renner, 1976.
[38]   See Santos, 1974, pp 74ff.

Rhetorical strategy and social structure account together for the dynamics of this complex social process.

4.2   The view from inside

A deep understanding of Pasargada law requires the analysis not only of its legal pluralist relations with the official legal system but also of its internal structure – ie, the inside view. In fact, the main goal of the case study presented in this chapter has been to capture Pasargada law in action, and both the research method – participant observation – and the analytical perspective – legal rhetoric and legal reasoning – have proved adequate for that purpose.

Though Pasargada law reflects the social stratification of the community and its ideology does not transcend the liberal legal tradition of capitalism, it seems to me that as a *functioning legal apparatus* it possesses some characteristics that would, under different social conditions, be desirable as an alternative to the professionalized, expensive, inaccessible, slow, esoteric and discriminatory state legal system in capitalist societies.

I cannot stress enough that my argument is not to be read as a romantic view of community life in capitalist societies in general, much less Pasargada life. This is a conclusion I explicitly want to avoid. Such romanticism has been a recurrent element of communitarian ideology, and has been present in such different realms of knowledge and social practice as psychiatric treatment, policing, crime and deviance policies, medicine, legal services, schooling and so on.[39] Pasargada is not an idyllic community. Like most urban squatter settlements throughout the world, it is the product of an uncontrolled process of urbanization that stems from the expropriation of peasants and savage industrialization. Because it is an open residential community significantly integrated into the asphalt society, it is not surprising that it reproduces the basic features of the dominant ideology and of the dominant social, economic and political structures. Its relative autonomy (as expressed in its law) derives both from its specific class composition and from its collective response to the brutalizing housing conditions imposed by capitalist development and translated into state policies such as the illegality of land tenure, social control of the community through the police and social work agencies, and the lack of basic public facilities.

The characteristics of Pasargada law that I identify below could never be fully developed within a *favela*, nor do they, in Pasargada, provide a sufficient guarantee against injustice, manipulation or even abuse. My contention is simply that some of these characteristics should be constitutive of an emancipatory legal practice in a radically democratic, socialist society. This contention, however, is central to the argument of

---

[39]   The mixed results of the 'back to the community' initiatives have been analyzed and exposed. One of the first critical analyses is in Scull, 1977.

this book, which is concerned fundamentally with envisioning legal theories and forms of law that further emancipatory social practices. Drawing on the study of Pasargada law, I claim that an emancipatory legal practice must comprise the following features.

4.2.1 NON-PROFESSIONAL

The *presidente* of the RA is a storekeeper who learned to read and write as an adult, and has no formal legal training. His daily work includes other activities besides preventing and settling disputes. Consequently, he performs law jobs in a non-professional manner. Legal skills in Pasargada are widely distributed. The fact that law jobs are not professionalized is associated with the structural weakness of the RA as a centre of modern political power and with the general pattern of atomized power prevalent in the community. However, we have observed that the rhetorical strategy of the settlement process may include an emphasis upon the nature and the quality of the legal knowledge possessed by the *presidente* and the RA about both asphalt law and Pasargada law. Moreover, this emphasis is reinforced by occasional references to the 'official quality' of the RA. The cumulative effect of this dramatization of the RA's position is to create the idea that it is endowed with quasiprofessional or quasiofficial knowledge. And this process is particularly visible in those situations in which the RA adopts a strategy of power restoration to counteract a perceived threat to its normal power position. This suggests that legal knowledge in Pasargada is given professional and official attributes by analogy when extra power is deemed necessary.

4.2.2 ACCESSIBLE

Pasargada law is accessible both in terms of its cost in money and time, and in terms of the general pattern of social interaction. Pasargada residents do not pay lawyers' fees or court costs, though they may be asked to join the RA if they are not already members, and to pay the membership fee. They do not have to pay for transportation or lose a day's salary, as they would if they had to consult a lawyer or attend the court in Rio. Furthermore, cases are processed very quickly. The *presidente* is proud of this contrast with the official courts: 'We decided the case right on the spot. If the resident had gone to the courts he would never get a decision on his case. It takes two or three years to get a decision on a simple case'. Delays are incompatible with the emergencies that usually are the stimulus for an appeal to the RA, and the latter tries in turn to respond to these emergency conditions, although the rhetorical argumentation necessary to achieve a compromise presupposes a rythm that cannot be hastened. But the time spent talking cannot be compared with the magnitude of the delays in an official court. Finally, the mode of social interaction within the RA is close to that of everyday life. People do not change clothes to go to the RA, or engage in ritualistic self-presentation, and they use ordinary language to convey the facts, values and arguments of the case. This does not mean, however, that Pasargada law is equally accessible to all. Not all Pasargadians are well informed about the dispute processing conducted by the RA. Not all feel the need to resort to the RA, since some may find alternative ways of solving conflicts within the community (friends, neighbours, religious leaders and so on). Moreover, in some 'bad neighbourhoods' of Pasargada, a form of 'tough justice' through violent means is still practiced. And though Pasargada law is not political justice in the same sense that asphalt law is, the fact that the *presidente* and directors of the RA are elected within the community means that residents will have differential incentives to use it, depending on their ties of friendship or politics. Finally, the legal process in Pasargada has developed what I have called a folk technical language. The barrier thus created may vary according to the rhetorical strategy of the case, but in any event it is not so high that it requires the help of professional legal knowledge. The seeds for differential accessibility do exist in Pasargada law, and they will germinate as social stratification and inequalities of power increase in the community.

4.2.3   PARTICIPATORY

Though closely related to accessibility – particularly as measured by the degree of homology between legal and social interaction – participation deals specifically with the roles played by the different people that intervene in the dispute process. The level of participation and the informality of the legal process are closely correlated, and in both Pasargada scores high. The parties present their own cases, sometimes helped by kin or neighbours. They are never represented by professional legal specialists. They are not confined in the strait jacket of formal rules, and can express whatever troubles them, since the criteria of relevance are broad. This does not mean that in Pasargada law the parties have full control of the process as they do in negotiation, where the third party is reduced to an errand boy or go-between. The *presidente* may interrupt the parties when this is required. These factors may also occasionally increase the formality of the process. Indeed, informality, by its very nature, allows for flexibility and gradation, and it is the rhetoric that activates the legal process in different directions. Moreover, the ratification process is permeated by formalism and by rituals of alienation through which the parties are confronted with a legal space that has meanwhile been created. It is as though legality, in the last instance, must mean the construction of alienation, the transformation of the familiar into the foreign, the horizontal into the vertical, the gift into the burden. The process of formalization is thus visible in Pasargada, but it does not approach the extremes that characterize the official legal system of the modern state.

4.2.4   CONSENSUAL

Mediation is the dominant model 'for dispute settlement in Pasargada law, so much so that adjudication may be disguised as mediation – a situation I have called false mediation. The attempt is always made to reach a compromise in which each party will give a little and get a little. In this respect Pasargada law differs from the official legal system, in which the model of adjudication – all-or-nothing decisions – prevails, although the extent of the differences must not be exaggerated. The predominance of mediation in a given setting may be due to several factors. It may be a reflection, in a legal context, of much broader cultural postulates – Japan is often offered as an illustration of this. It may be related to the type of social relations between the parties involved in the dispute; if they are bound by 'multiplex relationships', as Gluckman called them, involving different sectors of life, mediation is aimed at preserving the relationship. Finally, mediation may result from the fact that the dispute settler lacks the power to impose his decision, a situation which seems to prevail in loosely structured societies based on a plurality of groups, quasi-groups and networks, where a centre of power is either missing or very weak.

The first factor seems to be irrelevant to Pasargada, which is strongly imbued with the legal ideology of the West. But the others are important. Given the high density of population in Pasargada and the style of community life – street orientation, face-to-face relationships, gossiping, mutual gifts of use-values in knowledge and skills – neighbours interact intensely in public and private spaces and in the context of multipurpose relationships out of which disputes may occasionally arise. On the other hand, the RA has no formal sanctioning power, and the power to demolish illegal repairs is not exercised, since it collides with the overall interests of the community. For the same reason, the RA does not seek the informal support of the police. Threats are often used as intimidation arguments, but then the sanction is limited to the message. These factors, however, are mere preconditions. Mediation occurs through rhetoric, which creates the orientation toward consensus upon which the mediator builds.

What is the political meaning of Pasargada legal rhetoric? Throughout history rhetoric has flourished (both as a style of legal process and as an academic subject) in periods when the distribution of social and political power was relatively even among the members of the relevant community. The repressive component of law, by contrast, first came to dominate in situations where the legal system was used to pacify occupied countries defeated in war. It would, however, be both scientifically and politically naive to evaluate the social meaning of Pasargada rhetoric and orientation toward consensus in a social vacuum. The criterion of relevance in the 'relevant community' or 'relevant audience' reflects and reproduces unequal power relations. However widely shared, the power is exercised against someone: the irrelevant community. In the Athens of Ancient Greece slaves were not part of the relevant community. Consequently the law of the city-state, dominated by legal rhetoric, did not apply to them. They were merely objects of property relations among the free citizens. This means that a truly democratic legal order inside the relevant community may coexist with – and indeed be based on – the tyrannical oppression of the irrelevant community.

Although law has historically reflected and reproduced social processes of exclusion upon which social integration develops, the focus on legal rhetoric – and here lies its importance for the socio-historical analysis of the law – leads us to distinguish among different forms of social exclusion and mainly between external and internal inclusion. External exclusion is a social process by means of which a group or class is excluded from power *because it is outside* the relevant community, as illustrated by the law of Athens. Internal exclusion is a social process by means of which a group or class is excluded from power *because it is inside* the relevant community, as illustrated by the state law of modern capitalist societies.[40] In this case, the criterion of relevance of the relevant community is not evenly applied across the community. Vis-à-vis certain social groups or classes, the relevance is so thin or remote that they may be considered as excluded inside the community. There may also be mixed social processes in which elements of both external and internal exclusion are to be found in different degrees.

In Pasargada the use of legal rhetoric by the relevant community reflects a process of external exclusion, but one that is the reverse of the above-mentioned case of Athens. The irrelevant community in this case is the asphalt society, with respect to which Pasargada is powerless. Pasargada law is an underground law, the result of a process of social exclusion. But because the law of the excluded community stands in a relation of legal plurality with the law of the excluding community, we have a mixed social process of the type described above. Because they belong to the oppressed classes in a capitalist society, Pasargadians are internally excluded – as reflected, for instance, in the declaration by state law that their land tenure is illegal. However, the specific form of marginality to which they have been consigned through this process of internal exclusion has made possible alternative social action – Pasargada law – which points to a social process of external exclusion that however, is never attained. Nevertheless, as already suggested, the irrelevant community of Pasargada law is probably not only the asphalt society but also some areas or groups of residents inside Pasargada. And since Pasargada law is powerless with respect to both of these communities, it may be concluded that the rhetoric of Pasargada law is less the result of widely shared power than of widely shared powerlessness. The exercise of legal rhetoric directed by the relevant community is subject to certain constraints, illustrated in those cases in which the *presidente's* argumentation is imposed on the parties, rather than accepted by them, as a kind of non-repressive imposition. These limitations of legal rhetoric in Pasargada law are also related to social stratification in the community, as illustrated in some of the cases analyzed above.

Pasargada is not an idyllic community. Far from it. But this does not prevent its internal legality from hinting at some of the characteristics of an emancipatory legal practice. Although the risks of its emancipatory traits being co-opted or undermined are pervasive, the legal tools in Pasargada remain amenable to use in a radically democratic manner: wide distribution (non-monopolization) of legal skills as expressed in the absence of specialized professionalism; manageable and autonomous institutions as expressed in accessibility and participation; non-coercive justice as expressed in both the predominance of rhetoric and the orientation toward consensus.

---

[40]   On the conception of a multilayered, internally unequal civil society see Chapter Nine. See also Santos, 1974, pp 74ff.

Chapter 5

Globalization, Nation-States and the Legal Field: From Legal Diaspora to Legal Ecumenism?

I INTRODUCTION

In Chapter Four, the analytical focus was on legal particularism and legal locality in modern society. The analysis of Pasargada law illustrated how the modern state, far from having the monopoly of the production of law, shared the national legal field with other law-generating social forces operating at an infrastate level and entertaining with the state and the official legal system complex and multidirectional relations. Rather than as a monolithic entity, the national legal field was conceived as a quilt of legalities woven by a national-local dialectics that interlaced the hegemonic state legal thread with multiple local legal threads.

In the present chapter the analytical focus is, in a loose sense, the inverse of the previous chapter, ie, the global, suprastate time-space rather than the local, infrastate time-space. The phenomena analyzed here takes place mainly on a global-national axis, though at times also on a global-national-local axis. The national legal field is studied here as it interacts with multiple global legal fields. The focus is not on the interactions among different state legal systems – the traditional field of public international law – nor on the national legal regulation of private social relations touching upon the legal systems of different states – the traditional field of private international law. The focus is rather on (a) legal forms (regulations, institutions, cultures) which are transnational in origin or which, though national or even local in origin, reproduce themselves globally by mechanisms other than those typical of interstate relations; and on (b) national legal fields – eg, state legal orders and local, infrastate legal orders – as they are transformed by transnational social movements pursuing a legal strategy. In this chapter, therefore, the state monopoly of production of law is also questioned. But, unlike in Chapter Four, not because the national legal field comprises other non-state or infrastate forms of law, but rather because the national legal field is increasingly interpenetrated by transnational legal forms that unfold in complex relations both with the state legal order and the local legal orders.

In Chapter Four I felt the need to emphasize the fact that Pasargada law, far from being a residue of some pre-capitalist or pre-modern past, was an innovative, adaptive solution to the specific conditions of capitalist development or modernization in Brazil, and to that extent was constantly being reproduced and recreated. In this chapter the emphasis goes in the opposite direction. Indeed, in light of the dramatic intensification of transnational interactions in the last two or three decades and its impact on the legal field, one might be tempted to conceive of the 'globalization of the legal field' as a radically new phenomenon without any roots in the past. Though, in my view, such legal globalization or, at least, some aspects of it represent a qualitatively new development, it should be borne in mind that the modern world system, within which the globalization of social interactions occurs, has been in place since the sixteenth century, and that the roots of the most recent legal – as well as cultural, social, political and economic – transformations are to be located in this historical development. Moreover, the existence of a transnational legal culture antedates the modern world system, as is dramatically illustrated by the reception of Roman law in the twelfth century and onwards. Even at the end of the nineteenth century, at a time when liberal political theory had imposed the equation among nation, state and law, the idea of a global or world law continued to flourish as a legal sub-culture. Though cultivated at the time mainly by legal comparatists who were quite marginal to mainstream legal science, this legal sub-culture was part and parcel of a widely hegemonic cultural constellation based on the idea of the seamless and irreversible homogenization of the conditions of social life throughout the world, brought about by capitalism and progress associated with scientific and technological development.

The breakdown of national differences and of local confines as part of the unfolding of modernity itself, predicted in the *Communist Manifesto* of 1848, grounds both the idea of unified science propounded by the Vienna Circle and the proposal of a *droit commun de l'humanité* (*common law of humanity*) presented by Edouard Lambert in the course of the first International Congress for Comparative Law held in Paris in 1900, during the World Exhibition.[1] The epochal affinities between the *Manifesto* and Lambert's proposal are actually quite striking. According to Marx and Engels, '[n]ational differences and antagonisms between peoples are daily more and more vanishing, owing to the development of the bourgeoisie, to freedom of commerce, to the world market, to uniformity in the mode of the production and in the conditions of life corresponding thereto'.[2] For Lambert, 'comparative law must resolve the accidental and divisive differences in the laws of peoples at similar stages of cultural and economic development, and reduce the number of divergences in law, attributable not to the political, moral, or social qualities of the different nations but to historical accident or to temporary or contingent circumstances'.[3] Fourteen years later, World War I would put an end to the Utopian project of a world law, but in a more realistic version the idea continued to

---

[1]   In Zweigert and Kotz, 1987, I, p 3.
[2]   Marx and Engels, 1967, p 102.
[3]   In Zweigert and Kotz, 1987, I, p 3.

animate the study of comparative law, as shown in the latter's predilection for the unification of law and for model laws.

At the beginning of the twenty-first century, the globalization of the legal field assumes characteristics which, though seemingly rooted in the tradition of world law or of Feuerbach's *Universaljunsprudenz*,[4] depart from it in significant ways. Rather than being the product of an intellectual crusade by well-meaning jurists or philosophers, the globalization of the legal field is being promoted by practicing lawyers, state bureaucrats and international institutions, as well as by popular movements and NGOs. Far from being a monolithic phenomenon, it is extremely diverse, combining uniformity with local differentiation, top-down imposition with bottom-up creation, formal declaration with interstitial emergence, boundary-maintaining orientation with boundary-transcending orientation. Moreover, it cannot be accounted for by any mono-causal explanation, and defies integration in any uni-dimensional cultural postulate, be it the idea of progress or the critique of progress, capitalist mass culture or anti-capitalist folk culture, modern science or postmodern knowledge. It is, therefore, a highly complex and ambiguous phenomenon that mirrors the complexity and ambiguity of the much broader, seemingly all-encompassing process of globalization, of which it is only a very partial manifestation. For this reason, I will begin this chapter by briefly describing the main features of this process, moving then to analyze the most prominent instances of the globalization of the legal field.

2   THE GLOBALIZATION PROCESS

In the last three decades, transnational interactions have known a dramatic intensification, from globalization of production systems and financial transfers, to worldwide dissemination of information and images through the mass media and communication technologies, and to mass translocation of people, as tourists, as migrant workers or as refugees. The extraordinary range and depth of these transnational interactions has led some authors to see in them a qualitative departure from previous forms of worldwide relations, a new phenomenon designated as 'globalization',[5] 'global formation'[6] or 'global culture'.[7] Giddens defines globalization as 'the intensification of worldwide social relations which link distant localities in such a way that local happenings are shaped by events occurring many miles away and vice versa'; he also reproaches sociologists for the undue reliance upon the idea of 'society' as a bounded system.[8] Similarly, Featherstone challenges sociology to 'both theorize and work out modes of systematic investigation which can clarify these globalizing processes and

---

[4]   Feuerbach, 1989, p 618.
[5]   Among others, see Featherstone, 1990; Giddens, 1990; Albrow and King, 1990.
[6]   Chase-Dunn, 1991. But note that Chase-Dunn stresses the continuity of recent developments.
[7]   Appadurai, 1990.
[8]   Giddens, 1990, p 64.

destructive forms of social life which render problematic what has long been regarded as the basic subject matter for sociology: society conceived almost exclusively as the bounded nation-state'.[9] Robertson, who sees globalization as the unfolding of a temporal-historical path of ever higher degrees of global density and complexity, defines the current phase – which he calls Phase V, beginning in the 1960s, 'the uncertainty phase' – in a rather descriptive way as:

> 'Inclusion of Third World and heightening of global consciousness in the late 1960s. Moon landing. Accentuation of 'post-materialist' values. End of Cold War and spread of nuclear weapons. Number of global institutions and movements greatly increases. Societies increasingly face problems of multiculturality and polyethnicity. Conceptions of individuals rendered more complex by gender, ethnic and racial considerations. Civil rights. International system more fluid – end of polarity. Concern with humankind as a species-community greatly enhanced. Interest in world civil society and world citizenship. Consolidation of global media system'.[10]

Much to his credit, Immanuel Wallerstein has pioneered the critique of 'society' as a useful starting point for analysis. For three decades he has been propounding a sophisticated analytical framework, the modern world system, specifically geared to account for the ever expanding and deepening of transnational intercourse. Though both Giddens[11] and Robertson[12] criticize Wallerstein for the economic determinism underlying his approach, such a critique is more adequate when addressed to the earlier versions of the theory or to its more vocal followers[13] than when addressed to Wallerstein's more recent work.[14]

Be that as it may, an overview of the studies on the globalization process shows that we are before a multifaceted phenomenon with economic, social, political, cultural, religious and legal dimensions intertwined in most complex ways. Under such conditions, unilateral, explanatory or interpretative strategies seem least adequate. The more so in view of the fact that the globalization of the last three decades, rather than fitting the modernist pattern of globalization as homogenization or uniformization recurrently proclaimed from Leibniz to Marx and the developmentalist establishment, seems to combine worldwide sourcing and boundlessness with local diversity, national and ethnic identity, popular embeddedness and community grounding. Moreover, in view of its complexity, variety and amplitude, the globalization process is connected to other transformations in the world system that are nonetheless irreducible to it, such as growing world-level inequality, population explosion, environmental catastrophe,

---

[9]   Featherstone, 1990, p 2.
[10]   Robertson, 1990, p 27.
[11]   Giddens, 1990, p 69.
[12]   Robertson, 1990, p 16.
[13]   Chase-Dunn, 1991, for example.
[14]   Wallerstein, 1991a, 1991b; Balibar and Wallerstein, 1991.

proliferation of weapons of mass destruction, formal democracy as a political condition for international assistance to peripheral and semi-peripheral countries and so on.

Before attempting an interpretation of contemporary globalization, I will describe briefly its main features. In doing so, I will consider contemporary globalization not only as an economic process, but also as a political and cultural one. As for economic globalization, Fröbel, Heinrichs and Kreye speak of a new international division of labour[15] based on the globalization of production carried out by the transnational corporations (TNCs), which are, more prominently than ever, the key agents of the new world economy. The main features of this new world economy are: worldwide sourcing; flexible systems of production and low transportation costs allowing for the production of industrial components in the periphery and export to the core; the emergence of three great trading blocks – the US, based on privileged relations with Canada, Mexico and Latin America; Japan, based on privileged relations with the four little tigers and the rest of East Asia; and Europe, based on the EU and on privileged relations with Eastern Europe and North Africa. These transformations have been packaged throughout the world system and particularly in peripheral and semi-peripheral countries with a new political economy, which Barbara Stallings aptly calls the 'market-oriented development model'. The implications of these transformations for economic policy can be stated as follows: national economies should be open to trade, and domestic prices should conform to international market prices; fiscal and monetary policy should be prudently directed to the maintenance of price and balance-of-payments stability; private property rights should be clear and inviolable; state-owned productive enterprises should be privatized; private decision making, guided by undistorted prices, should dictate national patterns of specialization, resource allocation and factor returns, with minimal government regulation or sectoral policy; the residual government budget should be directed to targeted education programmes and social policy.[16] In countries of the South, the term 'neo-liberalism' aptly captured from the beginning the nature of such political economy, whose effects became painfully familiar as a result of structural adjustment programmes. Indeed, as worldwide criticism against neo-liberalism mounted, especially in the mid- and late 1990s, the term came to be adopted also by social movements and scholars in the North.[17]

The new international division of labour, coupled with the neo-liberal political economy, have also brought about some important changes in the interstate system, the political form of the modern world system. On the one hand, the hegemonic states, by themselves

---

[15] Fröbel, Heinrichs and Kreye, 1980. Walton, 1985, speaks of three successive forms of 'new international divisions of labor', the last and current one being characterized by the globalization of production carried out by transnational firms. A review of the different approaches to the 'new international division of labor' is in Jenkins, 1984; see also Gordon, 1988, Castells, 1996.

[16] Stallings, 1992b, p 3.

[17] The call of the Zapatistas for a worldwide crusade against neo-liberalism in January 1994 was a key factor in popularizing both the concept and its critique. Among the works produced in the North that theorize neo-liberalism, see the ones included in Comaroff and Comaroff, 2001.

or through the international institutions they control – particularly the international financial institutions – have strained the political autonomy and the effective sovereignty of peripheral and semi-peripheral states to an unprecedented extent, even though the capacity for resistance and negotiation on the part of the latter may vary widely. On the other hand, there has been a tendency towards regional, interstate, political agreements that may include forms of sovereignty pooling, as is the case of the EU. Last but not least, the nation-state appears to have lost its traditional centrality as the privileged unit of economic, social and political initiative. The intensification of cross-border interactions and transnational practices erodes the capacity of the nation-state to initiate, steer and control flows of people, goods, capital or ideas, as it had done in the past. As concerns socio-political relations, it has been claimed that, although the modern world system has always been structured by a world class system, a transnational capitalist class is emerging today whose arena of social reproduction is the globe as such, and which easily out-manoeuvres the workers' organizations that are still nationally based, as well as the externally weak states of the periphery and the semi-periphery.

The TNCs are the main institutional form of this transnational capitalist class, and the magnitude of the transformations they are bringing about in modern business is indicated by the fact that more than one third of the world's industrial output is produced by TNCs. Though the organizational novelty of the TNCs may be questioned from a world system perspective, it seems undeniable that their prevalence in the world economy, and the degree and efficacy of centralized direction they manage to achieve, distinguish them from older forms of international business enterprise.[18] The impact of TNCs on new class formations and on world-level inequality has been widely debated in recent years. Within the tradition of dependency theory, Evans analyses the 'triple alliance' of TNCs, elite local capital and what he calls 'state bourgeoisie', which he sees at the base of the dynamic industrialization and growth of a semi-peripheral country like Brazil.[19] Becker and Sklar, who propound a highly dubious theory of post-imperialism, speak of an emergent managerial bourgeoisie, a new social class emerging out of the relations between the state management sector and the large private enterprises. This new class consists of a local wing and an international wing. The local wing, the corporate national bourgeoisie, is a socially comprehensive category encompassing the entrepreneur elite, managers of firms, senior state functionaries, leading politicians, members of learned professions. For all their heterogeneity, these different groups constitute, according to the authors, a class, 'because its members, despite the diversity of their parochial interests, share a common situation of socio-economic privilege and a common class interest in the relations of political power and social control that are intrinsic to the capitalist mode of production'. The international wing, the corporate international bourgeoisie, is made of foreign nationals who manage the TNCs and the international financial institutions (IFIs).[20]

---

[18]   In this sense, see Becker and Sklar, 1987, p 2.
[19]   Evans, 1979, 1986.
[20]   Becker and Sklar, 1987, p 7.

On the issue of world-level inequality, the opinions vary widely. For Evans, the model of industrialization and growth based on the 'triple alliance' is inherently inequitable, and capable of only one kind of redistribution 'from the mass of the population to the state bourgeoisie, the multinationals and the state local capital. The maintenance of the delicate balance among the three partners militates against any possibility of dealing seriously with questions of income redistribution, even if members of the elite express support for income redistribution in principle'.[21] In more recent comparisons between Latin American and East Asian development models and patterns of social inequality, Evans has added other factors – the autonomy of the state, the efficiency of state bureaucracy, land reform, the role of TNCs, the existence of an initial phase of decoupling from metropolitan capital – that may account for the striking contrast between Brazilian and East Asian models of development.[22] On the other hand, Becker and Sklar emphasize the positive aspects of TNCs' operations, as follows:

> 'they offer the 'third world countries' access to capital resources, dependable markets, essential technologies and other services. . . . Beneath the usual differences regarding distribution of rewards, there lies a mutuality of interest between politically autonomous countries at different stages of economic development. At the deepest level, their interests are not fundamentally antagonistic and do not entail automatically the intensified domination of the less developed countries by the more developed'.[23]

But even they are forced to recognize that, given the centralized direction of TNCs, 'local concerns may be given short shrift. If, for instance, the corporate group's overall profitability would be enhanced by transferring an operation from one country to another, the *disposition* to make the shift probably will prevail within the managerial circles'.[24] Though Chase-Dunn indicates that 'it is by no means clear that there has been absolute immiseration over the long run',[25] the distribution of relative shares of world wealth has worsened in the last decades. Bouigorgnon found that the poorest 40 per cent of the world's population received 4.9 per cent of world income in 1950 but only 4.2 per cent in 1977.[26] Besides, there is dramatic evidence of the stagnation of many peripheral and semi-peripheral countries in the 1980s, as a result, in part at least, of the oil price shocks of 1973 and 1979 to 1981 and of the explosion of international debt. Latin American countries entered the 1990s with lower standards of living than they enjoyed in the 1970s. Between 1982, when the debt crisis first hit, and 1987, net resources flows (loans, grants and foreign direct investment) to peripheral and semi-peripheral countries fell by half. Due to sharp rises in the interest rates of the foreign

---

[21]   Evans, 1979, p 288.

[22]   Evans, 1987.

[23]   Becker and Sklar, 1987, p 6. For an opposite view, see Crotty et al, 1998.

[24]   Becker and Sklar, 1987, p.2.

[25]   Chase-Dunn, 1991, p 262.

[26]   Chase-Dunn, 1991, p 263. See also Kennedy, 1993, pp 193–228. According to Maizels, 1992, the primary commodities exports from the Third World increased in volume by almost 100 per cent in the period 1980 to 1988. But the revenue obtained was, in 1988, 30 per cent less than the one obtained in 1980. See also Singh, 1993; Becker, Epstein and Pollin, 1998; Chossudovsky, 1997.

debt (a 172 percent rise between 1970 and 1987) in many heavily indebted countries, the servicing of past loans still exceeds new revenues. For such countries as a whole, net transfers are in fact negative: 54 of the 84 less developed countries saw their GNP per capita decrease in the 1980s; in 14 of them the decrease was about 35 per cent; according to the estimates of the UN, around 1 billion people (one sixth of the world population) live in absolute poverty (with income of less than one dollar per day).

In the cultural field, the debate on globalization is equally intense. Indeed, the shifting emphasis in the social sciences in the last decades from socio-economic phenomena to cultural phenomena has reactivated the question of the causal primacy in the explanation of social life.[27] The issue is whether the cultural and normative dimensions of the globalization process play a primary or secondary role. While for some – Chase-Dunn among them – they play a secondary role, since the capitalist world economy is integrated more by political-military power and market interdependence than by cultural and normative consensus,[28] for others – John Meyer and Bergesen, for example – political power, cultural domination and institutionalized norms and values precede market interdependence in the development of the world system and in the stability of the interstate system.[29] Wallerstein has made a sociological reading of this debate, asserting that 'it is no accident... that there has been so much discussion these past 10 to 15 years about the problem of culture. It follows upon the decomposition of the nineteenth century double faith in the economic and political arenas as *loci* of social progress and therefore of individual salvation'.[30]

The most important debate in the cultural field centres on the question of whether a world or global culture has emerged in the recent decades. To be sure, it has been long recognized that, at least since the sixteenth century, the ideological hegemony of European religion, politics, economics and science has produced, by means of cultural imperialism, obvious similarities among the national cultures of the world system. But the question is whether, beyond that, certain cultural forms have emerged in recent decades that are originally transnational or whose national origins are relatively irrelevant as they circulate throughout the globe more or less disembedded from national cultures. Such cultural forms are identified by Appadurai[31] as mediascapes and ideoscapes, by Leslie Sklair[32] as culture ideology of consumerism, by Anthony Smith[33] as new cultural imperialism. From another perspective, the theory of international regimes has drawn our attention to the processes of consensus formation at the world

[27]   Featherstone, 1990; Appadurai, 1990, 1996; Berman, 1983; W Meyer, 1987; Giddens, 1990, 1991; Bauman, 1992. See also Wuthnow, 1985, 1987; Bergesen, 1980.
[28]   Chase-Dunn, 1991, p 88.
[29]   Meyer, 1987; Bergesen, 1990.
[30]   Wallerstein, 1991b, p 198.
[31]   Appadurai, 1990. See also King, 1986; Hall and Gleben, 1992.
[32]   Sklair, 1991.
[33]   Smith, 1990.

level and to the emergence of a global normative order.[34] And from still another perspective, the theory of institutional structure has emphasized the extent to which Western culture has created social actors and cultural meanings throughout the world.[35]

The idea of a global culture is, of course, one of the main projects of modernity. As Stephen Toulmin has brilliantly shown, it can be traced from Leibniz to Hegel and from the seventeenth to our own century.[36] The attention given by social scientists to this idea in the last three decades has, however, a specific empirical base. The dramatic intensification of cross-border flows of commodities, capital, labour, people, ideas and information is believed to have given rise to convergences, parallel developments and hybridizations among different national cultures, be they architectural styles, fashion, food habits or mass cultural consumption. Yet, most authors assert that, notwithstanding their relevance, these processes are far from leading to a global culture.

Culture is by definition a social process built in the intersection between the universal and the particular. As Wallerstein emphasizes, 'defining a culture is a question of defining boundaries'.[37] We might even say that culture is, if anything, a struggle against uniformity. The powerful and encompassing processes of diffusion, imposition, and imperialism of the recent – and not-so-recent – past have been confronted throughout the world system with multiple and resourceful processes of cultural resistance, identification and indigenization. Nonetheless, the debate on the issue of global culture has had the merit of showing that the political struggle over homogenization and uniformity has transcended the territorial mould in which it took place from the nineteenth century until very recently, that is, the nation-state. In this respect, nation-states have traditionally performed a rather ambiguous role. While externally they have been the champions of cultural diversity, of the authenticity of the national culture, internally they have been the champions of homogenization and uniformity, crushing the rich variety of local cultures coexisting in the national territory, whether by the power of the police, the educational system or the mass media, and most of the time by all of them in conjunction. This role has been played in very different forms by core, peripheral and semi-peripheral states, and may be changing now as part and parcel of the current transformations in the steering capacity of the nation-states. Under the conditions of the capitalist world economy and the modern interstate system, there seems to be room for only partial global cultures. Partial, that is, either in terms of the aspects of social life they cover or the regions of the world they encompass. Smith, for instance, speaks of a European 'family of cultures' consisting of overlapping and boundary-transcending cultural and political motifs and traditions – Roman law, Renaissance humanism, Enlightenment rationalism, Romanticism and democracy – 'which have surfaced in various parts of the continent at different times and in some cases continue to do so,

---

34   Keohane and Nye, 1977; Keohane, 1985; Krasner, 1983; Haggard and Simmons, 1987.
35   G Thomas *et al*, 1987.
36   Toulmin, 1990.
37   Wallerstein, 1991b, p 187.

creating or recreating sentiments of recognition and kinship among the peoples of Europe'.[38] Seen from outside Europe, particularly from regions and peoples intensively colonized by Europeans, this family of cultures is the quintessential version of Western imperialism in whose name so much cultural tradition and identity was destroyed.

In view of the hierarchical nature of the world system, it becomes crucial to identify the groups, classes, interests and states that define partial cultures as global cultures, thereby setting the agenda for political domination under the guise of cultural globalization. Even if it is true that the intensification of cross-boundary encounters and interdependency have created new terrains hospitable to tolerance, ecumenism, world solidarity and cosmopolitanism, it is no less true that new forms of intolerance, chauvinism and imperialism have likewise developed. Partial global cultures can thus be of a very different nature, range and political outlook. Under current conditions, nothing more than plural or pluralistic global cultures can be achieved.[39] That is why most authors assume a prescriptive or prospective posture whenever they speak of a global culture in the singular. For Hannerz, cosmopolitanism 'includes a stance toward the coexistence of cultures in the individual experience ... an orientation, a willingness to engage with the Other ... an intellectual and aesthetic stance of openness toward divergent cultural experiences'.[40] Chase-Dunn, on his part, while debunking Parsons's 'normative universalism'[41] as a crucial feature of the existing capitalist world system, propounds that such 'universalism' be carried forth 'to a new level of socialist meaning albeit with a sensitivity to the virtues of ethnic and national pluralism'.[42] Finally, Wallerstein would imagine a world culture only in a future libertarian-egalitarian world, but even there there would be a permanent place for cultural resistance: the constant creation and recreation of particularistic cultural entities 'whose object (avowed or not) would be the restoration of the universal reality of liberty and equality'.[43]

3   PARADIGMATIC AND SUB-PARADIGMATIC READINGS OF GLOBALIZATION

Having sketched the economic, political and cultural traits of the globalization process, in this section I will offer some interpretive orientations on such a process that will be instrumental for the analysis of the globalization of the legal field that will be carried out later on in this chapter. The intensification of transnational economic, political and

---

[38]   Smith, 1990, p 187.
[39]   Featherstone, 1990, p 10, Wallerstein, 1991b, p 184; Chase-Dunn, 1991, p 103. For Wallerstein, the contrast between the modern world system and earlier world empires lies in the fact that the former combines a single division of labour with a system of independent states and multiple cultural systems. Wallerstein, 1979, p 5.
[40]   Hannerz, 1990, p 239.
[41]   Parsons, 1971.
[42]   Chase-Dunn, 1991, p 105.
[43]   Wallerstein, 1991b, p 199.

cultural interactions of the past three decades has taken on such proportions that it is deemed to have inaugurated a new period of social development. The precise nature and duration of this period are at the centre of current debates on the character of the transformations under way in capitalist societies and in the capitalist world system as a whole. If scrutinized in light of the metatheoretical explanatory asymmetries put forward by Wright, Levine and Sober,[44] some of these debates are actually false debates, since they are not trying to explain the same thing, and hence may be fruitfully reconstructed as complementary readings of the current social transformations. The fact that such readings coincide in locating the beginning of the period in the late 1960s and early 1970s is significant in itself, but the type and the historical duration of the social dynamics then initiated will vary with the variations in the *explanandum*.

To my mind, there are two main readings of the nature and direction of globalization – *the paradigmatic reading* and *the sub-paradigmatic reading*. The relative merits of the two readings are today a topic of intense debate worldwide. The arguments they have generated derive from different rhetorical audiences in pursuit of alternative political agendas. Such audiences and agendas are associated with the different forms of globalization and transnational agency analyzed below. The contrast between these two readings may be identified in three different areas or levels: the epistemological, the socio-cultural and the socio-economic. At the epistemological level, the contrast concerns the nature and the magnitude of ongoing changes in science and in its relations with competing knowledges. I have dealt with this topic and will not pursue it here.[45] The socio-cultural level is the one in which modernists and postmodernists most characteristically clash. Finally, at the socio-economic level the contrast is between those that envisage futures beyond capitalism and those that conceive of the future as a playground of virtually infinite metamorphoses of capitalism. In what follows I characterize the two alternative readings mainly as they concern the socio-economic futures. I will offer a few comments on their rhetorical audience and political agendas.

The *paradigmatic reading* on the nature and future of capitalism asserts that the late 1960s and early 1970s inaugurated a period of transition from an old to a new paradigm in the world system, a period of final crisis and of radically new social and political creativity that point towards forms of societies and sociability that go beyond capitalism. As one might expect, this reading includes many different views. One that is particularly suggestive has been proposed by Wallerstein and his collaborators.[46] According to Wallerstein the modern world system has entered a period of systemic crisis which will stretch between 1967 and the middle or the end of the twenty-first century. In his view, the period between 1967 and 1973 is a crucial beginning, because it marks a triple conjuncture of breaking points (turns from A to B phases) in the world system: (a) the

---

[44] Wright, Levine and Sober, 1992.

[45] Santos, 1995, Chapter One.

[46] Wallerstein, 1991b. See also the research project on 'Hegemony and the World System, 1600–2025' directed by Wallerstein. Provisional results were presented at the Workshop on Trajectory of the World–System. Binghamton, 4–5 December 1992.

breaking point in a Kondratieff long wave (1945–1995?); (b) the breaking point in US hegemony in the world system (1873–2025?); (c) the breaking point in the modern world system (1450–2100?). Wallerstein cautions that the evidence is easier to assess for (a) than for (b), and for (b) than for (c), in part because the putative end point of each cycle is successively further into the future. In any case, it is suggested that we may have entered a period of bifurcation in Prigogine's sense. World economic expansion is coming close to the asymptotes of total commodification and total polarization (not merely quantitatively but socially) and, in consequence, is using up its last margin of rectification, and will soon exhaust 'its ability to maintain the cyclical rhythms that are its heartbeat'.[47] The breakdown of the structural adjustment mechanisms opens a wide terrain of social experimentation and real historical choices, by nature very difficult to predict.

Coming from the same school but with a different view, Arrighi argues that the course of capitalist history may be blocked given the crisis of capitalism in the West and the impossibility of the East Asian capital of benefiting from the state- and war-making capabilities that have accounted in the past for the enlarged reproduction of capital.[48] In a rather pessimistic tone, Arrighi offers some alternative scenarios as to how capitalism will come to an end. In the worst scenario '[w]hether this would mean the end of capitalist history or of all human history, it is impossible to tell'.[49]

On the other hand, the *sub-paradigmatic reading* sees the current period as a major process of structural adjustment within – rather than beyond – the confines of capitalism. The adjustment is a major one because it involves – as regulation theorists have argued – the transition from one regime of accumulation to another, from one mode of regulation to another.[50] From a quite different viewpoint – one that celebrates the advent of a capitalist 'network society' and that, in the face of increasing poverty and inequality, naively tauts the alleged progressive effects of global capitalism – Castells also has diagnosed a structural transformation of capitalist accumulation worldwide.[51]

Sub-paradigmatic readings of the current period of capitalist development put forth by regulation theorists show some consensus around the following issues. Given the antagonistic nature of capitalist social relations, the routine reproduction and sustained expansion of capital accumulation is inherently problematic. In order to be achieved, it presupposes (a) a dynamic correspondence between a given pattern of production and a given pattern of consumption (that is, a regime of accumulation); and (b) an institutional ensemble of norms, institutions, organizations and social pacts, which guarantees the reproduction of a whole range of social relations upon which the regime

---

[47]   Wallerstein, 1991b, p 134.
[48]   Arrighi, 1994, p 355.
[49]   Arrighi, 1994, p 356.
[50]   Aglietta, 1979; Boyer, 1986, 1990. See also Jessop, 1990a, 1990b; Kotz, 1990; Mahnkopf, 1988; Noel, 1987; Vroey, 1984.
[51]   Castells, 1996. A contrasting view by an insider: Stiglitz, 2002.

of accumulation is based (that is, a mode of regulation). There may be crises *in* and crises *of* either the regime of accumulation or the mode of regulation. Since the late 1960s, the core countries have been undergoing a crisis both of the regime of accumulation and mode of regulation. The regulatory role of the nation-state tends to be more decisive in crises *of* than in crises *in*, but the way it is exercised depends heavily on the international environment, the insertion of the national economy in the international division of labour, and the specific institutional capacities and resources of the state to articulate, under hostile conditions of crisis, accumulation strategies with hegemonic strategies and trust strategies.

My argument in this section is that the coexistence of the paradigmatic and sub-paradigmatic readings points to the crucial interpretive dilemmas of our time. Recognizing this will help us to understand the wide variety of adaptive and transformative practices and discourses as they emerge, spread and collapse across the globe, as well as the dramatic transformations in the legal field analyzed below. The paradigmatic reading is much broader than the sub-paradigmatic reading, both in substantive claims and in time-space range. According to the paradigmatic reading, the crisis of the regime of accumulation and mode of regulation are mere symptoms of a much deeper crisis: a civilizatory or epochal crisis. The 'solutions' of the sub-paradigmatic crises are the workings of the system's structural adjustment mechanisms; since the latter are being irreversibly eroded, such 'solutions' will be increasingly provisional and unsatisfactory. The sub-paradigmatic reading, on the other hand, is, at the most, agnostic in relation to the paradigmatic claims. It is either unconcerned with long-term developments, or dismisses their cognitive basis as unscientific. It claims that, if the past has one lesson to teach us, it is that, so far, capitalism has solved its crises successfully and always in a relatively short-term framework.

My suggestion is that the two readings are, in fact, two major arguments about our time, prompted by two major audiences. While the paradigmatic reading is prompted by the transformative audience, the sub-paradigmatic reading is prompted by the adaptive audience. These are ideal-typical audiences. Some social actors – individuals, groups, classes, organizations – participate in only one of them. But many of them participate in both, according to time or issue, moving back and forth between the two without pledging irreversible or exclusive allegiance to one or the other. Both audiences are constituted by heterogeneous and conflictual social bases, but the conflicts – be they class ethnic, or gender conflicts are played out differently in the two audiences.

The transformative audience is probably more apocalyptic in the evaluation of fears, risks, dangers and breakdowns emerging in our time, but it may also tend to be more ambitious as to the range of historical possibilities and choices that are being opened up. Depending on the issues and circumstances, the process of globalization may thus be seen either as highly destructive of irreplaceable identities and equilibriums, or as the propitious inauguration of a new era of global or even cosmic egalitarian solidarity. Conversely, for the adaptive audience the current global transformations in the economy, politics and culture are either to be resisted or encouraged, depending on the circumstances. But notwithstanding their undoubted relevance, they are forging neither a Brave New World nor a new Utopia. They merely express the transitory turbulence and partial chaos that usually accompany any change in routinized systems.

From a discursive and phenomenological point of view, the paradigmatic and the sub-paradigmatic readings are, thus, two lived experiences, two modes of social praxis. Different social actors in different times and spaces build their social experiences as constellations of practices, in which elements of the two archetypical interpretations of our time are combined in different ways. Some actors may experience the globalization of the economy in the sub-paradigmatic mode, and the globalization of culture in the paradigmatic mode. This is the case of most postmodern theorists and of cultural anthropologists. For instance, the Comaroffs speak of millennial capitalism as signaling the emergence of a new cultural and political form.[52] In turn, Appadurai sees in the emergence of global ethnoscapes a new form of imagination and subjectivity at work.[53] Others, on the contrary, experience economic changes as pointing to a paradigmatic shift while seeing in cultural changes variations of modernist culture. This seems to be the case of Wallerstein, for whom there will be no radical cultural shift as long as capitalism remains the dominant mode of production.

More importantly, some actors may conceive as economic the same processes of globalization that others conceive as cultural or political. This is the phenomenological side of the epistemic changes under way. The distinctions traditionally used to identify different sectors of social life, such as economy, politics, culture, have become increasingly problematic, as the new transnational practices are packaged in an infinite number of totalities in which economic, political and cultural dimensions are inextricably intertwined. For example, the ideology of consumerism is as cultural – in that it refers to symbols, values and lifestyles – as it is economic – in that there would be no consumerism without the possibility of mass production and consumption – and political. The quantity, the quality and the social distribution of mass consumption is one of the central political conflicts in any of today's nation-states, and consumerism is conceived as being an important ingredient of the 'new political culture', of political conformity and electoral abstentionism. For lack of better concepts, we may continue to resort to the old ones, provided that we keep in mind that they no longer correspond to real entities existing out there. They are, rather, different perspectives on the same phenomena that are socially constructed by actors clustering their social experiences around different archetypical readings of the social world.

The coexistence of paradigmatic and sub-paradigmatic interpretations is probably the most distinctive feature of our time. It endows it with a new and broader epistemological and social openness, a measure of chaos that measures both uncontrollable dangers

---

[52]   Commaroff and Commaroff, 2001.
[53]   Appadurai, 1996, 2001.

and unsuspected emancipations. For the time being, such openness and chaos are still interstitial and marginal, and coexist with a sense of global closure, blockage and even catastrophe. However, despite their marginal and interstitial character, they challenge entrenched epistemological and social determinisms. Some of the features of the globalization process, although connected with changes of regimes of accumulation, are not reducible to them. On the contrary, they represent logics of collective action that are the opposite of the capitalist logic. The coexistence of a paradigmatic mode and a sub-paradigmatic mode of living in and evaluating the social world manifests itself in central features of the globalization process. While some features have a predominantly subparadigmatic nature, others have a predominantly paradigmatic one, and the same is true of the different features of the globalization of the legal field. Before turning to the latter, I will briefly analyze the nature of globalization at large and the social basis of transnational agency. As will be apparent below, how the nature and the actors of globalization are conceived has a direct bearing on the view of the transformation of the legal field under the conditions of globalization.

4 THE NATURE AND TYPES OF GLOBALIZATION(S)

Far from being linear or unambiguous, the process of globalization is highly contradictory and uneven. It takes place through an apparently dialectical process, whereby new forms of globalization occur together with new or renewed forms of localization. Indeed, as global interdependence and interaction intensify, social relations in general seem to become increasingly deterritorialized, opening the way to new *rights to options*, crossing borders up until recently policed by customs, nationalism, language and ideology, and oftentimes by all of them together. But, on the other hand, and in apparent contradiction with this trend, new regional, national and local identities are emerging that are built around a new prominence of *rights to roots.* These localisms, both old and new, are often adopted by such varied translocalized groups of people as Islamic fundamentalist groups in Paris or London, Turkish migrant workers in Germany, and Latino-Latina migrant workers in the US. Therefore they cannot be traced back to a specific sense of place. But they are nevertheless always grounded on the idea of territory, be it an imagined or symbolic, real or hyper-real territory. This reterritorialization occurs usually at an infrastate level, but it can also occur at a suprastate level. A good example of the latter is the EU, which is in the process of deterritorializing social relations at the state level only to reterritorialize them at a suprastate level – the EU as a fortressed territory vis-à-vis the outside world.

The process of globalization is, thus, selective, uneven and fraught with tensions and contradictions. But it is not anarchic. It reproduces the hierarchy of the world system and the asymmetries among core, peripheral and semi-peripheral societies. There is, therefore, no genuine globalism. Under the conditions of the modern world system, globalism is the successful globalization of a given localism.

I shall start by specifying what I mean by globalization. Globalization is very hard to define. Most definitions focus on the economy, that is to say, on the new world economy that has emerged in the last three decades as a consequence of the globalization of the production of goods and services, as well as of financial markets – a process through which TNCs have risen to a new and unprecedented pre-eminence as international actors. For my analytical purposes I prefer a definition of globalization that is more sensitive to the social, political, and cultural dimensions. As I said above I start from the assumption that what we usually call globalization consists of sets of social relations. As these sets of social relations change, so does globalization. There is strictly no single entity called globalization. There are, rather, globalizations, and we should use the term only in the plural. Any comprehensive concept should always be procedural, rather than substantive. On the other hand, if globalizations are bundles of social relations, the latter are bound to involve conflicts, hence, both winners and losers. More often than not, the discourse on globalization is the story of the winners as told by the winners. Actually, the victory is apparently so absolute that the defeated end up vanishing from the picture altogether.

Here is my definition of globalization: it is the process by which a given local condition or entity succeeds in extending its reach over the globe and, by doing so, develops the capacity to designate a rival social condition or entity as local. The most important implications of this definition are the following. First, in the conditions of the Western capitalist world system there is no genuine globalization. What we call globalization is always the successful globalization of a given localism. In other words, there is no global condition for which we cannot find a local root, a specific source of cultural embeddedness. Indeed, I can think of no entity without such local grounding.

The second implication is that globalization entails localization. In fact, we live in a world of localization, as much as we live in a world of globalization. Therefore, it would be equally correct in analytical terms if we were to define the current situation and our research topics in terms of localization, rather than globalization. The reason why we prefer the latter term is basically because hegemonic scientific discourse tends to prefer the story of the world as told by the winners. Many examples of how globalization entails localization can be given. The English language, as *lingua franca*, is one such example. Its expansion as global language has entailed the localization of other potentially global languages, namely, the French language.

Therefore, once a given process of globalization is identified, its full meaning and explanation may not be obtained without considering adjacent processes of relocalization occurring in tandem and intertwined with it. The globalization of the Hollywood star system may involve the ethnicization of the Hindu star system produced by the once strong Hindu film industry. Similarly, the French or Italian actors of the 1960s – from Brigitte Bardot to Alain Delon, from Marcello Mastroiani to Sofia Loren – which then symbolized the universal way of acting, seem today, when we see their movies again, as rather exotic or parochially European. Between then and now, the Hollywoodesque way of acting has managed to globalize itself.

One of the transformations most commonly associated with globalization is time-space compression, that is, the social process by which phenomena speed up and spread out across the globe.[54] Though apparently monolithic, this process does combine highly differentiated situations and conditions, and for that reason it cannot be analyzed independently of the power relations that account for the different forms of time and space mobility. On the one hand, there is the transnational capitalist class of which Leslie Sklair has recently written about, really in charge of the time-space compression and capable of turning it to its advantage.[55] On the other hand, the subordinate classes and groups, such as migrant workers and refugees, are also doing a lot of physical moving, but are not at all in charge of the time-space compression. And there are also those who heavily contribute to globalization, but who, nonetheless, remain prisoners of their local time-space. The peasants of Bolivia, Peru and Colombia, by growing coca, contribute decisively to a world drug culture, but they themselves remain as 'localized' as ever; just like the residents of Rio's *favelas*, who remain prisoners of the squatter settlement life while their songs and dances are today part of a globalized musical culture.

In order to account for these asymmetries, I distinguish two forms of globalization. They may apply to different phenomena, but they may also be different dimensions of the same phenomena. The first one I would call *globalized localism.* It entails the process by which a given local phenomenon is successfully globalized, be it the worldwide operation of TNCs, the transformation of the English language into *lingua franca*, the globalization of American fast food or popular music, or the worldwide adoption of American copyright laws on computer software. The second form of globalization I would call *localized globalism.* It entails the specific impact of transnational practices and imperatives on local conditions that are thereby altered restructured in order to respond to transnational imperatives. Such localized globalisms include: free trade enclaves (eg, export-processing zones in semi-peripheral states); deforestation and massive depletion of natural resources to pay the foreign debt; use of historical treasures, religious sites or ceremonies, arts and crafts, and wildlife for tourism; ecological dumping; conversion of sustainability-oriented agriculture into export-oriented agriculture as part of 'structural adjustment' programmes; and the ethnicization of the workplace. In this context, the international division of the production of globalism assumes the following pattern: the core countries specialize in globalized localisms, while upon the peripheral countries is imposed the choice of localized globalisms. The world system and, more specifically, what in it is designated as globalization consist of a web of localized globalisms and globalized localisms. The dynamics of this web and the structural conflicts they create, express or reconstruct – class, national, gender, ethnic, religious, and generational conflicts – may be adequately captured by sub-paradigmatic analyses of the hierarchies of social production and reproduction on a world scale. In practice, the social relations constituted by both globalized localisms and localized globalisms tend to be adaptive and to be rendered intelligible by adaptive audiences dominated by sub-paradigmatic arguments.

---

[54]   Giddens, 1991b.
[55]   Sklair, 1998.

However, the intensification of global interactions entails two other processes that are not adequately characterized as either globalized localisms or localized globalisms, and that, in contrast with these, call for a paradigmatic reading of current worldwide transformations. The first one I would call *subaltern cosmopolitanism*. The hierarchy of the world system and the power relations and interdependencies it entails are played out in complex ways. The prevalent forms of domination do not exclude the opportunity for subordinate nation-states, regions, classes or social groups and their allies to organize globally in defense of perceived common interests, and use to their benefit the capabilities for transnational interaction created by the world system. Such organization is intended to counteract detrimental effects of hegemonic forms of globalization, and evolves out of the awareness of the new opportunities for transnational creativity and solidarity created by the intensification of global interactions. Cosmopolitan activities involve, among others, South-South dialogues and organizations; worldwide labour organizations – the World Federation of Trade Unions and the International Confederation of Free Trade Unions; North-South transnational philanthropy; international networks of alternative legal services, human rights organizations, transformative advocacy NGOs, literary and artistic movements in the periphery of the world system in search of alternative, non-imperialist cultural values and so on. As the growing visibility of the protests against the institutions promoting neo-liberal globalization – from Seattle in late 1999 to New York in early 2002 – and the consolidation of the World Social Forum – which in 2002 convened nearly 60,000 people in Porto Alegre – bear witness, cosmopolitanism has become a fundamental component of the global political agenda.

Even in the form of subaltern cosmopolitanism, the use of the term 'cosmopolitanism' to describe counter-hegemonic practices and discourses may seem inadequate in light of its modernist pedigree, so eloquently described by Toulmin,[56] as well as in light of its common usage to describe practices that are here conceived either as globalized localism or localized globalism – not to mention its usage to describe the worldwide operations of TNCs, as in the term 'cosmocorp'. I use it, nonetheless, for several reasons. First, I want to signal that, contrary to the modernist creed – particularly in its *fin de siecle* moment – cosmopolitanism is only possible interstitially, at the margins of the capitalist world system as a counterhegemonic practice and discourse. Secondly, cosmopolitanism is achieved by progressive coalitions of oppressed classes or groups and other classes or groups coalescing with them or acting in their name and/or in their interest. In this respect, cosmopolitanism may evoke Marx's belief in the universality of those who, under capitalism, have only their chains to lose. I do not dismiss such evocation, but I would nevertheless distinguish cosmopolitanism, as I use it, from Marx's universalism of the chained working class, if for no other reason, because the situation described by Marx is very different from the one we are experiencing today. The dominated classes of our world seem to fall into two categories, none of them reducible to the only-chains-to-lose class. On the one hand, sizable sectors of the

---

[56]   Toulmin, 1990.

working classes have more to lose than their chains, even if that 'more' is not much more, or is more symbolic than material. On the other hand, vast populations throughout the world do not even have chains, that is, are not even strong or 'useful' enough to be directly exploitable by capital and, as a result, the eventual occurrence of such exploitation would sound to them as liberation. In their enormous variety, the cosmopolitan coalitions aim at struggling for the true liberation of these two strata of oppressed classes, as well as of those strata that might eventually fit Marx's mould. Another, probably more important, difference between my conception of cosmopolitanism and Marx's universality of the oppressed is that the progressive, cosmopolitan coalitions have no essentialist class base. They can be rather mixed in their class composition and formed along non-class lines, such as ethnicity, gender or nationality. In part for this reason, the progressive character of cosmopolitan coalitions can never be taken for granted. It is, rather, intrinsically unstable and problematic, and can only be sustained through permanent reflexivity. Finally, contrary to Marx's conception, cosmopolitanism does not call for uniformity and the breakdown of local differences, autonomies and identities. Cosmopolitanism is nothing more than the networking of local progressive struggles with the objective of maximizing their emancipatory potential on the local scale through translocal/local connections.[57]

The second process that cannot be adequately described either as globalized localism or as localized globalism is the emergence of issues which, by their nature, are as global as the globe itself and which I would call, drawing loosely from international law, the *common heritage of humankind.* I said above that there is no genuine globalism. This, of course, does not apply to issues that only make sense as referred to the globe in its entirety: the sustainability of human life on earth, for instance, or such environmental issues as the protection of the ozone layer, the Amazon, the Antarctica or the oceans. Since nuclear weapons pose an indiscriminate and global threat to the survival of human and non-human life on earth, the struggle against the proliferation of mass destruction weaponry can also be conceived as being waged in the name of the common heritage of humankind. I would also include in this category the exploration of outer space, the moon and other planets, since the interactions of the latter with the earth are also a common heritage of humankind.

The concern with subaltern cosmopolitanism and the common heritage of humankind has developed considerably in the last decades. However, as we shall see below, it has also provoked powerful resistance. The common heritage of humankind in particular, which originated in public international law, has been under sustained attack by hegemonic countries, specially the US. The conflicts, resistances, struggles and coalitions clustering around subaltern cosmopolitanism and the common heritage of humankind show that these two forms of globalization are arenas in which adaptive practices and audiences collide with transformative practices and audiences, in which sub-paradigmatic readings of the issues involved collide with alternative paradigmatic

[57]   In Chapter Nine I elaborate on the concept of subaltern cosmopolitanism.

readings, in which both the negative and the positive horizons of expectations vary widely. While for some the issues calling for a cosmopolitan or a common heritage of humankind response can be adequately tackled by possible short- or middle-range measures – even if against much resistance within the current capitalistic world order – for others, on the contrary, such issues are constitutive features of the capitalist world (dis)order and, consequently, irresolvable as long as this order is in place. For this reason, subaltern cosmopolitanism and the common heritage of humankind, though obviously connected with the process of globalized localism and localized globalism, are irreducible to them. They, rather, create the space for social practices that transcend the hierarchies established by asymmetric globalisms, and for credible emancipatory discourses beyond the confines of capitalist reasoning and reasonableness.

As more social forces with different and even contradictory objectives define the scope of their activities in global terms, the global time-space becomes an important arena of political struggle. In light of the typology proposed above I submit that two kinds of globalization meet and clash in the global political arena: on the one hand, globalization from above, or hegemonic globalization comprising globalized localisms and localized globalisms, and, on the other, globalization from below or counter-hegemonic globalization comprising subaltern cosmopolitanism and common heritage of humankind. While hegemonic globalization is conducted according to sub-paradigmatic readings of our present time, in counter-hegemonic globalization coexist both paradigmatic and sub-paradigmatic readings.

5   THE SOCIAL BASIS OF GLOBAL AGENCY

The intensity and wide range of processes of globalization have resulted in the decline of forms of national or subnational collective action that up until now were considered of utmost importance and effectiveness, such as the organized labour movement. Moreover, out of the process of globalization have emerged new forms of collective action – local, national, international and transnational action. Some such forms are not new in and of themselves, but have assumed a new strength, range or efficacy. In the concomitant decline of old forms of collective action and the emergence of new ones lie the issue of transnational agency. In the preceding sections, I have already made some references to changes in class structures and strategies occurring in connection with globalization. Traditionally, class analyses have taken the national territory as the privileged if not the 'natural' unit of analysis. The only exception was the world system theory, according to which both the bourgeoisie and the proletariat were constituted by a single transnational division of labour. In its terms, the role of states in the interstate system and the uneven development of the world system accounted for the emergence and political relevance of nationally-based class struggles, but the full understanding of the latter would not be possible without considering the dynamics of the world system as a whole. In the last three decades, and mainly as a result of the globalization of production systems, the existence of a world capitalist class *in sich* has been widely accepted, and the question has in turn become whether this class has also become a class *für sich*. Through its privileged institutional form, the TNCs, the corporate transnational bourgeoisie I mentioned above has become the principal actor in the globalization of the economy. In fact, the transnational agency of this class takes place not just through an institutional form, the TNC, but rather through a network of institutions clustering around the TNCs. Among such institutions, the international financial institutions, such as the IMF and the World Bank, as well as the American corporate law firms loom large, though for different reasons. As Sassen has shown in her study of firms providing services to TNCs in 'global cities' and Dezalay and Garth have argued in their analysis of globalized law firms, the network formed by TNCs and such institutions constitute the engine of global economic transactions.[58]

But the question of transnational agency cannot be reduced to the transnational bourgeoisie. Worldwide capital does not exist without worldwide labour. As is well known, Marx's call for a world working class *für sich* has found little response. Indeed, capital has been far more successful than wage labour in uniting its forces on a global scale. In the twentieth century and particularly in core countries, the organizations of the working class grew more and more dependent on the nation-state, and their institutional settings, their struggles, their proletarian culture took the national territory as their unit of reference and their symbolic universe. Consequently, the relative strength of these organizations in the core countries has been of little use in promoting the transnationalization of labour militancy. In this respect, the labour organizations of the EU countries provide a striking illustration. So far, they have not been able to generate, collectively and at the level of the EU, the same organizational strength and the mobilization capacity that each one of them has in its own national space. Nevertheless, the transnationalization of labour organizations and mobilizations has some tradition, in spite of all the difficulties. As international labour organizations are part of the cosmopolitan globalization I mentioned above, so is the co-operation of different national labour unions in negotiations with and strikes against the same TNC operating in their respective countries. Moreover, the concept of 'global wage relation', however problematic, may point to a future reality, already surfacing in transnational regional agreements, be they the EU, NAFTA or the FTAA.

In light of the broad perspective on globalization I have been propounding in this chapter, it becomes evident that the issue of transnational agency cannot be reduced to the social actors clustered around the capital-labour relations. In the last two decades, new forms of transformative social action have emerged throughout the world. I mean popular movements or new social movements either with new political and ideological agendas – sometimes called 'post-materialist', such as ecology, peace, anti-racism, anti-sexism – or, particularly in peripheral countries, with old 'materialistic' agendas – around economic survival, housing, land, social welfare, education. In either case, forms of organization and mobilization are adopted that are very different from those typical of

---

[58]   Sassen, 1991; Dezalay and Garth, 1997; Crotty et al, 1998.

the labour movement (trade unions, political parties). These movements have been emphasizing democratic empowerment – human rights, collective or group rights, participatory democracy – institutional autonomy and equality, cultural (or grassroots) identity, the expansion of freedom against state authoritarianism or mass cultural domination. Most of these movements have been locally based, but have developed transnational ties of various sorts with movements in other parts of the world. Indeed, they constitute the backbone of the transnational agency clustering around the concerns with subaltern cosmopolitanism and with the common heritage of humankind.

This transnational agency has been furthered by a privileged institutional form which, though not new, has in the last three decades assumed an unprecedent prominence: the non-governmental organizations (NGOs) and, in particular, the transnational NGOs. By the designation of NGOs are meant institutions of the most varied nature and political or ideological outlook, some of them 'nongovernmental' only in name. They are described in general as non-profit or as private voluntary organizations, and as having emerged out of the social movements or being connected with them in more or less direct ways. Clark distinguishes six types of NGOs: (1) relief and welfare agencies; (2) technical innovation organizations; (3) public service contractors; (4) popular development agencies; (5) grassroots development organizations; and (6) advocacy groups and networks.[59] Focusing on the NGOs' connections with social movements and with social constituencies, Miller distinguishes between *democratic, voluntary membership associations*, on the one hand, and *social agencies* and *public interest organizations*, on the other.[60]

In view of my concern with transnational agency, I will concentrate on transnational NGOs. Transnational NGOs (TANGOs) – which are oftentimes also called INGOs (international NGOs) – may develop out of more or less formal transnational networks among local NGOs, or may be originally created with a transnational scope and with the purpose of collaborating with local NGOs and other social organizations or movements in different parts of the world – providing technical or legal expertise to popular social movements, representing social movements in international forums, forging lateral ties between social movements and offering expert testimony in international settings. Transnational NGOs have grown tremendously in the last two decades. In 1981 there were about 1,700 development-oriented NGOs in the OECD countries; in 1990 there were over 2,500. The World Resource Institute alone collects information by and about approximately 450 NGOs focusing on environmental issues, and about 3,300 organizations subscribe to its newsletter (the *NGO-Networker*). According to Cohen and Rai, the number of international NGOs increased fivefold between 1970 and 1995. By 1995, they estimate the number of such organizations at 23,000.[61] Also, the number of transnational NGOs with consultative status at the UN

---

[59]   Clark, 1990.
[60]   Miller, 1992, p 54.
[61]   Cohen and Rai, 2000, p 9.

increased five-fold in the period 1975-1995.[62] -The number of participants and the range of issues dealt with in the NGOs' global forum during the United Nations Environment Conference (Earth Summit) in Rio in June of 1992 is an eloquent demonstration of the dynamism of transnational NGOs. A simple enumeration of the alternative treaties elaborated by them shows how they are emerging as a global transformative audience in charge of the agendas of subaltern cosmopolitanism and common heritage of humankind: treaty on alternative economic models; citizens' commitment on biodiversity; treaty on '*cerrados*' (scrubland); climate change NGO treaty; communication, information media and networking treaty; treaty on consumption and lifestyle; NGO debt treaty; the earth charter; global forum '92 NGO treaty on energy; treaty on environmental education for sustainable societies and global responsibility; fisheries treaty; NGO food security treaty; NGO fresh water treaty; Rio framework treaty on NGO global decision making; NGO treaty on militarism, the environment and development; treaty for NGO cooperation and sharing of resources; treaty of the people of the Americas; treaty on population, environment and development; treaty against racism; NGO sustainable agriculture treaty; treaty on technology bank; NGO treaty on TNCs; democratic regulation of TNC conduct; alternative treaty on trade and sustainable development; treaty on urbanization; treaty on waste.[63]

The growing prominence of transnational NGOs has prompted research on both the factors behind it and the direction it will take. The new prominence of transnational advocacy NGOs is connected with recent trends in the world system and in particular with the collapse of the Communist regimes, the exhaustion of command-economy development models, the antistatist ideology associated with neo-liberal economic policy and crisis of the public sector in many states, the globalization of the economy, the political culture of neo-communitarianism and the new communication and information systems.[64] Indeed, as Kaldor[65] has recently argued, particularly since the 1980s the twin processes of the erosion of state power and increasing transnational interconnectedness has given rise to a 'transnational civil society', whose privileged actors are NGOs – which, unlike social movements, have organizational capacities (full time staff, offices, legal recognition, etc.) that allow them to be recipient of international funds. One of the consequences of the dramatic increase of the number of transnational NGOs is their enormous heterogeneity. Not all transnational NGOs are progressive, transformative or oriented toward paradigmatic change. Some of them are conservative, adaptive, oriented toward sub-paradigmatic change and indeed see themselves – and are seen and used by international agencies – as neo-liberal alternatives to the state. Indeed, as Stiles[66] argues, this has been the case oftentimes when NGOs aim at

---

[62]   Cohen and Rai, 2000, p 8.
[63]   UNCED Alternative Treaties, 1992.
[64]   Hunter and Trubek, 1992. A bibliography on TANGOs is in Hunter, 1992. See also Elkins, 1992; Slater, 1991; Boulding, 1991; Korten, 1990; Alger, 1990; Chekki, 1988; Drabek, 1987; Berg, 1987; Keck and Sikkink, 1998; Cohen and Rai, 2000; Brecher et al, 2000.
[65]   Kaldor, 1999.
[66]   Stiles, 2000, p 42.

substituting – rather than at pushing the reform of or creating a symbiotic relation with – states. As Kaldor puts it, in these circumstances NGOs come to embody 'a kind of social/political laissez-faire doctrine'.[67] The relations between transnational NGOs and local NGOs and social movements have also become problematic. For example, a report by an African regional NGO, the Zimbabwe Energy Research Organization (ZERO), assessing the regional NGOs in the development process, raises some important issues in this respect. It is argued that the unquestionable acceptance of NGOs as the panacea of rural development must be reviewed; that NGOs have little influence in the design of development policies; that the dependence of NGOs on international donor agencies has resulted in an identity crisis: they have been facing the dilemma of choosing between comfortable relations with donors, on the one hand, or enhancing an indigenous contribution and participation in development on the other. The report concludes that the role of NGOs as agents of change at the grassroots level may have been overstated and sometimes romanticized.[68]

Transnational NGOs have thus become a contested terrain. But the contestation also shows how successful has been the attempt to create a transnational agency alternative to the TNCs and their supporting institutions. Without pushing risky parallels too far, there is some evidence that transnational NGOs represent for the agendas of subaltern cosmopolitanism and common heritage of humankind what the TNCs represent for the agendas of localized globalism and globalized localism. It is therefore not surprising that one of the alternative treaties coming out of the Global NGOs Forum in Rio 1992, the treaty on the democratic regulation of TNCs, represents a direct confrontation between two alternative models of global development endorsed by two alternative transnational institutions. Notwithstanding the fact that many NGOs are active today in promoting hegemonic globalization – oftentimes by working in collaboration with such agencies as the World Bank[69] – we can still say that while hegemonic globalization is carried out by TNCs, counter-hegemonic globalization is carried out by NGOs. This is evident, for instance, in the contrast between the two fora that have come to represent the two types of globalization. On one hand, the World Economic Forum – currently held in New York – that brings together the top policy makers from core countries and top executives from TNCs. On the other hand, the World Social Forum – which has met in Porto Alegre but will be moving to India and then to other locations – that serves as a meeting point for progressive NGOs and also for representatives of social movements around the world.

---

[67]   Kaldor, 1999, p 202.
[68]   Moyo and Katerere, 1991. See also Shaw, 1990; Barrow, 1985. Drawing on examples from Kenya and Zimbabwe, Bratton, 1989, analyzes the strategies used by governments to exercise control over NGOs, and by NGOs to assert autonomy.
[69]   On recent collaborations between the World Bank and NGOs around the world – an alliance that the Bank has been actively seeking over the last few years – see World Bank, 1996.

6 THE GLOBALIZATION OF THE LEGAL FIELD: A MULTI-FACTOR ANALYTICAL FRAMEWORK

The globalization of the legal field is a constitutive element of the processes of globalization I have been dwelling on in this chapter. The analytical framework proposed here is a very broad one, not only because, as should be clear by now, globalization comprises, by its very nature, a very broad set of phenomena and dimensions, but also because it is my purpose to counteract a certain economistic bias that has been dominating the analysis of the globalization of legal phenomena. Far be it for me to say that the globalization of production and of market relations is not a key factor in recent changes in the legal field. I just want to argue that it does not cover the whole spectrum of global interactions, and that an exaggerated focus on it may lead us to disregard other equally important developments.

While some, admittedly the most significant, instances of the globalization of law can be directly traced back to the networking of globalized localisms and localized globalisms which go together with the transformations of capital accumulation and Western cultural imperialism on a global scale, other instances, although connected with these transformations – if for no other reason, to resist against them – stem from autonomous political and cultural reasons, such as those lying behind the agendas of subaltern cosmopolitanism and common heritage of humankind. And there are still other instances of legal change in which the four patterns of globalization – globalized localism, localized globalism, subaltern cosmopolitanism and common heritage of humankind – are present in complex combinations. The coexistence of equally credible paradigmatic interpretations and sub-paradigmatic interpretations of current global changes bears witness to the relative underdetermination of social practice in our time, and calls for multifactor analyses. As regards the transnationally-induced changes in the legal field, I start from the assumption that even the changes most closely associated with the accepted/imposed diffusion of the neo-liberal, market-oriented, development model, such as changes in corporate and labour laws in many different countries, must be analyzed within interpretive constellations of economic, political, historical, cultural and even religious factors.

Comparative analysis of the transformations of the legal fields throughout the world system have been far too narrow to capture diversity in historical temporality, social embeddedness and cultural identity, particularly when such diversity is hidden or declared irrelevant by the simultaneity and convergence of changes using the same transnationalized knowledges and discourses. The inadequacy of such comparisons is all the more evident in an analytical framework such as the one I am proposing here, based on a paradigmatic reading of our time and calling for the unthinking of law as a critical task for a transformative audience. Along these lines, I propose in the remaining of this chapter a research agenda comprising seven broad areas of legal globalization to be analyzed within the framework of a comparative approach based on three variables: the position of the country in the hierarchy of the world system, the historical trajectory of the country up to and through modernity, and the historical family or families of law and legal culture dominant in the country. A brief comment about each one of these factors is in order. Such threefold analytical framework provide us, I believe, with the adequate tools for undertaking the study of the seven forms of legal globalization that I will dwell on below, and of processes of globalization of the legal field at large.

6.1   The position of the country in the world system

The comparative analysis of socio-legal fields that the world system theory makes possible focuses mainly on the interstate system and on the relative strength of different nation-states. The world system theory claims that the world economy is constituted by a web of interlinked productive processes and commodity chains in which core processes are concentrated in core areas, whereas peripheral processes are concentrated in peripheral areas; the unequal exchange upon which this hierarchical division of labour is forged results in economic and political polarization between stronger states in core areas and weaker states in peripheral areas. According to Wallerstein, one state is stronger than another to the extent that it can maximize the conditions for profit-making by its enterprises (including state corporations) within the world economy.[70] Wallerstein's generalization that core states tend to be strong, both internally and externally (vis-à-vis other states), while peripheral states tend to be weak, has been criticized for its economism[71] and for the vagueness and problematic operationalization of the concept of state strength, both internal and external. Though agreeing with Wallerstein that not everything about political action and state structure can be explained by just knowing 'how and where a country is inserted into the world hierarchical division of labor', Chase-Dunn still considers that the question of internal strength is much more problematic than the question of external strength. 'It is generally agreed', he says, 'that in external state-to-state relations Wallerstein's generalization holds'.[72] As I will show below, the external strength of the state is of crucial importance in understanding some forms of legal globalization, especially that entailing the transformation of the nation-state's legal system under pressure from transnational forces and institutions.

6.2   Routes to and through modernity

I have been emphasizing that globalization should not be equated with homogenization, uniformization or unification. Globalization goes together with old and new forms of localization; deterritorialization of social relations coexists with reterritorialization of

[70]   Wallerstein, 1984, p 5.
[71]   Skocpol, 1977. Cochrane and Anderson, 1986, defend a *via per mezzo* between Wallerstein and Skocpol. See also Zolberg, 1981; Garst, 1985; Zeitlin, 1988; Evans, 1992; Haggard and Kaufman, 1992.
[72]   Chase-Dunn, 1991, p 111.

social relations; cultural diffusion is often confronted at the receiving end by syncretisms and creolizations. The explanation for these countervailing movements and their different combinations and articulations in different countries or areas of social praxis requires broad and complex explanatory strategies with wide-ranging time-space frameworks. The world system theory has made an important contribution in elucidating how, from the sixteenth century on, the different countries of the world were incorporated into the modern world economy. However, the quality of the economic historical analysis of the incorporation process has not been matched so far in depth and detail by its political and cultural historical analysis. In Chapter One I spoke of modernity as a vast, European, socio-cultural project whose ambitions and revolutionary promises have been curtailed, cancelled out or fulfilled in a perverse manner under the structural developmental limits imposed by world capitalism. I then tried in Chapter Two to trace this process in one of the two main motors of modern rationalization of social life, ie, modern law (the other one being modern science, which I have dealt with elsewhere).[73] Given the general theoretical level of the argument, I did not consider the historical specification of the diffusion of the project of modernity outside its European base. However, the globalization process analyzed in the current chapter calls for such specification, because the dramatic intensification of global interactions in the last three decades purports to represent the ultimate expansion of the modernity project, even if it is nothing more than the final unfolding of its historical inertia, the culmination of its excesses and deficits.

The historical unfolding of late modernity in each of the four processes of globalization distinguished above reveals how much destruction and marginalization is involved in the incorporation of the whole planet into the hegemonic forms of capitalist modernity. But it also reveals the contradictory encounters of modernity with other civilizing projects and the complex combinations that have emerged out of them, new constellations of civilizing meaning which, for the lack of a better name, we may call postmodern constellations. The most promising transformative practices in the agendas of subaltern cosmopolitanism and common heritage of humankind in recent decades have come from the 'South', the 'periphery' or the 'margins', from social actions and worldviews in which modern Western concepts, such as human rights, are combined with the struggle for modes of communal and cultural identity foreign to modernity, a struggle, indeed, to protect them from hegemonic projects of modernization. Learning from the South is thus no vain slogan. It is an invitation to a de-Westernized, decentred conception of globalization and what it means as a civilizing process. To learn from the South, however, it is necessary to know the historical trajectory of its encounter with Western modernity.

Following Therborn, I distinguish four passes of entry into modernity: the European gate, the New Worlds, the colonial zone, and modernization in the face of modernity as

---

[73]   Santos, 1995, Chapter One.

an external threat.[74] The European gate is 'the pioneering route', an endogenous process both in relation and in resistance to change. The New Worlds is the pass through transcontinental migration and genocide and through the independence proclaimed by settlers of a major part of North America, soon followed by that of the South and central parts of the hemisphere and also of Australia, New Zealand and Hawaii. The gate of the colonial zone runs from Northwestern Africa via the Indian subcontinent to the Archipelago of Southeast Asia, where modernity arrived by conquest, subjection and appropriation. Finally, the externally induced modernization is the gate of drastic, defensive change promoted by local elites who considered modernity a foreign menace, as in Japan's Meiji Restoration, in early nineteenth-century Egypt, and later on in China, Iran, and Thailand.

According to Therborn, the four routes to modernity can be conceived as ideal-types occurring historically in different combinations in different societies. From my perspective, however, a genuinely de-Westernized conception of the global process of modernization demands that the European route be conceived as non-symmetrical with all the other routes. Europe did not just enter modernity; it invented it and imposed it upon other civilizing projects throughout the world, with the exclusive purpose of extracting benefits thereby. For the non-European countries, modernity was never the broad socio-cultural project we have outlined in Chapters One and Two. It was rather a partial and, to a great extent, painful experience of unequal contact and exchange. Due to their position in the world system, such countries were not able, in general, to set the agenda or the pace of modernity, and only to a very limited extent could they modify it to their advantage. The success of Japan in the gate of externally induced modernization and of North America in the gate of New Worlds – where success involved the genocide of indigenous peoples – were exceptional and reproduced the same asymmetry in the surrounding regions. This original asymmetry lies at the heart of the asymmetries through which globalization unfolds today. The merit of this comparative dimension resides in the idea that the different entry routes into Western modernity conditioned the subsequent processes of social structuration, cultural development, nation-building and state-building. Such routes are thus historical marks that surface, sometimes unexpectedly, in the current globalization and legal transnationalization that the different countries of the world system are going through.

Such historical marks, however, should not be conceived as tattoos, as fixed entities impressed upon the social processes. The promise of the comparative analysis of the routes to and through modernity depends upon a reading of the latter that opens up rather than closes opportunities for social transformation. A historicist, determinist reading is out of the question. The routes into modernity are broad patterns that continue to unfold in a sea of contingent variables. Moreover, they are hermeneutic constructs that justify their explanation of the past as a choice of the present, which is also a normative consciousness of a future to build. In other words, to be fruitful, the history

[74]   Therborn, 1992.

of the routes into modernity must be conceived as a genealogy, following Nietzsche's and Foucault's metaphor, or as an archeology, following Freud's metaphor, or still as a Marxist history without determinism. In any case, it is a history that works backwards, from the present to the past.

6.3 Families of legal cultures and kinship ties

Besides the knowledge of the hierarchies in the political economy of the world system and the knowledge of the historical trajectories of the different routes to and through modernity, the full understanding of the processes of legal globalization under way requires the knowledge of the different historical legal cultures and legal styles prevalent in the different regions and countries of the world system. Some such legal cultures are part of Western modernity itself, while others existed long before their contact with it, and later evolved in conjunction or conflict with the Western legal cultures or as a complement to them. Like the broader cultural premises they are part of, legal cultures are deeply rooted in the history and social praxis of societies throughout the world system. They operate as filters – more selective or effective in some legal fields than in others – through which transnational influences get localized.

Aggregating the vast number of legal systems existing in the world into a small number of 'legal families' has been the traditional task of comparative law. Throughout our century several different criteria have been proposed to devise such groupings, each one of them leading to a different classification. Let me mention just a few: using the sources of law and general structure as a criterion, Esmein divided the legal world into the Romanistic, Germanic, Anglo-Saxon, Slav and Islamic families.[75] Based on the criterion of race, Sauser Hall distinguished Indo-European (subdivided into Hindu, Iranian, Celtic, Greco-Roman, Germanic, Anglo-Saxon and Lithuanian-Slav sub-groups), Semitic and Mongolian legal families, as well as, as one might expect, a residual family of 'uncivilized nations'.[76] Using the sources of law as the main criterion, Levy-Ullmann distinguished among the Continental legal family, the family of English-speaking countries and the Islamic family.[77] Based on what they called the substantive, internal characteristics of the law, Arminjon, Nolde and Wolff identified seven legal families: French, German, Scandinavian, English, Russian, Islamic and Hindu.[78] Resorting to ideology as his criterion, one of the most distinguished comparatists, René David, started out by distinguishing five legal families – Western systems (French group and Anglo-American group), socialist systems, Islamic law, Hindu law and Chinese law – which he later on collapsed into three major legal families – the Romanistic-German family, the common law family and the socialist family – alongside a loose group of 'other

75 Esmein, in Zweigert and Kotz, 1987, I, p 64.
76 Sauser-Hall, in Zweigert and Kotz, 1987, I, p 64.
77 Levy-Ullmann, in Zweigert and Kotz, 1987, I, p 64.
78 Arminjon, Nolde and Wolff, 1950, p 47.

systems', in which he included Islamic law, Hindu law, the law of the Far East, as well as a new group of African and Malagasy law.[79] Finally, based on the criterion of style – in which the following five factors are included: historical background and development; mode of legal thinking; distinctive institutions; legal sources; and ideology – Zweigert and Kotz propose to classify the legal world into eight legal families: the Romanistic family, the Germanic family, the Nordic family, the common law family, the socialist family, Far Eastern systems, Islamic systems and Hindu law.[80]

A sociology of the criteria used throughout the twentieth century by legal comparatists to classify legal families would show how their classifications tell us more about the ideology of Eurocentric comparative law than about the ideology of the different legal families (particularly the non-European ones). Although, since Rene David's *Traité*, legal comparatists have called for a contextual analysis of law, only very selectively have they incorporated the findings of legal sociology and legal anthropology in their analyses. Moreover, they have tended to assume a Eurocentric conception of law – usually reduced to state law – and to overvalue the social engineering, instrumentalist functions of law, oftentimes connected with a rather naïve readiness to promote or to legitimate the export or imposition of Western law in the peripheries of the world system. Despite all this, today – in a period of such intense legal globalization – the enterprise of legal comparison is more relevant and urgent than ever, and the wealth of knowledge accumulated throughout the century by legal comparatists cannot be dismissed out of hand.[81] On the contrary, once criticized and trimmed along the lines I have indicated, it remains an invaluable source of information in some areas. Once extracted from its ideological mould, the comparative law tradition can be reinvented with totally new emphases: the emphasis on the use-value of law, as a grounded phenomenon, rather than on the exchange-value of law; the emphasis on the diversity of the legal landscape and the articulation of diversity, rather than on absorption, unification and standardization, which are the avatars of the modernist tradition, from the *more geometrico* (Grotius) and the *ars combinatoria* (Leibniz), to the *Universaljurisprudenz* (Feuerbach) and the *droit commun de l'humanité* (Lambert); the emphasis on the plurality and diversity of laws (and conceptions of law) within the same geo-political space, rather than on the state and law equation; the emphasis on the contextual plasticity of law, rather than on monotonic instrumentalism; the emphasis on legal reasoning as the privileged meeting ground between 'values' and 'facts', rather than

---

[79]   David, 1950, pp 215–393; David and Brierley, 1978.

[80]   Zweigert and Kotz, 1987, p 75.

[81]   Supporters of the Law and Development Movement, who sought to export Weberian legal rationality throughout the world, would be less surprised with the 'irrational' outcomes of their undertaking if they had taken good cognizance of the work of legal comparatists. See Trubek and Galanter, 1974; Gardner, 1980; Snyder, 1980, 1982; van den Bergh, 1984; Benda-Beckmann, 1989. For a reassessment of Gardner in light of the new wave of law and development, see Heller, 1992. From a different perspective, Schmidhauser, 1992, examines the expansion of several major families of law as a concomitant of military conquest, colonial aggrandizement, and/or economic penetration. See also Sajo, 1990 and, lastly, Glenn, 2000.

on abstract norms which, particularly outside the Western legal families, are nothing more than legitimating abstractions of expedient, often oppressive, ruling systems; and, finally, the emphasis on the embeddedness of the legal processes in the political economy of the world system and in the trajectories to and through modernity, rather than on the abstract autonomy or autopoiesis of law.

This shift of emphases will permit us to combine a political economy of legal comparison with a cultural politics of legal comparison, without which the differentiated vibrations of legal transnationalization, across time and space, on different systems of law and on different legal fields within each system, will remain unaccounted for. Since, in order to build such analytical tools, we have to start from what exists, I suggest that we take, as a starting point, Zweigert's and Kotz's classification. In spite of its Eurocentric bias, it has greater openness than other classifications. It is based on a complex criterion in which legal reasoning plays an important role. It is sensitive to institutional specificity to differentiation among legal fields and historical periods, as well as to vertical and horizontal comparison. Because it distinguishes among a large number of legal families, it allows for the identification of more combinations of different legal traditions in a more vast number of legal fields within the same geopolitical legal pluralistic constellation.

In sum, an adequate understanding of the current processes of legal globalization is thus premised upon three explanatory factors: the position of the country in the hierarchy of the world system; the historical trajectory of entry and pass to and through modernity; and the specific kinship ties that link the different legal orders existing in the country with the larger families of the legal world. This multilayered comparative strategy is difficult to implement: three positions in the world system must be combined with four trajectories into modernity and with eight world legal cultures. This is the task for a research agenda that I will only outline in this chapter.

In what follows I will draw on the three-fold analytical framework just sketched to survey seven specific types of legal globalization that I deem particularly relevant: 1) the transnationalization of nation-state regulation; 2) the law of regional integration; 3) the re-emergence of *lex mercatoria*; 4) the law of people on the move; 5) the law of indigenous peoples; 6) subaltern cosmopolitanism and human rights; and 7) the law of the global commons. Given the overriding commitment of this book to unveil emancipatory possibilities upon which transformative audiences and transnational coalitions of oppressed groups struggles can be built, I will deal in greater detail with forms of cosmopolitan legal globalization, specially with the transnationalized, infrastate law of the indigenous peoples, the law of people on the move and the cosmopolitan law of human rights.

7   THE GLOBALIZATION OF THE LEGAL FIELD: A SURVEY AND A RESEARCH AGENDA

7.1   *The globalization of nation-state regulation*

7.1.1 THE HETEROGENEOUS STATE

I speak of the globalization of the nation-state legal regulation whenever it can be determined that the changes in the state law of a given country have been decisively influenced by formal or informal international pressures by other states, international agencies or other transnational actors. Such pressures tend to be exerted in similar ways or with similar goals in different parts of the interstate system. The impact of the international context on nation-state legal regulation, rather than being a new phenomenon, is inherent to the interstate system, and can be traced back to the Westphalia Treaty itself (1648). Nor is it new that the international context tends to exert a particularly strong influence in the field of legal regulation of the economy and commercial life, as witness the many projects for the unification of law and, restatement of laws, developed by legal comparatists, and carried out by international organizations and national governments. As the names of the projects themselves indicate, the international pulling effect has traditionally been in the direction of homogenization and standardization, best illustrated by the pioneering projects of Ernest Rabel, in the early 1930s, and the setting up of the International Institute for the Unification of Private Law (UNIDROIT) with the objective of unifying the law on the formation of international contracts, which led, for instance, to the Uniform Law on the Formation of International Sales Contracts (ULFIS, 1964) and the Convention on the International Sale of Goods (CISC, 1980).[82]

Despite this historical tradition, the current process of globalization of state legal regulation seems to be a qualitatively new phenomenon for two main reasons. First, it is a very broad and far-reaching phenomenon, covering a wide range of state intervention, and calling for drastic changes in the pattern of intervention. The core pressure is relatively monolithic, as it stems from the 'Washington consensus', in whose terms the market-oriented development model is the only feasible model for a new global regime of accumulation, and accordingly, the structural adjustment it calls for must be carried out worldwide. Combined with this core pressure, others are in place that, in a sense, reinforce it, such as the end of the Cold War, the dramatic innovations in communication and information technologies, the new systems of flexible production, the emergence of regional blocs, and a newly packaged ideological mix of economic liberalism and liberal democracy. The scope of these pressures is also wider ranging when compared with previous processes of globalization, because the current one takes place after decades of active state regulation of the economy in core, peripheral and semi-peripheral countries. The creation of the normative and institutional requisites

---

[82]   van der Velden, 1984, p 233.

for the operation of the neo-liberal model involves, therefore, such massive normative and institutional destruction, that it is likely to affect not only the accumulation strategies of the state, but also its hegemony and trust-creation strategies.

The second novelty of current legal globalization is that the asymmetries of transnational power between the core and the periphery of the world system, that is, between the North and the South, are more dramatic today than ever. Actually, the sovereignty of the weaker states is now directly threatened not so much by more powerful states, as used to be the case, but rather by international financial agencies and other 'private' transnational actors, such as the TNCs. The pressure is thus supported by a relatively cohesive transnational coalition, drawing on powerful and world-embracing resources.

Though not restricted to it, it is in the field of the economy that the globalization of state law assumes greatest salience. The policies of 'structural adjustment' particularly cover an enormous range of economic, commercial and social interventions of the state, provoking turbulence in wide legal fields and institutional settings. Trade liberalization, privatization of industries and services, agricultural liberalization, dismantling of regulatory agencies and licensing mechanisms, deregulation of the labour market and 'flexibilization' of the wage relation, reduction and marketization of social services (like cost-sharing mechanisms, more strict criteria for eligibility to social provision, social exclusion of most vulnerable groups, market competition among state institutions such as public hospitals), less concern with environmental issues, educational reforms geared to job training rather than to citizenship-building, family policies that further aggravate the condition of women and children – all these are intended/unintended features of the 'Washington consensus', and often require massive legal changes. Because these changes take place at the end of long periods of state intervention in economic and social life (notwithstanding sizable differences across the world system) the shrinking of the state cannot but be achieved by wide-ranging state intervention. Thus, the state must intervene in order not to intervene. One of the most striking instances of legal globalization in line with the neo-liberal approach, and connected with recent technological innovations, has occurred in the field of telecommunications. This is a domain in which, up until the mid-1970s, the legal field was absolutely dominated by the principle of the state. Most countries adopted the idea of a 'natural monopoly' over telecommunications, which operated as an extension of the respective government department. Monopoly of services and equipment, so it was believed, was the most efficient and equitable way of providing public service, both domestically and internationally. It was also believed that national security would be best served by such state controlled monopolies. Besides, politicians saw in the monopolies and in the corresponding control over national bureaucracies a virtually infinite source of political payoffs. As Peter Cowhey emphasizes:

'Since the most costly people to serve were in less densely populated areas and since these populations usually had disproportionate voting and political power in industrialized nations, it was attractive to politicians to build monopolistic systems that encouraged average cost pricing for a set of uniform services. Technological innovation kept absolute costs down, cross-subsidies kept key constituents happy, and the governments could point to their role in providing fairness, defined as universal service on roughly comparable terms throughout the nation. Over time, the special beneficiaries of the system could be counted on to rally quickly to attack any disturbing factor. No commercial player or politician could spot any conceivable benefits from questioning the telephone cartel, given the stiff political barriers to entry'.[83]

State control over domestic communications extended to international communications through jointly provided services, standardized networks and equipment and organized global commons. This mode of regulation, which lasted for over a hundred years, began to change in the 1970s, and the changes became dramatic in the 1980s and 1990s. At this point no unified mode of regulation has as yet replaced the old one, and the field of telecommunications is going through a period of great turbulence. The general trend consists in strengthening the principle of the market over the principle of the state, and entails pressures both by core countries and TNCs upon peripheral and semi-peripheral countries to adopt or comply with legal transformations occurring in the core. Two strategic factors seem to be behind this development. On the one hand, technological innovation and diffusion: the microchip revolution; satellite communications; the emergence of digital technology blurring the line between communications and data processing. On the other, the oligopsony structure of the telecommunications market and the political clout of the main actors: the largest users of communications are few in number and economically powerful; they can easily and efficiently organize political lobbying.

Not at all surprisingly, this legal transformation began in the US, and has been spreading throughout the globe. Having won the battle at home, the American telecommunications TNCs became the most prominent exponents of regulatory reform in many countries, using the US bargaining power to make global reform feasible. Two paths are being followed by the core countries to change the regime of telecommunications.[84] The first one is the 'big bang' path followed by the US, the UK and Japan, which together constitute 60 per cent of the world's telecommunications market. It consists in the overall, unilateral liberalization of telecommunications, including basic and enhanced services, equipments and facilities. The second one is the 'little bang' path followed by the other core countries, basically the European countries.[85] It consists in partial liberalization through various means such as: separating postal services from telephone services and basic services from enhanced services (for instance, express mail, electronic mail and video conferences) with the purposes of reducing cross-subsidies; creating

---

[83]　Cowhey, 1990, p 184. I follow Cowhey closely in the analysis of this example. See also Nutger and Smits, 1989.

[84]　Cowhey, 1990, p 188.

[85]　See also Riess, 1991; Huet and Maisl, 1989. Lastly, Eliassen and Sjovaag, 1999.

regulatory agencies with greater autonomy vis-à-vis the government; granting special rights and facilities to large users; reducing subsidies for average households and small businesses, though doing it very slowly so as not to alienate them politically. It is not relevant for my argument to inquire why some of the core countries follow the big bang and others the little bang path, or which of these paths will prevail in the future, if the trend is indeed toward homogenization. It suffices to note that, despite their differences, the two paths have much in common, and that their common features are being diffused throughout the world system. Since less than twenty industrialized nations constitute the overwhelming share of the world telecommunications equipment and service markets, they have clearly the market power to ensure major changes in the telecommunications regime.[86] This fact illustrates part of the dynamics of globalization outlined above. The reforms being promoted throughout the world system are successfully globalized local institutional solutions, that is to say, they are globalized localisms.

The transnational pressures for legal transformation are as strong as they are selective, in my judgment, and they are likely to reinforce the heterogeneity of state regulation. For instance, the states that have adopted the 'little bang' path are using two different logics of regulation within the same field of legal regulation of telecommunications: one, for small users, households and small business, in which the principle of the state seems to dominate, as the political use of the subsidies is retained, even if in an attenuated form; the other, for large users, in which the principle of the market appears to reign supreme through liberalization, competition and free entry, but indeed also compromising with the principle of the state, through the concession of special rights and the establishment of friendly specialized committees for policy grievances. As the provision of relatively similar services becomes the object of dualistic regulation, the principle of equality before the law is bent beyond recognition.

7.1.2 THE RELATIVE WEIGHT OF TRANSNATIONAL AND NATIONAL FACTORS

The debate on the relative weight of transnational and national factors in processes of social transformation is as old as social science itself, and this is not the place to review it in great detail. Without needing to go further back, it has been central to modernization and development theories since the 1950s. The initial emphasis of these theories on national factors led, in the seventies, to both the dependency and the world system theory, in which international factors were given primacy.[87] In the 1980s, the emphasis changed again in favour of national factors, this time as part of an analytical dislocation from class-centred to state-centred approaches, or from economy to politics. As Frieden says, with reference to the 'post-imperialist' approach of Becker and Sklar, 'politics remains primarily a national matter, despite the internationalization of investment and

---

[86] Cowhey, 1990, p 191.
[87] On dependency theory, see Cardoso and Faletto, 1979; Evans, 1979.

finance'.[88] But precisely for this reason the debate has been fueled by new issues in the most recent years. In view of the unprecedented increase in transnational productive interdependence and the continued (and even enhanced) relevance of political factors and state intervention in large investment or finance projects, a heightened contradiction between international or transnational variables, on the one hand, and national, domestic variables, on the other, seems to be evolving. While some authors continue to give primacy to national variables in the resolution of such a contradiction, others believe that, rather than a contradiction national and transnational factors increasingly complement each other, to such an extent that eventually the distinction between them will cease to make sense.[89] Other authors still think that the contradiction exists, but is being resolved by such a dramatic supremacy of transnational factors that the nation-states, particularly in the periphery and semi-periphery, lose control of their steering mechanisms, and in this sense become 'transnationalized' themselves (the 'transnational state').[90]

In my view, given the complexity and diversity of current transformations, unilateral and uni-dimensional explanations are totally inadequate. The ideology and practice of economic liberalism boosted by domestic and international political forces, combined with the practices of the TNCs, have indeed led to a relative decentring of the nation-state as an actor in the world system. Most authors tend to agree that, in decisive areas, the state is being uncoupled both from national capital and national labour, thereby losing the capacity to guarantee by itself the institutional arrangements needed for a stable reproduction of accumulation. This is, however, a very complex process that is full of contradictory developments. For one thing, much of the decentring of the state is indeed conducted by the state itself. For instance, the privatization of the state industrial sector requires a complex intervention of the state that extends far beyond the process of privatization. In such cases, the centrality of the state is somehow confirmed in the very process of its demise. On the other hand, state activity is increasingly becoming so heterogeneous, with different branches developing at different paces and sometimes in opposite directions, that sometimes a coherent pattern of state action can no longer be discerned. The decentring of state action in certain areas (labour relations, social welfare) may thus coexist with the recentring of state action in other areas (job training, criminal justice, political surveillance, immigration control, foreign policy geared towards the protection of TNCs' operations, etc).

Moreover, the relation between the nation-state and transnational capital varies not only from state to state but also, within the same state, from sector to sector – for example, from the extractive sector to the agro-industrial sector, from the industrial sector to the financial sector. It should be borne in mind that the externality of the state in relation to capital and the relations of production is as fundamental for transnational capital

---

[88]   Frieden, 1987, p 180. See also Boyer and Drache, 1996.
[89]   Picciotto, 1989, reaches that conclusion from another perspective. See also Picciotto, 1988.
[90]   McMichael and Myhre, 1990.

today as it was for national capital in the past. Only the nation-state can formulate credible nationalist ideologies to compensate for impossible nationalist practices, and a strong repressive state may often be needed to facilitate the requirements of global capital. Besides, the state can, according to the circumstances, either assimilate the transnational regulatory consensus – for example, by privatizing the national industrial sector under pressure from the IMF or stick to national differences – for example, by keeping wages and welfare benefits at lower levels than in competing states). There is room for opportunism, and only the nation-state can convert it ideologically into room for opportunity. This is especially evident in the area of social welfare, an area where the accumulation strategies of the state have traditionally been inextricably intertwined with hegemonic strategies. It is also an area that most clearly reveals how the vibrations of the transnational practices and pressures resonate unevenly throughout the whole spectrum of state regulation. Just one example: in a manner similar to what is happening with respect to the 'little bang' telecommunication reforms, in states where a national health service has been in place, the local 'reform coalition', usually in alliance with the medical equipment and pharmaceutical TNCs, rather than pretending a privatization across the board, is instead proposing a separation between basic services (primary medical care, labour intensive or hospital intensive care) and enhanced services (elective surgery, high-tech, capital-intensive care). As a result, the former will remain public and under state control, and the latter will be privatized, almost always through joint ventures between national and transnational capital. This example also illustrates the fact that, while the state showed in the past an indiscriminate capacity to cover the most different sectors of social practice, the market is highly discriminatory and selective, and by no means wants to be engaged in a generalized conflict with the state.

As research on this type of legal transnationalization progresses, the somewhat sterile debate on the relative weight of transnational and national factors will yield to a more promising one on the increasing internal heterogeneization of state regulation. Legal heterogeneity is a characteristic of state regulation as a whole, and can be said to exist whenever different political and ideological logics of regulation or different styles of law are identified in different areas of state intervention. Described in this way, legal heterogeneity is hardly a new phenomenon. It has always existed as a result of a plurality of factors, such as: the historical trajectories of state regulation in different areas of social life related in general to the trajectories of the country into modernity; the impact of religious or ethnic factors, greater in some areas than in others; the extent to which colonial legal heritage has been kept and in what combinations with new post-independence regulation; the differences in legal style in accumulation, hegemony and trust strategies. However, in my view, owing in great part to the intensity, selectivity and pace of the transnational pressures of the current period, the differentiated impact upon the state legal field, taken as a whole, is provoking a new and more accentuated heterogeneization of state regulation. The policies clustering around 'structural adjustment' programmes forced upon peripheral and semi-peripheral states are provoking drastic transformations in both state institutions and political pacts among sectorial interests. The changes called for have such a sense of urgency and single purposefulness that, in the areas affected by them, the state regulatory functions appear clearly as derivative, extraterritorially originated, a kind of political franchising or subcontracting, whereby 'semi-autonomous legal fields'[91] seem to be developing *inside* state law, rather than outside it, as used to be the case when the legal anthropological and sociological literature drew our attention to them. We may be witnessing the emergence of a new form of plurality of legal orders: partial legal fields constituted by relatively unrelated and highly discrepant logics of regulation coexisting in the same state legal system. As it loses coherence as a unified agent of social regulation, the state becomes a network of microstates, each one managing a partial dimension of sovereignty (or of the loss of it) with a specific regulatory logic and style.

As an hypothesis for future research I would suggest, drawing on the three elements of the analytical framework sketched above, that the heterogeneity of state legality will tend to be higher (a) in those states that occupy an intermediate position in the world system, the semi-peripheral states; (b) in states whose routes into modernity were the colonial gate and the gate of top-down modernization in the face of external threat; (c) in states whose dominant legal culture has traditionally been part of legal families with strong religious influence, such as Islamic and Hindu law, as well as, and to a certain extent, the Far Eastern systems.

7.2   The law of regional integration: the European Union

This type of globalization of the legal field occurs whenever a group of states comes together to create supranational institutions and legal competences which will assume direct regulatory functions that previously did not exist or, if they did, were performed by the individual states as prerogatives of their sovereign powers. Though there have been attempts at regional integration in different parts of the world system, in South and Southeast Asia, in the Middle East and the Magreb, and in the Americas (lastly, through NAFTA, Mercosur, and the FTAA project), the European Union remains so far the most advanced instance of regional integration and, for that reason alone, deserves to be singled out in the research agenda I am outlining here. Built over five decades – starting with the Paris Treaty of 1951 and the Rome Treaty of 1957 – by a mixture of diplomacy and interstate democracy, of intergovernmental politics and supranational institutionalism, the EU is today an innovative transnational entity both in political and legal terms. Comprising 15 member states with a population of 376 million citizens[92] and an institutional staff – Council, Commission, Parliament, Court of Justice, Court of First Instance, Court of Auditors, Economic and Social Committee, Committee of the Regions, European Investment Bank – of more than 25,000 people, of whom almost a quarter are involved in translation, the EU is the largest trading bloc in the world.

---

[91]   Moore, 1978, pp 54–81.
[92]   The fourth enlargement took place on 1 January 1995, when Austria, Finland and Sweden joined the EU.

Inducing astonishingly little political debate up until recently, over the years the EU developed a supranational legal and political system aimed at creating an internal market comprising the four freedoms of movement (of goods, persons, services and capitals) which is today already in effect and which, for all its ambitious goals, is only part of a broader process of economic and political integration to be culminated in a political union. After a period of 'Euro-pessimism' and 'Euro-sclerosis' in the late 1970s and early 1980s, the Single European Act, approved by the European heads of government in 1986, inaugurated a new period of 'Euro-phoria'. The liberalization of the market was linked to procedural and institutional reforms that included a new approach toward harmonization of standards for domestic economic regulations – known as 'mutual recognition' – and the expansion of the qualified majority voting in the Council of Ministers on matters pertaining to the internal market. Though neither of these reforms applied to other potential areas of European integration – such as political co-operation, social legislation, monetary policy, enlargement of EU membership – from then on, the broader political agenda lay at the core of the EU project. The 1990s were marked by the adoption of two important new treaties: the Treaty of the EU (or Treaty of Maastricht), that provides for the establishment of an Economic and Monetary Union; and the Treaty of Amsterdam, that extended the scope of the EU to foreign policy, security and defence, thus providing it with the political weight corresponding to the economic power of the EU deserves. Moreover, steps were taken in the direction of a political union: creating a concept of European citizenship parallel to and eventually replacing national citizenship; extending and improving EU policy competences, in the spirit of subsidiarity; increasing the democratic legitimation of EU decision making, primarily by upgrading the role of the European Parliament as a legitimate expression of the will of the people of Europe; improving effectiveness and efficiency of EC institutions, particularly through the extension of majority voting and improving co-operation between member states in the area of 'internal competences and the administration of justice'.

In 2001, the Treaty of Nice defined the principles and the methods for the institutional reform of the EU in view of its enlargement to Central and Eastern European countries planned for 2004. In December 2001, the EU proclaimed the Charter of Fundamental Rights of the European Union. Though not mandatory, this Charter was designed to pave the way for the future constitutionalization of human rights at the EU level. More recently, by the end of 2001, the European Summit, held in Leiken, created the European Convention with the objective of preparing proposals for the institutional restructuring called for by the next enlargement of the Union.

Culminating this ambitious political agenda, in a continent that has seen the modern nation-state arise, the Treaty of Maastricht finally sparkled a broad ideological and political debate throughout Europe. Even so, the debate was intense only in some member countries. On the other hand, although the political debate was kept latent for a long time, the EU, both as a transnational political field and as a transnational legal field, has been the object of much scientific discussion, and the bibliography meanwhile accumulated is immense.

Suffice it here to enumerate and consider briefly the topics that are more pertinent for the research programme outlined in this chapter: the national and the transnational; the state and the market; democracy, social cohesion and interest representation; Europe, the world system, and the history of Europe.

7.2.1 THE NATIONAL AND THE TRANSNATIONAL

The above-mentioned debate over the relative weight of national and transnational factors in the current processes of globalization assumes very specific characteristics in the case of the EU. The EU project started before such processes had gained much visibility in either political or scholarly circles. For almost five decades it has gone through periods in which national politics seemed to dominate and the theories of integration were in disarray (the periods of Euro-pessimism) and through periods in which the idea of the obsolescence of the nation-state and the uncontrolled growth of supranational institutionalism took centre stage (the periods of Euro-phoria). Some authors have emphasized the role of transnational factors in the development of the EU project. They consider, for example, pressures from EU institutions, particularly the Commission, the Parliament and the Court of Justice; lobbying by transnational business interest groups; or the political entrepreneurship of the Commission under the leadership of Jacques Delors. Other analysts, on the contrary, have put the emphasis on interstate bargains, intergovernmental institution-building, veto power, and national interests, particularly where core states are concerned (France, Germany and Britain).[93] While the first view runs against the evidence that, even as an idea, there is as yet no European state endowed with the political prerogatives and regulatory competences of the nation-states, the second view fails to explain adequately the emergence of a coherent and effective Community legal system, in which the EU law is a direct source of law within the member states and prevails over conflicting national laws. Analyzed by conventional concepts, the EU integration process seems inherently contradictory. If, on the one hand, the member states seem to determine essentially the Community decision-making processes, on the other hand, the EU legislation has detached itself from the kind of national political accountability that is applicable to national legislation. If, on the one hand, the member states may exert regulatory influence in the European standardization organizations which sometimes act as combinations of national organizations, on the other hand, the formation in the European context of private systems of government without transparency and public involvement cannot be further denied.

To my mind, the complexities of the EU integration as a legal and political transnational phenomenon call for an archeological excavation into the modern concepts of sovereignty, state and law. As the equation among nation, state and law gets eroded,

---

[93]   Among many others, Snyder, 1990; Weiler, 1981, 1991a, 1991b; Moravcsik, 1991; Joerges, 1991; Lodge, 1989; Mancini, 1989.

new political configurations emerge, not duly accounted for so far. First, the sharing of sovereignty is selective, and expands or retracts not only according to national or European conditions, but also to world system conditions. Secondly, not every sovereign power that is lost at the nation-state level can be reconstituted at the European level. What this means is that new, partial, shared, sovereignty paradigms may well be in the making, soon to be exported to other regions of the world system as the worldwide accumulation of capital so requires or recommends. Thirdly, the external sharing or pooling of sovereignty may go together with the increasing, rather than decreasing, centrality of the nation-state in the internal, domestic processes of social and political regulation. This has been particularly the case of the semi-peripheral member states, such as Greece, Ireland, Portugal and Spain.[94] In a kind of positive-sum game, the member nation-states become internally strengthened as the transnational field they integrate strengthens itself.[95] Fourthly, the concepts of 'national' and 'national interest' have been surreptitiously changing. As the concept of 'national' gradually concentrates on the political process (on an increasingly narrower conception of it, that is), economic and cultural relations become more and more denationalized, thereby opening spaces for nationalistic and even chauvinistic backlashes. Concomitantly, as a kind of a retroactive liberal entitlement, the state reassumes the representation of the national interest which it had lost in the period of organized capitalism. In the European context, the state presents, as national interest, a selective set of particularistic social, economic, cultural and political interests, sometimes with the support of the same national interests organizations, of capital as well as labour, which, in the past, had actively denied the delegation of the national interest to the state. Thereby, the state increases its 'relative autonomy' vis-à-vis the national civil society in a process that, apparently at least, is hyper-corporatist. Fifthly, the issue of the division of powers between the member states and the Community should not be viewed in quantitative terms. Powers change as they are divided, and so do the institutional mechanisms to exercise them. For instance, even if the member states remain key actors in the steering of the integration process, their institutional focus and strength may be dislocated from legislative initiative to control over the internal implementation of Community law and uniformization of national law, in conformity with Community guidelines and directives. Finally, the prospective political debate on the ideal-typical Europe of the future, that is to say, on the very ethos of European integration, is sometimes smuggled into the debate on the national-transnational explanations of the process of integration.[96] While the 'transnationalists', encouraged by the monetary integration represented by the adoption of the Euro in 2002, point toward a full political union, toward a federalist European state, the 'nationalists' favour the community, rather than the unity, 'premised on limiting or sharing sovereignty in a select albeit growing number

---

[94]   Santos, 1990c; 1993, pp 49–53.
[95]   This being the case, the EU integration process is a decisive modifying factor of the economical and political meaning of the above mentioned relative strength of the individual states in the interstate system, as elaborated by the world system theory.
[96]   Weiler, 1991a, p 2478.

of fields, on recognizing, and even celebrating, the reality of *interdependence* and on counterpoising to the exclusivist ethos of stated autonomy a notion of *community* of states and peoples sharing values and aspirations'.[97]

7.2.2 THE STATE AND THE MARKET

The Treaty of Rome, which created the European Economic Community, was based on a seemingly clear-cut distinction between the economic, on the one hand, and the social and the political, on the other. The economic, that is, the creation of the internal market, will be a matter for Community decision making, while the social and the political will be left to the sovereignty of the member states. This distinction, which is probably to be blamed for the relative poverty of the political debate about the European integration, has been shown to be increasingly artificial, if not outright false. The truth is that the disputes over the division of powers on economic policy between the EU and the member states have become political issues in themselves, and have resulted in decisions and non-decisions with important social and political consequences across the Community.

In terms of our research agenda, the most important issue here is the fate of regulation in the triple time-space of locality, nationality and transnationality. According to the original EC blueprint, the balance between the market and regulation was to be accomplished by the member states. The harmonization of laws that should have ensued failed, not only because the member states revealed a nationalistic bias, but also because the legislative processes at the European level (in the Council) suffered recurrent bottlenecks. As a consequence, the European Court of Justice, in co-operation with the Commission, had to assume the role of decision maker, a role that has been very active indeed. Performed both with a federalist and a deregulatory bias, particularly in the 1990s, it has favoured the Community to the detriment of individual members, and the market to the detriment of the state. This development is significant in itself, because it reveals a new dimension of the relations between the legal and the political fields. The judicial engineering carried out by the court from the 1960s onwards decisively affected the European integration process. Through the doctrines of direct effect and supremacy of the European law, the court 'constitutionalized' the Community legal structure as a legal order of its own. Much of this occurred without political debate, as a judicial rather than as a political process, which led Weiler to state the apparent paradox that while European law developed firmly in a continuing process of evolution, the EU went through one political crisis after another.[98]

The denationalization of regulation accomplished by the court is still going on in the new approach to harmonization policy known as mutual recognition. Contrary to the

---

[97]   Weiler, 1991a, p 2479.
[98]   Weiler, 1991a, p 2410. See also Snyder, 1996; Maduro, 1998.

'traditional' 'positive' harmonization policy, the new approach conceives of the regulatory process as a competition among national legislations founded on three bases: European legislation as mere basic standards or minimum requirements; mutual recognition of national legislations; acceptance of reverse discrimination (states can impose higher requirements on their nationals). The new approach aims at overcoming the legislation bottlenecks at the EU level by granting some measure of autonomy to the member states, in the anticipation that, through the competition between different national legislations, a better legislation will emerge.[99] Herein lies the relevance of the new approach for the issue of regulation in a transnational space. Since the states can impose their own regulations on in-state products but have to accept out-of-state products in accordance with other, eventually lower regulations, the pressure will be toward deregulation at the national level, that is, toward a race-to-the-bottom rather than a race-to-the-top. In a seemingly total subversion of the distinction between market and regulation, the market will be allowed to choose the best regulation to which it wants to be submitted, which means that the legislative competition will result in the best legislation not in regulatory, but in market terms. The integration at the European level seems to involve the disintegration at the national level. But it is not clear the extent to which the denationalization of regulation will amount to a global net decrease of transnational Community-wide regulation. It will all depend on how minimal the minimum standards to be established by the Community will be. With the regulatory powers entrusted to an ever-growing number of standard-setting organizations, as well as advisory, administrative and regulatory committees of all kinds, we may conclude that the deregulation at the national level is taking place alongside the re-regulation at the European level. Durkheim's idea that market relations will grow in tandem with state relations seems to be confirmed, except that the state is here a kind of suprastate. This is one of the main mechanisms through which the EU deterritorializes social relations in the national time-space, while at the same time reterritorializing them in the transnational time-space, as well as, eventually, in the local time-space (the so-called 'Europe of the regions').

7.2.3 DEMOCRACY, SOCIAL COHESION AND INTEREST REPRESENTATION

In recent years, the democratic deficit of the EU has become a topic for heated political debate. The relevance of this topic for the research agenda outlined here lies in the fact that it shows the extent to which the hegemonic model of modern democracy is tied up with national time-space and state action, making highly problematic both the extension of the model to transnational or local time-spaces, and the invention of other alternative models adequate to the latter. The democratic deficit has several dimensions, and only some of them have been actually debated. The most visible dimension is, of course, the fact that the only elected institution, the European Parliament, is not the legislative body of the EU. Even given that the Parliament's role in the decision-making process

---

[99]   Maduro, 1992; Reich, 1992; Charny, 1991; Sbragia, 1991.

has been increased by the European Single Act and the Maastricht Treaty, through the co-decision process involving the Council and the Parliament, the fact remains that the Council retains the last word in this process, and the Commission keeps the exclusive power to elaborate legislative proposals. The legitimacy of EU law is, therefore, grounded on the legitimacy of the member states. However, while at the national level the democratic control and legitimation is exercised by the national Parliaments, the latter have so far been unable to control effectively what their governments do in Brussels. On the other hand, and since there are no genuinely coherent European parties (the current political groups being nothing more than loose associations of national political parties), if more democratic control were to be granted the European Parliament, national parliaments would surely react negatively. The EU represents a loss of direct democratic control over (and participation in) the actual processes of governance. The probability that this loss brings with it the erosion of the legitimacy of the integration process as a whole depends to a great extent on whether a tangible and socially visible demonstration can be made that the total welfare of the citizenry has enhanced as a result of integration.[100]

Another dimension of democratic deficit which has received little critical attention (particularly before Maastricht) has to do with the above-mentioned growth of committees, the exact number of which is unknown, which operate without any kind of democratic control or public involvement. This 'commitology' is greatly responsible for the lack of transparency and bureaucratic overload in the process of EU policy implementation. Should the commitology syndrome expand (as is likely) and the enhancement of general welfare become problematic (as is also likely, at least in periods of recession), the legitimacy problems of the EU might be complicated by two further questions: economic and social cohesion, and interest representation. The first question refers to the economic and social disparities between the more and the less-developed regions or countries of the EU, an issue which has gained importance in view of the EU enlargement to Central and Eastern countries. In spite of the sizeable structural funds allocated to eliminate them, the disparities continue to exist, particularly those created by the last enlargement of the EU. The less-developed EU countries may end up concluding that, beyond the new physical infrastructures, the 'structural funds' have not at all closed the gap that separates them from the more developed countries, and furthermore, that the latter have overbenefited from the internal disintegration of the weaker national economies resulting from the integration process. On the other hand, incensed by chauvinistic regionalisms all too evident in the European scene, the more developed countries may well end up concluding that the social cohesion funds have been draining resources that might otherwise have been kept where they were generated. Since the nationalistic bias will continue to count on the member states to reproduce itself, it seems that, in terms of social cohesion and global welfare, only a positive-sum game will guarantee the legitimacy of the EU.

---

[100]   Weiler, 1991a, p 2471. On the European Community and human rights issues, see below, Section 7.6. On social cohesion, see, among many others, Schulte, 1991; Teague, 1989.

The question of interest representation has to do both with democracy and with social legitimacy. The role of European business interest groups in the development of integration is an object of dispute. Nevertheless, to the extent that both organizations of both capital and labour have played a role, the EU has undoubtedly been more of a capital game than of a labour game. With the unfolding of the integration process, the relative balance between capital and labour, which in some countries was achieved in the period of organized capitalism, has collapsed in favour of capital (in the southern European countries the balance was never consolidated). The shift of administrative competences to the Community level is bound to have effects on the organization of interest representation. It seems, however, that, as Streeck and Schmitter have argued, the forms of national corporatism are not likely to reproduce themselves at EU level, and that, instead, some kind of transnational pluralism will emerge.[101] If so, the preservation of the nation-states as key actors in the process of integration may provide, ironically enough, a safety valve against the consequences of greatly unbalanced representations of interests at the community level.

7.2.4   Europe, the world system and the history of Europe

This topic concerns me here only to the extent that it impinges upon the three-fold comparative analytical framework I have proposed for the study of the different forms that the globalization of the legal field is taking. The EU comprises core and semi-peripheral countries in the world system. I have argued elsewhere that the concept of semi-periphery should be regionalized in order to account for the social, historical and functional differences among the semi-peripheral countries in the European, American and Asian contexts.[102] The specific political shape of the EU would probably not have been possible if the semi-peripheral countries did not share with the core countries the same hegemonic route into modernity, that is to say, broadly speaking, the same modern history. Still, this same general history covers also different histories. Both Portugal and Spain entered modernity in a relatively subordinate position and at a later period. Although they did make pioneering and crucial contributions to the early phases of modernity (the overseas discoveries), they receded to the margins as the project unfolded. The case of Portugal is even more striking. It continued to be a colonial power until 1975, despite (or because of?) its semi-peripheral position in the world system, having acted as an intermediary between the periphery (the colonies) and the centre (England) for more than two centuries. What will be the impact of this complex history on EU integration in the future? I speculated above that integration may have contributed to the enhancement of the internal strength of the semi-peripheral states. In a sense, these states have been turned into core countries as a result of integration. But on the other hand, it seems that the economies of these countries continue to be as semi-peripheral as ever, even if the specific terms of this position are being drastically

---

[101]   Streeck and Schmitter, 1991. See also Sugarman and Teubner, 1990.
[102]   Santos, 1990c.

restructured. It might even be speculated that EU integration is contributing to turning semi-peripheral states into core states and to turning their economies into peripheral ones, thus giving rise to new articulations (both national and transnational) among the economic, the political and the cultural whose contours are hard to predict at this point in time.

Future enlargements of the EU, particularly to include the Central and Eastern countries,[103] will compound these issues, if for no other reason because the heterogeneity of the routes into modernity will increase. But issues will also be compounded by the increased heterogeneity of the families of laws and legal cultures in presence: the Romanistic, Germanic, Nordic, common law and socialist families. If it is true that the demise of the Communist regime has put an end to the reproduction of the socialist family, it should not be assumed that, after several decades of domination, such style of legality will disappear without a trace. As it disintegrates, it may reappear in unsuspected combinations in the new hegemonic legal culture. Moreover, to the extent that it disintegrates, it creates a void that must eventually be filled. Which of the European legal families will prevail in filling it? The problem is not completely new. As EU law evolves into a supranational legal order of its own, a *tertium genus* over and above the national legislations, the different legal families and legal styles that are superseded by the new legal order are still present in it, even if in unequal terms.

In a provocative analysis, in which he claims that 'the European community is not the true European community', Allott has cautioned against abstracting EU integration from the rest of European and world history and against reducing the process of integration to an aggregation of national interests devoid of historical, cultural and ethical depth.[104] Without subscribing to the idealistic tone of the argument or to its conclusion, I have proposed a comparative analytical framework that aims precisely at bringing to the foreground the diversity of the histories, spatialities and temporalities melted into the pot of the European Union. This diversity easily runs the risk of being swept under the carpet of legalistic, as well as realist or neo-realist, functionalist or neo-functionalist political analyses.

7.3   *Global capital's own law:* lex mercatoria

7.3.1   THE ORIGINS AND ELEMENTS OF *LEX MERCATORIA*

Understood as a set of customary principles and rules that are widely and uniformly recognized and applied in international transactions, *lex mercatoria* or *law merchant*

---

[103]   The new expansion will be decided upon requests made in the last fifteen years : Turkey (1987), Cyprus (1990), Switzerland (1992), Hungary (1994), Poland (1994), Romania (1995), Latvia (1995), Slovakia (1995), Lithuania (1995), Bulgaria (1995) Czech Republic (1996), Slovenia (1996) Estonia (1998) and Malta (request renewed in 1998). By mid-2002 the frontrunners are: Czech Republic, Cyprus, Poland, Hungary, Slovenia, and Estonia.

[104]   Allott, 1991.

is probably the oldest form of globalization of the legal field. Its origin can be traced back to the European urban uprisings of the eleventh century and to the growth of commerce that then started. Faced with the inadequacy of the local laws, the merchants – those '*pieds poudreux*' (dusty feet) who took their goods from town to town, from fair to fair, from market to market on foot or horseback – created for themselves a legal system that served their interests.[105] Laden with concepts of equity, or *ex aequo et bono, lex mercatoria* was a supranational law whose most distinct features were the following: the ease with which it permitted binding contracts; the stress on security of contracts; the speed of adjudication; the variety of mechanisms for establishing, transmitting and receiving credit; the normative value of customs and usages of the commercial world.

Medieval *lex mercatoria* underwent profound changes in the modern period, which indeed caused its seemingly irreversible decline. On the one hand, as trade expanded and more and more diverse trading communities emerged, customs changed and became more diversified. The diversity of customs made *lex mercatoria* less predictable, less transparent, and thus vulnerable to the critique of lacking impartiality. On the other hand, as the modern states gained control over their territories, the existence of a deterritorialized law, which did not derive its normative claims from treaties among sovereign states, was viewed as a threat. As a result, merchant courts were often either forbidden or assimilated into the domestic court system, and the transnational business customs were made to comply with national legislations. The expansion of transnational practices and the need to protect them legally led the states to develop a private international law. Since this was a national state law, and could therefore conflict with the private international law of other states, efforts were made to harmonize these bodies of laws through the creation of international uniform laws.

The scope of uniform laws has always remained very limited and unable to account for the tremendous growth, in number, complexity and variety, of transnational contracts and other business transactions, especially after World War II. These relationships, which committed generally larger amounts of money for longer periods than domestic relationships ever did, and engaged partners often separated by great distances and cultural and linguistic differences, had a greater degree of insecurity and required, therefore, a common normative foundation.[106] One solution might have been to choose the governing law from among different national laws. But because so much would depend on it, the choice of law was bound to be a sensitive issue: How to guarantee, for example, an equal footing between the parties? What to do if the chosen national law had been changed overnight to the disadvantage of one of the parties? Given these difficulties, the common foundation had to be sought elsewhere, in a deterritorialized set of normative principles and rules, expressed in such formulas as 'general common principles', 'principles of equity', 'principles of good faith and good will', 'principles

---

[105]   Tigar and Levy, 1977, p 4. Also Trakman, 1983; Mustill, 1988; Stoecker, 1990; Berman, 1988; Berman and Dasser, 1990; Draetta, Lake and Nanda, 1992.

[106]   Draetta, Lake and Nanda, 1992, p 5.

of international law', 'international trade usages', and so on. Because such normative references aimed at circumventing submission to national laws and to the traditional conflict of laws, transnational contracts were deemed to be self-regulatory, subjected only to their own provisions: *contrats sans loi, contratti senza legge, rechtsordnunglose Vertrage.* In fact, a new supranational legal order was emerging. It was the new *lex mercatoria*, which was to expand enormously in the period of disorganized capitalism, by reason of the sheer intensification of transnational transactions and in the wake of a new worldwide regime of accumulation in search of adequate institutional structures.[107] Indeed, during the last three decades – and especially in the late 1990s, after financial crises hit Southest Asia and Latin America – the call for the reinforcing of *lex mercatoria* has been been made by those who, like Harvard economist Jeffrey Sachs, consider it the requisite 'legal architecture' capable of holding together the global economy.[108]

The new *lex mercatoria* is comprised of several elements, including general principles of law recognized by commercial nations, rules of international organizations, customs and usages, standard form contracts, and reports of arbitral awards. Though this is disputed, *lex mercatoria* may be conceived of as also comprising uniform laws and public international law. Concerning the latter, though public international law governs the relations among nation-states, and not among private parties, *lex mercatoria* shares with it the 'general principles of law recognized by civilized nations', such as *pacta sunt servanda, rebus sic stantibus*, and the prohibition of undue enrichment. But the relation between *lex mercatoria* and public international law may also be conflictual whenever the first is used to create forms of immunity which operate both vis-à-vis the national law and the public international law.[109] As regards international uniform laws, once they have been adopted by the nation states and become part of the national law, they are not, in themselves, part of *lex mercatoria*. But before that process of adoption, and to the extent that they represent a crystallization of international trade usages, such laws are *lex mercatoria*.[110]

However informal, the new *lex mercatoria* is neither amorphous nor neutral, the customs and usages being not necessarily universal and much less traditional or immemorial. The new *lex mercatoria*, as an emerging transnational legal field, is a globalized localism, constituted by thick cognitive expectations and thin normative allegiances reproduced by the routine repetition of myriads of transnational contractual relations originally framed by transnational corporations and their lawyers, international banks and international organizations dominated by both. Depending on the power relations between the parties and their stakes in the transaction, the new *lex mercatoria* can operate in either a high rigidity mode (the iron cage mode) or in a high flexibility mode

---

[107]   B Goldman was one of the most influential jurists in the development of the notion of *lex mercatoria*. Goldman, 1964.

[108]   Sachs, 1998.

[109]   Farjat, 1982.

[110]   Muchlinski, 1997; Draetta, Lake and Nanda, 1992, p 13; Trakman, 1983, pp 23ff.

(the rubber cage mode): the first mode applies whenever the power differential between partners is high; the second mode, in the opposite case. Even in its rigidity mode, *lex mercatoria* is often ephemeral, an instantaneous customary law, so to speak, as in the case of a new type of contract drafted by a leading TNC and its lawyers, which must be accepted as drafted by the weaker partner, irrespective of the fact that such contract type may not be used again in its entirety. Within the research agenda I am outlining in this chapter, two issues raised by *lex mercatoria* deserve special attention: *lex mercatoria* and the world system, and *lex mercatoria* and legal cultures.

7.3.2 LEX MERCATORIA AND THE WORLD SYSTEM

It has been claimed that transnational contracts are purely contractual, in that they contain their own rules of recognition and validation and that, as a result, *lex mercatoria* is non-political, needing no reference to non-contractual elements to sustain itself as a normative order. Grounded on a legal formalistic reasoning, this conception unduly abstracts from the hierarchies and unequal exchanges that characterize the world system. A relative balance of power between partners in the transactions is only rarely obtainable. In most cases, the dominant practices at the basis of this global law are the practices of the dominant actors. The most prominent among these do indeed enjoy statelike political prerogatives, immunity privileges, special access to political resources – tax incentives, special rights on infrastructures and so on. And, indeed, they often negotiate directly with the host states the conditions under which the private transactions will be carried out. The political facilitation made possible by the state is a crucial non-contractual dimension of the transnational contracts. Moreover, this dimension can be found in the reports of the World Bank or IMF that, according to the specifics of the situation, open or close territories and areas for transnational transactions and *lex mercatoria*. The apparently infinite sea of global transactions is precisely mapped out by such reports and the 'dos' and the 'don'ts' they contain.

Another dimension of the relations between *lex mercatoria* and the world system, involving also the contractual/non-contractual dichotomy but rarely discussed in this context, concerns the international property rules. Since stable property rights are exceedingly difficult to establish across national boundaries, the international extension of capital, which is an original feature of the modern world system, has always been an inherently problematic activity. After the Treaties of Westphalia (1648), and particularly in the mid-nineteenth century, when foreign investments began to increase dramatically, European core countries effectively secured the economic rights of their subjects abroad through a network of treaty provisions that were then imposed on a global scale, from China to Latin America.[111] Their aim was to protect not only the personal safety and tangible property of their nationals but all their assets, including private

---

[111]   On the evolution of international property rules since the mid-nineteenth century, see Lipson, 1985.

debts.[112] This interstate legal field, created by the core states and imposed on the semi-peripheral and peripheral states, has changed substantially in the last 150 years, but has prevailed as a framing, boundary-setting legal and political structure, within which *lex mercatoria* has evolved apparently unencumbered by non-contractual constrains. The use of overt or covert intervention by force and economic sanctions by the core countries in the case of expropriations or debt renunciations in the periphery and semi-periphery has been for a long time an integral part of an 'international regime', closely reflecting the hierarchies in the world system.

The articulations of *lex mercatoria* with the world system thus illustrate how the dialectics of deterritorialization and reterritorialization operates in this legal field. The growth of deterritorialized legal relations entailed the reterritorialization of sovereign rights by core states beyond the national boundaries, whenever investors' rights were at stake. This hegemonic reterritorialization often sought to counteract subordinated reterritorialization, whenever peripheral and semi-peripheral states claimed the supremacy of sovereign rights over investors' rights, as was the case for the first time in a large scale in the first quarter of the twentieth century, with the Mexican Revolution, the Russian Revolution and the Turkish state-led industrialization. This dialectics goes on today in different forms, and not only at the macrolevel just mentioned, but also at the microlevel. The microlevel, which often goes together with the so-called 'micro *lex mercatoria*', comprises a myriad of instances of anticipated failures or inadequacies of *lex mercatoria* which are corrected by a complementary intervention of territorial, national law. One example of this occurs when the legal protection of deterritorialized global transactions demands the latter's fictive division into two territorialized national transactions, whereby an internationally legally unprotected relation is nationalized in order to become legally enforceable. Gessner and Schade offer an illustration[113] in the case of cross-border payments through documentary credit. In this case, a transnational legally unprotected contract between one seller and one buyer is divided into two nationally, legally protected contracts, one between the seller and a national bank and the other between the buyer and another national bank. The international relation thus created between the two banks is itself legally unprotected in terms of a national law, but it is covered by the *lex mercatoria* generated in the stable reproduction of inter-bank business relations. This example shows how the transnational legal system may benefit from keeping the national legal system as a reserve system.

7.3.3   LEX MERCATORIA AND LEGAL CULTURES

This issue deals with the relationship between *lex mercatoria* and the legal families we have identified above. Though more indirectly, it has also to do with the different routes into modernity. The internationalization of capital has always been the motor behind

---

[112]   Lipson, 1985, p 9.
[113]   Gessner and Schade, 1990.

the development of *lex mercatoria. Lex mercatoria* is, thus, basically a transnational business law or, more broadly, an economic law. Within the national legal field, economic law has traditionally been one of the laws most permeable to foreign influences and transplants, an area of law in which the ethos of the national legal cultures have always been less determinant. Not by mere coincidence has this area of law been the area of harmonization, homogenization and stardardization *par excellence.* For this reason, and also because of its deterritorialized character, *lex mercatoria* has often been considered as the expression of a 'global legal culture', a kind of 'third culture', independent of the various national legal cultures and hovering above them in its specific domain. This conception is flawed on many accounts. To begin with, the very existence of *lex mercatoria* is debatable, the debate being framed, in part at least, by rival presuppositions that can be traced back to the differences among the families of law. While the concept of *lex mercatoria* was developed by civil law scholars, its harshest critics seem to be scholars from a common law background. Draetta, Lake and Nanda have seen in this fact an interesting paradox: civil law lawyers, who are used to law being created by legislative authority and in a dramatic way, tend to view the legal nature of *lex mercatoria* with favour; whereas common law lawyers, who are used to law being developed by accretion and practice, have often rejected *lex mercatoria.*[114] Further research on legal cultures and styles is needed to explain this paradox, particularly because the conceptual debate seems to be totally at odds with the *lex mercatoria-in-action.* This law has expanded enormously in the last decades, mainly with the expansion of the global activities by TNCs, most of them of Anglo-American origin. Furthermore, the legal drafting of such transactions, in itself a major source of *lex mercatoria*, has been done for the most part by 'in-house' lawyers with a common law training or by American corporate law firms.[115]

I thus come to another argument against considering the new *lex mercatoria* as an expression of a global legal culture. If a new regime of global capital accumulation is indeed emerging, its most visible institutional features, aside from *lex mercatoria* itself, are the rise of TNCs and the international organizations that back up their activities, the adaptation of the nation-state regulatory legislation according to the transnational finance capital requirements, the globalization of the market for legal services promoted by the American or American-style corporate law firms, and the rise of international commerce arbitration. At the present transitional stage, the institutional devices of a predominantly suprastate nature, which will guarantee the stability of the new regime of accumulation, are yet to be developed. Of those already in place, one is particularly visible, though it is doubtful whether it is an institution of the new regime or rather an institution of the transition toward the new regime. I am referring to the American law firm. In terms of the conceptual framework advanced in this chapter, the American corporate law firm is one of the most striking globalized localisms in the current process

---

[114]   Draetta, Lake and Nanda, 1992, p 27.
[115]   Dezalay and Garth, 1997; Trubek et al, 1993.

of globalization of legal phenomena. Marc Galanter[116] and Yves Dezalay[117] have drawn our attention to them. According to the latter, '[t]he Wall Street firm, invented over a century ago in response to the demands of American finance and industry, has become a model for similar developments everywhere, as the local lawyers, in a struggle for survival, feel that they also must adopt the model of the corporate law firm'. This type of law firm is at the core of the new international market in consultancy, and its rise to prominence constitutes what Dezalay calls a 'big bang'[118] in the legal services, because the type of legal practice it produces is very much in line with the economic relations it deals with, and leads toward the infusion of high-level competition and market imperatives in the practice of law itself – and to a new generation of entrepreneurial lawyers.

In light of what I said above on the relations between *lex mercatoria* and the world system, the hegemony of the American corporate law firm is not a case of legal technological diffusion, as assumed by Dezalay. We are not simply before an organizational model and an experience particularly suited for the new conditions of transnational transactions. We are also before services provided to the actors that are shaping those conditions. The power of the model would be much less impressive if it were not backed by the power of the actors who impose it. As Gessner puts it, '[t]he world market dominated by the English language, American capital and common law reasoning is a home-match for American lawyers who in addition are organized much more in the entrepreneurial form needed for worldwide activities'.[119] The idea that a global legal culture is in the making is thus to be rejected, particularly if it is conceived as the ideal-typical culture of the big transnational economic actor who 'receives the advice of international banks and large law firms which use quasi-universal business language and which thrash out any differences on the level of interests rather than that of values, world views or social norms'.[120] The particularistic character of this 'global' legal culture becomes obvious when confronted with another (equally particularistic) global legal culture, also evidently in the making. I mean the international regime of human rights, which operates on the basis of an order or priorities – whereby values and worldviews have preference over interests – that is the obverse of that of *lex mercatoria*, as will be seen in greater detail below. Similarly, the character of the *lex mercatoria* as a globalized localism becomes particularly evident when it interacts with legal families with strong religious influences, and in countries whose route into modernity was the colonial gate or the top-down, externally induced modernization.[121]

In this latter respect, China is a telling illustration. Ever since Deng Xiaoping's 'open door' policy was adopted in 1978, the integration of China in the world economy has

---

[116]   Galanter, 1983.
[117]   Dezalay, 1990.
[118]   Dezalay, 1990, 1992. See also Trubek *et al*, 1993, pp 3–36.
[119]   Gessner, 1990, p 8.
[120]   Gessner, 1990, p 8. See also Gessner and Schade, 1990.
[121]   For the case of Indonesia, see Trubek *et al*, 1993, pp 50–65.

steadily expanded. The growth of foreign trade and investment and the development of international business transactions in China indicates an ever-greater presence of *lex mercatoria*. However, the 'universalistic' claims of *lex mercatoria* – meaning, to a great extent, the claims of US corporate firms – to predictable and secure transactions have necessitated a *modus vivendi* with two 'particularistic' conditions of 'Chinese capitalism' and 'Chinese modernization': the precedence of state policy over legality and the role of Confucian culture and *guanxi* relationships. Given the fact that China's traditional and, since 1949, Communist route toward modernity amounts to a top-down, state-led, authoritarian modernization, the state plays, in this case, a key role in the transition from command economy to market economy, to the extent that such a transition may itself be considered an expression of the command economy. Under such conditions, the predictability of commercial transactions and, in general, the certainty of the marketplace must be subordinated to overriding policy concerns of the state. As Jones points out, '[f]oreign lawyers used to a system of binding law in their own jurisdiction are surprised when Chinese partners break contracts or renege on deals whenever Party policy changes. . . . Since the right of interpretation of law remains with the National People's Congress, it is the Party which ultimately determines how and whether law will be enacted'.[122] The second particularistic condition has to do with the Confucian base of Chinese culture. The Confucian values of paternalism (subordination of the individual), social cohesion, strong familism, utilitarian discipline, self-confidence and so on, endow the commercial transactions with forms and resources of predictability and security, which are foreign to the universalistic (Western) principles of *lex mercatoria*. This is specially the case of the *guanxi* networks. *Guanxi* is an informal personalized system of connections based on the family, the clan or the friendship networks through which state favours are obtained and social relationships are lubricated with reference to a relational ethics (reciprocity, personal obligation, face and honor).[123] *Guanxi* operates, thus, both as a mobilizing and a stabilizing resource in social relationships in general and in business deals in particular. To the extent that partners in international transactions resort to *guanxi* to obtain or intensify business predictability and security, we may say that *lex mercatoria* is being guanxified. In other words, in China *lex mercatoria* and the old Confucian dimensions of Chinese legal culture interpenetrate.

7.4   Transnational third worlds: the law of people on the move

I am arguing in this chapter that the intensification of global interactions in the last three decades cannot be reduced to transnational business operations carried out by large and powerful world actors. In this period, cross-border interactions in general have expanded enormously for a whole range of reasons, of which only some have

---

[122]   See Jones, 1993, p 16.
[123]   Jones, 1993; Ghai, 1993c; Potter, 1993; Winn, 1993; Siu-Kai and Hsin-Chi, 1988; Wong, 1985.

directly to do with the increase in international trade. According to some estimates, on an average day more than seven million persons cross national borders by plane, train, bus, car or on foot.[124] People cross borders as tourists, on business or as migrant workers, and as scientists, students, consumers and refugees. These cross-border movements raise a myriad of different sociolegal issues, from international contracts, binational marriages, adoptions of foreign children, legal protection of tourists and cross-border consumer rights, to civil, political and social rights of legal and illegal foreign migrant workers, refugees and asylum seekers. In spite of this, however, the international community has paid relatively little attention to the movement of people across national borders, especially when compared with the elaborate sets of uniform laws, international conventions and *lex mercatoria* dealing with the movements of goods and services. Since the traditional international private law covers only a very small number of issues, the international flow of people is in many respects a legal no-man's land. As a result, the legal protection of human beings seems to be much more territorialized than the legal protection of goods and services. International movements and interactions of people thus imply a net loss of legal protection. In a world seemingly saturated with an ideology of rights, and undergoing a period of intense globalization, the challenges posed by this 'black hole' heavily underscore the sociological and political need to analyze the movements of people across national borders.

This analysis is as important as it is difficult, mainly because the movements of people across national borders encompass a wide variety of situations that is irreducible to a single theoretical explanation or policy orientation. As a starting point, and with the objective of identifying and classifying the major forms of movements, I suggest an analytical framework based on a double criterion: the degree of autonomy, and the level of risk involved in moving across borders. Tourists, for instance, have almost total autonomy over their movements, including the autonomy to decide the amount of risk to take – they may decide to go backpacking alone into the wilderness or join comfortably a tour organized by a travel agency.[125] Business people may have just a little less autonomy than tourists, particularly if they are employed but have full control over the personal risks involved – safe means of transportation, travel insurance, guaranteed labour rights and contracts. On the contrary, and though the situations may vary widely, migrants tend to move across borders with relatively little autonomy and with a great deal of personal risk. Finally, refugees are, generally speaking, the social group with least autonomy and highest degree of personal risk. International migrants and refugees are, therefore, the two most vulnerable groups of people moving across borders, and those whose legal protection is simultaneously most needed and most difficult to sustain politically. They thus deserve special attention in this section. Though I start by accepting as a given the distinction between international migrants (economically determined migration) and refugees (politically determined migration), I

---

[124]   Sohn and Buergenthal, 1992, p v.
[125]   Borocz, 1996.

will comment below on the reasons why the distinction has been blurred in the last decades.

7.4.1 INTERNATIONAL MIGRATION

According to Portes and Borocz, among the topics of interest to contemporary social science, few are more dynamic than international migration, especially as it has manifested itself in recent years.[126] In their view, rather than being the outcome of economic decisions governed by the law of supply and demand, international labour migration is a very complex social phenomenon, embedded in the political history of the relations between sending and receiving societies and in the networks constructed by the movement and contact of people across space, and whose basic dynamics lie in the labour needs of the world system as a whole. Such needs, as well as the means of fulfilling them, have changed over time. International migration is hardly a new phenomenon. From the very beginning, the modern world system relied on it, in the form of slavery. As Wallerstein has shown, capitalist development lies in the combination of free and coerced labour: 'Free labor is the form of labor control used for skilled work in core countries, whereas coerced labor is used for less skilled work in peripheral ones. The combination thereof is the essence of capitalism'.[127] From the sixteenth century on, unfree labour involved coerced labour flows under the slave trade from West Africa to the New World, where the indigenous populations had drastically declined in the aftermath of the conquest (in Mexico the population fell from 11 million in 1519 to 1.5 million in about 1650). With a wholly different context from that of classical slavery, the slave trade was the first major form of international migration in the modern world system.[128] This form of labour flow involved high-risk capital investment, and required the active support of the colonial state.[129]

From the nineteenth century on, and until the 1960s, a new major form of international migration emerged, based on migrant recruitment through economic inducements. This was a period of dramatic emigration from Europe. Between 1846 and 1930, over fifty million Europeans emigrated overseas. This migration occurred in the context of active recruitment practices – by the post-colonial states of the Americas, from the US to Argentina – which were again costly in terms of capital input, but required only passive support of the coercive bodies of the receiving states.[130] From this point of view, this form of international labour flow was at the midpoint between the coerced labour extraction of the slave trade and the self-initiated or spontaneous flows that came to dominate in more recent years. This third major form of international migration had its origins in the expectations raised by the cultural diffusion in the peripheral societies of

[126] Portes and Borocz, 1989, p 606. Also, Portes and Walton, 1981.
[127] Wallerstein, 1974, p 127. For a partial critique, see Cohen, 1987, pp 66ff.
[128] Cohen, 1987, p 4.
[129] Portes and Walton, 1981, Chapter 2; Portes and Borocz, 1989, p 608.
[130] Portes and Borocz, 1989, p 608.

the patterns of consumption typical of core societies: 'The fulfillment of such expectations becomes increasingly difficult under the economies of scarcity of the periphery and growing cross-national ties make it possible for certain groups located there to seek a solution by migration abroad'.[131]

The succession of these three forms of international migration represents only a general tendency. Given the historical capacity of capitalism to combine different forms of labour, different forms of international migration may be resorted to at a given point in time, and the combinations among them may vary according to the regions of the world system. The existence of pockets of slavelike labour flows – for example, sex tourism and prostitution rings – is recurrently a matter of international news,[132] while active labour procurement systems continue to exist under different forms.[133] One of such systems, the *Bracero* programme – an official agreement between the US and Mexico, established in 1942 – though officially brought to a halt in the period from 1965 to 1968, continued in reality under a different form as massive procurement of foreign workers by way of undocumented border crossers, at no risk whatsoever to the employers, and under conditions that facilitated ruthless exploitation.[134] Both in its formal and informal versions, this system had some features in common with the *Gastarbeiter* (guest workers) model that was targeted to the labour reserves of the Mediterranean Basin and adopted by the advanced European countries (especially Germany) throughout the 1960s and early 1970s.[135]

As forms of labour and of labour recruitment change over time, so do forms of settlement. Though the world labour market has always combined temporary migration and settlement with permanent migration and settlement, the end of the period of organized capitalism, in the early 1970s, seems to coincide with the demise of permanent migration and settlement. While only four countries (Australia, Canada, New Zealand and the US) can be said to accept permanent migrants today – such acceptance being defined as confirming rights of citizenship upon entry – virtually all countries are now participating in an international system of temporary migrations.[136] Though temporary migration has absorbed increasingly larger numbers of people in the last two decades, its internal dynamics is now changing, due to several economic, political and cultural factors that together create the context for the discussion of the two topics which, in

[131]   Portes and Borocz, 1989. Also Portes, 1979.
[132]   UN Chronicle, December 1992, p 72.
[133]   See Prothero, 1990, for an introductory analysis of labour recruiting organizations in the developing world.
[134]   Zolberg, 1989, p 407; Cohen, 1987, p 50.
[135]   The case of Germany is particularly striking. The federal labour office set up labour bureaux in the Mediterranean countries, encouraging German employers wanting labourers to pay this government agency a recruitment fee. The work of the FLO was supplemented by intergovernmental labour supply contracts with Greece (1960), Turkey (1961 and 1964), Morocco (1963), Portugal (1964), Tunisia (1965) and Yugoslavia (1968). See Castles *et al*, 1984, p 72. Also Cohen, 1987, p 157.
[136]   Basok, 2000; Salt, 1987, p 241.

the aspect of globalization dealt with here, I consider most important within the research agenda of this chapter: the role of the state in the regulation of international migration flows, and the legal protection of international migrants.

7.4.1.1   *State regulation of migration flows*

It is commonly agreed that one of the main features of the period of disorganized capitalism is a new international division of labour, in the terms of which industrial capital from the core is moving to the periphery, where cheaper labour is located, establishing factories to produce manufactured goods for export to the worldwide market.[137] Such factories and their contractors thus come to integrate what the recent literature in the sociology of development has called 'global commodity chains'.[138] This new division of labour involves a new spatial division of labour which, according to some authors, is producing some structural changes in the labour markets of the core countries, to the effect that the demand for massive industrial labour of the sort usually filled by immigrants will be substantially reduced.[139] It is further claimed that, in the future, the international migration flows will grow mainly in the South, among peripheral and semi-peripheral countries. Though this is disputed by other authors, for whom the bulk of industrial production continues to be located at the core and to feed the need for continuing international migration, it is evident that in recent years the core states have tightened the controls over entry, building imaginary fortresses or Walls of China around their national boundaries. This raises the issue of the role of the state in transnational flows of labour. A first observation is that the role of the state, no matter how drastically changed in its internal content over time, has always remained crucial in this field. Throughout the history of capitalism, labour flows have gone through time-spaces of intense deterritorialization and time-spaces of intense reterritorialization, but in either case the state has always played a crucial role. The three large forms of labour displacement mentioned above required from the states – from the receiving state but also from the sending state – the performance of important tasks with the purpose either of deterritorializing labour relations (opening up national borders) or reterritorializing them (closing down the national borders) according to the circumstances. Enforcing or relaxing border controls in the interests of capital as a whole has therefore been a major function of the modern state.[140]

But this is by no means the whole story. As the migration literature has emphasized, international migration is a complex social and political process that cannot be reduced to the operation of the laws of the market. Portes has drawn our attention to the creation and consolidation of migrant networks across space: 'More than individualistic calculations of gain, it is the insertion of people into such networks which helps explain

[137]   Fröbel, Heinrichs and Kreye, 1980.
[138]   Gereffi and Korzeniewicz, 1994.
[139]   Piore, 1986; Zolberg, 1989, p 410.
[140]   Petras, 1980, p 174. Also Cohen, 1987, p 175.

differential proclivities to move and the enduring character of migrant flows'.[141] The operation of such networks is partly responsible for the often-limited effectiveness of state efforts to regulate immigration. In West Germany, even though entries of migrant workers from outside the EU were banned in 1973, the number of foreign residents continued to grow due to family reunification. In spite of such limits, state control over national boundaries has been a crucial factor in the direction and intensity of international migration, and its operational logic cannot be reduced to that of world economy.[142] International migration has an inherent political element, in that it entails not only physical relocation, but a change of jurisdiction and social membership. In this respect, the policies of the receiving states are particularly important, because, after all, they determine whether the international movement, and of what kind, may or may not take place. In a world system characterized by widely varying conditions, international borders serve to maintain global inequality. State policies may aim at defending one fraction of capital to the detriment of another, or national capital to the detriment of foreign capital. They may also result from coalitions of capital and labour, particularly in core countries, as when organized labour is able to achieve some market protection by imposing limiting conditions on labour importation. [143] Furthermore, the state prerogative over national boundaries may be activated for reasons that, though related to economic factors, cannot be solely attributed to them. Racism, xenophobia and the social construction of codes of 'cultural incompatibility' between foreigners and nationals have a cultural and political leverage of their own, influencing migration policies autonomously.[144]

The state and the national boundaries it controls have thus performed crucial roles in the creation of international migration regimes throughout the history of modern capitalism. Even when the state control is limited either by global economic pressures or by global social networks of migratory movement and settlement, the state retains the control of the legal status of migrants, a detail that has a decisive impact on migrant life and experience in the host country. This control has become more central lately in light of the convergent impact of two recent trends: on the one hand, the trend of core states to favour, if at all, only temporary migration and only in restrictive terms – available only to those whose skills and expertise are in demand, like the prominent case of Indian computer engineers in the US bears witness[145] – with the consequent tighter control over borders; on the other hand, the increased pressure to emigrate and the potential for large-scale population movements motivated by the struggle for

---

[141]   Portes and Borocz, 1989, p 612. Also Portes and Zhou, 1992, pp 491–522. For a different view, Salt, 1989.

[142]   This fact has been emphasized, among others, by Zolberg, 1981; Zolberg, 1989, p 405.

[143]   In this perspective must be analyzed the opposition of the AFL-CIO against NAFTA. See Trubek *et al*, 1993, pp 37–49. In the late 1990s, however, the AFL-CIO adopted a more cosmopolitan position vis-à-vis immigration and has promoted the unionization of illegal immigrants. See AFL-CIO, 2000. See also Avci and McDonald, 2000.

[144]   Dijk, 1987.

[145]   Cheng, 1998.

survival resulting from the immiseration of significant regions of the world system and the growing disparities between the North and the South, hence the potential increase in illegal, clandestine or undocumented migration, and the consequent strengthening of the receiving states as monopoly holders of the legal status of migrants and of migrant life chances and expectations attached to it.

7.4.1.2   *The legal rights of migrants*

In general, states do not treat aliens, including legal resident aliens, the same way they treat citizens. They regularly reserve a variety of rights for nationals, and this is generally considered legitimate under international law. Thus, by definition, migrants are second- or third-class citizens, but their legal status varies considerably according to whether they are legal or illegal migrants. Concerning legal migrants, their legal status may still vary according to whether they are permanent immigrants – expected to settle in the host country – or temporary immigrants – seasonal migrants, 'guest workers', 'project-tied workers'. The legal status of illegal migrants, on the other hand, is the most precarious; accordingly, they are the most vulnerable class of immigrants, though they are also the fastest-growing class of immigrants.[146] The International Labor Organization (ILO) predicted that by 2010 there would be twenty-five million migrants in irregular situations throughout the world, not including refugees.[147] For these reasons, and also because they represent the highest social and political tension between national and transnational perspectives, between territorial sovereignty principles and human rights principles, I will focus briefly on the status of illegal migrants.

The undocumented migrants are the hardest working and lowest-paid labourers. They are specially vulnerable to arbitrary practices on the part of employers, landlords and merchants; they are afraid to avail themselves of the few rights they may enjoy for fear of exposure to immigration authorities and, above all, for fear of deportation. They are too culturally handicapped (including limited foreign-language-speaking ability) to have minimum access to the system, and are specially victimized by racial, class, ethnic and gender discrimination.[148] Some of their hardships are related to the specific work the undocumented migrants are engaged in. For instance, undocumented domestic workers – one fast-growing group in many European countries and in the US – often work without formal contracts; their working conditions are poorly enforced, due to the dispersed, isolated and private nature of work sites; they are often physically and sexually abused, due to close working quarters.[149]

In light of these multiple vulnerabilities, the extension of substantial human rights protection to undocumented immigrants seems particularly justified and necessary.

---

[146]   Rogers, 1992.
[147]   *Migration News Sheet*, February 1991, p 3.
[148]   Bosniak, 1991, p 747. Also Warzazi, 1986; Cohen, 1987; Selby, 1989.
[149]   Davis, 1993, p 14.

Nonetheless, protection is as problematic as it is urgent. The problems arise from the fact that illegal immigrants question, in a very direct way, one of the state's prerogatives most closely associated with territorial sovereignty: the state's powers to decide who will enter its territory, to refuse entry, and to expel unwanted aliens. The very existence of illegal immigrants demonstrates that such powers are being eroded and, with them, territorial sovereignty. In theory, the improvement of the legal status of illegal immigrants seems to be obtainable only at the cost of state sovereignty. From the latter's perspective, the sole logical way of dealing with illegal immigration is to prevent its occurrence. In practice, however, state policies vis-à-vis illegal immigration have varied widely, and in some periods they have been characterized by great tolerance toward unauthorized cross-border movements. I have already mentioned that in the US the *Bracero* programme continued informally after its official termination, without employers necessarily being punished or workers deported. In France, undocumented immigration, which constituted up to 80 per cent of all immigration until the early seventies, was described as 'spontaneous migration', and tolerated as such.[150] Today, in the periphery of the world system, irregular migration is a normal, often inconsequential occurrence, out of sheer incapacity on the part of the states to enforce border controls, or mere lack of political will. Only in the last three decades, as a result of economic deterioration and the rise of xenophobic anti-immigration movements, have states, particularly the core states, come to view illegal immigration as a threat to national sovereignty, indeed, as a legal, social and political problem of significant proportions. Many of these countries have introduced restrictive immigration legislation with the purpose of reasserting control over the borders and eliminating illegal immigration – the US, Canada, France, Australia, Japan, Germany, Argentina, Italy and, lastly, some European states in the ambit of the Schengen Agreements.

In spite of these legislative efforts, it is unlikely that illegal migration will diminish at any time soon. Many factors and indicators point, rather, to its substantial increase in the coming years, even after the tightening of border controls associated with the 'war on terrorism' declared after 11 September 2001. If this is the tendency, the principle of territorial sovereignty will appear increasingly at odds with the dynamics of transnational migration, and the tensions derived therefrom will accentuate. To a significant extent, these tensions are part of a much broader conflict between the core and the periphery of the world system, or between the North and South, and must be analyzed in this context, as I explain below . As things stand now, no international consensus has been reached on the possible terms of a compromise between the principles of international human rights applicable to nationals and non-nationals and to legal and illegal aliens, on the one hand, and the principle of territorial sovereignty, on the other. In other words, no international migration regime has come into existence.[151] The latent ideological and political conflict between these mutually inconsistent principles, both of them equally embedded in Western modernity, can be

[150]   Bosniak, 1991, p 744.
[151]   Rogers, 1992, p 45.

easily traced in the United Nations Convention for the Protection of the Rights of All Migrant Workers and Members of their Families, drafted in collaboration with the ILO, and adopted by the UN General Assembly of 1990.[152] Under the convention, it is the obligation of states to afford to documented as well as to undocumented workers a range of civil, social and labour rights, which include, among others, rights to due process of law in criminal proceedings, free expression and religious observance, domestic privacy, equality with nationals before the courts, emergency medical care, education for children, respect for cultural identity, rights to enforce employment contracts against employers, to participate in trade unions and to enjoy the protection of wage, hour and health regulations in the workplace. Yet, as Bosniak notes,[153] despite its laudable provisions, the Convention's treatment of undocumented immigrants is deeply ambivalent. While contracting states must meet a minimum standard of treatment of irregular migrants, the rights provided to these migrants need not be as extensive as those which must be afforded to legally admitted migrants. The states are thus entitled to discriminate against undocumented migrants in many decisive aspects, from rights to family unity and liberty of movement, to rights to social services, employment and unionization. Such discriminatory treatment is grounded on the Convention's overriding commitment to the principle of national sovereignty. Over and over again, the terms of the Convention state that the rights granted cannot be construed as an infringement on state power to exclude foreigners from its territory and to shape the composition of its national membership. 'The ultimate result', Bosniak concludes, 'is a hybrid instrument, at once a ringing declaration of individual rights and a staunch manifesto in support of state territorial sovereignty'.[154]

The tension between human rights and territorial sovereignty principles extends far beyond the migration context, and in a sense is constitutive of the modern inter-state system. But in the case of undocumented migrants it reaches a particularly high level, because the states here have no choice but to assert the prerogative of sovereignty against the recognition of their failure to assert it. Therefore, discrimination against undocumented migrants is a substitute for actual exclusion at the border. Under such circumstances, elimination of discrimination presupposes a radical transformation of the principle of sovereignty as we know it. Short of that, and irrespective of how many transnational migration movements, both regular and irregular, have contributed and will still contribute to world capitalist development, the situation of undocumented immigrants is bound to be structurally shaped by multiple and blatant violations of human rights.

The discrimination they suffer is double: on the one hand, their legal entitlements are very precarious; on the other, their social vulnerability makes the struggle for the

---

152   In the following analysis, I draw on Bosniak, 1991. See also Nafziger and Bartel, 1989; Martin, 1989; Fontenau, 1992; Goodwill-Gill, 1989.
153   Bosniak, 1991, p 741.
154   Bosniak, 1991, p 742.

enforcement of rights almost impossible and the impunity of violations a normal occurrence. To give just an example: according to the US Immigration Reform and Control Act of 1986, regardless of their legal status, undocumented workers are entitled to the federal minimum wage. If the employer pays them less than that – which occurs very often[155] – they are unlikely to complain about it to the authorities for fear of exposure to punishment or deportation; they are less likely to quit and risk unemployment since they are not eligible for unemployment benefits; and they are also less likely to organize in defence of their rights or to join existing labour unions for the same fear of public exposure. This is also today the lived experience of illegal immigrants in Europe, as Sassen's recent work has thoroughly documented.[156] Undocumented migrants are part of a growing, transnational Third World of people, a non-constituency for nationally-based political processes, moving around in a legal no-man's-land, living life experiences shaped by the dark side of a growing global economy whose inequities are in part guaranteed by the existence of national boundaries and the coercive powers of the states policing them. Thus, undocumented migrants reveal the innermost contradictions between the exclusionary powers of sovereignty and a cosmopolitan politics of rights called for to protect new transnational vulnerabilities against new transnational impunities.

7.4.2   REFUGEES AND DISPLACED PEOPLE

Though internally more diversified, another sector of the growing, transnational Third World of people are the refugees. As in the case of undocumented migrant workers, refugees concern me here insofar as they raise specific new issues in the broad conceptualization of the globalization of the legal field I am outlining in this chapter. Such issues have to do, in this case, with two clear-cut distinctions upon which the international refugee regime was built in the postwar period: between voluntary and involuntary international migration, on the one hand, and between economically motivated and politically motivated migration, on the other. I argue here that these two distinctions have collapsed in recent years, thereby producing new inadequacies between the hegemonic principles of territorial sovereignty and the dynamics of transnational movements.

The cumulative world number of postwar refugees has been estimated at around ninety million.[157] Massive refugee flows have marked the period since the end of the 1970s – starting with the dramatic situation of the Vietnamese 'boat people' in 1979 to 1981 – and have increased dramatically in the last few years. According to the UN High Commissioner on Refugees, in 2001 nearly twenty-two million people were seeking

---

[155]   In the mid-1980s, 24 per cent of illegal workers were paid less than the minimum wage. Friedman, 1986, p 1715.

[156]   See Sassen, 1999.

[157]   Hakovirta, 1993, p 37.

refuge across national borders.[158] Refugees are not evenly distributed around the world. Out of the nearly 22 million seeking refuge, roughly 8.5 million were in Asia, six million in Africa, 5.5 in Europe, one million in North America, 500,000 in Latin America and 70,000 in Oceania.[159] These numbers reflect a trend that began in the early 1980s, when the share of the South began to increase.[160] In the last decades, massive emergencies have forced hundreds of thousands of people to cross state borders in Jordan, Somalia, Eritrea, Vietnam, Ogaden, Sudan, Liberia, Mozambique, Cambodia, Laos, Iraq, Afghanistan, Sri Lanka, Lebanon, Uganda, Nicaragua, El Salvador and so on. The pressures on neighbouring countries have been enormous. Until very recently, there were one million Mozambican refugees in Malawi, whose native population is only seven times larger. In the last half-decade, refugees have become a serious problem in Europe, and they are likely to continue being seen as such in the coming years. The disintegration of the Soviet Union and Yugoslavia has already produced hundreds of thousands of displaced people. The spectre of massive flows of people within Europe is already transforming the European interstate system in significant ways. I mean 'Soviet-Poles' flowing into Poland, *Volksdeutsche* (German descendents) into Germany, Albanians into Italy, Transylvanian Magyars into Hungary, ex-Yugoslavians into Croatia and elsewhere, Pontic Greeks into Greece and so on.

But who is a refugee? According to the United Nations Convention of 1951 and 1967, a refugee is any person who:

> 'owing to a well-founded fear of being persecuted for reasons of race, religion, nationality, membership of a particular social group or political opinion, is outside the country of his nationality and is unable or, owing to such fear, is unwilling to avail himself of the protection of that country; or who, not having a nationality or being outside the country of his former habitual residence as a result of, such events, is unable or, owing to such fear, is unwilling to return to it'.[161]

Bearing in mind the reference above to the major refugee flows of our time, the above definition excludes most of the world's displaced populations, who are mainly victims of massive conflicts, human rights abuses, civil wars, external aggression and occupation, foreign domination and so on. Since they have not been personally persecuted, they are not entitled to refugee status, even though the political nature of the causes of their flight offers no doubt. They are considered 'displaced persons', and at the most may receive some humanitarian assistance. In the periphery and the semi-periphery of the world system, some regional inter-state agreements have taken some first steps to expand the concept of refugee in order to include the 'humanitarian

---

[158]   2001 Report of the UN High Commissioner for Refugees. http://www.unhcr.ch. Visited as of 22 May 2002.

[159]   2001 Report of the UN High Commissioner for Refugees. http://www.unhcr.ch. Visited as of 22 May 2002.

[160]   Hakovirta, 1993, p 37.

[161]   Sohn and Buergenthal, 1992, p 100.

refugee',[162] but the core countries have repeatedly expressed their opposition to such an expansion. In recent years, when confronted with the potential rise of applications for asylum, they have even adopted more restrictive legislation on (or rather, against) refugees and asylum seekers.[163] The most blatant examples are the Schengen countries in Europe (more on this below). The last two decades have witnessed other 'involuntary' flows of people still more at odds with international and domestic refugees legislation: hundreds of thousands of people fleeing from famine, starvation and natural disasters (droughts, earthquakes, volcanic eruptions). In may cases extreme poverty and environmental crises have acted together with civil war or political repression to provoke massive displacements of people, as in Haiti or Eritrea, in Mozambique or Cambodia. These are dramatic situations, apparently ever more recurrent, in which the distinction between economic and political factors have been blurred, if not totally dissolved; situations in which the calamitous deterioration of native survival systems turns the question of the voluntary or involuntary nature of the migration into a macabre exercise. The inadequacy and the inequity of an international system that fails to provide protection for millions of people in the most vulnerable of situations are thereby fully exposed. Notwithstanding the chauvinistic alarms in the core countries, the majority of these subordinate transnational migrant flows have taken place within the South, and have meant an enormous burden for neighbouring countries whose social conditions are often equally grim. Ought not burden-sharing be conceived on a global scale? And will this be possible in an interstate system based on state self-centredness?

Two types of 'involuntary' transnational migration are most likely to grow in the coming years. The first one will be caused by environmental catastrophes, directly or indirectly caused by anthropogenic climate changes and often coupled with overpopulation. Refugees will be environmental refugees, seeking ecological asylum.[164] Once again, most of these flows will take place in the periphery of the world system or, at least, will start from there. More stridently even than others, environmental refugee flows portray the dark side of capitalist world development and global lifestyles. They should, therefore, become the best candidates for the application of a new and more solidary transnational conception of burden sharing. It is, however, very doubtful that that may ever occur. Environmental refugees occupy the outer fringes of a generally precarious system of international protection. They fall outside the competence of the United National High Commissioner for Refugees, and their plight can be alleviated only to a very limited degree by the already-overcommitted resources of the United Nations Disaster Relief Co-ordinator. Furthermore, environmental refugees are most likely to collide with the territorial logic underlying social protection as a matter of right.

The second type of forced transnational migration likely to grow in the coming years is the most paradoxical form of migration because it consists of populations who stay

---

[162]   On the African refugees policy, Anthony, 1991.
[163]   Sohn and Buergenthal, 1992, p 102; Hathaway, 1991.
[164]   Wöhleke, 1992; Westing, 1992.

put and 'migrate' only because the political conditions in which they used to live 'migrate' themselves, so to speak. Over twenty-five million Russians who live outside Russia became minorities overnight when the USSR ceased to exist. In some cases they became even aliens in a quasi-refugee situation. The same happened in former Yugoslavia, with even more dramatic consequences. With the rise of ethnic nationalism – against the background of modern nation-state-building based on ethnic supremacy and ethnic suppression – it is not farfetched to predict new situations of standstill migration in other parts of the world, in Africa, in India, in China and so on. Unlike other forms of refugee situations, the fate of refugees is here determined by the weakness or even by the breakup of territorial sovereignty.

The high vulnerability of refugees derives from a double adverse condition. On the one side, international human rights applicable to them are very limited by a highly restrictive definition of refugees that leaves out most of the current and massive situations of forced migration. On the other side, the few rights they are entitled to are grossly violated with almost total impunity. Such rights have evolved both from international human rights law and international humanitarian law, and include the obligation of the states through which refugees and displaced people transit or seek asylum or durable settlement in, to uphold their rights to life, to personal property, to shelter, to food, to basic health care, to practice religion, to non-discrimination and so on. In reality, however, such rights are rarely respected. For alleged reasons of national security, refugees are often confined to camps and detention centres where, aside from the lack of freedom of movement and access to the outside world, refugees are subjected to the most degrading human conditions. I quote from the 1991 UNHCR Report which describes a situation that has not changed in the last ten years:

> 'In several countries, refugees and asylum-seekers were kept in closed camps as a matter of policy. Surrounded by barbed wire and surveyed by police and armed personnel, they were obliged to remain in such camps until either resettled elsewhere or returned to their respective countries of origin. Many have been kept in such camps for more than a decade. Such circumstances have led to severe strain among camp inhabitants and serious outbreaks of violence'.[165]

On the other hand, the discrepancy between the refugee politics of core countries – as is well illustrated by the Schengen Agreements[166] – and that of peripheral countries – as in the Organization of African Unity's broad definition of refugees, including those fleeing natural disasters, foreign intervention and civil unrest – is creating a tension which is likely to become another dimension of the North-South conflict. This is due mainly to the stability rent that core countries continue to collect directly or indirectly at the cost of the periphery in an historical continuity that can be traced back to European colonialism. Aside from recent upheavals in Central Europe, some of the

---

[165]   Sohn and Buergenthal, 1992, p 109.
[166]   Koser, 2001.

largest, most urgent and longest-lasting refugee situations have originated in countries where ethnic and/or religious cleavages overlap with regional inequalities, and where they possibly have a significant transboundary dimension.[167] These situations have predominantly occurred in the South, in most instances as part of the historical process of transition from decolonization to the conflicts of post-colonialism.

7.4.3 CITIZENSHIP, INTERNATIONAL MIGRATION AND COSMOPOLITANISM

I have focused on undocumented migrant workers and refugees because they constitute the two most vulnerable groups of subordinated transnational migration. Needless to say, many situations of often extreme vulnerability (poverty, starvation, repression) do not involve any massive movements of people or, if they do, such movements take place within the confines of national borders and for that reason have not been considered in this section. Migration literature and international relief agencies have coined the concept of 'internally displaced persons' to cover the situations in which the movement of people has kept within a given nation-state.[168] According to the estimates of the UN Representative for Internally Displaced Persons, in 2001 there were between twenty and twenty-five million internally displaced people worldwide, 'with major concentrations in Sudan, Angola, Democratic Republic of Congo, Eritrea, Afghanistan, Sri Lanka, Colombia, Bosnia-Herzegovina and countries of the former Soviet Union'.[169] The vulnerability of internally displaced people lies, among other factors, in that it remains for the most part beyond the purview of international organizations. In this situation, international human rights principles collide with special intensity with the principle of sovereignty. This conflict will be further considered from different perspectives in the context of my analysis of the forms of globalization of the legal field in the following sections.

Subordinate transnational migration is most likely to grow in the coming years. Three main factors account for this: the increasing inequality between the North and the South; the growing instability in the interstate system – including civil wars, ethnic infrastate nationalisms, boundary disputes and threat of nuclear holocaust – directly or indirectly related to the renewed struggle for supremacy among core states; the likelihood of a global environmental disaster due to the uncontrolled reproduction of anarchy in investment decision making and anti-ecological consumption habits and lifestyles. In themselves, and via the subordinate transnational movements of people that they will eventually generate, these factors will challenge in fundamental ways the principle of territorial sovereignty, as well as its satellite concepts of national community, citizenship and membership. It is therefore not by coincidence that the nation-states, especially the core states, are today in need of controlling one of the major effects of such factors,

---

[167]   Lohrmann, 2000; Hakovirta, 1993, p 45.
[168]   Copeland, 1992, p 995.
[169]   2001 Report of the UN High Commissioner for Refugees. http://www.unhcr.ch. Visited as of 22 May 2002.

ie, the dramatic increase in the migration potential and the likelihood of massive irregular transnational movements.

In fact, the control over national boundaries as a major prerogative of territorial sovereignty has been growing steadily since the mid-nineteenth century as a central dimension of the consolidation of the nation-states and of the modern interstate system. In Europe, in the second half of the nineteenth century, it was possible to travel from Portugal to Russia without passport or visa. Restrictions on movements of persons across borders were imposed mainly after World War I. From then on, wars and international tensions, disparities of economic development and standards of living, and differences in political and social regimes contributed together to build up restrictions and controls of cross-border movements. The general argument of this chapter – that globalization is a complex and even contradictory historical process that occurs both by deterritorializing and reterritorializing social relations – finds here an unequivocal confirmation. While in the above-examined forms of globalization of the legal field – transnational factors causing changes in domestic law; *lex mercatoria;* law of regional integration – the national state seems to have lost ground and become relatively obsolete, in the case of subordinate transnational movements, the state, particularly the core state, seems more affirmative and self-centred than ever.

The European states are in this respect specially revealing, because they are now in a double process of relinquishing the control over entry and membership in the national territory within the EU (the internal boundaries) and of strengthening it as far as non-EU countries are concerned (the external boundaries).[170] In terms of the Single European Act, the EU countries seem determined to guarantee the free movement of persons within its common borders. In spite of differences about who these persons are, and the political and institutional instruments that will guarantee such freedom in practice, this is a major political development, and entails a substantial transformation of a central prerogative of modern territorial sovereignty. This transformation is even more compelling within the fifteen Europeancountries that have signed the Schengen Agreements Concerning the Gradual Abolition of Controls at the Common Borders (1985, 1990). By 2002, 'Schengenland' was constituted by the joint territories of Austria, Belgium, Denmark, France, Finland, Germany, Greece, Iceland, Italy, Luxembourg, the Netherlands, Norway, Portugal, Spain and Sweden. One person authorized to enter at any external border of this transnational territory can move freely within it up to three months. To guarantee this freedom, an unprecedented system of international security co-operation is set up – police co-operation; court co-operation; the Schengen Information System and so on – in the 142 articles that comprise the 1990 Schengen Agreement, drawn upon for the purpose of 'executing' the 1985 Agreement.

[170]   For the recent trends in European immigration policy and the increasing integration within the limits of the EU, see Peixoto, 2001. A general overview of the EU migration policy is in Niessen, 1992, and of refugee policy in Boer, 1992. See also Heisler, 1992. A brief comparison between European and North American international migration is in Hammer, 1989.

The easiness with which one will be allowed to move within Schengenland is only matched by the difficulty in entering it. The refugee norms of Schengen, which are very strict, were replaced by the equally restrictive refugee legislation defined by the 1990 Dublin Convention Determining the State Responsible for Examining Applications for Asylum Lodged in One of the Member States of the European Communities. The latter entered into force in September 1997 in the 12 EU member states which had originally signed the instrument.[171] This convention, drafted in a moment of panic before the spectre of millions of refugees fleeing the disintegration of the Soviet Union,[172] not only sticks to the old, by now totally inadequate, concept of refugee, but also introduces numerous procedural and substantive controls which have led to the enactment, in the individual signing countries, of the most restrictive refugee legislation in their history. Increase in discretionary powers of the agencies in charge of asylum applications; elimination of judicial control over their decisions; granting transport carriers (almost always privately owned, like airlines); the public prerogatives (and obligations, subject to penalty if not fulfilled) of controlling entry on national borders; these are some of the features of this new antirefugee legislation. I am not concerned here with the problems deriving from the non-coincidence between the external borders of Schengenland and those of the EU, since the UK, Denmark and Ireland are not part of Schengen: in the future, some EU countries will be at the external borders of Schengenland. What I want to emphasize is that the deterritorialization of the internal borders goes together with the reterritorialization of the external borders. The principle of sovereignty is thus negated at the national level by the same process that confirms it with greater efficiency at the suprastate level. This enhanced confirmation and the democratic deficit that it implies are of consequence not only for asylum seekers but also for the nationals of this transnational space: the price of free movement will eventually be a greater vulnerability vis-à-vis globalized systems of repression and information.[173]

Though probably an extreme case, the European legal and political development epitomizes the ingenuity and resourcefulness of the principle of sovereignty, always ready to transform itself on the condition that it remains operative – and, if possible, with renewed efficiency – against the truly dangerous intruders, those that remain at the external borders. And these are, without exception, those that come from peripheral or semi-peripheral regions of the world system, and dare to benefit from the social

---

[171]   In Sweden and Austria, the Convention entered into force on 1 October 1997 and in Finland on 1 January 1998.

[172]   Curiously enough, for more than forty years, since the end of World War II, millions of refugees have fled from Eastern Europe because of the existence of the Soviet Union and the Communist bloc. During that period, Austria alone, as one of the adjacent countries, offered refuge to 2 million people. About two-thirds of them were subsequently resettled in third countries, primarily in traditional overseas immigration countries, like the US, Canada and Australia. Nonetheless, 600,000 refugees and displaced persons chose to settle in Austria. Kussbach, 1992, p 646. On the asymmetric axes of European migration policy, East-West and North-South, see Manfrass, 1992.

[173]   Bolten, 1992; Swart, 1992; Hoogenboom, 1992; Boeles, 1992.

amenities accumulated in the core, often at the expense of those same regions. The exclusionary virtuosity of the principle of sovereignty is not exercised in a social or political vacuum. The state, as a set of institutions, together with the political, social and cultural elites, are the cement with which the fortress of nationalistic chauvinism and ethnic panic are built. In an illuminating analysis of the widespread ethnic panic in the Netherlands created by the immigration of a group of Tamil refugees from Sri Lanka during the first months of 1985 – a potential minority group that up until then had been unknown to the population at large – van Dijk has found that ethnic prejudice is mainly preformulated in the prevailing discourse types of the elite – representatives of the national and local authorities, the judiciary, the police, welfare agencies, education and academic research – and that such discourse is publicly reformulated by the mass media.[174] In the last years, ethnic panic has spread throughout Europe as a kind of symbolic reterritorialization of national communities, which in a perverse way might have fed the contestation of the Maastricht Treaty.

This dialectics of deterritorialization-reterritorialization, which is observable at the macrolevel of policy, legislation and opinion making, can also be observed at the microlevel of sets of individual decisions by different state agencies. The European Court of Justice is one such agency. In my analysis of the transnational law of regional integration, I emphasized the prominent role of the court in deterritorializing the economic and commercial legislation of EU countries, creating in its stead a new, community-wide, supranational, legal order of its own, grounded on a new constitutional basis derived from the interpretation of the European treaties adopted by the court. In light of this, it is all the more symptomatic that the court has been extremely passive, restrictive and low-profile in interpreting the limits of its human rights jurisdiction in cases concerning non-EU nationals. As Weiler aptly notes, 'in relation to non-Community nationals the court has been ... particularly prudent and has eschewed the boldness which characterizes some of its jurisprudence in other areas'.[175] In my analytical framework, in this respect, the court has been acting in total consonance with the political project of EU member states, deterritorializing the internal borders in order to strengthen the position of Europe as a regional trading bloc in the upcoming struggle for supremacy in the world system, on the one hand, and, on the other, reterritorializing the external borders so as to prevent the strength of the position from being endangered by the disruptive presence of undesired and undeserving guests. The hard economic interest calculations that seem to fuel this dialectics are, however, in a collision course with the political and cultural principles that have been proclaimed as the essential ethos of the European project. Furthermore, the needs of electoral politics may at times require feeding on internal xenophobic sentiments, or at least, being ambiguous about them. The contradictory nature of such a course of action is well summarized by Weiler, when he speaks of:

---

[174]   Dijk, 1987, pp 81–122. In general, on minorities in Europe, see *L'evenement europeen*, October 1991, special issue on 'Minorities: What Chances for Europe?'

[175]   Weiler, 1992, p 70. See also Cassese, Clapham and Weiler, 1991a, 1991b.

'a delicate path to tread, one which is supportive of the process of European Union but acknowledges the dangers of feeding xenophobia towards non-Europeans and the even deeper danger towards one of the moral assets of European integration – its historical downplaying of nationality as a principal referent in transnational intercourse'.[176]

If the EU countries have lately become an extreme example of restrictive refugee policies, the US has been, and not only lately, an extreme example of political bias and discretionary selectivity in the application of refugee legislation formally informed by the principle of equal treatment. In 1965, Congress discarded favouritism by national origins in favour of the same immigration ceiling for every country; equal treatment was further extended in 1980 when, through the Refugee Act, the US redefined refugees as individuals fearing persecution not only from Communist systems, as had been the case before, but from any regime.[177] The Refugee Act established objective criteria for determining refugee admissions that would supposedly depoliticize the refugee policy. In practice, however, the Act's provisions have been easily circumvented by an executive branch with too much discretionary authority that has been exercised to fit overarching political objectives.

The Haitians' quest for political asylum illustrates best the strong bias in the implementation of US immigration laws. From June 1983 until March 1991, 74.5 per cent of refugees from the former Soviet Union were granted asylum, compared to 1.8 per cent of Haitians, and the discrimination is even more blatant when Haitians are contrasted with nationals from other American countries, namely with Cubans. As Little puts it, '[i]n many ways, immigration procedures towards Cubans and Haitians that seek entry into the US represent the extremes of United States' policy. Immigration policy towards Cuba tends to be generous and humanitarian; immigration policy towards Haiti tends to be stringent and inhumane'.[178] Soon after Fidel Castro took power in Cuba, the US enacted the Cuban Refugee Adjustment Act of 1966, enabling almost 800,000 Cubans to enter the US between 1966 and 1980.[179] During the same period, the government refused to admit refugees from Haiti, though they fled from one of the bloodiest and most repressive regimes of the world, the 'gangster government' of the Duvaliers. The truth of the matter lay in the fact that Haiti was anti-Communist and the Duvaliers supported the US's attempts to dislodge Communism in Cuba. For this reason, Haitian refugees were unwelcome. Discrimination against Haitians and in favour of Cubans has been a distinctive feature of the US refugee policy, and is pursued at different

---

[176]   Weiler, 1992, p 68. As reported by Clapham, 1991, p 84, at the discussion between ministers in the ACP (African, Caribbean and Pacific countries)/EEC Council of Ministers, on 28–29 March 1990, ACP states said they would have liked a joint expert group to be established to deliberate on how to combat racist attacks on their citizens in the Community. The Community opposed this idea on the grounds that these questions were of the competence of the member states. As Clapham commented: 'One cannot ignore the fact that community integration may exhibit nasty side effects which can rebound on "extra-communitari" in a particularly brutal way'.

[177]   Little, 1993, pp 270–271.

[178]   Little, 1993, p 290.

[179]   Lennox, 1993, p 712.

levels, for instance, in detention centres. During most of the time, Haitians have been the majority of the detainees in the best well-known INS detention facility, Krome North Service Processing Center located in Miami, Florida. In early January 1993, the Haitians detained here entered a nine-day hunger strike, following the arrival of 52 Cubans who had 'commandeered' a Cuban commuter flight from Havana to Varadero, Cuba, diverting it to Miami. They protested against another painful instance of the double standard: all the Cubans were released from the camp within 48 hours.[180] Plainly, the Refugee Act of 1980 has failed to eliminate ideological discrimination from immigration policy. Because the President selects the geographical locations and allotment of aliens who may enter, *de facto* discrimination based on geopolitical considerations has simply replaced *de jure* discrimination.[181]

For all their differences, recent immigration and refugee policies of the European countries and the US illustrate the extent to which the overriding commitment of core states to national interests – defined, in this instance, as territorial prerogatives – may lead to measures against non-nationals and to distinctions among non-nationals which, when viewed from a cosmopolitan human rights perspective, are arbitrary and discriminatory. The likely intensification of subordinate transnational migrations in the coming years, together with the increasing globalization of their root causes, are liable to raise the contradictions between their dynamics and the logic of territorial sovereignty to such a high level that current institutional and normative structures will collapse for lack of legitimacy and feasibility, calling for a new understanding and a new political approach. In my view, such a new departure will be built upon the following concerns, whose analytical and normative dimensions constitute the research agenda in the field of the subordinate global flows of people put forward in this chapter.

7.4.3.1. *A New historical epistemology of need and difference*

Whenever transnational migration is forced upon people, there is no justification to distinguish between nationals and non-nationals. In the light of international human rights principles, whenever people cannot choose to stay within their national boundaries except by risking their lives, they become *ipso facto* citizens of any other country. This is the basic premise of a new political and legal subaltern cosmopolitanism. It is cosmopolitan in that, to put it in Debra Satz's terms, from this perspective 'neither nationality nor state boundaries, as such, have moral standing with respect to questions of justice'[182] and thus are irrelevant as criteria for granting the benefits of citizenship. It is new to the extent that, rather than based on abstract principles of individualism, universalism and generality, it is historically grounded, culturally specific and politically discriminating.[183] In the same vein, Walter Mignolo has recently made a strong case for 'critical and dialogical cosmopolitan conversations, rather than blueprints or master

---

[180]   Little, 1993, p 289.
[181]   Lennox, 1993, p 711.
[182]   Satz, 1999, p 67.
[183]   A different conception of cosmopolitanism is in Pogge, 1992.

plans imposed worldwide'.[184] The history of the modern world system is a history of unequal exchanges that are at the roots of the war, starvation, oppression and ecological disaster that force people to migrate. Modern science has managed to separate the knowledge of this history from the history of this knowledge. For this reason, modern historical knowledge is ahistorical. Because this ahistorical knowledge benefits the countries that have benefited from the unequal exchanges, modern science is intrinsically territorial. To that extent, it is as great an obstacle to the development of a new cosmopolitan politics as the nation-state itself. Short of such a new subaltern cosmopolitanism, neither the needs nor the differences of transnational migrants can be properly addressed. As things stand now, the needs of migrants have been codified and ranked by criteria of nationality and territoriality that are inherently biased against them, while their differences have been codified and ranked by a hegemonic form of knowledge that cannot understand them except by what they are not.

Hegel conceived of modern science as a form of knowledge that progressed by distinctions, divisions and discriminations. He oversaw the fact that, in the real world, rather than calling for a philosophical *Aufhebung* (*supersession* or *sublation*), that form of knowledge became articulated with the modern state, whereupon scientific distinctions became social differences, which in turn engendered subordination. Subordinate transnational movements are movements of knowledges that have been suppressed and marginalized. Transnational Third Worlds of people are also transnational Third Worlds of knowledges, and they feed on each other. Learning from them, learning from the South, is one of the epistemological prerequisites of a cosmopolitan politics. Indeed, as I will argue in Chapter Nine, the view that results from such learning is the epistemological condition for engendering practices of counter-hegemonic globalization. Competition among different knowledges is a prerequisite to the transformation of the history of the modern world system into a tribunal to determine culpability and liability, grant entitlements to compensation, and establish the criteria for burden-sharing. It is also an epistemological condition to distinguish among differences that do not generate legitimate or occult subordination, and differences that do. Without alternative knowledges within the same hermeneutic constellation, it is not possible to sustain multicultural pluralism within the same territorial time-space.

.

7.4.3.2 *Community, membership, transnational advocacy*

Subordinate transnational migration represents a fundamental challenge to the concepts orbiting around the principle of territorial sovereignty, such as national community, citizenship, membership, and naturalization. It is today widely recognized that national boundaries are a major political device to maintain inequality across the world system, and that they do so by separating jurisdictions and defining membership. Control of entry and control over range of membership, though separate issues, are thus intimately

---

[184]   Mignolo, 2002, p 182.

interconnected. Whenever the state fails to control entry – as when illegal immigrants manage to settle inside the borders – it still can erect a wall against incorporation by virtue of the illegal status stamped on immigrant life experience. Illegal immigrants and asylum seekers thus doubly challenge the principle of territorial sovereignty, as they raise both the question of entry – to what extent does the denial of entry represent a violation of international human rights? – and the question of membership – to what extent can people already present in the national territory and, eventually, with significant ties to it, be denied full membership without thereby violating international human rights?[185] The second question deserves greater attention, because the social and political impact of decisions on entry is premised upon the quality and the range of membership they give access to.

The plight of illegal immigrants and asylum seekers is one of the most dramatic consequences of the impoverishment of the principle of community once it has been reduced to the national community, and the latter to the state and civil society as foils of one another. The legal and political overload of such a reduction disqualified at once both local communities and transnational communities. The concepts of citizenship, membership and, mediating between the two, the concept of naturalization, are the core of that overload, and have in recent years become the most contested terrain in a politics of belonging. Walzer has argued that the national community is the most comprehensive level at which human beings have been able to develop democratic forms of political organization and mechanisms for cultural understanding and for a fairer distribution of resources, and that for that reason it is legitimate to protect it as an established and functioning community against massive immigration. According to him:

> 'the idea of distributive justice presupposes a bounded world, a community, within which distributions take place, a group of people committed to dividing, exchanging and sharing, first of all among themselves.... At some level of political organization something like the sovereign state must take shape and claim the authority to make its own admissions policy, to control and sometimes to restrain the flows of immigrants'.[186]

This sophisticated defence of liberal political territoriality is a paradigmatic example of how an abstractly constructed and universally applicable principle of balanced relation between inclusion and exclusion may legitimize, under the conditions of the modern interstate system, a politics that in fact excludes the great majority of the world population from the goods that Walzer's national community is capable of delivering. Such national community is restricted to the core countries and, with the emergence of the interior Third World, will be increasingly restricted to a partial community inside them. The relatively high level of incorporation that it achieves within the national

---

[185]   Within the 'international regime' literature, see Hartigan's analysis of how nation–states attempt to match humanitarian norms with 'cold, hard [national] interests' (Hartigan, 1992).
[186]   Walzer, 1981, p 10. A contrasting view is in Satz, 1999; Nett, 1971.

borders, protecting one sixth of the world population, is the other side of the extremely high level of exclusion it commands outside those borders, where five-sixths of the world population lives.

Because illegal immigrants and asylum seekers are the most vulnerable social groups contesting national boundaries, they show most clearly the radical re-assessment of concepts of citizenship and membership required by a cosmopolitan politics. Conversely, they unveil the most resistant obstacles in building up a transnational coalition that would support and promote such a politics.[187] As Brubaker puts it, 'citizenship is at the vital centre of the political life of the modern nation-state'.[188] The ideal-type of citizenship, intrinsic to the ideal-type of Walzer's national community, is a form of membership characterized by being egalitarian, sacred, national democratic, unique and socially consequential.[189] This is not the place to analyze the 'deviations' of real citizenship in relation to this ideal type, even in core countries. For my argument here, it will suffice to mention that the modern concept of citizenship has always operated in articulation with a broader concept of membership that is also territorially based and intended to cover a whole range of statuses of people who are not full citizens. Legally admitted permanent immigrants are more members than seasonal workers, while illegal immigrants or asylum seekers are not members at all or, at best, vestigial members. By means of its territorial grounding, the concept of citizenship keeps its integrity only by creating, in sociological terms, second class, third class and even fourth class citizens. Millions of subordinate transnational migrants are generally deprived from getting beyond the first steps of the citizenship ladder. The legal disenfranchising of these people, together with the sociological disenfranchising of millions of nationals confined to the interior Third Worlds, show the discriminatory workings of modern politics of citizenship. The collision with international human rights is evident, and has been managed in different ways by different nation-states. Because such differences are very relevant, the creation of a cosmopolitan coalition – transnational networks of locally, nationally and globally embedded social relations of emancipation – must take them into account.

Moreover, they must be considered within the triple analytical framework I am propounding in this chapter: position in the world system, historical trajectory toward modernity, and prevalent legal culture. The bridge of naturalization between membership and citizenship is narrower and longer in some countries than in others. The fact that Canada entered modernity through the gate of the New Worlds (settlement) and Germany through the European gate explains, in part, the fact that the naturalization rate in Canada is more than twenty times higher than in Germany. The different traditions of nationhood in Portugal or France, on the one hand, and Germany, on the other, are, in part, explained by the fact that, while Portugal and France were colonial powers,

---

[187]   Who speaks for the undocumented immigrants, for instance? See Delgado, 1983.
[188]   Brubaker, 1989, p 14.
[189]   Brubaker, 1989, p 3.

Germany was not.[190] In countries whose legal culture is grounded on religion, as in the Middle East, citizenship is sacred, and its sacredness is reproduced by its unbridgeable reach, while in countries whose legal culture has been most pervasively secularized, as in the Nordic countries, short of naturalization, human rights can be granted more easily (for instance, in the form of the right to vote in local elections).

These differences must be analytically worked out before cosmopolitan coalitions can be built in this field. The networking of differences must be subjected to certain general orientations. A new theory of citizenship must be developed to account for the growing subordinate transnational movements and the challenges they pose to the international human rights regime.[191] Citizenship must be deterritorialized (less national and more egalitarian), so that the legal diaspora of millions of displaced people may come to an end. Citizenship must be decanonized – ie, it must become less sacred and more democratic – so that the passport and the visa cease to be a legal fetish upon which the life changes and human dignity of so many people depend. Citizenship must be socialistically reconstructed – ie, it must become more socially consequential and less exclusive – so that dual or even triple citizenship become the rule rather than the exception. The objective is to disperse both citizenship and territorial sovereignty, but in such a way that citizenship is thereby re-evaluated, while territorial sovereignty is devaluated. This is precisely the opposite of what is happening today in core countries, as I tried to show above. This general orientation must be institutionally grounded on a new global legal field, emerging out of a new balance between international human rights and the domestic legal statuses of persons (more on this in Chapter Nine). The new theory of citizenship is just a first step toward a new cosmopolitan consciousness and politics. It must be combined with a new theory of trust, globally conceived, which will replace the current paradigm of state-centred trust that is fortressed within national boundaries. The new historical epistemology of need and difference called for above will be the foundation of global trust. Since a great deal of forced transnational migration is taking place within the South, the new theory of citizenship, unaccompanied by a new theory of trust, could easily become another trap for the South. On the contrary, the cosmopolitan politics proposes that entry becomes irrelevant for membership. People enter specific countries, but they are members of all of them, and the guarantee of their human rights must be provided for by all countries according to their resources, that is to say, according to their historical responsibilities in the creation of worldwide inequalities.

7.5 Ancient grievances and new solidarities: the law of indigenous peoples

The legal constellation analyzed in this section has a long, social, if not sociological, tradition in all the societies whose route to modernity has been any of the three non-

---

[190] Brubaker, 1989, pp 6ff.

[191] For the prolegomena of a new theory of citizenship, see Chapter Nine, as well as Santos, 1995, Chapter Eight.

European routes. In general, it entails the coexistence, within the same geo-political territory, of a modern, Westernized, official, state legal order, with a plurality of local, traditional or recently developed, non-official, community-based, legal orders – in other words, the conventional situation of legal plurality. Due to its long standing, this legal constellation seems to have very little to do with what I have been calling in this chapter the globalization of the legal field. As I have argued in Chapter Four, far from being a sociological residue of pre-modern times in countries that have not yet completed the process of 'modernization', infrastate legal plurality is constitutive of the latter's unequal, uneven and exclusionary character, and for that reason is bound to be recurrently reinvented and reproduced as 'modernization' unfolds. The argument that I presented in that chapter, however, links infrastate legal plurality to capitalist modernity in general, and not specifically to the processes of globalization that I have been discussing in this chapter. Thus, this section seeks to make explicitly the linkage between infrastate and global legalities.

The legal constellations I have in mind here do not cover all the situations of infrastate legal plurality, but only those in which a specific global-local linkage can be identified. Without discarding the possibility of other legal constellations falling into this category, I will concentrate in this section on the *collective rights of indigenous peoples*, surely an old issue – at least as old as European expansion from the fifteenth century onwards – which has, however gained a new prominence in the last three decades. I will argue that this new prominence is due to a global-local linkage with two vectors, one older than the other, but both dramatically intensified in the last thirty years. The first vector has to do with the dialectics of globalized localisms/localized globalisms fueled by the emergence of worldwide outsourcing and the formation of production systems constituting global commodity chains, the most recent step of the secular trend of the capitalist world economy to incorporate the whole planet, even its most remote regions, in the process of capital accumulation. As a result, in the last two decades many indigenous peoples saw their traditional lifestyles, customary rights and peasant economies threatened by new or more powerful development claims by TNCs or the national state or, in most cases, the two combined.

For most of the indigenous peoples, particularly in the Americas, their founding memory is the memory of the violation of their rights throughout modern history and their resistance in very unequal conditions. What are seen (and they themselves see) today as their traditions, customs and economies are indeed the sedimentation of resistances, survival strategies and adaptive responses in the face of mass destruction of their ancestral communal life by modern conquerors and settlers of all denominations. In this sense, the 'contacts' of the last three decades are far from unprecedented. They merely represent another and probably more powerful wave of imperial globalization. One of its specific features is the extent to which the national state itself intervenes as a transnational actor. Pressed to conform to the 'Washington consensus' on debt, stabilization and structural adjustment, the peripheral and semi-peripheral states embark on new 'development projects', often in joint ventures with TNCs and with the support of international financial institutions, be they extractive, agro-industrial, road construction or hydro-electric projects. Some of these projects are to be carried out on indigenous lands, further destroying traditional lifestyles and economies, and forcing indigenous peoples into new and massive relocations.[192]

What is truly new in the new prominence of the indigenous question is the emergence of a transformative, transnational coalition involving indigenous and non-indigenous NGOs, which have been drawing the attention of world public opinion to the violations of indigenous historical rights, and pressing both international organizations and the national states to condemn the violations, stop the destruction and take active measures to effectively right (or begin to right) such massive historical wrongdoing. This is the second vector of the globalization of of the indigenous peoples' struggles. This global effort illustrates the process of globalization that I have called subaltern cosmopolitanism. Its reading of our time is paradigmatic in nature, its logic is anticapitalist, its politics is based on self-determination and autonomy, its ideology is emancipation from hegemonic 'development models'. The legal dimension of this transnational transformative action has some similarities with the one I will describe below as subaltern cosmopolitan law. But there is an important difference between the two. While under subaltern cosmopolitan law, as we shall see, the struggle is for access to nationally and transnationally established (but only selectively effective) systems of justice and universal individual human rights, in the case under analysis the struggle is for special collective rights and local autonomous legal regulation within clearly defined territories. In sum, while in the case of subaltern cosmopolitan law the emphasis is on universal rights and on general systems of globalized nation-state law, in this case of globalized infrastate law the emphasis is on the national and global recognition of local, community-based plurality of laws. In both cases, the national character of the 'nation'-state is questioned, but while in the first case it is questioned for its deficits, that is, for not being sufficiently developed according to its own political and legal claims, in the second case it is questioned for its excesses, that is, for being structurally flawed as a project of political and legal development.

[192] Examples of mass destruction of lifestyles and coercive resettlements as a result of 'development' projects abound in recent times: forest clearing in Canada and Malaysia; construction of hydro-electric plants in Mexico, Brazil, Bangladesh, Canada, Guyana, India, Malaysia, the Philippines, Norway, Sweden and the US; mining and extraction of oil in Brazil, Ecuador, Canada, Australia; oil exploration in Colombia. A few examples of sociological research in progress with a specific focus on the legal aspects: Lâm, 1985, 1991, has been studying the role of courts in dispossessing native Hawaiians from traditional land tenure. See also Lâm, 2000. Delaney, 1991, has done research on the contract between Conoco Oil Co (a subsidiary of DuPont) and the government of Ecuador for the exploration and extraction of oil from an area (called Block 16) located in Ecuadorian Amazon, land held since ancient times by the Huaorani people. Guevara Gil, 1992, does research on the impact of Peruvian development projects on the territorial and fishing rights of Quechua and Aymara people living on the shores of Lake Titicaca. Sánchez, 2001, and Arenas, 2002, have studied the combination of legal strategies and transnational political mobilization used by the U'wa people from Colombia in order to protect their sacred land from being turned by Occidental and the national government into an oil exploration site.

Though exact estimates are impossible in view of the nomadic existence of some indigenous peoples in inaccessible areas, the Secretary-General of the International Labor Organization estimates that '300 million indigenous tribal peoples of widely differing races live in just about every part of the world'.[193] While the interstate system is made up of roughly 170 independent states, 'educated estimates, based mainly on anthropological and linguistic criteria, would place the number of nations, peoples or ethnic groups at around five to eight thousand, the real figure probably being closer to the latter'.[194] In Latin America, it is estimated that there are four hundred indigenous peoples, comprising thirty million individuals, that is, ten per cent of the whole Latin American population.[195] Among the best-known indigenous peoples we should include the Native Americans or Amerindians, the Aborigines of Australia, the Inuit (Eskimos) of the Arctic, the New Zealand Maoris, the Scandinavian and Russian Sami (Lapps). Though in the South-East Asian and African countries the concept of indigenous peoples is not generally used, we should also mention the 'tribal people' in India (*adivasis*), the mountain people in the Philippines and Thailand, indigenous peoples in Malaysia and Sri Lanka and other Asian countries, and isolated ethnic groups in Africa.[196]

The best definition of 'indigenous peoples' has been formulated by UN Special Rapporteur, Martínez Cobo:

> 'Indigenous communities, peoples and nations are those which, having an historical continuity with pre-invasion and pre-colonial societies that developed on their territories, consider themselves distinct from other sectors of the societies now prevailing in these territories, or parts of them. They form at present non-dominant sectors of society and are determined to perceive, develop and transmit to future generations their ancestral territories and their ethnic identity, as the basis of their continued existence as people, in accordance with their own cultural patterns, social institutions and legal systems'.[197]

I shall rely on this definition to deal with the issues raised by indigenous peoples' rights that are most pertinent to outline the specific form of infra-state legal plurality they constitute. More specifically, I will deal with three issues: historical and cultural roots of indigenous rights; self-determination and the ethno-cratic state; and the formation of transnational coalitions.

---

193   Heintze, 1992, p 38.
194   Stavenhagen, 1990, p 2.
195   Stavenhagen, 1990, 1988. See also Brysk, 2000, p 301.
196   Stavenhagen, 1990, p 100.
197   Heintze, 1992, p 39.

7.5.1 HISTORICAL AND CULTURAL ROOTS OF INDIGENOUS RIGHTS

This issue raises a whole range of questions. The first one is the question of primordial identities in modernity, which, in turn, raises many issues: to start with, the conceptual issue of the relations between 'indigenous peoples' and 'ethnic minorities'. Ethnic groups are generally defined in terms of broadly defined cultural identity (of language, national origin, religion, race, social organization). They are considered minorities either because they are numerically so, or because they are discriminated against, socially excluded, or dominated in the countries they live in – ie, because they are sociological minorities. In at least one of these senses, indigenous peoples are ethnic minorities. They are, generally, both numerical minorities (though not in Bolivia, Guatemala, Peru, Ecuador and in the northern part of Canada) and sociological minorities.[198] According to the Aga Khan's report, indigenous peoples are:

> 'the most deprived and ill-treated groups in most countries . . . their average income is lower, their health is worse, they are disproportionately the subjects of arrest and imprisonment. Even in the richer countries, indigenous peoples live as second class citizens in conditions which often attract comparison with those existing among the poorest of the Third World'.[199]

With this in mind, some authors have argued that the recognition and protection of indigenous peoples' rights could be guaranteed by the same legal instruments developed by international law and many national laws to guarantee the protection of ethnic minorities. To be sure, indigenous peoples are a special case within a larger category: the ethnic minority. Both indigenous peoples and ethnic minorities are primordial social groupings, in Geertz's sense of groups bonded by congruities of blood, religion, speech, custom and other, 'first principles'.[200] They have also shared, for the most part, the same historical fate both as objects of the social sciences and victims of discrimination.

Being part of traditional collectivities – such as the church, community, neighbourhood, family – these primordial social groups fit Durkheim's concept of mechanical solidarity, which he conceived as a declining form of social solidarity in the process of being replaced by a new one, organic solidarity, based on social differentiation and complexity. After Durkheim, and for many decades, the social sciences, as well as liberalism and Marxism, predicted the gradual but inexorable disappearance of 'primordial' collective identities. Surveying some of the major social sciences, Stavenhagen rightly concludes

---

[198] There is a politics of classification underlying the demographic criteria to establish the size of the indigenous population. As Varese (1982), puts it, '[c]ensus statistics on Indo-ethnic populations are perhaps one of the areas of social knowledge and information which most clearly shows the reductive and manipulative intervention of the colonial mode of thought' (p 33).

[199] Heintze, 1992, p 59.

[200] Geertz, 1973. For a distinction between race and ethnicity, see Oommen, 1993.

that 'the paradigms of modern social theory have not included the ethnic factor as relevant to the questions they have asked of reality'.[201] For liberalism, primordial identities are pre-modern residues negatively interfering with the political obligation between individual citizens and the state, the latter viewed as the only legitimate foundation of political association. Throughout the nineteenth century, and up until the 1960s, this conception fitted the tasks of nation-state-building, whereby the 'nation', supposedly mono-ethnic, made possible the conversion of ethnic domination into nationalism. In Smith's words, 'ethnic nationalism has striven to turn the ethnic group into that more abstract and politicized category, the 'nation', and then to establish the latter as the sole criterion of statehood'.[202] For Marxism, primordial identities were subsumed within the analysis of class formation and class struggle and, more often than not, seen as obstacles to be overcome in the 'natural' unfolding of either of these social processes. Ethnic identities were more central in the analysis of the 'national question', but – except for the remarkable work of the Austro-Marxists – [203] this question received relatively little attention from Marxism.[204]

In the same way that they shared analytical neglect and political suppression in the past, indigenous peoples and ethnic minorities today also share the benefits of a cultural, political and scientific transformation under way. The shifts are evident in the transformation of multifarious symbolic universes: from the melting pot to multiculturalism, from functional and abstract identities to neo-primordial local identities, from class politics to ethnic politics, from modernization to ethno-development, from the quincentennial celebrations of the discoveries to the 1990 Declaration of Quito, proclaimed by the Indigenous Alliance of the Americas on 500 Years of Resistance. Needless to say, these shifts of analytical and political emphasis are not the outcome of unconditionally auspicious social processes. Some of the processes under way are, indeed, quite reactionary, as shown by the new rise of racism and chauvinistic nationalism, in the dramatic increase of refugee populations, in the proliferation of ethnic conflicts and in the new (and old) forms of ethnocide.

The legal and political claims of indigenous peoples and ethnic minorities, in general, have been at the centre of the debate over individual and collective human rights. According to the liberal political paradigm, rights are entitlements held by individuals, and only by individuals. Furthermore, since the 'universality' of human rights means both formal legal equality of all citizens, and non-discrimination – in the sense that no citizen can be excluded from the enjoyment of human rights – it has been claimed, within this paradigm, that collective human rights are either absurd or superfluous, as will be seen in detail in the next section of this chapter. As the argument goes, collective legal protection is the 'natural' result of universal individual protection. The fact that specified

---

[201]   Stavenhagen, 1990, p 6.
[202]   Smith, 1981, p xii.
[203]   Bauer, 1924. See also Bottomore and Goode, 1978, pp 102–135.
[204]   See Balibar and Wallerstein, 1991.

groups of people – children, workers, women, minorities – have been entitled to specific legal protection does not collide with the liberal principle, since rights pertain, in those cases as in general, to the individuals and not to the collective entities to which individuals belong.[205]

The liberal paradigm has been at the root of the states' aversion to recognizing collective rights of groups other than itself. Collective rights are viewed as threatening the principle of sovereignty and fueling domestic tensions: disruptive, at the internal level, of the political obligation that holds together citizens and the state, and, at the international level, of the normal operation of the interstate system. Against this liberal orthodoxy, an alternative view that has been defended by indigenous peoples and pioneering NGOs since the middle of the nineteenth century has recently been gaining wide acceptance in the international community, particularly in the last three decades. Such a view is based on two premises. First, in spite of the international recognition of universal human rights as a civilizing process, discrimination against indigenous peoples and ethnic minorities has been practiced and even legally supported over the years. To mention two striking examples: Australia did not grant civil rights to the Aborigines until the late 1960s, and in the earlier years of the UN, many Latin American states refused to admit that there were minorities in their territories, or that indigenous peoples were minorities in the UN's sense. Secondly, after a long history of genocide and ethnocide, of imposed policies of social exclusion or integration, the elimination of discrimination cannot be achieved by mere formal equality before the law. As the practice of both the United Nations' and the International Labor Organization's committees and working groups on ethnic minorities, indigenous peoples and racial discrimination clearly shows – whenever the testimonies of minorities are taken seriously – ethnic rights must be constructed and contextualized as rights of peoples and collectivities before they can adequately protect, as human rights, the individuals that belong to such peoples and collectivities. This is the position taken by ethnic minorities whose argument is that universal human rights are not enough, and that without specific provisos obligating the states not only to abstain from interfering with the collective rights of minorities, but also to provide active support for the enjoyment of such rights, minority groups will always be disadvantaged within the wider society. Following this line of argumentation, Stavenhagen justly emphasizes that 'the collective rights that ethnic minorities around the world have been demanding have to do with the survival of the ethnic groups as such, the preservation of ethnic cultures, the reproduction of the group as a distinct entity, the cultural identity attached to group life and social organization'. And he concludes: 'This is much more than expecting non-discrimination and equality before the law. It relates to the use of language, schooling and educational and cultural institutions, including religious institutions; frequently, with self-government and political autonomy'.[206]

---

[205]   Stavenhagen, 1990, p 55. For a comprehensive view of peoples and minorities in international law, see Anaya, 1996; Brolmann, Lefeber and Zieck, 1993.

[206]   Stavenhagen, 1990, p 65. A similar argument is made in Stavenhagen, 2002. See also *América Indígena*, 1989, p 1; Gros, 2000; Sieder (ed), 2002.

The struggle for collective rights is part and parcel of a politics of critical legal plurality, and has been understood as such by the nation-states, which tend to see in the recognition of collective rights the creation of internal legal competition, a challenge to the state monopoly of production and distribution of law. Linked to the right to self-determination, as we shall see below, collective rights are also likely to be viewed as obstructing the exercise of sovereign prerogatives and, ultimately, as undermining the survival of the nation-state itself. For these reasons, and having in mind the privileged position of states in the international system, international organizations have been quite slow and cautious, to say the least, in recognizing the collective rights of ethnic minorities. The only 'tangible result' of forty years of labour of the United Nations Sub-Commission on Prevention of Discrimination and Protection of Minorities has been the inclusion of Article 27 in the International Covenant on Civil and Political Rights, which states: 'In those states in which ethnic, religious or linguistic minorities exist, persons belonging to such minorities shall not be denied the right, in community with the other members of their group, to enjoy their own culture, to profess and practice their own religion or to use their own language'.

For reasons I cannot go into here, minority peoples have been quite disappointed and indeed felt cheated by this formulation.[207] However, as regards indigenous peoples more specifically, new international instruments have been recently produced which considerably strengthen their struggle for collective rights. In this respect, the ILO 'Convention 169' (Convention Concerning Indigenous and Tribal Peoples in Independent Countries) and the UN Draft Universal Declaration on Rights of Indigenous Peoples deserve to be mentioned. The latter includes the following rights:

3.   The collective right to exist as distinct peoples and to be protected against genocide, as well as the individual rights to life, physical integrity, liberty and security of person.

4.   The individual and collective right to maintain and develop their ethnic and cultural characteristics as distinct identity, including the right of peoples and individuals to call themselves by their proper names.

5.   The individual and collective right to protection against ethnocide.

In the same vein, the project of Paragraph 21 of the Draft Declaration states that indigenous peoples have 'the right to participate fully in the political, economic and social life of their state and to have their specific character duly reflected in the legal system and in political institutions, including proper regard to and recognition of indigenous laws and customs'.[208]

---

[207]   For an extended critical comment, see Stavenhagen, 1990 and 2002.

[208]   See UN–DOC E/CN.4/Sub.2/1991/40/Rev 1 of 3 October 1991.

By 2002, the Draft Declaration, after more than ten years of discussions and negotiations, was still working its way up to the UN General Assembly. However, the continued attention drawn by the indigenous question gave rise to the creation of a Permanent Forum on Indigenous Issues within the UN, a group of independent experts nominated in consultation with governments and indigenous organizations that meet yearly and serve as advisors to the UN Economic and Social Council.

The claim of collective rights by indigenous peoples and ethnic minorities is gaining strength in the international political agenda, supported by a broad and broadening global coalition. It is a claim for the legal recognition, both by national law and by international law, of situations of legal plurality that sociology and anthropology of law have vastly documented as social and political forms of resistance against internal legal colonialism. A full treatment of globalized infrastate legal plurality would thus require the analysis of collective rights claims by ethnic minorities in general. The reason why I concentrate on the claims of indigenous peoples is because they represent the most far-reaching challenge to the modern equation among nation, state and law that I dealt with at a theoretical level in Chapter Two, and also because they illustrate most eloquently and painfully the historical mass destruction, oppression and injustice upon which the routes to and through modernity were built outside Europe – though, of course, ethnocides within Europe, both ancient and modern, should not be forgotten.

Moreover, indigenous peoples' rights are different from the rights of ethnic minorities in two important counts, which together confer a specific profile to the situations of legal plurality they entail. First, because indigenous peoples are historically 'original' peoples and nations, their rights have a kind of historical precedence and, for that reason, the collective rights they struggle for are not conceived by them as rights to be granted to them, but rather as rights they had always enjoyed before they were taken away from them by conquerors, settlers, missionaries or merchants coming from afar.[209] Now, this historical precedence cannot be invoked by all ethnic minorities – for instance, by ethnic migrant communities. Secondly, among all the collective rights of indigenous peoples, the right to land, to their ancestral territory and its resources, is paramount. Therefore, legal plurality assumes in this case a distinct geo-spatial configuration. On the other hand, the claims of ethnic minorities may or may not include territorial rights, but they always include the right to cultural identity, with a symbolic autonomous territory within the broader mental maps of the culturally alien states in which they happen to be living for longer or shorter periods.

The territoriality of indigenous peoples' rights – combined with the fact that, by far, most indigenous peoples are peasants – has led some authors to believe that the issue of indigenous rights – particularly the collective right to govern their affairs through their own customary laws – should be subsumed under the issue of peasants' rights and laws – or, indeed, under the more general issue of the rights and laws of the

---

[209]   Stavenhagen, 1994.

oppressed or subordinate classes, of which Pasargada law, analyzed in Chapter Four, is an example.[210] Even though significant similarities between indigenous legal plurality, peasant legal plurality and even subordinate legal plurality can be identified, what is distinctive about indigenous legal plurality is the specific embeddedness of the legal dimension in broader, deep-seated, cultural, religious, linguistic, familial, and ethnic identities, to such an extent that the preservation of autonomous law becomes part and parcel of a politics of survival and resistance against 'assimilation' and ethnocide.[211] Indeed, the refusal by the state law and courts to recognize indigenous laws has been the central element of ethno-cratic domination throughout the centuries. In an eloquent analysis of the Peruvian criminal justice system, Aguirre has demonstrated how court decisions, more blatantly even than the Penal Code, express the ethno-centric bias of state legal domination. They do so by distinguishing, for instance, between 'civilized' and 'non-civilized' Indians in order to justify a humiliating 'special protection;' by showing their ignorance and arrogance vis-à-vis Indian culture; by subscribing to an uncritical and only apparently naïve equation between capitalist market and Western civilization; and by transforming prisons into spaces of Westernization.[212]

While the imperial ignorance of the indigenous laws and cultures has not been detrimental to those belonging to the majority, let alone the courts that bypass them altogether, the indigenous peoples' ignorance of the laws of the colonial or post-colonial state has always been severely punished. The indigenous peoples' ignorance has been made illegal by various means since the early times of the conquest, the *requerimento* being the most striking example. The *requerimento* was a formal document to be read to the indigenous peoples, 'informing' them that they were subjects of the Crown and should, therefore, adopt the Christian faith. They could not legitimately ignore this 'legal condition' from then on, even if they had understood nothing of what had been read to (against) them.[213] Throughout the centuries, ethno-cratic domination dealt with such disparate results of the ignorance of the law in different ways. If at times it conceived it as part of an unbridgeable cultural distance, at other times it viewed it as a transitory phenomenon, to be gradually superseded by cultural integration and assimilation under the supervision of the state. A good example of the latter are the 'indigenist policies' of many Latin American states in the 1930s and 1940s, with their characteristic paternalist and assimilationist tendencies.[214] Today, under the pressure

[210]   See, for instance, Brandt, 1986. For contrasting views, see Stavenhagen and Iturralde, 1990.

[211]   According to Stavenhagen (cited in Heintze, 1992, p 57), 'a principal factor which has enabled indigenous and tribal peoples to survive in the face of the persistent assaults against them by the dominant society, is their internal coherence, their social organization, as well as the maintenance of their own traditions, laws and customs, including local political authority'.

[212]   Aguirre, 1980; Cifuentes, 1993. Similar conclusions are found in studies of other jurisdictions: see, for instance, Gomez (ed), 1997; van Cott (ed), 1994, 2000; Sieder (ed), 2002; Sánchez, 2001 (Colombia); Marés, 2000 (Brazil); Dubly and Granda, 1995 (Ecuador).

[213]   Stavenhagen, 1988, p 19.

[214]   On the contrast between 'indigenism' (*indigenismo*) – as the philosophy underlying the neo-colonial state policies to deal with the 'Indian question' – and 'indianity' (*indianidad*) – as the philosophy underlying the Indian Liberation Movement on the American continent in the

of indigenous peoples' organization and mobilization, the national states are being forced into a more multicultural, polyethnic stance whose consolidation – as the indigenous organizations are well aware of – requires the state's recognition of collective rights and of a territorially-based plurality of legal orders. The resulting institutional innovations – from the inclusion of constitutional provisions establishing indigenous rights to ground-breaking judicial rulings recognizing the possibility of indigenous law coexisting with state law – have given rise, particularly in Latin America, to a dynamic practice of litigation and advocacy on behalf of indigenous groups that has continued into the new millennium. As Marés has claimed, based on the study of recent developments in Brazil, this has marked the 'renaissance of the indigenous peoples for law'.[215]

7.5.2 SELF-DETERMINATION VERSUS THE ETHNO-CRATIC STATE

The recognition of collective rights and autonomous laws of the indigenous peoples *qua* peoples raises the controversial issue of self-determination. The principle of self-determination of peoples is well established in international law, and was the guiding principle of decolonization, particularly after World War II. It granted the colonized peoples the right to independence, a right, therefore, to be exercised once and for all. The peoples were for the most part territorially defined according to colonial geography, and declared independent on its basis. In an attempt to link the right of self-determination clearly with the colonial situation, it was understood that the peoples to be granted independence were the ones that had been colonized by overseas colonial powers – the 'blue water' theory.

Once the colonized peoples became independent states, they considered that, *ipso facto*, there were no further grounds for the application of the principle of self-determination within their borders. For fear of chaotic secessions, the existence of indigenous peoples or ethnic minorities in the newly independent states was denied (and still is, in some cases). As Maivân Lâm puts it:

'Because the attainment of independence remains, for the present, the founding myth of the modern nation-states of the Third World, where the recall of national sacrifice and foreign perfidy respectively ennoble and enrage, counter-calls for independence, so to speak, easily suggest treason or complicity with foreign intervention which, because it continues to reproduce itself in the post-colonial age, if under different forms, sustains the myth, with extremely unfortunate results for indigenous peoples'.[216]

---

last two decades – see Varese, 1982, pp 29ff; Bataillon *et al*, 1982; and *América Indígena*, 1990.

[215]   Marés, 2000.

[216]   Lâm, 1991, p 21. See also Lâm, 2000.

In the field of international law, one such result has been the difficulty confronting the indigenous peoples of being recognized as peoples, that is to say, as collective entities with international legal personality and entitled to the exercise of self-determination.[217] In fact, in most documents of international organizations, they are described as persons, populations, groups of individuals. Only in more recent documents have they begun to be considered as peoples, due to the growing pressure of indigenous organizations. This is notably the case of ILO Convention No. 169, which, however, accepts the concept with a major restriction, prompted by the fear that the principle of self-determination attached to it might destroy the territorial integrity or the political unity of the sovereign states. Paragraph 3 of Article 1 states that 'the use of the term 'people' in this convention shall not be construed as having any implications as regards the rights which may attach to the term under international law'. The perceived need to compromise between the right to self-determination and state sovereignty has led to further specifications as, for instance, the distinction between external self-determination – which would involve secession and independence – and internal self-determination – restricted to the right to autonomy or self-government within the boundaries of the state and under the latter's sovereignty. These issues will be further discussed in the next section.

The fact of the matter is that, in most cases, the self-determination claimed by indigenous peoples has not entailed secession, statehood, or political sovereignty. Truly, indigenous peoples' organizations feel sometimes victimized by restrictive conceptions of 'colonialism' and of 'decolonization'. They think that, though 'external' colonialism ended, 'internal' colonialism continued and even thrived within the 'independent' states. Moreover, the general term of 'decolonization' hides strikingly different situations: while in Africa and Asia independence was granted to the colonized peoples, in almost all the countries of the Americas independence was granted to the European colonizers and their descendants – a difference that, as I have suggested above, was decisive in shaping the routes of these regions to modernity.

The indigenous peoples' claim to self-determination is focused on the right to their historical land and its resources, as well as to autonomous social organization and cultural identity – all of which can be made compatible with the sovereignty of the state in which they live. Either because they appreciate that to claim otherwise would be unrealistic within the interstate system as we know it (or even detrimental to their ultimate interests), or because statehood is to them a culturally alien concept, the indigenous peoples are basically claiming forms of ethnic equalization (not homogenization), ethnic federalism and ethno-development in order to protect themselves against always-recurrent dangers of ethnocide and corresponding new ethnographies of terror. Heintze cites a declaration by the Dene which graphically illustrates this:

---

[217]   Latin American Amerindians prefer the designation 'peoples', while the North American Amerindians or Native Americans also use the designation 'nations'.

'The Dene find themselves as part of a country. That country is Canada. But the government of Canada is not the government of the Dene. These governments were not the choice of the Dene, they were imposed upon the Dene. What we the Dene are struggling for is the recognition of the Dene nation by the governments and peoples of the world. And while there are realities we are forced to submit to such as the existence of a country called Canada, we insist on the right to self-determination as a distinct people and the recognition of the Dene Nation'.[218]

The struggle of the Miskitos for self-determination within the Nicaraguan state has been one of the most widely publicized indigenous mobilizations of the last decades and illustrates well the tensions I have tried to lay out in this section. The Miskito Indians are an indigenous people living in the Atlantic Coast of Nicaragua. Official records state that they number approximately 54,000, while other sources estimate their number at 120,000. Other, much smaller ethnic groups live in the area, such as the Rama, the Garifuna and the Sumu. For many decades, there was not much contact between the Atlantic and the Pacific coast until 1979, when the Sandinista Revolution took place. Throughout the twentieth century, the Miskito region was controlled by American TNCs and the Protestant Moravian Church without much interference from the central government (which was in the hands of the Somoza family since 1933). At first, and in line with their revolutionary ideology, the Sandinistas downplayed the ethnic component of social injustice in the Atlantic coast and saw the Miskitos' conditions, as with the conditions of Nicaraguans in general, as class-based and economically determined. Accordingly, in what was considered some years later a serious mistake,[219] the Sandinistas disregarded the Miskito organizations that already existed, and tried to replace them with Sandinist mass organizations. The confrontation between the government and the Miskitos broke out in 1981. Many Miskitos fled to Honduras and joined the contra-revolutionary movements, while the government decided to forcibly transfer ten thousand Miskitos living on the Honduras-Nicaragua border to new settlements located fifty km south of the border. This 'controversial decision' expressed a drastic incongruence between the progressive and liberating ideology of the Sandinistas and the reactionary, colonialist practice of forcible resettlement, justified rather unconvincingly by national security reasons. Confronted with international condemnation, and having also concluded that the Miskitos implicated in the counter-revolution had been manipulated or were simply aiding family members actually involved in it, in 1984 the Nicaraguan authorities radically changed their policies toward ethnic groups, acknowledging mistakes and actively seeking reconciliation. A general amnesty for Miskitos imprisoned or in exile was declared, and negotiations on autonomy for the Atlantic coast were held from 1984 until 1986. In September 1987, the Nicaraguan National Assembly ratified the law of autonomy for the Atlantic regions, whereby

---

[218]   Heintze, 1992, p 45.

[219]   See Roxanne Ortiz, 1987, p 49: 'The new revolutionary government, lacking experience and understanding of the Atlantic Coast region, initiated programs that were unrelated to the regional and ethnic reality'.

Nicaragua became the first formal, multi-ethnic, multicultural nation in Latin America. The main points of the law were the following:[220]

1. The authorities must show unconditional respect for the ethnic languages and the local culture.

2. The law guarantees local control over and the priority to the use of natural resources like land, forestry, mining and fishing.

3. Development projects must benefit the local population to a 'just degree' through agreements made between the regional council and central government in Managua.

4. Local authorities are to be elected directly. Two regional councils in the North and South, respectively, consist of 45 members for periods of four years. Each regional council elects a leader of the local government.

This law, which formalizes the right of Miskitos to self-determination, has been differently interpreted and evaluated, both within the indigenous communities and in international fora,[221] but it is generally agreed that the law has a potential for regional autonomy that far exceeds what ethnic groups in other parts of the world have achieved.[222] The defeat of the Sandinistas in the 1990 elections, combined with the structural adjustment programmes by Chamorro's government, made the real impact of the autonomy law even more problematic. The political context of the law – the recognition of multi-ethnicity as a means to strengthen national unity around the revolution and Sandinism – has changed radically, and this will definitely reverberate in the substantive, if not the formal, application of the law.

The Miskito case has been described here as a very recent illustration of some of the contradictions of nation-building in multi-ethnic societies and the difficulties faced by indigenous peoples and ethnic minorities in their struggle for the right to self-determination. Such contradictions and difficulties, far from being specific to the Americas, are to be found under different contexts in many other parts of the world, notably in South Asia.[223] Indeed, South Asia reveals very clearly how the equation between nation and state served to justify ethno-cratic rule in newly independent states, such as India, Pakistan and Sri Lanka. Often under apparently antagonistic legitimation principles – Islamic religion/Hinduism or, on the contrary, secularism and equal citizenship – and through a process of cajoling and coercing ethnic minorities, such

---

[220] In Hanne Bach, 1991, p 40.
[221] See, for different readings of the law of regional autonomy, Ortiz, 1987 (on the project of the law); Buvollen, 1989; and Bach, 1991.
[222] Bach, 1991, p 40.
[223] Among others, Tambiah, 1989; Sheth, 1989; and Ghai, 1993c, 2000a.

states sought to convert 'what was merely the political-cultural principle subscribed to by the ethnic majority into a universal principle for the nation as a whole'.[224] Based on the case of India, Sheth has argued that market and citizenship are not good enough bases for establishing a nation-state in multi-ethnic societies, and so calls for new political forms, for 'new relationships between the state and the society unmediated by the idea of a nation'.[225] Given that the nation-state is a political form that has contributed to too much ethnic conflict and ethno-cratic development, Sheth does not hesitate to call for a 'civil state' instead. Irrespective of its specific merits, this proposal signals the need for bolder political innovation well beyond the liberal paradigm, if the right of indigenous peoples and ethnic minorities to self-determination is to be fully recognized as the legal prerequisite for an autonomous and genuine political alternative to both integrationist and genocide policies.

7.5.3 BUILDING TRANSNATIONAL COALITIONS

The struggles of indigenous peoples for self-determination and, consequently, for infrastate, culturally autonomous, legal plurality are at the crossroads of such intense and contradictory processes of globalization that their conceptualization in this chapter as an instance of globalization of the legal field is fully justified. The well-known case of the Huaorani people[226] shows the complex web of globalization vectors involved in indigenous peoples' local struggles for land: on one side, a TNC (Conoco Oil Co) contracting with the national state with the accord of international financial institutions; on the other, the CONFENIAE (Confederation of Ecuadorian Indian Peoples), a national NGO that is also a member of a transnational NGO, the World Council of Indigenous Peoples, with the collaboration of a transnational advocacy NGO, the Sierra Club. The latter, through the Sierra Club Legal Defense Fund, submitted on 1 June 1990 a petition to the Inter-American Commission on Human Rights of the OAS on behalf of the Huaorani people .

A more recent case – the struggle of the U'wa people of Colombia to keep Occidental Petroleum Co from drilling for oil in their traditional, sacred territory in North Eastern Colombia – epitomizes the combination of legal and political strategies at the local, national and the global scales. Since 1992, the U'wa have adamantly opposed the drilling, invoking their ancient customs of respect for the sacred territory in which they have lived for centuries. First locally, then nationally with the support of the Colombian federation of indigenous peoples (ONIC) and, since 1997, with the active support of global NGOs devoted to indigenous and environmental issues – notably Amazon Coalition, the Earth Justice Legal Defense Fund, Oilwatch and Rain Forest Action

---

[224] Sheth, 1989, p 381. See also Breton, 1989 and Sheth and Mahajan (eds), 1999.
[225] Sheth, 1989, p 388. For a comprehensive socio-legal analysis of the 'untouchables' and tribal peoples in India, see Galanter, 1991.
[226] Delaney, 1991. See also Shutkin, 1991, pp 493–500.

Network – the U'wa have used multiple political strategies – from speaking tours around Europe and the US to civil disobedience vis-à-vis the decisions of the government granting Occidental the right to drill – to avoid the violation of their sacred land and, with it, their disappearance as a people.[227] They have also resorted to innovative legal tactics, from asking the Colombian Constitutional Court to stop the drilling to making their case before the Inter-American Human Rights Commission. The clash of forces operating at different scales and in different sites – the Colombian government and Occidental, on the one hand, and the U'wa and their support network, on the other – goes on today and has given rise to a temporary stalemate. By refusing to give up their culture and their sacred territory, and by doing it through multi-scale political and legal strategies, the U'wa people have demonstrated the potential of transnational mobilization for the cause of indigenous rights.

Using primarily political strategies, the Zapatista movement has also come to represent the possibilities of global action in the furthering of local struggles for the protection of indigenous rights. As several students of the movement have shown,[228] and as I will argue in detail in Chapter Nine, by combining the defence of such rights with resistance against other forms of oppression – from neo-liberal economic oppression to gender domination – and by eliciting the support of sympathetic movements, organizations and personalities ever since they made their first appeal from the mountains of Chiapas and on the Internet in January 1994, the Zapatistas have shown the potential of subaltern cosmopolitanism.

Indeed, according to Brysk's recent analysis of the globalization of indigenous people's struggles, such linkages between the local and the global, and between the indigenous cause and that of other subaltern groups, distinguishes successful from less successful indigenous movements. Based on her study of indigenous movements in Latin America, she concludes:

> '[G]reater impact is associated with stronger Indian rights movements that are engaged in identity politics and in internationalized situations and strategies. At the national level, the "identity plus internationalization" criterion has affected impact among the cases [...] and also distinguishes the group of high impact from "dogs that don't bark" [...]'[229]

Similarly, commenting on the Declaration of Quito of July, 1990, which resulted from the largest gathering of indigenous peoples of North, Central and South America in modern times, Maivân Lam stresses the expanded linkages and the improved organization of the indigenous political struggle in the Americas.[230] With roots in the

---

227   Arenas, 2002. For other cases of resistance of indigenous peoples against oil companies, see in general Gedicks, 2001.
228   Collier, 1995; Stephen, 1997. See also Holloway and Pedáez (eds), 1998.
229   Brysk, 2000, p 248.
230   Lâm, 1991, p 8.

nineteenth century – the Aborigines Protection Society was founded in 1837 – , the globalization of indigenous peoples' struggles has reached its highest point during the last three decades. According to Lâm:

'The ability to fight back, at least in the Western hemisphere, owed something to the American and European protest movements of the '60s, in which some indigenous young peoples cut their political teeth, thereby providing indigenous communities with new leaders who, equipped with extensive contacts to the outside world, could facilitate the banding together of indigenous communities into larger political organizations, and simultaneously link these up with strategically placed non-indigenous NGOs'.[231]

She then lists some of the transnational NGOs which, in the last decades, have taken up the defence of the indigenous peoples' rights, and integrated them in the progressive global political agenda: the International Working Group for Indigenous Affairs, Cultural Survival, Survival International, World Council of Indigenous Peoples, Comissão Pro-Indio, Consejo Indio de Sud America, Arctic Peoples' Conference, International Indian Treaty Council, Inuit Circumpolar Conference, West Papuan Peoples' Front, Karen National Union, Jumma Network in Europe, Indian Council of Indigenous and Tribal Peoples, Alliance of Taiwan Aborigines, National Federation of Indigenous Peoples of the Philippines, Lumad-Mindanao, Cordillera Peoples Alliance, Ainu Association of Hokkaido, Asia Indigenous Peoples Pact, Naga Peoples Movement for Human Rights, Homeland Mission 1950 for South Moluccas, Hmong People.[232] This incomplete list bears witness to the impressive transnational effort of the last decades to organize and mobilize the collective interests of indigenous peoples throughout the world. Moreover, part of this effort was the product of collaboration between indigenous NGOs and non-indigenous NGOs, such as the International Commission of Jurists, World Peace Council, World Council of Churches, Women's League for Peace and Freedom and the Fourth Bertrand Russell Tribunal. In Latin America, in the last three decades, the role of the Catholic Church in defence of indigenous peoples should also be mentioned. For instance, the Brazilian Conselho Indigenista Missionário, founded in 1971, has been very influential in denouncing ethnocidal policies (including those of missionization) and in facilitating the creation of leadership and organization among the indigenous peoples of Brazil.[233] It goes without saying that the transnationalization of the indigenous peoples' struggles was much helped by the information and mass communication revolution.[233a] The instant transmission of information and visual images across the globe has turned each one of us into an eyewitness of racial discrimination and ethnocide, thereby creating the contemporaneity of the non-contemporaneous, a new, layered synchronicity.

[231]   Lâm, 1991, p 15.
[232]   Lâm, 1991, pp 15, 34. See also Burger, 1987, p 206 Bataillon *et al*, 1982, p 352.
[233]   Bataillon *et al*, 1982, p 352.
[233a]   A recent overview in Haveman, 2000.

7.5.4   Learning from the South of the South

The struggles of indigenous peoples and ethnic minorities in general for the right to self-determination are relevant in more than one account for the analysis of the globalization of the legal field undertaken in this chapter. I have described them as an instance of globalized, infrastate, legal plurality. Their relevance, however, extends far beyond the issue of the globalization of the legal field, and I would like to mention here some of its broader dimensions. First, and as I have already indicated, the indigenous peoples' struggles bring to light the darkest side of modernity, the terror, oppression and destruction that was inflicted upon non-European peoples in order to pave the way for Western modernity. More than anything else, they symbolize the structural asymmetry between the European and the non-European routes to and through modernity. Secondly, they show the extent to which false equivalences among nationhood, ethnicity and statehood gave rise to ethno-cratic states, false national states, and, in some cases, doubly false national states, which is what Varese calls the Latin American states in which the indigenous peoples are the majority of the population.[234] Finally, indigenous struggles for legal autonomy illustrate the extent to which conventional comparative law and conventional taxonomies of world legal families have ignored important and deep-rooted legal traditions and legal cultures governing the social life of millions of people throughout the world. Without understanding them as integral parts of legal pluralistic formations, not even the official laws of the states with which they interact will be adequately grasped.

The dark-side relevance of indigenous peoples' struggles coexists with a bright-side relevance, which also must be highlighted. Throughout this book, I argue that, in order to build new emancipatory constellations in a period of paradigmatic transition, it is imperative to learn from the suppressed, marginalized traditions that, in most instances, are the traditions of suppressed or marginalized people. To use the metaphor of hierarchy in the world system, we have to learn from the South. What can we learn from the indigenous peoples who, in a sense, are the South of the South? To answer my question I suggest we consider three perspectives: neo-law, neo-community and neo-state. The prefix *neo* is meant to emphasize that we are not learning from the past 'as it really happened', but rather from the past as it is being reinvented or re-imagined by those entitled to it, the projection into the past of the self-determined future they want to live in and pass on to their children.

7.5.4.1   *Neo-law*

The indigenous struggle for legality is a double struggle: it is the struggle for a collective right to create laws and rights. On the one hand, indigenous peoples demand, both from international law and national state law, recognition of their collective rights as

---

[234]   Varese, 1982, p 36. See also Gros, 2000.

peoples, above all the right to self-determination. On the other, according to autonomous indigenous law, the paramount substantive content of such right is self-government. At both levels, indigenous law transcends the legal form of the modern nation-state, and points to new local-global legal linkages. For different reasons, both levels of legality are structurally characterized by a high degree of rhetoric and low degrees of bureaucracy and violence. At both levels, normativity is argumentative and thick, whereas enforcement mechanisms are thin. First-level legality (international legal recognition) depends heavily, both for its creation and enforcement, on public opinion and on the pressure exerted on governments and international organizations by global coalitions of indigenous and non-indigenous NGOs and social movements. Notwithstanding its extreme variation, second-level legality (the laws and customs within self-governed territories) tends to be informal, poor in bureaucratic and violent resources and rich in argumentative resources, bearing some structural similarities with Pasargada law. Both on account of the new local-transnational linkages they point to, and their legal style, centred on rhetoric, indigenous struggles for law enrich our views of the legal landscape, up until now so narrowly focused on the national frame of reference and on the bureaucracy-violence mix.

7.5.4.2   *Neo-state*

I have already suggested that at the roots of the struggle of indigenous peoples for self-determination lies a radical critique of the nation-state. Such a critique is so radical, indeed, that the self-determination sought for does not contemplate the typical attributes of statehood, such as independence or sovereignty. By denouncing the social exclusion and political suppression brought about in the name of false, abstract equivalences between nation, state and law, the indigenous struggles open the ideological space for a radical revision of the vertical political obligation that underlies the liberal state, and call for new conceptions of sovereignty – dispersed, shared, polyphonic sovereignty. Far from being pre-modern or pre-statist, the claim for collective rights and self-government points to postliberal or even postmodern state forms and political obligations, new non-corporatistic intermediations between citizens and state, and more equitable allocations of sameness and difference. In Tambiah's apt formulation, 'the time of becoming the same is also the time of claiming to be different'.[235] In the same line of reasoning, Varese also considers that 'unity does not imply uniqueness. This is the civilizing requirement par excellence, recognizing multiplicity as the framework of knowledge and of existence and the interaction of the differences as the only appropriate environment for the construction of civilization'.[236]

[235]   Tambiah, 1989, p 348.
[236]   Varese, 1982, p 40. On the articulaton of equality and difference, Santos, 2001b.

7.5.4.3   *Neo-community*

The indigenous peoples' claim to self-determination comprises the claims to self-government and local autonomy, and control over land and its resources, that is to say, claims to sustainable community life. Underlying these claims, there is the idea of a horizontal political obligation analogous to that which, in Chapter One, I considered to be characteristic of the principle of the community. Together with the principle of the state and the principle of the market, the principle of the community, we recall, constitutes the pillar of regulation of the socio-cultural project of modernity. It may seem absurd that the peoples most thoroughly victimized by modernity be converted, at the end of the twentieth century, into the guardians of one of the founding principles of modernity – indeed, the principle most neglected by the capitalist trajectory of modernity in the last two hundred years. It may also be argued that the community that the indigenous peoples struggled for is pre-modern or pre-Rousseaunian, since the political obligation upon which it is founded is ancestral and pre-given, and not the result of a social contract. Moreover, in a world of expanding deterritorialized social relations, an indigenous community seems anachronistic, with its hyperterritorial drive, its privileged anchorage in historical land and natural resources.

I would like to counterargue that, far from being a pre-modern relic, the community for which indigenous peoples are struggling is indeed a neo-community, a complex constellation of social and political meaning, in which pre-modern, modern and postmodern elements are tightly intertwined. In point of fact, the past that grounds such a community is a contemporary non-contemporaneity, a social construction designed to transform a past of oppression into a future of dignity, for that purpose using skillfully and innovatively the discursive and political resources of modernity and postmodernity. Just think of the wide variety of forms of organization and mobilization emerging everywhere, from grassroots movements to transnational NGOs, from local rallies to the Quito Declaration, from the use of mass media and the internet to participation in UN and ILO commissions and working groups. Most importantly, the neo-communitarian character of the indigenous quest for community lies in the fact that it links the local with the transnational community, thus providing an illuminating synthesis of the dialectics of reterritorialization-deterritorialization, which, as I showed above, underlies the current processes of globalization. Such a dialectics is clearly seen to be at work in the way the territorial dimension of the indigenous community is symbolically constructed. To be sure, the territory is historical and physical, but the transnational coalition organized in its defence makes it intelligible both to the coalition itself and to public opinion in general, by transforming it into a symbolic or even mythic territory. Thus transformed, the hyperreal territory is integrated into a symbolic universe, where it easily relates to such mental territories of romantic modernity as the promised land, the lost paradise or the frontier, which are likely to capture the imagination and motivation of highly heterogeneous transnational coalitions and world public opinions. Thereby, a common ground is created, an imagined community, in which the territories of history cohere with the territories of the mind.

Rather than an absurdity, it is probably mere cunning of historical reason if, as it withers away, modernity gets its last grain of truth or future precisely from those peoples whose truth and future it has savagely suppressed.

7.6   Cosmopolitanism and human rights

In the two previous sections I dealt with oppressed social groups whose oppression is closely linked to processes of economic, social and political globalization. In the case of undocumented immigrants, refugees and asylum seekers, vulnerability is expressed in the subordinate and forced character of their movements across national borders. They are made vulnerable both by the national and transnational factors that cause their moving, and by the effects of such moving in a world system structured by territorial sovereign states. In the case of indigenous peoples, the globalization of their oppression and suffering started very early, with the European expansion, and the genocide and colonial domination that came with it. Today, it is re-enacted in new forms in the escalating competition among core countries for the control of and access to raw materials, combined with the pressure in many a peripheral and semi-peripheral country to respond to the transnational imperatives of foreign debt and structural adjustment by further encroaching upon the ancestral territories and traditional livelihoods of indigenous peoples. In both cases, the prerogatives of territorial sovereignty constitute a powerful obstacle to the development of a cosmopolitan legal field that might provide for the effective protection of these transnational Third Worlds of people. The creation of a global progressive coalition – more visible at present in the case of the indigenous peoples than in the case of international migrants and refugees – is required in order to overcome such obstacles.

In this section, I broaden the scope of the inquiry to encompass subordinate classes and groups throughout the world. I mean victims of multiple forms of discrimination, privileged targets of massive violations of human rights, second and third class citizens or even pariahs, workers and peasants, women, ethnic and religious minorities, millions of undernourished and brutalized children, internally displaced people, gays and lesbians, sociological untouchables of all kinds. This is a very large social field, in which the social processes accounting for the forms of oppression, exploitation and domination are of the most diverse kind, some transnational, others local, some predominantly economic, others predominantly cultural, some centuries old, others very recent. Far from pretending to describe them all in detail, I am only concerned here with the emergence in the postwar period, and particularly in the last four decades, of a cosmopolitan legal culture that grew out of a transnational understanding of human suffering and the transnational constellation of progressive (legal, political, humanitarian) social actions devised to minimize it. Such a legal culture has gradually evolved into an international human rights regime supported by global coalitions of local, national and transnational non-governmental organizations, which have been growing dramatically in number, range and effectiveness in recent years.

The globalization of capitalist production; the enhanced competition of core countries and trading blocs for economic supremacy, and the increased inequalities between North and South associated with it; the hegemonic doctrines of national security, and the wars by proxy they have led to – all these factors have added, in the last three decades, new transnational dimensions to human suffering and social oppression. But they have also created the potential for the globalization of resistance. In a few instances, the link between the globalization of oppression and the globalization of resistance is very direct, as when workers employed by the same TNC in different countries act together to formulate their grievances and organize their struggles. Or when environmental groups from different countries (for instance, Mexico and the US) unite to fight against cross-border pollution (ie, against NAFTA's industrialization style).

In most cases, however, the impact of specific global practices is less direct and the networking of resistance much more difficult. Similar phenomena – be they massive violations of human rights, repression of unions, racial, ethnic and sexual discrimination, famine and starvation, destruction of the environment, or civil or cross-border warfare – occur in different parts of the world system as a result of different combinations of local, national and global factors. Irreversible destruction of the environment may result from the globally induced and intensified integration of one region into the world economy (for example, the Amazon); attacks on workers' rights and organizations may be justified in the name of a hegemonic global ideology such as neo-liberalism; civil or cross-border warfare may result from the confrontation between rival nationalisms exacerbated by interference of a globally or regionally hegemonic state; massive violation of human rights may take place through 'temporary' trade-offs between basic material needs, equality and freedom, on the one hand, and economic growth and competitiveness in the world economy as envisaged by political elites, on the other.

But in all these cases and in myriad similar ones, global factors operate alongside national and local factors, sometimes reinforcing the influence of the latter and sometimes countering it. Singling out the causes of the above phenomena – let alone finding someone responsible for them – becomes a difficult task. This sparks and exacerbates rivalry among subordinate classes or groups in different countries – despite the common roots of their plight – and the globalization of resistance and struggles for emancipation becomes very difficult, if not impossible. Moreover, the monopoly held by nation-states, as the only international political subjects, and the national basis of the 'old' social movements – labour unions and political parties – should caution us against triumphalist predictions of cosmopolitan politics and cosmopolitan legal fields resulting from the intensification of global practices, specifically from the new cross-border dimensions of human suffering and social oppression. For instance, in drawing conclusions from case studies on co-operation among labour unions from different countries, Gordon and Turner assert that logistical, cultural and economic obstacles have resulted in the fact that 'of the current strategies for [labour union] revitalization (including organizing, political action, partnership, mergers, and internal restructuring), international collaboration, although growing, remains the smallest'.[237] Similarly, in the above-quoted study on the globalization of the indigenous rights movement in Latin America, Brysk concludes that despite their remarkable legal and political achievements, the formidable obstacles the movement has faced has prevented it from developing the type of 'functional division of labor among disparate organizations: insiders and outsiders, local and global, spiritual and secular' that characterizes successful social movements.[238]

The emergence of an international human rights regime in the last four decades is nonetheless a major contribution to the development of a cosmopolitan legal field. It is a regime based on the UN but with wide regional differences – Europe and Asia as two extremes, one that, moreover, has been slowly undermining the monopoly of the states as international political subjects, challenging it through the growing strength of transnational advocacy NGOs and transnational networks of local and national NGOs devoted to the promotion of human rights on a world scale.

In this section, the international human rights regime will be critically analyzed and evaluated in light of the cosmopolitan legal culture I am envisaging, that is to say, as part of an emancipatory politics measuring up to the unprecedented challenges, risks and opportunities inherent to an increasingly globalized and interdependent but also increasingly unjust and eco-predatory world society. Given the research agenda put forward in this chapter, I will concentrate on three major topics that, though deeply interconnected, must be dealt with separately. In light of the three-fold comparative approach presented above, I will analyze in turn the following topics: national sovereignty versus international human rights advocacy; universalism versus particularism in human rights conceptions; and human rights and social development. Given the extreme complexity of each one of these topics, I will only touch upon the issues that I deem central to each one of them. At the end, I will present a few cosmopolitan policy orientations as they emerge from the analysis.

7.6.1 INTERNATIONAL HUMAN RIGHTS AND NATIONAL SOVEREIGNTY

The international human rights regime is built around three major documents and sets of standards: the Universal Declaration of Human Rights adopted on 10 December 1948; the International Covenant on Economic, Social and Cultural Rights opened for signature on 19 December 1966, which entered into force on 3 January 1976; and the International Covenant on Civil and Political Rights, opened for signature on 19 December 1966, which entered into force on 23 March 1976. Together they comprise

---

[237]   Gordon and Turner, 2000, p 261.
[238]   Brysk, 2002, p 298.

what Donnelly calls 'the global human rights regime',[239] a system of rules and implementation procedures centred on the UN, and whose main organs are the UN Commission on Human Rights and the Human Rights Committee. If we were to accept Chase-Dunn's[240] position that the capitalist world economy is held together by means of political-military power and market interdependence, rather than by means of normative consensus, it might be difficult to explain the emergence in the postwar period of an international human rights regime, based on an international consensus on substantive norms with high moral voltage. It is true that, for almost a century, between the consolidation of the liberal states and World War II, human rights were largely viewed as a domain in which only the state had competence, and that this situation could only change under the impulse of an exceedingly dramatic and atrocious violation of human rights – the Nazi horror – before which the democratic states had proved impotent.[241] Furthermore, in spite of strong moral and emotional demands for a new international interdependence in the area of human rights practices – turned into an extremely sensitive domain, with national violations becoming a matter of international concern – the new global human rights system started out as a rather weak regime in terms of enforcement, and so it remains today. Strong declarations and promotional activities have not translated themselves into strong implementation and enforcement practices. In other words, implementation and enforcement of international human rights were designed as largely a matter of national state action. The undisputed supremacy of the principle of national sovereignty saved the states from the threats and embarrassment that might derive from too effective an international scrutiny over human rights practices. Implicit here was the idea that an effective promotion of human rights would be at odds with the proper functioning of the states system.[242] The obligation to safeguard human rights was not in itself a collective one, let alone the institutional machinery to guarantee its fulfillment. In both regards, the collective vision was rather weak; it did not go beyond 'a politically weak moral interdependence,' as Donnelly puts it, and implied no significant limitation on national sovereignty. 'The result is a regime with extensive, coherent and widely accepted norms, but extremely limited international decision-making powers – that is, a strong promotional regime'.[243]

This global human rights regime allows for internal differentiation across the interstate system. Three or four regional sub-regimes are usually identified and ranked as follows, by decreasing order of strength: the European, the Inter-American, the African and the Asian and Middle Eastern (lack of) regime.[244] A brief comment on each one of them: what distinguishes the *European regime* – established by the members of the Council

239 Donnelly, 1989, p 206.
240 Chase-Dunn, 1991, p 88.
241 In the interwar period, the International Labor Organization (ILO) was a partial exception to the state-centred conception of human rights in the field of workers' rights.
242 On this topic, see in general Falk, 1981.
243 Donnelly, 1989, p 213. On human rights and social development, see lastly, Ghai, 2001.
244 Donnelly, 1989. Leary, 1990; Welch, Jr, 1990. On Asian perspectives on human rights, see Ghai, 1993a, 2000a.

of Europe in 1950 – is not so much the substantive human rights normativity, but the binding decision-making powers of the European Court of Human Rights, which were further strengthened with the entering into force of Protocol Eleven on 31 October 1998. This protocol eliminated the intermediary body that had hitherto screened the cases – the European Commission of Human Rights – and instead gave full powers to the court to decide directly on the admissibility of cases. Thus, currently any of the 41 contracting states or any individual claiming to be a victim of a violation of the Convention may lodge directly with the court in Strasbourg an application alleging a breach by a contracting state of one of the Convention rights. The complex legal and political relationships between this European regime, which comprises forty-one states (as of July, 2002), and another, narrower European regime constituted by the EU legal order and comprising fifteen European states, do not concern me here.[245] Nor am I concerned with the relationships between either regime and the strong human rights component of the Conference on Security and Co-operation in Europe established by the Helsinki Final Act, signed on 1 August 1975 by representatives of 35 states, comprising 32 European states, plus the Soviet Union, the US and Canada.[246] At this point I just want to emphasize two issues which, without questioning the overall strength of the European human rights regime when analyzed in comparative terms, nonetheless show some of its weaknesses, which are indeed bound to expand in the coming years. The first one, already touched upon in the section on refugees and non-EU immigrants, refers to the massive violations of human rights that may be in store for non-EU citizens, as the internal borders are eliminated and the external borders strengthened. Another dimension of this issue is the failure of the EU to define and comply with human rights criteria in decisions on foreign aid, international trade and restrictions on the international activities of European-based multinational corporations. The second issue relates to the net decline of human rights guarantees for European citizens as a side effect of the strengthening of the EU and specifically of the '1992' programme, the internal market of the four forms of free circulation and what will follow from them. As Clapham suggests:

> 'the drive towards '1992' and the changes which will continue way beyond "1992" mean that people in the Community will be subjected to new controls, new technology, new transnational actors, new forms of work, and continuing racial and sexual discrimination. Without new rights and remedies, some individuals and groups could find the negative effects of integration outweighing the positive opportunities which it claims to offer'.[247]

To the extent that it does not include the economic, social and cultural rights listed in the European Covenants, the *Inter-American regime* is substantively narrower than the European one. Similarly to the pre-1998 European regime (ie, the European regime in force before the adoption of Protocol Eleven), its main organs are the Inter-American Commission of Human Rights and the Inter-American Court of Human Rights. After a

---

[245]   Clapham, 1991, pp 54ff.
[246]   Clapham, 1991, p 82; Buergenthal, 1991, pp 333–386.
[247]   Clapham, 1991, p 103.

disappointing initial period – by 1992 the court had handed down decisions on only two cases – that raised serious doubts about their usefulness for the cause of human rights in the region, the Commission and the court have gradually become more professionalized – indeed, most of the current members of the court are former human rights activists or academics – and proactive. During the second half of the 1990s, the court ruled on cases involving torture, 'disappearances', and violations to freedom of the press. Particularly notable is a case decided by the court in 2001 in favour of the Mayagna (Sumo) indigenous group in Awas Tigni, Nicaragua. Based on a progressive interpretation of the right to property, the court ordered the Nicaraguan government to demarcate clearly and protect the ancestral territory of the indigenous community involved. However, this regime still suffers from a striking moral weakness – ie, the fact that the hegemonic power, the US, dominates the regime without being a party to the Convention that has created it (the American Convention on Human Rights of 1969). In a tremendous show of hegemonic arrogance, the US refuses to ratify the International Human Rights Covenants and other human rights treaties. Even more shocking is the fact that the US holds other countries to international human rights standards and procedures that it refuses to allow to be applied to itself. A simple illustration: while the State Department prepares an annual report on the human rights practices of most countries, the US refuses to submit reports on its own practices to international monitoring bodies.[248]

As to the *African regime*, the African Charter on Human and Peoples' Rights was adopted by the Organization of African Unity in Nairobi in June 1981. In terms of substantive normativity, this charter contains two major innovations: as the title of the charter itself indicates, to individual human rights it adds collective rights, as well as the right to development; it also introduces the concept of duty of individuals vis-à-vis the family, the community and the state. But the provisions that establish the African Commission on Human and Peoples' Rights are exceedingly vague, conferring on it no enforcement powers of any sort and only very modest investigative powers. To counter the African system's ineffectiveness, the Organization of OAU adopted in 1998 the Protocol on the Establishment of an African Court on Human Rights and Peoples' Rights. The establishment of the court is an important step towards the implementation of the Charter. However, as Orlu has recently pointed out, there are still fundamental shortcomings in the African system, two of which are particularly serious: 'the limitation of access of individuals and NGOs to the court, and the lack of provision for separate institutional roles for the Commission and the court'.[249] Even as a declaratory regime, the African regime is still rather weak, ridden by heated ideological confrontations.[250] For instance, the African Charter is often contrasted, in scholarly and political debates, with the Universal Declaration of the Rights of Peoples (known as the Algiers Declaration) adopted by a group of jurists, political scientists, sociologists,

---

248   Donnelly, 1992, p 265.
249   Orlu, 2001, p 328.
250   Two alternative African views: I Shivji, 1989; O Eze 1984.

representatives of trade unions and political parties of various countries, as well as members of several liberation movements, at a meeting held in Algiers on 4 July 1976. While the African Charter has been praised by some for establishing a new and higher standard for human rights politics, the peoples' rights, others have condemned it for its authoritarianism and opportunism.[251] For Issa Shivji, 'The Charter bears the birthmarks of essentially a neo-colonialist statist disposition', while, on the contrary, the Algiers Declaration is truly revolutionary, people-centred, anti-imperialistic and inspired by a global reflection on the real conditions in which people are actually living.[252]

If outside Europe the international human rights regimes are recognizably weak, in Asia and the Middle East no regime exists at all. Though in both regions the human rights debate is widening and deepening, there are, among other reasons, important cultural barriers to the establishment of a human rights regime. Human rights are often viewed as an exotic, foreign, Western conception whose worldwide circulation is nothing but a manifestation of the overall cultural imperialism of the West (more on this below).

International regimes refer to international normative consensuses among nation-states and, as such, they raise two interrelated questions: the extent to which the normative consensus collapses whenever the overriding imperatives of national sovereignty are considered to be better served by the violation of human rights; and the extent to which the inherent statism of implementation and enforcement mechanisms stays in the way of the emergence of new international legal subjects with a more cosmopolitan orientation and a transnational advocacy of greater efficiency.

The record of violations of human rights across the world system in the postwar period is a cruel comment on the human rights dominant discourse and a flat denial of the practical validity of international declarations on normative consensus. The optimist predictions in the last twenty years of a brighter future for human rights, in the wake of democratic transition in many countries ruled by dictatorial regimes, peace negotiations among nations, political factions or ethnic groups involved in civil and cross-border wars for many years, and, finally, the collapse of the Communist bloc, may prove to be wrong. Comparisons among regions of the world system are not very enlightening, and may be even misleading, as we lack accepted transregional criteria to assess differences and construct rankings.[253] Suffice it to acknowledge the disheartening fact that violations of human rights have been occurring everywhere. The following is just a brief overview.

Violations of human rights have been occurring in *Europe*, the region with the strongest international regime. According to the 2001 Amnesty International Report, the most

---

251 Howard, 1984, p 164.
252 Shivji, 1989, p 93; Falk, 1981, pp 185–195.
253 On the problematic nature of comparisons in this field, see Howard, 1984.

salient types of direct (active) violations of civil and political rights are related to the treatment of citizens by police or paramilitary forces, extra-judicial executions and disappearances by Russian and Chechen forces, widespread torture and ill treatment of men, women and children in Turkey, application of discriminatory legislation against linguistic and religious minorities, homosexuals and women, as well as promulgation of restrictive legislation against immigrants and asylum seekers – particularly on the basis of new anti-terrorist legislation passed in several countries, notably the UK, in the wake of the 11 September 2001, attacks. Indeed, according to the report, 'members of ethnic minorities and foreigners, including asylum seekers, were subjected to racist-related abuse and ill treatment in many countries in Western Europe including Austria, Belgium, Finland, France, Germany, Italy, Spain and Switzerland'.[254] Among indirect or passive violations of human rights there are justice delays, impunity, and failure to guarantee economic and social rights.

In the *Americas*, the last four decades were particularly tragic in terms of massive and often grotesque violations of human rights. Actually, in spite of the democratic transitions of the 1980s and 1990s, the perspectives for the near future are equally gloomy, in view of the general impoverishment of the region and the shocking growth of social inequality. In Latin and Central America, fragile political democracies (in some instances, no more than semi-democracies) have managed to put a halt to or at least reduce the brutality of politically motivated violations of some of the most fundamental human rights, such as the right to life and physical integrity. I have particularly in mind the torture inflicted on thousands and thousands of Brazilians, Chileans and Argentinians, the disappearance of more than ten thousand Argentinians, numberless extrajudicial executions in Guatemala, Haiti, El Salvador, Uruguay and so on.[255] But since these countries are now faced with the imminent failure to fulfill the most basic human needs of the large majority of the population – the right to food, shelter and health care, as the Argentinian crisis that started in 2001 dramatically illustrates – what happens is that different social and political processes again contribute, Sisyphus-like, to turning the people's right to life and physical integrity into an unfulfilled promise. The violence of parastate organizations in Colombia, the elimination of hundreds of opposition leaders in Mexico, mass killings of street children in Brazil, the violent 'structural adjustment' in Argentina and Peru, are some other dark sides of human rights practices in the subcontinent. Though North Americans like to believe that violations of human rights take place only to the South of them or, as Donnelly puts it, 'in places that must be reached by crossing large bodies of saltwater',[256] the truth of the matter is that police brutality, racial and sexual discrimination, homelessness, mass poverty and violence in the inner cities, health care crisis, obstruction to workers' unionization,

---

[254]   http://web.amnesty.org/ai.nsf/Index/REGIONS\EUROPE. Visited as of 4 July 2002.

[255]   See the South-South Conference on the Rule of Law and Human Rights: Exchanging Experiences and Breaking New Paths, Lund, 10–14 May 1993. Proceedings. Also, Lewellen, 1985; Bowen, 1985; Brockett, 1985; H Fruhling, 1992; Chomsky and Herman, 1979.

[256]   Donnelly 1989, p 268; 1992, p 265.

arbitrary treatment of prisoners, asylum seekers and undocumented immigrants, also constitute violations of human rights, even though they rarely find their way into international human rights reports.

In *Africa*, where, very early on, the Europeans set in motion massive violations of human rights through colonialism, slave trade, forced labour and apartheid, the historical and contemporary record of human rights violations is atrocious. Many examples contribute to the tragic portrait of the fate of human rights in Africa: the legal system of apartheid, up until recently in force in South Africa; millions of undernourished and starving people; more internally and internationally displaced people than in any other continent, fleeing from hunger, drought, civil wars and ethnic persecutions; ethnic slaughters of the Acholi and Langi in Uganda, of Igbo Biafrans in Nigeria, of ethnic Somalis in Kenya, of Eritreans in Ethiopia, of Ewe in Ghana; ethnic and, in the last decade, also religious conflicts in Sudan, where the civilian populations of the South are regularly bombed by the government, the death toll from war or starvation exceeding half a million since 1988; the denial of self-determination to the Casamanceans; the bloody dictatorships which for decades plagued the continent (Idi Amin, Bokassa and Mobutu); the ethnic bloodshed in Rwanda; the civil wars in Angola (1975-2002) and Mozambique (1985-1992), originally instigated by the superpowers and for many years fueled by South Africa.[257]

In the *Middle East*, the Palestinians and the Kurds have been the collective victims of the crudest violations of human rights in the region.[258] Particularly after the launching of the so-called 'war on terrorism' by the US in 2001 and Israel's massive attacks against Palestinian institutions and population in 2002, the Palestinians have become again the object of the crudest forms of repression and discrimination. In *Asia*, both ethnic and religious intolerance and/or dictatorial regimes have been at the roots of massive violations of human rights in India (starting with the Hindu caste system), Pakistan, Malaysia, Indonesia (with salience for the genocide of the Maubere people in East Timor), Sri Lanka (the persecution of the Tamil), Iran, Afghanistan, Bangladesh, the political repression in China, North and South Korea, Singapore, Burma, Thailand, the mass killings by the Pol Pot and so on.[259] It remains to be said that, in all these regions, there are other structural and more resilient violations of human rights, such as children's rights and, particularly in the Islamic regions, women's rights.

Even if one sticks to a conventional conception of human rights, as I did in the preceding survey, the global panorama of human rights practices is very sinister, and gives little room for optimism. In most instances, violation of human rights has its origin, directly or indirectly, actively or passively, in state actions or omissions that are justified as prerogatives of sovereignty, and in the name of state-defined national interests and

---

[257] See, among many others, R Howard, 1984; F Olaeghulom, 1985; Wright, 1985; Shivji, 1989.

[258] Zeidan, 1985; Donnelly, 1992.

[259] Thomas, 1985; Muzaffar, 1990; Joshi, 1990; Rubin, 1990; Jahangir, 1990; Feldman, 1990; Cascio, 1990; Galanter, 1991; Ghai, 1993c.

national security objectives. Given the fact that, in the current interstate system, implementation and enforcement of international norms is largely left to the initiative and political will of the individual nation-states, the existence of international human rights regimes has proved disarmingly impotent to prevent or punish major violations of human rights. It could, however, be imagined that, in conjunction with the international community and international organizations, the hegemonic democratic states of the global or regional human rights regimes might feel compelled to play a decisive role in forcing or inducing the compliance with human rights norms by externally weaker states. But in reality, even if sometimes proclaimed in abstract, such a role has been performed in a most disappointing way, precisely because its performance has been subjected to the same overriding commitment to national sovereignty that we have found to be responsible for so much violation of human rights.

The truth is that hegemonic states have subordinated the international human rights advocacy to their geo-political interests and objectives, defined in narrow national terms, with the result that recurrent and oftentimes shocking double standards continue to underline the moral weakness of official commitments to human rights. This is true of Europe, the US and Japan, but particularly blatant in the case of the US.

During the Cold War, the US repeatedly denounced violations of civil and political rights in the Soviet bloc countries, while condoning or even encouraging violations of the same rights in 'friendly countries'[260] (among the most grotesque cases: Duvalier in Haiti, Pinochet in Chile, Mobutu in Zaire, Marcos in the Philippines, Park in South Korea, the Shah in Iran, Stroessner in Paraguay, and Somoza in Nicaragua). Even when, after 1975, the US Congress linked foreign aid to human rights, the same overriding strategic interests continued to produce, to this day, otherwise unjustified double standards in Israel, Kenya, Egypt, Indonesia and so on. This duplicity reverberates in many policy areas, as witness the case of refugee policy and the different treatment given to asylum seekers from Haiti or from Cuba (section 7.4.3 above). The same reasons preside over swift changes in policy vis-à-vis certain leaders or countries where no corresponding changes in human rights practices have occurred: just think of Saddam Hussein and Khomeini, or China and Syria. The US has encouraged international violations of human rights, and then covered them up with outstanding geo-political reasons aired worldwide by a friendly mass communication system.

Writing in 1981 about the manipulation of the human rights agenda in the US in conjunction with the mass media, Richard Falk spoke of a 'politics of invisibility' and of a 'politics of supervisibility'. As examples of the politics of invisibility, he spoke of the total blackout by the media on news about the tragic decimation of the East Timorese people (taking more than three hundred thousand lives) and the plight of the hundred million or so 'untouchables' in India 'who suffer a daily existence, by and large, that is

---

[260]   Donnelly, 1992, pp 254–265; Nanda, Scarritt and Shepherd, Jr, 1981; Chomsky and Herman, 1979.

quite as humiliating as that endured by black South Africans'.[261] As examples of the politics of supervisibility, Falk mentioned the relish with which post-revolutionary abuses of human rights in Iran and Vietnam were reported in the US. He concludes: 'The poles of invisibility and supervisibility correlate closely with the American foreign policy imperatives of supporting certain repressive regimes and discouraging recourse to revolutionary politics. Human rights violations – keeping them hidden or magnifying their occurrence – became, then, part of the battle for the hearts and minds of Americans (and others)'.[262] Actually, the same could largely be said of the EU countries, the most poignant example being the silence that kept the genocide of the Maubere people in East Timor hidden from the Europeans throughout the decade, thereby facilitating the ongoing smooth and thriving international trade with Indonesia.

Writing at the end of the 1970s, Chomsky and Herman were even more radical in their critical assessment of the US' international human rights record. According to them, the massive US intervention in Latin America and Asia in the previous 25 years had been confined 'almost exclusively to overthrowing reformers, democrats and radicals', rarely 'destabilizing' right-wing military regimes, no matter how corrupt or terroristic they might have been. Their scathing conclusion was that 'for most of the sample countries, US-controlled aid has been positively related to investment climate and inversely related to the maintenance of a democratic order and human rights'.[263]

According to Donnelly, most of the structural factors that accounted for unimpeded or even promoted violations of international human rights during the Cold War continue in the post-Cold War period, and for that reason the impediments to establishing effective international human rights policies remain essentially unchanged.[264] Among such impediments there looms large a state-centred, sovereignty-based conception of international order, and the consequent absence of transnational enforcement capabilities. As the international regime depends largely on voluntary patterns of compliance, considerations of self-interest as perceived by the nation-states will continue to be the key factor. Enhanced competition for markets and for production niches in the current global restructuring of capital accumulation is likely to fragment the conceptions of national self-interest even further, and augment the political aggressiveness that defends them against competing states. The formation and consolidation of regional trading blocs, and mounting global competition among them, are likely to justify new trade-offs between commercial advantages and human rights issues, not only within the periphery but also within the core countries of each of the blocs. Under such circumstances, the continuation of a state-centred logic in the field of human rights will represent a growing impediment to an efficient and morally decent international human rights policy. This impediment will be mostly linked, from now on, to a double process. On the one hand, further colonization of conceptions of national

[261]   Falk, 1981, p 4.
[262]   Falk, 1981, p 5.
[263]   Chomsky and Herman, 1979, p 16.
[264]   Donnelly, 1992, p 258.

interest and security by the imperatives of the globalization of the economy according to the market-friendly development model will enhance the vulnerability of those human rights issues that might collide with such imperatives; therefore, national states will be expedient in invoking and strengthening the prerogatives of political sovereignty to justify human rights violations (which, indeed, both mirror and occult the weakening of economic sovereignty). On the other hand, the globalization of the economy is engendering global economic actors with tremendous economic and political clout. Because of their private character, these economic actors can commit massive violations of human rights with total impunity in different parts of the world, taking advantage of market-friendly expanded freedoms of movement and action in and out of the regional trading blocs. Because such actors are at the core of the loss in economic national sovereignty, their actions, no matter how offensive to human rights, are unlikely to collide with consideration of national interest or security that might otherwise prompt the corrective or punitive intervention of the state.

Once prisoner of a transnational capitalist order which, as a principle of social regulation, reorganizes in terms of global regulation what it disorganizes in terms of national deregulation, the state-centred logic must be transcended, if social emancipation is to be reinvented so as to measure up to the new authoritarianism of globally organized social regulation. To the extent that human rights belong to emancipatory agendas – though the fact that they have often been appropriated by regulatory agendas must not be neglected – they themselves must be reinvented.

To transcend the state-centred logic is, however, not enough. Above all, it is necessary to determine what alternative logic might replace it and the analytical tools that this task calls for. In the following I set out to contribute to such a task. My major concerns are the question of the problematic universality of human rights and the structural obstacles that the unequal exchanges in the world system pose to a radical emancipatory politics of human rights.

7.6.2 UNIVERSALISM VERSUS COSMOPOLITANISM?

Concrete violations of human rights or objections to human rights discourse are often justified by nation-states on grounds of national interest, national security and non-interference, as well as cultural specificity and development trade-offs. The first three grounds fall under the principle of sovereignty, already dealt with in the previous section. In the following sections I will concentrate on the last two grounds, the first one having a predominantly political-cultural profile, the other a predominantly political-economic profile.

One of the most heated human rights debates is whether human rights are a universal or rather a Western concept and, concomitantly, whether they are universally valid or not. Though closely related, these two questions are nonetheless autonomous. The first one deals with the historical and cultural origins of the concept of human rights, the second one with their validity claims at a given point in history. The genesis of a moral claim may condition its validity, but it certainly does not determine it. The Western origin of human rights may be made congruent with their universality if, hypothetically, at a given point in history they are universally accepted as ideal standards of political and moral life. The two questions are, however, interrelated, because the mobilizing energy that can be generated to make the acceptance of human rights concrete and effective depends, in part, upon the cultural identification with the presuppositions that ground human rights as a moral claim. From a sociological and political perspective, the elucidation of this linkage is by far more important than the abstract discussion of either the question of cultural anchorage or of philosophical validity. For this reason I will only review this discussion to the extent that it illuminates the sociological and political perspectives that concern me here.

Are human rights universal, a cultural invariant, that is to say, part of a global culture? I would suggest that the only transcultural fact is that all cultures are relative. Cultural relativity also means cultural diversity and incompleteness. From the (relative) point of view of a given culture, diversity is both experienced and denied as hierarchical differentiation, whereas incompleteness is both experienced and denied as a specific aspiration to completeness. Cultural relativity means, therefore, that all cultures tend to define as universal the values that they consider ultimate. What is highest is also most widespread. Thus, the specific question about the conditions of universality in a given culture is itself not universal. The question about the universality of human rights is a Western cultural question. Hence, human rights are universal only when they are viewed from a Western standpoint. The extent to which this standpoint can be shared, rejected, appropriated or modified by other cultures depends on the cross-cultural dialogues made possible by the concrete political and sociological power relations among the different countries involved.

Because the question of universality is the answer to an aspiration of completeness, and because each culture 'situates' such an aspiration around ultimate values and universal validity, different aspirations to different ultimate values in different cultures will lead to isomorphic concerns which, given the adequate hermeneutical procedures, may become mutually intelligible and mutually translatable. At best it is even possible to achieve a mixture and interpenetration of concerns and concepts. The more equal power relations among cultures are, the more probable it is that such *mestizaje* might occur. A balanced cross-cultural *mestizaje* of concerns and concepts is the multicultural correspondent of single-culture universality (more on this below).

We may then conclude that, once posed, the question of universality betrays the universality of what it questions, no matter what the answer may be. Other strategies to establish the universality of human rights have, however, been designed. For instance, human rights can be conceived as a cultural invariant whose universality derives from the fact that they are equally valid in any culture. Even so are they conceived by authors for whom human rights are universal because they are held by all human beings as human beings, that is, because independently of explicit recognition they are inherent to human nature.[265] This line of thought begs the question by dislocating its object. Since human beings do not hold human rights because they are beings – most beings do not hold rights – but because they are human, the universality of human nature becomes the unanswered question that makes possible the fictive answer to the question of the universality of human rights. There is no culturally invariant concept of human nature. Another possible way of establishing the universality of human rights might be through the concept of global culture, but I already expressed my reservations against this concept in this chapter, and so I will not pursue this line here.

The concept of human rights lies on a well-known set of presuppositions, all of which are distinctly Western,[266] namely: there is a universal human nature that can be known by rational means; human nature is essentially different from and higher than the rest of reality; the individual has an absolute and irreducible dignity that must be defended against society or the state; the autonomy of the individual requires that society be organized in a non-hierarchical way, as a sum of free individuals. Since all these presuppositions are clearly Western and liberal, and easily distinguishable from other conceptions of human dignity in other cultures, one might ask why the question of the universality of human rights has become so hotly debated, why, in other words, the sociological universality of this question has outgrown its philosophical universality.

To my mind, the answer must be sought in the historical trajectory of Western modernity after it merged with world capitalist development from the nineteenth century onwards. I argued in Chapters One and Two that the paradigm of modernity in Europe evolved from the sixteenth century onwards with wide-ranging revolutionary, regulatory and emancipatory claims, which were to be tailored to the needs of capitalist development only in the nineteenth century. I also noted that the consolidation of the liberal state played a decisive role in this political process. The asymmetry between the Western passage into modernity and all the others – the New Worlds, the colonial gate and the externally induced modernization – lies in the fact that all the others took place under the aegis of Western capitalism, and were similarly molded by the economic, cultural and political imperatives of the West. The regulatory and emancipatory claims of modernity, already tailored to fit capitalism in the West, were further retailored to fit Western capitalism as a global endeavour, that is to say, as imperialism. Like any other dimension of Western modernity, human rights were 'universalized' by sucessive processes of tailoring and retailoring.

---

[265] For two contrasting views, see Donnelly, 1989; Renteln, 1990. See also Schwab and Pollis, 1982; K Thompson, 1980; A Henkin, 1979; A Diemer, 1986; Ghai, 2000b; Mutua, 2001.

[266] A perceptive analysis from an Eastern perspective is in Panikkar, 1984, p 30.

Within the analytical framework I am adopting in this chapter, I would suggest that human rights have been universalized as a globalized Western localism. If we look at the history of human rights in the postwar period, it is not difficult to conclude that human rights policies, by and large, have been at the service of the economic and geo-political interests of the hegemonic capitalist states. In the previous section, I showed how the generous and seductive discourse on human rights has allowed for unspeakable violations, and how such violations have been evaluated and dealt with according to revolting double standards. But the Western mark in the dominant human rights discourse could be traced in many other instances: in the Universal Declaration of 1948, which was drafted without the participation of the majority of the peoples of the world; in the exclusive recognition of individual rights, with the exception of the collective right to self-determination which, however, was only applied to the peoples subjected to European colonialism and organized in colonial states; in the priority given to civil and political rights over economic, social and cultural rights; and in the recognition of the right to property as the first and, for many years, the sole economic right.

But this is not the whole history. Throughout the world, millions of people and thousands of non-governmental organizations have been struggling for human rights, often at great risk, in defence of oppressed social classes and groups that in many instances have been victimized by authoritarian capitalistic states. The political agendas of such struggles are usually either explicitly or implicitly anti-capitalist. A counter-hegemonic human rights discourse and practice has been developing, non-Western conceptions of human rights have been proposed, cross-cultural dialogues on human rights have been organized. Furthermore, Western modernity has unfolded into two highly divergent conceptions and practices of human rights – the liberal and the Marxist – and both of them, far from being monolithic, have given rise to very distinct human rights policies socially sustained by very different classes and social groups.[267] In sum, alongside the dominant discourse and practice of human rights conceived as a globalized Western localism, a counterhegemonic discourse and practice of human rights conceived as a cosmopolitan politics has been developing. The central task of emancipatory politics of our time, in this domain, consists in transforming the conceptualization and practice of human rights from a globalized localism into a cosmopolitan project.

What are the conditions for such a transformation? First of all, it is imperative to transcend the debate on universalism and cultural relativism. The debate is an inherently false debate, whose polar concepts are both and equally detrimental to an emancipatory conception of human rights. All cultures are relative, but cultural relativism, as a philosophical posture, is wrong. All cultures aspire genuinely to ultimate, universal concerns and values, but cultural universalism, as a philosophical posture, is wrong. Against universalism, we must propose cross-cultural dialogues on

---

[267]   See, for instance, Pollis and Schwab, 1979; Pollis, 1982; An-na'im, 1992.

isomorphic concerns. Against relativism, we must develop cross-cultural procedural criteria to distinguish progressive politics from regressive politics, empowerment from disempowerment, emancipation from regulation. Neither universalism nor relativism must be argued for, but rather cosmopolitanism, that is to say, the globalization of moral and political concerns with and struggles against social oppression and human suffering.

To the extent that the debate sparked by human rights might evolve into a competitive dialogue among different cultures on principles of human dignity and social emancipation, it is imperative that such competition induce cross-cultural dialogues and transnational coalitions to race to the top rather than to the bottom – What are the absolute minimum standards? The most basic human rights? The lowest common denominators? The often voiced cautionary comment against overloading human rights politics with new, more advanced rights or with different and broader conceptions of human rights,[268] is a latter-day manifestation of the reduction of the emancipatory claims of modernity to the low degree of emancipation made possible or tolerated by world capitalism.

Taking into account the incompleteness of each culture, a cross-cultural, *mestizo* conception of human rights is called for, implying that all cultures are problematic vis-à-vis human rights. In one way or another, to a lesser or greater extent, all cultures suffer from some fundamental weakness vis-à-vis a cosmopolitan politics of human rights. The cross-cultural dialogue is premised upon the reciprocal recognition of such weaknesses, its overall goal being their elimination. The most promising and cogent proposals for a multicultural dialogue on human rights, notably those produced by African scholars, point in this direction.[269]

How is such a dialogue to be built? Some of its sociological and political conditions will be briefly mentioned below. At this juncture, I am concerned with some of its epistemological conditions. The new rhetoric as a form of knowledge and as a means of communication, used in Chapter Four to understand the dynamics of Pasargada law, is called to task here. Discursive tolerance, readiness to incorporate alternative knowledges, preference for suppressed and marginalized knowledges, as well as for the hermeneutical circles, of victims and oppressed peoples, are some of the epistemological features of the dialogic rhetoric that are crucial to entertain, and indeed to build the will to entertain, a cross-cultural dialogue.

But this is only a starting point. In the case of a cross-cultural dialogue, the exchange is not only between different knowledges, but also between different cultures, that is to say, between different and, in a strong sense, incommensurable universes of meaning. Strong *topoi* within a given culture become highly vulnerable and problematic

[268]   As in Donnelly, 1989, pp 109–124.
[269]   See, for instance, Mutua, 2001; Obiora, 1997.

whenever used as premises of argumentation in a different culture. The best that can happen to them is to be moved 'down' from premises of argumentation into arguments, but they can also be excluded from the argumentation altogether. To understand a given culture from another culture's *topoi* may thus prove to be very difficult, if not at all impossible. I shall therefore propose a *diatopical hermeneutics*.[270]

Diatopical hermeneutics is based on the idea that the *topoi* of an individual culture, no matter how strong they may be, are as incomplete as the culture itself. Such incompleteness is not visible from inside the culture itself, since aspiration to the universal induces taking a part for the whole. Incompleteness in a given culture must be assessed from another culture's *topoi*. More than as an inadequate answer to a given problem, cultural incompleteness manifests itself as an inadequate formulation of the problem itself. The objective of diatopical hermeneutics is, therefore, not to achieve completeness – which is admittedly an unachievable goal – but, on the contrary, to raise the consciousness of reciprocal incompleteness to its maximum possible by engaging in the dialogue, as it were, with one foot in one culture and the other in another. Herein its *diatopical* character. To give an example: a diatopical hermeneutics can be conducted between the *topos* of human rights in Western culture and the *topos* of *dharma* in Hindu culture. According to Panikkar, *dharma:*

> 'is that which maintains, gives cohesion and thus strength to any given thing, to reality, and ultimately to the three worlds (*triloka*). Justice keeps human relations together; morality keeps oneself in harmony; law is the binding principle for human relations; religion is what maintains the universe in existence; destiny is that which links us with our future; truth is the internal cohesion of a thing. . . . Now a world in which the notion of *Dharma* is central and nearly all-pervasive is not concerned with finding the 'right' of one individual against another or of the individual vis-a-vis society but rather with assaying the *dharmic* (right, true, consistent) or *adharmic* character of a thing or an action within the entire theantropocosmic complex of reality'.[271]

Seen from the *topos* of *dharma*, human rights are incomplete, in that they fail to establish the link between the part (the individual) and the whole (reality), or, even more strongly, in that they focus on what is merely derivative, on rights, rather than on the primordial imperative, the duty of individuals to find their place in the order of the entire society, and of the entire cosmos. Seen from the topos of human rights, *dharma* is also incomplete, due to its strong undialectical bias in favour of harmony, thereby eventually occulting injustices and totally neglecting the value of conflict as a way toward a richer

---

[270]   See also Panikkar, 1984, p 28. In my view, the diatopical hermeneutics is the procedural solution for the debates going on, in the different cultural regions of the world system, on the general issues of universalism, relativism, cultural frames of social transformation, traditionalism and cultural revival. For the African debate, see O Oladipo, 1989; Oruka, 1990; K Wiredu, 1990; Wamba dia Wamba, 1991a, 1991b; H Procee, 1992; MB Ramose, 1992; Ibhawoh, 2001. A sample of the rich debate in India is in A Nandy, 1987a, 1987b, 1988; P Chatterjee, 1984; T Pantham, 1988. A bird's-eye view of cultural differences is in Galtung, 1981.

[271]   Panikkar, 1984, p 39. See also K Inada, 1990; K Mitra, 1982; R Thapar, 1966.

harmony. Moreover, *dharma* is unconcerned with the principles of democratic order, with freedom and autonomy, and it neglects the fact that, without primordial rights, the individual is too fragile an entity to avoid being run over by whatever transcends him or her.

At another conceptual level, the same diatopical hermeneutics can be attempted between the *topos* of the individual and the *topos* of *umma* in Islamic culture. The passages in the Qur'an in which the word *umma* occurs are so varied that its meaning cannot be rigidly defined. This much, however, seems to be certain: it always refers to ethnical, linguistic or religious bodies of people who are the objects of the divine plan of salvation. As the prophetic activity of Muhammad progressed, the religious foundations of *umma* became increasingly apparent, and consequently the *umma* of the Arabs was transformed into an *umma* of the Muslims. Seen from the *topos* of *umma*, the incompleteness of the individual lies in the fact that, on this basis alone, it is impossible to ground the collective linkages and solidarities without which no society can survive, and much less flourish. Conversely, from the *topos* of the individual, *umma*, like *dharma*, overemphasizes duties to the detriment of rights and, for that reason, is bound to condone otherwise abhorrent inequalities, such as the inequality between men and women and between Muslims and non-Muslims. As unveiled by this diatopical hermeneutics, the fundamental weakness of Western culture consists in establishing too strong a dichotomy between the individual and society, thus becoming vulnerable to possessive individualism, narcissism, alienation and anomie. On the other hand, the fundamental weakness of Hindu and Islamic culture consists in that they both fail to recognize that human suffering has an irreducible individual dimension, which can only be adequately addressed in a society not hierarchically organized. Since they are based on very different ontologies, the weaknesses of these two cultures manifest themselves differently, for instance, in the Hindu caste system in one case, and in the Islamic inequality between men and women and between Muslims and non-Muslims, in the other.

The recognition of reciprocal incompleteness and weaknesses is an essential condition of a cross-cultural dialogue. Diatopical hermeneutics builds both on local identification of incompleteness and weakness and on its translocal intelligibility. But why should cultures be interested in cross-cultural dialogue? Diatopical hermeneutics does not occur in a social void; rather, as a specific kind of new rhetoric, it shares with the latter a political bias in favour of emancipation. This will be further explained as I touch upon the other conditions for the transformation of human rights from a globalized localism into a subaltern cosmopolitan project.

7.6.3   Cultural embeddedness and cosmopolitanism

It may be contended that in a world in which more and more cultural processes are being globalized, diatopical hermeneutics rings like an anachronistic epistemology. My counter-argument is two-fold. First of all, I have already said that much of what presents itself as global culture is, in reality, a globalized localism, a cultural process whereby a hegemonic local culture cannibalizes and digests other subordinated cultures. The new wave of 'law and modernization' throughout the peripheral and semi-peripheral world, as the integration of these regions in the world capitalist economy widens and deepens, is a good manifestation of this phenomenon.

The resistance of the different legal cultures varies, but, aside from other political factors, it is likely to be higher in areas that touch upon ideals of morality and good conduct, human dignity and good life, as is the case of human rights. In this and similar legal areas, the cannibalization of the local cultures may lead to a whole range of 'deviant' results, such as: the opportunistic adoption of human rights policies to please foreign hegemonic powers or international agencies; extremely low and highly selective patterns of human rights enforcement; cultural distance and social apathy before violations of human rights, and the consequent difficulty in organizing social struggles and building coalitions to fight such violations and to bring about the punishment of violators.

In the area of human rights and dignity, the mobilization of social support for the emancipatory claims they potentially contain is only achievable if such claims have been appropriated in the local cultural context.[272] Appropriation, in this sense, cannot be obtained through cultural cannibalization. It requires cross-cultural dialogue and diatopical hermeneutics. A fascinating example of this in the field of human rights is offered by Abdullahi Ahmed An-na'im. There is a longstanding debate on the relationships between Islamism and human rights and the possibility of an Islamic conception of human rights.[273] This debate covers a wide range of positions, and its impact reaches far beyond the wide Islamic world.[274] Running the risk of excessive simplification, two extreme positions can be identified in this debate.[275] One, absolutist or fundamentalist, is held by those for whom the religious legal system of Islam, the Shari'a, must be fully applied as the law of the Islamic state. According to this position, there are irreconcilable inconsistencies between the Shari'a and the international human rights, but the Shari'a must prevail. For instance, regarding the status of non-Muslims, the Shari'a dictates the creation of a state for Muslims as the sole citizens, non-Muslims

[272] See R Falk, 1992a, p 45, for whom 'without mediating international human rights through the web of cultural circumstances, it will be impossible for human rights norms and practices to take deep hold in non-Western societies except to the partial, and often distorting, degree that these societies – or, more likely, their governing elites – have been to some extent westernized'. See also Pollis and Schwab, 1979.

[273] An-na'im, 1990, 1992; Dwyer, 1991; Mayer, 1991; Leites, 1991. See also Hassan, 1982; Al Faruqi, 1983. On the broader issue of the relationships between modernity and Islamic revival see, lastly, Sharabi, 1992. Also Shariati, 1986.

[274] According to reliable estimates, the Arab world is around one sixth of the world population and Muslims constitute at least 70 per cent of the total population in about forty countries. An-na'im, 1990, p xiu.

[275] In the review of the Islamic debate I follow closely An-na'im, 1990.

having no political rights; peace between Muslims and non-Muslims is always problematic, and confrontation may be unavoidable. Concerning women, there is no question of equality; the Shari'a commands the segregation of women and, according to some more strict interpretations, even excludes them from public life altogether. At the other extreme, there are the secularists or the modernists, who believe that Muslims should organize themselves in secular states. Islam is a religious and spiritual movement, not a political one and, as such, modern Muslim societies are free to organize their government in whatever manner they deem fit and appropriate to the circumstances. The acceptance of international human rights is a matter of political decision unencumbered by religious considerations. Just one example, among many: a Tunisian law of 1956 prohibited polygamy altogether on the grounds that it was no longer acceptable and that the Qur'anic requirement of justice among co-wives was impossible for any man, except the Prophet, to achieve in practice.

An-na'im criticizes both extreme positions in the many different versions they have assumed in the history of Islam. Against secularism, he argues:

> 'Unless one is advocating the abandonment of Islam itself, Shari'a will continue to be extremely important in shaping the attitudes and behavior of Muslims even if it is not the public law of the land. So long as the Muslim population continues to associate its religious beliefs with the historical Shari'a at the psychological and private levels, Shari'a will have a strong impact on the nature and policies of the state'.[276]

Real secularism, An-na'im further argues, is unlikely to receive broad and lasting support in the Muslim world and, in view of recent developments, is indeed increasingly on the defensive and actually receding.[277] On the other hand, against the absolutists he holds that the adoption of the Shari'a as the law of the state in countries such as Iran, Pakistan and Sudan has created more problems than it has solved. The Shari'a has been proposed as a miraculous cure for all the ills of Muslim societies, but it is in fact a manipulation of the sentiments of the masses to protect vested interests and justify highly unjust societies. Furthermore, the implementation of historical Shari'a in areas of conflict with universal standards of human rights implies that Muslims cannot exercise their right to self-determination without violating the rights of others.

The middle-ground solution proposed by An-na'im aims at establishing a cross-cultural foundation for human rights, identifying the areas of conflict between Shari'a and 'universal standards of human rights', and seeking a reconciliation and positive relationship between the two systems.[278] This is a difficult task, because each religious and cultural tradition has its own internal frame of reference and derives the validity of its precepts and norms from its own sources. In order to overcome the hostility thereby developing among cultures, it is imperative to find one common cross-cultural principle,

[276]   An-na'im, 1990, p 42.
[277]   An-na'im, 1990, p 62.
[278]   An-na'im, 1990, p 161.

shared by all the major cultural traditions, which, if construed in an enlightened manner, may be capable of sustaining universal standards of human rights. An-na'im sees such a golden rule in the principle of reciprocity, according to which 'universal human rights are those which a cultural tradition would claim for its own members and must therefore concede to members of other traditions if it is to expect reciprocal treatment from the others'.[279] For example, the problem with historical Shari'a is that it excludes women and non-Muslims from the application of this principle. Thus, a reform or reconstruction of Shari'a is needed, which must satisfy two conditions if it is to be effective in changing Muslim attitudes and policies: first, constructing the other person in such a way as to encompass all human beings, regardless of gender, religion, race or language, must be valid and credible from the Islamic point of view also; secondly, other cultural and religious traditions must undertake a similar process of enlightened construction.[280]

The method proposed for such 'Islamic reformation' is based on an evolutionary approach to Islamic sources that looks into the specific historical context within which Shari'a was created out of the original sources of Islam by the founding jurists of the eighth and ninth centuries. In the light of such a context, a restricted construction of the other was probably justified. But this is no longer so. On the contrary, in the present different context there is, within Islam, full justification for a more enlightened view. Following the teachings of *Ustadh* Mahmoud, An-na'im shows that a close examination of the content of the Qur'an and Sunna reveals two levels or stages of the message of Islam, one of the earlier Mecca period and the other of the subsequent Medina stage. The earlier message of Mecca is the eternal and fundamental message of Islam, and it emphasizes the inherent dignity of all human beings, regardless of gender, religious belief, or race. Under the historical conditions of the seventh century (the Medina stage) this message was considered too advanced, was suspended, and its implementation postponed until appropriate circumstances would emerge in the future. The time and context, says An-na'im, are now ripe for it.

Far be it for me to evaluate the specific validity of this proposal within Islamic culture. What I find remarkable about it is the attempt to transform the Western conception of human rights into a cross-cultural one that vindicates Islamic legitimacy rather than relinquishing it. In abstract and from the outside, it is difficult to judge whether a religious or a secularist approach is more likely to succeed in an Islamic-based cross-cultural dialogue on human rights. However, bearing in mind that Western human rights are the expression of a profound, albeit incomplete, process of secularization which is not comparable to anything in Islamic culture, I would be inclined to suggest that, in the Muslim context, the mobilizing energy needed for a cosmopolitan project of human rights will be more easily generated within a religious framework. If so, An-na'im's approach is very promising. But its relevance is more general, in that it is a true *exemplar* of diatopical hermeneutics, albeit conducted with unequal consistency. In my view,

[279]   An-na'im, 1990, p 164.
[280]   An-na'im, 1990, p 165.

An-na'im accepts the idea of universal human rights too readily and acritically. Besides, although he conditions the success of his cross-cultural project to a symmetrical reconstruction of rights on the part of the other cultures with which Islam entertains dialogue, in actual fact he does not go very far in relation to the Western conception of human rights. Furthermore, even though he subscribes to an evolutionary approach and is quite attentive to the historical context of Islamic traditions, An-na'im becomes surprisingly ahistorical and naïvely universalist as far as the Universal Declaration goes. But he should not be heavily charged on this account. Diatopical hermeneutics is not a task for a single person writing within a single culture. It requires not only a different kind of knowledge, but also a different process of knowledge creation. It requires a production of knowledge that must be collective, interactive, intersubjective and networked.

7.6.4 CULTURAL IMPERIALISM AND THE POSSIBILITY OF COUNTER-HEGEMONY

An idealist conception of cross-cultural dialogue will easily forget that such a dialogue is only made possible by the temporary simultaneity of two different contemporaneities: the one of social action (the encounter among the partners converging in the dialogue) and that of social meaning and intelligibility (the cultures and traditions they bring to the encounter). The partners in the dialogue are contemporaneous; but so are each of them and the historical tradition of their respective cultures that brings them *now* together into dialogue. The latter form of contemporaneity tends to subvert or obstruct the former, whenever to be contemporaneous with one's past implies the denial of the other as being entitled to be contemporaneous with a past of his/her own. This is most likely the case when the different cultures involved in the dialogue share a past of interlocked unequal exchanges. What are the possibilities for a cross-cultural dialogue when one of the cultures *in presence* has itself been moulded by massive and long-lasting violations of human rights perpetrated in the name of the other culture? When cultures share such a past, the present they share at the moment of starting the dialogue is at best a *quid pro quo* and at worst a fraud. The cultural dilemma is the following: since in the past the dominant culture rendered unpronounceable some of the aspirations of the subordinate culture to human dignity, is it now possible to pronounce them in the cross-cultural dialogue without thereby further justifying and even reinforcing their unpronounceability?

Cultural imperialism and the destruction of cultures and knowledges that results from it (which I call epistemicide) are part of the historical trajectory of Western modernity. After centuries of unequal cultural exchanges, is equal treatment of cultures fair? Is it necessary to render some aspirations of Western culture unpronounceable in order to make room for the pronounceability of other aspirations of other cultures? Paradoxically – and contrary to hegemonic discourse – it is precisely in the field of human rights that Western culture must learn from the South, if the false universality that it attributed to human rights in the imperial context is to be converted into the new universality of cosmopolitanism in a cross-cultural dialogue.

Learning from the South is only a starting point, and it may actually be a false starting point if it is not borne in mind that the North has been actively unlearning the South all along. As Said has frequently pointed out, the imperial context brutalizes both the victim and the victimizer, and induces in the dominant as well as in the dominated culture 'not just assent and loyalty but an unusually rarified sense of the sources from which the culture really springs and in what complicating circumstances its monuments derive'.[281] Monuments have, indeed, messy origins. Viewing the pyramids, Ali Shariati observed once:

> 'I felt so much hatred toward the great monuments of civilization which throughout history were praised upon the bones of my predecessors! My predecessors also built the Great Wall of China. Those who could not carry the loads were crushed under the heavy stones and put into the walls with the stones. This was how all the great monuments of civilization were constructed – at the expense of the flesh and blood of my predecessors'.[282]

In my view, the same could be said about human rights as one of the greatest monuments of Western civilization. The clean, clear-cut, ahistorical formulations to which they have lent themselves hide their messy origins, ranging from the genocides of European expansion, to the Thermidor and the Holocaust. But this rarification of cultures occurs in the subordinate cultures as well, as Said has shown:

> 'Young Arabs and Muslims today are taught to venerate the classics of their religion and thought, not to be critical, not to view what they read of, say, Abbasid or *nahda* literature as alloyed with all kinds of political contests. Only very occasionally does a critic and a poet like Adonis, the brilliant contemporary Syrian writer, come along and say openly that readings of *turath* in the Arab world today enforce a rigid authoritarianism and literalism which have the effect of killing the spirit and obliterating criticism'.[283]

To recognize the reciprocal impoverishment of victim and victimizer alike, however asymmetrical, is the most basic condition for a cross-cultural dialogue.[284] Only the knowledge of history permits us to act independently of history. Scrutiny into the relationships between victim and victimizer cautions us against too strict distinctions among cultures, a caution that is particularly relevant in the case of the dominant culture.

---

[281] Said, 1993, p 37. Gilroy, 1993, criticizes the 'overintegrated conceptions of pure and homogeneous cultures which mean that black political struggles are construed as somehow automatically *expressive of* the national or ethnic differences with which they are associated' (p 31).

[282] Shariati, 1982, p 19.

[283] Said, 1993, p 38.

[284] The cross-cultural reconstruction of human rights is particularly problematic in the cases in which the reciprocal impoverishment of victim and victimizer has occurred within an historical process of extremely brutal asymmetries as, for instance, in the case of 'contacts' between Western culture and the cultures of indigenous people. On North American Indians, see Zion, 1992; specifically on Canadian aboriginal peoples, A McChesney, 1992; on Brazilian Indians, M Cunha, 1992; on Australian indigenous peoples, P Hyndman, 1992; on the Sami people in Scandinavia, T Svensson, 1992.

According to Pieterse, Western culture is neither what it seems, nor what Westerners tend to think it is: 'What is held to be European culture or civilization is genealogically not necessarily or strictly European'.[285] It is a cultural synthesis of many elements, and currents, many of them non-European. Bernal has undertaken a deconstruction of the concepts of 'classical civilization' to show its non-European foundations, the contributions of Egypt and Africa, Semitic and Phoenecian civilizations, Mesopotamia and Persia, India and China, regarding language, art, knowledge, religion and material culture. He also shows how these Afro-Asiatic roots of Ancient Greece were denied by nineteenth-century European racism and anti-Semitism.[286]

In line with this inquiry, the messy origins of human rights, as a monument of Western culture, can be seen not only in the imperial and domestic domination they once justified, but also in their original composite character as cultural artifacts. The presuppositions of human rights, which were indicated above in their clear-cut, Enlightenment, rational formulations, echo vibrations of other cultures and their historical roots reach far beyond Europe. The cross-cultural dialogue must start from the assumption that cultures have always been cross-cultural; but also with the understanding that exchanges and interpenetrations have always been very unequal and inherently hostile to the cosmopolitan dialogue that is here being argued for. Ultimately, the question is whether it is possible to construct a post-imperial conception of human rights. Put differently, the question is whether the vocabulary or the script of human rights is so crowded with hegemonic meanings as to exclude the possibility of counter-hegemonic meanings. Although I am fully aware of the almost insurmountable barriers, I give a positive answer to my basic question. In the following I try to specify the conditions under which the possibility of counter-hegemony can be actualized.

7.6.5 Human rights as an emancipatory script

The history of human rights is complex and contradictory. Its imperial dimension, decisive as it may be, is not exclusive. In the European context, human rights were at the core of the emancipatory developments of modern law analyzed in Chapter Two – from the reception of Roman law to rationalist natural law and the theories of the social contract. Conceptually, therefore, human rights symbolize the highest emancipatory consciousness of modern law and politics, and are inherently Utopian. They were culturally constructed at a moment in which law was at the core of the conversation of humankind, and they reinforced and expanded that position by being themselves at the core of the emancipatory dimension of modern law.

---

[285] Pieterse, 1989, p 369.
[286] Bernal, 1987.

However, the fact that their historical deployment in political practice is tainted with blood illustrates cogently the dialectics of regulation and emancipation in the paradigm of modernity. Any cursory analysis of human rights across generations will show beyond any doubt that they were put at the service of the regulatory needs of the state. But they were also the framework for the progressive politics of the popular classes, whose struggles in fact contributed greatly toward all the major advances in human rights politics. Being an inherently contested terrain, human rights were not monolithically conceived. On the contrary, within the European context there were many different conceptions fighting for hegemony – namely the liberal and the socialist, the reformist and the revolutionary conceptions.

The consolidation of the liberal state from the mid-nineteenth century onwards brought a renewed cogency to the idea of human rights, in that they were conceived then as a weapon against the state, to keep it under democratic control and prevent the authoritarian hubris. This dimension of human rights struggles has since prevailed. The gradual incorporation of human rights policies within state action was part of a broader political process of social incorporation. Such a process was, however, highly ambivalent because, due to the conversion of modern law into a monopoly of the state, the rights against the state were granted by the state itself. When the so-called second generation of human rights – ie, economic and social rights entered the political agenda, the ambivalence of the process became even more apparent, because the implementation of such rights depended on the positive action of the state. The oppositional strength of human rights struggles was thus tailored to fit the boundaries and capabilities of state action.

But, at any given moment, the performance of regulatory functions by human rights policies was but the crystallization of a conflict with the oppositional, progressive struggles of the popular classes fighting for the effective enforcement of existing rights, the expansion of the reciprocity range of existing rights – as in the laws of suffrage – and, finally and foremost, the promulgation of new rights. The emancipatory energy of human rights struggles has always lain in the ever-incomplete list of granted rights and, consequently, in the legitimacy of the claim to new rights. The open-endedness of human rights struggles has also kept their Utopian character alive. For more than a century this utopia was a luxury of the core countries. Vast colonial populations – including populations subjected to internal colonialism, like African-Americans in the South of the US and Native Americans throughout the continent – were left out of the principle of reciprocity, at first because they were not considered full human beings, and later on because they were not considered civilized (*assimilados*). Thus, the incorporation of labour rights in European legal systems did not collide with the existence of the institution of forced labour in Africa until the 1940s.

The quest for a counter-hegemonic politics of human rights amounts to asking if and how it is possible to recuperate the emancipatory potential and the Utopian character of human rights. After such a prolonged and violent period of imperial domination, can human rights still adequately represent human suffering across the world? Are they still part of the conversation of humankind? Is it possible to speak and act progressively in the name of human rights? My answer is a qualified 'yes'. Yes, it is possible, but the conditions are stringent. It is my contention that, once cross-culturally reconstructed, human rights are one of the most powerful factors in bringing about the unthinking of modern law and politics, thereby generating the emancipatory energies necessary to face the challenges of the new times ahead. Human rights are the privileged ground upon which the uncoupling of law from the state and the recoupling of law with polity and revolution must be pursued on a global scale. Why should human rights be elected as the language and code of the emancipatory conversation of humankind on a global scale, rather than any other principle of human dignity found in any of the major world cultures? The answer epitomizes the dilemmatic situation we are in.

The subaltern cosmopolitan politics I have been calling for cannot occur but in an imperial context, though hopefully carrying with itself the transition toward a post-imperial context. To a certain extent it will therefore be, of necessity, a product of the empire. One of the main political features of the empire has been to organize the world system in a system of sovereign states, the so-called interstate system. The same modern state form has been accordingly ascribed to the most diverse nations and cultures. In a more or less restricted or fraudulent manner, human rights discourse was incorporated into the constitution of virtually all the nation-states across the globe. Parallel to this development, an international regime of human rights gradually emerged in the postwar period, and most members of the interstate system subscribed to it.

A post-imperial cosmopolitan politics must start from what exists. What exists is, on the one hand, the nation-state as the still prevalent political form vis-à-vis which human rights politics seems to be the most adequate one to trim off the excesses of authoritarian rule; on the other hand, an interstate system that has adopted human rights as a kind of international code of moral conduct. The contradictions in the regulatory functions of human rights must therefore be taken as the starting point for an emancipatory politics. Because they are experienced worldwide, albeit very differently, such contradictions bear the seeds of translocal intelligibility and the formation of cosmopolitan global coalitions. In their conventional conception, human rights are falsely universal because they are oblivious to the inequalities in the world system, the double standards, the multiple forms of gender domination and the different ways (and degrees) in which human rights are embedded in different cultures. It is up to cosmopolitan politics to transform such false universality into the new universality of cosmopolitanism. Human rights are a political Esperanto, which cosmopolitan politics must transform into a network of mutually intelligible native languages.

In what follows, I explore the three conditions that, to my mind, are crucial for such a transformation to take place. First, I discuss the issue of global subjects, ie, the actors likely to be either responsible for or the beneficiaries of a cosmopolitan human rights discourse and practice at the global level. Secondly, I tackle the difficult question of cultural relativity and the possibilities for a cross-cultural reconstruction of human rights. Thirdly, I deal with the conception of the world system as a single human rights field.

7.6.5.1   *Global subjects*

The nation-states will remain, in the foreseeable future, a major focus of human rights struggles, both as violators and as promoters-guarantors of human rights. However, in light of recent changes in the principle of sovereignty, whose erosion is highly selective and tends to be hostile mainly to the interests of the popular classes, it is imperative to challenge the nation-states and the monopoly of international legal subjectivity in order to make room for more and more powerful global advocacy by human rights non-governmental organizations. Related both to increasing inequalities in the world system and to the activities of TNCs, the most serious violations of human rights have nowadays a distinctive global dimension. To that extent, violations of human rights are what I call a localized globalism, that is to say, the locally specific and organized impact of global capital operations. A clear example of this is the detrimental – and often disastrous – effects of neo-liberal globalization on civil and social rights in countries subject to 'structural adjustment' programmes. For instance, in his recent analysis of the impact of neo-liberal globalization on East Asia, Yash Ghai concludes that '[i]t is evident that human rights have not fared well by economic globalization' in the region, since, despite the fact that 'economic growth has raised standards of education, health and nutrition', 'these benefits have not accrued to all, certainly not to all equally. The market has created large disparities of wealth and income. In the midst of incredible affluence, there is appalling poverty', as demonstrated by the effects of marketization in China.[287]

States – when they are not themselves the violators of human rights – are relatively impotent to counteract human rights violations originated in the operation of the global economy – and to counteract localized globalisms in general. As Falk has stressed: 'Most states, even when allowedly concerned about human rights, often lack capability and credibility, having too much to hide themselves and generally subordinating and eroding the credibility of their human rights concerns by according priority to geo-politics'.[288] By the same token, Falk insists, the state is too small to constitute a protective enterprise against localized globalism, 'in the sense that it cannot extend its authority far or effectively enough to control the flow of entropic forces in the world or to fashion suitable regimes for handling global scale problems'.[289] If this is the case, then it is imperative to strengthen the extant forms of global advocacy and promotion and protection of human rights – as well as to create new ones.

[287]   Ghai, 1999, p 258.
[288]   Falk, 1992, p 55.
[289]   Falk, 1992, p 55. See also Falk, Kirn and Mendlowitz, 1982.

In the postwar period, advocacy of human rights has been the most prominent field of the activities of transnational NGOs, first in Europe and the US, and then, in the 1970s and 1980s, in Latin America and Asia, with Africa lagging behind.[290] The progressive roles they have been playing, both nationally and globally, have been widely recognized, and indeed the emergence of a cosmopolitan consciousness on human rights must be largely credited to them. Their brave denunciation of massive and gross violations of human rights under Latin American dictatorships in the 1970s and early 1980s is particularly admirable, in view of the intimidations, reprisals and all kinds of abuses inflicted on their members.[291]

Much of the efficacy of NGOs in the future will depend on their capacity to network grievances and struggles across the globe. The obstacles are gigantic, however. To begin with, and in line with what I have already said on global agency in general above, human rights NGOs are very heterogeneous politically and socially. While some operate securely in core democratic countries, others operate at great risk in peripheral authoritarian countries.[292] While some are deeply embedded in grassroots movements, others are external missions or services provided by committed experts or intellectuals. While some are crisis-oriented, focusing on violations and disregarding the analysis of the underlying causes of repression, others focus instead on the understanding of structural causes and seek wide-range institutional transformation. While some subscribe to a liberal, individualistic conception of human rights, others promote a socialist conception of human rights. In sum, there are profound positional, organizational and ideological differences among human rights NGOs. 'An NGO established in the Western world only to deal with the problem of political prisoners', says Shepherd, 'operates within the individualist paradigm and performs a limited service. It is not comparable to an NGO that, in a Third World state, supplies support to a liberation movement. One seeks amelioration while the other is aimed at revolutionary change'.[293]

Within the Third World itself, the diversity is also enormous. In Africa, Shivji criticizes African NGOs for not addressing the issue of imperialism, for collaborating with non-democratic states and for distancing themselves from the grassroots movements: 'African NGOs that are set up, it would seem, are institutional mechanisms by which to obtain foreign funds: they are what might be called FFUNGOS (foreign funded NGOs) rather than grass-roots organizations of the intellectuals and the people to struggle for rights'.[294]

---

[290]   K Sikkink, 1992.
[291]   On the 'Latin American human rights network', see Sikkink, 1996 and Keck and Sikkink, 1998.
[292]   On the unbalanced regional distribution of NGO activity in the world system, see Blaser, 1985. See also Nanda, Scarritt and Shepherd, Jr, 1981.
[293]   Shepherd, 1985, p 214. See also Nanda, Scarritt and Shepherd, Jr, 1981, Part 3.
[294]   Shivji, 1989, p 61.

In Latin America,[295] but also in Asia[296] and elsewhere, the profound differences among NGOs are particularly striking in the field of legal services. Some of them focus exclusively on individual legal conflicts purported to be apolitical, and accept uncritically the laws and the judicial institutions within which they operate. This is still the case, for instance (despite notable exceptions), of most NGOs receiving funds from such sources as the Ford Foundation – which, as a recent survey of the law-related work of its grantees claims explicitly, since the mid-1990s has concentrated its support on NGOs devoted to delivering legal services.[297] Others, on the contrary, perform alternative legal services, grounded on non-liberal assumptions, inasmuch as they conceive law as politics, give priority to public interest or – as Baxi has called it, 'social action litigation'[298] – promote forms of collective citizenship, fight for legal and institutional transformation, and, in general, organize the legal services as part of broader social and political emancipatory movements.

As will become clear below, the cosmopolitan politics of human rights I am proposing here is part of much broader political transformations called for in the period of paradigmatic transition we are now entering. In such a context, the demands on global subjectivities and coalitions are very high, and run along the following lines. First, the cross-cultural reconstruction of human rights I am arguing for is premised upon the centrality of the link between local embeddedness and grassroots relevance and organization, on the one hand, and translocal intelligibility and global repercussion, on the other. Secondly, in the paradigmatic transition, social and political activism must be grounded on a deep archeological understanding of Western modernity and its imperial expansion throughout the world. The unthinking of dominant institutional and normative practices and discourses thus produced will open the cosmopolitan legal field upon which new, paradigmatic human rights can be reinvented, adequate to the emancipatory traversing of the paradigmatic transition. Finally, the new legal status of local, national and global cosmopolitan coalitions must be inscribed both in domestic and international law. The dispersal and multiplication of citizenship in different social fields is premised upon the emergence of new subjects besides the monolithic liberal individual and state. Herein lies the ideal of a new polity and civil society. The critique I have levelled against civil society as the symmetrical counterpart of the nation-state opens the space for a new conception of civil society, a global civil society thought of as the global networking of subaltern cosmopolitan social practices. As I will explain in greater detail in Chapter Nine, there are clear signs and examples of the emergence of subaltern cosmopolitanism that bear directly on the field of human rights.

---

[295]   See, among others, Rojas, 1986.
[296]   See, among others, Lev, 1990. See also, for India, Baxi, 1982; Galanter, 1991.
[297]   McClymont and Golub, 2000.
[298]   Baxi, 1982.

7.6.5.2   *Cross-cultural reconstruction*

In the transition from imperial to post-imperial conditions, the cross-cultural reconstruction of human rights must involve some measure of *mestizaje*. *Mestizaje* operates through the creation of new constellations of meaning, which are truly unrecognizable or blasphemous in light of their constitutive fragments. *Mestizaje* resides in the destruction of the logic that presides over the formation of each of its fragments, and in the construction of a new logic. What An-na'im has attempted for Islamic culture vis-à-vis Western culture – ie, re-reading the Islamic tradition in such a way that the latter build bridges with the Western culture – must be also attempted for Western culture vis-à-vis all the other major world cultures – ie, re-reading the Western culture as a particular culture whose own intelligibility calls for the recognition of alternative cultural meanings and conceptions of human dignity.

The general profile of such *mestizaje* must be provided by the following orientations. First, the peculiarity of Western experience must be fully recognized and historically contextualized. For instance, the idea of generations of human rights – the first generation consisting of civil and political rights, the second of economic and social rights, etc – has some plausibility as a reading of the historical experience of some core European countries, but makes no sense whatsoever elsewhere, not even in Southern Europe. Secondly, the possessive individualism that bedevils the Western conception of human rights must be fully recognized, and the incompleteness and bias of such a conception must be addressed and transcended through the acceptance of collective rights. In this context, the right to self-determination must be given a new prominence (more on this below). Thirdly, the precedence given to the individual to the detriment of the community, and to rights to the detriment of duties in the Western conception of human rights, has destroyed the capacity for compassion and fellow feeling, and has blocked the development of a principle of responsibility capable of adequately accounting for massive human starvation and suffering and ecological depredation on a global scale. Neither is humankind a mere sum of free and autonomous individuals nor is human nature totally separable from nature as a whole. Nature is the second nature of society; to apply to nature the liberal symmetry between rights and duties is an invitation to ecocide. Even if we grant that it has no rights, nature is entitled to our duty to secure its sustainability – which is also our sustainability as a global community. Fourthly, cross-cultural reconstruction must be fully aware of the asymmetries among the different historical routes into modernity and of all the different legal cultures existing in the world. The different routes into modernity that different regions and countries took explain, for instance, why the issue of universalism/particularism of human rights is so important in Africa and Asia, but not in Latin America. They also explain, in part at least, why core countries with specific, non-Western, legal cultures, which have undergone top-down, externally induced modernization, like Japan, tend to adopt blatantly opportunistic policies vis-à-vis human rights with no major political costs. They will, finally, help to explain why post-colonial states in Africa have ended up destroying communal forms of life and environment sustainability, without providing the modern alternatives that were available, in part at least, to the European states.

There is a growing and vibrant literature on the potential of cultural dialogue and crossbreeding as a means to a truly cosmopolitan discourse and practice of human rights. For example, along the same lines that I have been arguing, Makau Mutua has recently claimed that '[t]he relentless efforts to universalize an essentially European corpus of human rights through Western crusades cannot succeed'. Thus,

> '[t]he critiques of the corpus from Africans, Asians, Muslims, Hindus, and a host of critical thinkers from around the world are the one avenue through which human rights can be redeemed and truly universalised. This multiculturalization of the corpus could be attempted in a number of areas: balancing between individual and group rights, giving more substance to social and economic rights, relating rights to duties, and addressing the relationship between the corpus and economic systems'.[299]

My quest for a cross-cultural reconstruction of human rights is grounded on the idea that the lack of cultural legitimacy is one of the major causes of violations of human rights. As it stands now, the global human rights regime is overly embedded in Western culture, and appears as relatively foreign or exotic to other cultures. In order to become more acceptable to other cultures, it may have to be rewritten.[300] This is, as I am well aware, a highly controversial position. Many authors think that the question of a cross-cultural conception of human rights is a false problem. Like Donnelly, whose position I have already cited,[301] Howard also maintains that human rights principles are very recent and have been specifically designed to deal with the advent of the nation-state and to curb its power.[302] Since the nation-state is today the central actor on the contemporary political stage, human rights principles are applicable around the globe wherever the nation-state has entrenched itself. From a very different perspective, the Marxist conception of human rights tends to minimize the interest of cross-cultural reconstruction since, according to it, the most massive and serious violations of human rights have been directly related to the impositions of capitalist development, most recently the international debt crisis and structural adjustment.[303]

In my analytical framework, all these structural factors are of the utmost importance in understanding the map of human rights violations across recent history and across the globe. It seems to me, however, that cultural factors are equally decisive, at least from the perspective of a social action that aims at understanding social apathy or indifference, indignation or revolt, vis-à-vis violations of human rights, as a first step to promote vigorous social mobilization against such violations. Culture is, after all, where structure and agency meet. Lindholm is right when he asserts 'that cultural determinants shape and constrain people's understanding and value commitments,

---

[299]   Mutua, 2001, p 243.
[300]   In the same sense, An-na'im, 1992, pp 1–43.
[301]   Donnelly, 1989, pp 109–124.
[302]   Howard, 1992.
[303]   See Lindholm, 1992. Two sophisticated discussions on human rights from a Marxist perspective are in L Oliveira, 1989; R Nordahl, 1992.

and in particular their reasons for action and inaction, even when structural explanations apply and people are trapped by unintended consequences and impersonal social forces'. According to him, therefore, '[t]he study of the cultural legitimacy of human rights is one major concern, because human rights violations and compliance spring from human action informed by cultural determinants'.[304] Lindholm's approach to cross-cultural reconstruction of human rights is nonetheless problematic. It consists in re-interpreting the Universal Declaration of 1948 as evolving from specific, global, societal circumstances and as embodying a situated geo-political moral rationality which does not depend on any particular theology or metaphysics, and which, for that reason, can be cross-culturally appropriated. Specifically in relation to the classical Western tradition – ie, natural rights theory – he maintains, the '"official" UN foundation of the internationally acknowledged system of human rights is a more complex, more realistic, and more "open-ended" scheme of justification'.[305] In my judgment, cultural disembeddedness is not a prudent strategy for a cross-cultural dialogue where, on the contrary, the specificity of the different cultures must be fully acknowledged. With the best of intentions, Lindholm may end up presenting as the profile of a global human rights culture what, in reality, is nothing more than a reductionist version of Western culture.

As a final note on the guiding principles of cross-cultural reconstruction of human rights, let us be reminded that diatopical hermeneutics is an exercise in cultural tolerance. In order to maximize its efficacy, it must privilege, in each individual culture, the versions that are in themselves most tolerant, more open-ended, and promote wider ranges of reciprocity. That cultures are not monolithic entities, and allow for much internal differentiation and confrontation, cannot be sufficiently emphasized. Openness toward other cultures is often to be found in non-hegemonic, marginal, oppositional, transgressive versions that, because they are more distant from the cultural core, evolve at the borders, that twilight zone where cultures mix and give rise to intercultural symbolic universes. Since within Western culture the liberal conception of human rights – itself not monolithic – has been hegemonic by far, it may not be the ideal starting point for a cross-cultural dialogue. Precedence should perhaps be given to non-hegemonic conceptions instead. For instance, given its critique of property rights and its notion of the inherently restricted range of reciprocity of all the other rights in capitalist societies, the Marxist version of human rights may offer a partial contribution to the cross-cultural dialogue, particularly as regards the cultural politics of rights in peripheral countries or regions of the world system facing the cruel reality of mass starvation and economic immiseration. On the other hand, communitarian, personalist and feminist conceptions of human rights may contribute even more decisively toward a new understanding of collective or group rights. In this respect, global advocacy of indigenous peoples and ethnic minorities rights, and the conceptions of self-determination and cultural identity that have evolved therefrom, may also be of

---

[304]   Lindholm, 1992, p 391.
[305]   Lindholm, 1992, p 397.

importance. Radical social democratic conceptions of human rights also provide a rich framework for the legal and political linkages between individuals and the different communities they belong to, particularly at a moment in which the state provision of trust seems to be declining. The ecological conceptions of human rights – specifically the eco-socialist conceptions – furnish the intellectual parameters for the incorporation of nature in a politics of rights *and* duties. Finally, in connection with the politics of duties, participatory democracy conceptions of human rights should be assigned the important task of showing that duties vis-à-vis communities or nature must be assumed democratically, lest they become subterfuges for old or new tyrannies.

7.6.5.3 *The world system as a single human rights field*

As I have already indicated, states continue to be both the major violators and guarantors of human rights, and so they will also continue to be a major focus of human rights struggles. However, the conditions underlying both violations and guarantees of human rights seem to be increasingly beyond the reach of the nation-state. The interstate system has for a long time hidden the workings of the world system. Recent transformations in the world system, some of which I have been analysing in this chapter, have made such occultation increasingly unconvincing. A new approach to human rights is thus needed to confront the new globally organized violations, no matter how locally they are felt, and to explore possible new opportunities to mount global struggles against them. This topic deserves special attention and, for that reason, I deal with it separately in the following.

7.6.6 HUMAN RIGHTS, DEVELOPMENT AND PARADIGMATIC TRANSITION

If lack of cultural legitimacy is today one of the major causes of human rights violations in the world, the other is the unequal exchanges that constitute the capitalist world economy and world system. People are not poor, they are impoverished; they do not starve, they are starved; they are not marginal, they are marginalized; they are not victims, they are victimized. With its exclusive reliance on capitalist accumulation, market relations and property rights, the world capitalist economy is structurally unjust, in the sense that its normal operation breeds social injustice both internally and internationally.

The interstate system and the nation-states have here played a decisive double role, both in guaranteeing the smooth operation of the capitalist economy, and in correcting some of its grossest excesses. I have been arguing in this chapter that, in light of worldwide changes in capitalist accumulation in the last three decades, the first role of the state has become a political imperative of the highest priority – which marks the rise of business's welfare state – while the second role has been eroding – thus bringing about the crisis of people's welfare state. Therefore, as the last legal form of apartheid fades away in South Africa, a new global social apartheid is emerging between rich countries and poor countries, and, within the national societies, between the rich and the poor. This situation, however novel in some of its features, has been known for a long time in the peripheral and semi-peripheral countries. The postwar period, which early on became also the post-colonial period, witnessed the simultaneous emergence of an expanded interstate system, comprising countries and sovereign states of very unequal development, and a global regime of human rights, a moral and legal yardstick for political processes across the interstate system.

The economic, social, political and cultural conditions for the effective enforcement of this new normative consensus were not stipulated – they were left to the states – nor was the extent to which the favourable conditions in some countries related to the unfavourable conditions in others ever subject to serious scrutiny. Therefore, the universality of human rights was superimposed not only on different cultures connected and disconnected by a long past of unequal exchanges (cultural imperialism), but also on different states and societies tied together by unequal relations of imperialism, neo-colonialism, and geo-politics – the Cold War, areas of influence, patron-client relationships, etc.

Under these circumstances, it should come as no surprise that the question of the articulation between human rights and development issues would sooner or later be raised. Indeed, for the last forty years, throughout the periphery and semi-periphery of the world system this question has been seen in two contradictory ways: on the one hand, development, or rather, lack of development, has been seen as an excuse for the violation of human rights; on the other, development has been considered a human right in and of itself. The first perspective was particularly popular in the 1960s and 1970s in Latin American countries under military dictatorship, and is now being raised in some Asian countries, particularly in China. The second has been informing the African debate on human rights with particular cogency. A brief reference to each of these perspectives is in order at this juncture.

7.6.6.1 *Trade-off between development and human rights*

The idea that, in order to achieve rapid development, it is necessary to accept short-run and even medium-run sacrifices of human rights lurked behind the conventional theories on 'law and development' and 'law and modernization' of the 1960s and the 1970s – indeed, to such an extent that it might be considered to have been the reigning orthodoxy of the times, at least in Latin America.

The democratic transitions of the 1980s and 1990s challenged this idea, but probably less radically than might have appeared. In fact, the critique was mainly focused on civil and political rights, leaving aside economic and social rights, which were considered merely as programmatic principles to become enforceable rights only inasmuch as economic and social development allowed for them. In recent years, incorporated in the conventional wisdom of the new wave of 'law and development' theories, the idea of the trade-off between development and human rights has assumed a new prominence in the Asian context – China, Malaysia, Indonesia, Thailand, and also India and Bangladesh.[306]

According to Donnelly, the idea of a trade-off between development and human rights has been advocated in three main forms: the needs trade-off; the equality trade-off, and the liberty trade-off.[307] The needs trade-off implies that, rather than devoting scarce resources to social programmes that satisfy basic human needs, relatively high levels of absolute poverty must be accepted in order to maximize investment. According to the equality trade-off, inequality of income distribution is a necessary condition for a rapid transition from a traditional economy (both with low income and low income inequality) to a modern economy. In terms of the liberty trade-off, the exercise of civil and political freedoms may create social unrest, exacerbate labour activism, obstruct necessary but unpopular sacrifices, all of which are susceptible of disrupting the development plan, and must for that reason be temporarily suspended. Underlying all these trade-offs is the idea that the Western model of human rights is a luxury that developing countries cannot afford, at least for a while.

Supported by abundant scholarship produced mainly in the 1960s and 1970s, the idea of trade-offs has been expounded by many peripheral and semi-peripheral states. Indeed, as a recent collection on the topic shows, states in East Asia have oftentimes embraced such view, which, coupled with the argument of incommensurable cultural difference, have promoted the idea of 'East Asian exceptionalism' vis-à-vis the implementation of democracy and human rights.[308] But it has also found some of its most dedicated supporters among TNCs. Given the new prominence of TNCs, and the growing impact of their operations on human rights, a brief reference to their conception of the trade-offs is justified. It is today widely recognized that the activities of TNCs often result in direct or indirect violations of civil, political, economic and social rights.[309] To the extent that their (export-oriented) policies contribute to increasing unemployment, food and nutrition shortages, high levels of unmanageable urbanization and the siphoning off of natural resources to generate foreign exchange, TNCs may be said to violate human rights indirectly in the 'host countries'. But, in many instances, they violate the human rights directly, with the connivance of the host states:

'by pursuing policies which violate freedom of association (opposition to unionization), which perpetuate racial discrimination (support for apartheid) and which may result in genocide (support for policies which result in destruction of aboriginal peoples), by

---

[306] On this topic and in general on 'the East Asian challenge to human rights', see lastly Bauer and Bell (eds), 1999.

[307] Donnelly, 1989, p 164.

[308] Donnelly, 1989; Ghai, 1993a and Bauer and Bell (eds), 1999.

[309] See Lippman, 1985; T Donaldson, 1989. A critique of Donaldson is in G Brenkert, 1992.

engaging in activities harmful to the health and welfare of individuals (marketing toxic drugs) and by interfering with the civil and political freedom of individuals (subsidization of repressive regimes and support for the overthrow of regimes perceived as antimultinational)'.[310]

When forced to respond to public criticism against some of these forms of active violation of human rights, and whenever incapable of negating violations that are far too obvious, TNCs argue in their own defence that the activities under scrutiny: (1) create employment opportunities and integrate disadvantaged groups in the economy; (2) help to develop a technological elite that can act as a force for social change; (3) introduce liberal ideas of equal opportunity and market efficiency that will generate social welfare in the future; (4) integrate the host country in world politics and put pressure on the government to act as a responsible member of the international community; (5) increase the leverage of the democratic parent country of the multinational corporation upon the host government.[311] As can be easily observed, all these lines of defence echo the idea of trade-off in one way or another.

Donnelly has presented a forceful critique of the idea of trade-offs. To his way of thinking, trade-offs are almost always unnecessary and often positively harmful to both development and human rights.[312] Comparing the development experiences of Brazil ('the tragedy of success') and South Korea ('a more successful success story'), he concludes for the superiority of the 'redistribution first' over the 'growth first' strategy. In his view, the latter strategy, which has lain at the heart of conventional wisdom, implies major sacrifices for literally hundreds of millions of people: 'We should be particularly wary of tradeoff arguments in environments of despotism and oligarchy, for under such conditions "tradeoffs" tend to involve people *being* sacrificed, rather than *making* sacrifices... The standard arguments for economic tradeoffs require magnified sacrifices from those least able to sacrifice'.[313] After reviewing the debate on trade-offs, Nanda also concludes that '[a]lthough the debate on human rights-economic development tradeoffs is likely to continue, it seems fair to observe that the proponents of economic growth at the cost of civil and political liberties have failed to prove the soundness of their position'.[314]

In recent years, this conventional wisdom dating from the 1960s has been re-invigorated by the neo-liberal economic development model put forward by international agencies like the World Bank and the IMF in the context of structural adjustment and foreign debt crisis, but with a twist in relation to the original formulation: the 'growth first' strategy must be made compatible with democratic rule – the so-called 'political conditionally'. This means basically that gross violations of economic and social rights

[310]   Lippman, 1985, p 254.
[311]   Lippman, 1985, p 262.
[312]   Donnelly, 1989, p 166.
[313]   Donnelly, 1989, p 180.
[314]   Nanda, 1985, p 295.

are to be tolerated as a trade-off for a certain measure of compliance with civil and political rights. Such is the compromise built into the neoliberal creed in its newest version. This has led Baxi recently, in his assessment of 'the future of human rights', to assert that the paradigm of the Universal Declaration of Human Rights is 'steadily, but surely, supplanted by that of trade-related, market-friendly human rights'.[315] The trade-off inherent in the neoliberal paradigm consists, for him, in the demand the latter makes that we 'shed the fetishism of human rights and appreciate that in the absence of economic development human rights have no future at all'.[316]

Two interrelated ideas guarantee the global reach of the neoliberal view of rights. On the one hand, peripheral and semi-peripheral countries must adopt the principle of the generations of human rights – civil and political rights first, economic and social rights later – followed by core countries since the mid-nineteenth century. On the other hand, core countries are suffering from an overload of economic and social rights derived from the fact that the levels that were reached in the last two or three decades were the product of an irreproducible conjuncture. Neither in the core nor certainly in the periphery or semi-periphery will the conditions ever again materialize that make that kind of social welfare boom possible.

The fraudulent character of this 'wisdom' resides in the fact that it postpones the economic and social rights for a future which, given the insurmountable barriers in its way, will never happen – and, to the extent that it may have already happened, it must soon be stopped. It also wilfully disregards one of the most solid tenets of human rights practices in the postwar period: that human rights are indivisible, and that economic and social rights are conditions for the enjoyment of civil and political rights, and vice versa. Alternatively, it may be argued that such a tenet is not in the least disregarded by the neoliberal 'Washington consensus', herein lying the explanation for the latter's adoption of a rather minimalist concept of democracy (low-intensity democracy): a regime is democratic if it upholds some kind of formal elections and tolerates no shockingly visible violations of civil and political rights. Under the aegis of such a diminished conception of democracy, civil and political rights will be drawn down the drain along with economic and social rights.

7.6.6.2   *The right to development*

The current re-invigoration of the conventional wisdom on trade-offs between development and human rights, and the growing inequality and social injustice in the world system confer a new urgency to the issue of the right to development. The right to development is considered a specifically African contribution to international human

---

[315]   Baxi, 2002b, p 132.
[316]   Baxi, 2002b, p 152.

rights discourse.[317] Proposed for the first time in 1972 by Keba M'Baye, it found a formal recognition in the African Charter of Human and Peoples' Rights, and was adopted in the Declaration on the Right to Development of the UN General Assembly (resolution 41/128 of 4 December 1986).[318]

M'Baye starts from a comprehensive concept of development, in light of which the condition of underdevelopment in itself constitutes a violation of human rights, and, as a collective condition, undermines the universalism of human rights. Without condoning the use of the imperative of development as an excuse for the violation of human rights, M'Baye sees an antinomy between underdevelopment and human rights in the fact that developing countries are not in a position to guarantee compliance with economic and social rights.[319] Such an antinomy is not insurmountable, however, and the right to development is precisely the link connecting and reconciling development and human rights. The right to development is simultaneously an individual and a collective right. It is, as M'Baye says, 'the prerogative of all human beings, and of all human beings collectively to have an equal right to the enjoyment, in a just and equitable proportion, of the goods and services produced by the community to which they belong'.[320] It includes both civil and political rights, on the one hand, and economic and social rights, on the other. Its foundation is international and national solidarity; its justification, the safeguard of peace.[321]

In the 1970s and 1980s the debate on the linkages between development and human rights took place both in the UN and its agencies (UNCTAD, ILO, UNESCO and so on) and in several non-governmental organizations (International Commission of Jurists, Brandt Commission and so on). The International Commission of Jurists has proposed the most encompassing conception of the right to development as follows:

'Article 1

1. The right to development is a right of individuals, groups, peoples and states to participate in and benefit from a process of development aimed at realizing the full potentialities of each person in harmony with the community.

2. The right to development recognizes that the human person is the subject as well as the object of development, its main participant as well as its beneficiary.

Article 2

All human rights, economic, social and cultural as well as civil and political are interdependent and inseparable elements of the right to development.

[317]   Shivji, 1989, p 29.

[318]   See lastly, M'Baye, 1991.

[319]   A strong emphasis on the right to development as a defensive argument in light of international criticism of human rights violations is the touchstone of Chinese human rights diplomacy nowadays. See Li Daoyu, 1992.

[320]   M'Baye, 1991, p 220.

[321]   For other positions on the right to development, see Shepherd, Jr and Nanda, 1985.

Article 3

The right to development applies to all levels, community, local, national, regional and global'.

It should come as no surprise that a right to development of such a scope would be an easy target of criticism within the hegemonic discourse on human rights. Donnelly criticizes it as 'entirely pointless', confusing rights with moral claims, and indicating no specified right-holders or duty-bearers.[322] According to Howard, on the other hand, the 'right to development touted by African elites as a prerequisite to the more traditional human rights, may well be merely a cover for denial of those basic civil and political liberties which will allow the dispossessed masses to act in their own interests'.[323]

But the right to development has also been criticized from the left. For Shivji, the question is whether the right to development does serve the interests of people in Africa. In his view, this right has very weak conceptual foundations, because it can either be expanded so as to include everything or, more often, narrowed down to economic development alone.[324] Furthermore, the right to development is state-centred, since, in all the declarations that have adopted it, development appears both as a primary right and as a primary responsibility of the states. Finally, Shivji adds, 'underlying the right to development is a conception which sees development/democracy as a gift/charity from above rather than the results of struggles from below'.[325] Inspired by the Algiers Declaration of 1976 (Universal Declaration on the Rights of People), Shivji proposes, in its stead, as one of the central rights in the present African conjuncture, the right to self-determination which, according to him, expresses the principal contradiction between imperialism and the people on the international plane.[326] With partially similar concerns, but inspired mainly by liberation theology, Shepherd proposes self-reliance as the basic human right, a kind of a right to rights focused on the needs of the people, on redistribution before growth, and on political participation.[327]

7.6.6.3 *Human rights in the paradigmatic transition*

If the world system is indeed entering a period of paradigmatic transition, as I have been arguing all along, then a new politics of rights is needed – a fresh approach to the task of empowering the popular classes and coalitions in their struggles for emancipatory solutions to the final crisis of modernity. A new architecture of rights, based on a new foundation and with a new justification, is called for. Since my purpose

---

[322] Donnelly, 1984, p 261.
[323] Howard, 1983, p 478.
[324] Shivji, 1989, p 82.
[325] Shivji, 1989, p 82.
[326] Shivji, 1989, p 72. A different African view of the right to self-determination is in Eze, 1984, pp 65–102.
[327] Shepherd, 1985, pp 13–25.

in this chapter is only to propose a new research agenda, I will limit myself to some exploratory remarks and general guiding principles.

The new architecture of rights must go to the roots of modernity, not in order to restate above-the-roots – for that is fairly well known – but to inquire into below-the-roots, turn the roots upside down, so to speak, and locate there the new construction site. This inquiry and building plan is a genealogy, in that it looks for the hidden transcript of the origins, inclusions as well as exclusions, legitimate as well as bastard ancestors. It is also a geology, because it is interested in sedimentation layers, gaps and fault lines – which cause social and personal earthquakes. It is, finally, an archeology as well, in that it is interested in knowing what was once legitimate, proper and just, and then discarded as anachronistic, suppressed as deviant or hidden as shameful. While for centuries modernity was taken to be universal from an assumedly Western point of view, from the nineteenth century onwards, it was reconceptualized as universal from a supposedly universal point of view. From then on, a totalizing relationship between victimizers and victims evolved which, however unequal in its effects, brutalized both of them, forcing them both to share a common culture of domination in their acceptance of simplistic and impoverished versions of their own cultures. Modern social sciences are the most sophisticated forms of epistemology of such reductionism and impoverishment.[327a]

In the paradigmatic transition, a politics of rights is basically a politics of rights to roots and rights to options.[327b] This means that all human rights are potentially both individual and collective. It is up to the individuals to decide democratically whether they want to exercise their rights as collective rights – ie, as rights to roots – or as individual rights – ie, as rights to options. There should be no collectivity in relation to which the individual would have no right to opt out.

The first central right in the paradigmatic transition is the *right to a solidarity-oriented transformation of the right to property.* Though conceived as an individual right in the Western conception of human rights, this right is one of the key collective rights that have been violated by the North in victimizing the South and destroying nature. With great forethought, Rousseau saw, in the right to property conceived as an individual right, the seeds of war and all human suffering, and the destruction of community and nature; the problem rested, as Rousseau clearly saw, in the dialectics between individual holding and collective consequences. This dialectics has reached a climax in recent decades, with the rise of the TNCs to world economic prominence. Though constituted by large collectivities of stockholders and managers, with resources exceeding those of many nation-states and operating worldwide, TNCs are nevertheless considered rightholder individuals, and are dealt with as such by both domestic and international law. However extreme, this example illustrates very well the exclusion of the principle of the community as one of the pillars of modern regulation from the

---

[327a] See Santos, 2001c.
[327b] See Santos, 1998c.

nineteenth century onwards, with the ensuing recognition of only two forms of property, state property and individual property, a dualist conception of property that is shared both by liberalism and Marxism. In the period of paradigmatic transition, it is up to the cosmopolitan politics of human rights to recuperate the principle of the community and the forms of property legitimated by it. Between the state and the market, a third social domain must be reinvented: a collective but not state-centred, private but not profit-oriented, new, social domain in-which the right to a solidarity-oriented transformation of property rights will be socially and politically anchored.

The second core human right in a paradigmatic transition is the *right to grant rights to entities incapable of bearing duties, namely nature and future generations.* The Western conception of rights is based on a symmetry between right-holders and duty-bearers, in whose terms only those susceptible of being duty-bearers are entitled to be right-holders. This symmetry narrowed down the scope of the principle of reciprocity as to leave out children, nature and future generations. Once left out of the reciprocity circle, they could easily be excluded from both economic calculations (cost-benefit analysis) and political calculations (the electoral cycle) as well. The tragic result of these arbitrary exclusions is today too obvious to be swept under the rug of cynicism. The sustainability of life and environment – whether as mere survival or improvement – has become undeniably problematic. If it is not already too late, restoring it requires no less than upsetting the symmetry of rights and duties.

The third central human right in the paradigmatic transition is the *right to democratic self-determination.* With a long tradition both in liberal and Marxist versions of Western modernity, this right legitimated all the democratic revolutions of the eighteenth and nineteenth centuries, as well as the independence of Latin American colonies, and was proclaimed almost at the same time, as the right of nations to self-determination, by both Woodrow Wilson and Lenin.[328] In the postwar period, it presided over the process of decolonization, and, as I have shown above, it is now being invoked by indigenous peoples in their struggle for social, political and cultural identity. Though the strength of this tradition is undoubtedly a progressive historical fact, it may also become a serious barrier to the radical reconceptualization of the right to democratic self-determination called for in the paradigmatic transition. A brief note on the conventional international understanding of this right is therefore in order. There is nowadays a consensus that the self-determination of peoples can be either 'external' or 'internal'. According to Cassesse,

> '"External" self-determination refers to the ability of a people or a minority to choose freely in the field of international relations, opting for independence or union with other states. "Internal" self-determination usually means that a people in a sovereign state can elect and keep the government of its choice or that an ethnic, racial, religious

[328]   See Wallerstein, 1991b, p 5. An extended analysis of the rights of peoples in our century is in J Crawford, 1992.

or other minority within a sovereign state has the right not to be oppressed by central government'.[329]

Reviewing, at the end of the 1970s, the trajectory of the right to self-determination during the previous forty years, Cassesse notes that the moderate and relatively ambiguous formulation of this right in the United Nations Charter was soon superseded by the strength of the anti-colonialist movement (the Bandung Conference was held in 1955) and the predominance of the socialist doctrine of self-determination over that of the Western world.[330] While expanding the concept of self-determination to mean liberation from colonialism, racist domination (South Africa and Southern Rhodesia) and foreign occupation (Arab territories occupied by Israel), socialist countries, together with Arab and African countries, restricted its use to external self-determination: for sovereign independent states, self-determination was tantamount to the right to non-intervention. On the contrary, Western countries maintained that self-determination should also be understood as internal self-determination, that is to say, as the right of peoples against sovereign states that massively violate human rights – meaning the totalitarian regimes of the Communist bloc. Normative developments in the UN system, particularly after the International Covenants of 1966, have persuaded Cassesse that the UN has been one-sidedly concentrated on 'external' to the detriment of 'internal' self-determination.[331]

In my analysis of the indigenous peoples' struggles above, I tried to lay bare the almost insurmountable barriers raised by the principle of sovereignty against the recognition of 'internal' self-determination. Although the priority given to 'external' self-determination might have been justified during the anti-colonialist process, it has since lost all justification. As Cassesse puts it, 'new forms of oppression are developing and spreading – neo-colonialism, hegemonic oppression, domination by multinational corporations and transnational repressive organizations – and minorities are awakening from secular oppression to a more vital sense of freedom and independence'.[332] The continued priority given to 'external' self-determination has thus been the other side of the international supremacy of the principle of sovereignty. Hence the special significance, in the European context, of the Helsinki Declaration of 1975, which firmly established the principle of internal self-determination: 'All peoples always have the right, in full freedom, to determine when and as they wish, their internal and external political status, without external interference and to pursue as they wish their political, economic, social and cultural development'.[333] Today, more than a decade after the collapse of the Communist bloc, this formulation has a renewed significance. For many years, cases of external self-determination in Europe seemed to be confined to colonial

---

[329]   Cassesse, 1979, p 137.
[330]   Cassesse, 1979, p 139.
[331]   Cassesse, 1979, p 157.
[332]   Cassesse, 1979, p 148.
[333]   For an analysis of the Helsinki Final Act and the Conference on Security and Co-operation in Europe (the CSCE rights system), see Buergenthal, 1991.

British rule in Northern Ireland and Gibraltar, divided Germany, and the occupation of Cyprus; whereas the internal self-determination issue concerned basically, from the Western point of view, the Communist bloc. Today, however, the explosive cauldron of ethnic nationalism in the former Soviet Union and Yugoslavia shows how internal and external self-determination have both become part of European politics.

In a broader international context, a special reference must be made to a non-governmental document which has gained worldwide moral authority, and in which the right to self-determination of peoples receives the fullest recognition. I am referring to the Algiers Declaration of the Rights of Peoples of 1976, and specifically to its Articles 5, 6 and 7.

'Article 5

Every people has an imprescriptible and unalienable right to self-determination. It shall determine its political status freely and without foreign interference.

Article 6

Every people has the right to break free from any colonial or foreign domination, whether direct or indirect, and from any racist regime.

Article 7

Every people has the right to have a democratic government representing all the citizens without distinction as to race, sex, belief or color, and capable of ensuring effective respect for the human rights and fundamental freedoms of all'.

The merit of these provisions is two-fold. On the one hand, they focus on the collective rights of peoples both to internal and external self-determination, thus relativizing the prerogative of national sovereignty and even the state's right to non-intervention:[334] in the terms of Article 30, 'the re-establishment of fundamental rights of peoples, when they are seriously disregarded is a duty incumbent upon all members of the international community'. On the other hand, the link between collective and individual human rights is established by an emphasis on democratic forms of government (Article 7). In view of the erosion of some modern nationally-based safety nets (the 'pathologies' of democratic representation, the crisis of the welfare state) and the emergence of new forms of global political domination (by non-political, private, global, economic actors), which together question both external and internal self-determination and, in fact, blur the distinction between them altogether, the Algiers Declaration provides, in my judgment, an adequate foundation for a broader and deeper conception of the right to self-determination, as required by the paradigmatic transition.

Shivji has proposed the right of people to self-determination as one of the central rights in the African context, a collective right 'embodying the principal contradiction between

---

[334]   See Falk, 1981, pp 185–194.

imperialism and its compradorial allies vis-à-vis people on the one hand, and oppressor vis-à-vis oppressed nations, on the other'.[335] According to him, the right-holders of this right are dominated/exploited people and oppressed nations, nationalities, national groups and minorities, and the duty-bearers are states, oppressor nations and nationalities and imperialist countries. Although basically in agreement with Shivji, I would like to stress that, in my conception, the right to self-determination can be exercised both as a collective and as an individual right: at the core of any collective right is the right to opt out of the collectivity. Furthermore, unlike Shivji, I put an equal emphasis on the political outcome of self-determination and on the participatory democratic processes towards self-determination. Peoples are political entities and not idealized abstractions, they do not speak with one voice, and when they do speak, it is imperative to establish participatory democracy as the criterion for the legitimacy of the positions voiced.

The fourth central human right in the paradigmatic transition is the *right to organize and participate in the creation of rights*. The paradigmatic transition characterizes itself by relatively unmapped and totally uninsurable risks of oppression, human suffering and destruction, as well as by new, unsuspected possibilities and opportunities for emancipatory politics. Herein lies the characteristic deficit of determinism in the paradigmatic transition I alluded to above. The risks feed on the atomization, depoliticization and apartheidization of people deriving from the downward spiraling of old forms of organization (the vicious circle between declining mobilizing energies and increasingly pointless organizations). Far from being an 'organic' process, such spiraling down is actively provoked by repressive measures and ideological manipulation. For instance, in the core countries, particularly in the US (but also in Europe and Japan), the right of workers to organize in labour unions has been undermined by union-bashing, while their interests have been ideologically miniaturized as 'special interests' and, as such, equated with any other special interests – for instance, those of the US National Rifle Association. On the other hand, the opportunities for emancipatory politics depend, according to the circumstances, either on the invention of new forms of organization specifically targeted to meet the new risks, or on the defence of old forms of organization, which are then reinvented to measure up to the new challenges, new agenda and new potential coalitions.

The right to organize is in a sense a primordial right, without which none of the other rights can be minimally achievable. The specific breadth and depth of the basic human rights of the paradigmatic transition listed above must be matched by a correspondingly broad and deep right to organize. It amounts to the right to organize all possible solidarities against all existing colonialisms.[336] In one of its dimensions, the right to organize is a metaright, a right to create rights. Paradoxically, the expansion of the circle of reciprocity can only be genuinely accomplished by those that have been kept outside

---

[335]   Shivji, 1989, p 80.

[336]   Shivji, 1989, p 83, subscribes to a more restricted conception of the right to organize.

it. To be sure, the analysis of the struggles of indigenous peoples to conquer the right to create their own rights, which I offered above, can be expanded to cover other social forms of exclusion. In much the same way, Falk argues for the relevance of exclusion/inclusion to evaluate the normative adequacy of human rights as a protective framework at a given time and place: 'Those *excluded* from rights-creating processes are only likely to be taken into account, if at all, in a partial and paternalistic manner'.[337]

The right to organize and the right to create rights are thus two inseparable dimensions of the same right. According to the vulnerabilities of specific social groups, the repression of human rights is targeted against either the creation of rights or the organization to defend or to create rights. The specific vulnerabilities of the growing interior Third World (the poor, the permanently unemployed, the homeless, the undocumented migrant workers, the asylum seekers, the prisoners and so on), as well as the social fragility of workers, women, ethnic minorities, children, gays and lesbians, clearly show the extent to which a paradigmatic politics of rights is deeply interlocked with the politics of participatory democracy, and calls for the theoretical reconstruction of democratic theory. Inadequate representation or even exclusion from membership, lack of meaningful political participation, repression of organization and demobilization are different dimensions of the same deficit of democracy that foster the violations of human rights and guarantee their impunity.

Given the wide-ranging destructuring that goes together with the paradigmatic transition, more violations and more impunity are to be expected. To counteract them and make room for the emancipatory opportunities likewise opened, I have proposed a cosmopolitan politics of rights. The rights I have proposed are not enforceable under the current political and legal system. Indeed, to the extent that they are adopted by cosmopolitan coalitions and their advocacy is transposed to the concrete political domain, these rights will have a profound destabilizing impact on current political and legal systems. In fact, they fit the category of 'destabilization rights' in Unger's conception of rights, except that, for Unger, the scope of such rights is more narrowly defined, and the extent to which they can be exercised as collective rights is not clear.[338] As conceived here, destabilization is not the privilege of abstract citizens, but rather the responsibility of cosmopolitan coalitions of exploited and dominated social classes and groups in their struggles for paradigmatic rights. I will turn to this issue in Chapter Nine where I present the theoretical and political blueprint of a new conception of law that I call subaltern cosmopolitan legality.

7.7 The *global commons*: jus humanitatis

Of all forms of transnational legality, *jus humanitatis* is the one that pushes the idea of globalization further, for it takes the globe itself as the object of its regulation. Since

---

[337] Falk, 1992a, p 48.
[338] Unger, 1987, p 530.

neither the capitalist nor the interstate system allows for a genuine globalization of social practices, *jus humanitatis* is potentially the privileged field of the struggles between capitalist forms of globalization (globalized localisms and localized globalisms), on the one hand, and forms of globalization pointing towards the emergent paradigm (cosmopolitanism and common heritage of humankind), on the other. We might assume, then, that the advances and setbacks of *jus humanitatis* are a good gauge of the advances and setbacks of the paradigmatic transition. Since it covers a very wide field of analysis, and we are just now beginning to enter the paradigmatic transition, the contours of *jus humanitatis* are as yet but all too vague. I will limit myself here to describing briefly its present profile, identifying at the same time some obstacles to its development, and stressing its paradigmatic potential.

As I conceive of it here, *jus humanitatis* expresses the aspiration to a form of governance of natural or cultural resources which, given their extreme importance for the sustainability and quality of life on earth, must be considered as globally owned and managed in the interest of humankind as a whole, both present and future. In this sense, *jus humanitatis* clashes with two fundamental principles of the dominant paradigm: property, upon which the capitalist world system is based; and sovereignty, upon which the interstate system is based. Little wonder, then, that its application has been so little so far. Nevertheless, its prolegomena are already quite visible in the doctrine of the common heritage of humankind that has been adopted by international law for the last few decades. Though the doctrine has its own limitations, it is grounded on principles which, were they to be fully developed, would bring about the bankruptcy of the dominant paradigm, and hence of international law itself as it is conceived today. As we can see, therefore, the doctrine of the common heritage of humankind has many virtualities for the development of the emergent paradigm. I use the concept, similarly to my use of the concept of cosmopolitanism, as a form of juridical globalization that transcends the limits of capitalist globalization. As a matter of fact, there is a deep complicity between cosmopolitanism and the common heritage of humankind: while cosmopolitanism signifies the struggle of oppressed social groups for a decent life under the new conditions of globalization of social practices promoted by the capitalist world system, the common heritage of humankind signifies the idea that such a struggle will be fully successful only in terms of a new pattern of development and sociability that will necessarily include a new social contract with the earth, nature and the future generations.

The concept of the common heritage of humankind was formulated for the first time in 1967 by Malta's Ambassador to the UN, Arvid Pardo, in relation to UN negotiations on the international regulation of the oceans and the deep seabed. Pardo's purpose was:

> 'to provide a solid basis for future worldwide cooperation ... through the acceptance by the international community of a new principle of international law . . . that the seabed and ocean floor and their subsoil have a special status as a common heritage of

mankind and as such should be reserved exclusively for peaceful purposes and administered by an international authority for the benefit of all peoples'.[339]

Since then, the concept of the common heritage of humankind has been applied not only to the ocean floor but also to other 'common areas' such as the moon and outer space. The idea behind this concept is that these natural entities belong to humankind in its entirety and that all people are, therefore, entitled to have a say and a share in the management and allocation of their resources. Five elements are usually associated with the concept of the common heritage of humankind: non-appropriation; management by all peoples; international sharing of the benefits obtained from the exploitation of natural resources; peaceful use, including freedom of scientific research for the benefit of all peoples; conservation for future generations.[340]

Although it was formulated by international lawyers, the concept of the common heritage of humankind transcends by far the field of traditional international law. International law deals traditionally with international relations among nation-states, which are supposed to be the main beneficiaries of the regulation agreed upon. Such relations are based chiefly on reciprocity, that is, granting advantages to another state or states in return for equivalent advantages for oneself.[341] The concept of the common heritage of humankind is different from traditional international law on two accounts: as far as the common heritage of humankind is concerned, there is no question of reciprocity; and the interests to be safeguarded are the interests of humankind as a whole, rather than the interests of states. To be sure, as Kiss points out, since the nineteenth century, states have been signing conventions containing no implication of reciprocity (prohibition of slave trade, freedom of navigation, regulation of labour conditions and so on), and whose concern is to safeguard 'a benefit for all mankind which can be obtained only by international co-operation and the acceptance of obligations by all governments, even if they receive no immediate return'.[342] But the concept of the common heritage of humankind reaches much further, inasmuch as both its object and subject of regulation transcend the states. Humankind emerges, indeed, as the subject of international law, entitled to its own heritage and the autonomous prerogative to manage the spaces and resources included in the global commons.[343]

The Law of the Sea Convention, signed in Montego Bay on 10 December 1982, contains, in its Part XI, the most developed formulation of the concept of the common heritage

[339]   Pardo, 1968, p 225–226.
[340]   Pureza, 1993, p 19, 1998a, 1998b; Payoyo, 1997; Baslar, 1998; Zieck, 1992, pp 177–197; *Pacem in Manbus XX*, 1992; Blaser, 1990; Weiss, 1989; Joyner, 1986; Kiss, 1985; White, 1982; Dupuy, 1974.
[341]   Kiss, 1985, p 426.
[342]   Kiss, 1985, pp 426–27.
[343]   Pureza, 1993, p 19. An overview of recent transformations of international law is in Bilder, 1992.
[344]   In what follows, I draw on Kiss, 1985, pp 432–435.

of humankind to date.[344] The Law of the Sea Convention asserts that the seabed, the ocean floor and its subsoil beyond the limits of national jurisdiction are the common heritage of humankind, the implication being that all rights on the resources in question are vested in humankind as a whole. No state shall claim or exercise sovereignty or sovereignty rights over any part of the area or its resources; no state or natural or juridical person shall appropriate any part of it. Activities in the area shall be carried out for the benefit of humankind as a whole, regardless of the geographical location of the states; but the interests and needs of developing countries must be taken into particular consideration. Marine scientific research in the area, as well as any other activity, will be carried out exclusively for peaceful purposes. All the activities in the area are to be organized, carried out and controlled by an international authority with three main organs: an assembly, a council and a secretariat. The role of this international authority is to grant the right to explore and exploit the resources of the area, but the fundamental principle is that all benefits must be shared by the international community, with a bias in favour of developing countries.

As far as traditional international law is concerned, the Law of the Sea Convention is truly a 'marine revolution'. It should therefore not be surprising that it clashes with the interests of some states, particularly those that have the technological capacity and financial means to engage in the exploration of the ocean floors – the core countries. As might be expected, the reservations of core countries, particularly the US, about the Convention concern both the control of the authority to grant rights of exploration and exploitation of seabed minerals, and the principle of equal sharing of profits and other benefits from seabed mining. Benefit- and profit-sharing are especially problematic for core countries, in that they must take 'into particular consideration the interests and needs of developing states and peoples who have not attained full independence or other self-governing states'[345] (Chapter 3.C.2). The US has read into this recommendation echoes of the 'New International Economic Order' (NIEO) that 'Third World countries' brought to the forefront in the UN in the seventies. The position of the US on this issue is quite clear in a statement of the White House Office of Policy Information, dated 15 April 1983: the Law of the Sea Treaty would:

> 'transfer control of the ocean's minerals to an international authority dominated by Third World states, which are largely hostile to free market approaches and to the interests of the industrialized nations of the free world.' . . . The LOS treaty is viewed by the [developing countries] as a significant step toward . . . the establishment of a NIEO, ... a scheme for restructuring the international economy along the socialist lines of the world's centrally managed economies and for redistributing the world's wealth'.[346]

Curiously enough, in the early 1980s the demands for an NIEO had already quieted down. What was really at stake was, rather, the opposition of mining companies, as

---

[345] Janis, 1988, p 156; Kimball, 1983.
[346] Kimball, 1983, p 41. On the relations between NIEO and the common heritage of humankind, see Joyner, 1986, p 192. See also Baslar, 1998, pp 205-242.

well as the free enterprise and deregulation orientation of the Reagan Administration. According to the latter, the International Seabed Authority made deep seabed mining too burdensome and unrealistic, as well as unjust, insofar as it allowed benefits to be shared by peoples who had not contributed to obtaining them. The issue was not one of principle, but of interests already deeply rooted at the time that the convention was signed. The truth is that, though the commercial feasibility of deep seabed mining was then still highly problematic, the technology to undertake it was available, and long-term profit seemed promising enough. The principal known deep seabed resources at issue are manganese nodules that lie in great quantities at depths of twelve to twenty thousand feet. The nodules vary greatly in size and composition, but many of them contain rich amounts of minerals like manganese, nickel, copper and cobalt. When the convention was signed, four major ocean mining consortia were in operation; their estimated expenditure was 300m dollars, and they were headquartered in the US and involved corporations from such countries as (besides the US itself), Italy, the UK, Japan, Belgium, former West Germany, Canada and the Netherlands.[347] Even though the Convention was originally signed by 159 states, it took 12 years to be ratified by 60 states, the number of ratifications needed to bring the Convention into force. The implementation of the Convention started in November 1994. Due to the pressure of the industrialized countries to correct some of its 'imperfections',[348] the Convention will be implemented with an annex agreement, which in fact will neutralize or subvert some of the most innovative features of the common heritage of humankind regime (UN Resolution 48/263, 28 July 1994).

Another area in which the common heritage of humankind regime has been consecrated is the outer space. I have in mind the Moon Treaty of 1979 which entered into force on 11 June 1984.[349] In its Article XI, the Moon Treaty states unequivocally that the moon and its natural resources are a common heritage of humankind. Article VI is particularly explicit about the practical implications of such a statement. In its terms, 'the exploration of the moon shall be the province of all mankind and shall be carried out for the benefit and in the interest of all countries, irrespective of their degree of economic and scientific development'. Unlike the Outer Space Treaty of 1967, the Moon Treaty explicitly adopts the principle of the common heritage of humankind, though not to the same extent as the Law of the Sea Convention; but like the latter it too denounces obvious clashes with the interests of core countries. Neither the US nor the former Soviet Union, China, Japan and the UK are signatories or parties, with the result that none of the major 'space powers' is legally obliged by the Treaty. Again, one of their main reasons for not participating in the international regime is economic.

As an example, let us consider studies undertaken by the US on the use of the deuterium (D) and helium-3 (He^3) fuel cycle as the major source of energy in the twenty-first

---

347 Kimball, 1983, p 16.
348 Pacem in Manbus XX, 1992, p 1.
349 Joyner, 1986, p 196; Williams, 1981; Baslar, 1998, pp 159–204.

century. Now, while there are no large identifiable sources of He³ on earth to be obtained economically, the Apollo mission of 1970 revealed that there is a large source of He³ on the surface of the moon. NASA studies, in fact, indicate that it could be as large as one million metric tons (which is equivalent in energy content to ten times all the economically recoverable coal, oil and natural gas on earth). Furthermore, it seems that He³ can be extracted and transported to earth with existing technology at an 'attractive economic profit'. Such studies show that the He³ is worth at least a billion dollars per ton, and as such would be competitive with oil at seven dollars per barrel. A study on legal regimes for the mining of He³ from the moon, conducted by the Wisconsin Center for Space Automation and Robotics,[350] states clearly that '[t]his is the first time in history that we have looked to the moon as a possible solution to our future energy problems and to alleviate pollution here on earth'. The question that this study proposes to give an answer to is, accordingly, '[u]nder what legal regime could such a major undertaking be accomplished and what should the US be doing now to insure that if we choose to pursue this energy form in the 21st century, we will be able to do so without severely disrupting international order?' Besides helium-3, other key resources such as magnesium, aluminum, iron and silicon seem to be available on the moon. In addition, the moon has potential as a base from which further space exploration might take place.[351]

As we can see, it is not difficult to understand why the common heritage of humankind regime, once applied to the moon, clashes with the interests of the leading space powers. As might be expected, opposition is particularly strong concerning international management and benefit-sharing. The latter is particularly relevant for peripheral and semi-peripheral societies with no exploration or extractive capacities, and whose fear is that the use of enormous and still untapped resources may become in the future the most powerful source of hierarchy and domination in the world system. According to Blaser, the US Senate failed to ratify the Treaty, due in part to an intensive lobbying campaign by the space industry. A United Technologies advertisement captured beautifully the fears of the Americans who were against the Moon Treaty: it expressed opposition to 'socializing the moon', giving in to the Third World majority in the UN, and creating an 'OPEC-like monopoly'.[352] Ultimately, the aim of such strong opposition was to prevent the application to the moon of the regime already established for the deep seabed. According to its critics, this regime fostered inefficient production and reduced the real income of most Third World countries. Using the standard trick of the 'trickling-down' benefits, they suggested that even Third World states would benefit from unregulated access to ocean and space resources.

The lunar future envisaged by the leading space powers seems to be geared more to the condominium principle (two or more states govern and share control over a particular

---

[350]   Bilder *et al*, 1989, p 1.
[351]   Blaser, 1990, p 79.
[352]   Blaser, 1990, p *91.*

area) than to the principle of the common heritage of humankind. The advocates of condominium proposals claim that they are based on merit, but it is not hard to see that, as Blaser explains, such proposals 'will promote a tipping effect whereby the "meritorious" will acquire an ever greater advantage, and Third World representatives will be less and less able to participate'.[353] From the point of view of the common heritage of humankind regime, the 1980s were a sombre decade, particularly as concerns the US outer space policy. It was a decade of militarization and commercialization of outer space. In 1982, US military expenditures in space exceeded spending for civilian purposes for the first time, and by the end of the decade, military spending was more than double civilian spending. In the process, the peaceful use of outer space has been reinterpreted to include non-aggressive military uses. On the other hand, while military spending has not increased significantly lately, the commercialization of space programmes continues to be strongly emphasized.[354]

The huge inequalities thus created between countries with and without space capability are also obvious in a related field: the field of telecommunications. An interpretation of the Outer Space Treaty on the basis of the common heritage of humankind underlies the plan adopted in 1988 by the World Administrative Radio Conference on the Use of Geostationary Orbit to provide 'equitable and guaranteed access by all countries of the world to the Geostationary-Satellite Orbit (GSO) and the space services utilizing this orbit'. Nevertheless, the 'information gap' between the North and the South, which was at the origin of proposals regarding a New World Information and Communication Order, has increasingly widened, and the tendency is believed to continue as the Integrated Services Digital Network (SDN) and information satellites become implemented. In sum, this is another domain that seems to be lost for the doctrine the common heritage of humankind.[355]

The information gap resulting from technological development in the field of telecommunications is not just a gap between the North and the South, but, within each country, between the state and the citizens, and between dominant and subordinated classes. Information has become a crucial question of human rights. Though formulated at the state level, this question has a global reach, thereby taking humankind in its entirety as the recipient of human rights. Suffice it to mention remote sensing satellites. It is today acknowledged that reconnaissance satellites have the capability of photographing, with distinguishable quality, the faces of individuals on the ground. There is, therefore, nothing far-fetched about imagining situations in which remote sensing will violate the right to privacy. The development of space technology and the emergence of spatial capital will undoubtedly engender new risks for the global commons and new inequalities and power structures in the world system.[356]

[353]   Blaser, 1990, p 98.
[354]   Jasentuliyana, 1990.
[355]   Pureza, 1998a, p 257.
[356]   Potter, 1989.

Besides the seabed and outer space, the other common space in relation to which the application of the common heritage of humankind regime has been considered is the Antarctic region. Ever since exploration was started in the Antarctic region, its territorial status has been a source of potential conflict. While some countries take Antarctica to be *terra nullius* – that is to say, land belonging to no one, and thus capable of appropriation by the traditional methods of territorial acquisition (discovery, exploration, effective occupation, or geographic continuity or contiguity) – others have asserted that the continent is the common heritage of humankind. Amongst the former, some have actually made territorial claims (Argentina, Australia, Chile, France, New Zealand, Norway and the UK), while others consider themselves to be potential claimants. This is the case of the US and the former Soviet Union, which agree that Antarctica is *terra nullius*, though without recognizing the specific territorial claims of the above-mentioned countries, rather reserving the right to make claims of their own.

In 1959 the Antarctic Treaty was signed to take effect on 23 June 1961 upon ratification by the twelve participating states.[357] Since then, the number of participant states increased to 26. By its very elitist nature – that is, reserved to participant states, the so-called 'Antarctic aristocracy' – the Antarctic Treaty does not consecrate the common heritage of humankind principle. It is focused on three major issues: Antarctica (defined as the area south of 60 degrees south geographic latitude) is to be a zone of peace; while not restricting the types of peaceful activities that may be conducted in Antarctica, the Treaty emphasizes the importance of scientific research; the treaty does not attempt a final resolution of territorial claims, but puts the issue on hold. We might say that the Antarctic regime tries to reconcile the condominium with the common heritage of humankind principle.[358] That much it accomplishes by excluding from the Antarctic 'club' the great majority of peripheral countries.

The regime of the common heritage of humankind is thus evolving unevenly and slowly, and the times ahead may not be very promising. 'The negotiating histories of the Moon, Antarctica, and Law of the Sea Treaties', White points out, 'reveal the principle of the "common heritage of humankind" in three distinct phases of implementation'. White then proceeds to identify the phases of uneven implementation of the common heritage of humankind:

> 'It is firmly entrenched in the developing law of the sea, where it covers both the International Seabed Area and its resources, and provides for an international regime to implement the principle. It is articulated in limited form in the Moon Treaty, where it will apply to celestial bodies but not to resources extracted from them, when exploitation becomes feasible. It has not yet been formally extended to Antarctica, though certain elements – international management and sharing of benefits – have long been part of the relevant agreements'.[359]

[357]   Lanzerotti *et al*, 1993, pp 32–46; Grolin, 1987; Thakur and Gold, 1983.
[358]   Lanzerotti *et al*, 1993, p 34.
[359]   White, 1982, p 541. See also Baslar, 1998, pp 243-276.

Besides the common spaces and resources that are directly integrated in the global commons, other spaces and resources, both natural and cultural, quite often under national jurisdiction and even objects of private property, have been increasingly regarded as susceptible of being regulated by the principle of the common heritage of humankind, broadly conceived. I mean monuments, groups of buildings, natural features, geological and physiological formations, and natural sites or precisely delineated areas of outstanding universal value from the point of view of history, art, science, natural beauty or conservation. Such objects are protected by the UNESCO Convention for the Protection of World's Cultural and Natural Heritage, dated 1972. 'According to the Convention', writes Kiss, 'the contracting parties recognize that their duty is to ensure the identification, protection, conservation, presentation and transmission to the future generations of that heritage and that such a heritage constitutes a world heritage for whose protection it is the duty of the international community as a whole to cooperate'.[360] Finally, the International Ocean Institute, during its twentieth Pacem in Maribus Conference (Malta, 1 to 5 November 1992) studied the possibility of extending the common heritage of humankind or its elements to five sectors of global concern: energy, food, outer space, atmosphere and science and technology. The purpose is to turn the common heritage of humankind into the congregating concept for the quest for a new sustainable world order, which was the focus of all the debates at the United Nations Conference on Environment and Development held in Rio de Janeiro in June 1992.

The expanded application of the principle of the common heritage of humankind shows the potential of this concept in the paradigmatic transition. Against capitalist expansionism, it proposes the idea of sustainable development; against private property and national appropriation, the idea of shared resource management, rational use and transmission to the future generations; against nation-state sovereignty, the idea of trust, management by the international community or under its control on behalf of humankind as a whole; against the hubris of the pursuit of power that so often leads to war, the idea of peaceful use; against the political economy of the modern world system, the idea of equitable redistribution of the world's wealth, including resources still untapped. In sum, the principle of the common heritage of humankind points forward to *jus humanitatis*, a law of and for humanity as a whole, the law of a decent human condition in a non-dualist, but rather mutualist, interaction with nature. Given its paradigmatic potentialities, it is hardly surprising that the principle of the common heritage of humankind has so little application in our time, and that all attempts to extend it to areas susceptible of affecting significantly hegemonic capitalist and state-centred prerogatives are met with fierce opposition, and end up failing altogether.

The new *jus humanitatis* breaks with the basic premises both of nation-state law and traditional international law in many different ways. To begin with, it creates a new spatiality. Beyond local, national and international, it creates global legal spatiality.

---

[360] Kiss, 1985, p 433; 1989, pp 67–103.

For this reason, we could characterize it as a fourth-dimension law. This social perception of globality may be facilitated by the so-called 'overview effect' produced by space exploration. In the space age, humankind has had the haunting experience of viewing the earth in its entirety for the first time. Indeed, from the perspective of outer space, we are enabled to see the arbitrary borders that separate nations, and we become keenly aware of a single delicate ecological system. The same kind of 'overview effect' may underlie some of the theoretical and epistemological reflections that I analyzed in Chapter One as prefiguring a new epistemological paradigm. Such is particularly the case of the Gaia hypothesis formulated by Lovelock. The Gaia hypothesis is the conception of an all-encompassing natural system, or, as Lovelock himself puts it, 'a complex entity involving the earth's biosphere, atmosphere, oceans and soils; the total constituting a feedback or cybernetic system which seeks an optimal physical and chemical environment for life on this planet'.[361] Informed by such an overview effect, *jus humanitatis* departs from the individualistic microethics of liberal tradition, and takes humankind as a whole as a recipient of human rights. Moreover, while adopting a non-capitalist conception of property, *jus humanitatis* breaks with the conventional reciprocity between rights and duties. The seabed, outer space and Antarctica have rights of their own that do not depend on any private or international property rights over them. A global duty to respect their rights is the only way of sharing the right to the common heritage of humankind that they constitute.

Jus humanitatis is transtemporal; it is grounded on the idea of intergenerational responsibility. The unilateral rights of the global commons are proclaimed in the name of the continued sustainability of life on earth. The basic principle of *jus humanitatis* is the principle of sustainability and responsibility, rather than the principle of expansionism. For this reason, trust, which, together with accumulation and hegemony, is a major strategy of the modern state (see Chapter Two above), has to be exercised on behalf of humankind in a non state-centred framework. The transtemporal character of *jus humanitatis* is reinforced by another overview effect, perhaps more problematic but certainly equally important – the overview effect of tradition. The idea of transmitting the world's cultural and natural heritage to future generations is central to *jus humanitatis*. This transmission presupposes a simultaneous view over two or more different yet closely related temporalities. Such is the simultaneity of tradition. Tradition is constituted of two elements: the act of transmitting (*tradere*) and its content (*traditum* or *tradendum*). By virtue of these two elements, all tradition is creative, dynamic and, in a sense, also invented, but by no means totally arbitrary, rather, based on a certain continuity and stability (the heritage). Hence, *jus humanitatis* implies both creativity and heritage.

Thus conceived, *jus humanitatis* is Utopian without apology. Analyzed in light of the three regulatory principles that underlie modern law, *jus humanitatis* represents the re-emergence of the principle of the community in a new mould. This is a highly

---

[361]   Lovelock, 1979. Also Goldsmith, 1988 and Taylor, 1998.

conflictual process. As we saw above, the principle of the market has prevailed in the restrictive interpretation of the common heritage of humankind, as witness the extension of the entitlement to mine the moon to private entities, and the commercialization of outer space in general. By the same token, the principle of the state has prevailed regarding the formulation of territorial claims, the role of the states in the negotiations leading to the treaties, the militarization of outer space and the regulation of its commercial use. In all instances, the role of the US has been quite instrumental. Curiously enough, however, this highly conflictual arena is being disputed in the language and rhetoric of the principle of community, as is intimated by the use of such phrases as 'global commons', 'global village', 'common heritage', 'world community' and so on. True enough, neither the principle of the market nor the principle of the state can provide adequate semantics and rhetoric. Indeed, both the language of the market and the language of the state are in the antipodes of *jus humanitatis*.[362] The fact that the principle of the community, one of the unfinished representations of modernity, provides the language of a law that points clearly to the paradigmatic transition, is significant in itself. To be sure, it may conceal a manipulative rhetoric through which the principle of the state and the principle of the market try to survive in a field whose language they do not master. But this very concealment is relevant for what it, in turn, reveals about the linguistic bankruptcy of the hegemonic principles of modern regulation, which find themselves unable to name such crucial topics as humanity, human condition, global sustainability and transmission to future generations. The task of emancipatory coalitions is precisely to denounce such concealment, and to highlight its subversive hidden transcript.

---

[362]   It is true that the principle of the state has provided some linguistic innovation ('world state', 'world government'), but as *topoi* for the new spatiality these terms are much less credible than those provided by the principle of the community.

Chapter 6

Law and Democracy: The Global Reform of Courts

I INTRODUCTION

In Chapter Five I set out to offer an analytical framework and a research agenda for understanding the changes of law in the context of globalization. Given the broadness of the agenda and the need to develop an overarching theoretical framework, I only mapped the central issues and did not seek to offer a detailed analysis of each of them. This is particularly true as regards the impact of globalization upon legal institutions such as courts. In this chapter I focus on one of the most puzzling phenomena of sociology and political theory at the beginning of the twenty-first century – ie, the greater social and political visibility and protagonism of courts in several countries and the global call for the rule of law and the reform of the judicial system – in order to offer a more detailed account of the processes at work, thus engaging in the type of grounded theorizing on law that this book aims to further. This phenomenon is puzzling because in the modern state, with the possible exception of the US, courts have had a fairly uneventful existence. Marginalized by the executive and legislative powers and far more impotent than them, courts have become a mere accessory of the other branches of government or paid for its institutional independence with insulation and irrelevancy vis-à-vis society. It is, therefore, hard to understand why, since the late 1980s, courts have become so prominent in the daily newspapers of many countries of Europe and Latin America, Africa and Asia, why so many projects for judicial reform have been started in different countries of the various continents, and why multilateral agencies and foundations for international aid have been giving priority to judicial reform and rule of law programmes in such diverse countries as Russia, Guatemala, Colombia, Sri Lanka, Philippines, South Africa, Mozambique, Nigeria, Uruguay, China, Argentina, Cambodia and so on, and so forth.

Does the fact that this phenomenon is occurring in different countries make it a global phenomenon? Can it be explained in all cases by the same causes? Does it have a univocal political meaning? In terms of the typology of globalization laid out in Chapter Five, is this new global interest on courts part and parcel of hegemonic globalization or rather of counter-hegemonic globalization? I shall try to answer these questions by focusing on three issues. First, I will consider the global political, economic and ideological context in which the consensus of the rule of law and judicial reform and activism has developed. Secondly, I will examine whether the role played by courts in the modern state is linked to the transformations undergone by the state itself. Thirdly, I will assess the prospects for democracy deriving from the worldwide focus on the rule of law and court reform.

2   THE FOUR DIMENSIONS OF THE GLOBAL HEGEMONIC CONSENSUS

According to hegemonic political thinking, we live in a period of vanishing deep political cleavages within nations and among nations. In this view, despite more or less intense warfare going on in some peripheral countries, and even among semi-peripheral countries, very often because of ethnic or religious conflicts, the world is evolving in the direction of global consensus. The East/West conflict is a remnant from the past and the North/South division is not really a cleavage. It is rather an axis of increasing interconnectedness and interdependence leading eventually to a global economy, a global civil society, and even a global polity.

Such consensual view and practice is based upon four main liberal consensuses, which constitute the ideological basis of hegemonic globalization: the neo-liberal economic consensus; the weak state consensus; the liberal democratic consensus; and the rule of law and judicial reform consensus. *The neo-liberal economic consensus*, also known as the 'Washington consensus', sealed in the electoral victories of Thatcher and Reagan, has been so pervasively with us for the past twenty years that I will not dwell on it here. It concerns a global economy, including both global production and global markets of goods, services, and finance, and is based on free market, deregulation, privatization, state minimalism, control of inflation, export orientation, cuts in social expenditures, reduction of the public deficit, concentration of market power in the hands of transnational corporations and of financial power in the hands of transnational banks. For my purposes I wish merely to emphasize three institutional innovations brought about by the neo-liberal economic consensus: (1) new legal restrictions on state regulation; (2) new international property rights for foreign investors and intellectual creators; (3) subordination of the nation states to multilateral agencies: the World Bank, the IMF, and the WTO. These institutional innovations have been put into effect in various supranational agreements with considerable variation: from the hyper-liberal NAFTA and Uruguay Round to the social democratic or socio-liberal EU. On the other hand, the developmentalist states of Asia had much greater leverage in adapting the neo-liberal economic consensus to their perceived needs than the developmentalist states of Latin America. Ambiguity in the underlying consensus made it possible for its recipes to be applied now with extreme rigidity (iron cage model) now with extreme flexibility (rubber cage mode). For instance, it is little known that Pinochet, for all his iron-cage like applications of the neo-liberal medicine in Chile, managed to keep the copper mines in state hands throughout the period.

The weak state consensus is intimately related to the neo-liberal economic consensus but is conceptually autonomous. Of course, favouring market-based rather than state-managed economic strategies implies a preference for a weak state. But the consensus in this case is much broader and goes beyond the economic or even the social realm. It sees the state, rather than as the mirror of civil society, as the opposite of civil society. The strength of the state, rather than a consequence of the strength of civil society or, alternatively, a compensation for the weakness of civil society, is seen as the cause of the weakness of civil society. The state, even the democratic state, is seen as inherently oppressive and must therefore be weakened as a pre-condition of the strengthening of civil society. This liberal consensus is plagued by a dilemma: since only the state can produce its own weakness, it takes a strong state to produce it efficiently and sustain it coherently.

The liberal democratic consensus was sealed with the fall of the Berlin Wall and the collapse of the Soviet Union. Its antecedents were the democratic transitions of the mid-1970s in Southern Europe (Greece, Portugal, and Spain), of the early or mid-1980s in Latin America (Argentina, Chile, Brazil, Uruguay, Bolivia), and of the late 1980s and early 1990s in Central and Eastern Europe, Africa (Cape Verde Islands, Namibia, Mozambique, Congo, Benin, South Africa), the Philippines, Nicaragua, Haiti. The convergence between the neo-liberal economic consensus and the liberal democratic consensus has been emphasized and may be traced back to the origins of liberal representative democracy. Free elections and free markets were always seen as the two sides of the same coin: the collective good to be achieved by utilitarian individuals engaged in competitive exchange with minimal state interference. But here, also, there has been much room for ambiguity. While nineteenth-century democratic theory was equally concerned with justifying sovereign state power both as a regulatory and as a coercive capability, and with justifying the limits of that power, the new liberal democratic consensus is concerned only with coercion; sovereignty is no concern at all, particularly in the case of peripheral and semi-peripheral states and the regulatory functions are dealt with as a state incapacity rather than a state capacity.

Moreover, if we look at the cluster of normative and institutional features of liberal democratic theory, it is evident that the political realities of the beginning of the century around the globe are still at arms' length from this model of government. Following David Held, I will identify the following main features of liberal democratic theory: elected government; free and fair elections in which every citizen's vote has equal weight; right to suffrage enjoyed by all citizens irrespective of distinctions of race, religion, class, sex, and so on; freedom of conscience, information and expression on all public matters broadly defined; the right of all adults to oppose their government and stand for office; and associational autonomy, that is to say, the right to form independent associations including social movements, interest groups, and political parties.[1] Judged by these standards, one may easily conclude that most democracies, even in the West, are still today low intensity democracies. However, the consensus is not thereby disturbed, either because this cluster of features is conceived as an ideal type or as comprising a maximalist conception out of which it is possible to 'extract' a less ambitious one, or because the consensus is being constructed with the recognition that there is no alternative to the democratic model of government and that the different empirical polities will gradually approximate the model.

The *rule of law/judicial consensus* is the fourth pillar that supports hegemonic globalization. This consensus derives from the other three consensuses. The neo-liberal development model, with its greater reliance on markets and the private sector, has changed the ground rules of both private and public institutions, calling for a new legal framework for development conducive to trade, financing, and investment. The provision of such a legal framework and the responsibility for its enforcement is the new central role of the state that is allegedly best fulfilled in a democratic polity. The rule of law is thus quintessential in development: 'the development potential of law lies in that law is not only a reflection of the prevailing forces in society; it can also be a proactive instrument to promote change.'[2] There is, supposedly, no alternative to law but chaos. This, however, will only be possible if the rule of law is widely accepted and effectively enforced. Only then are certainty and predictability guaranteed, transaction costs lowered, property rights clarified and protected, contractual obligations enforced, regulations applied. To achieve all this is the crucial role of the judicial system: 'a well-functioning judiciary in which judges apply the law in a fair, even, and predictable manner without undue delays or unaffordable costs is part and parcel of the rule of law.'[3] The judiciary is responsible for delivering equitable, expeditious and transparent judicial services to citizens, economic agents, and the state.

But inasmuch as the role of the state has been reformed to serve the new global consensus, the judicial system must be reformed as well. The judicial reform is an essential component of the new model of development and the basis of good governance, the provision for which is the priority of the non-interventionist state. Administration of justice is essentially a service delivered by the state to the community in order to preserve social peace and facilitate economic development through the resolution of disputes. As the World Bank officials confess – and 'confess' sounds right since they seem to be atoning for old sins – 'it has taken failures of government in Africa, the collapse of dictatorships in Latin America and profound transformations in Central and Eastern Europe to manifest that without a sound legal framework, without an independent and honest judiciary economic and social development risk collapse.'[4]

[1]   Held, 1993, p 21.
[2]   Sihata, 1995 p 13.
[3]   Shihata, 1995, p 14.
[4]   Rowat *et al*, 1995, p 2.

Given that, out of the four consensuses, the rule of law/judicial reform consensus is the one most closely related to the global legal field that concerns me in this and the previous chapter, I will devote the remainder of this chapter to its study.

3 THE RULE OF LAW/JUDICIAL CONSENSUS

Of all the liberal global consensuses, the one of the rule of law and judicial reform is by far the most complex and ambiguous. If for no other reason, because its focus is on the institution (courts) which better than any other represents the national character of modern institution-building and which, on this account, one might expect to resist globalizing pressures most effectively. Notwithstanding some high profile international courts in the past, and the European Court of Justice and the European Court of Human Rights today, the judicial system remains the quintessential national institution, and it has been far more difficult to internationalize it than the police or the armed forces.[5] Though my initial formulation of the judicial consensus may have suggested that the focus on the judicial system is imposed on nation-states around the world by global hegemonic institutions and countries – ie, the type of externally-induced institutional convergence that I will call throughout this chapter 'high-intensity globalization' – in fact such focus is the result also of parallel and partially convergent judicial transformations cropping up in different countries across the globe and, in part at least, in response to national needs and expectations – ie, the type of spontaneous institutional convergence around the globe to which I refer as 'low-intensity globalization'. The analysis must therefore be sensitive to the diversity of national developments and their causes, rather than hastily producing monolithic global explanations.

One of the most striking features of the focus on the judicial system is that the attention given to courts lies, now in the recognition of their function as the ultimate guarantors of the rule of law, now in the denunciation of their incapacity to fulfill such function. In other words, the judicial system gains social and political visibility for being simultaneously part of the solution and part of the problem of the enforcement of the rule of law. When it is viewed as part of the solution, the focus is on judicial power and judicial activism; when seen as part of the problem, the focus is on judicial crisis and the need for judicial reform. However, in the latter case, the features or conditions that are now the object of criticism and reform were previously tolerated or ignored. The critical attention they now get is a product of the new role attributed to courts as a key instrument of good governance and law-based development.

---

[5] The current debate on the autonomy and jurisdiction of the new permanent International Criminal Court which entered into force in 2002 is illustrative of the tensions and constraints confronting the internationalization of the judicial system.

4   THE GLOBALIZATION OF THE RULE OF LAW AND JUDICIAL REFORM

The 1990s witnessed the increasing social and political visibility of the judicial systems across the globe, the rising protagonism of courts, judges, and prosecutors in public life and the mass media, and the transformation of the once exoteric judicial affairs and proceedings into frequent topic of conversation among lay citizens. All this has been seen as evidence that we are entering a period of global expansion of judicial power. Is that so? And if so, what is its sociological and political explanation and meaning? Before trying to answer these questions, let us scrutinize the empirical evidence at hand. For analytical purposes, as I have been doing throughout this book, I shall distinguish among core, semi-peripheral, and peripheral countries, according to their position in the world system – although my study will concentrate on core and semi-peripheral countries. Based on the three-fold analytical framework I laid out in Chapter Five, this criterion will be combined with two others: the different legal cultures and institutional traditions, and the different trajectories through which the various countries entered modernity and thus legal modernity.

4.1   *The judicial system in core countries*

Concerning the core countries of Europe and North America, the most striking fact of the last decade is the large-scale battle of the Italian courts against the political corruption that devastated the political class that had dominated Italian politics since World War II, and indeed shattered the basic foundations of the Italian political regime. This battle, known as *Mani Pulite* (Clean Hands) started in Milan in April 1992. The whole process of corruption cases in the city came to be known as *Tangentopoli* (Kickback-City) and spread to other cities later on. Charges, arrests, and measures of preventive custody were issued against ministers, party leaders, members of parliament – at one time as many as one third of them were under investigation – civil servants, businessmen, financial journalists, and members of the secret services. They were accused of bribery, corruption, abuse of public office, fraud, criminal bankruptcy, false accounting, and illicit political funding. Two years later 633 arrests had been ordered in Naples; 623 in Milan; 444 in Rome.[6]

The political turmoil was so vast and deep that many saw emerging in its aftermath a new political regime, the Second Republic, a product of an extreme form of judicial activism and of judicialization of politics, derogatorily called by some the 'Republic of Judges'. However unique in its radicalism, the Italian judicial protagonism does not stand alone in Europe. High-profile abuse of power charges, charges against members

---

[6]   For this description I rely heavily on Nelken, 1996. On the political impact of corruption in Italy, see Della Porta and Di Tella, 1997. On corruption in Europe, see Della Porta and Meny, 1997. On the economic and politics of corruption in general, see Heywood, 1997.

of the government, as well as corruption charges against politicians and businessmen have been brought to court in France, Belgium, Holland, Germany, Greece, Spain, and Portugal. In Spain the judicial investigation came very close to the then Prime Minister, Felipe González, in a case of alleged abuse of power, the funding of death squads against the militants of ETA, the armed organization of basque nationalists.

But the expansion of judicial protagonism in Continental Europe is not limited to criminal justice. It occurs in three other instances. First, the new activism of the constitutional courts in Germany, Italy, Spain, and Portugal in cases of separation of powers or of distribution of competences among levels of government (local, regional, national), and in cases of human rights guaranteed by the Constitution. Secondly, an emerging assertiveness of regular and administrative courts against the abuse of administrative power by state institutions in favour of judicial guarantee of individual and collective rights in the field of consumer and environmental protection. Thirdly, the high-profile role played by the European Court of Justice, a key institution in the creation of the European legal system, often forcing member states to change their policies in line with its rulings.[7] At a different level, and on a much smaller scale, the same has also been the case of the European Court of Human Rights.

But the social visibility of the courts in Europe resides as much in their accomplishments as in their failures. Indeed, the high-profile interventions of courts in high-profile and political cases – what I shall call dramatic justice – have contributed to sharpen the contrast with the everyday functioning of courts – routine justice – the judicial activity that is most likely to affect ordinary citizens. Particularly in Italy, France, Portugal, and Spain, the courts have been harshly criticized for their inefficiency, inaccessibility, unreasonable delays, high expenses, lack of transparency and accountability, corporatist privileges, the large numbers of prisoners awaiting trial, investigative incompetence, and so on and so forth. In a study I conducted with a research team regarding the uses of courts in Portugal, a clear picture emerges of the citizens' great distance and diffidence vis-à-vis the judicial system and their relatively low degree of satisfaction whenever they have been involved in court proceedings.[8]

If we turn to the North American countries, the US has been the motherland of legal and judicial activism,[9] to such an extent that Shapiro refers to the recent judicial trends in Europe as 'Americanization'.[10] Curiously enough, for the last decade such a distinctive feature of American society has been under attack: the so-called litigation explosion, the public and political denunciation of excessive litigiousness and of the costs of litigation, the call for less active court intervention in policy-making, the changes

---

[7] On the evolution of the European Court of Justice and its contribution to the emergence of a 'European Union rule of law,' see McCormick, 1999. See also Chapter Five.

[8] Santos *et al*, 1996.

[9] Galanter, 1992.

[10] Shapiro, 1993.

in the Supreme Court, etc. Moreover, while the call for the new centrality of the judicial system in social and political development across the globe seems to echo the American experience, in the US the role of courts in bringing about progressive social change has been highly questioned in recent times.[11] These developments have led some to believe that the US 'may have passed the peak of judicial policy-making in both constitutional and administrative judicial review.'[12] In Canada the judicial power seems to be on the rise, particularly after the adoption of the Charter of Rights of 1982, which granted the Supreme Court a major influence on the policies of provincial and cultural autonomy.

The global picture of courts in the core countries is thus one of expansion of judicial power, with a probable counterbalance in the country traditionally with the highest level of judicial power. Though identified in several countries, this process seems to respond to internal specific conditions in each one of them. In all of them, however, the higher visibility of courts has involved heightened criticisms of the courts' limitations and inefficiencies or, in the case of the US, criticisms of lawyers held responsible for the dysfunctional excesses of litigation. In any case, in all the countries in question, these criticisms have been less harsh than those addressed at government and elected politicians. Indeed, the growing distrust of the latter is believed to have led to the judicialization of politics. Before engaging in a detailed analysis of this phenomenon, I will examine the recent judicial trends in the semi-peripheral countries.

4.2   The judicial system in semi-peripheral countries

4.2.1   THE DEMOCRATIC TRANSITION AND THE FIGHT AGAINST CORRUPTION

Semi-peripheral countries tend to be highly unstable polities. Their intermediate position in the world system, their class structure, the conflictual coexistence of an active civil society, however fragmented and poorly organized, with a strong state, often a developmentalist state varying widely in legitimacy, coercive capacity and efficiency – all these features make social conflicts particularly complex in these societies and social compromises more difficult to achieve. That is why these countries have tended to undergo more or less long periods of authoritarian rule alternating with periods of more or less consolidated democratic rule.

Concerning the semi-peripheral countries of Europe, Portugal and Spain lived under an authoritarian regime for four decades and, during that period, the judicial system was either reduced to an appendage of the government – in politically sensitive areas such as political crimes and labour disputes – or kept a low-profile independence and remained utterly isolated from society. The democratic transitions of the mid-1970s

---

[11]   Rosenberg, 1991 argues that the idea that judicial activism promotes social change is a myth.
[12]   Shapiro, 1993, p 64.

brought with them large institutional changes in the judicial system. It took a decade for the courts to vindicate a more active role in society. Today, what distinguishes these two countries from the European core countries is that in them the judicialization of politics coexists with a greater distance and higher diffidence of citizens vis-à-vis the judicial system. The discrepancy between the dramatic justice of high profile judicial activism and the routine justice of everyday operations of the judicial system is accordingly wider.

The semi-peripheral countries of Central and Eastern Europe underwent democratic transitions in the late 1980s.[13] During the communist period, and even though the situation varied from country to country, there was very little room for the rule of law or independent judiciary. Probably for this reason, the judicialization of politics through judicial review became a central issue early in the transition period. The Russian case is particularly telling in this respect because the autocratic traits of Russian political culture antedate 1917 and have fostered a deep-seated resistance against a strong independent judiciary. In the late 1980s the *glasnost* media started reporting extensively on such a phenomenon as the 'telephone law' in which party officials would telephone a judge and 'advise' him on what the outcome of a particular case ought to be.[14] In 1989 the Soviet Committee on Constitutional Supervision was established. The committee had the power to declare as invalid laws, presidential decrees and other normative instruments.[15] In the two years of its existence it struck down many laws and decrees. The political incongruence of this Committee was that it coexisted with the Soviet Constitution of 1977, the Brezhnev Constitution, which was utterly hostile to the idea of the judicialization of politics. Indeed, the same incongruence continued after the coup of August 1991, when the Soviet constitutional committee was replaced by the Russian Constitutional Court. This court had increased powers of judicial review, and its first chairman, Valery Zvorkin, made it clear that the court's dual mission was to create the rule of law and to prevent the relapse into totalitarianism.[16] The not unexpected clashes between the court and President Yeltsin led to its suspension and to a new Constitution with a revised regime of judicial review that same year.[17]

---

[13] Transitional justice has become the object of a very dynamic area of interdisciplinary legal research. For an overview see Elster, 1998.

[14] Thomas, 1995, p 425.

[15] Kitchin, 1995, p 443.

[16] Kitchin 1995, p 446.

[17] The Russian Constitutional Court was suspended for more than a year. It resumed its activities in March 1995 and it was immediately thrust into the public spotlight. According to Pomeranz, 1997, one of the most controversial cases that the Constitutional Court has dealt with since its 1995 reinstatement has been the Chechen case, which revolved around President Yeltsin's decision to send federal troops into the Chechen Republic without first seeking legislative consent. For Pomeranz this controversial case on the division of powers represented the opportunity for the new Constitutional Court to dispel the activist image that it had acquired during the previous period, before suspension.

Other countries in the former communist Europe have been successful in instituting judicial review through the establishment of constitutional courts. The most remarkable example is probably Hungary where the Constitutional Court – established when the parliament adopted a highly revised version of the old socialist constitution in October 1989 – has played a crucial role in shaping the political system of the country and has become the most credible institution of the new democratic regime in light of its advanced human rights jurisprudence.[18]

Aside from the Constitutional Court and judicial review, the other major focus of the rule of law and judicial reform in Central and Eastern Europe has been the creation of a legal framework and a judicial system suited to promote and consolidate the sweeping transition from an administrative-command economy to a market economy. The assumption – a distinctly Western law-and-modernization assumption – is that privatization of the immense state sector and the consequent massive expansion of contractual relations will both presuppose and induce an increasing reliance on law and judicial institutions.[19] Without this, there will be neither stability nor predictability, which are the prerequisites of a healthy economic environment based on the market and the private sector. These concerns have been paramount in the international assistance provided to Central and Eastern Europe by the World Bank, the USAID, and various American Foundations. In the early 1990s the USAID announced its purpose to invest more resources in democracy and rule-of-law programmes in the region, particularly in view of the fact that the countries under consideration were 'advanced developing countries,' that is to say, semi-peripheral countries.[20]

Though the programmes are still going on, the most recent assessments of the legal and judicial reforms in this region, and particularly in its most important country, Russia, are now less enthusiastic than before. For instance, Hendley concedes that her hypothesis that the combination of privatization and political differentiation in post-Soviet Russia might serve as a catalyst for a profound change in Russian legal culture was overly optimistic. According to Hendley, the Soviet past weighs too heavily on the Russian present; managers do not believe in the enforceability of contracts through legal means and try to achieve the basic purpose of contracts (ensuring their supplies) by other means.[21] Under these circumstances, the distrust of law and legal institutions cannot be remedied with quick-fix reform: 'The patron-client networks that characterized the prior system [the authoritarian policies of the ruling Communist Party] may be more easily taken over by private law enforcers, namely the mafia, than by formal legal institutions.'[22]

---

[18]   Zifzak, 1996, p 1.
[19]   Hendley, 1995, p 41.
[20]   USAID, 1994, p 2.
[21]   Hendley, 1995, p 63.
[22]   Hendley, 1995, p 48. Over the years Hendley has offered us a sustained analysis of the evolution of legal and judicial reform in Russia. See Hendley, 1996, 1997, 1998, 1999, 2001.

The recent rule of law and judicial trends in Central and Eastern Europe offer two sharp contrasts with the situation in Western Europe. In the first place, the increased judicial protagonism in Western Europe has derived above all from the campaign against political and business corruption. In Russia, as in other Eastern European countries, the Constitutional Court has been a major focus of attention; and on the other hand, though corruption has been rampant with the proliferation of mafias filling the void of power and command once exerted by the Communist Party, it has caught little judicial attention. The focus has been rather on the legal consequences of economic reform, privatization, marketization, and contractualization. This has been particularly the case of the foreign legal assistance in which the US has played a pivotal role. And this leads me to the second contrast with Western Europe. The legal and judicial reforms undertaken by the Southern European countries during their democratic transitions in the mid-1970s were carried out with domestic resources, in response to internally defined needs and aspirations, and with the purpose of re-integrating their legal and judicial systems in the democratic tradition and the continental European legal culture. In Central and Eastern Europe, the legal and judicial reforms are being driven by strong international pressures – a form of high-intensity globalization, for which, especially in the economic legal field, American law, rather than continental European law, provides the model. Between 1993 and 1998, the US spent 970m dollars in foreign aid for legal reform in 184 countries. Although in this period the region of the world that received most funds was Latin America and the Caribbean (349m dollars), the amount of money given to Europe increased throughout the period and in 1998 represented a third of the funds distributed that year. Central Europe – which includes, among others, Bosnia-Herzegovina, Croatia, Slovenia, Hungary, the Czech Republic, Poland, Macedonia and Romania –, along with the newly independent countries – in which, curiously enough, Russia is included together with Armenia, Azerbaijan, Kazakhstan, Ukraine, Moldavia, Byelorussia, etc – received 287.3m dollars between 1993 and 1998.[23]

I turn now to some semi-peripheral countries of Latin America. Rule of law and judicial programmes in Latin America, as much as in Central Eastern Europe, have a strong international component. They are a domain of high-intensity globalization in which the US plays the leading role followed at a distance by some countries of the EU. In some Latin American countries more than in others, there are strong internal forces driving the reforms, at times in tandem with the globalizing pressures, at times in collision with them. There are also strong internal resistances to reform. In the countries that were ruled until the 1980s by an authoritarian regime – such as Argentina, Chile, Brazil, El Salvador, Honduras – the internal impulse for judicial reform in the democratic transition focused more on the independence of the judiciary, due process guarantees, judicial review, and far less on access to justice.[24]

---

[23]   GAO/NSIAD-99-158-5.

[24]   In Argentina, during the presidency of Carlos Menem the focus was on access rather than on independence, as shown below.

During the dictatorship, judges – generally viewed in Latin America as a conservative body who systematically favoured the propertied classes and the rulers of the day – were either sympathetic to the military *juntas* (as in Argentina) or easily neutralized by them (as in Brazil).[25] This was even the case of the Chilean judicial system, which had reputation for conservatism but also for probity and seriousness. The activism of the Chilean judicial system against the democratic socialist measures of Salvador Allende in the early 1970s, which closely resembled the activism of the US Supreme Court against the New Deal, became a landmark of conservative judicial protagonism in Latin America. The Truth Commissions that were established to investigate the violations of human rights and the crimes perpetrated by the *juntas*, such as those in Argentina, Chile, El Salvador, and Honduras, recommended thorough judicial reforms.[26] Indeed, the first test for the new judicial system – which in most cases remained very much the same as the old one – was the trial of the dictators and the torturers at their orders. The test failed, either because of the political compromises between the outgoing and incoming political class (the cases of Brazil and Chile), or because of the instability caused by the trials forced the government to retreat (the case of Argentina).

The other major focus of the judicialization of politics in the last decade in Latin America has been judicial review, that is, the power of the courts to declare a law or other normative decree null and void on the ground that it violates the Constitution. In some countries judicial review is the responsibility of the Supreme Court (Argentina); in others it is the responsibility of constitutional courts (Brazil and Colombia) or even on lower courts with possibility of further review by the higher court (Colombia). The effective exercise of this power and its contribution to the consolidation of democracy varies widely from country to country.

On one extreme we may find the Argentinean Supreme Court. According to Carlos Nino, since its independence some 160 years ago Argentina has lived under open and genuine democracy for more than twenty years and the Supreme Court has been more than anything else an impairment of the democratic process.[27] By way of example, Nino mentions a long-standing judicial doctrine, the 'doctrine of the *de facto* law,' that ascribes validity to the laws enacted by regimes that come to power by force. The vicissitudes of this doctrine in recent times show how far the political control of the judiciary by the government can go. One of the first measures of President Alfonsín after he took office in 1983 was to send a law project to Congress asking for the nullification of the so-called self-amnesty law, a law which the military had enacted right at the end of their period to cover the abuses of human rights committed under their rule. The nullification was unanimously approved by Congress, the law was subsequently upheld by the Supreme Court, and thus breaking away from the doctrine of the *de facto* law for the first time in more than a century. After taking office in 1991, President Menem, not

[25]   Osiel, 1995.
[26]   Popkin and Roht-Arriaza, 1995.
[27]   Nino, 1993, p 317.

happy about the Supreme Court, hastened to pass a law to increase the number of Supreme Court judges and fill the new positions with people loyal to his ideas.[28] In the same year, the Supreme Court resumed the old doctrine with the positivist argument that the laws enacted by the Congress should be deemed valid regardless of the 'affective or ideological evaluation' that can be made of military regimes. This leads Nino to the conclusion that 'the Supreme Court and in fact the judicial system as a whole fell short during most of Argentina's history of realizing its responsibility as custodian of the democratic system.'[29]

At the other extreme, we might consider the Colombian Constitutional Court created by the Constitution of 1991. The Colombian Constitution has the broadest system of constitutional control. At the request of any citizen, it grants to the lower courts the power to suspend a decision or measure by any public or private authority on the ground that it violates fundamental rights and the ruling may be reviewed on appeal by the Constitutional Court. Judicial review is vested upon the Constitutional Court, which has intervened in some high-profile cases regarding the protection of human rights and cultural diversity[30] and has even nullified government decrees declaring the state of exception.[31] In an interview the President of the court confided that the court was walking a tight rope, since the government, unhappy about the show of judicial independence and having the majority in Congress, could at any moment propose the revision of the Constitution to abolish the court or reduce its review powers.[32] Such risk has only increased with the advent of a right-wing government in 2002.

The high-profile interventions or omissions of the highest courts in Latin America have been very controversial and often in collision course with the executive or the legislature. Their contribution to the consolidation of democracy is ambiguous and cannot be established in general. This protagonism of the judicial system has, however, been upset by a kind of negative protagonism: the increased and ever more publicized dissatisfaction of the citizenry with the inefficiency, slowness, inaccessibility, elitism, arrogant corporatism and even corruption of the judicial system in its everyday functioning. The dual image of courts already identified in Southern Europe is much more striking in Latin America. To continue with the case of Colombia, the activism and protagonism of the Constitutional Court stands in stark contrast with the routinization of civil courts, which devote most of their time and effort to debt collection

---

[28] Stotzky and Nino, 1993, p 8; Nino, 1993, p 319. With the same purpose of keeping the judicial system under political control, several judges of the Constitutional Court of Peru were dismissed by the Government in 1997. See Pastor, 1998: p 22.

[29] Nino, 1993, p 321.

[30] García-Villegas and Rodríguez, 2001.

[31] García-Villegas, 1993, p 139; 1996.

[32] The interview was given to the author on 10 September 1996, as part of a research project on the landscape of justices in Colombia.

on behalf of banks and other financial corporations.[33] Moreover, the Latin American judicial system seems to be very timid in bringing corruption charges against government officials. Cases of corruption are reported daily in the mass media but very little judicial investigation takes place. In Brazil, President Collor de Mello, who was impeached by the Congress on corruption charges, was acquitted in court. In this regard, and for reasons mentioned below, Colombia seems to be a partial exception. In the late 1990s, the Attorney General's Office (*Fiscalía*) conducted a high-profile battle against political corruption, particularly relating to organized crime and drug trafficking. Ministers and other high-ranking party officials were arrested and half of the members of Parliament were under investigation.

4.2.2 COURT REFORM IN THE SEMI-PERIPHERY: A CASE OF HIGH-INTENSITY GLOBALIZATION

The most notorious feature of the focus on rule of law in the developing world from the mid-1980s onwards is the high-intensity globalization character of the reformist pressure on the judicial system. In Latin America, the institutions that exert such pressure are the USAID, the World Bank, the Inter-American Development Bank, the US Justice Department, the Ford Foundation, and the EU (collectively or through some of its members). I cannot go into great detail here about the multiple features of this pressure. I will limit myself to commently briefly on some of them. As far as the USAID is concerned, since the early 1990s, support for the rule of law has become a major component of its assistance programmes. Although, – as César Rodríguez has shown in his study of the two waves of 'law and development' in Latin America[34] – USAID investments in law programmes date back to the 1960s – ie, the first wave of law and development focusing on legal education – the current resurge of activities in this area began in the mid-1980s with the USAID Administration of Justice programme in Latin America, which marks the beginning of the second wave, focusing on judicial reform. According to an internal assessment, Latin America was the testing ground for the law programmes that since the 1990s have spread to Asia, Africa, Eastern Europe, and the newly independent countries.[35]

The USAID distinguishes four generations of law programmes since the early 1960s. The first generation focused on legal education and law reform; the second, on basic needs legal aid; the third, on court reform. The current fourth generation is the most ambitious and political in the Agency's terms because it encompasses all the concerns of the three previous generations of programmes and broadens their scope while including them in the design and implementation of country democracy programmes.[36]

---

[33]   On this contrast, see Rodríguez, 2001b (on Colombian civil courts) and Rodríguez, 2001c (on Colombian labour courts).

[34]   Rodríguez, 2001a.

[35]   USAID, 1994; VII.

[36]   USAID, 1994, p 4.

In the latest generation, unlike in the previous periods, assistance is conceived as political and not merely as technical. The objective is to promote democracy even against the resistance of the host country. In the latter case, resistance must be overcome through coalition and constituency-building strategies to forge elite commitment to law reform.[37] In the Agency's jargon, such strategy 'facilitates host country demand.'[38] In a recent assessment of six rule-of-law programmes, four of them in Latin America, the Agency concedes that this strategy was successful only in one of them, Colombia.[39]

The constituency-building strategy is considered the most important of all the strategies used because it is the most political. Indeed, the approaches adopted in the previous periods are criticized for being narrowly defined as technical assistance conducted by 'planners accustomed to thinking bureaucratically rather than politically.'[40] And yet, the Agency recognizes that the technical approach was suited to the political conditions of the cold war motivated by:

> '[...] the concern that mobilizing citizen pressure groups for reform might inflame national sentiments over US involvement in a sensitive political area ... and in some instances there was apprehension (particularly in the cold war era) that encouraging grassroots demands for reform might overwhelm fragile democratic institutions and open the way to the ascendance of antidemocratic political movements from either the left or the right.'[41]

This concern with the right being a potential source of instability sounds utterly cynical since the USAID co-operated with all the military *juntas*. In any case, the inference is that in a post-cold war period the strategies of the Agency must be overtly political, meaning that the law reforms must be understood as part of a political project for the consolidation of democracy.

The ROL (rule of law) programmes are wide-ranging and involve the following strategies: coalition and constituency-building, structural reform of laws and institutions, access to justice and legal system strengthening. A closer look at the deployment of these strategies shows that from country to country they vary in scope and emphasis. Among Latin American states, Colombia, El Salvador, Guatemala, Honduras and Panama were the main recipients of USAID 'legal aid' funds, according

---

[37]　USAID, 1994; VIII.

[38]　One cannot help tracing in this 'new' strategy the same imperialistic posture that led in a very recent past the USAID and the US government to collaborate with military *juntas*, when they were not directly involved in their coming to power.

[39]　Other evaluations of the rule of law and judicial reform movement in Latin America mention Chile and Costa Rica as successful cases and Mexico and Argentina as failures. See Carothers, 1998, p 101.

[40]　USAID, 1994, p 19.

[41]　USAID, 1994, p.18.

to a 1999 General Accounting Office Report.[42] Since the early 1990s, the USAID and the Department of Justice granted more than 160m dollars for legal aid programmes.[43] In all of those countries, except Colombia, this period witnessed the transition from dictatorship to democracy, as well as intense violent political conflicts, which in Colombia deteriorated further. It comes as no surprise, then, that most legal aid funds were aimed at criminal justice reform. In Colombia, USAID invested 2.7m dollars between 1986 and 1991. In the 1991–1999 period alone, 39m dollars were invested: 18.5m through USAID and the remainder through two programmes funded by the US Department of Justice – 7m through the International Criminal Investigative Training Assistance Program (ICITAP)[44] and 3.5 million through the Overseas Prosecutorial Development Assistance and Training (OPDAT). El Salvador, which received 13.7m dollars between 1984 and 1992 from USAID, has received 54m dollars since – 18m from USAID and 36m from ICITAP. In Guatemala, foreign aid for criminal justice reform programmes rose from 6.1m dollars in 1987–1993 to 17 m in 1993–1999. In Honduras, USAID spent 8m dollars between 1987 and 1998 and planned to grant 7m between 1999 and 2002. Also, between 1994 and 1999 ICITAP invested 4m dollars in the creation of the Honduran police force. In Panama, since 1990 the US have invested 43.3m dollars – 9.6m through USAID and 33.7m through ICITAP, the latter for 'strengthening the national police force'.

While in these countries the legal aid programmes were sizable, in others the programmes were rather modest. For instance, USAID's assistance programme in Argentina between 1989 and 1993 involved less than 2m dollars, and in Uruguay only 850,000 dollars. However, it is important to note that in the period 1993–1998 the country that in the region – and indeed in the world – received the most funds for rule of law programmes was Haiti, due to the role of the US in the dismantling of the Haitian army after the concerted intervention of 1991. Almost all the funds (137.9m dollars) were invested in the creation of the national police.[45] According to the same report by the General Accounting Office, assistance programmes in Latin America and the Caribbean were focused on criminal justice (to which 57 per cent of the funds were devoted), including

---

[42]   GAO-NSIAD-99-195.

[43]   It is not easy to determine precisely the amount of legal aid funds involved. Even when the same source is used, different reports present different data. Compare, for instance, the August 1999 GAO report (GAO/NSIAD-99-195) with the July 1999 report by the same source (GAO/NSIAD-99-158).

[44]   Despite being rather unknown, ICITAP is nowadays essential in the US programs of bilateral assistance regarding police and criminal investigation reforms. Created in 1986 in order to cater to Latin America and the Caribbean, ICITAP expanded very quickly in the 1990s, both in budget and geographical scope. Between 1986 and 1996 its administrative budget increased twenty-fold – by 1996 it was 30m dollars. Countries in which ICITAP has been an active player include Panama, El Salvador, Bolivia, Colombia, Haiti, Guatemala and Honduras. In 1996 new projects were approved to be carried out in South Africa, Liberia, Belize and Brazil. Projects were being considered also for Albania, Cambodia, Estonia, Jordan, Mexico and Lebanon. See Call, 1998.

[45]   GAO/NSIAID-99-158-10.

assistance to the police, prosecutors, investigators and other actors involved in anti-drug and anti-terrorism activities. The other programmes concerned infrastructure (21.3 per cent of the allocated funds), the reform of government and the army (13.6 per cent), and human rights and democracy promotion (6.3 per cent).[46] While the USAID proclaims today the political character of its law and judicial reform programmes, the World Bank prefers to emphasize the need to foster the legal and judicial environment conducive to trade, financing, and investment, justifying its position with the Bank's charter, which defines the promotion of economic development as the Bank's principal mandate and does not include political reform.[47] This mandate is very broad indeed: 'it encompasses everything from writing or revising commercial codes, bankruptcy statutes and company laws through overhauling regulatory agencies and teaching justice ministry officials how to draft legislation that fosters private investment.'[48] The increasing interest of the World Bank in court reform is thus justified because 'experience has shown that such reform cannot be ignored in the process of economic development or adjustment.'[49] That this interest in the role of law and courts is only apparently apolitical or depoliticized is clearly shown in the philosophy underlying one of the areas of intervention that in previous periods was considered more political, the area of access to justice. In a conference organized by the Bank, Bryant Garth argued that the constitutionalization of human rights had made possible a more neutral stand on the question of gaining access to justice and, therefore, a 'depoliticized' legal aid: 'instead of seeing legal aid as the cutting edge of a political movement, it can now be considered a fundamental right of citizenship under the rule of law.'[50]

The Bank's intervention in this area is worldwide and may be very wide-ranging in scope. In Laos, for instance, it has addressed the country's legal system as a whole because, since it had embarked on a complete change of its economic and social system, the country 'needed a parallel overhaul of its legal system.'[51] In Latin America the Bank has provided, among others, grants or loans for legal and judicial reform in Venezuela (1992, 30m dollars),[52] in Bolivia (1995, 11m dollars), in Ecuador (1996, 10.7m dollars) and Peru (1997, 22.5m dollars).[53]

---

[46] GAO-NSIAD 99-158-11.

[47] The USAID sees itself as an experimental risk-taking innovator in developing approaches, with modest funding, that can then be taken over by other donors willing to make more substantial investments (USAID, 1994).

[48] Messick, 1999, p 118.

[49] Shihata, 1995, p 14.

[50] Garth, 1995, p 90.

[51] Shihata, 1995, p 14.

[52] The total investment of Venezuela in judicial reform, in particular, in the reform of penal justice, amounts to 120m dollars. According to recent official data, of the 23,379 detained in Venezuelan prisons, only 7,945 have been convicted. These and other similarly disquieting data have led the president of the Judicial Council to consider that the judicial and legal reform is a question 'of survival of democracy'.

[53] A recent and persuasive analysis of the failures of the judicial reforms in some Latin American countries (El Salvador, Brazil, Argentina and Chile) can be read in Prillaman, 2000.

Outside Latin America the concern with the rule of law and judicial reform is also very much present. In peripheral countries, such as Mozambique or Cambodia, and in spite of the abysmal social problems that afflict their populations, this concern is often part and parcel of painful and fragile democratic transitions after years or even decades of civil war and dictatorship.[54] The problematic nature of these transitions is further compounded by the hardships imposed on popular classes by the neo-liberal economic recipes that usually accompany such transitions. In these countries the rule-of-law/ court reforms tend to be extreme instances of high-intensity globalization, in that, the reforms are mainly driven by donor countries, international assistance agencies, and international financial institutions. They define the priorities, impose the orientation and the sequencing of the reforms and, of course, provide the resources to bring them about.

Concerning the semi-peripheral countries the situation is very different. In many of them the interest in rule-of-law and court reform runs very high but internal developments, rather than globalizing pressures seem to explain it. In some countries the judicial system is assuming a more prominent role and consequently becoming more controversial and inviting debate on the expansion of the judicial power and the judicialization of politics. In Africa, South Africa is a particularly interesting case. As Heinz Klug has pointed out, having emerged from a long period of authoritarianism and apartheid, South Africa has shown a striking faith in the judicial system to mediate in the construction of a post-apartheid political order (1996). The Constitutional Court, established under the 'interim' constitution of 1993, was assigned the role of reviewing the final 1996 Constitution enacted by the Constitutional Assembly. The court performed that role in very concrete terms, nullifying some of the provisions of the document initially submitted to it by the Assembly, and the latter subsequently made the changes according to the court's ruling. The South African, as well as the Russian, Hungarian and Colombian cases, show the extent to which constitutional courts and judiciary review in general have contributed towards the judicialization of politics during the last decade. In the South African case, Klug argues, the faith in the judiciary to uphold the new democratic order 'is particularly striking given the past failure of the judiciary to uphold basic principles of justice in the face of apartheid policies and laws.'[55]

As a matter of fact, the South African judicial system is facing a challenge similar to the one faced by Latin American courts in the aftermath of the democratic transition: the

---

[54]   In Cambodia see Lorenz, 1995. The Kmer Rouge literally liquidated the judicial system as a whole. Only one judge with legal training remained in the country after that. In the case of Mozambique, after centuries of colonialism and thirty years of war, the few able lawyers of the country are justices of the Supreme Court or practice law in Maputo. In the rest of the country, the judicial system, in the liberal modern sense, hardly exists. The Danish international aid agency (DANIDA) and the Portuguese government have recently provided the funds to rebuilt (or rather to build anew) the judicial system. See Santos and Trindade, 2002.

[55]   Klug, 1996, p 2. See also Klug, 2000a.

challenge of submitting to trial and punishment the politically motivated murders and tortures committed by the apartheid rulers or at their service. The acquittal in October 1996 of apartheid-era Defence Minister Magnus Malan and 15 others involved in the death squad massacre of 1987 might indicate that, in this instance, the South African courts will probably not fare better than the Latin American ones. Furthermore, the post-apartheid access to justice is still to be built, and that is another great challenge. What distinguishes South African courts from Latin American courts is the former's greater efficiency in dealing with the judicial affairs of the business world. Probably for this reason, contrary to what is happening in Latin America, the judicial reforms in South Africa are being carried out with internal resources and according to needs and expectations defined domestically.

Two other semi-peripheral countries, both in Asia, reveal interesting trends towards a greater political protagonism on the part of the judicial system. In India, the judicial system has been recently at the centre of the political debate, pressed or encouraged by a strong public opinion against political corruption. The indictment of the former Prime Minister PV Narasimha Rao on forgery charges and of many other politicians and high state officials on corruption charges was viewed as a test case of the courts' integrity and independence.[56] In South Korea, the judicial system has traditionally been an appendage of authoritarian government, first Japan's colonial rulers, then a succession of military rulers. Moreover, corruption in the judicial system has been pervasive all along. Today, however, in tandem with the democratization process, the judicial system has begun to assert its independence, starting with a set of proposals put forward by the chief justice of the Supreme Court, Yun Kwan, soon after his confirmation in 1993, which have sparked public attention and political debate.[57] Since then two former presidents have been convicted in corruption cases.

4.3 USAID in Colombia: a case study of high-intensity global legal reform

To further ground my argument on the globalization of the legal field as it is played out in the domain of legal reform, in this section I offer a brief case study of the role of USAID in Colombia. As I mentioned above, Colombia is one of the countries in Latin America where USAID has been most involved in programmes of legal aid. USAID's activities in Colombia can be divided into three periods: 1986–1991, 1992–1996, and 1997–1999.[58] The first phase was exploratory in nature and focused on supporting the investigative apparatuses of the police and the judiciary. As mentioned above, the funds invested in this period were considerably lower than those invested in the

---

[56] The cover story, titled 'Steely Resolve', of *India Today*, 31 October 1996 is dedicated to the courts' determination to uphold accountability at all costs: 'A judicial coup d'etat? Hardly. The growing assertiveness of the higher judiciary over the past year in meting out corruption in public life has caused near hysteria amongst politicians' (p 20).

[57] Hoon, 1993.

[58] For an analysis of these periods, especially the first two, see Arenas, 1998; Rodríguez, 2001a.

subsequent periods. Due to disagreements between the Colombian Secretary of Justice and the judiciary as to who should manage the funds, USAID decided to entrust the management of the project to a private foundation by the name of FES (*Fundación para la Educación Superior* – Foundation for Higher Education). The programme thus created was dubbed Program for the Modernization of the Administration of Justice (PMAJ for its acronym in Spanish). In 1990, with the arrival of César Gaviria to the presidency – who would later become Secretary General of the OAS – USAID's intervention took a dramatic turn, as shown by the fact that USAID funds available for legal reform projects in Colombia increased 50 per cent. In fact, the sums of money granted in 1990 (1.1m dollars) are equal to the amount granted in the previous two years.

The appointment of Jaime Giraldo Angel – the 'main spokesperson for the judicial reform programmes promoted by USAID through FES'[59] – as Secretary of Justice raised considerably the political profile of the programmes. According to the 1992 report of the General Accounting Office, 'FES representatives became experts on judicial reform and, in recognition of their performance, President Gaviria appointed some of them in positions within his government. Thus the bridge that made possible the transition to large-scale projects was built.'[60]

Thereafter, the scale and scope of USAID-funded programmes increased. They focused on two main areas: creating specialized courts responsible for handling 'public order' cases – ie, those involving drug trafficking, terrorism and other types of highly destabilizing criminal activities – and supporting the government's draft of a new Constitution, which was submitted to the newly elected constitutional assembly in 1991. As for the first area, among other initiatives, FES sent a commission to Italy to study the strategies that the criminal justice system had pursued against organized crime.

However, the war against drugs quickly occupied all of the attention and resources of the USAID programmes. The single-minded focus on the fight against drug trafficking thus came to dominate the second phase of the programmes. As I mentioned above, USAID's intervention was complemented by programmes funded by ICITAP and OPDAT. On this front, USAID's priority was to get the Attorney-General's Office (*Fiscalía*) – created by the new 1991 constitution – established in order to improve the investigation and prosecution of crimes.

Although it proclaimed itself as a replica of the US prosecutorial system, the *Fiscalía* is in fact a hybrid institution, since its officials carry out both prosecutorial and judicial activities. In order to further strengthen the tools to fight drug trafficking, USAID also supported programmes aimed at bolstering the above-mentioned 'public order' courts – known otherwise as 'faceless courts' because their judges, for security reasons, remain anonymous even to the parties to the trial. Such courts were deemed by USAID to be

59   Arenas, 1998, p 16.
60   GAO/NSIAD-92-269-3.

successful institutional innovations, but have been subject to intense criticism by Colombian and international human rights circles. In addition to the fact that the anonymous nature of the judges violates due process rights, most of the defendants in these courts are not drug traffickers but rather poor peasants caught in the cross-fire between drug traffickers, paramilitary groups, the army and the guerrilla groups.

As USAID's intervention increased, the autonomy and room for manoeuvre of the Colombian government shrank, as shown by two events that took place during the Gaviria administration. First, the proposal made by the government to get drug traffickers to turn themselves in in exchange for milder penalties was not approved by the US. Thus, the proposal was quickly replaced by an all-out repressive strategy aimed against the Cali Cartel. Secondly, the Colombian Attorney General, Gustavo de Greiff, who had some sympathy for the debate on the legalization of drugs as a means to eliminate the economic incentives that make the drug business profitable – a position that went directly against US prohibitionist policies – was marginalized and harshly criticized by the Colombian government.

Colombian legal reform programmes and foreign policy became increasingly dependent on the imperatives of the drug war dictated from Washington during the Samper administration (1994–1998). As Uprimny argues:

> 'Despite the nationalist rhetoric, both the government and Congress carried out all the tasks laid out in the agenda of the US war on drugs: going after major drug traffickers, increasing prison penalties for certain crimes, stepping up the aerial spraying of coca fields with chemicals, re-establishing the extradition of drug traffickers to the US, and putting in place legal mechanisms against money laundering.'[61]

With the increase in USAID funds during the second phase came the intervention of other multilateral agencies. Thus, in May 1995 the Inter-American Development Bank (IDB) announced the donation of 1.2m dollars to a programme for strengthening private arbitration and conciliation mechanisms for solving commercial disputes managed by the Bogota Chamber of Commerce. In December 1995 the IDB approved a 9.4m dollars loan to Colombia for a programme aimed at bolstering the Attorney-General's Office.[62] This loan further focused legal aid programmes in Colombia on the war on drugs, to the detriment of other reforms aimed at improving access to justice and the protection of human rights.[63]

The third phase of the USAID legal aid activities in Colombia is basically the continuation of the programmes from the second period. This was made possible by an agreement signed between the Colombian government and USAID in September

---

[61]   Uprimny, 2001, p 290.
[62]   Arenas, 1998, p 30.
[63]   On this asymmetry within legal reforms programs in Colombia and in Latin America at large, see Rodríguez, 2001c.

1997, which was in force until August 1999. The emphasis in this phase was again criminal justice reform to continue waging the drug war. Five areas of reform were the centre of this period: (1) support to prosecutors; (2) support to judges; 3) support to public defenders in criminal trials; (4) support to the three main investigative bodies: the Police, the investigative branch of the *Fiscalía* (CTI) and the special investigative force (DAS); and (5) improvement of mechanisms of access to justice and of the judiciary's image, through programmes organized by the Colombian Department of Justice and local NGOs.

In this phase, FES – the private foundation that participated in the previous two periods – no longer managed USAID's funds. Instead, USAID handled the projects either directly or in collaboration with ICITAP or OPDAT.[64] The latter became an active player in the so-called National Training Program, which sought 'to create "special units" made up of prosecutors and investigators working together permanently and carrying out investigations swiftly through the use of team work methodologies and the application of the new criminal laws.'[65]

US intervention has dominated legal reform in Colombia to such an extent that it would be more appropriate to speak of Americanization rather than of globalization of such a reform. However, it makes sense to continue to speak of globalization because US conceptions regarding legal reform have also dominated programmes promoted by other countries and regions – eg, those of some European countries and of the EU itself. We are thus witnessing a process of high-intensity globalization – or even one of extreme-intensity globalization, as the description I just offered of the Colombian case shows. Such extremely high pressure on the Colombian judicial system is legitimated by a hegemonic conception promoted by the US on the unconditional prohibition and repression of production, sale and consumption of some drugs. Since this is a US conception that has been gradually globalized, in terms of the typology of globalization I laid out in Chapter Five it amounts to a globalized localism.

Over the last few years, such a conception has dominated completely US criminal justice policy in Latin America in general and in Colombia in particular. Such a hegemonic form of globalization has prevented Colombia – despite the utter failure of the prohibitionist approach – from trying or experimenting with other alternatives and exploring forms of international co-operation to implement them. Among such alternatives would be some that the US itself has adopted vis-à-vis other substances that are likely to produce dependence. For instance, in the case of tobacco – which,

---

[64]   According to GAO, between 1996 and 1997 ICITAP funded and provided technical support for the training of 3,500 investigators. OPDAT funded training programs for 2,500 prosecutors and 800 judges (GAO/NSIAD-99-195-22).

[65]   Project No 514-9002; Appendix II, Part IV, 3). Compared with the criminal justice programs, the access to justice projects – represented by the creation of multi-purpose legal aid centers called 'casas de justicia' (houses of justice) located in marginalized urban areas– as well as those dealing with the promotion of human rights and NGO's working on judicial issues, were marginal.

unlike cocaine and heroin, is produced in the US – the US government has privileged strategies centred on consumption. In theory, there is no reason why such a strategy may not be adopted also in the case of other drugs.

The tragedy of this story is that, after more than fifteen years of intervention and investments of hundreds of millions of dollars, the results of the prohibitionist strategy and the judicial reform that has accompanied it have been very modest. As the report produced by the General Accounting Office itself in 1999 put it, 'the Colombian judicial system continues to be weak and inefficient' in fighting organized crime. According to the report, the main problems are arbitrary detention, court backlogs, intimidation against judges and judicial employees, corruption and impunity.[66] The report also states that, according to USAID, the implementation of the new criminal procedure legislation would take between three and five years, but that – due to the unclear division of labour between the government organizations responsible for carrying out such a task – the new legislation may also prove ineffective.

In presenting the Colombian case, my aim has been – rather than questioning the need for reforms to the judicial system – to highlight the extreme intensity of the globalizing pressure to which the Colombian government and judiciary have been subjected. Such pressure, as some of the agencies and individuals involved acknowledge, has contributed decisively to the failure of most of the reforms.

5   STATE WEAKNESS, THE JUDICIALIZATION OF POLITICS AND THE EXPORTATION OF THE RULE OF LAW

In the remainder of this chapter I shall try to analyze the sociological and political meaning of the rising interest in courts and of the rule-of-law/judicial reform movement across the globe. I will try to answer two questions in turn: What type of state form is both presupposed and produced by the expansion of judicial power? What are the prospects for democracy? In this section I take up the first question.

One of the striking features of the focus on law and the courts is, as I have already indicated, its global reach. In light of the extreme diversity of concrete instances and conditions, it is highly improbable that they can be brought together under the same causal explanation. In the preceding sections, I organized my analytical description according to two main factors: the position of the country in the world system (core, periphery, semi-periphery) and the nature of the driving force behind the increasing role of law and the courts (high-intensity global pressure or mainly internal dynamics). My working hypothesis is that there is an intimate link or correlation between the legal and judicial reform, on one side, and the state, both as political system and as an

[66]   GAO/NSIAD-99-195-20.

administrative apparatus, on the other. What this means is that the question of judicial reform, though being a judicial question, is, above all, a political question. By the same token, the judicialization of politics entails the politicization of the judiciary. The way this phenomenon is occurring all over the world is, however, very diverse.

In core countries the rising protagonism of courts, particularly in continental Europe, is above all the symptom of a failure of the state as a democratic state. This failure is the result of the public perception of a loss of transparency, accountability, and participation in government. Judicial activism against political corruption and the expanded judicial review of the separation of powers and state competences are the responses to such perception. It should be borne in mind that, in the case of corruption, the mass media and civic organizations have performed a decisive role in pressing the judicial system to act. Though the judicial system is considered to be, in general, a reactive institution – that is to say, it waits for citizens to request its services – prosecutors, who are part of the system, are supposed to be proactive and launch criminal investigations. But the truth of the matter is that, in most countries, prosecutors have acted only after reports from the media, indeed oftentimes limiting themselves to following leads offered by the media. The reasons why some cases are brought to the attention of the media and others not are often mysterious. According to Zaffaroni, behind the media attention are conflicts among powerful economic or political groups in which the losers are publicly exposed.[67]

To a lesser extent the judicial activism is related to the perceived failure of the state as a welfare state. The moderate growth of litigation in the fields of administrative law, social and economic rights, torts, consumer and environmental protection, occupational health and safety has been prompted by a growing distrust of the state – a loss of confidence in the capacity or willingness of the state either to act positively to implement the rights and policies that guarantee the well-being of citizens or to protect them against the wrongdoing of powerful private actors. In this respect, the European countries in the postwar period offered a sharp contrast with the US. Stronger and more developed welfare states provided efficient protection and reduced the impact on citizens whenever protection failed, thus making litigation unnecessary or keeping it at much lower levels than in the US. Current legal and judicial changes in Europe, which as I mentioned above some see as the Americanization of Europe, are in part a direct effect of the crisis of the welfare state.

The double failure of the democratic and welfare features of the state, which has been associated with the legislature and the executive, has induced a dislocation of the legitimacy core of the state from the legislature and the executive to the judiciary. The extent of this dislocation and its potential to avert a crisis of legitimacy of the state as a whole is an open question. But the very fact that this dislocation has occurred is in and of itself remarkable and intriguing. After all, the judicial system is part of the state

---

[67]   Zaffaroni, 1997, p 10.

and as such should be regarded as part of the problem, rather than part of the solution. On the other hand, as I have already mentioned, the increasing protagonism of courts has also drawn attention to their own inefficiency, particularly in areas in which there is potential high judicial demand on the part of the citizens. That courts can be easily put on the defensive, and that the promises they make may exceed by far what they deliver, adds another element of perplexity to the current dislocation of legitimacy. But the most disturbing element is probably that, by such dislocation, democratic legitimacy may henceforth lie in the only non-elected branch of government.

Since it is far from obvious that a more central role should be assigned to courts, we must ask ourselves why this has happened. In order to find an answer we must go back to nineteenth-century political theory of the liberal state, or perhaps even further back to Montesquieu. Of the three powers or branches of government, the judiciary is by far the least powerful or, as Alexander Bickel would have it, the least dangerous.[68] The judiciary is a reactive institution with no enforcement powers, which must apply the pre-existing law when asked to do so by disputing individuals. US constitutionalism with judicial review by the Supreme Court is the exception rather than the rule.[69]

In Europe, the independence of the courts has been premised upon their social insulation and political neutralization. In late nineteenth century, Europe was immersed in unprecedented social disorganization and conflict generated by the capitalist revolution. This raised new problems that were bundled together under the umbrella of 'the social question': explosive urbanization and the sub-human housing conditions; rampant anomie, crime, and prostitution; degraded health and life conditions of uprooted peasants; industrial child labour and malnutrition. The judicial system stood aloof of all this turmoil, quietly defending property rights and adjudicating contractual obligations among individuals, mostly members of the bourgeoisie.

In our century, collective conflicts, if certainly not solved, were institutionalized via the class compromises promoted by social democracy and leading to the welfare state. The political cleavages remained deep, particularly in the context of the cold war, but this underlying consensus became the basis of governability, which consisted in transforming social problems into rights effectively enforced. Since courts were kept away from all this political process, probably precisely for this reason, their independence was not tampered with. On the contrary, it was rather strengthened, in part as a result of the general corporatist defence of professional interests, in part as an indirect result of the contamination of the judiciary by the political cleavages in society, as happened most notably in Italy. Indeed, the highly politicized atmosphere, both inside and outside the judicial system, made corporatist independence the common ground for the very governability of the judicial system.

[68] Bickel, 1962.
[69] According to Tushnet, 1993, p 506, the example set by the United States is itself more ambiguous than has often been supposed since the successes of judicial review are concentrated in the recent past, from roughly 1940 to the present.

For the last two decades, the economic and social basis of the class compromises underlying the welfare state have been eroding and with them the nature of the democratic political obligation. Resentful and distrustful citizens have been claiming redress for the violation of their rights and the punishment of an all too promiscuous intimacy between state officials and politicians, on the one side, and the corporate world, on the other. The independence of the judiciary, once premised upon its low profile and passivity, has become the necessary condition of the public pressure on it to become more active and high-profile. For how long, we might well ask. Nobody really knows. The contrast between Europe and the US should be pointed out again in this context. Granted that it is very difficult to compare patterns of judicial independence, it is unquestionable that political control over the judiciary, particularly as concerns the higher courts, has been greater in the US than in Europe: courts in the US are more politically controlled and more active; courts in Europe are less politically controlled and less active. It shouldn't be surprising if the increased protagonism of courts in Europe were to be met by attempts to tighten the political grip on them. In Italy, at least, there are some signs that this may occur.

The phenomenon may be transient but it points to a new state form. In fact, we seem to be heading towards a post-welfare state form – the core countries version of the weak state consensus. It will remain a regulatory and interventionist state, strong enough to produce its weakness efficiently, opening the space for partial replacement of the political obligation with contractual relations among citizens, corporations, NGOs, and the state itself. Because the direct provision of welfare services will diminish, more intermediaries will be at stake and, consequently, the provision will become more controversial. This would explain why the downsizing of the welfare administrative sector may lead to the upsizing of the judicial system, a phenomenon that is indeed already occurring as witnessed, for instance, in the recent explosion of the numbers of judges or courts in some countries.[70] Because they act in individual, not collective, disputes, and because they are ambiguous given the relative unpredictability of their rulings, courts tend to depoliticize public life. The activism of courts in the US may have something to do with the extent to which real political cleavages have been smoothed out in this country.

By criminalizing certain previously accepted political behaviour – I mean the fight against corruption – the judicial system contributes to regulating the turbulence and bouts of state anomie that tend to occur in periods of transition from one state form to another. On the other hand, by becoming more active in the area of administrative law and the protection of rights, courts contribute to diffusing the conflict that may arise in the process of dismantling the welfare state. The judicial system thus injects legitimacy into the democratic social pact of a state enfeebled by the erosion of the conditions that had hitherto sustained it. This judicialization of politics is not without problems: caught in the dilemma of having all the independence to act but no powers to enforce,

---

[70]   In the Portuguese case see Santos et al, 1996.

the promise of court activism may soon prove to exceed by far its delivery. When that occurs, if it occurs, courts will cease to be part of the solution to become precisely part of the problem.

The political nature of the growing focus on the rule of law and the judicial system renders more complex and ambiguous its impact on the form of the state, if for no other reason because the polities and societies we are dealing with are very distinct. Some of them have recently emerged from long-term dictatorships of various sorts and the high profile of courts is part and parcel of the democratic transition. Very often such judicial protagonism is mainly due to the activism of the constitutional courts. Their role is a regime-building role, as by defining the boundaries among the various branches of government, allocating competences among central and regional and local authorities (South Africa, Hungary, Portugal). The ambiguous, relatively unpredictable and piecemeal character of the courts' intervention is particularly functional whenever the political forces have not been able to reach a political compromise. In such cases, the Constitution acknowledges the differences, rather than settling them. It is up to the constitutional court to arbitrate the differences, often by political experiment through trial and error.

Leaving aside the constitutional courts, what has brought the courts into the spotlight particularly in semi-peripheral countries is the highly contrasting dual image I mentioned above. Mobilized by the mass media and NGOs, in recent years courts have shown in some countries a greater activism as regards human rights, protection against injuries provoked by powerful actors (consumer and environmental cases), and against corruption. This intervention, however timid, has raised the expectations vis-à-vis courts, and consequently made all the more visible their poor performance. Hence the focus on judicial reform. In this respect, two main contrasts must be noticed between trends in core countries and trends in semi-peripheral countries. On the one hand, while in core countries the reforms under way seem to respond to internal dynamics, even if conditioned by global trends, in some semi-peripheral countries of Central and Eastern Europe and Latin America the reforms are being conducted under high-intensity globalizing pressure, a pressure dominated by US institutions and US legal models. On the other hand, while in core countries the focus is mainly on courts, since the rule of law is taken for granted and legal reform is an established political process, in most semi-peripheral countries the focus is much broader, contemplating the rule of law and legal reform, as well as judicial reform.

In my view, both contrasts are explained by the more far-reaching political reforms deemed necessary in the semi-peripheral countries. What is really at stake here is the creation of the post-structural adjustment state. Most semi-peripheral countries have been ruled for the past forty years, for shorter or longer periods, by authoritarian regimes and strong interventionist states. The communist states of Central and Eastern Europe ruled an administrative-command economy; the developmental states of Latin America and Asia based their rule on a strong nationalized economic sector and on a tight, mostly protectionist, regulation of the economy as a whole. Neither the communist nor the developmentalist states were welfare states, but both developed schemes of social protection in health and social security, far more advanced in the communist states than in the developmentalist states. In different ways, the neo-liberal consensus presiding over the expansion of global market capitalism contributed to the downfall of both state forms. They were to be replaced by weak states, acting as facilitators of the new model of development based on the reliance of markets and the private sector.

In the communist states, and in view of their total collapse, the building of the post-structural adjustment state is an all-encompassing task. It involves not just institution building of different kinds but also the building of a legal culture capable of sustaining the legal reforms called for by the new economic environment. In the developmental states the situation is very different because although the democratic transitions changed the political regime, they did not by themselves change the state institutional structure significantly. These changes were to be carried out within the framework of the existing state. The neo-liberal dilemma in this regard became apparent in the early 1990s. It can be formulated as follows. Only a strong state can produce its own weakness efficiently but once this weakness has been produced it has spillover effects that go beyond the intended reach, to the point of endangering the performance of the tasks assigned to the state in the new model of development.

One such spillover effect is, for instance, the manner in which the constructed weakness of the state facilitates the public diffusion of a neo-utilitarian conception of the state that basically sees it as a rent-seeking set of institutions and agents, thus discrediting state action altogether and converting state officials into exemplars of cynical reason. In other words, the weak state cannot control its own weakness. The pathologies of state weakness became apparent in the early 1990s: massive tax evasions, widespread corruption, withering away of a public service culture, loss of control over the national territory, the emergence of mafias and paramilitary groups disputing the state monopoly of violence, abysmal mismanagement of development grants and loans, etc.

In recent years the World Bank has started to lament the fact that the state has become too weak to perform the new but equally central role assigned to it by the neo-liberal development model. In one of its reports, the Bank emphasizes that the state cannot be just the facilitator of market economy, it must also be its regulator.[71] Significantly, the Bank's 1997 World Development Report is entitled *The State in a Changing World* and is dedicated to rethinking the state, refocusing on its effectiveness and on re-invigorating its institutional capability.[72] The priority the Bank now gives to the rule of law, and legal and judicial reforms stems from the need to restore the regulatory capacity of the state in new terms: the post-developmental state. The state continues, of course, to be involved in development, but because the state has ceased to be the

[71] Rowat, 1995, p 17.
[72] World Bank, 1997.

very engine of development, social transformation is not a political problem any more; it is merely the economic and technical problem of bringing about a better life for all citizens. The rule of law and the judicial system are thus conceived of as principles of social ordering, as instruments of a depoliticized conception of social transformation. In terms of the argument I have been making in this book about modern law, this means the streamlining of the emancipatory potential of the rule of law and the conversion of the latter into just one more technique of regulation.

The depoliticization of social transformation may, however, prove to be a very problematic endeavour. Concurrent with it is the dramatic growth of poverty and social inequality across the globe, as well as the gradual erosion of the fragile safety nets once provided by the welfare state no matter how incomplete or embryonic. To address this issue with a combination of liberal democracy rule of law and judicial activism seems utterly insufficient. Contrary to European experience, where democracy has always flourished at the cost of economic liberalism, in both peripheral and semi-peripheral countries today democracy is offered as the political counterpart of economic liberalism. Not surprisingly a press release on building democracy by the USAID states as being one of the major problems to be addressed by its programmes: 'misperceptions about democracy and free-market capitalism.'[73]

Contrary to the experience in core countries, democracy is being promoted by the USAID and the international financial institutions as the socially more acceptable version of a weak state. As we have already seen above, the rule-of-law and judicial reform programmes are conceived by the USAID as political rather than technocratic in nature. Without ideological competition, the hegemonic political globalization can thus engender depoliticization without having to compromise the benefits of presenting itself as political.

When we compare these trends in semi-peripheral countries with similar trends in peripheral countries, the first contrast is that, in the latter, both the internal demand for and dynamics of the rule of law and judicial activism are very weak. In these countries the reforms are almost exclusively the product of high-intensity globalization pressure. Moreover, notwithstanding regional differences, leverages and linkages varying from country to country, whatever economic growth has been made possible in these countries by the globalization of the economy, it was made possible at the cost of tremendous social inequalities and effective social exclusion of the majority of the population.

Namely in Africa, globalization has meant economic decline and general destitution. For the majority of the population of these countries social exclusion is a euphemism for the predatory effects of neo-liberal economic globalization. Structural adjustment and foreign debt have pushed some countries to the brink of collapse. Under such

[73]   USAID, 1996.

circumstances, democracy programmes and the rule of law programmes have become one more foreign imposition, a political conditionality for assistance that the 'host' countries are in no condition to resist. In some cases, particularly when the countries have been devastated by long civil wars, a democratic transition may correspond to a national aspiration, as in Mozambique. In other countries, the imposition of democracy may indeed lead to ethnic civil war, as the case of Congo illustrates. At its best, the legal and judicial reform aims at building or restoring the minimal state capacity. Beyond this, it seeks to secure legal stability and predictability for the internationalized sector of the economy by concentrating legal investments in the capital city of the country: mainly through the professionalization of the Supreme Court and the training of a few lawyers in business law.

6   PROSPECTS FOR DEMOCRACY

In this section I will try to give an answer to the question on the prospects for democracy deriving from the global reliance on the rule-of-law and judicial activism. Two cautionary notes are in order. First, in a world increasingly dominated by globalized forms of power and of unequal exchanges, the prospects for democracy will heavily depend on the possibility of democratizing global interactions and social relations. Democracy has always been conceived as a national political form congruent with both the national economy and the national culture. Consequently, democratic theory assumed, in David Held's formulation, 'A "symmetrical" and "congruent" relationship between political decision-makers and the recipients of political decisions.'[74] Hence, political accountability, transparency, protection and participation have always been basically national problems. This symmetry and congruence have been shattered by economic and cultural globalization. As long as symmetry and congruence are not re-established at a global level, national democracy will be an endangered species.

The second cautionary note is that the prospects for democracy cannot be identified without specifying what we mean by democracy. There are different models of democracy. Even liberal democracy may be defined differently. I shall distinguish between two ideal-types of democracy, which I shall call representative democracy and participatory democracy. Both subscribe to the basic features of democracy stated in the Introduction to this chapter, but, while representative democracy ranks them according to their capacity to deliver governability and gives priority to the value of freedom over the value of equality, participatory democracy ranks them according to their capacity to empower citizens and achieve social justice, thus seeking a dynamic equilibrium between freedom and equality.

Both forms of democracy conceive national societies as open societies. However, while for representative democracy such 'openness' is premised upon free markets and the

[74]   Held, 1993, p 25.

neo-liberal economic globalization, for participatory democracy the fate of the open society is linked to the outcomes, risks and opportunities, emerging from the conflict between hegemonic globalization and counter-hegemonic globalization. While representative democracy accepts world capitalism as the final and highest criterion of modern social life and consequently accepts the precedence of capitalism whenever the latter feels threatened by democratic 'dysfunctions', participatory democracy conceives of itself, rather than capitalism, as the final and highest criterion of modern social life and therefore sees itself as taking precedence over capitalism whenever threatened by it.

As discussed below, in concrete political processes the two types of democracy are never present in their ideal-typical forms. Truncated versions, loose combinations of heterogeneous elements, hybrid forms of representative democracy and participatory democracy, make the real life of our polities. For analytical purposes, however, I will start by discussing the possible political roles of courts within the framework of each ideal-type of democracy.

I have argued that after two decades of engendered failure and engendered weakness of the state we are entering a new phase, the phase of the reconstruction of the state suited to the regulatory needs of the new neo-liberal development model in the meantime consolidated. Such reconstruction involves the political and institutional design of the post-welfare state in the core countries and of the post-developmentalist state in the semi-peripheral countries. I have also argued that the focus on the rule of law and judicial system is a major component of the reconstruction of the state underway.

6.1   The role of law and courts in representative democracy

Taking representative democracy as our model to ask about the prospects for democracy as deriving from legal and court reforms amounts to asking about the contribution of the latter to strengthen the capacity of the emerging state form to bring about the compatibility between economic liberalization and political liberalization, that is to say, between capitalism and democracy. The overarching liberal consensus referred to in the introduction presupposes such compatibility. However, in light of the recent past, the compatibility between capitalism and democracy has become an open question. In their systematic comparison of a series of semi-peripheral countries, some of which undergoing democratic transition and/or structural adjustment, Haggard and Kaufman conclude that even if there is support for the compatibility assumption, there are nonetheless important tensions between capitalism and democracy, particularly when the former produces highly unequal distributions of assets and income, abrupt social dislocations and, above all, severe rural inequalities.[75] The effects of these distributional conflicts on democratic stability remain an open question. In fact, this impact is mediated

---

[75]   Haggard and Kaufman, 1992, p 342. For the incompatibility assumption, see Wood, 1996.

by a complex set of factors, such as the economic performance in itself, the political institutions, the organization of civil society, the capacity of the state to sustain order, etc, etc. The role of law and the judicial system in this context is two-fold.

First, it may increase the stability and predictability of economic transactions, promote social peace, and improve the administrative capacity of the state. In this case, the rule of law and the courts contribute directly towards the economic performance and indirectly towards the democratic stability. The second role consists in dispersing the social conflicts emerging from social dislocations and the distributive inequalities produced by global capitalism. As the rule of law transforms social problems into rights and courts transform collective conflicts into individual disputes, they tend to discourage collective action and organization. Moreover, the judicial tempo, the relative unpredictability of judicial decisions and even the judicial inefficiency if not too high may have a cooling effect on social contestation, lowering social expectations without, however, nullifying them altogether. By all these mechanisms, law and courts promote governability by preventing the overload of the political system and expanding the boundaries of public toleration, particularly in those countries in which the rule of law and the independent courts are part and parcel of recent democratic transitions.

This analysis so far fails to consider the effects of the performance of these roles upon the judicial system itself. The prevention of the political overload may lead to judicial overload. The latter is being anticipated by the agencies in charge of the global court reform, and to prevent it they are increasingly including models of alternative dispute resolutions (ADR) in their reform projects. Another impact of the focus on courts upon the courts themselves is the possible rise of corporatist independence, that is to say, the emergence of a conception of judicial independence less concerned with the democratic potential of independent courts to enfranchise people and bring about honest government than with the unaccountability and the professional privileges that independence secures.

Representative democracy is by far the dominant conception of democracy today. It is also the conception that is being globalized in the hegemonic programmes of political liberalization across the globe. It is in fact an instrumental conception, a means to stabilize economic liberalization and prevent the complete decay of state institutions and the usual 'pathologies' that go with it. Its weakness lies in not guaranteeing its own survival in the case of a conflict with economic liberalization. But short of complete collapse, representative democracy may be contracted in different ways in order to accommodate the political needs of global capitalism. Many semi-peripheral countries, not to mention the peripheral ones, live under different versions of contracted or restricted democracy. In these situations the rule of law and the judicial system perform ambiguous and often contradictory roles. On the one hand, the high-profile interventions of courts function as symbolic amplifiers of the democratic rule in that they dramatize the democratic competition among the political elites or factions, or among state institutions or branches of government. This symbolic amplification of democracy within the inner circle of the political system is usually the other side of the contraction of democracy in the outer circle of the political system, that is, in the relations between citizens and their organizations on the one side, and the state and the political class on the other. Such contraction manifests itself in many different ways, as a deficit of representation, as a deficit of participation, and very often as the emergence of violent and corrupt political actions. Rather than being a countervailing force, the rule of law and the judicial system may reproduce such contraction by reinforcing the distinction between enfranchised and disenfranchised citizens.

But on the other hand the judicial system may find itself in the front line of the struggle between democratic and anti-democratic forces. In Colombia, around three hundred judges were assassinated between 1979 and 1991. They were investigating or trying cases involving individuals or organizations that felt powerful enough to attack the system head on rather than using it to their benefit, for instance, by manipulating procedural guarantees and legal loopholes. Colombia is probably the only country in the world with a philanthropic organization devoted to providing welfare assistance for the widows and children of assassinated judges. This philanthropic organization (FASOL) is an interesting case of internationalist judicial solidarity, in that it is funded in part by German judges, who contribute to it a day's salary per year. In such a situation of contracted democracy, one may well wonder where the protection function of the judicial system lies when the system cannot even protect itself.

Short of such a violent intrusion, the contraction of democracy may impinge upon the judicial system in various other forms. The most common one is the judicial reform itself, as a way of tailoring the activity of the courts to the coercive needs of the state or as a way of securing the non-interference of the courts in the areas in which the state operates in a distinctly authoritarian way. As an illustration, in Colombia, one of the most successful judicial innovations according to the USAID has been the creation of the so-called public order courts to fight organized crime and terrorism. But, as I mentioned above, these courts, staffed by faceless judges and operating under special procedural rules violate basic due process guarantees, and their activity has been targeted mainly against poor peasants caught in the middle of the struggle among *terratenientes* (large land owners), drug dealers, the military, paramilitary groups and the guerrilla. On the other hand, the executive has been pressing the legislature to pass a reform that curtails significantly the judicial review power of the Constitutional Court.

6.2 The role of law and courts in participatory democracy

Participatory democracy is a counter-hegemonic conception of democracy. In its perspective, representative democracy is seen as an incomplete conception of democracy, rather than a wrong one. Participatory democracy accepts, therefore, representative democracy as a starting point. Its difference from representative democracy is that it does not believe that the compatibility of world capitalism with democracy can be sustained forever, while maintaining that, in the case of collision between democracy and capitalism democracy must prevail.

The core idea of participatory democracy is that global capitalism inflicts systematic harm upon the majority of the populations of the globe, as well as upon nature and the environment. Only unified opposition to global capitalism can reduce, if not eliminate, such harm. 'Democratic' can be said of any peaceful, but not necessarily legal, struggle that seeks to reduce systematic harm by empowering the populations systematically affected by it. Participatory democracy is, therefore, less procedural and more substantive than representative democracy and its focus is less on governability than on citizen empowerment and social justice. The criteria for the rule of law and the judicial system to meet the demands of participatory democracy are, thus, much more stringent than those applying to representative democracy. A number of complex issues must be addressed in this regard. Here I mention briefly four of them.

The first one concerns the political orientation of judicial activism. Judicial activism or protagonism is not in itself a good or bad thing for participatory democracy. It must be evaluated in terms of its substantive merits. For instance, up until recently the best-known instances of court activism were politically conservative, if not reactionary. Just think of the German courts in the Weimar Republic and their scandalous double standards punishing extreme right and extreme left violence; the rulings of US Supreme Court against New Deal legislation; the opposition of Chilean Supreme Court to the democratic socialist measures of Salvador Allende. More recently, Italian prosecutors benefited from special procedural laws that had been approved by the political elites to expedite criminal prosecution of the leftist organization known as the Red Brigades. In Portugal, the first high-profile judicial intervention in the post-1974 democratic period was the indictment of an extreme left organization known as the FPs 25. The punishment of violent political organizations is as much of an asset for participatory democracy as it is for representative democracy. But it is an unconditional asset only to the extent that the extreme right and the extreme left are treated equally. This, however, has rarely been the case.

The second issue refers to the ways the judicial system addresses the large-scale, collective or structural conflicts. Structural conflicts are the social sites of the systematic harm produced either directly or indirectly by global capitalism in its interactions with local, regional or national societies. Their symptoms or manifestations may be very diverse. The massive occurrence of disputes among individuals or organizations is one of them, as, for instance, the exponential growth of consumer bankruptcy cases, consumer or environmental protection cases, or even tort liability cases. The usual responses to judicial overload caused by these types of litigation have been restriction of demand, routinization or simplification of procedure, diversion to alternative dispute mechanisms, etc. In the perspective of participatory democracy, courts may have here a democratic contribution only if, rather than trivializing such disputes, they make the connection between individual disputes and the underlying structural conflicts. This will involve a far-reaching post-liberal reform in substantive law as well as in procedural law and court organization: class actions, broad standing, proactive judicial system, greater lay participation on the part of citizens and NGOs, radical politics of individual and collective rights, progressive multiculturalism, etc and none of this will be possible without a vast reform of legal education. In sum, in order to meet the criteria of participatory democracy the judicial system must see itself as part of a political coalition that takes democracy seriously and gives it precedence over markets and an individualist, possessive conception of property.

This leads me to the third issue, which concerns the access to law and justice. Contrary to the recommendations of the World Bank, from the perspective of participatory democracy it is imperative to repoliticize the question of the access to law and justice by questioning not only the pool of citizens, grassroots movements, and NGOs that must have access, but also the kind of law and justice to which access is struggled for.

I mentioned above that one of the common manifestations of structural conflicts is the massive proliferation of individual disputes in a given area of social life. As common, however, is the opposite manifestation: the systematic suppression of individual disputes or their resolution by extrajudicial violent means. By way of example I mention the capital/labour conflict. Such indicators as the growth of structural unemployment in many countries, the declining share of salary income in the national income, and the proliferation of the so-called atypical work relations and of jobs so badly paid that the workers holding them cannot get above the poverty line, show that the structural conflict between capital and labour on a global scale is intensifying rather than diminishing. Nevertheless, in many core and semi-peripheral countries labour litigation has been sharply declining for the last decade. The increased vulnerability of workers and labour unions in the post-Fordist era has acted as a deterrent to resorting to courts to defend labour rights.

Just to give an example of what I mean by structural conflicts, in my research on Colombia I have identified five of them. First, the land conflict involving *terratenientes* (large land owners), poor and dispossessed peasants, the guerrilla and paramilitary groups. Secondly, the capital/labour conflict involving rural and urban workers and employers. Thirdly, the conflict over biodiversity and natural resources involving the state, the multinational corporations, and the indigenous and black communities. Fourthly, the conflict over cultural diversity involving the state, people of European descent and their organizations and the indigenous and black communities. Fifthly, the conflict over the state's monopoly of violence, involving the state itself, the guerrilla, the paramilitary groups and the drug cartels. In a collective research project, we analyzed the level and content of judicialization in each one of these conflicts.[76]

Whenever the political and social conditions are such that structural conflicts suppress rather than provoke judicial disputes, access to law and justice according to participatory democracy involves the active promotion of disputes. In other words it must address

[76]   See Santos and García-Villegas, 2001.

the suppressed demand of justice. In this case, a post-liberal judicial system must be socially constructed as much as a mechanism of dispute settlement as a mechanism of dispute creation. Whenever litigation stems from structural conflict and not, for instance, from lawyers' market needs, the struggle against suppressed judicial demand may be a form of political enfranchising of politically excluded populations.

And thus I come to my last issue concerning the conception of the rule of law and judicial system from the perspective of participatory democracy. To the extent that the sustainability of democracy at the local and national level will increasingly depend on the democratization of international and transnational political relations, it is conceivable that the democratic potential of the judicial system will increasingly depend on the emergence of forms of international justice more adequate to confront the systematic harm produced by structural conflicts at the level at which it is produced – the global level. One may think of institutions similar to the European Court of Justice, but premised, rather, on the principle of democracy first, and capitalism (markets and property) second and not the opposite, as is the case of the European Court.

The ideal-typical contrast between representative democracy and participatory democracy is useful only to identify clearly two possible and opposite political roles to be performed by the courts in democratic societies. In fact, the social and political processes are much messier. Partial versions of both types of democracy may be coexisting side by side, supported by different social groups, or articulate, interpenetrate or fuse in complex, hybrid political constellations. Thus, in real social processes the political role of courts is inherently ambiguous, undetermined, open-ended and, above all, in itself an object of social struggle. Different political groups will struggle to control the nature, orientation or interpretation of court rulings. The attempt by dominant groups to keep the judicial activism within the boundaries of representative democracy – restricting it to promote governability and facilitate economic transactions – will be met with resistance by subordinate groups trying to expand judicial activism into the areas of citizens' empowerment and social justice. The relative strength of these groups will dictate the overall political profile of the courts' roles.

The scale, time frame and context of political struggles also condition the nature of judicial intervention. Taken in isolation at a given point in time, an individual court ruling cannot be said to promote (or hinder) unequivocally either representative democracy or participatory democracy. Let us take the example of judicial rulings against political corruption. It is today consensual that political corruption is detrimental to representative democracy. On the one hand, by transforming rights into favours and by engendering inefficiency and unpredictability in public administration, it erodes the confidence in the state, thereby bringing about ungovernability.[77] On the other hand, by undermining the conditions of market competitions, elevating costs, and having a negative impact on investment, political corruption is impairment to an efficient

---

[77]   Della Porta and Vannucci, 1997, p 114.

and open market economy.[78] A few court rulings against political corruption do not necessarily contribute to the end of corruption. They may even function, by its sporadic nature, as a cover up, whitewashing and legitimating the political system that goes on producing political corruption in a systematic fashion. In a time dominated by media politics and by politics as spectacle, the courts' intervention in high-profile cases – usually, the cases involving powerful, high-profile individuals – performs a symbolic function which we could call the judicial carnivalization of politics: a 'ceremony' through which, for a brief period, the powerful are treated as ordinary citizens like anyone of us.

On the contrary, a systematic judicial campaign against political corruption, particularly if complemented by a high-profile, aggressive judicial intervention in the public sphere, specially in the mass media will, as has happened in Italy, contribute decisively to eradicate corruption, thus strengthening representative democracy.[79] In a longer time frame, however, this effect may have very different and contrasting consequences for democracy, depending on the overall political, social and cultural context. Given the curative, rather than preventive, character of judicial action, the political system may find other ways, less amenable to judicial scrutiny, to reconstitute systematic corruption. Or it may design and bring about a judicial reform aimed at reducing the possibility of judicial protagonism in politically loaded cases. In such cases, the positive impact of the judicial activism against political corruption will, in the long run, be neutralized or even turned into a negative impact. But, on the contrary, in a country with an active, well-organized civil society, the democratic impulse, provided by judicial intervention, may ignite the initiative of active citizens to develop mechanisms of participatory democracy designed to achieve a corruption-free and redistributive allocation of public funds. In such case, the empowerment of citizens and the social justice made possible by an articulation of representative democracy and participatory democracy will point to a democracy of higher intensity, participatory democracy. The emergence of participatory democracy is thus related, even if remotely, to the initial democratic impulse provided by judicial activism.

On the other hand, although, as we saw above, courts tend to disperse social conflicts and, consequently, to reduce the social mobilization around them, it is not to be excluded that the opposite effect might occur. This will be the case if the social groups systematically harmed by the capitalist 'solutions' of the structural conflicts are strong enough to reorient judicial activism and put it at the service of more advanced social goals. Similarly, though the consolidation of representative democracy, as the hegemonic conception of democracy, may tend to render participatory democracy as either unnecessary or dangerous, it may also unleash democratic energies and impulses which it cannot contain or control, thereby opening up political space for participatory democracy.

[78] Ades and Di Tella, 1997, p 98.

[79] In Italy, the judges helped to open up the political system allowing for the emergence of new opposition parties but, at the same time, they also contributed to a new wave of populism, a 'virtual democracy', using the media to appeal directly to the people.

The global focus on the role of law and the judicial system is part and parcel of the hegemonic type of democracy, representative democracy, and, as such, it is a form of hegemonic globalization. However, to the extent that subordinate groups across the globe manage to intensify social struggles in such a way as to inscribe the goal of participatory democracy in the political agenda and resort, for that purpose, among other means, to the intervention of courts, the latter will operate as a form of counter-hegemonic globalization.[80] The reason why this possibility seems nowadays remote lies in the fact that the political forces engaged in struggles geared to participatory democracy have not yet been willing or able to identify the full democratic potential of the indeterminacy and ambiguity of the judicial activism within the confines of representative democracy.

Such unwillingness or incapacity stems not only from the fact that high-profile judicial activism is in most countries a novelty at best and, as such, an unfamiliar political tool, but also from the fact that in pro-participatory democracy social struggles the role of courts tends to be much less central, its political weight being premised upon complex articulations with many other forms of political action. The constitutional status of the judicial system and its institutional insulation does not facilitate the emergence of constellations of political action in which resorting to courts is part of a broader political strategy. Depending on the circumstances, such an encompassing political strategy may indeed dictate either the intensive use of courts or, on the contrary, the systematic avoidance of courts. Among the circumstances, we can list the political content of the laws to be implemented and the degree of freedom of the judges to interpret them, the patterns of training and recruitment of judges and prosecutors, and the vulnerability of courts to political patronage or to corruption.

From another perspective, the determination of the hegemonic or counter-hegemonic character of judicial activism is subjected to the same difficulties discussed above in identifying and distinguishing traits of representative democracy and of participatory democracy in concrete political processes. Assuming that hegemonic liberal globalization involves a total priority of freedom over equality, whose social cost is the promotion of unprecedented exclusionary policies, we can establish, as a kind of rule of thumb, that the counter-hegemonic value of court activism is premised upon the latter's capacity to block the race to the bottom across the globe. Such capacity is to be tested and exercized against powerful actors – eg, in cases aiming at the protection of labour, minority, women's, consumer, sexual orientation and environmental rights – against the state – in cases involving seeking the protection of citizens against illegal, discretionary or otherwise unpredictable acts of public administration – or against political power in a broad sense – like in cases aiming at punishing cases of abuse of state power and of political corruption (more on this in Chapter Nine).

---

[80]   I will explore this possibility in Chapter Nine.

7 CONCLUSION

The focus for the last decade on the rule of law and the judicial system across the globe is a major transnational political phenomenon of our time. Now a product of internal dynamics, now a product of high-intensity globalization pressure, now still, more often than not, a product of a combination of both, this trend, known as the judicialization of politics or as the expansion of judicial power, is intimately related to the construction of a new state form. Such state form can be characterized as post-welfare (in core countries) or post-developmentalist (in semi-peripheral countries) – an efficient weak state suited to complement the efficient regulation of social and economic life by markets and the private sector. This new model of development, which seems to be the object of a global consensus – how strong, genuine or well-informed this consensus is remains an open question – is premised upon the idea that social transformation has ceased to be a political issue. The rule of law and the judicial system appear to be the ideal instruments of a depoliticized conception of social transformation.

Concomitantly, democracy has been promoted as the political regime best suited to guarantee the stability, governability, and social legitimacy of an efficient weak state as well as a depoliticized capitalist social transformation. The rule of law and the courts have been called upon to be the main pillars of such a democratic project.

This hegemonic project, the ideal-type of which I have designated as representative democracy, is based on the assumption that capitalism and democracy are compatible and even interdependent. Such an assumption has been highly problematic in the past, and nothing has changed in the last decade to make it less problematic now. Nothing has changed in the recent past to eliminate or even reduce, in the framework of this democratic project, the precedence of capitalism over democracy, particularly now that capitalism is global and democracy continues to be national. It is highly improbable that, against past experience, the rule of law and courts will sustain democracy against capitalism.

The vulnerability of this democratic project is two-fold. First, democratic stability is dependent upon not letting social inequalities go too far. Now, they have actually been increasing dramatically for the past decade. It is quite an open question, mediated by many political factors, when such dramatic increase will reach the breaking point beyond which turbulence will take over democratic stability. Secondly, liberal democratic public sphere presupposes the rule-based equality of all citizens and the equal accountability of the government towards them. Under the neoliberal model of development, powerful social agents are emerging in command of such an economic and political leverage that they can easily circumvent the laws or change them to suit their interests. The principle of equality is thereby manipulated beyond recognition. On the other hand, the same development model makes the nation states tightly accountable to global capitalist enterprises, at the same time that it forces them or allows them to be more and more vaguely accountable to national individual citizens. The combination of these two trends may contribute to turning capitalist democratic societies into ever shrinking islands of democratic public life in a sea of social fascisms.[81]

Both vulnerabilities of the representative democracy project are the product of or are compounded by structural conflicts and therefore can only be effectively neutralized by political action addressed to the democratic settlement of such conflicts. Under representative democracy, the rule of law has done little to address structural conflicts, when in fact it has not exacerbated them, while the judicial system, by its very liberal institutional design, has in general stayed away from such conflicts. In this respect, the political role of courts is as determined by the disputes that are selected to be processed by them as by the disputes that are suppressed or selected out. Thus perceived, the political role of courts is rather disquieting. For courts, by their actions or omissions, tend to hide or negate the very existence of systematic harm; or else, that not being at all possible, they tend to divide those who might otherwise unite to fight against such harm.

The analysis of recent judicial experience shows that the rule of law and the judicial system are a central component of representative democracy and crucial to sustain it short of a situation of incompatibility vis-à-vis the accumulation needs of global capitalism. It seems, therefore, that democracy can only be effectively defended in such a situation if the assumption of the taken-for-granted compatibility between capitalism and democracy is rejected, and if democracy is conceptualized as taking precedence over capitalism, should a situation of incompatibility among them arise. This is the project of what I have called participatory democracy. In this project, the rule of law and the judicial system are as important as in representative democracy. They are, however, less central because they must be conceived as part of a much broader set of participatory institutions and social movements, pluralistically organized and networking around a simple but crucial principle: democracy first, capitalism second.

---

[81]   On the concept of social fascism and the different forms it assumes, see Chapter Nine and Santos, 1998a.

Chapter 7

On Modes of Production of Law and Social Power

I INTRODUCTION

As I argued in Chapters One and Two, the development of an oppositional postmodern view of law capable of furthering emancipatory struggles requires both innovative theorizing aimed at the repoliticization of legal thought, and empirical research into the local, national and global conditions under which such repoliticization must take place. Grounded theory is thus the key analytical tool of the view of law that I advance in this book. Thus, in Chapters Four and Five I sought to flesh out – based on the examination of legal practices at the local and global level – the pluralist theory of law sketched in the previous chapters. Such empirical inquiry allows us to return in this chapter to theory with a richer understanding of the aim of the view on law I put forward and the practical challenges it seeks to face up to.

My main objective in this chapter is to put forth a theoretical framework for understanding the relationship between law, power and knowledge. Specifically, I address the following three issues. First, the critique of modern science and modern law that I offered in Chapters One and Two leads to the recognition of a plurality of legal orders, forms of power and forms of knowledge. But merely to recognize the existence of a plurality of legal orders, without grounding it theoretically, implies a triple fallacy: the fallacy of descriptivism, ie the idea that a given list of pluralities is as complete as any other alternative list; the fallacy of triviality, ie the idea that, even assuming that there are lists that are more complete than others, the more complete the list, the greater the probability that it will be useless as a description of reality: if law, power and knowledge are everywhere, they are nowhere; and finally, if I may borrow Sartre's term,[1] the fallacy of seriality – ie, the list is practico-inert, the relationship among its elements – irrespective of their number – is never more complex than the relationship between people in a queue waiting for the

---

[1] Sartre, 1976.

bus. In order to avoid these fallacies, the recognition of pluralities of laws, powers and knowledges must be theoretically reconstructed – a reconstruction that must be self-reflexive also. As an alternative to dominant paradigms, the theoretical work to be done ought to be particularly aware of the likely risk that the development of its principles might betray the principles of its development. In my view, two such principles deserve equal attention. On the one hand, the plurality of forms of law, power or knowledge, far from being chaotic or infinite, is structured and relational. On the other hand, the recognition of such pluralities, far from denying the centrality of state law, state power and scientific knowledge in contemporary societies, confirms and relativizes it at the same time by integrating these hegemonic forms in new and broader constellations of laws, powers and knowledges.

The second main issue to be addressed in this chapter is the question of the orientation of and obstacles to transformative agency. Critical theory has traditionally tended to be vulnerable to two opposite risks: voluntarism – ad hoc self-justification for any possible course of action – and passivity – immobility induced by the realization of a too great discrepancy between the small scale of human action and the big scale of the transformations aimed at. There is a thin line to be walked between these two risks. Among the many available theories designed to keep us on track, Bourdieu's theory of practice[2] and Giddens's theory of structuration seem to me to be the most useful ones.[3] Thus, a few brief comments on these theories as they serve the purpose of this chapter are in order before I offer my own alternative below.

My first comment is that a theoretically controlled proliferation of structures is quite adequate to ground transformative agency. Since structures are nothing more than provisional sedimentations of successfully reiterated courses of action, the proliferation of structures broadens the context within which determinations and contingencies, constraints and opportunities are played out, thereby facilitating the formation of multiple coalitions. My second comment is that neither the distinction between structure and agency nor the distinction between underlying phenomena and surface phenomena should be overstressed. To use a physical metaphor, structures are solid moments or marks in the flowing currents of practice, and their (measure of) solidity can only be determined in concrete situations and is bound to change as the situations unfold. Moreover, an underlying phenomenon is not necessarily an unconscious or unaccounted-for component of situational practice. An underlying phenomenon may be so because it has been made to lie under through silencing and forgetting, through different means of knowledge and action suppression. In some situations, such as revolutionary or, more generally, emergency situations, underlying structures are excavated by collective agency and become themselves the surface of practice. A third comment is that structures are not incompatible with a rhetorical conception of knowledge. Indeed,

---

[2]   Bourdieu, 1980.
[3]   Giddens, 1979, 1984.

in the following I shall designate structures as *structural places*. Without being necessarily common places, structures are sites of production of common places. As I will show below, they are sites of production of *topoi* and common sense. Once rhetorically reconstructed, structures may be either arguments about solidity and resistance in social practice (about major obstacles which, once overcome, allow for major changes) or premises of argumentation, zones of strong consensus about possibilities of action. My fourth and final comment is that structures are places not only in rhetorical terms but also in socio-geographical terms. Each structural place is constitutive of a specific spatiality; the social interactions it calls for and makes possible have a locational reference that gets inscribed in what, through them, is done or thought. In the last two decades, geography has firmly established not only that spaces are socially constituted, but also that social relations are spatially constituted.[4] This much is taken for granted in this chapter. The double sense in which structures are places – ie, the rhetorical and the socio-geographical sense – suggests an unsuspected complicity between geography and rhetoric, but so far this complicity has not caught the attention of either geographers or rhetoricians.

The third main issue to be addressed in this chapter deals with the relations between national societies, the interstate system and the global economy. Thus, I will theorize in this chapter at a more abstract level, many of the insights or conclusions presented in Chapter Five. I have argued that the erosion of state power – specifically in the economic field – does not make the state form less fundamental to the political functions required by the world system, if for no other reason because the erosion of state power is, more often than not, brought about by state action. I have also argued that the richness of the legal landscape – which includes not only state legal field but also local and global legal fields – should not be understood as minimizing the centrality of state law in national societies or the centrality of international law in the interstate system. Thus, the theory to be developed should be able to relate national societies and the world system not as parts of an overarching totality but as a system of partial totalities. Such an approach will allow for cogent analytical descriptions *both* of the national societies *and* the world system, thereby overcoming one of the most resilient dilemmas of current social theory.

In the following, my argument will unfold as an explicit or implicit dialogue on law, power, and knowledge with Marxism, Foucault and feminist theory. Before venturing to offer a theoretical alternative, however, I will present a critique of the conceptual orthodoxy that is to a great extent shared by classical liberalism and Marxism. But since in the previous chapters I devoted more attention to law and knowledge than to power, a few notes on power and its modes of production are in order here.

---

[4]   See Blomley *et al* (eds), 2001; Massey, 1984; Gregory and Urry (eds), 1985; Peet and Thrift (eds), 1989.

2   POWER, EMPOWERING, DISEMPOWERING

2.1   *The contributions of Foucault and feminist theory*

The relative uncoupling of law and the state argued for throughout this book makes the coupling of law with social power all the more central. For this purpose, a preliminary dialogue with Foucault seems appropriate at this point.[5] The outstanding contribution of Foucault's analysis of power is two-fold. First, drawing on a tradition shared by radical (Nietzsche) and conservative (Burke and the historical school) political thinking, Foucault dislocates power from its liberal niche, the state. Since the eighteenth century, says Foucault, the most important form of power circulating in society is produced by society itself, not by the state, and according to rules, principles and mechanisms totally autonomous from the state: this he calls the disciplinary power of modern science, and distinguishes from the juridical power of the modern state. Secondly, drawing once more on a tradition with a radical (Gramsci) and a conservative (Parsons) side, Foucault conceives of disciplinary power as being in total contrast with juridical state power: disciplinary power is a non zero-sum power, not exercised from the top down nor from a centre to a periphery, not based on the distinction of ruler/ruled or master/servant, not based on negation, prohibition or coercion. It is a form of power without centre, exercised horizontally, through its own subjects (beginning with the human body). The subjects of such power cannot desire or know but the desires, knowledge or truths of the disciplinary institutions – public and private, schools and hospitals, barracks and prisons, families and factories – which are created as the subjects (not objects) of their own subjection.

As I have already pointed out in Chapter One, though Foucault is rather confusing about the relationship between these two forms of power, it is clear that, in his view, they are incompatible, and that the scientific, normalizing power of the disciplines has become the most pervasive form of power in contemporary societies. I also indicated that Foucault overstates the incompatibility between the two forms of power, thereby ignoring the complex circulations of meaning and the possible complicities, articulations and interpenetrations between them. Power is never exercised in a pure, exclusive form, but rather as a power formation, that is, as a constellation of different forms of power combined in specific ways. I would now like to add two further criticisms of Foucault that are especially relevant for the argument of this chapter.

First, although Foucault is correct in positing the existence of power forms outside the state, and in considering them as political in nature as state power, he goes too far in stressing their dispersion, fragmentation and decentred character. In his view, disciplinary powers are everywhere, and they operate in the same way everywhere. Only in a trivial sense is the school different from the hospital, or the hospital from the factory. All of them operate by creating docile bodies and actively desiring and knowledge-seeking

---

[5]   Foucault, 1976, 1977, 1980.

subjects. Foucault thus combines an extremely fragmented conception of disciplinary power with an utterly monolithic one. As I said above, if power is everywhere, it is nowhere. If there is no principle of structuration and hierarchy, there is no strategic framework for emancipation. Indeed, Foucault's conception of power offers itself to both blind voluntarism and hyperlucid passivity. In my view, Foucault is forced to think of resistance to power outside his overall conception of power and power relations, as a kind of ad hoc afterthought. In his conception, resistance to power is the ultimate exercise of power. Empowering people is always a way of intensifying their participation in the mechanisms of subjectivity/subjection that subjugate them. For Foucault, then, to empower means ultimately to disempower.

My second criticism of Foucault is that his conception of state juridical power is as monolithic as his conception of disciplinary power. In the previous chapters, I reached two conclusions that go directly against the core of this conception. On the one hand, it is wrong, and indeed amounts to falling into the liberal trap, to equate the juridical with the *étatique*. As the conception of legal pluralism put forward in Chapter Three shows, various non-state juridical powers circulate in society that actually show better than state juridical power the subtle interpenetrations between juridical and disciplinary power. On the other hand, far from being monolithic, state juridical power is highly heterogeneous and internally differentiated – and indeed, as I showed in Chapter Five, such heterogeneity is increasing under the impact of globalization – its plasticity being both the symptom and the measure of its articulation with other forms of power circulating in and constituting social practice

These criticisms notwithstanding, Foucault's contribution to our understanding of power in contemporary societies has been invaluable. In the last three decades, the impact of his thought has continued to reverberate, particularly in feminist theories.[6] Indeed, the idea of power relations disseminated in society, acted out in non-dualistic forms, and exercised mainly through the naturalization of hegemonic representations and identities, was congenial to the radical revision of social and political theory – of liberalism and Marxism, functionalism and positivism – undertaken by feminism in its multiple facets and currents. But feminism, in its turn, has expanded and enriched the Foucaultian conception of power in many ways, two of which are particularly relevant for the theoretical perspective developed in this chapter.[7] First, by focusing on gender power or gendered forms of power, and their articulation with other forms of power (class, race, age, nationality), feminist theory drew our attention to the internal

---

[6] Foucault is pervasively present in feminist theorists. Some examples are Young, 1990; Connell, 1987; Cocks, 1989; Fraser and Nicholson, 1990. In Butler and Scott, 1992, Foucault shares with Derrida and Freud the biggest number of references, and exactly the same occurs (if we exclude the references to feminist theorists) in Hirsch and Keller, 1990.

[7] A third form of enrichment and expansion of Foucault by feminism is of an epistemological nature: the critique of the multiple vectors of sexism in modern science undermines the latter's foundationalism, and shows the extent to which scientific truth is nothing but a discourse of truth. I deal with this topic in Santos, 1995, Chapter One.

differentiation of disciplinary power – that is to say, with what Iris Young calls the multiple 'faces of oppression'.[8] It thus called for richer and more open interfaces of structure and agency, as well as for a sense of directionality which the power-knowledge strategies of Foucault lacked. Secondly, feminism showed that a general form of power, such as gender power, could be exercised in very different and interlocked forms, some of which were direct emanations of state power, through action or inaction, through decisions or non-decisions, through the exercise of violence or through tolerance in the face of violence, through the command of distributional resources (gendered welfare state) or through the state's general preponderance over Adorno's 'administered world' – ie, the increasing interference of the state in social relations. Furthermore, feminism showed that some of the power formations mixed state and non-state power forms until they became indistinct. In general, we might say that the expansion and enrichment of Foucault's ideas by feminism have been more significant when feminist theories engage with Marxism, rather than when they discard the latter altogether.

2.2 *Power, constellations of power and social emancipation*

What then, is power? At a very general level, power is any social relation ruled by an unequal exchange. It is a social relation because its persistence lies in its capacity to reproduce inequality through exchange, rather than by external diktat. Exchanges may encompass virtually all the conditions determining action and life, personal and social trajectories and projects, such as goods, services, assets, resources, symbols, values, identities, capacities, opportunities, skills, and interests. In terms of power relations, what is most characteristic of our societies is that material inequality is deeply interwoven with non-material inequality particularly with unequal opportunities for learning and unequal representational/communicative skills, on the one hand, and unequal conditions and capacities for organizing to defend common interests and for participating autonomously in meaningful decision-making processes, on the other.[9]

It is not easy to measure the inequality of an unequal exchange, and to evaluate how determinant it is in affecting the life conditions and trajectories of the people or groups involved in it. This is so mainly because power relations do not occur in isolation, but rather in chains, sequences or constellations. In a given situation of exercise of power, links in the chain of inequality as diverse as race, sex, class, age, nationality, educational assets and so on, may converge. And although the situation tends to be organized and discursively framed by the nearest link or by the link operating on a high tension mode (more on this below), the nearest link may not necessarily be the most unequal or the most determinant in the set of inequalities that constitute the life trajectory and chances of a given person or social group. For instance, a situation framed as an

---

[8]   Young, 1990, pp 39ff. See also Bartky, 1990; Townsend et al, 1999.

[9]   I disagree with Young's restricted conception of distribution – ie, restricted to the distribution of material goods – for the reasons stated below.

intergenerational conflict may be a symptom of an underlying unequal sexist relationship between father and daughter. For the same reason, what appears interactionally as an external diktat over a given, otherwise power-free, relation is more often than not a manifestation of the same power constellation in one of its previous and more remote links. That is why people frequently accept as equal what in fact is an unequal exchange.

Of course, this disguise of power as equality is an illusion; but because it is necessary as an illusion, it has its grain of truth. This can be observed in two different but convergent types of social process. In one type, power is inherently distributional, but because it is exercised in constellations of power relations that either reinforce or neutralize each other, unequal exchange is, in general, the end result of an unequal distribution of equal (or more or less equal) exchanges. For instance, male and female workers belonging to the same ethnic minority are equal in their relations – that is, they are equal (or more equal) both as members of the same ethnic minority and as workers – but they are unequal (or less equal) in that they belong to different genders. Yet this combination of equality/inequality is changed into a new combination whenever they relate with male/female workers belonging to an ethnic majority. Moreover, both combinations may change again as they overlap with a third combination emerging out of the relations between all the workers (ethnic minority/ethnic majority, male/female) and their employers who, in turn, may be ethnic majority or ethnic minority, male or female. Actually, the employers' ethnic or gender identity may end up having a much lesser weight in the third combination than the ethnic or gender identity of the workers in the first two combinations. Furthermore, inequalities among workers are experienced by them as being independent of their unequal relations with employers, even though, from a structural point of view, relations among workers, as workers, are premised upon them. As I suggest below, mutually reinforcing or neutralizing inequalities create a pattern of unequal distribution that is difficult to confront precisely because, interactionally, inequalities are often made of unequally relevant equalities.

The second type of social process in which power is disguised as equality relates to the fact that power constellations are as much boundary-setting and path breaking as distributional. As boundary-setting they are constraining, as path breaking they are enabling. All the dualisms anchored in power relations have this double character: thinkable-unthinkable, knowable-unknowable, possible-impossible, allowed-forbidden, desired-rejected, legitimate-illegitimate, included-excluded and so on. The first pole of any of these dualisms is path breaking, enabling, while the second pole is boundary-setting and constraining. All relations of power operate both in the *path-breaking mode* and in the *boundary-setting mode*, but they do not operate always in both modes simultaneously, or with the same relative intensity. Because they are exercised while integrated in constellations of power, and never overlap completely, power relations invest the same situation of power exercise with an asymmetric mixture of constraining and enabling features. A male worker fighting for a better salary, but finding it absurd that a female worker may get the same salary, is thereby exercising (and being exercised upon by) class power in the path-breaking mode, and gender power in the boundary-setting mode. Conversely, the female worker who fights for equal pay but thinks it absurd or impossible to join forces with male workers in pursuance of common interests against capital, is thereby exercising (and being exercised upon by) gender power in the path-breaking mode, and class power in the boundary-setting mode. Therefore, the same constellation of power allows for multiple situations and contexts, in which empowering exercises combine with constraining exercises. The disconfirmation or dislocation of constraints is only likely to occur when, in a given social situation like the one used as an example here, different power relations – eg, class and gender relations – are set in the path-breaking mode. Such convergence is, in part, made possible by questioning and confronting what makes a given course of action seem impossible, unthinkable, or out of the question.

Given the intricacy and complexity of power constellations in our societies, it is difficult to think of emancipation in emancipatory terms: more equal exchanges seem to go along with and indeed to confirm unequal exchanges; more empowering exercises seem only to be possible by accepting and indeed reiterating constraints. But there is nothing mechanical, impeccably functional or fully determined in this. Power constellations are clusters of relations among people and among social groups. Rather than machines, they are like rivers: according to the season or the stretch, they are now dangerous, then amenable, now navigable, then not, now fast, then slow, now flowing, then ebbing, and sometimes changing courses. They are, however, irreversible, never returning to the source. In sum, they are like us, neither chaotic, nor totally predictable.

What makes a social relation an exercise of power is the extent to which the interests of the parties in the relation are unequally dealt with or, more blatantly, the extent to which *A* affects *B* in a manner contrary to *B's* interests. After having thus defined power, Lukes concludes that 'any view of power rests on some normatively specific conception of interests'.[10] This is, for Lukes, the reason why the concept of power is one of the 'essentially contested concepts'.[11] For a critical theory, however, the concept of power must rest on a concept of emancipation from power relations. Emancipation is as relational as power. There is no emancipation as such. There are, rather, emancipatory relations, relations that create an ever greater number of ever more equal relations. Thus, emancipatory relations develop inside power relations – not as the automatic outcome of any essential contradiction, but rather as created and creative outcomes of created and creative contradictions. Only through the cumulative exercise of the enabling mode of power relations – the path-breaking mode – is it possible to alter constraints and change distributions, that is, to transform capacities that reproduce power into capacities that undo it. In order to be effective and non self-defeating, emancipatory relations must therefore congregate in constellations of emancipatory practices and relations.

---

[10]   Lukes, 1974, p 34.
[11]   Lukes, 1974, p 26.

The articulation among different emancipatory relations is no easy task, mainly because the empowerment they aim at involves increasing equality in some relations and the increasing difference in others. To give an example: in South Africa today, black Africans see their liberation in the right and power to decide in which respects they want to be equal to white Africans and in which respects they want to be or remain different. There are, therefore, empowering and disempowering differences, as there are empowering and disempowering equalities, and the criteria to distinguish amongst them tend to be in practice highly contested, if not obscure. There is an inevitable asymmetry between differences and equalities as concerns their relations to emancipation: it is easier to identify an equal exchange of equalities than an equal exchange of differences. For instance, class related exchanges among people belonging to the same class are more easily identified as equal exchanges than identity related exchanges among people belonging to different ethnic groups. Furthermore, because emancipatory relations, like power relations, operate in constellations, people involved in concrete emancipatory struggles may have to face the task – in general, a highly contested one – of establishing hierarchies among discrepant or even antagonic clusters or chains of empowering equalities and differences. For instance, indigenous people organizations often find themselves in the position of having to decide whether to press for policies that enhance the equality among the members of a given ethnic group or for policies that strengthen the identity of the group vis-à-vis other ethnic groups. The same is likely to occur within the feminist, ecological or labour movements. As usual, this task is immensely simpler in theory than in practice. An overarching principle of equality – one that is not just procedural – is needed to allow for empowerment not only through equality but also, just as importantly, through difference. I mean a principle of distribution in the widest sense, along the lines of the very broad conception of unequal exchange presented above.

Though I agree with Young that emancipation is enabling justice, I disagree with her criticism of an expanded conception of distribution. She is critical of 'the logic of distribution' because it 'treats non-material goods as identifiable things or bundles distributed in a static pattern among identifiable, separate individuals', and argues that 'the concept of distribution should be limited to material goods' and not to 'other important aspects of justice [which] include decision-making procedures, the social division of labour and culture'.[12] In my view, the risk of reification and individualism is much higher once we confine distribution to material goods, in particular at a time in which the world system seems to have reached full commodification of social life. Without subscribing to the extreme positions of Baudrillard,[13] it must be recognized that it is increasingly problematic to distinguish between material and non-material goods, and if such a distinction must be upheld – as I think it must – it is theoretically unsound and politically risky to derive from it fundamentally different claims or criteria. Leslie Sklair has convincingly shown that the culture-ideology of consumerism is today deeply entrenched in social groups and societies with no monetary capacity to engage

[12]   Young, 1990, p 8. A different view in Fraser, 1999.
[13]   Baudrillard, 1981.

in the practice of consumption.[14] The truth is that the same basic principle of unequal exchange that presides over the uneven distribution of material goods throughout society and the world system also presides over the uneven distribution of material and non-material dimensions of goods in general. As a result of this, large social groups are confined to the consumption of non-material dimensions of goods only. The ideology of consumerism without the practice of consumerism – consumption *in absentia*, so to speak.

Distribution and empowering are, thus, the two sides of emancipation: without changes in distribution, there will be no changes in empowering, and vice versa.[15] Thus broadly defined, emancipation runs the same risk of trivialization as the concept of power: if emancipation is everywhere, it is nowhere. This highlights the need for a theory attentive to specific practices, hierarchies and the interaction of structure and agency in both in conceptualizing power and in thinking about emancipatory relations.

In an attempt to respond to this need, I present below a theoretical model that entails a structure-agency map of contemporary capitalist societies as they make up the modern world system. The model identifes six structural clusters of social relations within which six main forms of power, law and commonsense knowledge are produced in capitalist societies. These structural places are orthotopias – that is, core sites of production and reproduction of unequal exchange in capitalist societies. But they are also susceptible of being converted, through transformative agency, into heterotopias – ie, core sites of emancipatory relations. This model aims at replacing the dualism state/civil society and all its corollaries, like the distinction between public and private sphere, the conception of politics as a specialized sector or dimension of social life identified with the state, the reduction of law to state law and the concomitant separation of law from politics. This dualism and its corollaries, which are the core of liberal political thought, and have been accepted in a modified version by classical Marxism, I designate as 'conceptual orthodoxy', to signal that its predominance in contemporary political thought is compatible with its theoretical bankruptcy. I will start by presenting a critique of this conceptual orthodoxy, elaborating on Chapter Two.

---

[14]   Sklair, 1991.

[15]   Distribution and capacitation are also the two sides of rights, when conceived from a radical perspective. In this context, the juridical roots of the concept of emancipation are worth noting, and semantic history may be helpful here. In classical Roman law, *emancipatio* was the juridical act by which the child was released from paternal power (*patria potestas*). Later on, it came to mean the freeing of slaves and, in an even broader sense, the lifting of legal restrictions on certain social groups, as when we speak of the emancipation of Jews in eighteenth- and nineteenth-century Europe, of serfs in nineteenth-century Russia, or of Roman Catholics in early nineteenth-century England, or still of women, at least in the early and first-wave feminist movements, for whom the concept of emancipation was central in their campaigns for equal rights. For Roman law, see, among others, Berger, 1953, p 451. For the feminist movement, see Humm, 1990, p 61; and Smith-Rosenberg, 1985.

3   THE STATE AND CIVIL SOCIETY

It has been said that the dualism state/civil society is the greatest of all dualisms in modern Western thought.[16] In this conception, the state is a contrived reality, an artificial, modern creation, when compared with civil society. In our century, no one has expressed this idea better than Hayek: 'Societies form, but states are made'.[17] Culminating the historical process of state formation that started in the post-Westphalia period, the modernity of the nineteenth-century constitutional state was featured in the latter's formal organization, internal unity, absolute sovereignty in a system of states and, above all, in the unified and centralized legal system, conceived as the universal language through which the state communicated with civil society. In contrast with the state, civil society was viewed as the realm of economic life, of spontaneous social relations guided by private, particularistic interests.

Despite its apparent self-explanatory character, the dualism state/civil society was never unequivocal; rather, it was from the start pregnant with contradictions, and bound to be in permanent crisis. The principle of the separation between the state and civil society encompassed both the idea of a minimum and a maximum state, to the same extent that state action was simultaneously conceived as a potential enemy of individual freedom and as the condition of its exercise. The state as a contrived reality was the necessary condition of the spontaneous reality of civil society. Eighteenth-century thought is saturated with this contradiction, since freeing economic activity from the corporatist regulations of the *ancien regime* by no means implies that modern economy will dispense with enlightened state action. Take the Scottish enlightenment thinkers who were converted into doctrinaires of laissez-faire by nineteenth-century thought. The Scottish enlightened thinkers were not doctrinaires of laissez-faire. At most, they may be so viewed only retrospectively, that is, vis-à-vis the corporatist regulations of the feudal state. They were, on the contrary, keenly aware that the modern economy would lead to the emergence of a state with an incommensurably higher potential to influence the lives of people than that of the feudal state. This explains why they were so concerned with developing political arrangements that would prevent the abuse of power, '*les grands coups d'authorité*', in Montesquieu's words.[18]

This concern pervades the work of Adam Smith,[19] for whom the idea that commerce generates freedom and civilization goes hand in hand with the defence of political institutions that secure a free and civilized commerce. The state is assigned a very active and, indeed, a crucial role in creating the institutional and legal conditions for the

16   Gamble, 1982, p 45.
17   Hayek, 1979, p 140.
18   Montesquieu, 1989.
19   Smith, 1937.

expansion of the market.[20] As Billet has justly emphasized, from the first to the last chapter of *An Inquiry Into the Nature and Causes of the Wealth of Nations*, 'one is struck by the idea, crucial to Adam Smith's thought, that the character of a nation's political institutions and practices decisively affects its capacity for sustained economic development'.[21] As an example, comparing Portugal and Spain with Britain, Adam Smith considers the despotic nature of the first two states, their 'violent and arbitrary government', as responsible for their stagnant economies and relative poverty: 'Industry is there neither free nor secure and the civil and ecclesiastical governments of both Spain and Portugal are such as would be alone sufficient to perpetuate their present state of poverty'.[22] Still more striking is that, for Smith, despotism may be either the result of an arbitrary government, ruling by force and unrestrained by institutional or legal constraints, or the result of a weak government, an unstable authority incapable of maintaining law and order and performing the regulatory functions required by the economy.[23]

The idea of the separation of the economic from the political, based on the state/civil society distinction and expressed in the laissez-faire principle, seems to be fraught with two insoluble contradictions. The first one is that, given the particularistic nature of interests in civil society, the principle of laissez-faire cannot be equally valid for all possible interests. Its internal coherence is premised upon an accepted hierarchy of interests, candidly implied in John Stuart Mill's dictum that 'every departure from laissez-faire, unless required by some great good, is a certain evil'.[24] The discussion of the principle always takes place in the shadow of the discussion of the interests to which the principle is to be applied. Thus, the same legal measure may be the object of opposing but equally consistent interpretations. To give an example, the joint stock legislation of 1825 to 1865 was viewed by some as a good example of laissez-faire, in that it removed restrictions on the mobility of capital, and by others as a clear violation of laissez-faire, in that it accorded privileges to corporate enterprises which were denied to the individual entrepreneurs.[25] This explains why Victorian England has been portrayed by some as the age of laissez-faire, and by others as the embryo of the welfare state.[26] The second contradiction concerns the mechanisms by which the principle of laissez-faire is socially activated. The state is a condition of existence and reproduction of capitalist relations

---

[20]   There has been some debate about the role of political and legal institutions in A Smith's thought. Against what is becoming a widely accepted view (Viner, 1927; Billet, 1975; Samuels, 1979), Hirschman tends to minimize such a role. But he also recognizes that 'it appears that Smith advocated less a state with minimal functions than one whose capacity for folly would have some ceiling' (1977, p 104).

[21]   Billet, 1975, p 430.

[22]   Smith, 1937, p 509.

[23]   Viner, 1927, p 218; Billet, 1975, p 439.

[24]   Mill, 1921, p 950.

[25]   Taylor, 1972, p 12.

[26]   It should therefore not be surprising that the current 'crisis of the welfare state' or the 'crisis of the regulatory state' is viewed by some as a return to laissez-faire (free trade fundamentalism) and by others as the emergence of a new, more authoritarian state form (the new welfare state as guarantor of the welfare of business rather than people).

that operates through the externality of the state vis-à-vis production. Rather than an omission, this externality is the result of active state-building and state intervention, laissez-faire being one of their possible outcomes. Nineteenth-century England witnessed not only the growth of legislation on social and economic policy, but also the rise of a wide range of new state institutions, such as the Factory Inspectorate, the Poor Law Board, the General Board of Health and so on, some of which were explicitly intended to carry out laissez-faire policies. As Dicey noted, 'sincere believers in laissez-faire found that for the attainment of their ends the improvement and the strengthening of governmental machinery was an absolute necessity'.[27] As laissez-faire policies were carried out through active state intervention, the state, then as now, had to intervene in order not to intervene.

In view of all this, the following question emerges: if the state/civil society distinction has always been so pregnant with contradictions, why is it so widely accepted, so self-evident and even commonsensical? Before trying to answer this question, and because the issue is important for the development of my argument, I would like to illustrate briefly the weight of this conceptual orthodoxy within Marxism itself. Leaving aside eighteenth-century English and French liberal political theory, and focusing solely on the nearest background of Marx's thought, the German context, it might be useful to recall that, according to Hegel[28] in his most Hegelian moment, civil society – rather than being the opposite of the state – is a transitional stage in the development of the idea, the final stage being the state. The family is the thesis, civil society is the antithesis, and the state is the synthesis. Civil society is the 'system of needs', the destruction of the unity of the family and the atomization of its members. In sum, the realm of particularistic interests and of egotism, a stage to be superseded by the state as the ultimate unifier of interests, the universal idea, the most final completion of moral consciousness.[29]

There are, thus, two lines in Hegel's thought about the state and civil society. One, very much subsidiary to English and French liberal thought, is the conceptual distinction between state and civil society in terms of contradictory entities. The other, distinctively Hegelian, is the idea that the concept of civil society is not on an equal footing with (ie, on the same speculative level as) the concept of the state. It corresponds to a lesser-developed stage of consciousness actually to be superseded by the state, which means that the dichotomy of state and civil society as two autonomous, self-identical concepts is theoretically untenable. Though the latter line, in spite of its idealistic and ideological content, is still, in my view, very important today to understand some of the historical and social processes of capitalist societies, it was abandoned in the philosophical and historical controversies that followed Hegel's work. The reification of the dichotomy

[27]   Dicey, 1905, p 306.
[28]   Hegel, 1981.
[29]   Hegel, 1981, p 140.

state/civil society was soon accomplished, mainly through the writings of Lorenz von Stein II.[30]

Notwithstanding the brilliant rescue attempt undertaken by Max Adler,[31] I believe that Marx accepted the reified version of the state/civil society distinction. He inverted but did not supersede it. He discovered that the allegedly 'natural' laws of classical economy hid social relations of exploitation, which the state, only apparently neutral, had the function to guarantee. Rather than universal social interest, the state represented, according to Marx, the interest of capital in reproducing itself. However, because he was concerned with confronting classical economy on its own terms, Marx ended up trapped in the distinction between economy and politics – or, at least, he did not push the critique of this distinction to its conclusion, and indeed tended to reduce politics and law to state action. What Marx failed to see was the real (and not merely metaphorical) sense in which 'economic relations' were not only social, but also distinctively political and legal relations in their structural constitution. Thus, the metaphor of the economic base grounding the political and legal superstructure is not a complete distortion of Marx's thought, as can be demonstrated by its remarkable resilience in subsequent attempts to reconstruct the question it meant to address.

One of such attempts, by far the most influential within Western Marxism in the 1970s and 1980s, is the French structuralist Marxism of Althusser and his group – with its theory of relatively autonomous instances (the economic, the political, the ideological), the concept of overdetermination and the principle of economic determination in the last instance. The bias of economism is still present in this school, and it is visible in the work of Poulantzas,[32] who is without any doubt the most brilliant analyst of law and politics in this school. In his analysis of the relation of property as one of the elements of the economic instance, for example, Poulantzas says: 'It should be noted that [the relation of property] belongs strictly to the region of the economic and that it should be clearly distinguished from the juridical forms with which it is invested, ie from juridical property'.[33] He also criticizes Maurice Godelier for ignoring that 'the relations of production and the productive forces belong to the same combination/ structure of the economic whereas private (juridical) ownership of the means of production belongs to the superstructure'.[34] Though Poulantzas changed his view on this in his later work,[35] this formulation, which first appeared in 1968, remained by far the most influential.

How to explain the self-evidence of the conception of the economic as a separate and autonomous realm and of the correspondent conception of the political and legal as an

[30]   Stein, 1888.
[31]   Adler, 1922.
[32]   Poulantzas, 1978a.
[33]   Poulantzas, 1978a, p 26.
[34]   Poulantzas, 1978a, p 67.
[35]   Poulantzas, 1978b.

exclusive attribute of the state? How to explain the persistence of the state/civil society dichotomy in spite of its internal contradictions and permanent crises? As with any other social doctrine, this conceptual orthodoxy has a shred of truth. In feudalism, necessary labour – that is, the labour required for the subsistence of the serfs – and surplus labour – that is, the labour performed by the serfs to guarantee the subsistence and accumulation of the feudal lords – were separate both in time and in space. Because feudal lords did not own the means of production, they had to rely on the political and legal institutions of the state to extract the surplus labour from serfs. In a way, since feudal lords had no private ownership of the means of production, their social power was most directly linked to their private ownership of the state. In capitalism, on the contrary, necessary and surplus labour take place within the same labour process, given the control over the latter by capitalists as an attribute of their ownership of the means of production. Once the state guarantees the enforcement of the law of property, class relations occur and reproduce themselves in the private realm of the factory. It seems, therefore, that the externality of the state vis-à-vis the relations of production is the correlate of the view of production relations as an economic, private affair between private individuals within the civil society.

On further reflection, this derivation is not logically necessary. Without questioning the externality of the political and legal institutions of the state vis-à-vis the relations of production, it should be equally logical to conceive these relations inside the factory as a set of political and legal social processes taking place outside the state, under the direct control of capital. And indeed, it would not be difficult to detect legislative bodies, power blocs, coalitions, legal regulations, dispute settlement mechanisms, positive and negative sanctions, police surveillance and so on inside the factory, or, more generally, in any type of labour process. Why was this alternative conceptualization of the factory and the labour process not adopted? Why was this extreme variety of social processes lumped together in the amorphous concept of 'economic relations?' To my mind, the separation of the economic from the political made possible both the naturalization of capitalist economic exploitation, and the neutralization of the revolutionary potential of modernity as a political project – two processes that converged to consolidate capitalist social relations. If by way of a mental experiment we compare social relations across time, we will find that it is in the field of political relations that capitalist societies most unequivocally represent civilizing progress. For the first time in history, the constitutional state has become truly public, that is, not the private legal possession of any specific group.[36] The formal universalization of citizenship through equal civil and political rights made the state, in all its theoretical attributes, the ultimate embodiment of

---

[36]   I mentioned in Chapter Two how gradual and difficult it was to conceptualize the conversion of the state into a *republica* between the twelfth and eighteenth centuries. A remarkable residue of such difficulty can be seen in the 'theory' of the 'King's Two Bodies', as divulged by English jurists of the Tudor period and thereafter. See Ernst Kantorowicz, 1957. The 'privatization' of the preconstitutional state was not only political, but also bureaucratic. One of the best examples of the latter was the sale of offices, pervasive until the eighteenth century. See Swart, 1949.

the democratic ideal of equal participation in social affairs. If, on the contrary, we take production relations in capitalist societies, the picture is almost the obverse of the one just described. We may still grant to capitalism having achieved tremendous progress in terms of technology of production, but concerning the social relations in production we are led to conclude, with Meiksins Wood, that 'in no other system of production is work so thoroughly disciplined and organized, and no other organization of production ... so directly responsive to the demands of appropriation'.[37] This unprecedented control over production is what Marx called the despotism of the workshop,[38] and Braverman the degradation of the labour process.[39]

In my view, and as I will further argue below, the economy/politics dichotomy was essential to keep these two pictures incomparable or incommensurable. It kept them separate in such a way that the political form of social relations could never become the model for the economic form of social relations. Confined to the public place, the democratic ideal was neutralized or strongly limited in its emancipatory potential. On the other hand, the conversion of the public place into the exclusive site of law and politics performed a crucial legitimation function, by obscuring the fact that the law and the politics of the capitalist state could only operate as part of a broader political and legal configuration in which other contrasting forms of law and politics were included. In the periphery of the world economy – in the colonies first, and later in the newly independent, less-developed, peripheral countries – the shred of truth of the dichotomy state/civil society was even smaller. Here, civil society was, from the start, a product of the state in the most direct sense. Even more than in the metropolitan countries, the creation of the labour force was an administrative issue for the colonial state or for the quasi-state colonial companies. Moreover, the persistence of pre-capitalist modes of production, submitted to capital through market mechanisms but autonomous in terms of the organization of production, called for the direct political control of surplus appropriation, and thus for the privatization of state power and state functions, as illustrated in *coronelismo* (in Brazil) and *caudillismo* (in Spanish-speaking Latin America). Notwithstanding these differences, the state/civil society dualism, whenever proclaimed, tended to perform basically the same function throughout the world system: as the production of politics got confined to the state, the politics of production could be pursued unencumbered by the juridical and political principles that purported to inform the public sphere. Thereby, the publicization of the state, which was the other side of the privatization of production, became incommensurable with the latter. Because the state and private production operate in autonomus social fields, the former in the political field and the latter in the economic field, it becomes impossible to determine how economic is the state or how political is the system of production.

This analysis should not, however, be understood in functionalist terms. Often, particularly in the periphery and semi-periphery, the state/civil society dualism has been

[37]   Wood, 1981, p 91.
[38]   Marx, 1970.
[39]   Braverman, 1974.

used for progressive purposes, namely as an ideological tool against the authoritarianism of the state. What is at stake here is not the reproduction of specific political regimes, but rather the reproduction of the regime of the autonomy of autonomy of politics vis-à-vis everything else. In light of the crisis of the welfare state in the core of the world system, the collapse of Communist or state-socialist regimes in the semi-periphery and periphery, and the rise of neo-liberalism on a global scale, it is today more imperative than ever to present a credible alternative to the conceptual orthodoxy of the state/civil society dualism. This is no easy task. The resilience of a given conceptual orthodoxy is that it overflows beyond its boundaries and in different directions, creating loyalties both on the right and on the left of the political spectrum. The most characteristic feature of any orthodoxy is to naturalize itself, to become evident, commonsensical knowledge. Any posited alternative is bound to be less than credible. Alternatives tend to be viewed as unrealistic, either because they are outright Utopian, or because they are, on the contrary, so infiltrated by the dualism they criticize that they reproduce it in a different way. In either case, alternatives are considered to be highly political and essentially contested. Aware of these difficulties, I present the following model as an attempt to contribute to the creation of a new legal, political and epistemological common sense.

4 A STRUCTURE-AGENCY MAP OF CAPITALIST SOCIETIES IN THE WORLD SYSTEM

My main argument in this section runs as follows. First, capitalist societies are *political* formations or constellations, constituted by six basic modes of production of power articulated in specific ways. These modes of production generate six basic forms of power that, though interrelated, are structurally autonomous. Secondly, capitalist societies are *legal* formations or constellations, constituted by six basic modes of production of law articulated in specific ways. These modes of production generate six basic forms of law that, albeit interrelated, are structurally autonomous. Thirdly, capitalist societies are *epistemological* formations or constellations, constituted by six basic modes of production of knowledge articulated in specific ways. These modes of production generate six basic forms of knowledge that, though interrelated, are structurally autonomous.

Basic to this argument is the idea that the political nature of power is not the exclusive attribute of any given form of power, but rather, the global effect of the combination of different forms of power and of the modes of production thereof. Power forms never operate in isolation. For instance, sexism or patriarchy never operates in an exclusively sexist setting. Thus, the political meaning of a given power form depends on how the operation of that power form is supplemented, neutralized or transformed by the operation of other power forms operating in tandem with it. Similarly, the legal nature of social regulation is not the exclusive attribute of any form of law, but rather the global effect of the combination of different forms of law and of the modes of production thereof. We would not be able to adequately characterize the legal regulation of the family by looking exclusively at the official family law. To do so we would have to look at other realms of official law such as labour law or inheritance law as well as at other non-official laws such as domestic law or community law (on these latter forms of law see below). Finally, the epistemological nature of knowledge practices is not the exclusive attribute of any given epistemological form, but rather the global effect of the combination of different epistemological forms and of the modes of production thereof. In spite of the epistemological privilege held by modern science in our society, the practice of science calls upon other kinds of knowledges such as local knowledges and trust relationships typical of community culture and competitiveness and individualism as inhering in productivism (on the latter forms of knowledge see below).

Table 2 (opposite) shows in a synoptic form the structure-agency map of capitalist societies as integrating the world system. I distinguish six structural places: the householdplace, the workplace, the marketplace, the communityplace, the citizenplace and the worldplace. I understand by structural places the most basic and most consolidated clusters of social relations in contemporary capitalist societies. The differentiation and the autonomy of the six structural places are the result of a long historical process, and even today they present themselves differently in the core, the periphery and the semiperiphery of the world system due, to a great extent, to the different historical trajectories into Western modernity.[40]

The identification and characterization of the structural places are guided by a few theoretical insights that must be mentioned at this juncture. The first one is an analytical emphasis on the questions of power, law and knowledge. The social contexts of these phenomena, their internal differentiation, and the articulations among them must be highlighted. Critical sociological theory has rarely tried to study these three macro-phenomena of our time in conjunction and within the same theoretical analytical framework. Foucault was, of course, the social theorist who made the most sustained effort in the right direction, but even he decided to leave out or, at least, neglect law. His narrow conception of law as state law led him to see it as an anachronistic phenomenon, a residue of past forms of domination. The analytical framework presented in this chapter is an attempt at a more inclusive approach, one that includes power, law and knowledge on an equal analytical footing, without collapsing them into simplistic totalities – as has happened in so much critical social theory. Instead, the framework

---

[40]   As is well known, the separation of the workplace from the householdplace was a direct result of capitalist development. In the early stages, the workplace collapsed partially with the 'citizenplace' (before the emergence of the liberal state there is no citizen-place in the modern sense). In the sixteenth century, textile workers in Milan worked under oath, sanctioned by the state, that they would not abandon the city, and in 1682 Colbert sentenced to death the workers who abandoned France to work abroad (Adler, nd, pp 72–73). This complex intertwining of the coercive apparatus of the state with that of production prompted Adler (nd) and later on Rusche and Kirchheimer (1968) to argue for the original twin functions of the prison and the factory. A restatement of this argument can be found in Melossi and Pavarini, 1981. In the colonial periphery of the world system, this functional promiscuity continued well into the twentieth century.

TABLE 2. STRUCTURE-AGENCY MAP OF CAPITALIST SOCIETIES IN THE WORLD SYSTEM

Dimensions / Structural Places	Social Agency	Institutions	Developmental Dynamics	Power Form	Legal Form	Epistemo- logical Form
Household-place	Gender, generation	marriage, family, kinship	Maximization of affection	patriarchy	domestic law	familism, familial culture
Workplace	class, nature as 'capitalist nature'	factory, corporation	Maximization of profits and of the degradation of nature	exploitation, 'capitalist nature'	production law	productivism, technologism, professional training, corporate culture
Marketplace	consumership	market	maximization of utility and of the commodific- ation of needs	fetishism of commodities	exchange law	consumerism, mass culture
Community-place	ethnicity, race, nation, people, religion	community, neighbour- hood, region, grassroots organizations, church	maximization of identity	unequal differentiation	community law	local knowledge, community culture, tradition
Citizenplace	citizenship	state	maximization of loyalty	domination	territorial (state) law	educational and cultural nationalism, civic culture
Worldplace	nation-state	interstate system, international agencies and associations, international treaties	maximization of effectiveness	unequal exchange	systemic law	science, universal progress, global culture

seeks to capture the range of differentiation and fragmentation of and links between varieties of law, power and knowledge.

The second theoretical insight guiding the framework is that the characterization of the structural places must emphasize the multiple dimensions of inequality and oppression in contemporary capitalist societies and in the world system as a whole, so as to map out new possible fields for relevant emancipatory struggles. Privileged sites of inequality and oppression must, accordingly, be identified and conceived as impure, unstable, incomplete, asymmetric and heterogeneous.

Closely connected with the previous guiding postulate, the third one is that the centrality of state power, state law, and modern science must neither be neglected nor mistaken as a totality or as a monopoly. The three are pervasive in the respective constellations of power, law and knowledge that emerge in concrete social fields, but they always operate in articulation with various non-state forms of power and law, and with various forms of non-scientific knowledge. The final theoretical insight is that the analytical framework must avoid focusing on the core or the West as much as possible and, instead, promote genuine comparisons across the world system. Marxist and critical social theory in general were for many decades focused on core capitalist societies, having created an impressive body of knowledge on what, in my analytical framework, is designated as the workplace and the citizenplace. As we well know today, the exclusive concentration on these two clusters of social relations – without any doubt crucial to understand capitalist societies – left out of the analytical scope other equally important aspects of capitalist social production and reproduction. Critical feminist theory is to be credited for bringing the householdplace into consideration, and for offering a radical revision both of the workplace and the citizenplace. This significant analytical expansion has, however, been largely confined to the analysis of national societies in core capitalist societies.

Dependency theory, first, and the world system theory, later, broke with this status quo by drawing our attention to peripheral societies and their integration in a world system comprising peripheral, core and semi-peripheral societies ordered according to a major hierarchical principle – the international division of labour. With its emphasis on global interactions and hierarchies, the world system theory has, however, tended to provide relatively crude and reductionist analyses of individual national societies and locally or nationally based social processes. To counteract this tendency, the world system, in the form of the worldplace, is conceived here as an internal structure of national societies. The worldplace of a given society is the specific way in which the world system becomes embedded in national social relations through pertinent effects. Such effects are the sum total of globalized localisms and localized globalisms analyzed in Chapter Five. This internalization of the world system, I believe, allows for a more productive dialogue between the theoretical perspectives and analytical insights developed by the world system theory and those traditionally developed by the social theories specifically concerned with the other structural places.

Furthermore, the analytical framework proposed here is not only designed to account for the multiple inequalities of today's world system, but also for the different and unequal historical trajectories into modernity. Accordingly, I identify the communityplace as one of the structural places. It may be surprising to consider the communityplace, which is grounded on the idea of physical or symbolic territory, as an autonomous structural place. It is usually argued that, in light of its territoriality, the hegemonic claim of the modern state to exclusive control over a given territory has brought about the collapse of the communityplace into the citizenplace. In light of the historical processes of state formation in most peripheral and semi-peripheral societies, I argue alternatively that the communityplace has remained, throughout the world system, as an autonomous site of social relations irreducible to the social relations clustered around the citizenplace.

This is quite evident in the case of multinational states emerging out of European colonialism, but is also visible elsewhere. Even in Western core societies, the communityplace has remained as subtext of the citizenplace, surfacing in periods of crisis of the state. In Islamic states organized on the basis of a fundamentalist interpretation of the Qu'ran, it can even be argued that, in opposition to the Western experience, the citizenplace has collapsed into the communityplace.[41] Throughout the world system, the communityplace entertains complex relations with all the other structural places. For instance, in societies in which Hinduism or Confucionism is the organizing principle of the communityplace, the latter is deeply intertwined with the householdplace (to tender the domestic altar).[42]

As I suggest below, while my conception of the communityplace pertains mainly to the historical and social realities of the periphery, my conception of the marketplace relates chiefly to the historical and social realities of the core. However mistaken in some fundamental ways, the different theories that describe the dramatic transformations of core capitalist societies in the last three decades in terms of post-capitalism, post-industrialism, postmodernism or consumer society can be said to have a grain of truth. They have drawn our attention to the ideological expansion of the fetishism of commodities as a form of power leading to a new form of hegemony. This new hegemony somehow inverts the logic of capitalist accumulation by converting commodities into something more through ideological surplus values generated by the compulsive practice of commodification of needs and of the satisfaction of the latter. In my opinion, the relatively autonomous social production of consumption and consumerism has not structurally changed capitalist societies, but it has made them more complex. Consumption is no longer an epiphenomenon. It is, rather, an autonomous structural site of social relations, a new form of power, legality and knowledge. This structural feature, however grounded in the social practices of core societies, is also present, in modified or selective forms, in peripheral and semi-peripheral societies: the culture-ideology of consumerism is already much more widely distributed throughout the world system than the practice of consumption, and indeed seems to go on expanding even as the latter shrinks.

5   READING THE STRUCTURE-AGENCY MAP

Social interaction in capitalist societies centres around six modes of production of social practice – that is, the six structural places. At the most abstract level, a mode of production of social practice is a set of social relations whose internal contradictions endow it with a specific endogenous dynamic. It is, therefore, a complex field of interaction having six dimensions: social agency, institutions, developmental and interactional

41   See Ghai, 1993c, for an excellent overview of the ongoing tensions and conflicts between the citizenplace (state governance) and the communityplace (ethnicity) in Asia. Also Ghai (ed), 2000.

42   An excellent account of women in Korean ritual life is in Kendall, 1985. See also Bynum, Harrell and Richman, 1986.

dynamics, and a privileged form of power, law and epistemology. Below I define and explain briefly each structural place and its dimensions. For now, it is important to bear in mind that the specificity of each structural place lies in the form of unequal exchange that is the specific form of power in action that marks the social relations it constitutes. As it unfolds, this relational inequality produces a specific form of capital (in Bourdieu's use of the term) whose reproduction invests the social field with an interaction style and sense of directionality of its own. Though it is specific and endogenous, this logic is, not self-contained, insofar as social relations are as determined by their structural location as by their articulations – combinations, mutual interferences, interfaces and interpenetrations – with social relations in other structural locations. Phenomenologically speaking, the developmental logic of a specific structural place is but a sustained form of hybridization. In other words, the lived experiences of individuals and groups always mix structurally different logics even if specific courses of action are dominated by specific logics. Such hybridization is neither chaotic nor infinite, because the structural places are limited in number and concrete in internal specification. In other words, each structural place opens up a specific horizon of possibilities and, as such, it precludes any possibilities falling outside it. Before elaborating further on the problem of structural determination, I will describe in some detail the nature of the social relations constitutive of each one of the structural places.

5.1   The structural places and their dimensions

The *householdplace* is the cluster of social relations of production and reproduction of domesticity and kinship, between husband and wife – or otherwise-defined partners in comparable types of relations – between either and the children, and among kin.[43] The *workplace* is the set of social relations clustered around the production of economic exchange values and of labour processes, relations of production *strictu sensu* – between direct producers and appropriators of surplus value, and between both and nature – and relations in production – between workers and management and among workers. The *marketplace* is the cluster of social relations of distribution and consumption of exchange values whereby the commodification of needs and means to satisfy them is produced and reproduced. The *communityplace* is constituted by the social relations clustered around the production and reproduction of physical and symbolic territories and identities. The *citizenplace* is the set of the social relations that constitute the 'public sphere' and, in particular, the relations of production of the vertical political obligation between citizens and the state.

---

[43]   This structural place is defined in terms of the household, rather than in terms of the family, in order to stress the multiple sharing relationships (namely, the income-pooling practices). Since the institutional and ideological reproduction of the household occurs mainly through the family, I use the latter to define the institutional and epistemological form of the householdplace. With similar purposes, Michele Barrett speaks of 'households' and of 'familial ideology' 'as terms that avoid some of the naturalism and mystification engendered by the 'family'' (1980, p 199). See also Donzelot, 1977.

In Chapter Two, in analyzing the pattern of normal change, I described the citizenplace in detail through the operations and strategies of its institutional form, the state. Finally, the *worldplace* is the sum total of the impact upon a given society of the social relations through which the global division of labour is produced and reproduced – what I have called in Chapter Five globalized localisms and localized globalisms. The view of the worldplace as an internal structure of a given (national, local) society aims at rendering theoretically consistent the interactions between the global dynamics of the world system, on the one hand, and the extremely diverse and highly specific conditions of national or subnational societies across the globe, on the other. The worldplace is, therefore, the organizing matrix of the pertinent effects of world conditions and world hierarchies upon the household-, work-, market-, community- and citizenplace of a given society.

Each of these six structural places is complex, and consists of six dimensions laid out in Table 2. Since in any concrete social field the structural places always operate in constellations, each dimension of each structural place is in some way present in any other correspondent dimension of any other structural place. For instance, the privileged form of agency in the householdplace is gender and generation – in that the core struggles in the householdplace take place between members of different genders and generations – but this, of course, does not mean, as feminist theories have so persuasively shown, that gender and generation are confined to the householdplace. On the contrary, gender, for instance, combines specifically with class in the workplace, with consumer agency in the marketplace, with race, ethnicity or religion in the communityplace, with citizenship in the citizenplace and with nation-state agency in the worldplace. The same can be said of any other dimension of the structural places. Although the state is the privileged institutional form of the citizenplace, it is present in different ways in all the other structural institutions, be they the family, the corporation, the market, the community, or the interstate system. And the same is true of any of them vis-à-vis the state. Some states are run as extended families, particularly in countries in which *coronelismo* or *caudillismo* and other forms of privatization of the state are prevalent – as, for instance, in the Middle East dynastic regimes. When, for instance, the public health system of a given core country undergoes reforms that aim at creating internal markets within the state bureaucracy as is the case in the UK and, in a different form, in the US – the new institutions are combinations of market and state. In countries of the periphery of the world system in which foreign aid constitutes a disproportionate percentage of national income the state is, for most relevant purposes, an institutional mix of state and international agencies.

In the following, I will engage in a brief general description of the different dimensions of the structural places, paying closer attention to those whose identification seems more problematic. Those with greater analytical interest for this chapter – that is, forms of power, law and knowledge – will be also stressed below.

Social agency is the active dimension of the structural place, the privileged organizing principle of collective and individual action, the main criterion of identity and identification of individual and social groups engaged in social relations clustering around that particular structural place. In going through the forms of social agency of each structural site in Table 2, it may seem surprising that I identify the social agency of the workplace as both class exploitation and exploitation of nature ('capitalist nature'). Elsewhere I have made an epistemological critique of modern science and its conception of nature as *res extensa* with no subjectivity or dignity, a spontaneous mechanism regulated by mechanical laws, an infinite resource to be explored/exploited at human will. I also pointed out that, as modern science became interlocked with industrial capitalism and was converted into a force of production, such a conception of nature legitimated ideologically the conversion of nature into a condition of production, both as 'natural resources' and 'natural environment'.[44] That epistemological critique must now be complemented by a theoretical alternative.

Though the 'robbing' of the earth was considered by Marx as one of the conditions of capitalist wealth, the other being the exploitation of labour, and though the destruction of the environment has long been recognized as an inevitable consequence of capitalist accumulation and market expansion,[45] Marxists have, until recently, paid little attention to the ecological hubris of capitalism – or at least they have found its integration in the political economy of capitalism difficult to figure out. This oversight or difficulty is, of course, not fortuitous. It is anchored in the ideology of productivism, scientism and progress as infinite economic expansion, which has dominated both classical Marxism and classical liberalism. In the last three decades, however, some efforts have been made to integrate the exploitation of labour and the destruction of nature within the same contradictory developmental dynamics of capitalism.

One of the most sustained efforts has been made by O'Connor.[46] Following an approach that he himself defines as 'Polanyist-Marxist',[47] O'Connor claims to develop an 'ecological Marxism' as a method to theorize the new social movements within a broad Marxist framework. In his conception, capitalism, as a mode of production, unfolds through two contradictions. The first contradiction is symbolized by the rate of exploitation, and expresses capitalism's social and political power over labour, as well as capitalism's inherent tendency toward a realization crisis (a crisis of overproduction). The second contradiction centres around the category of 'the conditions of production', meaning by that 'everything that is treated as if it is a commodity even though it is not produced as a commodity in accordance with the law of value or law of markets'[48]; such a broad definition enables O'Connor to discuss labour power, land, nature and urban space under the same general category. The second contradiction, which manifests itself as an underproduction crisis of capital, resides in the tendency of capital to impair or destroy

44   Santos, 1995, Chapter One.
45   Karl Polanyi, 1944, insistently called attention to the destructive features of capitalist development (destruction of both the social and the natural environment).
46   O'Connor, 1988, 1991a, 1991b.
47   O'Connor, 1991b, p 2.
48   O'Connor, 1991b, p 1.

its own conditions of production, whereby the recurrent crises of the cost-push type lead to further attempts to restructure the conditions of production in order to reduce costs: 'when individual capitals lower costs, ie externalize costs on to nature (or labour or the urban) with the aim of defending or restoring profits, the unintended effect is to raise costs on other capitals (at the limit, capital as a whole) and lower profits'.[49] Capitalism has thus a tendency to appropriate, and use self-destructively, labour power, space, and external nature and environment. Though the second contradiction must be theorized in its own terms, it is clear that it is dependent on the first one:

'if we regard the rate of depletion and pollution of nature as dependent on the rate of accumulation and rate of profit, increases in the rate of labor exploitation will increase the profit and accumulation rates, and hence the rates of depletion and pollution. The more capital exploits labor, the more it exploits nature and vice versa'.[50]

O'Connor's reconstructive attempt raises several problems: is the second contradiction a real contradiction? Are the two contradictions not rather two aspects of the same contradiction? and so on, but its general outlook and direction are basically sound. It calls for a deeper understanding of emancipatory anti-capitalist struggles in which the 'subjectification of labor' cannot be achieved with the 'subjectification of nature' and vice versa. Accordingly, in order to account for a more complex understanding of capitalism and of anti-capitalism, the social agency of the workplace is conceived here as consisting both of class and of 'capitalist nature', that is, of class relations and of capitalist relations of and over natural use values.

The *institutional* dimension of the structural places refers to the organization of repetition in society, that is to say, to the forms, patterns, procedures, apparatuses or schemes which organize the constant flow of social relations in repetitive, routinized and normalized sequences, whereby interaction patterns develop and are 'naturalized' as necessary, irreplaceable and commonsensical. The different institutions in Table 2 are relatively straightforward, and need not be elaborated on here.

The *developmental dynamics* refers to the direction of social action, the local principle of rationality that defines which social relations belong (and to what degree) to a particular structural place. The developmental dynamics of the householdplace is one of the most central cathectic orientations in society, that is, an orientation that is invested with especially great emotional energy. The reproduction of gender and generation relations is achieved by the concentration of emotional energy (maximization of affection) on ideas and stereotypes of family life and family relations. On the contrary, the internal principle of the workplace is arguably the most anti-cathectic orientation in social relations. The logic of capital accumulation involves the maximization of surplus values extracted both from labour power in wage relations, and from nature as a

---

[49]   O'Connor, 1991b, p 4.
[50]   O'Connor, 1991b, p 9.

condition of production. In the marketplace, the incommensurability between needs and the means to satisfy them is eliminated by the potentially infinite commodification of both, however regulated by the reduction of demand to solvent demand. This logic has also a cathectic component, operating through the transformation of things into surrogate personalities, which are then objects of emotional investment. The developmental dynamics of the communityplace shares with that of the householdplace a strong cathectic dimension and, indeed, in some societies the two dynamics are hardly distinguishable. The former is based on a potentially endless excavation into primordial communalities and roots, upon which radical claims for inclusion (and, conversely, for exclusion) are formulated. The developmental dynamics of the citizenplace shares some features with that of the communityplace, and the competition between them underlies the most intractable tensions in the interstate system. Both dynamics operate by defining membership, drawing circles of reciprocity in bounded physical or symbolic territories. But while the citizenplace dynamics is organized by the vertical political obligation, the communityplace dynamics tends to be organized by the horizontal political obligation. The citizenplace, though grounded on coercion, maximizes its potential development through legitimation and hegemony, whereas the communityplace is endowed with original legitimacy, but often resorts to coercion to maximize its development potential. While the cathectic component of identity maximizing tends to abound, the cathectic component of loyalty maximizing is inherently lacking, and must be constantly reproduced by the symbolic state – nationalist civic culture; the flag, the national anthem, national holidays; subliminal or explicit transfusions of identity maximizing into loyalty maximizing. Finally, the developmental dynamics of the worldplace and the workplace are symbiotic and reciprocal. One presupposes the other. Indeed, they are two relatively autonomous aspects of the same logic of capital accumulation: the hierarchies established in the workplace by the extraction of surplus values are unevenly distributed throughout the world system by virtue of the global division of labour. They thus also become hierarchies among countries, societies, regions and peoples. The relative autonomy of the two aspects derives from the specific political form of the world system, an interstate system of sovereign states, whereby states cannot extract surplus values from other states. Leverage – that is, the relatively stabilized unequal capacity to transform national interests into international imperatives – permits the smooth unfolding of the global division of labour and the unequal exchanges that keep the hierarchies of the world system in place.

Since the structural places only operate in constellations, social actions are often informed by different and mutually incongruent logics, which means that each developmental dynamic is partial. Each one of them is also grounded on a specific contradiction, a relation between entities that tend to negate each other, and whose unfolding generates, for that reason, inescapable asymmetries and inequalities: between genders and generations; between employers and workers, and between both and nature; between commodification of needs and solvency; between inclusion in and exclusion from the community and the reciprocity circle; between private and public interests; between individuality and mass loyalty; between one state national interest and another (creditors and debtors, the core and the periphery). Partial contradictions constitute concrete social fields by coming together into constellations in different ways, normally around one particular contradiction, but involving all the others. Depending on the country or the moment, the developmental logics of the communityplace and citizenplace may now coalesce, now conflict; the householdplace and the workplace logics may be more or less deeply intertwined; the citizenplace logic may support, supplement or contradict the logic of any of the other structural places. His populist scientism put aside, Engels was not totally off the mark when he suggested in the *Anti-Dühring* (a mere suggestion, not a 'general law') that opposites interpenetrate and that, as a result, any entity is constituted by an unstable unity of contradictions.[51] For our purposes here, it is necessary to analyze in greater detail the ways in which partial contradictions express themselves in forms of power, law and knowledge.

5.3   Forms of power

All forms of power constitute unequal exchanges. Different forms of unequal exchange give rise to different forms of power. I distinguish six forms of power circulating in capitalist societies (see Table 2). All of them tend to be present, in one way or another, in concrete social fields and the different constellations of power they form, but each one of them has a privileged niche in one of the six structural places. *Patriarchy* is the privileged form of power of the householdplace. This means that, though they are always constellations of power, the social relations clustered around the householdplace – housework, reproduction, mutual care, property management, child-rearing, leisure and so on – tend to be organized by patriarchy as a system of male control of women's social reproduction. But it does not imply that the householdplace is necessarily the most important site of the oppression of women in capitalist societies. This may be the case in some societies during certain periods, but not in other societies or in other periods. Though it is the privileged form of power in the householdplace, patriarchy is also present in the constellations of power of social relations clustered around the workplace, the marketplace, the communityplace, the citizenplace and the worldplace, and its strongest impact on the life experiences of household members may occur, according to specific circumstances, in either of these structural places. For Saudi Arabian women it may be located in the householdplace, for North American women in the workplace[52] and marketplace, for Swiss women in the citizenplace, for Indian and African women in the communityplace.[53]

---

[51]   Engels, 1966.

[52]   According to Tickner, 'even in the United States, where considerable advances have been made in the economic position of women, full-time working women in 1987 earned an average of 71 percent of the earnings of full-time working men ... women frequently experience harassment and intimidation in the workplace and taking time off for bearing and raising children may impede opportunities for promotion' (1991, p 200). Also Kessler-Harris, 2001.

[53]   Connell (1987), shows that feminist thought, which around 1970 commonly identified the family as the strategic site, the key to the oppression of women, moved subsequently to

Exploitation, as defined by Marx, is the privileged form of power of the workplace. However, to signal the double contradiction in capitalist production (exploitation of labour and degradation of nature), to exploitation I add 'capitalist nature' – that is, nature as a historical and social construction jointly 'produced' by modern science and capitalism. The articulation between this form of power and other forms of power, namely patriarchy[54] and domination, is one of the core debates in social theory today. In general, what was just said about constellations of power with reference to patriarchy can equally be said with reference to exploitation, but the issue of structural determination will call for further specification below. At this point, in order to illustrate the advantages of an expanded conception of exploitation that includes capitalist nature, I would like to draw attention to the emergence of new links between the degradation of nature and the degradation of women's lives, that is to say, between (expanded) exploitation and patriarchy. Studies on specific exploitation of poor and tribal women in non-Western societies[55] and, more generally, studies on eco-feminism have convincingly demonstrated that capitalist nature, be it in the form of the massive use of chemical materials in agriculture, deforestation, dam construction, privatization of water resources, water scarcity and so on, victimizes and excludes women in a particularly intense way.[56] Furthermore, the social construction of woman as nature or as close to nature (corporeality, sensuousness) allows for an insidious isomorphism between domination of nature and domination of women.[57]

Fetishism of commodities is the form of power of the marketplace. I use it in much the same way as Marx. As they acquire autonomous qualities and meanings that reach beyond the narrow economic sphere, commodities tend thereby to negate the consumers who, as workers, are also their creators. Because the autonomy of commodities is obtained at the cost of the autonomy of the consumer as a social actor (both as creator of commodities and as a free consumer), the consumer is transformed, through the fetishism of commodities, from a subject of consumption into an object of consumption, from a creator into a creature. As Marx says, 'the consumer is not freer than the producer. His judgment depends on his means and his needs. Both of these are determined by his social position, which itself depends on the whole social organization'.[58] In a commodity-producing society, such social organization engenders both the 'reification of persons' (labour power as a commodity) and the 'personification of things'. By personification of things is meant the fact that, as workers become subordinate to market relations, commodities become godlike fetishes, thereby transforming their own creators into their creatures. Market domination and control is possible because commodities function as fetishes. Thus fetishism of commodities is

emphasize other sites of oppression and comments: 'If anything the pendulum has now swung too far the other way' (p 110). On non-Western women and the worldplace, see, Rao, 1991. See also Boserup, 1970; Beneria and Sen, 1981. Lastly, Layton, 2001.

54   Vogel, 1983; Westlund, 1999.
55   Rao, 1991; Tickner, 1991, pp 204–205.
56   Mies and Shiva, 1993; Kuletz, 1992; Mellor, 1992. Also Diamond and Orenstem (eds), 1990.
57   See B Holland-Cunz, in Kuletz, 1992, pp 64ff; Gaard, 1998; Salleh, 1997; Bravo (ed), 1999.
58   Marx, 1963, p 41.

intimately interlocked with exploitation, and the type of alienation it gives rise to may be simply viewed as the 'qualitative side' of exploitation. But, to my mind, it must be considered as a separate form of power. On the one hand, through its cultural transformation, the fetishism of commodities reaches far beyond exploitation. Converted into a semiotic system globally diffused by cultural imperialism, fetishism of commodities is often an outpost of capitalist expansion, the messenger of incoming exploitation.[59] On the other hand, and in part for this reason, the process of consumption is today too complex to be grasped in terms of Marx's dichotomy of individual consumption and productive consumption. The relative autonomy of relations of consumption is still to be fully explored.

Unequal differentiation is the privileged form of power of the communityplace, and probably the most complex and ambiguous form of power. It operates by means of the creation of otherness, and the exercise of difference on the basis of more-or-less deterministic criteria. Essential to this form of power is the dualism of inclusion (in-group) and exclusion (out-group) that allows it to be exercised in a Janus-faced mode: rubber power (soft power, shared power, non-power) vis-à-vis the in-group, and iron power (naked power, terror) vis-à-vis the out-group. This form of power centres around the privilege to define the other. Now, as Edward Said has eloquently shown, those who are defined as the other are also defined as incompetent to define or represent themselves.[60] For those supposedly incompetent to define themselves, the question of identity is therefore a question of cultural resistance, of making the subaltern speak. As a consequence, this form of power is acted out through struggles between imperial definitions of identity and subaltern definitions of identity. In its most pervasive form, unequal differentiation involves the attribution of social meaning to particular patterns of ethnic difference, and the negative evaluation of real or imputed characteristics ascribed in a determinist fashion to groups defined as different. This form of power is racism in the broadest sense, and is acted out in society in a wide variety of forms, such as discrimination, ethno-centrism, prejudice, xenophobia, stereotyping, racial profiling, scapegoating and so on.

The relation between this form of power and the other structural forms of power is very complex, and it is the object of ongoing debate, particularly regarding its relation to patriarchy and exploitation. The analytical difficulties arise out of the ever-shifting interpenetrations between them, but they are also the result of the crudeness of our analytical tools, of accumulated theoretical neglect about a form of power considered for decades to be anachronic, residual, pre-capitalist, in sum, condemned by history. Nowadays, however, the restructuring of capital accumulation on a world scale is forcing us to sharpen our analytical tools, and to reinvent modern history in order to understand the new (and old) constellations of power, some of which I analyzed in Chapter Five,

---

[59]   Baudrillard, 1981.
[60]   Said, 1985; Sklair, 2001.

such as re-ethnicization of the labour force as a way of devaluing labour power below 'normal' capitalist levels; super-exploitation of undocumented migrant workers; social distribution of minority groups into specially degraded workplaces (seasonal labour, hazardous work); ethnically biased criteria and decisions over refugees; the commodification of indigenous peoples' natural resources by TNCs, and so on.

Domination is the privileged form of power of the citizenplace. It is the only form of power that both liberal political theory and classical Marxism view as political power, that is, power generated in the political system and centred around the state. It is conceived here within the critical tradition, though considered as only one among other forms of power circulating in society. There is, however, one striking peculiarity of domination that must be mentioned at this point. Of all forms of power, domination is the most institutionalized, the most self-reflexive – it 'thinks of itself' as the exclusive form of power – and also the most widely diffused, at least in core societies. Accordingly, it tends to be the most pervasive form of power in the multiple constellations of power generated in society, even though the quality and the degree of its presence vary enormously. This peculiarity expresses a profound contrast between domination and all the other forms of power. I distinguish between domination, as *cosmic power*, and all the other forms of power, as *chaosmic power*. By cosmic power, I mean centralized power, exercised out of a high-voltage core (the state) and reaching out to formally defined limits through institutionalized sequences and chains of bureaucratic intermediation. By chaosmic power, in contrast, I mean decentralized and informal power, exercised by multiple microcores of power in chaotic sequences without predefined limits. All constellations of power combine a cosmic component with a plurality of chaosmic components. The heterogeneity between cosmic and chaosmic components is responsible for the phenomenological opacity of power relations in society: as lived experiences, the constellations of power tend to be reduced either to their cosmic or their chaosmic components, thereby affecting the struggles of resistance against power, and eventually causing them to fail.

As to *unequal exchange*, the form of power of the worldplace, there is also a long tradition of analysis, namely in theories of imperialism, dependency and the world system. Although, in the conception adopted in this book, all forms of power involve an unequal exchange, the term unequal exchange is used here *strictu sensu*, as a specific form of power, and with reference to the work of A. Emmanuel.[61] According to Emmanuel, the core-periphery hierarchy in the world system is the result of unequal exchange, a mechanism of trade imperialism by means of which surplus-value is transferred from the periphery to the core. It operates not only because core productions have, on average, a higher organic composition (a higher ratio of capital to labour in the production process), but also, and above all, because workers in the periphery receive, on average, lower wages than workers in core countries for similar work. A carpenter in the US may earn ten times more than a carpenter in Mexico, despite their use of similar work

[61]   Emmanuel, 1972.

technology.[62] Wage differentials are way beyond differences in productivity. Because they conceal a transfer of surplus-value from low-wage periphery to high-wage core, market exchanges are described as 'unequal exchanges of equals. Other economic unequal exchanges relating to trade composition – raw materials from the periphery to the core, manufactured goods from the core to the periphery – have increased dramatically in the last decades. According to Maizels, in the period from 1980 to 1988, primary commodities exports from the periphery increased in volume by almost 100 per cent, but the total revenue obtained was, in 1988, 30 per cent less than that obtained in 1980.[63] Throughout the 1990s the terms of trade of the exports from the periphery continued to deteriorate. Concerning certain products like steel and fruits, the deterioration of the terms of trade has been compounded by the new (and old) protectionism of the core countries. The details of Emmanuel's theory do not concern me here, though I would suggest that a more inclusive conception of unequal exchange is necessary to account for the multiple inequalities between the core, the periphery and the semi-periphery of the world system, not only regarding economic but also political and cultural exchanges. The virtue of Emmanuel's conception is, however, that it stresses the fact that the mechanisms that reproduce these hierarchies are inherent in the relations themselves between the core and the periphery: unequal exchange as the source of uneven development.[64]

As I have already suggested, unequal exchange comes together in constellations with other forms of power, namely with exploitation and fetishism of commodities. But it also converges with domination in some crucial ways, as my analysis of the relations between the globalization of the economy and the nation-states in Chapter Five clearly shows. For peripheral and semi-peripheral states, one of the fundamental dimensions of such a constellation lies in the ways in which these states impose on their citizens the structural adjustment policies of the World Bank and the IMF, which are the worldplace institutions under the control of core states. Unequal exchange constellates with unequal differentiation as well when, in instances also described in Chapter Five, TNCs extract raw materials in ancestral indigenous territories under contracts with nation-states – in which case the constellation of power involves domination too. Last but not least, unequal exchange also constellates with patriarchy in multiple and cross-cutting forms. The interaction between unequal exchange and patriarchy seems to be governed by two main mechanisms, whose unfolding may be either convergent or divergent. On the one hand, the expansion of capital accumulation across the world system relies heavily on non-wage labour, particularly as performed in the household under the aegis of patriarchal power; this reliance tends to increase as we move from the core

---

[62]   Chase-Dunn, 1991, p 231.

[63]   Maizels, 1992 and 1999.

[64]   After summarizing a wide variety of theories that have been elaborated to account for the hierarchy between the core and the periphery of the world system, Chase-Dunn points in the right direction by identifying a set of economic, social and political factors – power-bloc formation, state formation, unequal exchange and class struggle – whose interaction produces and reproduces the core/periphery hierarchy. Chase-Dunn, 1991, pp 238ff.

to the periphery. On the other hand, world capitalism is driven by a tendency to multiply the commodification of human needs and everyday life in such a way as to force core as well as peripheral and semi-peripheral families to become income pooling units,[65] thereby changing the conditions of exercise of patriarchy in significant ways.[66] Such changes become more dramatic as we move from core to peripheral families. As we see, this constellation is extremely complex, in that it mixes unequal exchange, exploitation, patriarchy and fetishism of commodities. In the case of indigenous or tribal families – the peripheries of the peripheries – unequal differentiation also enters this constellation of power in significant ways.

5.4   Forms of law

The analytical framework proposed in this chapter allows us to go back to law, the central topic of this book, with additional theoretical tools. The same broad conception of law that was presented in Chapter Two is adopted here: law is a body of regularized procedures and normative standards, considered justiciable in any given group, which contributes to the creation and prevention of disputes, and to their settlement through an argumentative discourse, coupled with the threat of force. Granting, once again, that this very broad conception of law can easily lead to the total trivialization of law – if law is everywhere, it is nowhere – I wish to argue that of the great variety of legal orders circulating in society, six are particularly relevant, in that they are anchored in, constituted by, and constitutive of the six structural clusters of social relations in capitalist societies integrating the world system. As it generates (and is generated by) a specific form of power and specific epistemological form, each structural place also generates (and is generated by) a specific form of law. Although forms of power, law and knowledge tend to operate either as means or conditions of the exercise of each other, the way they do so may be more or less congruent and, consequently, more or less functional to the developmental logic of the different structural places. Actually, this is one of the main reasons why the reproduction of the structural places is inherently problematic and calls for constant structural adjustment both 'horizontally', among its different dimensions, and 'vertically', among each one of the dimensions of the six structural places.

As in all the other dimensions, in concrete social fields the forms of law operate in constellations of legality: different forms of law combining in different ways according to the specific social field for which they provide the normative ordering. There are, however, some specificities in the constitution of constellations of legality (or rather, legalities) and in the ways they operate in conjunction with the other dimensions of the structural places. First, in contrast with power and epistemological forms, whose operation tend to be more diffuse and free-floating, legal forms tend to operate within the confines of the core institutions of a given structural place. Secondly, the legal form is a doubly

[65]   In the same sense, Wallerstein, in Balibar and Wallerstein, 1991, p 112; Kessler-Harris, 2001.

[66]   As exploitation of women increases (paid labour in the factory and unpaid labour at home), it seems that patriarchy decreases or, at least, loses some of its most traditional forms of exercise.

contested terrain because, while framing disputes arising in social relations, it is likewise reframed by them through rival interpretations. What is disputed is always, in part, the law of the dispute. Thirdly, although all legal forms integrate constellations of legalities, territorial state law, that is, the legal form of the citizenplace, shows a peculiarity that is in fact quite symmetrical with the one noted above with reference to domination, that is, the power form of the citizenplace. On the one hand, it tends to be more spread out across social fields than any other legal form, even though its presence in the concrete constellations of legalities is very uneven. On the other hand, since it is the only self-reflexive legal form, that is, the only legal form that thinks of itself as law, the law of the territorial state tends to conceive of the legal field as exclusively its own, thus refusing to recognize its operations as integrating broader constellations of laws. This tendency accentuates as we move from the periphery to the core of the world system. Let us now examine in turn the forms of law corresponding to each of the six structural places.

Domestic law is the 'native' law of the householdplace, the set of rules, normative standards and dispute settlement mechanisms both resulting from and in the sedimentation of social relations in the household. It comprises a wide variety of rules, from the informal norms of respect for the parents to the implicit or explicit norms regulating the distribution of housework between men and women. Domestic law tends to be very informal, non-written, and so deeply embedded in family relations that it is hardly conceivable as an autonomous dimension thereof. It is an interstitial legality. It is also an unequal law to the extent that it is grounded on patriarchy-based inequalities among the different members of the household. It varies widely across time and space in the world system, according to class, race, culture, religion and so on. Its variation, combined with its elusiveness, raises enormous obstacles to sociological analysis. What follows are some hypotheses for a contextual comparative analysis, focused on three structural features of law I have elaborated on in previous chapters: rhetoric, violence and bureaucracy. In spite of its extreme variation, domestic law tends to have a structural profile in which bureaucracy is almost totally absent, while rhetoric and violence are both pervasive and combined in intricate interpenetrations. Domestic legal rhetoric may be based on a greater or smaller polarization between the speaker and the relevant audience. In the patriarchal family, polarization is high and the argumentative discourse is dominated by the husband/father. Polarization and the inequality it reflects and reproduces express themselves in the asymmetry of the arguments, and consequently in the inequality of discursive exchanges. Inequality – in the antipodes of Habermasian 'ideal speech situation' – turns domestic legal rhetoric into manipulation, into an exercise of symbolic violence, indeed one of the most pervasive forms of interpenetration between rhetoric and violence. But interpenetration occurs in many other instances, such as unilateral decisions about the range of the argumentative field, occasions on which argumentation may actually take place, sequencing and ordering of arguments and speakers, and, above all, unilateral impositions of silence and speech. As we move from the Western core of the world system to the non-Western peripheries, this mix of rhetoric and violence may be compounded with more formalistic procedures, which we could call ritualistic bureaucracy. These general hypotheses notwithstanding, both in core and in periphery householdplaces, the mixes of rhetoric, violence and bureaucracy may be dominated by any one of the structural elements of legality. Wife-battering and child abuse are the most common expressions of domestic law combinations dominated by violence.

Like all the other dimensions of the structural places, domestic law operates in concrete social fields in constellation with other legal forms. In the social fields clustered around the householdplace, the constellation of legalities tends to be dominated by domestic and territorial state law, combined in a variety of forms and degrees. Inspired by Foucault's pioneer work, Donzelot, among others, has shown how the modern state, particularly in the core of the world system, has gradually 'policed the families' by a whole range of legal and institutional interventions.[67] The sum total of such interventions, consolidated in different layers in the course of the last two hundred years, is what we call family law, and, to a great extent, welfare or social law as well. The range of these interventions, combined with the positivist equation of law with state law, led to the idea that state family law is the only law of the householdplace. Leaving aside the fact that many other state legal fields not usually considered as family law for example, laws regulating mortgages or health services – do operate in the householdplace, my central argument in this chapter is that householdplace relations are legally constituted by combinations of domestic and territorial (state) law. Rather than a *tabula rasa* upon which the state inscribes its legality, the householdplace is a complex social field in which state and domestic legality engage in a constant process of interaction, negotiation, compromise, conflict, mutual reinforcement, mutual neutralization.

The fact that this articulation remains socially invisible, particularly in the Western core of the world system, is the result of two convergent factors. First, this is the region of the world system in which the positivist reduction of law to state law has gone further, both as regards scientific legal knowledge (turned into a learned orthodoxy) and as regards common social practices (turned into a legal common sense). Secondly, this is the region in which stronger states have so permeated the householdplace, and for such long periods, that the rules and principles of domestic law have been significantly changed in accordance with the rules and principles of territorial law. In this case, the invisibility of domestic law is the result of its isomorphism with state family law. More recently, however, in the aftermath of the crisis of the welfare state, the manifestations of an underlying constellation of legalities in the householdplace have resurfaced, due to the attenuation of the monopoly claims of state law over the legal character of householdplace relations. The reduction and degradation of welfare services and payments have correspondingly shrunk the range and intensity of state legal penetration in the householdplace. A legal vacuum seems to have emerged, as if the erasure of the welfare state inscriptions had really created a *tabula rasa*, this time ready for new, post-welfare inscriptions. Nevertheless, within the alternative framework of analysis I here propose, we can see that what is changing are the boundaries and the

[67]   Donzelot, 1977.

combination between the state law of the household and domestic law. What appears to be a delegalization or a deregulation of the householdplace is in fact a replacement of state law by domestic law, the emergence of a new constellation of legalities in which domestic law assumes a stronger role than before.

In the periphery and semi-periphery of the world system, state legal intervention in the household has always been weaker and less diversified, and the absorption of domestic law into state family law has been correspondingly less credible. Furthermore, the state legalization of the householdplace, besides being less pervasive, has also oftentimes contradicted domestic law. As a result, there have been recurrent conflicts between state family law and domestic law. These conflicts have been particularly intense in periods of revolutionary state transformation, in which the lack of isomorphism between domestic law and the revolutionary law of the state has been quite extreme. For example, when Bolshevik family laws in Tashkent collided with the domestic legality of peasant families shaped by Islamism, the resulting social conflicts, as well as the perverse or counterproductive effects of the revolutionary laws, forced the Bolsheviks to adopt a more compromising position.[68] A less extreme case concerns the transformations of family law in the aftermath of the Carnations Revolution in Portugal in 1974 to 1975, which swerved somewhat from the traditional domestic law of Portuguese households, particularly in rural areas. As a consequence of the clashes between the new state family law and domestic law, the enforcement of the new state legality has remained very selective to this day, while domestic law has also changed in significant ways.[69] In this case, as in general in all situations of discrepancy between the two legal orders, what appears on the surface as a gap between law in books and law in action is, in fact, the ongoing process of struggle and negotiation between the state law of the family and domestic law.[70]

This alternative approach to the legal construction of the householdplace is less focused on core countries and the West than the conventional one and, therefore, more adequate to critical comparative research – that is, to a comparative strategy that avoids the trap of characterizing semi-peripheral and peripheral, non-Western societies for what they lack. The conception of constellations of legalities enables us to hypothesize, in general, articulation and hybridization among legal orders, and then inquire about the specific forms they may assume: for example, whether some combinations may be more complex or more balanced than others, or whether a given society lacking in one type of law may abound in another and so on. Moreover, my alternative approach is equally promising for the analysis of core or Western households, particularly inasmuch

---

[68]   Massell, 1968.

[69]   Santos, 1993.

[70]   Dahl and Snare (1978) use the concept of 'coercion of privacy' to highlight the persistence of women's subordination in spite of the laws passed to eliminate some forms of sexual discrimination; a forceful argument on the social construction of victims of sexual discrimination can be read in Bumiller, 1988. In my conception, the coercion of privacy is the realm of domestic law.

as the so-called crisis of the welfare state unfolds, and we enter a post-welfare state legality. In such a period it will be important, both analytically and politically, to reconstruct the legal transformations in the householdplace in ways that allow us to evaluate the extent to which the retrenchment of (conceivably more progressive) welfare state legality coexists with the expansion of (conceivably more retrogressive) domestic legality – for example, new child care duties imposed on the housewife – or the extent to which more authoritarian state legality engenders a new isomorphism with domestic law by nurturing its more authoritarian traits or roots.

Production law is the law of the factory, the law of the corporation, the set of regulations and normative standards that rule the everyday life of wage labour relations (both relations of production and relations in production), factory codes, shop floor regulations, codes of conduct for employees and so on. Production law may be imposed unilaterally by the employer or management, or result from negotiation with labour unions or other workers' representatives, but in any case it is marked by the power prerogatives inherent to the ownership of the means of production. This form of law varies widely, both in the core and in the periphery and semi-periphery of the world system, according to productive sector, firm size, business cycle, political environment, workers' organization, corporate culture and so on. In general, it establishes the routines within the enterprise, and the punishment for their violation, governing tightly and in great detail the lives of workers and managers during the working day, and sometimes even beyond that. It may include the disciplining of human movements and rhythms, interactions and conversations, appearances, ways of dressing and talking, body language and the like. Most regulations are confined to the workplace, but some of them may reach out into family life, leisure time, public interaction and even political activities. It may further impose restrictions on freedom of speech – silencing, keeping secrets, distorting information, repeating public relations formulas and so on.

Production law may be written or unwritten, formal or informal. However, contrary to domestic law, its artificiality, arbitrariness and external imposition tend to be recognized as such in the everyday life experiences of those ruled by it. Structurally speaking, production law has chameleon-like features that make its characterization a very difficult task. Rhetoric, violence and bureaucracy may be combined in the most intricate ways, and while in some instances the combinations are stable – for instance, because they are embedded in the normative style and corporate culture of a given firm – in other instances they change rapidly, or are so elusive as to escape description. As a general hypothesis, I would suggest that rhetoric plays a lesser role in this case than either bureaucracy or violence. Production law is, rather, a command law with some military-law-like features. Co-management – a form of production law that relies on argumentation and persuasion – is a rare phenomenon.[71] Rhetoric tends, therefore, to be congealed in

[71]   According to Weber, 1948 and Hobsbawm, 1975, given the incapacity of precapitalist family-based industries to establish the organizational model for the large enterprises emerging in the eighteenth century, such a model was sought in the military organization and in the emerging state bureaucracy, a transplant particularly evident in the case of railways.

clearly defined hierarchies and strict obedience rules. Despite the much-touted rise of high-tech enclaves of co-operative labour relations along the lines of 'flexible specialization',[72] control, bureaucracy and violence continue to dominate even in such production sites, as Moody has shown in his study of lean production.[73] Moreover, argumentative discourse has a *tempo* which is incompatible with the production rhythm and the productivist cognitive maps that orient interaction inside the corporation. Violence and bureaucracy vary widely, as witness the vast bibliography on control over the labour process (more on this below).

In practice, production law is a very complex social phenomenon. Although it is embedded in production relations, its artificial and externally imposed character tends to surface clearly (and sometimes, brutally) in the life experiences of workers. Its despotism makes it excessive as law: it is too despotic to be law. While domestic law appears as too weak to be law lacking in bureaucracy and, often, overt violence – production law appears as too strong to be law – too violent, whether bureaucratically or not: 'the rules of the game', 'the boss is the boss', 'who sells labor sells freedom'. In the lives of wage labourers, rather than being independent, these two images feed upon each other. On the one hand, domestic law may seem more benevolent, partly because life in the workplace is so despotically ruled by production law. But on the other, the despotism of production law may also affect working-class households, whenever the male worker – who is, of course, ruled by production law in the workplace – uses his ruling privileges in domestic law to impose production-like imperatives in the household relations.

Working-class households tend, therefore, to be ruled by complex combinations of domestic law, production law, and state family and welfare law, which vary widely across the world system. In the periphery, and particularly in rural areas, domestic law and production law are so deeply intertwined in the everyday life of peasant communities that it may be difficult and even inadequate to distinguish them. Whenever social production and social reproduction occur within the same social field, the constellations of legalities must be reconstructed in order to capture highly flexible transitions and subtle sequencings among aspects or moments of self-identical practices. Curiously enough, the expansion of flexible, post-fordist, production systems both in the core and the periphery of the world system are creating new constellations of legalities between domestic law and production law which also tend to involve a much deeper intertwining of the two forms of law. The new 'putting-out' systems and the consequent proliferation of homework – that is, the sub-contracting of production down global commodity chains that go from the contracting TNC to sub-contractors in the North or the South who in turn contract labour-intensive tasks out to homemakers – are blurring the distinction between householdplace and workplace. As Sassen has cogently argued, these new developments associated with economic globalization and the expansion of the informal

---

[72]   Piore and Sabel, 1984.
[73]   Moody, 1997.

economy have created 'regulatory fractures'[74] which, I would argue, are often sites of combination of different forms of laws – as the convergence of production law and domestic law in this case shows. As non-wage capitalist work (homework) combines in the same social field (the household) with wage capitalist work, the interfaces between domestic law and production law expand enormously, and so do the vectors of interpenetration and contamination among them. Given the fact that much of the paid homework is informal – ie, not regulated by state labour law – the intensification of the articulations between these two forms of law goes hand in hand with their relative uncoupling from state law.

The constellation of production law with territorial state law – for instance, labour law and economic law – is probably the key constellation of legalities in capitalist societies. Part of what I said about the constellation between domestic law and state law applies here as well, since in both cases the constellation of legality grew in complexity as the core states evolved from a liberal state form to a welfare state form. In more recent times, the relative weakening of state law (the crisis of the regulatory state) combines with a relative strengthening of the 'native' laws of the structural places, especially production law in the workplace and domestic law in the householdplace. As in the case of the household-place, the 'deregulation' of the workplace is the surface image of a transfer of regulation from state law to production law. In spite of these general similarities, there are many differences between the constellations of legality around domestic law and production law, resulting largely from historical and political differences of state 'penetration' in the householdplace and in the workplace.

The other forms of law were to some extent dealt with in Chapters Two and Five so I will mention them only briefly here. *Exchange law* is the law of the marketplace – trade customs, rules and normative standards that regulate market exchanges among producers, between producers and merchants, among merchants, and between producers and merchants on the one side, and consumers on the other. To the extent that it was the first legal field to break away from medieval state legality and to develop autonomously, this legal form pioneered the emergence of modern legality. In the wake of this tradition, *lex mercatoria* thrives in world economy today, regulating market exchanges with great autonomy vis-à-vis the nation-states. As a matter of fact, the existence of an informal, unofficial, exchange law has been long established in the sociology of law, as Stewart Macaulay's pioneering study on the topic so well illustrates.[75] In general, exchange law is very informal, flexible and finely tuned to the interests and needs of the participants and the power relations among them. As we saw in Chapter Five, it may operate in a rubber cage or an iron cage mode, according to whether the parties have more or less the same power or, on the contrary, very unequal power. As an informal law, it tends to be low on bureaucracy, and high on rhetoric and violence. Whenever the asymmetries of

---

[74]   Sassen, 1998, p 155.
[75]   Macaulay, 1963.

power between the parties are very high, rhetoric and violence may converge so as to become indistinguishable.

This legal form constellates with all the others, in particular with state law – as in contract law and consumer law. While the legal constellations of the marketplace vary widely across the world system, the level of correspondence between the territorial state law of market exchanges and exchange law are of specific comparative interest. As the commodification of needs expands, a certain cross-national convergence among the constellations of legality around the marketplace might be expected, and it is in fact occurring in the areas covered by *lex mercatoria.* Since the operation of exchange law is closely tuned to the power differences between the parties, whenever such differences are structural (as between producers and consumers), exchange law operates almost as despotically as production and domestic law.

Like the communityplace itself, *community law* is one of the most complex legal forms, in that it covers extremely diverse situations – from dispute resolution rules in marginalized communities like Pasargada to norms of loyalty within gangs or mafias to the ancestral laws of indigenous peoples. As these examples illustrate, community law may be invoked either by hegemonic or oppressed groups, may legitimize and strengthen imperial aggressive identities or, on the contrary, subaltern, defensive identities, may arise out of fixed, unbridgeable asymmetries of power or regulate social fields in which such asymmetries are almost non-existent or merely situational. As a result, the constellations of legality to which it contributes are very diverse; for example, those that also involve state law tend to have a great impact on the lives of people, particularly on those belonging to out-groups. In some societies – often (but not always) peripheral societies coming out of colonial domination – hegemonic identity groups have managed to convert, to a greater or lesser extent, their community law into the law of the state. Islamic states are an extreme example of this process. In other societies, in India, for instance, the articulations between community law and state law are far more contradictory.[76]

As regards groups with subaltern identity, I have offered an analysis of Pasargada law (Chapter Four) and the laws of indigenous peoples (Chapter Five). In spite of the striking differences between these two instances of community law, they have in common the fact that the social construction of an alternative legality arises out of an unequal differentiation that defined them as out-groups. Furthermore, in both cases, the alternative law, as part of a broader social and political process, aims at reducing this exclusion by creating or recreating an alternative identity, even though subaltern. The different sociological profiles of the two cases, the different historical roots of the social identities underlying them, and the different political processes that sustain the struggles in both cases account for the different constellations of legality with state law in the two cases. While in the case of Pasargada, the precarious exercise of self-government

---

[76] Galanter, 1991; Mendelsohn and Baxi (eds), 1994.

is a product of official legal exclusion, and is premised upon its continuation, in the case of the indigenous peoples, the struggle for self-determination is a struggle for official legal recognition by both the constitutional law of the (multinational) state and international law.

Territorial law or *state law* is the law of the citizenplace and, in modern societies, is central to most constellations of legalities. For the past two hundred years, it has been constructed by political liberalism and legal science as the only form of law existing in society. In spite of its original arbitrary character, in the course of time this construction has invaded commonsense knowledge, and has become part of the legal habitus of individuals and social groups. As so conceived, state law is self-reflexive – it is, in other words, the only form of law that 'thinks of itself' as law. For this reason, although the conception of different modes of production of law and constellations of legalities I advance here is sociologically more adequate and politically more progressive (more on this below), it may appear to run against common sense and carries, therefore, a heavy burden of proof. At stake is precisely the construction of a new legal common sense, the task that I have set out to contribute to and that has given the title to this book.

The strategic value of territorial state law in constellations of legality in modern capitalist societies resides in the pervasiveness of its presence in the different structural places, even though the range and nature of this presence may vary widely across social fields and across the world system. Pervasiveness is important in itself, since it enables the state law to conceive of the different structural places as an integrated whole. In modern capitalist societies, state law is the only form of law capable of thinking the legal field as a totality, even if an illusory one. The strategic value of state law resides also in the power of the state backing it. In contrast with the other forms of power, in terms of the above-mentioned distinction between cosmic and chaosmic powers, domination is cosmic, inasmuch as it is a highly organized and specialized type of power driven by a claim to monopoly, and commanding vast resources in all the structural features of law (violence, bureaucracy and rhetoric). Though firmly embedded in the social relations clustered around the citizenplace, in contrast with other forms of power it operates as if disembedded from any specific context, with potentially infinite mobility and infinite potential for diffusion in the most diverse social fields. Thus backed by a form of power with such features, state law tends to overestimate its regulatory capacities, to claim more than it can deliver. But, on the other hand, and for the same reason, it also guarantees an organizational priority in the constellations of legalities, since all the other forms of law tend to take its presence for granted, and to organize and maximize their own regulatory intervention and efficacy around the limits, gaps and weaknesses of state law. Just as domination is a cosmic form of power, so is state law a cosmic law; it operates cosmically by constellating with all the chaosmic laws.

Finally, *systemic law* is the legal form of the worldplace, the sum total of rules and normative standards that organize the core/periphery hierarchy and the relations among the nation-states in the interstate system. Above, I alluded to the debate on the role of normative integration as the glue holding together the world system. Even assuming, as Chase-Dunn does, that such a role is relatively secondary in comparison with market interdependence and political military power, inasmuch as they are social relations the latter generate their own normativity, clusters of rules and normative standards that distinguish between legitimate and illegitimate expectations and discipline behaviors. No matter how unilaterally imposed by imperial states, dominant partners or core controlled international organizations, such rules and normative principles are invoked and applied to strengthen or stabilize the always-problematic coherence of the world system; for this reason I call them systemic law. International regimes are systemic law. Systemic law tends to be strong on rhetoric and violence, and weak on bureaucracy. *Lex mercatoria* operates, in general, either as a mixture of exchange law and production law or as a mixture of exchange law and systemic law. As is the case of other structural forms of law (with the exception of state law), systemic law is not socially constructed as law by the parties involved or affected by its normative claims. Depending on the position or the location of the parties, it is either constructed as '*realpolitik*', and 'business as usual', or else as 'naked oppression', 'imperialism' or 'abuse of power'. Systemic law is to international law what domestic law, production law, exchange law and community law are to territorial state law. It exists on the reverse of the official legality that governs the relations among nation-states, sometimes complementing it, sometimes conflicting with or undermining it. The forms of cosmopolitan law analyzed in Chapter Five are global emancipatory struggles for the rights of oppressed social groups throughout the world and tend, therefore, to challenge the form of power that sustains systemic law (unequal exchange *strictu sensu*). To that extent, cosmopolitan law is an anti-systemic law.

A final note on legal constellations. Due to its cosmic character, which relies on the legal activism and sanctioning power of the state, territorial law is a highly diversified legal field. It encompasses a multiplicity of sub-fields, a variety of modes of juridicity, each one with its own character and its historical trajectory, from contracts to criminal law, from labour law to consumer law, from torts to environmental law. In my analysis of state strategies in the world system in Chapter Two, I described in some detail the pattern of normal change grounded on the potentially infinite availability of territorial law to bring forth a societal transformation through repetition and amelioration. I saw this legal Utopia, as I called it, as involving a complex distribution of legal resources by the three major strategies of the state: accumulation, hegemony and trust strategies. Each sub-field of territorial state law tends to constellate differently with the different chaosmic legal forms. For instance, the way in which state family law constellates with domestic law differs from the way in which labour or business law constellates with production law; and state welfare law constellates differently with domestic, production or community law. Because of their social and political impact, the constellations of state criminal law with the other structural laws are particularly striking. What is declared criminal or non-criminal by state criminal law, for instance, is the result of complex negotiations, confrontations, complicities or compromises by state law in the process of constellating with the other structural laws. From this perspective, many more criminal courses of action occur in society than those so declared by state criminal law. Since inherent to each structural place is a form of power conceived as a specific unequal exchange, then crime is any course of action in which the exchange is so seriously unequal that it may even be considered physically or symbolically violent. In crime the polarity between power and powerlessness reaches its highest level. The level of polarization is in itself the result of the negotiation of meaning, which in turn reflects the prevalent power relations in the specific cluster of social relations. As Henry and Milovanovic put it, 'crimes are nothing less than moments in the expression of power such that those who are subjected to these expressions are denied their own contribution to the encounter and often to future encounters. Crime then is the power to deny others'.[77]

Legal constellations around crime vary widely. To the extent that chaosmic legal forms are more despotic than territorial state law, their detection and regulation thresholds are higher than those of state law. Accordingly, they may consider legal or even obligatory a given course of action that state law considers criminal. For instance, in many societies, wife-battering and child abuse are considered legal by domestic law, in spite of the fact that they are declared criminal by state criminal law. In areas of high incidence of undetected or unreported crime, the legal constellation manifests itself in the highly selective way in which state criminal law is enforced. A second type of constellation takes place in the inverse situation: when any of the structural laws deems criminal an activity that state criminal law considers legal or even obligatory. To continue with the example of domestic law, certain particularly vehement forms of confrontation of patriarchal power by the wife or the children may be considered criminal by domestic law – in that they are conceived as reducing the power-holder to powerlessness – while they are legal from the point of view of state law. The constellation in this case assumes several forms. It may express itself in the way state law defines its jurisdiction in order not to collide with domestic law. And if the collision cannot be avoided, it may express itself in highly selective enforcement, as in the first type of constellation.

In the two types of constellations analyzed so far there is an incongruence or conflict between cosmic and chaosmic legality which may be managed in various ways, from confrontation to mutual accommodation. But the most common situations by far, and often with the greatest social and political impact, are those in which there is congruence or complicity between cosmic and chaosmic legality. Legal constellations assume here two basic forms: one, when both state law and any other structural law consider crime what, from the point of view of the weaker party in the power relation, is resistance against crime; the other, when both state law and any other structural law consider legal or outside their respective jurisdictions a course of action which, from the point of view of the weaker party in the power relation, is criminal. In either case, the complicity or similarity between cosmic and chaosmic law puts the weaker party in the power relation, that is, the party most likely to be the victim, in a particularly vulnerable position. To

[77] Henry and Milovanovic, 1993, p 2.

recognize the existence of legal constellations at work in the process of vulnerabilization has crucial value, both sociologically and politically, because it underscores the fact that resistance against doubly legitimized exercises of power must take place against all the legal orders involved. One mere change in state law may change very little if the other legal orders are in place and manage to re-establish their constellations with state law in new ways. Furthermore, the recognition of legal constellations amounts to the recognition of the fact that emancipatory practices and struggles must also network and constellate if they are to succeed at all. Otherwise, one isolated struggle against a given form of regulation may unintentionally reinforce another form of regulation.

5.5   Forms of knowledge

In terms of the rhetorical view of knowledge and law that laid out in Chapters One and Four, I see the six structural places as topic fields, argumentative circles and audiences held together by clusters of local *topoi*. Each structural place is a set of widely shared arguments, counter-arguments and premises of argumentation, by which courses of action and interactions fall into a specific topic field. The coherence, sequencing and networking among arguments, together with the specific polarities between speakers and audiences, configure a local rhetoric, a specific style of reasoning, persuading and convincing. Each structural place is, therefore, a specific common sense, a local hegemony.[78] All social interaction is an epistemological interaction, an exchange of knowledges. What is distinctive about structural places is that they are privileged epistemological locations, specifically powerful and shared symbolic fields, widely used maps of meaning. Their imprint on knowledge practices in general is very intense and pervasive, even though different life experiences and trajectories generate different exposure to and expertise in one or another form of commonsense knowledge.

The core tenet of the epistemological framework I am presenting is that there is not one single common sense, but rather six major common senses circulating in society – six modes of production of knowledge-as-regulation, through which individuals and groups know what they are doing and saying by doing and saying according to what is supposed to be done and said in the specific structural place where the course of action or of communication takes place. Each form of knowledge establishes boundaries of reasonableness, symbolic demarcations for ordered action and communication. Cognitive claims are thus deeply intertwined with normative claims (more on this below). In Table 2, I identify these six structural epistemological forms by resorting, as the designations chosen indicate, to studies on sociology of culture and cultural studies in general, which were already used in Chapters One and Five. I will confine myself to commenting on some of the more problematic features of this framework.

---

[78]   Though in a different sense, Hunt also uses the concept of local hegemony (1993, pp 227–248).

First, a conceptual note. Central to my argument is the idea that all forms of knowledge are partial and local. They are contextualized, and thus limited by the clusters of social relations of which they are the epistemological 'consciousness'. There is, therefore, no specific epistemological reason to designate as local knowledge the common sense of the communityplace. I use this designation to relate the concept of this form of knowledge to Geertz's analyses of community-based 'local knowledges'.[79] The 'location' of science in the worldplace may be disputed. Indeed, bearing in mind that, since the mid-seventeenth century, and particularly after the mid-nineteenth century, modern science consolidated its hegemony by benefiting from increasing state protection to the point of becoming the official knowledge taught in the public educational system and developed in research institutions set up or financed by the state, it could be argued that science is the epistemological form of the citizenplace. As a matter of fact, in my analysis of the state strategies in the interstate system (pattern of normal change) in Chapter Two, I consider science to be the privileged form of knowledge of state action, a productive force in accumulation strategies, a discourse of truth sustaining the educational system in hegemony strategies, and and a national resource in trust strategies. It could be alternatively argued that, since the first industrial revolution, modern science has gradually been transformed into a force of production, to the point of being today the force of production *par excellence*, and that, accordingly, it should be conceived as the epistemological form of the workplace.[80]

Without questioning the facts supporting the arguments above, I prefer to conceive of modern science as the epistemological form of the worldplace in order to emphasize the fact that modern science is one of the earliest and by far the most successful globalized localism of Western modernity, and that its success lies in part in not letting itself be reduced either to a force of production or to an official knowledge. The universalism of the scientific ethos as conceptualized by Merton, though mystifying, does have a grain of truth.[81] Of course, as I suggest in Chapter One, modern science is a Western cultural artifact, whose 'universal' diffusion in the world system has been uneven, and has reproduced asymmetries and hierarchies among the core, the periphery and the semi-periphery. There is, however, a grain of truth in science's 'universalism': scientific knowledge is today a worldwide argumentative audience, a highly stratified audience to be sure, with a great polarization between speakers (concentrated in the core countries) and non-speakers, but still an audience reaching far beyond the national boundaries, and endowed with a high level of transnational intelligibility (the 'scientific community'). This conception of modern science as the epistemological form of the worldplace permits us to see both the range of its audience, and the ways in which it reproduces and reinforces the hierarchies of the world system. Indeed, modern science, in constellation with the epistemological form of the workplace (productivism,

79   Geertz, 1983.

80   With Taylorism, the workplace itself became a scientific endeavour in the form of scientific management. To quote Taylor himself, 'best management is a true science, resting upon clearly defined laws, rules and principles' (1911, p 1, in Clegg and Dunkerley, 1980, p 87).

81   Merton, 1968.

technologism, professional training and corporate culture), is today the key factor of the international division of labour, contributing decisively to accentuate the unequal exchanges in the world system.

As the common sense of scientists or *ideologie des savants*, modern science is the hegemonic form of knowledge in contemporary societies, which constellates with the other common senses produced in society through powerful means of diffusion. It is, therefore, a highly pervasive form of knowledge, a cosmic form of knowledge. However, in contrast with the cosmic form of power (domination) and the cosmic form of law (state law), science does not rely exclusively on a national, centralized and bureaucratic institution (the state) for its cosmic operation. Though the state is an essential facilitator through scientific research and development policies, science operates cosmically because it is an organized, specialized, professionalized knowledge susceptible of being produced *ad infinitum* in apparently context-blind settings, according to formalized and replicable methodologies. It is a form of knowledge capable of powerful and drastic interventions in nature and society, whereby its instrumental efficacy is in turn reinforced and dramatized.

In spite of its cosmic character, and in much the same way as domination and state law, modern science only operates in constellation with other, chaosmic, forms of knowledge. Two of the most strategic constellations in the reproduction of capitalist societies have already been mentioned: science and citizenplace knowledge (science as official knowledge and measure of national advancement); and science and workplace knowledge (science as force of production). But science also constellates with all the other structural common senses, in either conflictual or complementary relations. For instance, the constellation of science and communityplace knowledge is a tense one. On the one hand, in its hegemonic drive, science aspires to dismiss and replace local knowledges altogether. The very idea of a 'scientific community' suggests that science considers itself the only modern identity-value on which basic communitarian ideals can flourish. On the other, whenever science is operative in concrete social fields (other than the scientific community), it resorts to other local knowledges in order to pre-empt conflicts, facilitate interventions, lower costs and so on. Whenever such complementary relation fails to happen, the constellation becomes conflictual, and scientific knowledge is likely to be confronted, obstructed or subverted by communityplace knowledge. These complex articulations are particularly visible, and sometimes become even dramatic, as we move from the core to the periphery of the world system.

The constellations of science with familism and familial culture are equally complex. In the core countries, from the mid-nineteenth century onwards, many transformations of household relations were promoted by the state in the name of science, and for the progress of the nation. They represented complex knowledge formations of family culture, civic culture and science. Today, the campaigns for the vaccination of children or for the sterilization of women throughout the periphery constitute similar constellations. As science constellates with other knowledges, it is also transformed by them; by means of interpenetration or contamination, it assumes partial characteristics of other knowledges.

I am not speaking of gross manipulations of science in order to yield to other knowledges, as in the case of the Lysenko *affaire*, when science was made to yield to cultural nationalism.[82] I am speaking of spontaneous, interstitial, relatively chaotic processes, by means of which science is mixed with mass culture as the epistemological form of the marketplace – for instance, in popular science and science fiction – or with the epistemological form of the communityplace – for instance, the sense of community among groups of scientists, the creation of scientific traditions and scientific identities. In each knowledge formation, science is the context-blind component of cultural contexts, herein lying the deepest roots of its cosmic operation. But because this context-blindness can only affirm itself in cultural contexts, it becomes necessarily contextualized by the chaosmic knowledges with which science constellates.

Such contextualized context-blindness is most visible in the articulations between cognitive and normative claims. All epistemological forms combine, albeit very differently, these two types of claims. Each form of knowledge is also a moral code in Wuthnow's sense: 'a set of cultural elements that define the nature of commitment to a particular course of behavior'.[83] Familial culture is deeply intertwined with family values; corporate culture with the values of achievement and discipline; consumerism and mass culture with individualism and with what Wuthnow calls the 'morality of the marketplace';[84] local knowledge with the precedence of primordial identities and roots; civic culture with national identity and civic values. What is specific of science is that it denies the possibility of cognitive and normative claims coexisting in the same epistemological form. It thinks of itself as making only cognitive claims – the truth. In light of the epistemological critique hinted at in Chapter One and developed elsewhere,[85] and bearing in mind that science operates in knowledge formations, it should be clear by now that the specific normative claim of science is to purport to make no normative claims. By the same token, it should be also clear by now that its truth is but a discourse of truth.

As in the case of forms of power and law, I have concentrated here on the hegemonic forms of common sense in capitalist societies, that is to say, on knowledge-as-regulation. But if structural places are indeed clusters of social relations, then they are also clusters of knowledge relations. Inasmuch as they are fields of social struggles, they are also fields of struggles among knowledges. Thus, in concrete social practice, the regulatory rhetorics are often confronted with emancipatory rhetorics. The task of oppositional postmodern critical theory in general and of the legal theory that results from it in particular is to promote, through dialogical rhetoric, in each one of the six clusters of social relations, the emergence of emancipatory *topoi* and arguments or counter-hegemonic common senses which will expand along with the argumentative audiences created around them, eventually to become hegemonic knowledges-as-emancipation.

82 Lecourt, 1976.
83 Wuthnow, 1987, p 69.
84 Wuthnow, 1987, Chapter 3.
85 Santos, 1995, Chapter One.

These knowledge struggles must be conducted in all six clusters of social relations. Like knowledge-as-regulation, knowledge-as-emancipation only operates in constellations of knowledges. To disregard this fact amounts to running the risk of having the emancipatory rhetoric conquered in one of the epistemological forms constellate 'naively' with the regulatory rhetoric of another epistemological form.

6 ON STRUCTURAL DETERMINATION: ASYMMETRIES AND BIFURCATIONS

What characterizes capitalist societies is not so much the structure of determination, but the horizon of determination, that is, the outer boundaries of structural limitation. In Wright's conception, structural limitation is a pattern of determination in which some social structure establishes limits within which some other structure or process can vary, and establishes probabilities for the specific structures or processes that are possible within those limits.[86] Unlike Wright, I do not think that only some of the relevant structures provide structural limitation, nor that it is possible in general to establish any form of structural determination. In abstract, none of the structural places separately establishes more or more important limits than the other. The six structural places taken together as constellations of social actions establish the horizon of determination, the outer structural limits of social life in capitalist societies. Within the structural limits there is a sea of contingency. The different structural forms of social power, law and knowledge, unfold in the two contrasting modes that I have already identified: *boundary-setting* and *path breaking*. As boundary-setting, they establish limits, as path breaking, they create contingency and may dislocate the limits. Insofar as they are inhabited by partial contradictions (the systematic production of a certain form of inequality), the structural places also unfold in a contradictory manner. Hence their functional reproduction cannot be guaranteed *a priori* or forever; on the contrary, it is inherently problematic. Furthermore, besides unfolding as path breaking or boundary-setting (qualitative dimension), structural forms of power also unfold in *high-tension mode* or in *low-tension mode* (quantitative dimension). When unfolding in a high-tension mode, the form of power provides the matrix for organizing the concrete social field; when unfolding in a low-tension mode, it facilitates or obstructs, consolidates or disrupts, expands or contracts, supplements or subverts such a process of organization.

Structural places are well-established locations of social agency – gender and generation; class and 'capitalist nature'; consumership; citizenship; community and ethnicity; nation-state. To unfold in constellations means that, in concrete social action, agency is always a constellation of some or all the different forms of agency. Since in abstract it is impossible to judge which constellations of agency will be more pervasive or determinant, let us think of a concrete example. Social relations between a working-class couple in which husband and wife have different ethnic backgrounds may, in 'normal

---

[86]   Wright, 1978; p 594.

times', be organized around the householdplace, that is, by gender relations. The fact that they are both workers and citizens of the same country and, at the same time, members of different ethnic groups, may now facilitate or consolidate, now disturb or obstruct the dominant pattern of relations. In 'critical times', however, when, for instance, one or both of them has lost their job, their relations will be drastically reorganized by the workplace, whereas gender or ethnic relations may either attenuate or further aggravate the costs of such reorganization. In still other instances of 'critical times', as when there is an outbreak of ethnic violence in the neighbourhood or in the country, their social relations as a couple may be further drastically reorganized by the communityplace, particularly as regards their relations with their children and their upbringing – the language they will learn as their first language, the school they will attend, the religion they will profess, the way they will dress and so on. In such a situation, gender, class and citizen relations may either supplement or subvert, facilitate or obstruct such reorganization.

If we move from the microlevel of interactions to the macrolevel of national societies in the world system, the above-mentioned example of free trade fundamentalism and hegemonic demands for structural adjustment, stabilization and foreign debt payment indicates very clearly that the worldplace of peripheral societies is drastically reorganizing all the other structural places, even though the range and the depth of the reorganization may change enormously across social fields. It seems reasonable to hypothesize that the worldplace will have a much higher-tension presence in social relations clustered around the workplace, the marketplace and even the citizenplace than in social relations clustered around the householdplace or the communityplace.

How might one account metatheoretically for a scheme of structural limitation, itself constituted by a plurality of partial structures, within whose boundaries, never fixed or stable, social fields are played out in open-ended contingency and indeterminate social relations, and thus not amenable to being explained by causal primacies defined generally for social relations of a given type? To answer this question, it may be useful to confront the conception adopted here with those of two authors who in recent years have reformulated their structural theories, in both cases by softening somewhat their deterministic claims. I am referring to Erik O Wright (in collaboration with Levine and Sober), well known for his model of structural determination based on the causal primacy of the class structure,[87] and I. Wallerstein, equally well known for his theory of the world system, according to which causal primacy is attributed to the unequal economic exchanges inherent to the global division of labour.[88] Both have recently presented metatheoretical proposals – in Wright, Levine and Sober's case, a fully developed reconstruction,[89] in Wallerstein's, some innovative suggestions[90] – which deserve attention and help to shape the proposal I myself am presenting in this chapter. Both

---

87   Wright, 1989.
88   Wallerstein, 1974.
89   Wright, Levine and Sober, 1992.
90   Wallerstein, 1991a, pp 228ff; Wallerstein, in Balibar and Wallerstein, 1991.

proposals are metatheoretical, one in the tradition of the philosophy of science (Wright, Levine and Sober's) and the other with Kuhnian and Prigoginian traits (Wallerstein's).

Wright, Levine and Sober's proposal is born of the need of 'reconstructing Marxism' in dialogue with other influential and highly revisionist reconstructions of the last decade, namely by Giddens[91] and Habermas,[92] as well as with important theoretical work (for example, GA Cohen[93] and J Elster[94]) and historical work by Marxists, neo-Marxists and post-Marxists (specially Skocpol[95]). They propose a 'weak historical materialism' and a pragmatic re-evaluation of the 'methodological distinctiveness' of Marxism. They start out by acknowledging that many debates in the social sciences revolve around issues of causal primacy and causal asymmetry:

> 'Often, proponents of contending positions agree that certain causes are relevant for explaining some phenomenon but differ in their assessments of the relative importance of these causes (*quantitative asymmetry*) or in their understanding of the qualitatively different ways in which they enter into particular causal processes (*qualitative asymmetry*)'.[96]

The debates Wright, Levine and Sober have in mind are basically those, within and without Marxism, which engage the relative explanatory importance of class, gender and the state, only to proceed onto a careful and detailed specification of different forms of causal asymmetry. Some of their conclusions are of particular interest for the argument of this chapter. First, many of the explanatory disputes are not genuine, because even if they address the same topic, they do not have the same *explanandum* – it is one thing to explain why social insurance was introduced in Britain in 1904, in Canada in 1922 and in the US in 1933, and another thing to explain why no capitalist country had a social insurance in 1850 and why all developed capitalist countries had some form of social insurance by 1950.[97] Shifts of *explananda* are particularly evident in discussions of the relation between class and gender and between class and the state. Secondly, causal primacy claims are difficult to sustain with precision, and amount to assertions of one or another kind of quantitative asymmetry. The relation between explanatory importance and asymmetry is, however, problematic. The distinction between dynamic and non-dynamic systemic causes provides a good illustration of the difficulties. In a synchronic ('static') analysis of capitalist societies, it is impossible to sustain, in general, a causal primacy claim between state, class and gender, since each one of them imposes structural limits on any of the others. On the contrary, according to Wright, Levine and Sober, in a dynamic analysis, that is, in an analysis of the internal developmental dynamics of capitalist societies, there is a causal asymmetry between the state, class and gender since, of the three, only class has internal dynamics: 'the

91   Giddens, 1981.
92   Habermas, 1978.
93   Cohen, 1978.
94   Elster, 1985.
95   Skocpol, 1979,1985.
96   Wright, Levine and Sober, 1992, p 129.
97   Wright, Levine and Sober, 1992, p 150.

trajectory of development of the state [and also of gender] and the economy would be driven by dynamic causes operating in the economy, but not by dynamic causes endogenous to the state [or to gender]'.[98] Nevertheless, this asymmetry cannot be considered enough basis for a claim of causal potency: 'there is no reason to consider dynamic endogenous processes more important than contingent causes or synchronic systemic causes *simply because they are dynamic and endogenous*'.[99] Again, the causal primacy can only be established in light of the precise characterization of the *explanandum.* Thus, Wright, Levine and Sober's conclusion turns out to be a rather weak version of structural determination. Though they assume that there are asymmetries among causes, including asymmetries that justify causal primacy claims, 'there is no principle that warrants the conclusion that class considerations always comprise the primary determinants of social phenomena', and for this reason, 'the sweeping, global claims to causal primacy characteristic of much of the Marx tradition are unsustainable'.[100] The causal pervasiveness of class should therefore be much more important than its causal primacy.[101]

Wright, Levine and Sober's concern with the precise description of *explananda* is the most innovative and promising feature of their metatheoretical reconstruction of Marxism. The problem with this reconstruction is that, being formulated within the tradition of epistemological realism, it assumes that the precise description of the *explanandum* is possible without resorting to the theory that will then explain it as a kind of pre-understanding. In light of my epistemological argument in Chapter One,[102] this is highly problematic.[103] As the deep problems of realist epistemology become increasingly evident, the relation between facts and theories also becomes more complex. Facts and theories simply represent different perspectives and different degrees of vision within the same epistemological field.[104] An exclusive emphasis on causal analysis is therefore misplaced, and the precise description of the *explanandum*, rather than adjudicating among competing theories from 'the outside', so to speak, can only signal theoretical preferences in intelligible ways. In other words, the concern with the *explanandum* does not solve the metatheoretical problem, it merely displaces it.

---

[98]   Wright, Levine and Sober, 1992, p 170.
[99]   Wright, Levine and Sober, 1992, p 172.
[100]   Wright, Levine and Sober, 1992, p 174.
[101]   In a study on the empirical relationship between the location of households in class structure and gender inequalities in performance of housework, Wright *et al* found that class location is not a powerful or systematic determinant of variations in the gendered domestic division of labour (1992).
[102]   For a more detailed presentation of such a critique, see Santos, 1995, Chapter 1.
[103]   Wright, Levine and Sober, 1992, also presuppose that synchronic and dynamic analyses may generate different and logically unrelated causal asymmetries and causal primacy claims, which is also highly problematic.
[104]   This conception is also more congruent with the rhetorical reconstruction of scientific knowledge for which facts and (theoretical) truths are different arguments within the same discourse.

In the conception I am proposing here, we go a step further in softening structural determination. Since assessments of relative importance even among 'important causes' are unsustainable, the analytical focus turns to the identification and enumeration of important factors (the six structural places) rather than to their rankings; to horizons of determination rather than to road maps of determination. Within such a horizon, contingency and creativity are both lived experiences, and conditions of intelligibility of what happens to people and of what people make happen. This leads me to Wallerstein's metatheoretical insight. Economic determinism is one of the basic tenets of world system theory. Its most recent and articulate formulation is Chase-Dunn's conception of the world system as a social system whose historical specificity lies to a great extent in being held together and integrated through a division of labour, that is, through 'the interdependence produced by a market-mediated network of economic differentiation', rather than through cultural and normative integration.[105] Consequently, for world system theory, culture and normative integration play secondary rather than primary roles in the reproduction of contemporary world order.[106] The epiphenomenal character of culture and even of politics in the world system theory has been widely criticized. Since the mid-1980s, Wallerstein himself has felt the need to stress the political[107] and cultural[108] dimensions of the world system. Indeed, in response to Balibar's critique of his determinism,[109] Wallerstein has most recently suggested that structural determination is itself a dependent variable that must be evaluated in conjunction with Braudel's multiplicity of social times:

> '[W]hen an historical system is functioning normally – whatever the system and thus including the capitalist world-economy – it seems to me that, almost by definition, it operates overwhelmingly as something that is determined. . . . But every historical system moves eventually towards its end via the working-out of the logic of its contradictions. At that point, the system goes into a 'crisis', enters a period of 'transition' which leads to what Prigogine calls a 'bifurcation', that is to say, to a highly fluctuating situation in which a slight push can lead to a very large deviation. In other words, it is a situation in which freewill prevails. It is exactly for that reason that it is almost impossible to foresee the outcome of the transformations'. Ibid, p 231.

In other words, in such a situation, the claims of determination must be scaled down and, even though it is possible to continue to speak of mechanisms, structures, constraints and limits, the social transformation must be thought of more in terms of 'utopistics'[110] than in terms of the workings of primary causes: 'We are approaching the end of the system – that long moment which, I believe, we have in fact already entered

---

[105]   Chase-Dunn, 1991, p 94.
[106]   Chase-Dunn, 1991, p 88.
[107]   Wallerstein, 1984.
[108]   Wallerstein, 1991b.
[109]   Balibar and Wallerstein, 1991.
[110]   Wallerstein, 1991a, p 270.

and thus we need to think about the possible leaps we might make, the Utopias that are now at least conceivable'.[111]

Ours is a time of paradigmatic, epistemological and, though less visibly or more embryonically, sociocultural-political transition as well. I therefore join Wallerstein in his call for scaling down determination claims and indeed going beyond the limits of the world system theory as it currently stands. Rather than relying on one macrostructure, the worldwide division of economic labour, I propose a constellation of six structural places of which this macrostructure is one (the worldplace). Among them, no asymmetries, hierarchies or primacies can be established in general, which is the same as saying that there is no 'natural' or 'normal' constellation of structural places. The development of capitalist societies and the capitalist world system as a whole are grounded on such constellations, and not on any one of the structural places individually. Conversely, the success of anti-capitalist, anti-systemic struggles depends upon their capacity to organize in constellations of emancipatory social agencies, that is, in constellations of equal exchanges against constellations of powers, in constellations of radical democratic legalities against constellations of despotic legalities, in constellations of emancipatory knowledges against constellations of regulatory knowledges. To account for such an agenda, theoretical reconstructions must be far more demanding and innovative, and the social practice they call for, more creative and complex (as well as aware of limits as of possibilities). Such theory and practice must be less dogmatic and, in view of the partial nature of all relevant forms of agency, willing to forge alliances to overcome incompleteness. Finally, they must be epistemologically more tolerant in the face of the various local and partial knowledges and common senses involved in them.

7   EXPANDING THE LEGAL AND THE POLITICAL FIELDS

I argue in this chapter that, as power formations, capitalist societies are constituted by six forms of power and, as legal formations, by six forms of law. This is, however, only one side of my argument. The other side is that only one of the six forms of law is officially recognized as law (state law) and only one of the six forms of power is recognized as political power (domination). The two sides of the argument must always be considered together.

The analysis above suggests that, of the six forms of power, domination is, in liberal democratic societies, the least despotic, in that it is a form of power whose exercise is limited by certain democratic rules and controls, and allows for a certain measure of citizens' participation and citizens' welfare in light of the civil, political and socio-economic rights guaranteed by the constitution of the state. It also suggests that, of

---

[111]   Balibar and Wallerstein, 1991, p 232. See also Wallerstein, 1991a, p 254.

all the six forms of law, the state law is, in liberal democratic societies, the least despotic, because it is promulgated by democratic processes, exercised according to procedural rules (the rule of law) that protect the weaker part against arbitrary decisions and applied by bodies of professionals trained to separate the legal from the political and decide with impartiality. But, as we have seen, the very broad claims for democratic power and rule of law of Western modernity were drastically reduced from the mid-nineteenth century onwards. As capitalism became the exclusive development model of modern societies, most social relations could not possibly be governed according to the radical democratic claims of modernity. Indeed, as I explained above, in some social fields, capitalism would necessarily generate despotic social relations – more despotic, in fact, than pre-capitalist ones.

To solve this antinomy without thereby undermining the credibility of the liberal project, the universal character of the democratic claims was upheld by converting a relatively restricted field of social relations – the citizenplace – into the universe of entitlement to such claims. As a consequence, only the rules and normative standards emanating from the state and exercised by it would be considered legal. Similarly, only the power exercised by the state or centred around it would be considered political. Beyond this, neither law nor political power would be recognized as such.

This arbitrary reductionism produced two forms of occultation, both crucial for the legitimation of capitalism as a global social relation. First, it obfuscated the fact that the relatively democratic power of the state could only operate in constellation with other forms of power, in general more despotic than itself. Secondly, it obfuscated the fact that the democratic rule of law could only operate in constellation with other forms of law, in general more despotic than itself. Once this double occultation was successfully inculcated throughout society by a whole range of hegemonic strategies – from legal science to mass media and the educational system – , there was no point in extending the legal and political principles of modernity beyond the citizenplace to the remaining five forms of law and power – in spite of their being, when taken together, a much larger body of law and power, governing a much wider range of individual and social life. As a result, the despotism of these forms of law and power remained invisible as legal and political despotism, and consequently could not be compared or contrasted with the relatively democratic character of the law and power of the citizenplace.

In order to illustrate this process, I will briefly review Marx's analysis of the emergence of the factory acts in nineteenth-century England in the first volume of *Das Kapital* (Chapter Ten). I will then offer a re-interpretation of Marx's findings in light of the alternative framework that I have proposed in this chapter. The reason why I choose Marx is because, even though he was the most radical and lucid critic of the liberal capitalist project, he nevertheless surrendered to the project's legal and political common sense, which, in itself, bears testimony to the latter's resilience and pervasiveness. As described by Marx, this historical example does not allow us to view the interaction among the six structural places but, at least, the interaction between the workplace and the citizenplace emerges very clearly, and though very weakly (due to Marx's analytical preferences), we can also 'feel' the presence of the householdplace, the marketplace, the communityplace and the worldplace.

The crucial role of the state and state legislation in the creation of the labour force required by the emerging capitalist mode of production is today well documented. This is a long historical process that, in England, lasted from the fifteenth to the eighteenth century. As Marx puts it in the *Grundrisse*, 'the annals of English legislation contain the bloody handwriting of coercive measures employed to transform the mass of the population, after they had become propertyless and free, into free wage laborers'.[112] Marx analyses then, in *Das Kapital*, the 'bloody legislation against vagabondage' at the end of the fifteenth century and during the sixteenth century throughout Europe.[113] These were the laws that created the labour force, and were an essential factor of so-called primitive accumulation. Once this stage was concluded and the labour force was created, one would think that capitalist relations of production would develop by themselves. In capitalism, 'surplus labor and necessary labor glide one into the other',[114] and, as a result, 'the dull compulsion of economic relations'[115] operates by itself, making superfluous any direct intervention of the state in the appropriation of the surplus labour by capitalists. Indeed, this is only part of the picture, as Marx also recognizes, for three reasons. First, because the 'dull compulsion of economic relations' was in fact constituted by the state law of property and the law of contract. Secondly, because, whenever the economic compulsion failed (as in the case of destruction of machinery or of strikes), its operation could only be restored by state coercive intervention. Third, because the state intervention in the reproduction of the labour force went far beyond coercive measures against workers in exceptional situations, the Factory Acts on the working day being a good illustration of such an intervention.[116] Marx insists that given 'the passion of capital for an unlimited and reckless extension of the working day',[117] 'the factory legislation was the first conscious and methodical reaction of society against the spontaneously developed form of the process of production'.[118]

Were these laws against the interests of capital? 'No', Marx replies, because the 'unrestricted waste of human life'[119] resulting from the 'unnatural extension of the working day'[120] would in the end paralyze the mechanism of exploitation. But the truth

---

[112]   Marx, 1973, p 769.
[113]   Marx, 1970, p 734.
[114]   Marx, 1970, p236.
[115]   Marx, 1970, p 737.
[116]   As late as 1949, Kahn-Freund could say that: 'the regulation of hours of work by legislation or collective agreements was the earliest and remains the most notable restriction of the command power which is the concomitant of the ownership of means of production' (in Renner, 1976, p 161).
[117]   Marx, 1970, p 298.
[118]   Marx, 1970, p 480.
[119]   Marx, 1970, p 475.
[120]   Marx, 1970, p 266.

of the matter is that capitalists fought as much as they could against the promulgation of the Factory Acts, and they used the most diverse devices to evade their enforcement once they were passed.[121] On the contrary, workers fought for those laws, and Marx concluded that 'the establishment of a normal working day is the result of centuries of struggle between capitalist and laborer',[122] the product of a 'protracted civil war'.[123]

Marx's analysis of the Factory Acts suffers from a certain ambiguity. If the Factory Acts furthered the interests of capital, why did capitalists fight against them? Why did the workers fight for them? If they were in favour of the interests of capital, were they necessarily detrimental to the interests of the workers? Marx did not adequately answer these questions. Nor are they being properly answered in the current discussions of the rise and demise of the welfare state or of the regulatory state. In my view, the Factory Acts symbolize an historical turning point in the articulation of citizenplace and workplace. The Factory Acts were an absolute gain for the workers at the level of the citizenplace. The corresponding absolute loss for capital at that level was, however, compensated for by the gains it did obtain at the level of the workplace, within the new parameters established by the laws. Marx and social historians of the period emphasize that the Factory Acts contributed decisively to the restructuring of capital: they accelerated the transition from the manufacture system to the factory system, and they changed the conditions of competition in favour of the most productive and technically advanced factories and industries. The gains for capital were thus an increase in the control over the social relations in the workplace through the intensification of the labour process – speedups, introduction of piece wages, mechanization and so on. These gains could not be extended to all capitals and capitalists. They were allocated to those that could convert the losses in the citizenplace into gains in the workplace. All others would disappear or become members of the proletariat. For those capitalists that succeeded, the loss in the citizenplace was compensated for or neutralized by the gain in the workplace. For the workers the inverse was true.

But the most important feature of this transaction is that, due to the autonomy of the structural places, it remained invisible, it remained below the threshold of social consciousness. This game of gains and losses was socially constructed not as a positive-sum game between the workplace and the citizenplace, but as two separate zero-sum games – one in the workplace, the other in the citizenplace – whose results could not be measured one against the other. It entailed gains for workers and losses for capital in the citizenplace, and gains for capital and losses for workers in the workplace.

---

[121] Marx describes in great detail the different forms of resistance against the laws: frontal violation; the relay system, making it difficult for faculty inspectors to detect violations; restriction of the inspectors' access to the factories; wage cuts; changes in the legal concept of 'child' (what Marx calls 'capitalist anthropology': 1970, p 280); the use of the 'economic crisis' as a justification for not enforcing the laws; the denial of responsibility; the negotiation over the range and degree of violation. See also Carson, 1979.

[122] Marx, 1970, p 270.

[123] Marx, 1970, p 299.

Put differently, the gains and losses were not compensated for at the same level, nor were they perceived as results of reciprocal developments, and as such their structural combination remained hidden. Capital's loss of political power within the citizenplace could not be measured against its gain of political power in the workplace. In other words, its loss of control over state law could not be measured against its gain of control over production law.

The incommensurability of gains and losses was crucial in the consolidation and legitimation of capitalist social relations because it reinforced the differences between the workplace and the citizenplace. It made clear that the distribution of social power and legal competence to the workers in the citizenplace could never expand to the workplace in the same way or by the same process, and that this fact would not be conceived as the result of a political decision, but rather as the natural and necessary outcome of the structural autonomy of the two places. In other words, under capitalist social relations, the worker would always be less a citizen of his or her factory than of his or her country. Moreover, such a discrepancy would be considered to be not only inevitable but also natural. The fact that the worker's gains were obtained in the citizenplace was important in itself. They were translated into state law, a form of law based on general, universal rights. Given their institutional separation from the workplace, rights were relatively stable entitlements. They were not strictly tied to the fluctuations of the economic cycle. This lack of reciprocity with production reinforced the developmental dynamics and rationality of the citizenplace (loyalty maximizing), and by the same token stabilized its form of power (domination). However, this relative stability was obtained through a process which simultaneously obtained the consent of the workers to be subjected, within the workplace, to production law, a form of law based not on universal rights but on production interests. And since interests were defined by the rationality of profit maximizing, they were precarious entitlements, strictly tied to the fluctuations of production and as unstable as production itself. In other words, the Factory Acts legitimated the state before the workers-as-citizens and, by the same process, they legitimated the factory before the workers-as-a-class-of-wage-labourers. This laid out the structural foundation for the types of class compromises that were later on achieved most notably by social democracy in the core countries.

By now it should be clear that, contrary to what is commonly assumed, the 'false consciousness' of law in capitalist societies does not lie as much in the discrepancy between law in books and law in action as in a well-knit social construction that converts state law into the exclusive form of law, thereby presuming to suppress domestic, production, exchange, community and systemic law. Without this crucial move, state law could not possibly operate as it does in our societies. Sociology of law, no matter how critical, has done nothing since the nineteenth century but consolidate and legitimate this suppression of dimensions of the legal formation. Capitalist societies are less than democratic, not because the law of the citizenplace is less than democratic, but rather because this form of law, no matter how democratic, must coexist with five other forms of law that are more despotic, and operate in constellation with it. This explains why all the attempts to create industrial citizenship, under conditions of capitalist appropriation of the means of production, are always bound to fail whenever they come into conflict with the logic of profit maximizing.[124]

Marx was acutely aware of the changes in the regulation of labour taking shape in his time. Indeed, he established the material base for the articulation among different political and legal forms when he distinguished between the division of labour in society at large and the division of labour in the workshop, and related one to the other:

> 'The division of labor in the workshop implies concentration of the means of production in the hands of one capitalist; the division of labor in society implies their dispersion among many independent producers of commodities ... in a society with capitalist production, anarchy in the social division of labor and despotism in that of the workshop are mutual conditions, the one of the other'.[125]

But he failed to see in these changes the dynamics of the articulation among political and legal forms and institutions throughout society. When he uses the terms *political* and *legal* in the context of the workplace, he does so in an analogical or metaphorical sense: 'that a capitalist should command on the field of production is now as indispensable as that a general should command on the field of the battle'.[126] However, this power of command is not merely a technical function, it is rather, and at the same time, a 'function of the exploitation of a social labor process'.[127] The political analogy is taken to the extreme when Marx says that: 'This power of Asiatic and Egyptian kings, Etruscan theocrats, etc, has in modern society been transferred to the capitalist, whether he be an isolated or, as in joint-stock companies, a collective capitalist'.[128] As to the legal analogy or metaphor, the factory code is conceived as a 'caricature', a code 'in which capital formulates like a private legislator and at his own good will, his autocracy over his work people, unaccompanied by the division of responsibility, in other matters so much approved of by the bourgeoisie, and still unaccompanied by the still more approved representative system... '[129]

The main point of my argument is that the power of command in the workshop is not political power in any metaphorical sense. It is as political as the power of the citizenplace, the power of the householdplace, the power of the worldplace or the power of any other structural place. They are different in their forms, as they derive from different modes of production – exploitation, domination, patriarchy, unequal exchange, fetishism of commodities and unequal differentiation – but this does not alter their

---

[124] The history of this failure is well documented at least since Gramsci's workers' councils in 1919 Turin. See, for an overview, Clegg and Dunkerly, 1980, p 512.
[125] Marx, 1970, pp 355ff.
[126] Marx, 1970, p 330.
[127] Marx, 1970, p 331.
[128] Marx, 1970, p 334.
[129] Marx, 1970, p 424.

political nature. On the contrary, such nature is not an attribute of any of them taken separately; it is, rather, the aggregate effect of the articulations among them. Similarly, the factory code is not law in any metaphorical sense. It is law, just as the law of the state is law. Moreover, the fact that it is unhampered by the representative system of the citizenplace does not make it a caricature. The despotic law of production is a necessary condition of democratic state law.

The idea of conceiving regulation of labour in the factory as a form of law was originally hinted at by the Austrian Marxists, particularly by Max Adler[130] and K Renner.[131] Adler is mostly concerned with the functional and structural relations between the prison and the factory, thus inaugurating a line of research that was later on pursued by the Frankfurt School through Rusche and Kirchheimer,[132] and most recently by Foucault[133] and Melossi and Pavarini.[134] Closer to my concerns here is Renner's political and legal conception of the organization of production. Renner is best known for his theory of property. According to him, the law of property originated in Roman law as 'a person's all-embracing legal power over a tangible object',[135] but changed completely its social function in the transition from feudalism to capitalism, when the means of production became an object of private appropriation. While previously property rights granted to the proprietor a mere control over things, with the emergence of capitalism and the private appropriation of the means of production, the control over things was transformed, surreptitiously as it were, into a control over people, that is, a control over the workers operating the means of production through the contract of labour:

> 'In the eyes of the law, the property-subject is related to the object only, controlling
> matter alone. But what is control of property in law, becomes in fact man's control of
> human beings, of the wage-laborers, as soon as property has developed into capital. The
> individual called owner sets the tasks to others, he makes them subject to commands

---

[130]   Adler, nd.

[131]   Renner, 1976.

[132]   Rusche and Kirchheimer, 1968.

[133]   Foucault, 1977.

[134]   Melossi and Pavarini, 1981. Though M Adler is one of the most innovative Marxist thinkers, nobody, to my knowledge, has acknowledged his original contribution to the analysis of the articulation between economic production and punishment. The most influential analysis has remained Rusche's and Kirchheimer's. It has been critically assessed and expanded in different directions (Foucault, 1977; Jankovic, 1977; Melossi, 1978; Ignatieff, 1978; Melossi and Pavarini, 1981). In general, the functionalist and economicist biases in Rusche's analysis have been transcended by an emphasis on structural correspondences or homologies, which is particularly the case of Foucault and of Melossi and Pavarini. But, in my view, these authors exaggerate such an emphasis by collapsing the mechanisms of social power of the workplace with those of the citizenplace. I will come back to Foucault later on in the text. As to Melossi and Pavarini, they try to combine Rusche and Kirchheimer with Pashukanis (1978) and derive the structural isomorphism between prisoners and workers from the logic of capital: 'If the punishment as deprivation of liberty is structured, then, on the model of "exchange" (in terms of retribution by equivalent), its execution (read: penitentiary) is modeled on the hypothesis of manufacture, of the "factory" (in terms of discipline and subordination' (1981, p 186).

[135]   Renner, 1976, p 81.

and, at least, in the initial stages of capitalist development, supervises the execution of his commands. The owner of a *res* imposes his will upon *personae*, autonomy is converted into heteronomy of will'.[136]

According to Renner, the most relevant aspect of this transformation is that the right of ownership assumes a new social function without any change in the norm itself. As the literal formulation of the norm does not change, the change in its social function remains ideologically hidden. This social theory of property is complemented with a political and legal conception of the organization of production, a lesser-known aspect of Renner's work, but particularly relevant for my argument here. In his view, the regulation of labour inside the factory under the command of capital is a delegated public authority, since 'the institution of property leads automatically to an organization similar to the state'.[137] Accordingly, 'the factory is an establishment with its own code with all the characteristics of a legal code'.[138] Renner sharply criticizes lawyers and legal doctrine for not taking into due account this legal reality: 'we see further that this regulation of power and labour remains concealed to the whole of bourgeois legal doctrine which is aware of nothing but its most formal, general and extraneous limitations'.[139]

Despite the fact that it points in the right direction, Renner's conception must be criticized on three accounts. First, he takes too far the identification of law and power of the state with law and power of the factory. He fails to recognize the structural differences between the state and the factory as two institutional forms and, consequently, the structural differences between the two forms of law and social power through which they operate. In my view, such differences and their articulation are the specific characteristics of the legal field in capitalist societies. Secondly, Renner conceives power and law in the factory as exclusively coercive. It is true, as I have already mentioned, that production and labour are tightly organized and disciplined in capitalism, as never before. This, however, does not mean that such organization and discipline are only made effective through coercion. Thirdly, Renner neglects the historical specificity of capitalism, as when he says that 'the employment relationship is ... a public obligation to service, like the serfdom of feudal times'.[140] This is obviously not true. What differentiates capitalism from feudalism is precisely the privatization of the political power over production, which separates the control over production from the performance of public functions and communal services typical of feudalism.[141]

In more recent times, Burawoy has presented the most forceful argument for a broad political conception of the labour process. Resorting to the Gramscian concept of hegemony, Burawoy shows that the specificity of the capitalist organization of

---

[136] Renner, 1976, p 106.
[137] Renner, 1976, p 107.
[138] Renner, 1976, p 115.
[139] Renner, 1976, p 114.
[140] Renner, 1976, p 115.
[141] Brenner, 1977; Wood, 1981, p 86.

production is that it must elicit, in order to be efficient, the active consent to and the participation of workers in their own exploitation.[142] This conception is based on the idea of the factory as an 'internal state' – an idea that, as we saw, goes back to Renner, at the same time that it echoes explicitly Selznick's theory of industrial justice.[143] Burawoy's main thesis is that the despotic form of production relations in the phase of competitive capitalism has evolved, in the phase of large corporations and trade unionism, into a hegemonic form, resting 'on a limited participation by representatives of labor in the government of industry'.[144] This evolution is captured by the concept of the 'internal state', by which he means: 'the set of institutions that organize, transform or repress struggles over relations in production and relations of production at the level of the enterprise'.[145] The most important among such institutions are the collective bargaining and grievance procedures.

I would like to qualify this stimulating analysis of the labour process with two critical observations. First, though Burawoy, in contrast to Selznick, emphasizes that the politics of production is subjected to the logic of securing and obscuring the extraction of surplus value, he takes too far, in a direction opposite to Renner, the identification of the politics of production with global politics or, in my conception, the politics of the workplace with the politics of the citizenplace. The structural difference between the two lies precisely in the presence in only one of them of the logic of securing and obscuring the extraction of surplus. Such is the difference which, to my mind, accounts for the despotic nature of the political and legal forms of the workplace.[146] This by no means contradicts the presence of hegemonic or consent components, which, as we well know, after EP Thompson[147] and Douglas Hay,[148] were also present in the despotic laws of the *ancien regime*. Coercion and consent, though present in both the workplace and the citizenplace, are different in their form and mode of production, and combine in the two structural places according to different logics. There are different hegemonies in society – family hegemony, state hegemony, factory hegemony, market hegemony, community hegemony, national hegemony and world hegemony – and they are not necessarily congruent.[149] Neither Burawoy nor Meiksins Wood,[150] who has also argued for a political reading of production relations, theorizes the specificity of state law in

---

[142]   Burawoy, 1979, p 27.
[143]   Selznick, 1969.
[144]   Burawoy, 1979, p 110.
[145]   Burawoy, 1979, p 110.
[146]   Edwards and Scullion have criticized Burawoy for focusing mainly on the creation of consent (1982, p 9). Based on broader empirical data, they try to analyze how the control in the workplace relates to both consent and resistance.
[147]   Thompson, 1975.
[148]   Hay, 1975.
[149]   High wages and 'work humanization' have been the two most important factors of factory hegemony. Their strict dependence on the production cycle distinguishes them from the factors of the other forms of hegemony.
[150]   Wood, 1981.

adequate terms. While Burawoy accepts implicitly the base/superstructure framework, Wood relapses into it by locating hesitantly part of state law in the base, and part in the superstructure.[151] The second critical observation is that, due to the relative collapsing of the different power forms, Burawoy neglects the central question of the articulations and constellations among them.

The re-interpretation of the legal and political nature of the workplace undertaken in this section on the basis of Marx's analysis of the factory laws and its prolongations in the work of the Austro-Marxists (Adler and Renner) and of Burawoy only illustrates, as I cautioned at the outset, some very partial aspects of the alternative framework presented in this chapter. To be sure, factory laws would invite a much wider view of the interplay among the six structural places, but Marx's analytical priorities did not favour such a view. Here are just a few glimpses at the wider panorama. First, the special legislation on women's and children's labour presupposed a new articulation between the householdplace and the workplace. Secondly, the fraction of capital that benefited most from the factory legislation was the most active in the world expansion of British capitalism; it was therefore interested in shaping the workplace (and indirectly all the other structural places) in ways congruent with the worldplace they wanted for British capitalism and for British society as a whole. Today, under the conditions of globalized production – through transnational outsourcing along 'global commodity chains' – production law is increasingly the result of a mixture of factory law, national labour laws, international (ILO) conventions, and state-less systems of enforcement of corporate codes of conduct. As César Rodríguez has shown in his work on the interpenetration of these regimes in zones of Mexico and Central America with high concentrations of factories producing for export (maquiladoras), labour conditions in such factories are regulated by a pragmatic mixture of different legal regimes – a paradigmatic example of the type of legal plurality that I have argued characterizes the global legal field.[152] Third, even a quick visit to the new industrial cities – from São Paolo to Shangai to Delhi – would show that class exploitation went hand in hand with nature degradation, which confirms that the social construction of the capitalist wage worker and of 'capitalist nature' are the two sides of the same historical process. Fourthly, the fact that the workers were not yet consumers of the products they produced was a determinant of the marketplace relations and of its interplay with the other structural places. As an example, the coexistence of 'pre-capitalist' markets (household or community based) with 'post-capitalist' markets (workers' consumer co-operatives and international solidarity exchanges) reveals how, in a highly turbulent context, the marketplace manages to constellate household and community relations

---

[151] Wood, 1981, pp 79ff. One of the most stimulating aspects of Burawoy's research is his concern with the comparative analysis of the labour process (US, Zambia, Hungary and Russia). His empirical research is particularly relevant to determine the impact of the worldplace upon the workplace in any given country.

[152] Rodríguez, forthcoming.

with international anti-systemic relations.[153] Finally, the massive dislocations of workers and their families in search of work, the uprooting of traditional communities and their devaluation in a (multi)national territory symbolically consolidated by the ideology of nationalism, on the one hand, and the regionalist resistances beyond many of the workers' struggles, as well as the reinvention of communal values, practices and identities in the new settlements, on the other, signal confrontations and new constellations of social practice between the community place, the citizenplace and the workplace.

8   CONCLUSION

In this chapter I have presented an alternative theoretical framework to the conceptual orthodoxy centred around the state/civil society dichotomy. The main features of this framework are the following. Capitalist societies within the world system are constituted by six structural places, six basic clusters of social relations, which define the horizon of relevant determination. This horizon establishes both outer limits and possibilities, thereby allowing for a minimalist order, a chaos-friendly order, an ordering principle that operates through complexity, fragmentation, hybridization and, above all, through constellation. Within this structural horizon there is contingency and creativity.

The structural places are complex relational entities, constituted by six dimensions. The structural places are autonomous, and have specific developmental dynamics. But each partial dynamics can only be set in motion in social practice, in articulation or constellation with all the other partial dynamics. This does not mean that the structural places, when taken individually, are partially dynamic. Rather, it means that in concrete social fields their dynamics always transcend them, and therefore cannot be controlled in any one of them separately. Not all structural places are always present in the same quantitative or qualitative way in all constellations of social relations or in all social fields. Constellations vary widely across the social fields – according to their privileged relation with or proximity to a specific structural cluster – and across the world system – according to the core/ semi-periphery/periphery hierarchy.

In this chapter I drew attention to three such dimensions – power form, legal form and epistemological form – and dealt with the first two in greater detail. In the course of my analysis I tried to isolate what I believe to be the two main characteristics of capitalist societies. On the one hand, capitalist societies are political constellations of six main forms of power, legal constellations of six main forms of law, and epistemological

---

[153]   For a discussion of the coexistence of pre-capitalist and post-capitalist markets, especially in the semi-periphery, see Santos and Rodríguez, 2002; Santos (ed), 2002. An illustration of such coexistence is offered in Rodríguez, 2002, based on a case study of co-operatives (ie, post-capitalist organizations) of garbage recycling founded and run by communities of homeless garbage pickers working on the streets of Colombia – ie, communities that are subject to the worst kind of social exclusion and who are usually relegated to the most precarious niches of the market.

constellations of six main forms of knowledge. On the other, capitalist societies are characterized by a hegemonic, ideological suppression of the political character of all forms of power except domination, of the legal character of all forms of law except state law, and of the epistemological character of all forms of knowledge except science.

These two characteristics are equally crucial for the normal reproduction of capitalist societies in the world system. My argument is that the political character of social relations of power does not lie in one particular form of power, namely citizenplace power (domination), but rather in the aggregate power resulting from the constellations among the different forms of power in different social fields. Similarly, the legal character of social relations of law does not derive from one single form of law, namely from citizenplace law (state law), but rather from the different constellations among different forms of law. Finally, the epistemological profile of social relations is not provided by one specific epistemological form, namely the epistemological form of the worldplace (science), but rather by the different constellations of knowledges that people and groups produce and use in concrete social fields.

The political, legal and epistemological constellations have two features that I have specifically emphasized. The first one is that the different forms of power, law and knowledge that integrate them respectively are structurally autonomous, each one irreducible to any one of the others. My major criticism of Renner and Burawoy was that it is as important to recognize the legal and political nature of workplace relations as it is to recognize that their (partial) legal and political character is structurally different from the legal and political character of citizenplace relations. The second feature of the political, legal and epistemological constellations is that, in the immense variety of concrete constellations they give rise to in concrete social fields, one specific form tends to be more pervasive and more widely diffused: domination in the power constellations, state law in the legal constellations, and science in the epistemological constellations. The centrality of domination, state law and science in capitalist societies does not derive from their exclusivity over specific social relations, but rather from the pervasiveness of their presence in social relations as a result of the development of capitalist modernity. They are cosmic forms whose cosmic operation is premised upon their virtuosity in constellating with chaosmic forms.

The second structural characteristic of capitalist societies is that the existence of these constellations of power, law and knowledge is ignored, occulted, suppressed by a whole range of hegemony strategies which convert the reduction of politics to the citizenplace into political common sense, the reduction of law to state law into legal common sense, and the reduction of knowledge to scientific knowledge into epistemological common sense. These multiple hegemonic reductions are not just illusions, manipulations that are easy to discredit or to dismiss. Once they become common sense, they are not just necessarily illusory; they also become necessary as illusions. They become embedded in the social, political and cultural *habitus* of people and of social scientists as well, and as such, they guide social practice, create comforting order, produce reassuring labels for self-mapped spaces – politics here, law there, science over there. The political, legal and epistemological reproduction of capitalist societies depends heavily on these hegemonic evidences.

If it wants to be socially effective, critical theory cannot rest content with merely identifying the structural map of capitalist societies, nor with unveiling the mystifying nature of the common sense that both lubricates and occults (and lubricates by occulting) the complex constellations of power, law and knowledge. It must rather become a new, emancipatory, common sense. The difficulty, however, is that it is not through theory that theory can become common sense. And the difficulty is all the greater (even greater) because social theorists rarely recognize it. The idea that critical theory does not need to become common sense in order to be socially validated is one of the most entrenched and mystifying common senses of critical theory. It is indeed this common sense that makes modern critical theory modern. Oppositional postmodern critical theory, on the contrary, starts from a kind of preposterous self-critique, with the purpose of bringing its emancipatory claims down to adequate proportions. Only by fighting its own common sense does it discover the other common senses it must fight. Its contribution to a new, emancipatory, common sense – or rather to new, emancipatory, common senses – resides, first of all, in identifying and characterizing the constellations of regulation, that is, the multiple sites of oppression in capitalist societies and the linkages among them. It lies also in identifying and characterizing the plurality of social agents, social tools and social knowledges susceptible of being mobilized into constellations of emancipatory relations. The inventions of meanings emerging out of these constellations are the seeds of new common senses.

In this chapter I was mainly concerned with the constellations of the modern pillar of regulation as it is embedded not only in law but also in power and knowledge. In the following chapters, in line with the goal of the book, I focus my argument on law and turn to emancipation. In Chapter Eight I elaborate on an oppositional postmodern view of law. In Chapter Nine I conclude by looking into the current possibilities and signs of the emergence of an emancipatory legal common sense.

Chapter 8

Law: A Map of Misreading

I   INTRODUCTION

The idioms of regulation and emancipation are inextricably linked together. The structural places analysed in Chapter Seven are orthotopias, in that they are hegemonic modes of production of social action, power, law and knowledge, through which social, political and cultural inequality is reproduced and justified. But, as I have already mentioned, and will argue in greater detail in the last chapter, they are also heterotopias or even Utopias, that is to say, sites of revolt, resistance and emancipation. The contradiction between regulation and emancipation – which manifests itself as latent or overt conflicts among concrete social groups – runs through even the most hegemonic constellations of power, legality and knowledge. There is no global or definitive *Aufhebung* (supersession) for this contradiction. As a result, neither regulation nor emancipation will ever be complete or everlasting. There will always be social struggles between regulatory powers, laws and knowledges, on the one hand, and emancipatory powers, laws, and knowledges, on the other.

After having focused on regulation in Chapter Seven, and before focusing on emancipation in the concluding chapter, it makes sense to pause for a close-up view of the intrinsic limits and possibilities of forms of power, law and knowledge as they become idioms of contradiction in regulation/emancipation struggles. In this chapter I will concentrate on forms of law, using them as revolving doors through which different forms of power and knowledge circulate. The type of close-up view I am calling for can only be obtained in the context of concrete struggles as they unfold, mobilizing, inventing, confronting, appropriating or rejecting different forms of legality and illegality. In the analysis that follows I will therefore draw on some of my own previous empirical studies of concrete social processes and legal struggles, some of which were already presented in the preceding chapters. I hope to show how this analysis might apply to the six structural forms of law once the research agenda laid out in Chapter Seven has been carried out in concrete empirical studies.

The idea of space and spatiality is central to the theoretical construction I am presenting in this book. Needless to say, spaces are time-spaces, as spatialities are also temporalities. The focus on space is preferred only because it highlights co-presence and simultaneity as necessary conditions of social struggles, without thereby forgetting that encounters are always relatively asymmetric, inasmuch as simultaneous occurrences are always made of different temporal experiences and expectations. A legal system is a more or less sedimented terrain, a geological construct made of different laws composing different layers, all of them in force together but never in a uniform fashion, all of them in the same moment but always as a momentary convergence of different temporal projections. Koselleck's conception of 'the contemporaneity of the non-contemporaneous', which is derived from Heidegger and Gadamer,[1] may be useful to capture the complexity and unevenness of social, political, legal, or epistemological co-presence. From a sociological perspective, however, the analytical potential of this conception is maximized, once it is made self-reflexive, complex, uneven and open to sociological variation itself. Indeed, although in general all social processes bring together in a given time-space different temporalities and spatialities, some social processes – which we may call performative – emphasize the contemporaneity, that is to say, the uniqueness of the encounter, while others – which we may call self-reflexive – emphasize the non-contemporaneous roots of what is brought together. Social struggles, whether they constellate around power, law or knowledge, tend to be performative, as they actively produce – rather than merely reproducing – the forms of power, law or knowledge that best suit their horizons of expectations. Whatever is brought into conflict (issues, social groups, cognitive maps, normative orderings) is somehow pulled by the roots, so as to become coeval with whatever else is brought together into conflict. The momentary and pragmatic suspension of non-contemporaneity favours the elimination of hierarchies among social temporalities, thereby pre-empting the possibility of one temporality absorbing other competing temporalities.[2] Not all social struggles achieve such pragmatic suspension of non-contemporaneity, and indeed, many of them convert such suspension into the main object of struggle, but it is only through coevalness that social struggles mark their uniqueness and their irreversibility, in sum, their historicity.

The emphasis on spatiality in this chapter and the previous one is, therefore, also a temporal emphasis, an emphasis on coevalness. The identification of multiple sites and idioms of social struggles, constellating around forms of power, forms of law and forms of knowledge, suits my analytical purposes, but it is also adequate to the broader epistemological claims formulated in Chapters One, Two and Three. The recognition of the rhetorical nature of legal knowledge, and the quest for a new rhetoric, a dialogic rhetoric that is self-reflexively aware of its own limits (the unspoken, the unspeakable, silences, silencings) call for coeval and spatialized interpretive communities and rhetorical commonplaces (or *topoi*) through which structural locations become cultural belongings. In Chapter Seven, I conceive of the six structural places as social relations

---

[1]   Koselleck, 1985.
[2]   In a somewhat different sense, see Fabian, 1983.

endowed with specific spatialities, sites of production and reproduction of social agency, and institutions, of power, legality and knowledge; but also as rhetorical places or *topoi*, around which different common senses are built, ideological orthodoxies that, very much like moral codes, define symbolic boundaries and invite commitments from those located inside them.

This multilayered conception of structural places, that is, their multiplicity and mutual articulations, inspired me in Chapter Seven to speak metaphorically of the structure-agency map of capitalist societies in the modern world system. In this chapter, I will try to take this metaphor as seriously as possible, to the point of literalizing it. As I cautioned above, the analysis will focus on forms of law; only latterly will the forms of power and the forms of knowledge be brought into the picture (or rather, into the map). The purpose of my analysis is to show that, since the struggles on regulation/emancipation are never fought in general but rather in specific social sites, involving specific issues and social groups, and drawing on specific instrumental and expressive resources, it is of crucial importance and strategic value to understand the limits and the possibilities of the different contexts of struggle, in this particular case, social struggle centred around law, legality and illegality.

The central argument of this chapter is that laws are literally maps. Maps are ruled distortions of reality, organized misreadings of territories that create credible illusions of correspondence. By imagining the unreality of real illusions we convert illusory correspondences into pragmatic orientation, making true William James's dictum that 'the important thing is to be guided'.[3] Just like maps, laws are ruled distortions or misreadings of social territories. They share this characteristic with poems. According to Harold Bloom's theory of poetic creation – formulated in a book from whose title the title of this chapter was taken[4] – in order to be original, poets (poems) must misread the poetic tradition that comes down to them through the generations and generations of poets (and poems) that preceded them. Poets suffer from the anxiety of influence, and poetry is always the result of the poet's attempt to deny it. Poets overcome the anxiety of influence by misreading (or distorting) poetic reality.

Though for different reasons, maps, poems and laws all distort social realities, traditions or territories, and all according to certain rules. Maps distort reality in order to establish orientation; poems distort reality to establish originality; and laws distort reality in order to establish exclusivity. As far as laws are concerned, for example, irrespective of the plurality of normative orders circulating in society, each one of them, taken separately, aspires to be exclusive, to have the monopoly of regulation and control of social action within its legal territory. This is most patently the case with state laws. In order to operate adequately, a given labour law, for instance, not only must negate the existence of other normative orders or informal laws (such as factory codes, production laws and

---

[3]   James, 1969.
[4]   Bloom, 1973.

so on) that might interfere in its realm of application, but must also revoke all the state labour laws that have previously regulated the same labour relations. This is, as we well know, a double misreading of reality. On the one hand, as I argue in Chapter Seven, other normative orders do operate, and are effective in the same legal territory. On the other hand, since law and society are mutually constitutive, the previous labour laws, once revoked, nevertheless leave their imprint on the labour relations they used to regulate. Though revoked, they remain present in the memories of things and people. Legal revocation is not social eradication.

This misreading of reality is not chaotic. It occurs through determinate and determinable mechanisms and operations. Leaving aside poetic misreading, I intend to show in this chapter the parallels or isomorphisms between the rules and procedures of cartographic misreading and the rules and procedures of legal misreading. In my view, the relations laws entertain with social reality are very similar to those between maps and spatial reality. Indeed, laws are maps; written laws are cartographic maps; customary, informal laws are mental maps. This is a strong metaphor, and as such it will be taken literally, hence the subtitle of this chapter could very well be: 'on taking metaphors literally'. In the following, I will draw extensively on the work of cartographers, and I will try to show to what extent sociology of law may learn from cartography. As Josef Konwitz rightly notes, 'it is a supreme irony that maps, though they are one of the most common cultural metaphors, are still far from occupying the place they deserve in the history of mentalities'.[5] I will deal with the structural features of maps and mapmaking, as well as with the practice of using maps.

2   UNDERSTANDING MAPS

The main structural feature of maps is that, in order to fulfill their function, they inevitably distort reality. Jorge Luis Borges told us the story of the emperor who ordered the production of an exact map of his empire. He insisted that the map should be exact to the most minute detail. The best cartographers of the time were engaged in this important project. Eventually, they produced the map and, indeed, it could not possibly be more exact, as it coincided point by point with the empire. However, to their frustration, it was not a very practical map, since it was of the same size as the empire.[6]

---

[5]   Konwitz, 1980, p 314. On maps as *the* fundamental analogy, see Robinson and Petchnik, 1976, p 2. In epistemological terms, cartography is a very complex science, in that it combines 'features' of the natural and the social sciences. The paradigmatic transition from modern science to postmodern knowledge, mentioned briefly in Chapter One and developed in Santos, 1995, Chapter One, is likely to reverberate a great deal in cartography, a scientific field in which technological progresses have a very direct political and ethical impact. See McHaffie *et al*, 1990; Monmonier, 1991a, 1991b; see also, Harley, 1989, 1990. My use of cartography in this chapter is due to the virtuosity of cartographic analytical tools; but also, more importantly, because cartography is a science in which modern science's epistemological foundationalism and the correspondence theory of truth are bound to be 'naturally' disproved.

[6]   Borges, 1970, p 90.

To be practical, a map cannot coincide point by point with reality. However, the distortion of reality thus produced will not automatically involve inaccuracy, if the mechanisms by which the distortion of reality is accomplished are known and can be controlled. And, indeed, that is always the case. Maps distort reality through three specific mechanisms which, since they are used systematically, become intrinsic or structural attributes of any map. Such mechanisms are: *scale, projection* and *symbolization*. They are autonomous mechanisms that involve different procedures and require separate decisions. But they are also interdependent. As Monmonier puts it:

> '... all advantages and limitations of maps derive from the degree to which maps reduce and generalise reality, compress or expand shapes and distances and portray selected phenomena with signs that communicate without necessarily resembling visible or invisible characteristics of the landscapes. The three elements of a map are interdependent. Scale influences the amount of detail that can be shown and determines whether or not a particular kind of symbol will be visually effective'.[7]

Maps should be convenient to use, but there is a permanent tension in maps between representation and orientation. These are contradictory claims between which maps are always unstable compromises. Too much representation may hinder orientation, as we saw in Borges's map. Inversely, a very accurate orientation may result from a rather poor and elementary representation of reality. When we are invited to a party in a house whose location we do not know, the host will probably draw a map which will be very effective in orienting us, though very inaccurate in representing the features of the environment along the way to our destination. Another example might be seen in the medieval *portolans*, the maps of ports and coasts well known in the Middle Ages which, though very poor as far as representation of the globe goes, were very effective in orienting navigators at sea.[8] There are maps that solve the tension between representation and orientation in favour of representation. These I would call, borrowing from French cartography, *image maps*. Other maps solve the tension in favour of orientation. These are *instrumental maps*.[9]

Since I would like to suggest that this dialectic of representation and orientation applies to law as much as it applies to maps, and consequently that, in the analysis of 'law in society', we should substitute the complex paradigm of scale/projection/symbolization

---

[7] Monmonier, 1981, p 1. On limits of maps, see also Monmonier, 1993 and MacEachren, 1994.

[8] See Hodgkiss, 1981, p 103. In the sixteenth century, Mercator, the famous Flemish geographer who developed the type of map projections that now bears his name, wrote the following instruction on his famous chart of 1569: 'If you wish to sail from one port to another, here is a chart, and a straight line on it, and if you follow carefully this line you will certainly arrive at your port of destination. But the length of the line may not be correct. You may get there sooner or you may not get there as soon as you expected, but you will certainly get there.' Quoted in Jervis, 1936, p 27. On the history of maps, see, among others, MJ Blakemore and JB Harley, 1980.

[9] See Wahl, 1980, p 42.

for the simple paradigm of correspondence/non-correspondence (law in books/law in action), I will now proceed to analyze in more detail each one of the procedures through which maps distort reality.

The first procedure is *scale*. Scale, as Monmonier has defined it, 'is the ratio of distance on the map to the corresponding distance on the ground'.[10] Scale involves, then, a decision on more or less detail. 'Since large-scale maps represent less land on a given size sheet of paper than do small-scale maps, large-scale maps can present more detail'.[11] Since maps are 'a miniaturised version' of reality,[12] mapmaking involves the filtering of details, 'the selection of both meaningful details and relevant features'.[13] As Muehrcke puts it, 'what makes a map so useful is its genius of omission. It is reality uncluttered, pared down to its essence, stripped of all but the essentials'.[14] One easily understands that the decision on scale conditions the decision on the use of the map, and vice versa: 'Small-scale maps are not intended to permit accurate measurements of the width of roads, streams, etc, but rather to show with reasonable accuracy the relative positions of these and other features'.[15]

Geography, which shares with cartography the concern for spaces and spatial relations, has also contributed important insights on scales, both scales of analysis and scales of action. As to the former, there are phenomena that can only be represented on a small scale, such as climate, while others, like erosion, for instance, can only be represented on a large scale.[16] This means that the differences in scale are not simply quantitative but also qualitative. A given phenomenon can only be represented on a given scale. To change the scale implies a change of the phenomenon. Each scale reveals a phenomenon and distorts or hides others. As in nuclear physics, the scale creates the phenomenon. Some of the fallacious correlations in geography derive from the superimposition of phenomena created and analyzed on different scales. The scale is 'a coherent forgetting' that must be carried out coherently.[17] Mediating between intention and action, scale applies also to social action. Urban planners as well as military chiefs, administrators, business executives, legislators, judges and lawyers define strategies on a small scale and decide day-to-day tactics on a large scale. Power represents social and physical reality on a scale chosen for its capacity to create phenomena that

---

[10]   Monmonier, 1981, p 4.
[11]   Monmonier, 1981. In non-technical discourses, large scale and small scale are usually understood in ways opposite to the technical meaning, eg when we designate as large-scale an analysis covering a large, wide-ranging object, however, not in great detail. Elsewhere in the book I use large scale/small scale in this more conventional meaning. In this chapter I will follow the technical meaning.
[12]   Keates, 1982, p 73.
[13]   Monmonier, 1981, p 4.
[14]   Muehrcke, 1986, p 10.
[15]   Monmonier, 1981, p 4.
[16]   See Lacoste, 1976, p 61; 1980, p 17.
[17]   See Racine, 1982, p 126.

maximize the conditions for the reproduction of power. The distortion and concealment of reality is thus a presupposition of the exercise of power (more on this below).

The second mechanism of representation/distortion of reality is *projection*. To be useful, maps must be easily carried about and stored away. Flat maps can be rolled and folded. It is by means of projection that the curved surfaces of the earth are transformed into planes. The most convenient transformation cannot yield flat maps without distorting shapes and distance relationships. I will not elaborate on the specifics of projection, different types of projection and the distribution and degrees of distortion characteristic of each of them.[18] I will only make a few general remarks that are relevant to my argument. The first remark is that, as we might expect in light of the preceding, projections do not distort reality at random. Each type of projection creates a field of representation within which forms and degrees of distortion are unequally but determinably distributed. For instance, some projections distort the equatorial regions more than the polar regions, while others do the opposite. Moreover, the different projections distort the different features of the space differently. Some projections – called conformal projections – preserve areas but distort angles and shapes and directions, while other projections – called equivalent projections – do the inverse. We cannot get the same degree of accuracy in the representation of all the different features, and whatever we do to increase the accuracy in the representation of one given feature will increase the distortion in the representation of some other feature. It is very much like the Uncertainty Principle of Heisenberg in quantum physics, according to which we cannot measure the velocity and the position of the particles simultaneously and with the same degree of precision, and whatever we do to increase accuracy in determining the position will distort the measurement of velocity. Every map projection is thus a compromise. The decision on which kind of distortion to prefer is conditioned by precise technical factors, but it is also based on the ideology of the cartographer and on the specific use intended for the map. For instance, during the Cold War, the Western mass media used to show the Soviet Union on a world map designed according to the cylindrical projection of Mercator. Since this kind of projection exaggerates the areas in high and median latitudes to the detriment of those in intertropical latitudes, such a map would inflate the size of the Soviet Union, thus dramatizing the extent of the Communist threat.[19]

The second remark on projection is that each map, each historical period or each cultural tradition of mapmaking has a centre, a fixed point, a physical or symbolic space in a privileged position, around which the diversity, the direction and the meaning of other spaces are organized. For instance, medieval maps used to put a religious site at the centre

---

[18]   See, among others, Monmonier, 1981, p 15; Keates, 1982, p 72; Muehrcke, 1986, p 456; Muracciole, 1980, p 235; Hodgkiss, 1981, p 32.

[19]   On the use of maps for propaganda purposes, see Monmonier, 1981, p 43; Hodgkiss, 1981, p 15; Muehrcke, 1986, p 395; Riviere, 1980, p 351; Speier, 1941, p 310; Quam, 1943, p 21; Boggs, 1947, p 469; Sharkey, 1984, p 148.

– Jerusalem in European maps, Mecca in Arab maps.[20] The same happens with mental maps, that is, with the cognitive visual images we have of the world around us. As Muehrcke puts it, 'most of our mental maps would emphasize our own neighbourhood, with its environments assuming less significance'.[21]

Symbolization is the third mechanism of map representation/distortion of reality. It refers to the representation of selected features and details of reality in graphic symbols. Without signs the map will be as unusable as Borges's map. Such is the case of the captain's map in Lewis Carroll's *Hunting of the Snark:*[22]

> '...one could see he was wise
> The moment one looked in his face!
>
> He had brought a large map representing the sea,
> Without the least vestige of land:
> And the crew were much pleased when they found it to be
> A map they could all understand.
>
> "What's the good of Mercator's, North Poles, and Equators,
> Tropics, Zones and Meridian lines?"
> So the Bellman would cry; and the crew would reply,
> "They are merely conventional signs!"
>
> "Other maps are such shapes with their islands and capes!
> But we've got our brave captain to thank".
> (So the crew would protest) "that he's brought us the best,
> A perfect and absolute blank!"'[23]

Cartographic language is a fascinating theme, and semiotics has provided its research with new analytical tools. The sign systems have evolved over time, and still today different systems may be chosen according to the specific cultural context of mapmaking or according to the purposes of the maps. In a study on this topic, JS Keates, drawing

---

[20] See Hodgkiss, 1981, p 29. For a slightly different view, showing the way the map centre changed as the Middle Ages developed, see Woodward, 1985, p 510. Henrikson, 1980, p 73, shows how the progressive shift of the US from the periphery to the centre of world affairs – a shift completed with World War II – resulted in changes in the types of map projections adopted or favoured: 'The relationship of the United States to the major theatres of battle was such that a new picture of the world – a new global strategic map – was needed. Cylindrical map projections, such as the conventional Equator-based Mercator, failed to show the continuity, unity, and organisation of the 'world wide arena' as Roosevelt called it. Hence, other map projections came into fashion, notably the North Pole-centered azimuthal projection.... The position of the United States on these polar maps was usually a central one.' (p 83). See also, Henrikson, 1975, p 19. On propaganda and cartography, see Burnett, 1985. See also Reitan, 1986.

[21] Muehrcke, 1986, p 6.

[22] Carroll, 1976, p 757.

[23] Carroll, 1976, pp 760–61.

from semiotics, distinguishes between *iconic signs* and *conventional signs*.[24] Iconic signs are naturalistic signs that establish a relation of likeness with the reality represented (for instance, a bunch of trees to designate a forest), while conventional signs are far more arbitrary: 'Convention holds that certain types of symbols are appropriate for certain types of phenomena; for instance, linear symbols for roads and boundaries and graduated circles for cities and towns'.[25] If we look at the historical record we will see that the sign systems used in maps were initially more naturalistic, and gradually became more conventional.[26] But even today, depending on many circumstances, maps may be more figurative or more abstract; they may rely on emotive/expressive signs or on referential/cognitive signs; they may be more readable or more visible.[27]

This digression on maps and on cartographic imagination will make it possible to compare, in the following section, cartographic imagination with legal imagination.[28] There are, in fact, striking similarities between laws and maps – both concerning their structural features and their use patterns. Obviously, laws are maps only in the metaphorical sense. But, as rhetoric also teaches us, the repeated use of a metaphor over a long period of time may gradually transform the metaphorical description into a literal description.[29] Today, laws are maps in a metaphorical sense. Tomorrow they may be maps in a literal sense.

3 A SYMBOLIC CARTOGRAPHY OF LAW

I will now present the outline of what I would call a symbolic cartography of law. As I indicated above, my examples will be drawn from my own empirical research conducted in Portugal, Brazil and the Cape Verde Islands. The research in Portugal deals with the contradictions between democratic legality and revolutionary legality during the revolutionary crisis of 1974 to 1975, in the aftermath of the fall of the dictatorial regime that ruled the country for almost fifty years.[30] The research conducted in Brazil deals with the social and legal battles of squatter settlers in the northeastern city of Recife, against the state and private landowners, to obtain a legal title over the land they had invaded, and upon which they had built their shacks and organized their urban lives.[31] The research in the Cape Verde Islands, conducted in 1984 and 1985, is concerned with the popular courts that have been created by the state since independence from

---

24   Keates, 1982, p 66.
25   Monmonier, 1981, p 6.
26   See Caron, 1980, p 9.
27   See Keates, 1982, p 69.
28   Geertz, 1983, p 232, refers to law as a way of imagining the real.
29   See Perelman, 1951, p 405.
30   Santos, 1982a, p 251; Santos, 1985, p 45; Santos, 1979, p 151.
31   For a detailed presentation of this study, see Santos, 1995, Chapter Five.

Portuguese colonialism in 1975. These are non-professional courts organized on a residential basis and with jurisdiction over small civil disputes and petty crimes.[32]

3.1 *Law and scale*

One of the main reasons for recommending the symbolic cartography of law is its ability to analyze the effect of scale on the structure and use of law. I argued in Chapter Two that the modern state is based on the assumption that law operates on a single scale, the scale of the state. In Chapters Three through Seven, I presented, as an alternative conception, a complex and internally diversified legal landscape, consisting of a plurality of legal orders including, besides national or state law, local or infrastate as well as global or suprastate laws. Within this conception, we can therefore distinguish three major legal spaces: local, national and global legality.[33] My suggestion is that the analysis of these spaces in terms of scales of legal regulation will illuminate some black holes in the sociology of legal pluralism, particularly the existence of internal asymmetries in constellations of legalities whenever the different, competing, legal forms purport to regulate the same, or seemingly the same social process or action.

Let us assume that local law is a *large-scale legality*, nation-state law, a *medium-scale legality* and global law, a *small-scale legality*. This means, first of all, that since scale creates the phenomenon, the different forms of law create different legal objects upon the same social objects. In other words, laws use different criteria to determine the meaningful details and the relevant features of the activity to be regulated, that is to say, they establish different networks of facts. In sum, different forms of law create different legal realities.

This may be illustrated with the analysis of a given labour conflict in a factory producing for a TNC through franchising or sub-contracting. The factory code, that is, the production law of the workplace, as a form of local legality, regulates the relations in production in great detail, in order to maintain workplace discipline, to prevent labour conflicts, to reduce their scope whenever they occur and eventually to settle them. The labour conflict is the nuclear object of the factory code, because it confirms, *a contrario*, the continuity of the relations in production, which are the *raison d'etre* of the factory code. In the wider context of national state labour law, the labour conflict is only a dimension, however important, of industrial relations. It is part of a broader network of social, political and economic facts in which we easily identify, among others, political stability, inflation rate, income policy and relations of power among labour unions, business and government. In the even wider context of the global legality of international

---

[32] Santos, 1984.

[33] In Chapter Three, I designate the spaces of legality as time-spaces to emphasize the fact that different spatialities are also different temporalities. In this chapter I am primarily concerned with the spatial dimension.

franchising or sub-contracting, the labour conflict becomes a minute detail in international economic relations, hardly worth mentioning. Thus, the different legal orders operating on different scales translate the same social objects into different legal objects.

However, since in real socio-legal life, the different legal scales do not exist in isolation but rather interact in different ways – in our example the regulatory purposes of the three legal scales converge in the same social event – there may be the illusion that the three legal objects can be superimposed point by point. In fact, they do not coincide; neither do their 'root images' of law and the social and legal struggles they legitimate coincide. Workers and sometimes the employer tend to have a large-scale view of the conflict, with all its details and relevant features, a concept moulded by local legality. Union leaders and sometimes the employer tend to see the conflict as a crisis in a process of continuous industrial relations. Their view is predominantly moulded by national state legality; consequently, their actions in the conflict aim at a compromise between the medium-scale and the large-scale view of the conflict. For the multinational corporation, the labour conflict is a tiny accident in a globally designed investment and production system; if not promptly overcome, it can be easily circumvented by moving the production to another country.

To analyze such discrepancies and unevenness exclusively in terms of conflicting interests or degrees of class consciousness is to ignore the fact that law creates the reality that fits its application. Such a creation is, among other things, a technique that operates according to certain rules, one of them being the rule of the scale. That is why we can really compare or contrast only social interests and degrees of class consciousness within the same legal space. The difficulty lies in the fact that socio-legal life is constituted by different legal spaces operating simultaneously on different scales and from different interpretive standpoints. To that extent, in terms of socio-legal practice, and as a result of interaction and intersection among legal spaces, one cannot properly speak of law and legality, but rather, of interlaw and interlegality. More important than the identification of the different legal orders is tracing the complex and changing relations among them. But if while doing this we forget the question of scale, we may find ourselves in the same distressing situation as a tourist who forgot to pack the voltage transformer that would enable him to use his electric razor in a foreign country.

While doing my research on popular justice in the Cape Verde Islands, I was confronted with an intriguing fact. The philosophy underlying the organization of popular justice entailed integrating local customary laws as much as possible. This integration was facilitated by the fact that the judges were laypeople, members of the local communities; the written laws governing the procedures and decisions of the courts were few and vague, and very often unknown to or disregarded by the judges. However, both the state and the ruling party (the PAICV) took great care in selecting the judges, and tended to favour young or middle-aged males considered politically reliable, a fact that was sometimes a source of tension in the local communities, for whom the exercise of justice was in general associated with old wise folks. It would seem that, while the state felt unable to control the creation of law and sought to compensate for that by tightening the control of the application of law, the local communities paid no attention whatsoever to the creation of law, and sought to keep control of its application – which for them, in fact, was nothing but its creation. On further reflection, this was a case of interlegality – a case of a complex relation between the customary law and the state law, using different scales. For the local communities, the customary law was the local law, a large-scale legality well adapted to prevent and settle local disputes. For the state, the customary law was part of a broader network of social facts that included the consolidation of the newly independent state, the unity of the state legal order, political socialization, and so on. On this smaller scale, the customary law became part of state law, and the latter became an instrument, though a specific one, of political action.[34]

The first implication of a scale conception of law is that it draws our attention to the phenomenon of interlegality and the complex mechanics of its operation. The second implication has to do with what I call *regulation patterns* and *action packages* that are associated with each scale of legality. I will start by illustrating different *regulation patterns*, which have basically to do with the dialectical tension between representation and orientation. Representation and orientation are two antagonistic modes of imagining and constituting reality, one geared to identify position, the other geared to identify movement. Large-scale legality is rich in details and features; describes behaviour and attitudes vividly; contextualizes them in their immediate surroundings; is sensitive to distinctions (and complex relations) between inside and outside, high and low, just and unjust. This applies to any social object of legal regulation, be it labour conflicts, family relations, contractual terms, crimes or political rights. What I mean is that this form of legality favours a pattern of regulation based on (and geared to) representation and position. On the contrary, small-scale legality is poor in details and features. It captures only the skeletons of behaviours and attitudes, and reduces them to general types of action. But, on the other hand, it determines with accuracy the relativity of positions – the angles between people and between people and things – provides sense of direction and schemes for shortcuts and, finally, is sensitive to distinctions (and complex relations) between part and whole, past and present, functional and non-functional. In sum, this form of legality favours a pattern of regulation based on (and geared to) orientation and movement.

When I studied the informal law of the squatter settlements in Rio (see Chapter Four), I had occasion to observe how adequately such local legality represented the socio-legal reality of urban marginality, and how it contributed to maintaining the status quo of the squatters' social positions as precarious inhabitants of shacks and houses built upon invaded land. When later on I studied the legal battles of squatter settlers in Recife that aimed at securing land tenure or, at least, a legal lease, the form of law resorted to was primarily the state law, a smaller-scale law that represented the socio-legal position of the squatter settlers very roughly but, on the other hand, a law that very clearly defined

---

[34]   See Santos, 1984, p 33.

the relativity of their positions, the angles of their relations vis-à-vis the landowners and the state, and, lastly, a law that was the shortest path to move from a precarious to a secure position under the social and political circumstances of the time.[35]

Besides having different regulation patterns, different scales of legality also condition different *action packages*. An action package is a connected sequence of actions structurally determined by pre-defined boundaries. I identify two kinds of boundaries: those defined by range and those defined by ethics. According to range, we can distinguish two ideal types of action packages: the *tactical* and the *strategic action package*. According to ethics, we can also distinguish two ideal types of action packages: the *edifying* and the *instrumental action package*. In the light of the previous examples, I would suggest that large-scale legality invites tactical and edifying action packages, while small-scale legality invites strategic and instrumental action packages. Social groups or classes that are predominantly socialized in one of these forms of legality tend to be specifically competent in the type of action package associated with it. In a situation of interlegality, that is, in a situation in which large-scale legality and small-scale legality intersect, the large-scale action package tends to be defensive and to regulate normal, routine interaction or, at the most, molecular struggles, while the small-scale action package tends to be aggressive and to regulate critical, exceptional situations, triggered by molar struggles.[36] These tendencies may hold true irrespective of the class nature of the social groups involved in the specific action package.

The third and last implication of the scale analysis of law is the least developed, but potentially very important. It refers to what I would call *regulation thresholds*. Irrespective of the social object it regulates and the purpose of regulation, each scale of legality has a specific regulation threshold which determines what belongs to its realm of law and what does not. This threshold is the product of the combined operation of the three thresholds: the detection threshold, the discrimination threshold and the evaluation threshold. The *detection threshold* refers to the smallest details of the social object that will be considered for regulation; it distinguishes between relevant and irrelevant issues. The *discrimination threshold* refers to the minimum detectable differences in the description of the social object that may justify qualitative differences in regulation; it distinguishes between the same – that which deserves equal treatment – and the different – that which deserves unequal treatment. Finally, the *evaluation threshold* refers to the minimum detectable differences in the ethical quality of the social object; it distinguishes between the legal and the illegal.

During the revolutionary crisis in Portugal in 1974 to 1975, a rural worker was indicted for the murder of a big landowner. In his defence, the worker invoked provocation and

---

[35]   Nevertheless, it should be pointed out that, whenever they felt the need to represent their life experiences, and in defining their positions, the squatter settlers relied on local legality, that is to say, on the internal normative orderings of social interaction in the squatter settlements.

[36]   For the distinction between molar and molecular struggles, see Miller, 1972, p 59.

a long list of arbitrary and violent actions perpetrated by the *latifundiário* (a large land owner) against the rural workers during the many years in which the Salazar dictatorship allowed him to rule the community despotically. From the point of view of 'democratic legality' – as the sum total of state laws in force throughout the revolution was called by rightist, centrist and social democratic parties – the two sets of action – that of the rural worker and that of the landowner – were very different, both in structural and ethical terms. From the point of view of revolutionary legality, championed by leftist parties, and in light of its lower discrimination and evaluation thresholds, the two sets of actions were similar, in that they were both illegal. While for democratic legality, the rural worker, irrespective of past grievances, had committed an unpardonable murder, for revolutionary legality, the murder, though not a legitimate revolutionary act, could, as a reaction against the landowner's past arbitrariness, be justified, and accordingly, pardoned.[37]

The three thresholds vary according to the scale of the legal form, but the same scale of law may allow for internal differences in its regulation threshold. It may, for instance, have a high detection threshold but a low evaluation threshold, or vice versa, and the discrepancies may also occur across legal realms – for instance, state labour law may have a higher regulation threshold than criminal or social welfare law. Moreover, the regulation threshold is not a fixed entity. It may move up and down within certain limits. But its movement is always the result of the combined movements of the different thresholds that constitute it. In the current social and political context, calling for the deregulation of the economy and social interaction, the regulation threshold of state legality moves up as a result of higher detection and discrimination thresholds. But since, in practice, socio-legal practice always involves interlegality, the deregulation within state legality may be counteracted or compensated for by the increase of regulation within other forms of legality.

3.2 Law and projection

Legal orders can also be distinguished by the type of projection they use. Projection is the procedure by which the legal order defines the limits of its operation, and organizes the legal space inside them. Like scale, and for the same reasons, projection is not a neutral procedure. Different types of projections create different legal objects upon the same social objects. Each legal object favours a specific formulation of interests and a specific concept of disputes and of modes of settling them.

Each legal order stands on a grounding fact, a *superfact* or a *supermetaphor*, as I would call it, which determines the specific interpretive standpoint or perspective that characterizes the adopted type of projection. The private economic relations in the market are the superfact underlying capitalist state legality, while land and housing, conceived as extra-economic, social and political relations, are the superfact underlying the law of Pasargada. According to the type of projection adopted, each legal order has a *centre*

---

[37]   See Santos, 1982a, p 272.

and a *periphery*. This means, first of all, that, as in the case of money capital, the legal capital of a given legal order is not equally distributed across the latter's legal space. The central regions are those in which the legal capital is more concentrated and owns greater returns. Here the space is mapped in greater detail, and absorbs greater inputs of institutional resources – legal professions, courts and so on – and symbolic resources – legal science, legal ideology and culture and so on. Conversely, the peripheral regions are those with less legal capital and lower returns. Here the legal space is only roughly and scarcely mapped, and absorbs meagre institutional resources – inaccessible justice, understaffed courts, underfunded legal aid, third-class lawyers – and symbolic resources – less prestigious legal practice, less sophisticated legal theorizing, less quoted legal precedents.

The second implication is that theories, ideological configurations and interpretive styles and techniques that are dominant at the centre, tend to be taken out of the context in which they originate and to be exported to (and imposed upon) the periphery. They are then applied in the legal periphery with little attention to local regulatory needs, since such needs are always interpreted and satisfied from the point of view of the centre. It is very much a symbolic transfer of technology. Sticking to my examples, it is clear that the centre of capitalist state legality is occupied by contracts, as witness the codification movement and, particularly, the Napoleonic Code. Contracts – their types, concepts, theories, interpretations, general principles – have been the centre of modern legislation, legal training and legal ideology. Moreover, the contractual perspective has been exported to other legal fields, be they constitutional, administrative or even criminal law. In spite of an alleged return from contract to status in late capitalism, contracts remain the privileged archaeological site and, indeed, the ground metaphor of modern state law. The emergence, in recent years, of neo-contractualism in political philosophy and constitutional law is a good illustration. Similarly, in Pasargada law, land and house transactions and the disputes they originate occupy the centre of the legal space. As we saw in Chapter Four, whenever the Residents' Association ventures into criminal, public order or family matters, it always seeks a connection with land and housing matters, and applies to the former the popular legal technology and legal competence gained in the latter. The center/periphery effect of projection shows that the legal mapping of social reality is not equally distorting. It seems to become more distorting as we move from the centre to the periphery. The periphery is also the legal region where the interpenetration between different legal orders is most frequent. It creates a twilight zone where the shadows of different legal orders converge.

The second effect of projection refers to the type of features of the social object that tend to be privileged no matter how central or how peripheral the social object. According to this effect, two general types of projection can be distinguished: the egocentric and the geocentric.[38] The *egocentric projection* favours the representation of personal and particularistic features, voluntary or consensual social action. The *geocentric projection*

---

[38]   This distinction is also used, in a slightly different sense, in the analysis of cognitive mapping (egocentric and geocentric mental maps). See Muehrcke, 1986, p 4.

favours the representation of objective and generalizable features, patterned, bounded or conflictual social action. According to the dominant type of projection, two general forms of law can be distinguished: the *egocentric legality* and the *geocentric legality*.

In light of these categories, it is illuminating to analyse some recent trends in legal change, as well as some long-range developments in legal history as described by Max Weber. While analyzing, in *Economy and Society*, the forms of creation of rights, Weber drew our attention to the long and sinuous historical process by which geocentric legality gradually substituted for egocentric legality. In the past, Weber said, law arose as 'volitive' and as 'particularistic' law, based on the agreed enactment of consensual status groups. There were different legal communities, constituted in their membership by personal characteristics such as birth, political, ethnic or religious denomination, mode of life or occupation, and so on. Individuals or groups of individuals had their own personal legal quality, and carried their law, their *professio juris* (legal quality or status), with them wherever they went.[39] The *jus civile* in Rome was the personal law of Roman citizens, and the *jus gentium* was created to cater for the legal needs of non-citizens. The idea of a law of the land developed only very gradually – the *lex terrae*, which was applicable to everyone regardless of personal characteristics, and imposed as a heteronomous law, that is, a law that cannot be claimed as someone's law and is rather generally valid within the boundaries of a given territory. In the development of a geocentric form of law, the extension of the market economy and the bureaucratization of consensual groups played a decisive role: 'The ever-increasing integration of all individual and all fact situations into one compulsory institution which today, at least, rests in principle on formal "legal equality" reached its climax in the French Revolution, after which the state appears as the all-embracing coercive institution'.[40] Max Weber was aware that in modern society there are also volitive and particularistic laws but, unlike those in pre-modern times, they are based on economic or technical grounds, are never defined in terms of personal group membership, and are effective within the boundaries set by the national general law.[41]

In my view, this historical interplay between geocentric and egocentric legality cannot be definitely decided in favour of geocentric legality. Some recent trends in legal development seem to witness the emergence of new legal particularisms, that is to say, forms of egocentric legality that, by creating personal legal 'enclosures', empty or neutralize the conditions for the application of the law of the land. To illustrate this, I resort to the new *lex mercatoria* analyzed in Chapter Five. I mean the new international commercial contracts, as well as a proliferation of charters, codes of ethics, codes of conduct or fair practices, which cover the activities of multinational corporations, and international economic and professional associations, in fields so diverse as transfers of technology, stock markets, advertising, sales promotion, market studies, insurance, technical assistance, turnkey contracts and so on. All these new forms of global legality

---

[39]   Weber, 1978, p 695.
[40]   Weber, 1978, pp 698, 724.
[41]   Weber, 1978, p 697.

create a global legal space that often conflicts with the national state legal space.[42] Such conflicts take several forms: the conception of liability in the new contracts is autonomous vis-à-vis national laws; the contracts introduce vague clauses on applicable law such as the general principles of law, the usages of commercial life, the only purpose being to eliminate or evade the application of state law; the arbitration system is often resorted to with the same purpose; commercial partners enter gentlemen's agreements or protocols that openly violate national laws (particularly those on fair competition); the national legislation enacted to police the contracts of transfer of technology has little efficacy; powerful multinational corporations impose their laws on the states. The violation of national state law is so widespread that a proposed code of ethics for multinational corporations included the astonishing clause that 'the multinational corporation will respect the laws of the state where it operates'.[43]

All these latent or manifest conflicts are symptoms of a tension between the geocentric legality of the nation-state and the new egocentric legality of international private economic agents. Indeed, as already suggested in Chapter Five, we are witnessing the emergence of a new particularism that echoes the personalist laws of the ancient and medieval world described by Weber. Like the old status groups, each transnational corporation or international economic association has its own personal legal quality, and carries its law wherever it goes. The new personalism derives also from the fact that this legality is closely tailored to the interests of the most powerful companies or banks. Goldman found that many 'standard contracts' were created by a single corporation powerful enough to impose them on its partners.[44] This explains why a new economic practice by a powerful corporation may become an instant custom. This new form of status privileges (corporation privileges) can also be found in the codes of international professional associations (for example, the International Franchising Association), because in general, as Farjat notes, there is a coincidence between the powerful economic agents and the professional authorities that write the codes.[45]

To conceive of the tension between nation-state law and the new global legality as deriving from two forms of law, anchored in two different types of projection of social reality, prevents us from falling into a reductionist view – be it economistic or otherwise – of the conflicts they express. To be sure, there are conflicting interests and power relations, but they are played out through the intermediation of specific projective devices with their hermeneutic logic. The legal forms thus ensuing have an autonomy of their own, and an efficacy that extends beyond the stakes of the conflicting interests or power positions. For instance, attention to types of projection shows the relativity of the distinction between law and fact. Clifford Geertz has reminded us of such relativity

[42] For an analysis of conflicts between the new global legal space and the national legal space, see, among others, Kahn, 1982; Farjat, 1982; Wallace, 1982; Marques, 1987. More recently, see the articles included in Teubner (ed), 1997.
[43] See Farjat, 1982, p 65.
[44] See Goldman, 1964, p 180.
[45] See Farjat, 1982, p 57.

when different legal cultures are compared.[46] But even within the same general culture, the distinction between law and fact seems to be largely an effect of projection. Because of its emphasis on objective and generalizable features of reality, geocentric law tends to polarize law and fact, and to be stronger on norms than on facts. Overridden by the fear of fact, it reacts by sterilizing or by reducing it to its skeleton. As Geertz has put it, facts became 'close edited diagrams of reality'.[47] In Pospisil's terms, it results in 'a justice of law'.[48] On the contrary, egocentric law tends to soften the distinction between law and fact, and to be stronger on facts than on norms. It allows for the explosion of facts, as the case of instant customs mentioned above well documents. It results in a 'justice of fact'.

3.3   Law and symbolization

Symbolization is the visible side of the cartographic and legal imagination of reality. It is the most complex procedure, because it operates on the basis of, and conditioned by, scale and projection. Rhetoric, semiotics and cultural anthropology have contributed important insights into the complexities of the legal symbolization of reality. From the synthetic perspective in which these contributions merge with that of literary criticism, I shall distinguish two contrasting, ideal-typical modes of legal Symbolization: *the Homeric style of law* and *the biblical style of law*. These metaphorical designations refer to two polar ideal-types, which concrete legal orders approximate in different degrees. The designations are borrowed from Auerbach, in his classical account of the different forms of representation of reality in Western literature.[49]

Auerbach identifies two basic types of literary representation of reality in European culture. He exemplifies the opposition between these two types by contrasting the *Odyssey* of Homer with the Bible. The *Odyssey* describes the tragic and sublime nature of heroic life: a fully externalized description, uniform illumination, uninterrupted connection, all events in the foreground, displaying unmistakable meanings, and few elements of historical development and of psychological perspective. On the contrary, the Bible represents the sublime and the tragic in the context of commonplace and everyday life, a description attentive to the multi-layeredness of the human predicament – in which certain parts are brought into high relief, others left obscure – and to the multiplicity of meanings, the need for interpretation and the development of the concept of historical becoming.

I would like to suggest that this basic contrast in the literary representation of reality may also be found in the legal representation of reality. Accordingly, I identify two ideal-typical sign systems by means of which law symbolizes reality. I shall speak of a

[46]   Geertz, 1983, p 167.
[47]   Geertz, 1983, p 173.
[48]   Pospisil, 1971, p 23.
[49]   Auerbach, 1968, p 23.

Homeric style of law when the legal symbolization of reality has the following characteristics: the conversion of the everyday continuous flux of reality into a succession of disparate solemn moments (contracts, legal disputes and so on), described in abstract and formal terms through conventional cognitive and referential signs. This style of symbolization invites an instrumental mode of operation (instrumental legality). In contrast, what I call the biblical style of law invites an expressive mode of operation (image-based legality) characterized by a preoccupation with inscribing the discontinuities of legal interaction into the multilayered contexts in which they occur, and with describing them in figurative and informal terms through iconic, emotive and expressive signs. The biblical style of law is probably older than the Homeric, but in each historical period, no matter which one dominates, there is a tension between the two. For instance, the modern state legal order is predominantly a Homeric style of law, but the biblical style of law shows its vitality in many ways. Going back to the example of the particularistic law created by the new global legal subjects, it is apparent that this emerging global legality tends to be formulated in a biblical style of law. Some specialists have called attention to the moralistic rhetoric in the use of non-cognitive, emotive and expressive signs in codes of ethics and standard contracts drawn by them, as illustrated in the recurrent use of expressions like concertation, common interest, reciprocal trust, trustworthiness, co-operation, assistance and so on.[50]

But the contrast between the two types of legal symbolization is most visible in those situations of legal pluralism in which social practice is a constant bridging between legal orders with different styles of symbolization. All of my case studies mentioned above involve situations of this type. In the case of popular justice in the Cape Verde Islands there is an attempt at a fusion between local customary law and nation-state law. The tensions between the two contrasting sign systems manifest themselves in the way judges settle the disputes. While some – generally older – judges adopt a local, image-based view of law, describing law and fact without much distinction, in figurative and informal terms, resorting to verbal and gestures and signs of the iconic, expressive and emotive type, other – and generally younger – judges seek to impersonate the professional judge or even the political *cadre*, hence adopting an instrumental view of law that distinguishes law from fact, and describes both in abstract and formal terms by means of verbal and gestures and signs of the conventional, cognitive and referential type. But the same judge may, in different situations, adopt different styles of law. Nha Bia, for instance, a remarkable woman judge presiding over the popular court of Lem Cachorro in the outskirts of the capital city of Praia (Santiago Island), adopts a biblical style of law in those cases she is most familiar with, and when she feels more autonomous to deliver justice 'in her own way'. These are, for example, the water disputes involving women – disputes usually occurring in water lines over the order of the women in the line to fill the water cans at the public fountains, or over the water supply to be used daily. Since droughts often last for several years, this is a very common type of dispute. On the other hand, Nha Bia tends to adopt a Homeric style of law whenever the dispute is less common,

---

[50]   See, for instance, Farjat, 1982, p 65.

or in cases in which her legal competence or jurisdiction may be challenged, such as those with political overtones or involving powerful members of the community.[51]

In the case of the social struggles in Recife, both the urban poor, and the Catholic Church on their behalf, seek a momentary and unstable complementary relation between the unofficial law of the squatter settlements and the state official law. The social construction of reality in the two legal orders follows different sign systems, the biblical and the Homeric style respectively. Community leaders and lawyers hired by the church to represent the squatter settlers often find themselves in the position of having to translate one sign system into the other before the relevant audience of the moment – whether the audience is the people from the community, the state court or the state administrative agency for housing affairs. It may also occur that the two sign systems interpenetrate or superimpose, as when large groups of squatter settlers, attending the trial of one of the land disputes in the state court, start shouting slogans and singing religious songs.[52]

In the case of popular justice during the revolutionary crisis in Portugal, there is neither an attempt to fusion nor an effort to turn the two forms of law – in this case, between democratic legality and revolutionary legality – into mutual complements. Rather, there is an open contradiction between those two forms of law. Democratic legality tries to insulate the legal representation of reality from the everyday experience of a revolutionary crisis, and for that purpose it stresses the distinction between law and fact, and resorts to a formal and abstract description of reality in which the sign system characteristic of a Homeric style of law dominates. On the contrary, revolutionary legality tries to integrate and even dissolve the legal representation into the social and political context in which it occurs, and for that purpose it softens the distinction between law and fact, thus allowing for the explosion of facts as a mechanism of law creation, and privileges a figurative and informal description of reality.[53] In sum, it is a biblical style of law.

4   SYMBOLIC CARTOGRAPHY AND OPPOSITIONAL POSTMODERN LAW

Chaim Perelman wrote, in his treatise on the new rhetoric, that while classical thought favoured spatial metaphors, modern thought has favoured temporal ones.[54] It seems to me that postmodern thought will return to spatial metaphors, even though inspired by new spaces and spatialities, and aware of the fact that spatialities express the measure of coevalness among temporal differences.[55] In light of the analysis in the preceding chapters, the theory of symbolic cartography of law sketched in this chapter may be

---

[51]   See Santos, 1984, p 105.
[52]   See Santos, 1995, Chapter Five.
[53]   See Santos, 1982a, p 254.
[54]   Perelman, 1951, p 390.
[55]   It is not by accident that postmodernism started as a debate within architecture, the art of space created by people. See, among others, Jameson, 1984, p 53; C Jencks, 1987.

considered a further step in the construction of an oppositional postmodern conception of law – or, as I have called it in Chapter Five and will explain in more detail in Chapter Nine, a subaltern cosmopolitan legality.

Scale, projection and symbolization are not neutral procedures. The choices made within each of them promote the expression of certain types of interests and disputes, and suppress that of others. We can only speak of the autonomy of law, as a specific way of representing, distorting and imagining reality, in relation to these procedures and the choices they make possible. The symbolic cartography of law, particularly when combined with a legal pluralist conception of law, as is the case here, allows us to deal with the question of the specificities of legal imagination and legal construction of reality with greater analytical depth, and without falling into the traps of either legal fetishism or legal essentialism. More specifically, the symbolic cartography of law reinforces the conception of legal plurality that I have been presenting throughout this book – not the legal pluralism of traditional legal anthropology, in which the different legal orders are conceived as separate entities coexisting in the same political space, but rather, the conception of different legal spaces superimposed, interpenetrated and mixed in our minds, as much as in our actions, either on occasions of qualitative leaps or sweeping crises in our life trajectories, or in the dull routine of eventless everyday life. We live in a time of porous legality or of legal porosity, multiple networks of legal orders forcing us to constant transitions and trespassing. Our legal life is constituted by an intersection of different legal orders, that is, by *interlegality*. Interlegality is the phenomenological counterpart of legal plurality, and a key concept in an oppositional postmodern conception of law.

Interlegality is a highly dynamic process, because the different legal spaces are non-synchronic, and thus result in uneven and unstable combinations of legal codes (codes in a semiotic sense). The mixing of codes is visible in all the case studies I mentioned. It is also visible in the ways in which the emerging global legal space appropriates local legal vernaculars.[56] As I have shown, small-scale global legality mixes the telescopic view of reality with a moralistic rhetoric typical of large-scale legality. While broadening the legal space to a world or even planetary scale, it creates new particularisms and new personalisms, echoing the medieval privileges of the different *professiones juris*. The mixing of codes is still visible in popular images of law. In a study on images of law in the mass media, Macaulay has shown how the mass media, and particularly television, promote a fragmented and inconsistent view of law – a view of overlapping and contradictory legal messages, rules and offsetting counterrules, inciting both to obedience and disobedience, legal and illegal action.[57]

---

[56] For a sympathetic view of the concept of interlegality as I have proposed it and of its potential for analyzing the interface between global, national, and local legalities, see Twining, 2000, p 230.

[57] Macaulay, 1987, p 185.

Such a conception of legal pluralism and interlegality calls for complex analytical tools. Those presented here, together with the ones presented in Chapter Seven, intend to show not only that the fragmentation of legality is not chaotic, but also that each legal construction has an internal coherence. It is a construction built according to the rules of scale, projection and symbolization. In a polycentric legal world, the centrality of the state law, though increasingly shaken, is still a decisive political factor. But above all, it is reproduced by multiple mechanisms of acculturation and socialization. As there is a literary canon that establishes what is and what is not literature, there is also a legal canon that establishes what is and what is not law. Because people are permanently (even if inconsistently) socialized and acculturated in the types of scale, projection and symbolization that are characteristic of the national state legal order, they refuse to recognize as legal those normative orders that use different scales, projections and symbolizations. They are beyond the minimum and the maximum threshold of legal cognition. Some (infrastate, local) legal orders are too close to everyday reality to be viewed as a fact of law (a *legal* fact), while other (suprastate, global) legal orders are too remote from everyday reality to be viewed as a law of fact (a legal *fact*). The symbolic cartography of law, using as a metaphor such commonplace and vulgar objects as maps,[58] contributes to the creation of a *new legal common sense*, another key component of the postmodern conception of law advanced in this book.

---

[58]   On the vulgar and trivial nature of our daily encounters with maps, see Hodgkiss, 1981, p 11: 'It is difficult to avoid being confronted by at least one or two maps during the daily routine. Perusing the morning paper in the commuter tram we are likely to see small black-and-white maps serving to locate and explain some significant contemporary event. At home, in the evening, similar maps face us on the television screen, as a feature of the television news. The current state of the weather is indicated in the press and on television with the aid of satellite photographs and maps which have been specially designed so that their meaning should be clear to the untrained map user.' The new, legal, common sense aims at equally trivializing our daily encounters with the laws, so that their meaning becomes clear to the untrained law user.

Chapter 9

Can Law Be Emancipatory?

I INTRODUCTION

Throughout this book I have been arguing that we live in a period overwhelmed by the question of its own relativity. The pace, the scale, the nature and the reach of social transformation are such that moments of destruction and moments of creation succeed each other in a frantic rhythm without leaving time or space for moments of stabilization and consolidation. This is precisely why I characterize the current period as one of transition.

It is characteristic of transitional periods that the nature of the transition is discerned by the fact that the complex questions it raises fail to find a social or cultural environment conducive to their answer. On one side, those – usually small, dominant social groups – that lead the sequences of social destruction and social creation are so absorbed in the automatism of the sequence that questioning what they are doing is at best irrelevant and at worst threatening and dangerous. On the other side, the overwhelming majority of the population that experience the consequences of intense social destruction and creation are so busy or pressed to adapt, resist, or simply survive that they fail to ask, let alone answer, complex questions about what they are doing and why. Contrary to what some authors have claimed[1] this is not a period conducive to self-reflexivity. Probably the latter is confined to those privileged enough to attribute it to others.

This is a very complex period to analyze. In the previous chapters, I have dwelt on such complexity as it relates to law. Paradoxically, however, the meaning of such complexity as an orientation for action is not most effectively addressed by complex questions but rather by simple questions. A simple, elementary question is one that reaches, with the technical transparency of a sling, the deepest magma of our individual

---

[1]   Beck, Giddens and Lash, 1994.

and collective perplexity – which is nothing else than unexplored complexity. In a period not unlike ours Rousseau, in his *Discourse on the Sciences and Arts* (1750), asked and answered a very simple question that in his view captured the complexity of the transition under way. The question was: does the progress of the sciences and the arts contribute to the purity or to the corruption of manners? Or in another even simpler formulation: is there a relationship between science and virtue? After a complex argumentation, Rousseau answers in an equally simple way: a resounding 'no'. In this chapter I will conclude the exploration into law, globalization and emancipation undertaken in this book by trying to respond to an equally simple question: can law be emancipatory? Or: is there a relationship between law and the quest for a good society? Unlike Rousseau, however, I don't think I will be able to answer with a simple no or with a simple yes.

In the first section of the chapter I will provide the historical and political background of the question I am trying to answer. In the second section I will analyze the situation in which we are now. Finally, in the third and fourth sections I will elaborate on the conditions under which a highly qualified yes can be given to the question being asked. I will specify some of the areas in which a relationship between law and social emancipation seem to be most urgently needed and possible.

2   SETTING THE CONTEXT FOR THE QUESTION

As I argue in Chapter Two, once the liberal state assumed the monopoly of law creation and adjudication – and law was thereby reduced to state law – the tension between social regulation and social emancipation became one more object of legal regulation. In the terms of the distinction between legal and illegal social emancipation – which then became a crucial political and legal category – only those emancipatory practices and objectives sanctioned by the state and therefore consistent with the interests of the social groups behind it were to be allowed. This regulated dialectics turned gradually into non dialectical regulation whereby social emancipation ceased to be the other of social regulation to become the double of social regulation. In other words, rather than being a radical alternative to social regulation as it exists now, social emancipation became the name of social regulation in the process of revising or transforming itself.

With the triumph of liberalism in 1848 the central concern of the liberal state ceased to be to fight against the *Ancien Régime* but rather to counter the emancipatory claims of the 'dangerous classes' which, however defeated in the revolution of 1848, kept pressing the new political regime with growing demands for democracy (Wallerstein, 1999, p 90). From then on the struggles for social emancipation were expressed in the language of the social contract, as struggles against exclusion from the social contract and for inclusion in it. The strategies differed between those that sought to struggle within the legal confines of the liberal state – the demoliberals, and later, the demosocialists – and those for whom such confines were set to frustrate any emancipatory struggle worth the name and had therefore to be overcome – various kinds of radical socialists.

This duality came to characterize left politics in the last one hundred and fifty years: on one side, an emancipatory politics obtained by legal parliamentary means through incremental reformism; on the other, an emancipatory politics pursued by illegal extra-parliamentary means leading to revolutionary ruptures. The first strategy, which came to dominate in Western Europe and the North Atlantic, assumed the form of the rule of law and translated itself into a vast programme of liberal concessions that aimed at expanding both the ambit and the quality of the inclusion in the social contract without threatening the basic structure of the economic and political system in force – that is, capitalism and liberal democracy. The expansion of political citizenship – universal suffrage, civil and political rights – and social citizenship – welfare state, social and economic rights – was the political outcome of this strategy. The second strategy, inspired by the Russian Revolution, which came to dominate in the periphery of the world-system, assumed the form of illegal, violent or non-violent confrontation with the liberal state, the colonial or the post-colonial state and the capitalist economy, leading to the creation of socialist states of different kinds. As I said before, the Russian Revolution was the first modern revolution that rather than being conducted in the name of law was conducted against law.

These two strategies were internally very diverse. I already mentioned that the revolutionary strategy, however predominantly enclosed in the same political theory – Marxism – covered different politics carrying different means and goals competing among themselves often fiercely if not outright violently. Similarly, the legal or reformist camp was split between those that gave priority to liberty over equality and were in favour of the most feasible minimal concessions (demoliberalism) and those that refused to establish a hierarchy between liberty and equality and were in favour of the most feasible maximal concessions (demosocialism). Both strands of legal politics fought against conservatism, adamantly opposed to concessions to the excluded from the social contract. Although they were all framed by the liberal state, those different political strategies led to different politics of law which in turn were at the source of transformations of the liberal state in different directions – strong welfare states in Europe, weak welfare states in North America, especially in the US, etc.

As I have been arguing, in the last twenty years this political paradigm entered into a crisis that impacted both the reformist and the revolutionary strategy. In the core countries the crisis of reformism took the form of the crisis of the welfare state and in the peripheral and semi-peripheral countries, the form of the crisis of the developmentalist state, through structural adjustment and drastic cuts in the incipient state social expenses. It meant, in political terms, the re-emergence of conservatism and an ideological tide against the agenda of a gradually expanding inclusion in the social contract which, in different forms, was common to demo-liberalism and demo-socialism. Thus, the legal avenue towards social emancipation seemed (and seems) to be blocked. Such an avenue is admittedly structurally limited – an emancipatory promise regulated by the capitalist state and therefore consistent with the ceaseless and inherently polarizing accumulation needs of capitalism. In the core countries, however, and during many decades, it accounted for the compatibility between capitalism – always hostile to social redistribution – and democracy based on either demoliberal or demosocialist policies of redistribution. The collapse of this strategy led to the disintegration of the already highly attenuated tension between social regulation and social emancipation. But because this tension inhabited the political model as a whole, the disintegration of social emancipation carried with it the disintegration of social regulation. Hence the double crisis of regulation and emancipation in which we are now, a crisis in which conservatism thrives under the misleading name of neo-liberalism. Neo-liberalism is not a new version of liberalism but rather a new version of conservatism. What is intriguing, however, is the fact that the collapse of the political strategies that guaranteed in the past the compatibility between capitalism and democracy, far from leading to the incompatibility between the two, has seemingly strengthened such compatibility and, moreover, has extended it beyond the core countries to which in the past it was mostly confined.

About the same time, the revolutionary avenue towards social emancipation entered an equally serious crisis as the nation-states that had emerged from successful struggles against colonialism and capitalism collapsed. Of course, just as had happened with the reformist strategy, the 'quality' of social emancipation brought about by the revolutionary strategy had been called into question long before. Notwithstanding the crucial differences between them, both the liberal states and the socialist states had put forward a state-promoted, heavily regulated tension between social emancipation and social regulation through which structural exclusions – be they political, economic, or social–crystallized if not deepened.

This way of thinking about social transformation – ie, in terms of a tension between social regulation and social emancipation – is a modern one. In a situation, such as ours, in which we experience a crisis both of social regulation and social emancipation one may wonder whether such formulation should not be simply abandoned as it fails to capture in positive terms any aspects of our life experiences. If not all is wrong with our life experiences, something is wrong with the conception that renders them in unconditionally negative terms. Similarly, if both the overarching strategies to bring about modern social transformation, legal reformism and revolution, are in crisis – law abounds but apparently not for social reform purposes, while revolution is simply not there anymore – it is legitimate to ask whether we should not look for new conceptions to make sense of social transformation, if the latter is to be kept at all as a way of describing aggregate changes in individual and collective life experiences.

As I have been arguing in this book, we are in a transition period that can be best described in the following way: we live in a period in which we face modern problems for which there are no modern solutions. The ideas of a good order and of a good society go on haunting us if for no other reason because of the nature of the (dis)order that prevails in our evermore unequal and excluding societies, precisely in a moment of history when technological progress seem to exist for our societies to be different and better. To abandon the tension between social regulation and social emancipation or the very idea of social transformation altogether – which, as I showed in Chapter One, is the proposal of celebratory postmodernists – seems thus a politically risky proposition not only because it coincides with the conservative agenda but also because there are not in the horizon any new conceptions with the potential to capture the political aspirations condensed in the modern concepts. Reinventing the tension between social regulation and social emancipation seems therefore a better or more prudent proposition than throwing it together into the dustbin of history.

The same is true of the political strategies that in the past embodied the tension between social regulation and social emancipation: law and revolution. The reinventing in this case is particularly complex since while revolution seems definitely discarded, law is more pervasive than ever, indeed filling the social and political spaces opened up by the collapse of revolution. For conservatives there is nothing to be reinvented here, except ever more subtle (and not so subtle) ways of dismantling the mechanisms through which both liberals and demosocialists turned law into an instrument of social change. The scientific and political task ahead may be thus formulated: how to reinvent law beyond the liberal and demosocialist model without falling into the conservative agenda – and indeed, how to do it so as to combat the latter more efficiently.

most feasible concessions

3 THE WESTERN BIAS AND THE PLAUSIBILITY OF THE QUESTION

Can law be emancipatory?

Before trying to answer this question it is imperative to ask whether it adequately addresses the issues that concern progressive politics and legal practice at the beginning of new millennium. Because, if the answer is no, the question of the reinvention of law should be reformulated before we proceed. The narrative above is a Western narrative that started out with a quintessentially Western question: can law be emancipatory? This question, apparently all-encompassing, makes a number of assumptions that are specific to Western culture and politics. It presupposes that there is a social entity called law susceptible of being defined in its own terms and of operating autonomously. It also assumes that there is a general concept of social emancipation, different and separate from individual emancipation and from particular emancipatory projects by different social groups in different historical contexts. Moreover, it takes for granted that there are social expectations above and beyond current social experiences and that the gap between experiences and expectations can and must be filled.

All these assumptions are highly problematic when seen from beyond the boundaries of Western modernity. After 500 years of European expansion and an extremely diverse geography of contact zones where a myriad forms of hybridization and creolization took place, it is still problematic in many non-Western cultures and societies to identify law as a separate social field and much less an autonomous and homogeneous social field. Instead, in addition to state law – which has some formal affinities with the Western liberal concept of law – there is a vast array of normative structures anchored in non-state entities and agencies. Such structures are fully embedded in sets of social practices that cannot be adequately described as legal, political, economic or religious fields because they seem to be all that at the same time. Moreover, in these societies, though the cultural and political elites formulate the gap between social experiences and social expectations as a problem to be overcome by social emancipation, there is no collective memory of struggle or of movements carried out in the name of 'social emancipation'. In most instances the only collective memory that approximates this idea relates to the anti-colonial struggles. The idea of good order and good society are often couched in religious terms, and they involve religious law rather than secular law, revelation rather than revolution.

If the question I am asking is, in the above formulation, a distinctively Western one, the same can be said of the historical narrative of the fate of the tension between social regulation and the role played by law in it. I argued in Chapter Two that the reception of Roman law in the twelfth century marks the first modern presence of law in the tension between social regulation and social emancipation, the development of a legal form suited to serve the progressive interests of the emergent merchant class. This is, of course, a Western narrative. On the twelfth century and indeed much earlier there were thriving merchants that populated the commercial routes uniting China and India to the Mediterranean and many others around Eastern Africa, Western Africa and North Africa, but their legal history has nothing to do with the history of the urban commercial classes in Medieval Europe fighting against feudal rulers with the intellectual weapons provided by Roman law. Moreover, after 1848 the world was much larger than the limited geographical space occupied by the Western European liberal states. There were ancient states from Egypt and Ethiopia to Central Africa, Persia, China and Japan. There were European colonies in Africa and Asia and the second wave of colonialism was still to begin. There were post-colonial states in Latin America served by liberal constitutions but with political practices that, among other things, condoned slavery and intensified the genocide of the indigenous people. Throughout the nineteenth and twentieth century these states oscillated between periods of minimal democratic rule and periods of dictatorship, as indeed was the case of some Western Europe states, such as Portugal, Spain and Greece. The compatibility between democracy and capitalism sought by both demoliberalism and demosocialism was indeed exclusive to a few countries – and, even in Europe, had to yield to fascism in Italy, to Nazism in Germany, to Franquism in Spain, to Salazarism in Portugal, etc. Inclusive forms of political and social citizenship (welfare states) have been by far more an exception than a rule. In the same way, on a global scale, law, as state law, has played a minimal role in managing the tension between social regulation and social emancipation. By far, revolution, both as an oppositional political strategy and as a non-liberal state form, played a much bigger role throughout the twentieth century.

The historical peculiarity of my apparently all-encompassing question and inquiry should by now be evident. Why should I proceed then? And if so, how? First, why to proceed. It is my contention that the history of my question is probably more Western than its future. In the last twenty years, neo-liberal hegemonic globalization and the demise of the socialist bloc have in different ways interrupted both the Western and the non-Western legal and political histories, thus creating an institutional void that is being globally filled by a specific version of Western politics – conservatism. Both legal reformism and social revolution have been discredited as well as other legal and political forms existing outside Western Europe and North Atlantic. Moreover, any attempt at articulating alternatives to the hegemonic consensus has been swiftly and efficiently suppressed. Such consensus, as I showed in Chapters Five and Six, is in fact constituted by four sectoral and interrelated consensuses: the neo-liberal economic consensus, the weak state consensus, the liberal-democratic consensus, and the rule of law and judicial reform consensus.

For the development of my argument here – that is, to answer the question why to proceed with the inquiry: can law be emancipatory? – it is important to bear in mind that – as shown in those chapters – the neo-liberal legal globalization under way is replacing the highly politicized tension between social regulation and social emancipation with a depoliticized conception of social change whose sole criterion is the rule of law and judicial adjudication by an honest, independent, predictable and efficient judiciary. The law that rules in this model is not the reformist law in either a demo-liberal or demo-socialist version. The neo-liberal, conservative law simply establishes the framework within which a market-based civil society operates and flourishes, while the judiciary guarantees that the rule of law is widely accepted and effectively enforced. After all, the legal and judicial needs of the market-based development model are quite simple: transaction costs have to be lowered, property rights must be clearly defined and protected, contractual obligations must be enforced, and a minimalist legal framework has to be put in place.

In sum, neo-liberal hegemonic globalization has advanced a political and legal paradigm that is global in scope. Inspired by a highly selective view of the Western tradition, it is being imposed throughout the world system. This means that the question of the relationship between law and social emancipation, albeit historically a Western one, may now become a global question – one that fits in the political and scientific agenda of both Western and non-Western countries, and of core, semi-peripheral and peripheral countries.

Of course, for that to occur, it is necessary to reach beyond the confines of neo-liberal globalization. While the role of law, and the judicial reform are today topics of debate throughout the world system, any discussion about social emancipation is being suppressed by neo-liberal globalization since in its terms the good order and good society are already here with us and only need to be consolidated. The question of the role of law in bringing about social emancipation is today a counter-hegemonic question to be pursued by the social forces that across the world system fight against neo-liberal hegemonic globalization. Indeed, the latter – while propagating throughout the globe the same system of domination and exclusion – has created the conditions for the counter-hegemonic forces, organizations and movements located in the most disparate regions of the globe to visualize common interests across and beyond the many differences that separate them and to converge in counter-hegemonic struggles embodying separate but related emancipatory social projects.

Since, as shown in Chapter Five, my inquiry is premised precisely upon the distinction between hegemonic neo-liberal globalization or globalization from above, on one hand, and counter-hegemonic globalization or globalization from below, on the other, I believe that the question on the emancipatory potential of law can be adequately tackled by looking into the legal dimension of such counter-hegemonic global struggles. This is the task that I undertake in the last part of this chapter. Thus, the question is plausible and its answer may be a promising means for rethinking the emancipatory potential of law under the conditions of globalization.

It remains to be seen, however, how the question should be addressed. Here also it is crucial for my argument to distinguish between hegemonic and counter-hegemonic forms of legal globalization. To formulate the question in such a way that it does not frustrate the possibility of counter-hegemonic legal globalization it is imperative to de-Westernize the conception of law that will lead the inquiry. This involves the radical unthinking of law that I proposed in Chapters Two and Five – that is, reinventing law to fit the normative claims of subaltern social groups and their movements and organizations struggling for alternatives to neo-liberal globalization.

As I will show below, such reinvention of law involves a search into subaltern conceptions and practices, of which I distinguish three types: 1) conceptions and practices that though being part of the Western tradition and evolving in Western countries were suppressed or marginalized by the liberal conceptions that came to dominate; 2) conceptions that evolved outside the West, mainly in the colonies and later in the post-colonial states; 3) conceptions and practices that are today being proposed by organizations and movements which are active in advancing forms of counter-hegemonic globalization. In sum, in a period of paradigmatic transition away from dominant modernity, subaltern modernity provides some of the instruments that will allow us to transit along in a progressive direction, that is, in the direction of a good order and of a good society that is not yet here.

To fully capture both the potential of and the obstacles to the consolidation of such subaltern cosmopolitan practices, it is necessary to look briefly into the social, political, and economic context that neo-liberal globalization has produced and in which subaltern practices have to be deployed. To this task I turn in the following section.

4 THE DEMISE OF THE SOCIAL CONTRACT AND THE RISE OF SOCIAL FASCISM

4.1 *Social exclusion and the crisis of the modern social contract*

As I claimed in Chapter Two, the social contract – with its criteria of inclusion and exclusion, and its metacontractual principles – has presided over the organization of the economic, political, and cultural life of modern societies. In the last twenty years, this social, political, and cultural paradigm has been undergoing a period of great turbulence that affects not only its operative devices but also its presuppositions. Indeed, the turbulence is so intense that it has produced a veritable crisis of the social contract. Such a crisis is one of the most distinctive features of the pradigmatic transition.

As I have argued elsewhere,[2] the social contract is based on three presuppositions: a general regime of values, a system of measures and a privileged time-space. The crisis of the social contract can be detected in each one of these presuppositions. The *general regime of values* is based on the idea of the common good and general will. These are principles through which individual sociabilities and social practices are aggregated. Thus, it becomes possible to designate as 'society' the universe of autonomous and contractual interactions between free and equal subjects.

Such a regime seems today unable to resist the increasing fragmentation of society, divided into many apartheids, polarized along economic, social, political, and cultural axes. The struggle for the common good seems to be losing its meaning and consequently the same happens to the struggle for alternative definitions of the common good. The general will seems to have become an absurd proposition. Under these circumstances, some authors even speak of the end of society. Ours is a post-Foucaultian world, and we suddenly realize, in retrospect, how organized Foucault's world was. As we saw in Chapter One, according to Foucault, two main modes of social power coexist in modern societies; on one hand, disciplinary power, the dominant one, centred around the sciences, and, on the other, juridical power, centred around the state and the law and in a process of decline. Nowadays, these powers coexist with many others – in Chapter Seven I identified six different forms of power – and they themselves are fragmented and disorganized. Disciplinary power is increasingly a non-disciplinary power, to the extent that the sciences lose their epistemological confidence and are forced to share the field of knowledge with rival knowledges – such as indigenous knowledges in the case of contemporary struggles around biodiversity – which are in turn capable of generating different kinds of power and resistance. On the other hand, as the state loses its centrality in regulating society its law becomes

---

[2]   Santos, 1998b.

labyrinthian. State law becomes disorganized as it is forced to coexist with the non-official law of multiple de facto non-state legislators, who, by virtue of the political power they command, transform facticity into norm, vying with the state for the monopoly of violence and law. The seemingly chaotic proliferation of powers renders difficult the identification of the enemies, sometimes even the identification of the victims themselves.

Moreover, the values of modernity – liberty, equality, autonomy, subjectivity, justice, solidarity – as well as the antinomies amongst them remain, but are subjected to an increasing symbolic overload, in that they mean increasingly more disparate things to different people or social groups, with the result that the excess of meaning turns into trivialization, and hence into neutralization.

The turbulence of our present time is noticeable particularly in the second presupposition of the social contract, the *common system of measures*. The *common system of measures* is based on a conception of time and space as homogenous, neutral, linear entities that function as the minor common denominators for the definition of relevant differences. Starting from this conception, it is possible, on the one hand, to separate nature from society and, on the other, to establish a quantitative means of comparison between overall and widely distinct social interactions. Their qualitative differences are either ignored or reduced to the quantitative indicators that can account for them approximately. Money and commodities are the purest concretizations of the common system of measures. Through them, labour, wages, risks, and damages are easily measurable and comparable.

But the common system of measures goes way beyond money and commodities. By virtue of the homogeneities it creates, the common system of measures even allows for the establishment of correspondences amongst antinomic values. For instance, between liberty and equality it is possible to define criteria of social justice, redistribution, and solidarity. The assumption is that the measures be common and function by correspondence and homogeneity. That is why solidarity is only possible among equals, its most perfect concretization being solidarity among workers.

Neutral, linear, homogenous time and space have long disappeared from the sciences but only now has their disappearance begun to make a difference at the level of everyday life and social relations. In Chapter Eight I have alluded to the turbulence affecting today the scales in which we are used to seeing and identifying phenomena, conflicts, and relationships. Since each one of them is the product of the scale in which we observe them, the turbulence of scales produces strangeness, defamiliarization, surprise, perplexity, and invisibility. To my mind, a clear example of the turbulence of scales is found in the phenomenon of urban violence in Brazil, which can be found also in other places around the world.[3] When a street child looks for shelter to spend

---

[3]   Santos, 1998b.

the night and is, as a consequence, killed by a policeman, or when someone who is solicited on the streets by a beggar, refuses to give alms and is, as a consequence, killed by the beggar, what happens is an unforeseen explosion of the scale of the conflict: a seemingly trivial phenomenon is suddenly escalated up to another level and turned into a dramatic phenomenon that has fatal consequences. This abrupt and unpredictable change of scale of phenomena occurs nowadays in the most diverse domains of social practice. Following Prigogine (1979; 1980), I believe that our societies are undergoing a period of bifurcation, that is to say, a situation of systemic instability in which a minor change can bring about, in an unpredictable and chaotic way, qualitative transformations. The turbulence of scales destroys sequences and means of comparison, thereby reducing alternatives, creating impotence or promoting passivity.

The stability of scales seems to be confined to the market and consumption – and even there with radical mutations of rhythm and ambits that impose constant transformations of perspective on the acts of commerce. The hyper-visibility and high speed of heavily advertised commodities turns the intersubjectivity demanded from consumers into the interobjectuality among acts of consumption. In other words consumers become nomadic supports of commodities. The same constant transformation of perspective is also occurring in information and telecommunication technologies, where indeed scale turbulence is the originating act and condition of functionality. Here, the increasing interactivity of technologies dispenses more and more with the inventiveness of the users, the consequence being that interactivity surreptitiously slides into interpassivity. Zapping is probably a telling example of interpassivity under the guise of interactivity.

Finally, the *national state time-space* is losing its primacy because of the increasing importance of the global and local time-spaces that compete with it. This destructuring of the national state time-space also occurs at the level of rhythms, durations, and temporalities. The national state time-space is made up of different but compatible and articulated time frames: the time frame of the elections, the time frame of collective bargaining, the time frame of courts, that of the welfare bureaucracy, the time frame of the national historical memory, etc. The coherence amongst these temporalities is what gives the national state time-space its own configuration. Now, this coherence is becoming more and more problematic because the impact produced by the global and local time-space varies from one time frame to another. For instance, the time frame of courts tends to be less affected by the global time-space than the time frame of collective bargaining. On the other hand, the local time-space is, in the US, affecting more the time frame with which the welfare system works – given the recent 'devolution' of welfare functions to the states and local comunities – than the time frame of electoral politics, while in Europe the inverse seems to occur, as illustrated by new local democracy initiatives in Spain, France or Germany.

Furthermore, time frames or rhythms that are quite incompatible with the national state temporality as a whole become increasingly more important. Two of them are worth specific mention. The *instant time* of cyberspace, on the one hand, and the *glacial time* of ecological degradation, the indigenous question and biodiversity, on the other. Either temporality collides head-on with the political and bureaucratic temporality of the state. The instant time of the financial markets precludes any deliberation or regulation on the part of the state. The slowing down of this temporality can only be obtained at the level of the scale in which it occurs, the global scale, and hence through international actions.[4] On the other hand, glacial time is too slow to be compatible with any of the national state time frames – particularly with those of courts and electoral politics. Indeed, recent juxtapositions of state time and glacial time have been little more than attempts on the part of state time to cannibalize and decharacterize glacial time. One has only to consider how the indigenous question has been handled in many countries,[5] or the quite recent global wave of national laws on patents and intellectual property rights having an impact on the question of biodiversity.

Since it has been so far the hegemonic time-space, the national state time-space configures not only the action of the state but also social practices in general, upon which the competition between instant time and glacial time rebounds as well. For instance, both the volatility of the financial markets and global warming give rise to crises that impact state politics and state legitimacy precisely because of the inadequacy of the state's responses. As in the case of scale turbulence, both instant time and glacial time converge, in different ways, to reduce alternatives, generate impotence, and promote passivity. Instant time collapses the sequences into an infinite present which trivializes the alternatives by their techno-ludic multiplication, fusing them into variations of the same. Glacial time, on the contrary, creates such a wide distance between real alternatives – from alternative models of development to alternatives to development – that they stop being commensurate and susceptible of being counter-weighed, and end up wandering in incommunicable systems of reference.[6] The same confrontation between glacial time and national state time both creates the urgent need of a global alternative to capitalist development and makes it impossible to envision it, let alone to opt for it.

It is, however, at the level of the operational devices of the social contract that the signs of the crisis of this paradigm are more visible. Nevertheless, at first sight, the present situation, far from prefiguring a crisis of social contractualism, is rather characterized by an unprecedented consolidation of the latter. Never before has there been so much talk about the contractualization of social relations, labour relations, welfare relations and partnership of the state with social organizations. But this new contractualization has little to do with the contractualization founded on the modern

---

[4]   With the specific purpose of slowing down the instant time of financial markets in order to create time for democratic deliberation, the social movements pursuing counter-hegemonic globalization have been proposing the adoption of the Tobin Tax.

[5]   On this topic, see Chapter Five.

[6]   On this topic in general and on the possibilities of imagining alternative development and alternatives to development, see Santos and Rodríguez, 2002.

idea of the social contract. First, unlike the social contract, the new contractual ties have no stability and can be broken at any time by any of the parties. It is not a radical option; it is rather a trivial option. The 'historical bloc' once needed to sustain the conditions and objectives of the social contract is now set aside and replaced by a multitude of contracts whose conditions and objectives remain a private matter. Secondly, neo-liberal contractualization does not recognize conflict and struggle as structural elements of the social pact. On the contrary, it replaces them by passive assent to supposedly universal conditions deemed to be unsurpassable. Take the so-called Washington Consensus. If indeed it is a social contract, it occurs only amongst the core capitalist countries. For all other national societies, it appears as a set of inexorable conditions for acritical acceptance under pain of implacable exclusion. What later sustains individual contracts of civil law are precisely these insurmountable, uncontractualized global conditions.

For all these reasons, the new contractualization is a false contract, a mere appearance of a compromise constituted by conditions, as costly as they are inescapable, imposed without discussion upon the weaker party. Under the appearance of a contract, the new contractualization prefigures the re-emergence of status, that is, of the principles of pre-modern hierarchical order in which the conditions of social relations were directly linked to the position of the parties in social hierarchy. But there is no question of a return to the past. As a matter of fact, status is now merely the consequence of the enormous inequality of economic power amongst the parties – be they states or individuals – in the individual contract, as well as the capacity with which such inequality – in the absence of the state's corrective regulation – endows the stronger party to impose without discussion the conditions that are most favourable to it. The new contractualism reproduces itself through extremely unfair contract terms.

The crisis of modern contractualization consists in the structural predominance of exclusion over inclusion processes. The latter are still in force and even assume advanced forms that allow for the bare reconciliation of the values of modernity, but they confine themselves to increasingly more restrictive groups which impose abysmal forms of exclusion upon much larger groups. The predominance of exclusion processes takes on two, apparently contradictory, forms: post-contractualism and pre-contractualism. Post-contractualism is the process by means of which groups and social interests up until now included in the social contract are excluded from the latter without any prospect of returning. The rights of citizenship, hitherto considered unalienable, are confiscated and, without them, the excluded turn from citizens into serfs. This is the case, for example, of those excluded from the shrinking welfare systems in core countries. Pre-contractualism consists in blocking access to citizenship to social groups that before considered themselves candidates to citizenship and had the reasonable expectation of acceding to it. This is the case, for instance, of the popular classes in the semi-periphery and the periphery.

The exclusions thus brought about both by post-contractualism and pre-contractualism are radical and insurmountable, to such an extent that those who suffer them, though being formally citizens, are in fact excluded from civil society and thrown into a new state of nature. In postmodern society at the beginning of the century, the state of nature consists in the permanent anxiety vis-à-vis the present and the future, imminent loss of control over expectations, permanent chaos concerning the simplest acts of survival and conviviality.

Whether by way of post-contractualism, or by way of pre-contractualism, the deepening of the logic of exclusion creates new states of nature: the precariousness of life and the servitude generated by the workers' permanent anxiety concerning the amount and continuity of work, by the anxiety of the unemployed in search of jobs or of those who don't even have conditions to search for jobs, by the anxiety of the self-employed regarding the continuity of a market which they themselves have to create every day to assure the continuity of their income, and finally by the anxiety of the undocumented migrant workers, who have no social rights at all. The stability referred to by the neo-liberal consensus is always the stability of market and investment expectations, never of the expectations of working people. Indeed, the stability of markets and investments is only possible at the cost of the instability of the expectations of people.

For all these reasons, work increasingly ceases to sustain citizenship, and vice-versa, increasingly citizenship ceases to sustain work. By losing its political status as both a product and a producer of citizenship, work is reduced to the pain of existence, both when it is available – in the form of stressful work – and when it is not – in the form of stressful unemployment. This is why work, even though it dominates people's lives more and more, is disappearing from the ethical references that sustain the subjects' autonomy and self-esteem.

In social terms, the cumulative effect of pre-contractualism and post-contractualism is the emergence of an underclass of excluded, which is smaller or larger according to the central or peripheral position of a given society in the world system. This underclass is constituted both by social groups trapped in downward social mobility – unqualified workers, unemployed, migrant workers, ethnic minorities – and social groups for which the possibility of work has ceased to be a realistic expectation, if it ever was – eg, the permanently unemployed, youths unable to enter the labour market, disabled people, large numbers of poor peasants in Latin America, Africa, and Asia.

This excluded class assumes in core countries the form of an internal Third World, the so-called lower third in the two-third society. In Europe, there are 18 million unemployed and more than 52 million people below the poverty line; 10 per cent of the population have physical or mental disabilities that make their social integration very difficult. In the US, the underclass thesis has been articulated by William Julius Wilson to characterize African Americans in the urban guettos, affected by the decline of industry and the economic desertification of the inner cities.[6a] Wilson defines underclass according to six main features: residence in spaces socially isolated from the other

[6a]   Wilson, 1987.

classes; lack of a long-term job; monoparental families headed by women; lack of professional qualification or training; long streches of poverty and dependence on welfare; and tendency to engage in criminal activity, such as street crime. This class expanded considerably from the 1970s to the 1980s and, tragically, is increasingly made up of young people. The percentage of the poor less than 18 years old was 15 per cent in 1970 and 20 per cent in 1987, the increase of child poverty being particularly dramatic. The structural character of exclusion, and hence of the obstacles to inclusion to which this class is subjected, can be observed in the fact that, though African Americans show remarkable intergenerational educational improvement, such an accomplishment has not resulted in regular, full-time jobs. According to Lash and Urry, three main factors are responsible for this: the decline of industrial jobs in the economy in general; the flight of the remaining jobs from the inner cities to the suburbs; and the redistribution of jobs according to different types of metropolitan areas.[7] In the periphery and semi-periphery, the class of the excluded amounts to more than half of the countries' population, and the causes of exclusion are even more tenacious: apart from a small elite with ever weaker roots in their countries, those spared the breakdown of expectations are only those with no expectations at all.

The structural growth of social exclusion, whether by way of pre-contractualism or post-contractualism, and the resulting expansion of the state of nature, which allows for no individual or collective opting out, signals an epochal, paradigmatic crisis, which some designate as demodernization or counter-modernization. This situation entails, therefore, many risks. This is indeed the phenomenon that Beck has referred to as the rise of 'the risk society'[8] or the 'Brazilianization'[9] of the world. The question is whether it contains any opportunities for the replacement of modernity's old social contract by another one, less vulnerable to the proliferation of the logic of exclusion.

4.2 *The emergence of social fascism*

Let us first take a look at the risks. Actually, I think they can be summarized in one alone: *the emergence of social fascism*. I do not mean a return to the fascism of the 1930s and 1940s. Unlike the earlier one, the present fascism is not a political regime. It is rather a social and civilizational regime. Rather than sacrificing democracy to the demands of capitalism, it trivializes democracy to such a degree that it is no longer necessary, or even convenient, to sacrifice democracy in order to promote capitalism. It is a type of pluralist fascism produced by the society rather than by the state. The state is here a complacent bystander if not an active culprit. We are entering a period in which democratic states coexist with fascistic societies. This is therefore a form of fascism that never existed.

---

[7]   Lash and Urry, 1996, p 151.
[8]   Beck, 1999.
[9]   Beck, 2000.

I distinguish four main forms of social fascism. The first is the *fascism of social apartheid*. I mean the social segregation of the excluded through the division of cities into savage and civilized zones. The savage zones are the zones of Hobbes' state of nature. The civilized zones are the zones of the social contract, and they are under the constant threat of the savage zones. In order to defend themselves, the civilized zones turn themselves into neo-feudal castles, the fortified enclaves that are characteristic of the new forms of urban segregation – private cities, enclosed condominiums, gated communities. The division into savage and civilized zones in cities around the world – even in 'global cities' like New York or London that, as Sassen[10] has shown, are the nodes of the global economy – is becoming a general criterion of sociability, a new hegemonic time-space that crosses all social, economic, political, and cultural relations, and is, therefore, common to state and non-state action. As far as the state is concerned, the division amounts to a double standard of state action in the savage and civilized zones. In the civilized zones, the state acts democratically, as a protective state, even if often inefficient and unreliable. In the savage zones, the state acts in a fascistic manner, as a predatory state, without the slightest regard, not even in appearance, for the rule of law.[11]

The second form of social fascism is *parastate fascism*. It concerns the usurpation of state prerogatives (such as coercion and social regulation) by very powerful social actors, often with the complicity of the state itself, which now neutralize, now supplement the social control produced by the state. Parastate fascism has two dimensions: contractual fascism and territorial fascism.

Contractual fascism occurs in the situations, already described, in which the power discrepancy between the parties in the civil contract is such that the weaker party, rendered vulnerable for having no alternative, accepts the conditions imposed by the stronger party, however costly and despotic they may be. The neo-liberal project of turning the labour contract into a civil law contract like any other foreshadows a situation of contractual fascism. This form of fascism occurs today frequently in policies aimed at 'flexibilizing' of labour markets or privatizing public services. In such cases, the social contract that presided over the production of public services in the welfare state and the developmentalist state is reduced to the individual contract between consumers and providers of privatized services. This reduction entails the elimination from the contractual ambit of decisive aspects of the protection of consumers, which, for this reason, become extracontractual. These are the situations in which the connivance between the democratic state and parastate fascism is clearest. By claiming extra-contractual prerogatives the fascist, parastate agencies take over functions of social regulation earlier carried out by the state. The state, whether implicitly or explicitly, sub-contracts parastate agencies for carrying out these functions and, by so doing

---

[10]   Sassen, 1991.

[11]   A good illustration of this dynamics is Caldeira's study on the geographic and social cleavages in São Paulo. See Caldeira, 2000.

without the participation or control of the citizens, becomes complicit with the production of parastate social fascism.

The second dimension of parastate fascism is *territorial fascism*. It occurs whenever social actors with enormous amounts of capital dispute the control of the state over the territories wherein they act, or neutralize that control by co-opting or coercing the state institutions and exerting social regulation upon the inhabitants of the territory, without their participation and against their interests. These are the new colonial territories inside states that are very often post-colonial states. Some of these territories are reinventions of the old phenomena of *coronelismo and caciquismo* while others are new territorial enclaves sealed of autonomous state intervention and ruled by pacts among armed social actors.[12]

The third form of social fascism is the *fascism of insecurity*. It consists in the discretionary manipulation of the sense of insecurity of people and social groups rendered vulnerable by the precariousness of work, or by destabilizing accidents or events. This results in chronic anxiety and uncertainty vis-à-vis the present and the future for large numbers of people, who thus reduce radically their expectations and become willing to bear huge burdens to achieve the smallest decrease of risk and insecurity. As far as this form of fascism is concerned, the *Lebensraum* – the 'vital space' claimed by Hitler for the German people, which justified annexations – of the new *Führer* is the people's intimacy and their anxiety and uncertainty regarding the present and the future. It operates by putting in action the double play of retrospective and prospective illusions, and is today particularly obvious in the domain of the privatization of social services, such as health, welfare, education, and housing. The retrospective illusions consist in underscoring the memory of insecurity in this regard and the inefficiency of the state bureaucracy in providing social welfare. The prospective illusions, in turn, aim at creating expectations of safety and security produced in the private sector and inflated by the occultation of some of the risks and the conditions for the provision of services. Such prospective illusions proliferate today mainly in the form of health insurance and private pension funds.

The fourth form of social fascism is *financial fascism*. This is perhaps the most vicious form of fascist sociability and requires, therefore, more detailed analysis. It is the type of fascism that controls the financial markets and their casino economy. It is the most pluralist in that the flows of capital are the result of the decisions of individual or institutional investors spread out all over the world and having nothing in common except the desire to maximize their assets. Precisely because it is the most pluralist, it is also the most vicious form of fascism, since its time-space is the most averse to any form of democratic intervention and deliberation. Highly significant in this regard is the reply of that stock market broker when asked what he considered to be the long

---

[12]   This is the case, for instance, of popular militias in Medellín (Colombia), and of the groups of emerald miners in the western part of Boyacá, Colombia. See Gutiérrez and Jaramillo, 2002.

term: 'for me, the long term is the next ten minutes'. This virtually instantaneous and global time-space, combined with the speculative logic of profit that sustains it, confers a huge discretionary power to financial capital, strong enough to shake, in seconds, the real economy or the political stability of any country. The exercise of financial power is totally discretionary and the consequences for those affected by it – sometimes, entire nations – can be overwhelming.

The viciousness of financial fascism consists in that it has become the model and operative criterion of the institutions of global regulation. I mention just one of them: the rating agencies, the agencies that are internationally certified to evaluate the financial situation of the different states and the risks or opportunities they may offer to foreign investors. The grades conferred – which, in the case of Moody's go from Aaa to C, with 19 grades in between – are decisive for the conditions under which a given country or a firm in such a country may be eligible for international credit. The higher the grade, the better the conditions. These companies have extraordinay power. According to Thomas Friedman, 'the post-cold war world has two superpowers, the United States and Moody's'.[13] Friedman justifies his statement by adding: 'if it is true that the United States of America can annihilate an enemy by using its military arsenal, the agency of financial rating Moody's has the power to strangle a country financially by giving it a bad grade'.[14] These agencies' discretionary power is all the greater because they have the prerogative of making evaluations not solicited by the countries or firms in question.

In all its forms, social fascism is a regime characterized by social relations and life experiences under extremely unequal power relations and exchanges which lead to particularly severe and potentially irreversible forms of exclusion. Such forms of social exclusion exist both within national societies (the interior South) and in the relations among countries (the global South). The quality of sociabilities that societies allow or grant to their members depends on the relative weight of social fascism in the constellation of different social regimes present in them. And the same may be said for the relations among countries.

4.3   Social fascism and the production of a stratified civil society

How to confront social fascism? Which political and legal strategies will be most effective in eliminating it? Before addressing these questions, I will briefly characterize the impact of social fascism on the liberal dichotomy state /civil society – since, as will be apparent below, such dichotomy underlies both the problems of and the potential solutions to social fascisms. In Chapter Seven I advanced an overarching and long-

---

[13]   Moody's is one of the six rating agencies certified by the Securities and Exchange Commission; the others are Standard and Poor's, Fitch Investors Services, Duff and Phelps, Thomas Bank Watch and IBCA.

[14]   In Warde, 1997, pp 10–11.

term conceptual alternative to the state/civil society dichotomy. In the current chapter, in which my argument is more focused and short-term, and intended to provide political orientations, I resort for a moment to the dominant conceptual framework while swerving from it in significant ways. I distinguish three types of civil society: the intimate civil society, the strange civil society, and the uncivil civil society. If only for graphic purposes we can locate the state at the centre of a given society, the *intimate society* is the inside circle around the state. It consists of individuals and social groups that enjoy high levels of social inclusion (hyperinclusion). Assuming that the idea of the three generations of human rights – civil and political, socio-economic, and cultural rights – is adequate, those included in the *intimate civil society* enjoy all the gamut of rights. They belong to the dominant community that is tied up very closely with the market and the economic forces that run it. Indeed their intimacy with the state is so great that those included in this tier of civil society have access to state or public resources above and beyond what can be obtained by any politics of rights. The relation of this civil society with the state can be described as the privatization of the state.

The *strange civil society* is the intermediate circle around the state. The social classes or groups included in it have mixed life experiences of social inclusion and of social exclusion. Social inclusion is of a low or moderate quality and correspondingly social exclusion is attenuated by some safety nets and is not viewed as irreversible. In terms of the three generations of human rights, it can be said that those in the strange civil society may exercise more or less freely the civic and political rights but have little access to the social and economic rights, not to speak of the cultural or 'post-materialist' rights.

Finally, the *uncivil civil society* is the outer circle inhabited by the utterly excluded. They are mostly socially invisible. This is the circle of social fascism and in rigor those who inhabit it do not belong to civil society, since they are thrown into the new state of nature. They have no stabilized expectations because in practice they have no rights.

This multiple stratification of civil society has always characterized modern societies. They have distinguished (and distinguish) themselves by the relative size of the different circles of civil societies. While in the core countries the wider circle has tended to be the intermediate circle (the strange civil society), which in class terms has been occupied by the middle and lower middle classes, in peripheral countries the outer circle (the uncivil civil society) has tended to cover the majority of the population. In the last twenty years the neo-liberal hegemonic globalization has produced a double decisive impact on the dynamics of the multi-layered civil society. On the one hand, the intermediate circle, the strange civil society, has been narrowing down across the world system as a few of those living in it have moved up to the inside circle while the vast majority has moved down or see themselves as being in the process of moving from the intermediate circle to the outer circle, to the uncivil civil society. As a result, both core and peripheral and semi-peripheral countries, irrespective of the many differences that separate them, have become more and more polarized between forms of social hyperinclusion and forms of social hyperexclusion. On the other hand, as the neo-liberal model of development is imposed throughout the world system, the dynamics behind both hyperinclusion and hyperexclusion is more and more a global one. The exclusion of today is probably more directly linked to policies originated in countries in the West (and in international institutions controlled by them) than it was the case with colonialism or imperialism. The intervention on the economies and polities of both peripheral and semi-peripheral countries conducted by neo-liberal globalization is unprecedented in terms of its scale and intensity and also in terms of the vast global hegemonic coalition that controls it. This fact explains why the Western based view of social political reality, exported as a globalized localism across the globe, is an evermore 'adequate' view of the dominant power structures in different countries. However, as I claim below, this also means that the subaltern West can more easily ally itself to the subaltern 'rest'. Only through such alliances will it be possible to overcome the 'West/rest' hierarchy.

The typology of civil societies above allows us to show that, despite the ideological rhetoric to the contrary, the political and legal discourses and practices allowed by neo-liberal globalization are incapable of confronting social fascism and therefore of addressing the 'social question' of the dramatic growth of the uncivil civil society. Indeed, the aggressive re-emergence of conservatism has had a decisive impact on the two other ideologies sanctioned by the liberal state, liberalism and demo-socialism, as I showed in the first section. It has led to the merging of the two, under the aegis of liberalism. The doctrine that expresses that kind of political hybridization is what I call demo-liberalism. The best expression of such a hybrid is the so-called Third Way, as propounded by the British Labour Party and theorized by Anthony Giddens.[15] In fact, though presented as the renewal of social democracy, the Third Way recuperates most of the liberal agenda and abandons most of the demo-socialist agenda.

As I will argue in the next section, to confront social fascism successfully and address the needs of the uncivil civil society another law and another politics are necessary: the law and politics of counter-hegemonic globalization and subaltern cosmopolitanism.

5   ON SUBALTERN COSMOPOLITANISM

I have argued throughout this book, especially in Chapter Five, that neo-liberal globalization, although being the hegemonic form of globalization, is not the only one. Throughout the world, local, national and transnational social groups, networks, initiatives, organizations and movements have been active in confronting neo-liberal globalization and in proposing alternatives to it. Aside from struggles that are originally

---

[15]   Giddens, 1998.

transnational, I include in this vast set of confrontational politics social struggles that, though local or national in scope, are networked in different ways with parallel struggles elsewhere. Together they constitute what I call counter-hegemonic globalization.

They are counter-hegemonic not just because they fight against the economic, social and political outcomes of hegemonic globalization but because they challenge the conception of general interest underlying the latter and propose an alternative conception. For hegemonic globalization the unfettered expansion of global capitalism is the general interest and as such legitimized to produce vast, unavoidable and in the end positive (because growth-promoting) forms of social exclusion. On the contrary, counter-hegemonic movements and organizations claim that such massive social exclusion bears witness to the fact that the interests of global capital, far from being the general interest, are indeed inimical to the latter, since social exclusion and particularly its most extreme form, social fascism, deny basic human dignity and respect to large parts of the population across the globe. Treatment with dignity and respect are due to humankind – and for some, to nature as well. As such, the idea of general interest calls for social inclusion and cannot be reconciled with processes of social transformation premised upon the inevitability of social exclusion.

Counter-hegemonic globalization is therefore focused on the struggle against social exclusion, a struggle which in its broadest terms encompasses not only excluded populations but also nature. The eradication of social fascism is thus the primary objective and therefore the uncivil civil society is the privileged social base of counter-hegemonic struggles. The latter aim at reaching out to what I have called the strange civil society, where less extreme forms of social exclusion prevail.

Social exclusion is always the product of unequal power relations, that is, of unequal exchanges. Since several forms of power circulate in society it is as unfeasible to produce a monolithic theory of social exclusion as it is to bring all the struggles against it under a single banner. Counter-hegemonic globalization is therefore a plural project. Herein lies both its strength and its weakness. Such plurality and diversity does not preclude the possibility of communication, mutual understanding and co-operation among the different struggles. Indeed, the potential and viability of counter-hegemonic globalization revolves around such a possibility. Nevertheless, whatever is achieved through collaboration among progressive movements and organizations is less the result of a common starting point than of a common point of arrival. I call this rather loose bundle of projects and struggles subaltern cosmopolitanism, or cosmopolitanism of the oppressed.

The current debates on cosmopolitanism do not concern me here. In its long history cosmopolitanism has meant universalism, tolerance, patriotism, world citizenship, worldwide community of human beings, global culture etc., etc. More often than not, when this concept has been used – either as a scientific tool to describe reality or as an instrument in political struggles – the unconditional inclusiveness of its abstract formulation has been used to pursue the exclusionary interests of a particular social group. In a sense cosmopolitanism has been a privilege of those that can afford it.

There are two ways of revisiting this concept, one by asking who can afford it, the other by asking who needs it. The first question is about social practice. It entails the singling out of those social groups who have managed to reproduce their hegemony by using to their benefit concepts like cosmopolitanism that would seem to run against the very idea of group benefits. This question has thus a critical, deconstructive stance. The second question is about social expectations. It entails the identification of groups whose aspirations are denied or made invisible by the hegemonic use of the concept and may be served by an alternative use of it. This question has a post-critical reconstructive stance. This is the question I ask here.

Paraphrasing Stuart Hall, who raised a similar question in relation to the concept of identity,[16] I ask: who needs cosmopolitanism? The answer is simple: whoever is a victim of intolerance and discrimination needs tolerance; whoever is denied basic human dignity needs a community of human beings; whoever is a non-citizen needs world citizenship in any given community or nation. In sum, those socially excluded, victims of the hegemonic conception of cosmopolitanism, need a different type of cosmopolitanism. Subaltern cosmopolitanism is therefore an oppositional variety. Just as neo-liberal globalization does not recognize any alternative form of globalization, so also cosmopolitanism without adjectives denies its own particularity. Subaltern, oppositional cosmopolitanism is the cultural and political form of counter-hegemonic globalization. It is the name of the emancipatory projects whose claims and criteria of social inclusion reach beyond the horizons of global capitalism.

Since there is no unified theory, and much less a unified strategy underlying these projects, subaltern cosmopolitanism is best rendered by reference to those projects that provide specially cogent or exemplary illustrations of the struggle against social exclusion in the name of an alternative globalization. In my view, the Zapatist movement is one such project. Thus, I will now move to identify the major political features of subaltern cosmopolitanism through a theoretical reconstruction of the Zapatista movement. This theoretical reconstruction by far transcends the Zapatistas themselves and, I believe, its relevance will survive the future vicissitudes of its protagonists of today.

What is most striking about the Zapatistas is their proposal to ground the struggle against social exclusion in a new civilizing horizon. By focusing on humanity, dignity and respect, they go way beyond the progressive political legacy we have inherited from the nineteenth and twentieth centuries. In my view, the novelty of their contribution to subaltern thought and struggles is fourfold.

---

[16]   Hall, 1996. On different conceptions of cosmopolitanism, see Breckeridge et al (eds), 2002.

The first novelty concerns the conception of power and oppression. Neo-liberalism, more than a specific version of the capitalist mode of production, is a civilizing model based on the dramatic increase of inequality in social relations. Such inequality takes on multiple forms that are as many faces of oppression. The exploitation of workers is one of them, but there are many other kinds of oppression affecting women, ethnic minorities, indigenous peoples, peasants, the unemployed, immigrants, ghetto underclasess, gays and lesbians, the young and children.

All these kinds of oppression bring about exclusion, and that is why at the core of the Zapatista struggle there are not the exploited but rather the excluded, there is not class but rather humanity: 'Behind our 'pasamontañas'. . . there are all the simple and common men and women of no account, invisible, nameless, without future'.[17] The emancipatory nature of social struggles resides in all of them as a whole and not in any one of them in particular. The priority to be given to one or the other does not stem from any theory but rather from the concrete conditions of each country or region in a given historical moment. The struggle to which, under these conditions, is given priority, assumes the task of opening up the political space for the remaining struggles. Thus, for example, the concrete conditions of Mexico at this moment give precedence to the indigenous struggle. However, it was not accidental that the Zapatista leader that addressed the Mexican Congress on 28 March 2001 was Comandante Esther. With her impressive speech, the Zapatista movement sealed its alliance with the women's liberation movement.

The second novelty concerns the equivalence between the principles of equality and difference. We live in societies that are obscenely unequal, and yet equality is lacking as an emancipatory ideal. Equality, understood as the equivalence among the same ends up excluding what is different. All that is homogeneous at the beginning tends to turn eventually into exclusionary violence. In as much as they carry alternative visions of social emancipation, differences must, therefore, be respected. It is up to those who claim them to decide to what extent they wish to hybridize or de-differentiate. This articulation between the principle of equality and the principle of difference requires a new radicalism in the struggles for human rights. Regardless of the concessions made to workers, and later to other excluded from the social contract, political liberalism neutralized the radically democratic potential of human rights by imposing worldwide a very restrictive European historical reality. In legal and political terms this is embodied in the concept of different generations of human rights and the idea that the first generation (civil rights) prevails over the second one (political rights) and both prevail over the third one (social and economic rights). The radical novelty of the Zapatista proposal in this regard lies in formulating their claims, which by and large concern human rights, in such terms as to avoid the trap of generations. Considered separately, the eleven Zapatista claims are far from being path breaking or revolutionary: work, land, housing, food, health, education, independence, freedom, democracy, justice,

---

[17]   Sub-commandante Insurgente Marcos, cited by Ceceña, 1999, 102-102.

peace. Together, they make up a 'new world', a civilizing project that offers an alternative vis-á-vis neo-liberalism.

The third novelty concerns democracy and the taking over of power. If the forms of power are many, and if society is not globally changed in the direction of the protection of dignity and respect, it is useless to take over : 'To seize power? No, simply something far more difficult: a new world'.[18] The stress is not on the destruction of what exists rather on the creation of alternatives. As the faces of oppression are multiple, so are the struggles and proposals for resistance varied. So varied are they that no vanguard will unify them: 'We do not wish, nor can we, occupy the place that many expect us to occupy, the place whence emanate all opinions, all answers, all truths. We won't do it'.[19] Rebellion must find itself from below, from the participation of all. Violence is no alternative – indeed organized violence is a 'prerogative' of the dominant classes or social groups – and representative democracy only fails because it is corrupt and because it does not accept the challenges of participatory democracy.

What is at stake is the constitution of a counter-hegemonic globalization encompassing several worlds, several kinds of social organizations and movements, and several conceptions of social emancipation. The political obligation that unites such diversity is a horizontal political obligation that feeds on the substitution of relations of shared authority for relations of power. But such an obligation is as fundamental in relations among organizations or movements as inside each of them. Internal democracy is the golden rule, not to be confused with democratic centralism, of a Leninist bent, which was only justified, if ever, in the context of clandestine struggles against dictatorships – amongst recent examples, the case of the ANC against apartheid in South Africa must be highlighted.

The low-intensity democracies in which we live are trapped by the spaces of political action they open and are unable to fill up. Filling them up is a task for the counter-hegemonic forces. These can show that democracy, when taken seriously, has little to do with the caricature into which liberalism, not to mention neo-liberalism, has turned it. What is essential is to understand that, contrary to what the modernist vanguards wanted, 'one must walk along with those that walk more slowly'.[20] Since there is no goal but rather a horizon, what matters is that we walk together. The strategic role of communication and information consists in showing that you are not alone in the struggle.

The fourth novelty of the contribution of the Zapatistas to subaltern cosmopolitanism is that rebellion and not revolution is the key issue. Since taking over state power is not an immediate objective, rebellious actions have a vast social field of operation –

[18]   Sub-comandante Insurgente Marcos, cited by Ceceña, 1999, p 103.
[19]   Sub-comandante Insurgente Marcos, cited by Ceceña, 1998, p 145.
[20]   Ceceña, 2001, p 28.

the vast set of social interactions structured by power inequalities. Different movements or struggles may be interested in confronting different social interactions and the struggle has to be conducted in light of the specific conditions at hand in that particular social field at that precise historical conjuncture. This means that an old canonical sequence of revolutionary Marxism in the twentieth century, which was put forward most eloquently by Althusser: 'Marxists know that no tactic is possible which does not rest on some strategy and no strategy which does not rest on some theory'[21] is thereby abandoned or completely subverted. Under Zapatism what is tactics for a movement may be strategy for another and the terms may mean different things for different struggles in different parts of the world and in some of them may even be utterly meaningless. Moreover, no unified theory can possibly render the immense mosaic of movements, struggles and initiatives in a coherent way. Under the modern revolutionary paradigm the belief in a unified theory was so entrenched that the different revolutionary movements had to subscribe to the most simplistic descriptions of their empirical reality, so that they fit the theoretical demands.[22]

From the point of view of subaltern cosmopolitanism, such effort is not only ludicrous but it is also dangerous. The theory, whatever its value, will always be last, not first. Instead of theory that unifies the immense variety of struggles and movements, what we need is a theory of translation – that is, a theory that rather than aiming at creating another (theoretical) reality over and above the movements, seeks to create mutual understanding, mutual intelligibility among them so that they may benefit from the experiences of others and network with them. Instead of our rarified descriptions the procedure of translation rests on thick descriptions. Indeed, there is never enough specificity in the accounts of two or more movements or struggles to guarantee an unproblematic translation among them.

Another old idea of twentieth century revolutionary politics that is abandoned here is the idea of stages of struggle – ie, the idea of the passage from the phase of the coalitions with democratic forces to the phase of socialist takeover – which consumed so much of the time and energy of the revolutionaries and was responsible for so many splits and fratricidal confrontations. Given the mosaic of subaltern cosmopolitan movements at work under such different circumstances around the globe, it makes no sense to speak of stages, not only because there is no end point or final stage because also there is no general definition of the initial conditions that are responsible for the first stage. Instead of an evolutionist modernist paradigm of a transformative movement, subaltern cosmopolitan struggles – as illustrated by Zapatismo – are guided by a pragmatic principle based on commonsensical rather than theoretical knowledge: to make the world less and less comfortable for global capital. The idea of stages is replaced

---

[21]   Debray, 1967, p 27.

[22]   The most salient and nonetheless brilliant manifestation of this theoretical work was Regis Debray's analysis of social revolution in different Latin American countries in the 1960s. See Debray, 1967. On the Zapatistas, see Holloway and Peláez (eds), 1998.

by the idea of destabilizing potential, a potential which, irrespective of the scale of the movements, is strengthened by the networking among them. A given local struggle may be the 'small motor' that helps the larger motor of a global movement to get started. But, conversely, a global movement may equally be the small motor that helps the larger motor of a local struggle to get started.

Finally, in subaltern cosmopolitanism the question of the compatibility of a given struggle or movement with global capitalism, which in the past led to heated debates, has become a moot one. Since taking over state power is not a privileged objective and since there is no organization unifying the mosaic of counter-hegemonic movements under a single banner, all cosmopolitan initiatives are allowed to engage without apology with their particular roots and their empirical reality. As they live in a world largely governed by global capital they are per definition compatible with the latter, and whenever they represent a more radical break with a given state of affairs, they may be easily dismissed as an island of difference, as a microcosm of social innovation which is easily accommodated within the overall picture of hegemonic governance. The question of compatibility is then the question of whether the world is made less and less comfortable for global capitalism by subaltern insurgent practices or whether, on the contrary, global capitalism has managed to co-opt the latter and transform them into means of its own reproduction.

The question of compatibility is for all practical purposes replaced by the question of the political direction of the cumulative processes of mutual learning, reciprocal adaptation and transformation between dominant hegemonic social practices and subaltern, insurgent practices. This is a crucial question indeed as the future of the competing globalizations will depend on the answer to it. The form of globalization that will learn more and faster will fare better in the confrontation. If history repeated itself one could predict that hegemonic globalization would more likely learn more and faster from counter-hegemonic globalization than vice versa. Indeed, notwithstanding the difference in context, times and interests at stake, it is useful to recall here Debray's admonition that the US and its counter-revolutionary strategy in Latin America in the 1960s learned faster from the Cuban Revolution than the other revolutionary groups that were active at the time in other parts of the continent – Venezuela, Brazil, Bolivia, Argentina, Peru, etc.[23]

The features of the new paradigm of a subaltern cosmopolitanism as theoretically reconstructed here on the basis of the Zapatista movement open space for a great deal of political creativity on the part of movements and organizations. The evaluation of such creativity will be guided by the same pragmatic principle that has replaced the idea of stages of struggle. Thus, the question to be asked is whether such creativity has rendered the world less comfortable for global capitalism or not. As regards any other paradigm, the features of the new political paradigm are not entirely new. Above

---

[23]   Debray, 1967.

all, they are too vague. They must, therefore, be reflected upon, considered in detail and adapted by the different organizations and movements to the historical realities of each country or local. Only thus will they contribute effectively to broaden the paths of counter-hegemonic globalization.

6 SUBALTERN COSMOPOLITANISM AND LAW: THE CONDITIONS FOR COSMOPOLITAN LEGALITY

Subaltern cosmopolitanism, as understood here, is a cultural, political and social project of which there are only embryonic manifestations. Accordingly, an inquiry into the place of law in subaltern cosmopolitanism and the nascent practices that may embody a subaltern cosmopolitan legality must be done in a rather prospective and prescriptive spirit. This is the spirit that animates the remainder of this chapter, which aims at laying out – rather than fully fleshing out – a research agenda on subaltern cosmopolitan legal theory and practice and at mapping some of the key sites in which such theory and practice are currently being tried out.[24]

To this purpose, the approach I adopt here is, as I have it done elsewhere,[25] a sociology of emergence, which entails interpreting in an expansive way the initiatives, movements or organizations that resist neo-liberal globalization and social exclusion, and offer alternatives to them. The traits of the struggles are amplified and elaborated upon in such a way as to make visible and credible the potential that lies implicit or hidden in the actual counter-hegemonic actions. The symbolic enlargement brought about by the sociology of emergence aims to analyze the tendencies or possibilities inscribed in a given practice, experience or form of knowledge. It acts upon both possibilities and capacities. It identifies signals, clues, or traces of future possibilities in whatever exists. This approach allows us to identify emergent qualities and entities at a moment and in a context in which they can be easily discarded as having no future-bearing quality, as being insignificant, or indeed as being past oriented. This approach corresponds in prospective analysis to the extended case method in sociological analysis.

Given my concern with law in this book, I am not going to deal with the whole spectrum of initiatives or movements but rather only with those whose legal strategies seem more prominent. Indeed I am going to deal with the legal strategies themselves – that is, with subaltern cosmopolitan legality (in short, cosmopolitan legality). Cosmopolitan

---

[24]   In presenting the research agenda and mapping the sites of subaltern cosmopolitan legality, I draw heavily on the results of an ongoing collective research project that – under my direction and with the participation of more than sixty scholars and activists from India, Brazil, Portugal, South Africa, Mozambique and Colombia – has been exploring forms of counter-hegemonic globalization in the South. The case studies and the overall results of the project are published in Portuguese (Santos, org 2002a, 2002b, 2000c, 2002d, 2002e) and will be also available in English and Spanish. See also the project's website at http://www.ces.fe.uc.pt/emancipa/.

[25]   See Santos, 2001a.

legality furthers counter-hegemonic globalization. And since in our current conditions counter-hegemonic globalization is a necessary condition of social emancipation, the inquiry into cosmopolitan legality is my way of responding to the question I started out with: can law be emancipatory?

I will start out by presenting, in the form of theses accompanied by brief explanatory notes, the conditions or presuppositions of subaltern cosmopolitan legality.[26] They are in a condensed form the main results of the sociology of emergence. Together they form an ideal typical image of cosmopolitan legality. I will then move on in the next section to offer some illustrations of struggles against neo-liberal globalization in which law has been a significant component. It will become clear that the concrete illustrations represent different degrees of approximation to cosmopolitan legality.

As for the conditions for cosmopolitan legality, they can be summed up in the following eight theses.

6.1 *It is one thing to use a hegemonic instrument in a given political struggle. It is another thing to use it in a hegemonic fashion*

This applies both to law and the politics of rights. As I will show below, according to subaltern cosmopolitanism, law is not reduced to state law nor rights to individual rights. This, however, does not mean that the state law and individual rights are to be excluded from cosmopolitan legal practices. On the contrary, they may be used if integrated into broader struggles that take them out of the hegemonic mould. This mould is basically the idea of autonomy and the idea that rights are both means and ends of social practice. In this view, law and rights are autonomous as their validity is not contingent upon the conditions of their social efficacy. They are autonomous also because they operate through specific sets of state institutions established for this purpose – courts, legislatures, etc. Moreover, law and rights are conceived of as pre-empting the use of any other social tool. Laws are authoritative state-produced normative standards of social action, while rights are authoritative state-guaranteed individual entitlements derived from laws. Thus conceived law and rights determine their own boundaries and beyond them nothing can be claimed either as law or as right. Because they are produced and guaranteed by the state, the latter has the monopoly over the declaration of legality or illegality, of right or wrong.

---

[26] For decades US scholars have debated the question of whether rights strategies facilitate 'progressive social change' or whether they legitimate and reinforce social inequalities. A good overview can be read in Levitsky, 2001. In the narrow terms in which it has been discussed – as a debate within demo-liberalism – this debate is undecidable. I offer an analytical and political alternative in this chapter.

In opposition to this conception, cosmopolitanism makes two assertions: first it is possible to use these hegemonic tools for non-hegemonic objectives; secondly, there are alternative, non-hegemonic conceptions of such tools. To this I turn in the following thesis.

6.2 A non-hegemonic use of hegemonic legal tools is premised upon the possibility of integrating them in broader political mobilizations that may include legal as well as illegal actions

Contrary to the critical legal studies movement, cosmopolitan legality subscribes to a non-essentialist view of state law and rights. What makes the latter hegemonic is the specific use that the dominant classes or groups make of them. Used as autonomous exclusive instruments of social action they are indeed part of top-down politics. They are unstable, contingent, manipulable and confirm the structures of power they are supposed to change. In sum, conceived and utilized in this way they are of no use to cosmopolitan legality.

There is, however, the possibility of law and rights being used as non-autonomous and non-exclusive. Such a possibility is premised upon the 'integration' of law and rights in broader political mobilizations that allow for the struggles to be politicized before they are legalized. Once law and rights are resorted to, political mobilization must be intensified, so as to avoid the depoliticization of the struggle which law and rights, left alone, are bound to produce. A strong politics of law and rights is one that does not rely solely on law or on rights. Paradoxically, one way of showing defiance for law and rights is to struggle for increasingly inclusive laws and rights. Manipulability, contingency and instability from below is the most efficient way of confronting manipulability, contingency and instability from above. A strong politics of rights is a dual politics based on the dual management of legal and political tools under the aegis of the latter.

The most intense moments of cosmopolitan legality are likely to involve direct action, civil disobedience, strikes, demonstrations, media-oriented performances, etc. Some of these will be illegal, while others will be located in spheres not regulated by state law. Subaltern illegality may be used to confront both dominant legality and dominant illegality. The latter is particularly pervasive and aggressive in the case of the parallel state to which I referred above. In societies with some historical experience of demo-liberal legality, state law and rights, once viewed from the margins – from the viewpoint of the oppressed and excluded – are contradictorily both sites of exclusion and sites of inclusion. The nature and the direction of political struggles will determine which will prevail. In societies with little or no historical experience of demo-liberal legality it is highly improbable that hegemonic laws and rights be put to a non-hegemonic use.

6.3 Non-hegemonic forms of law do not necessarily favour or promote subaltern cosmopolitanism

The question of non-hegemony in the realm of law is today a rather complex one. Demo-liberal legality has traditionally been understood as state law or state sanctioned law and such has been the hegemonic concept of law. Today, in a period of intense globalizations and intense localizations there are multiple sources of law and not all of them can be said to be sanctioned by the state. Non-hegemonic forms of law are not necessarily counter-hegemonic ones. On the contrary, they may rather be at the service of hegemonic law contributing to its reproduction under new conditions and indeed accentuating its exclusionary traits. The new forms of global legality 'from above', produced by powerful transnational actors, such as the new *lex mercatoria* analyzed in Chapter Five, are a case in point as they combine or articulate with state legality in a kind of legal co-management that furthers neo-liberal globalization and deepens social exclusion.

There is also much legality being generated from below – traditional law, indigenous law, community law, popular law, etc. As is the case with non-state legality from above, such non-hegemonic legality is not necessarily counter-hegemonic as it may be used in conjuncture with state law to pursue exclusionary purposes. But it may also be used to confront demo-liberal state legality and to fight for social inclusion and against neo-liberal globalization, in which case it assumes a counter-hegemonic political role. In this case, non-hegemonic legalities from below are part and parcel of cosmopolitan legality.

Legal pluralism plays a central role in cosmopolitan legality but must be always subjected to a kind of litmus test to determine which forms of legal pluralism are conducive to cosmopolitan legality and which are not. The test consists in evaluating whether legal pluralism contributes to reducing the unequality of power relations, thereby reducing social exclusion or upgrading the quality of social inclusion or whether, on the contrary, it rigidifies unequal exchanges and reproduces social exclusion. In the first case we are before cosmopolitan legal plurality.

6.4 Cosmopolitan legality is voracious in terms of the scales of legality

Cosmopolitan legality takes seriously the idea put forth in Chapter Eight that law is a map of misreading. Accordingly, for cosmopolitan legality the forms of political mobilization and their concrete objectives will determine which scale must be privileged (local, national, global). The privilege granted to a given scale does not mean that the other scales will not be mobilized. On the contrary, cosmopolitan legality tends to combine different scales of legality and indeed to subvert them in the sense of targeting the global in the local and the local in the global. It is a transcalar legality.

6.5 Cosmopolitan legality is a subaltern legality targeting the uncivil and the strange civil society

Cosmopolitan legality targets first and foremost the uncivil civil society as it aims to eradicate social exclusion, particularly its most extreme form – social fascism. But it reaches out also to the lowest strata of the strange civil society in which often massive social exclusion takes place. While fighting social exclusion cosmopolitan legality is aware of the danger of thereby confirming and legitimating the modern liberal social contract and therefore also the systematic exclusion it produces, as happens with demo-liberal legality and the latter's selective concessions to selected excluded groups. To avoid this, cosmopolitan legality seeks to address systematic harm and not just the victim/perpetrator relationship as is the case with demo-liberal legality. This explains why political mobilization and confrontational, rebellious moments are not complements but rather intrinsic components of cosmopolitan legality. To address systematic harm involves claiming a new radically more inclusive social contract. Restorative justice, which is the demo-liberal conception of justice *par excellence*, must therefore be replaced by transformative justice, that is, by a project of social justice that reaches beyond the horizon of global capitalism. Here lies the oppositional and counter-hegemonic character of cosmopolitan legality.

6.6 As a subaltern form of legality cosmopolitanism submits the three modern principles of regulation to a hermeneutics of suspicion

Contrary to demo-liberal legality, cosmopolitan legality conceives of power relations as not being restricted to the state but rather 'inhabiting' both the market and the community. Accordingly, it distinguishes between dominant market and subaltern market, and between dominant community and subaltern community. The objective of cosmopolitan legality resides in empowering subaltern markets and subaltern communities. Together they are the building blocs of subaltern public spheres.

6.7 The gap between the excess of meaning and the deficit of task is inherent to a politics of legality. Cosmopolitan legality is haunted by this gap

Even if cosmopolitan legality, whenever it resorts to state law, it does so in the context of a counter-hegemonic strategy, the fact remains that the gap between excess of meaning (symbolic expansion through abstract promises) and the deficit of task (the narrowness of concrete achievements), referred to in Chapter Two, may end up discrediting the cosmopolitan struggles as a whole. The crisis of the modern social contract resides in the inversion of the discrepancy between social experience and social expectation. After a long period of positive expectations about the future, at least in core and semi-peripheral countries, we have entered a period of negative expectations for large bodies of populations around the world. The cosmopolitan project consists precisely in restoring the modern discrepancy between social experiences and social expectations even if through oppositional postmodern practices and pointing to radical political transformations. In light of this, however, a tension may develop between cosmopolitanism as a whole and cosmopolitan legality. Indeed in a period in which social expectations are negative when compared with current social experiences, cosmopolitan legality may find itself in the position of being most effective when defending the legal status quo, the effective enforcement of laws as they exist in the books. The dilemma for cosmopolitanism lies in having to struggle both for deep social transformation and for the status quo. Once again, the way out resides in a strong political mobilization of law that uses law's excess of meaning to turn a struggle for status quo into a struggle for deep social transformation; and law's deficit of task to turn a struggle for social transformation into a struggle for the status quo.

6.8   *In spite of the deep differences between demo-liberal legality and cosmopolitan legality, the relations between them are dynamic and complex*

Demo-liberal legality makes a hegemonic use of hegemonic conceptions of law and rights. It has no place for political infringements of law's autonomy and much less for illegal actions. It targets both the intimate and the strange civil society, and the concessions it makes to the severely excluded (the uncivil civil society) are made in such a way as to confirm and legitimate the social contract and its systemic exclusions. It gets its regulatory resources from the state, where according to it all the relevant power relations reside, and from the dominant market and the dominant community. Finally, since it does not aspire to any form of deep, structural social transformation, it excels in restorative justice and uses the gap between excess of meaning and deficit of task to advance adaptive manipulations of the status quo.

This shows how much cosmopolitan legality differs from demo-liberal legality. However, in spite of these differences, cosmopolitan struggles may profitably combine cosmopolitan legal strategies with demo-liberal strategies, thus giving rise to political and legal hybrids of different sorts. Human rights struggles offer themselves to this kind of legal hybridization. Emancipatory projects, guided by principles of good order and good society, always combine different sets of objectives, some of which may be pursued within limits through demo-liberal strategies when they are available. It may also happen that the political, cultural and social context in which cosmopolitan struggles take place forces the latter to formulate themselves in demo-liberal terms. This is likely to occur in two contrasting situations in which more radical struggles may be met with efficient repression: in societies in which a strong political and legal demo-liberal culture coexists with overarching conservative ideologies as is most notably the case of the US; and in dictatorial or quasi-dictatorial regimes, and, more generally, in situations of extremely low intensity democracy as is the case of many peripheral countries and some semi-peripheral countries. In both situations, transnational coalitions and transnational advocacy will be often necessary to sustain cosmopolitan legality.

But the legal hybridization between cosmopolitanism and demo-liberalism has a deeper source. It stems from the concept of social emancipation itself. Substantive concepts of social emancipation are always contextual and embedded. In any given context, however, it is possible to define degrees of social emancipation. I distinguish between thin conceptions and thick conceptions of social emancipation, according to the degree and quality of liberation or social inclusion they carry. The thin conception of social emancipation underlies, for instance, the struggles by which vicious forms of oppression or extreme forms of social exclusion are replaced by milder forms of oppression or by non-fascist forms of social exclusion. As illustrated below with the case of San José de Apartadó in Colombia, sheer physical survival and protection against arbitrary violence may be the only and simultaneously the most cherished emancipatory objective. On the other hand, the thick conception of emancipation entails not just human survival but human flourishing guided by radical needs, as Agnes Heller has called them. According to Heller, radical needs are qualitative and remain unquantifiable; they cannot be satisfied in a world based on subordination and superordination; they drive people toward ideas and practices that abolish subordination and superordination.[27] Although the distinction between thin and thick conceptions of social emancipation may be made in general tems, the kinds of objectives that fall in one or the other term of the distinction can only be determined in specific contexts. It may well be the case that what counts as a thin conception of emancipation for a given cosmopolitan struggle in a given society and historical moment may count as a thick conception for another cosmopolitan struggle in another geographical and temporal context.

In light of this distinction, it can be said that cosmopolitan and demo-liberal legal strategies are more likely to be combined whenever thin conceptions of social emancipation tend to dominate the emancipatory projects of cosmopolitan groups and struggles. This will be, for instance, the case of cosmopolitan groups fighting for basic civic and political rights without which they can neither mobilize nor organize.

7   COSMOPOLITAN LEGALITY IN ACTION

In the following I will briefly mention some instances in which legal practices and claims are constitutive components of cosmopolitan struggles against neo-liberal globalization and social fascism. As I said above, rather than an exhaustive analysis of the myriad manifestations of legal cosmopolitan practices around the world, I seek to map some of the most salient and promising ones as a way to lay out a research agenda on

[27]   Heller, 1976, 1993.

cosmopolitan legality and spot the potential for linkages among seemingly disparate struggles.[28] Specifically, I will deal with five clusters of cosmopolitan legalities: law in the contact zones, law and the democratic rediscovery of labour, law and non-capitalist production, law for non-citizens, and the law of the state as the newest social movement.

7.1   *Law in the contact zones*

Contact zones are social fields in which different normative life worlds meet and clash.[29] Cosmopolitan struggles often take place in such social fields. Normative life worlds, besides providing patterns of authorized or legitimate social, political and economic experiences and expectations, appeal to expansive cultural postulates and therefore the conflicts among them tend to involve issues and mobilize resources and energies far beyond what seems to be at stake in the manifest version of the conflicts. The contact zones that concern me here are those in which different legal cultures clash in highly asymmetrical ways, that is, in clashes that mobilize very unequal power exchanges. For instance, as I showed in Chapter Five and will comment on below, indigenous peoples enter asymmetric encounters with dominant national cultures, as do illegal immigrants or refugees trying to survive in a country not their own.

Contact zones are therefore zones in which rival normative ideas, knowledges, power forms, symbolic universes and agencies meet in unequal conditions and resist, reject, assimilate, imitate, subvert each other, giving rise to hybrid legal and political constellations in which the inequality of exchanges are traceable. Legal hybrids are legal and political phenomena that mix heterogeneous entities operating through disintegration of forms and retrieval of fragments, giving rise to new constellations of legal and political meaning. As a result of the interactions that take place in the contact zone both the nature of the different powers involved and the power differences among

---

28   As I said above, in mapping cosmopolitan legal practices I draw heavily from the research project 'Reinventing Social Emancipation', which I directed between 1998–2002 and whose results have been published as Santos (org), 2002a, 2002b, 2002c, 2002d, 2002e. Although the project did not have an explicit socio-legal dimension to it, many of the case studies carried out by the project's participants from Brazil, India, Colombia, Mozambique, South Africa and Portugal document subaltern struggles in those countries that resort to cosmopolitan legal strategies.

29   Mary Louise Pratt, 1994, p 4, defines contact zones as 'social spaces where disparate cultures meet, clash and grapple with each other often in highly asymmetrical relations of domination and subordination – like colonialism, slavery or their aftermaths as they are lived out across the globe today'. In this formulation contact zones seem to involve encounters among cultural totalities. This does not have to be the case. The contact zone may involve selected and partial cultural differences, the ones that in a given time-space find themselves in competition to provide meaning for a given course of action. Moreover, as I have been claiming in this book, the unequal exchanges extend today far beyond colonialism and its aftermath even though, as post-colonial studies have shown, the latter continues to play a much more important role than one is ready to admit. See lastly Mignolo, 2000.

them are affected. The latter may indeed intensify or attenuate as a result of the encounter.

Complexity is intrinsic to the definition of the contact zone itself. Who defines who or what belongs to the contact zone and what does not? To whom belongs the line that delimits the contact zone both externally and internally? Indeed, the struggle for the appropriation of such line is the meta-struggle for cosmopolitan legality in the contact zone. Another source of complexity lies in that the differences between cultures or normative life worlds present in the contact zone may be so wide as to be incommensurable. The first task is then to approximate the cultural and normative universes, to bring them so to say, 'within visual contact' so that translation among them may begin. Paradoxically, because of the multiplicity of cultural codes in presence, the contact zone is relatively uncodified or sub-standard, a zone for normative and cultural experimentation and innovation.

The question of power is the central one for cosmopolitan struggles as the subaltern groups fight for equality and recognition against the dominant groups. Cosmopolitan legality is thus the legal component of struggles that refuse to accept the power status quo and the systematic harm it produces and fight them in the name of alternative cultural and normative legitimacies. Cosmopolitan legality in the contact zone is anti-monopolistic in that it recognizes rival legal claims and organizes the struggle around the competition among them. Legal plurality is therefore inherent to the contact zone.

What is at stake in the contact zone is never a simple determination of equality or inequality since alternative concepts of equality are present and in conflict. In other words, in the contact zones the law of equality does not operate in separation from the law of recognition of difference. Cosmopolitan legal struggle in the contact zone is a pluralist one that fights for transcultural or intercultural equality of differences. This equality of differences includes the transcultural equal right of each group involved in the contact zone to decide whether to remain different or mix with other and form hybrids.

Cosmopolitan legal struggles in the contact zone are particularly complex and the legal constellations that emerge from it tend to be unstable, provisory and reversible. Cosmopolitan legal struggle is not, of course, the only type of legal struggle that may intervene in the contact zone.

The contrast between demo-liberal legality and cosmopolitan legality is best highlighted by the types of contact zone sociability that each legal paradigm tends to privilege or sanction. I distinguish four types of sociability: violence, coexistence, reconciliation, and conviviality. *Violence* is the type of encounter in which the dominant culture or normative life world vindicates full control over the contact zone and as such feels legitimated to suppress, marginalize or even destroy the subaltern culture or normative life world. *Coexistence* is the sociability typical of cultural apartheid in which different cultures are allowed to unfold separately and in which contacts, intermingling or hybridizations are strongly discouraged if not outright forbidden. *Reconciliation* is the type of sociability based on restorative justice, on healing past grievances. It is a past-oriented rather than a future-oriented sociability. For this reason the power imbalances of the past are often allowed to go on reproducing themselves under new guises. Finally, *conviviality* is, in a sense, a future-oriented reconciliation. Past grievances are settled in such a way as to make possible sociabilities grounded in tendentially equal exchanges and shared authority.

Each of these sociabilities is both the producer and the product of a specific legal constellation. A legal constellation dominated by demo-liberalism tends to favour reconciliation and, whenever impossible, coexistence or even violence. A legal constellation dominated by cosmopolitanism tends to favour conviviality.

In the following, I identify the main instances in which cosmopolitan legal strategies intervene today in the contact zones. In most cases such interventions take place through legally hybrid strategies, in which cosmopolitanism combines with demo-liberalism. As mentioned above, depending on the direction of political mobilization, such strategies may end up favouring cosmopolitan or demo-liberal outcomes.

7.1.1 MULTICULTURAL HUMAN RIGHTS

The crisis of Western modernity has shown that the failure of progressive projects concerning the improvement of life chances and life conditions of subordinate groups both inside and outside the Western world was in part due to lack of cultural legitimacy. I argued in Chapter Five that this is the case with human rights and human rights movements since the universality of human rights cannot be taken for granted .The idea of human dignity can be formulated in different 'languages'. Rather than being suppressed in the name of postulated universalisms, such differences must be mutually intelligible through translation and what I called diatopical hermeneutics.[30]

Human rights are an issue that transcends the law in the contact zone. In the contact zone what is at stake is the encounter between human rights as a specific cultural conception of human dignity and other rival or alternative conceptions. While demo-liberal legality will defend, at best, a sociability of reconciliation premised upon the superiority of Western human rights culture, cosmopolitan legality will seek, through diatopical hermeneutics, to build a sociability of conviviality based on a virtuous hybridization among the most comprehensive and emancipatory conceptions of human dignity subscribed both by the human rights tradition and by the other traditions of human dignity present in the contact zone.

---

[30]   I will not dwell on human right and multiculturalism here, as I have discussed this issue in detail in Chapter Five. On the Zapatistas' concept of dignity, Holloway, 1998.

This cross-cultural reconstruction is premised upon a politics of recognition of difference able to link local embeddedness and grassroots relevance and organization, on one hand, and translocal intelligibility and emancipation, on the other. One of such linkages lies in the issue of group rights or collective rights, an issue that is suppressed or trivialized by demo-liberal legality. Cosmopolitan legality propounds a politics of rights in which individual and collective rights, rather than cannibalizing each other, strengthen each other. As is the case with all the other instances of cosmopolitan legality, cosmopolitan human rights in the contact zone are to be carried out or struggled for by local, national and global actors capable of integrating human rights in more encompassing cosmopolitan emancipatory projects.

7.1.2 THE TRADITIONAL AND THE MODERN: THE OTHER MODERNITIES OF INDIGENOUS PEOPLES AND TRADITIONAL AUTHORITIES

This is another contact zone in which the politics of legality plays an important role and in which demo-liberalism and cosmopolitanism offer alternative conceptions.

The politics of legality in this contact zone expresses itself through alternative conceptions of legal plurality. As I mentioned above, the first and probably the central issue concerning the contact zone is who defines the external and internal boundaries of the contact zone and with which criteria. This is a particularly burning issue in this contact zone since in the last two hundred years Western modernity has claimed for itself in practice the prerogative of defining what is modern and what is traditional. As such the traditional is as modern as modernity itself. It is the other of modernity. Thus constructed this dichotomy was one of the main organizing principles of the colonial rule and has continued so under different forms in the post-colonial period. As has happened with other empirical dichotomies, it has often been appropriated by subordinate groups to resist against colonial or post-colonial oppression, and it has also resulted in different kinds of legal hybrids.

Based on my own field research I identify two instances in which the dichotomy traditional/modern is played out in legal strategies. The first concerns the role of traditional authorities in Africa today.[31] For instance, in Mozambique, during the post-independence revolutionary period (1975–1989) traditional authorities were viewed as remnants of colonialism and as such marginalized. In the following period, the adoption of liberal democracy and the imposition of structural adjustment by the IMF converged to open the space for a new role for the traditional authorities. The internal transformations they underwent to respond to new tasks and adjust to new roles such as participation in land management bear witness to the possibilities underlying the

---

[31] See Santos and Trindade, 2002.

invention of tradition. The second instance of the unfolding of the traditional/modern dichotomy through legal strategies is the struggle of indigenous people for the recognition of their ancestral political and legal systems in Latin America.[32] This topic was analyzed in some detail in Chapter Five and thus I will not dwell on it here.

In both cases, despite the difficult conditions in which the struggles unfold, there is room for cosmopolitanism. In both cases, though in different ways, the traditional has become a successful way of claiming modernity, another kind of modernity. Under the violent impact of neo-liberal globalization and in light of the collapse of the state, it has come to symbolize what cannot be globalized. In its own specific way it is a form of globalization that presents itself as resistance against globalization.

Thus reinvented, the dichotomy between the traditional and the modern is today more crucial than ever. This is a privileged field for the emergence of legal hybrids. In different regions, such hybrids display different traits. For instance, legal hybrids moulded by traditional authorities in Africa differ from those resulting from the interaction between national state laws and indigenous legal systems in Latin America as well as in Canada, India, New Zealand, and Australia. Indeed, as shown in Chapter Five, in Latin America the rise of multicultural constitutionalism has become a privileged ground for the disputes in the contact zone between demo-liberalism and cosmopolitanism.

7.1.3   Cultural citizenship

This is a contact zone of great importance in which different political and legal strategies have been fiercely disputing the terms of conflict and negotiation between principles of equality (citizenship) and principles of difference (cultural identities). Though thus far theorized to convey critically the experience of Latinos in general and Mexicans in particular in the US in their struggle to claim belonging without surrendering cultural identity, the concept is of a much broader scope and is relevant to describe similar struggles throughout Europe, and indeed in all continents.

In the US, the growing LatCrit literature has cogently articulated the central issues of cultural citizenship as they relate to Latino migrants and their descendants. Central to this literature are legal struggles located at the intersection – indeed, 'intersectionality' is a key concept in this body of literature – of Latino and North American cultures and life experiences, such as those revolving around immigration, education, and language.[33] In Europe, as Sassen[34] has shown, regulations and legal struggles on immigration and cultural citizenship are no longer played out exclusively at the national level. Instead,

---

[32]   See Santos and García-Villegas, 2001.

[33]   A useful survey of these and other topics within the LatCrit debate can be found in Stefanic, 1998.

[34]   Sassen, 1999.

the 'de-facto transnationalization of immigration policy making' resulting from globalization, on the one hand, and 'the growth of a broad network of rights and court decisions', on the other, mean that today cultural citizenship is increasingly a site of legal struggles at the regional scale.[35]

This site of cosmopolitan legality thus entails a cultural and political process by means of which oppressed, excluded or marginalized groups create subaltern public spheres or insurgent civil societies out of the uncivil civil society in to which they have been thrown by the dominant power structures. Herein lies the oppositional character of the quest for cultural citizenship and its success depends on the capacity of subaltern groups to mobilize cosmopolitan legal and political strategies. The objective is to promote sociabilities of conviviality between different cultural identities as they meet in and dispute a potentially common ground of inclusion and belonging. Through conviviality, the common ground, while becoming more inclusive, becomes also less common in the sense of less homogeneously common to all those claiming to belong to it.

7.1.4   INTELLECTUAL PROPERTY RIGHTS, BIODIVERSITY AND HUMAN HEALTH

The discussion on the meaning of intellectual property rights is today the epicentre of a debate about the roots of modern knowledge. By transforming one among many worldviews into a global, hegemonic view, Western science localized and condensed the remaining forms of wisdom as 'the other'. Thus, these other forms became indigenous – because distinct – and particular – because located. In this paradigm, knowledge and technology are things – objects which can be valued and traded. To allow for this valuing and trading, knowledge and technology must be regarded as property, and orthodox intellectual property rights are the rules for the ownership of this form of property.

This topic constitutes today the battleground for one of the most serious conflicts between the North and the South.[36] It covers multiple issues, each with a variety of legal, political and cultural ramifications. Under this heading I will deal exclusively with those that involve the contact zone. The contact zone here is the time-space where alternative and rival knowledges meet: on one side, the Western-based modern science and technology; on the other side, the local, community-based, indigenous, peasant knowledges that have been the guardians of biodiversity. This is not a new contact zone but it is one that has gained great prominence in recent years due to the microchip and biotechnology revolution. This scientific innovation has made it possible to

---

[35]   Sassen, 1999, p 156.

[36]   The literature on this topics is immense. See, for example, Brush and Stablinsky (eds), 1996; Shiva,1997; Visvanathan, 1997; Posey, 1999. Different case studies of conflicts and possible dialogues among knowledges can be found in the results of the project 'Reinventing Social Emancipation' See www.ces.fe.uc.pt/emancipa/ and Santos, 2002c and 2002d.

develop in a short time new pharmaceutical products out of plants known to cure certain diseases. Mostly beyond the reach of biotechnological and pharmaceutical industries, the knowledge of the therapeutic value of plants is in the hands of *shamans, mamos, taitas, tinyanga, vanyamusòro, curandeiros* or traditional healers. In sum, it is a non-Western knowledge which, because not produced according to the rules and criteria of modern scientific knowledge is conceived of as traditional. The key question in this area is the following: While biotechnology and pharmaceutical firms claim intellectual property rights over the processes by which they obtain the active ingredient in plants, can the holders of traditional knowledge equally protect, in ways that suit them, their knowledge of the curative properties of the plants without which biodiversity cannot be put to industrial use?

In this contact zone, the clash is therefore a double one, between distinct knowledges and between rival conceptions of property. The dichotomy traditional/modern is very much present in this contact zone. What is 'traditional' about traditional knowledge is not the fact that it is old, but the way it is acquired and used, that is, the social process of learning and sharing knowledge, which is unique to each local culture. Much of this knowledge is very often quite new, but it has a social meaning and legal character, entirely different from the knowledge that indigenous peoples have acquired from settlers and industrialized societies.

The contact zone between traditional herbal knowledge and modern scientific knowledge of biodiversity is a social field of fierce political and legal disputes. Since most of the biodiversity exists in the South, particularly in indigenous peoples' territories, the legal and political issue that arises is under which conditions can access to biodiversity be granted, as well as what type of compensation must be awarded to the concerned states or communities for the knowledge – given the huge profits made by biotechnology and pharmaceutical firms through the exploitation of biodiversity. Even assuming that traditional knowledge must be protected, who will protect it and how? With which kinds of controls over the protection mechanisms?

The stakes for indigenous and local communities have risen dramatically as a result of the growing use of biotechnology in production of goods for export and the adoption of the 1995 WTO Agreement on Trade Related Aspects of Intellectual Property Rights (TRIPs).[37] These two factors have created a large potential market for the knowledge and resources of indigenous and local communities and raised significant fears that these resources will be misappropriated. As a consequence, indigenous and local knowledge is receiving increasing international attention – not only because of its relationship to indigenous and communal struggles for self-determination and group rights, but also because of its linkage with the clash between traditional knowledge and modern science. Recent high-profile cases involving ayahuasca (a traditional herb used as medicine and hallucinogen) from South America, turmeric from India, and the

---

[37]   See Correa, 2000; The Crucible Group, 1994.

soapberry from Africa, for example, have drawn international attention and have put the topic on the agenda of cosmopolitan social movements and organizations around the world.[38]

The resolution of the conflict will depend on the type of legal paradigm that prevails and will give rise to a certain type of sociability in the contact zone. So far demo-liberalism has been the dominant paradigm engendering a sociability of violence which in this case assumes the form of biopiracy[39] or at best reconciliation. Some indigenous leaders have called for coexistence – ie, granting access to indigenous knowledge subject to conditions established by the indigenous peoples – a proposal which, except in some restricted cases, seems quite unrealistic given the pressure, coming from opposing sides, for hybrid sociabilities which in these cases mean often informal arrangements which that are easily manipulated by the stronger partner. Whenever reconciliation is favoured, a past-oriented settlement is reached that, through compensation (monetary or otherwise), makes some concessions to indigenous/traditional knowledge while confirming the overriding interest of biotechnological knowledge.

The subaltern cosmopolitan agenda calls for conviviality ruled both by the principle of equality and the principle of difference. In its terms the cultural integrity of non-Western knowledge should be fully respected through the recognition on an equal basis of the rival knowledges and rival conceptions of property at play. The indigenous movements and allied transnational social movements contest this contact zone and the powers that constitute it, and fight for the creation of other, non-imperial contact zones, where relations among the different knowledges may be more horizontal, bringing a stronger case to the translation between biomedical and traditional knowledges. Accordingly, it would be up to the indigenous/traditional communities to determine the conditions under which a possible entry in the sphere of modern capitalist economy might further their communitarian interests in the future. In this and similar struggles[40] undertaken by movements confronting the global orthodoxy of intellectual property rights and the monopoly of scientific modern knowledge, subaltern cosmopolitan legality has a key role to play.

Finally, another instance of cosmopolitan legality in the field of intelectual property rights has arisen over the last few years. Here the contact zone is not as visible, although the clash between different conceptions of property and of health indeed is. It relates to the global HIV/AIDS pandemic. According to Klug, HIV/AIDS activists and non-government organizations such as Medecins Sans Frontieres and Oxfam have identified patent protection as one of the core causes of the high drug prices that effectively

---

38 Kothari, 1999.
39 Shiva, 1997.
40 Case studies of such struggles can be found in Posey, 1999; Meneses, 2002; Xaba, 2002; Escobar, 2002; Flórez, 2002; Coelho, 2002; Santos, 2002 (under Laymert Santos); Randeria, 2002.

deny access to life-saving medicines to millions of poor people in developing countries. Thus, their campaigns have now focused on the newly patented medicines to treat opportunistic infections and the retro-viral drugs that have made HIV/AIDS a chronic illness in the developed world rather than a death sentence.[41] It seems that the counter-hegemonic global coalitions against intellectual property rights in this field are yielding some fruits. Klug reports on the withdrawal of two major legal cases at the root of which is HIV/AIDS – one against South Africa, in a South African court, based on a complaint by the pharmaceutical industry, and the other against Brazil, in the WTO dispute settlement panel, brought about by the US.[42] Moreover, due to international pressure the WTO, in its annual meeting in Doha, Quatar (November, 2001), has agreed that the TRIPs agreement ' does not and should not prevent members from taking measures to protect public health…[and] that the agreement can and should be interpreted and implemented in a manner supportive of WTO members' rights to protect public health and, in particular, to promote access to medicines for all'. In light of this Klug concludes that 'the recognition that international economic law, and TRIPs in particular, may have profound implications for a country's public health strategy has re-opened the debate over the impact of trade rules on human rights and public policies aimed at addressing issues of poverty, inequality and health'.[43]

7.2   Law and the democratic rediscovery of labour

The democratic rediscovery of labour is a central factor in the construction of cosmopolitan sociabilities. Labour is for that reason one of the social fields in which the clashes between demo-liberalism and cosmopolitanism are most violent at the local, national and global levels. The disembedding of the economy from society brought about by neo-liberal globalization, which reduces labour down to a mere factor of production, has curtailed the possibility of labour to sustain and be a conduit for the enjoyment of rights of citizenship even in the core countries. This has involved a massive intervention of neo-conservative legality against the labour laws and labour rights that liberalism and demo-socialism had promoted under the pressure of labour movements.

Most particularly in this area, demo-liberalism has been in recent years unable or unwilling to confront the neo-conservative tide. It has mostly surrendered to it. This has occurred mainly through drastic changes in the relevant scales of political and legal intervention. Neo-liberal globalization has managed to move the nerve system of labour regulation to the global scale and has delivered it to unfettered neo-conservative politics and legality. As demo-liberalism has remained a national politics and legality, its credibility has been eroded as the national scale of labour regulation has yielded in to the global scale. This is, therefore, a field in which the confrontation in the years to come will most likely be between conservative demo-liberalism and cosmopolitanism.

Contrary to the expectations of the nineteenth-century labour movement, capitalists of the entire world, not the workers, have united. While capital globalized itself, labour unions built their strength at the national level. In order to confront global capital, the labour movement must restructure itself profoundly. It must incorporate the local and the transnational scales as efficiently as it once incorporated the national scale. It is also the new task of the union movement to reinvent the tradition of workers' solidarity and the strategies of social antagonism. A new, wider circle of solidarity must be designed in order to meet the new conditions of social exclusion and the forms of oppression existing in relations *in* production, thus going beyond the conventional scope of union demands – ie, those concerning the relations *of* production, that is, the wage relation. On the other hand, the strategies of social antagonism must be reconstructed. A more political labour movement is called for to fight for a civilizing alternative, where everything is connected to everything else: work and the environment; work and the educational system; work and feminism; work and collective social and cultural needs; work and the welfare state; work and the elderly, etc. In a word, the workers' demands must not leave out anything affecting the life of the workers and the unemployed. This is the spirit, for instance, of the type of 'social movement unionism' that, as Moody[44] has shown, has slowly emerged in some countries of the global South.[45]

The most sustained instances of cosmopolitan legality in place today can be brought together under the same normative idea – ie, the idea that labour must be democratically shared on a global scale. The permanent technological revolution in which we find ourselves allows for the creation of wealth without creating jobs. The available stock of work must, therefore, be redistributed on a world scale. This is no easy task for, even if labour, while a factor of production, is today globalized, the wage relation and labour markets are as segmented and territorialized as before. Four initiatives seem most promising. They are all of global dimension, even if unequally distributed in the global economy.

The first initiative entails the *reduction of working hours*. Although this is a crucial initiative to redistribute labour, it has so far had very little success except in a few European countries. For that reason I will leave it as an item on the agenda of cosmopolitan legality without pursuing it any further here.

The second initiative concerns the implementation of *international labour standards*, that is, the definition of basic rights that must be guaranteed to workers around the

---

[44]   Moody, 1997.
[45]   For a discussion of strategies for forging links of solidarity among unions around the world, see in general Gordon and Turner, 2000.

world and whose protection is a pre-requisite for the free circulation of products in the global market. The issue of international labour standards constitutes today a fascinating site of scholarly discussion and political mobilization. It comprises a wide range of proposals and alternatives aimed at stopping the race to the bottom in which countries in the South are forced to engage in in the absence of international labour regulation. Some of the strategies being discussed and developed around the world include the reinforcement and effective application of ILO conventions, the inclusion of social clauses in global trade agreements like the WTO or in regional ones like NAFTA, the adoption of codes of conduct by transnational corporations under pressure from consumers in the North and the creation of mechanisms for monitoring compliance with such codes, and the use of unilateral sanctions against countries sponsoring exploitative work conditions.[46]

In order not to generate discriminatory protectionism, international labour standards must be adopted alongside alongside two other initiatives: the aforementioned reduction of working hours, and the flexibilization of migration laws with a view to the progressive denationalization of citizenship. The latter will encourage a more egalitarian sharing of labour worldwide, promoting population flows from the peripheral regions to the core regions. Nowadays, and contrary to what the propaganda of xenophobic nationalism in core countries, such flows take place predominantly between peripheral countries and constitute for them an unbearable burden. Against the social apartheid to which pre-contractualism and post-contractualism subject immigrants, citizenship must be denationalized in order to grant the immigrants conditions that guarantee both equality and respect of difference, so that the sharing of labour may also become a multicultural sharing of sociability.

The third initiative, very much connected with the previous one, concerns the *anti-sweatshop movement*. The movement is based on a network of different organizations, rather than on a centralized body. It has thus far focused on raising consumer consciousness and creating consumer pressure against firms that have been found to violate workers' rights in their offshore facilities or to tolerate such violations in factories with which they sub-contract. Through consumer pressure, anti-sweatshop organizations have been pushing for the adoption of codes of conduct by large firms, particularly in the apparel and footwear industries.[47] Currently, transnational cosmopolitan coalitions for the elimination of sweatshops include labour unions, consumers' organizations, religious groups, human rights NGOs, independent monitoring agencies, students' organizations, umbrella agencies like the Workers Rights Consortium and the Fair Labor Association – and, though still with notorious

---

[46]   For a survey of these different strategies, see Compa and Diamond, 1996.
[47]   See Ross, 1997, for a survey of the political and legal stategies undertaken by transnational coalitions for the defence of workers' rights. For a discussion of codes of conduct as means to stem sweatshops, see Fung *et al*, 2001; Rodríguez (forthcoming)

reluctance, some transnational corporations.[48] In light of the aggressive and pervasive impieties of global neo-liberalism and the incapacity or unwillingness of demo-liberal state legality, wherever still present, to offer any credible resistance, cosmopolitan struggles in this area must give a special priority to the political and ethical construction of the conflict before any legal strategy is attempted. Such strategy will have a double focus.

First, the subaltern groups involved in this struggle and their allies know by experience how unreliable demo-liberal politics and legality is today in the social field of labour and labour relations. On the other hand, given the unfavourable conditions, the movement cannot afford not to use whatever legal tools are available. However, to avoid the frustration caused by unjust defeats and the negative impact it may have on the motivation of activists, it is imperative that the cosmopolitan groups try to mobilize demo-liberal legality in a non-hegemonic fashion by putting pressure on courts and legislators through innovative political mobilization. The main objective of such mobilization resides in the symbolic amplification of the violation of labour rights by transforming the legal matter at hand into a moral one – the moral and unjust denial of human dignity. This has indeed been the tactic used in the most visible successful struggles against sweatshops, which have managed to combine legal strategies in local courts with constant international pressure from sympathetic organizations and social movements.[49]

The second focus of cosmopolitan legality resides in the subaltern global legality as it is emerging from the abovementioned struggle for international labour standards and also from a new convergence between human rights and labour rights which by now is very embryonic and full of ambiguities. The objective here is to explore the extent to which what has been lost, in terms of labour rights, at the national scale, can be recovered at the global level. Recent discussions within the ILO to define a list of 'core labor rights' to be protected as basic human rights around the world go in this direction, although which rights are to be included in such a list is a matter of contention.

Finally, the fourth initiative toward a rediscovery of labour resides in the *recognition of the polymorphism of labour*, that is, the idea that the flexibility of work designs and labour processes does not necessarily entail the precariousness of the labour relation. A regular full-time job for an indeterminate period of time was the ideal type of labour that has guided the workers' movement since the nineteenth century. However, such an ideal type has some sort of equivalent in reality only in the core countries, and only during the brief period of fordism. To the extent that the so-called atypical forms of labour proliferate and the state promotes the flexibilization of the wage relations, this ideal-type is getting farther and farther away from the reality of labour relations. The

---

48 The operation of such coalitions in Central America has been studied, among others, by Anner, 2000.

49 Anner, 2000.

atypical forms of labour have been used by global capital as a means of transforming labour into a criterion of exclusion, which happens whenever the wages do not allow workers to rise above the poverty line. In such cases, recognizing labour polymorphism, far from being a democratic exercise, foreshadows an act of contractual fascism. In this domain, the cosmopolitan agenda assumes two forms. On the one hand, the recognition of the different types of labour is democratic only in so far as it creates for each type a minimal threshold of inclusion. That is to say, labour polymorphism is acceptable only to the extent that labour remains a criterion for inclusion. On the other hand, professional training must be incorporated in the wage relation no matter what the type and duration of the job.

7.3   Law and non-capitalist production

A market economy is within limits desirable. On the contrary, a market society, if possible, would be morally repugnant and most probably ungovernable. It would amount to generalized social fascism. This is, however, the project that neo-liberal globalization is trying to put into practice on a global scale. Global capitalism is not just the global extension of free markets and the production of goods and services as unrestricted as possible from state regulation but also the commodification of as many aspects of social life as possible. Commodification means both the creation *ab ovo* of commodities – that is, the creation of products and services valued and exchanged according to market rules, and the transformation into commodities of products and services which have been produced and distributed before on a non-market basis. The latter case means, for instance, that social institutions – such as education, health care or social security – are converted into and treated as service commodities often to competitive forces and the dictates of the market and commercial interests.

In the social field conventionally known as the economy, cosmopolitanism has a four-fold objective. The first one refers to the conditions and relations of production of commodities, namely the wage relation. This is the focus of the strategies aimed at the democratic rediscovery of labour analyzed above. The second objective is decommodification, that is, seeking that public goods and services and social institutions are not privatized, or if privatized, are not fully subjected to the capitalistic market rules. This is the struggle, for instance, of impoverished communities around the world – most notably in recent times in Bolivia – against the takeover of communal and affordable forms of water distribution by TNCs. The third objective is the promotion of subaltern non-capitalistic markets, that is, markets run by solidarity rather than by greed. Finally, the fourth objective is to further alternative systems of production, non-capitalistic production for either capitalistic or non-capitalistic markets. As I have argued elsewhere in surveying case studies on initiatives undertaken along these four lines,[50]

---

[50]   Santos and Rodríguez, 2002. This and the other papers from the 'Reinventing Social Emancipation' project are available in English at www.ces.fe.uc.pt/emancipa/.

alternative economies currently combine ideas and practices taken from multifarious traditions, from cooperativism to alternative development to market socialism.

The second objective has been the ground for progressive alliances of cosmopolitanism with demo-liberalism. The third and fourth aims (together with the first one) are those most characteristic of cosmopolitanism and probably the most promising in spite of the odds against them. As it is the case in general with cosmopolitanism, law is here a subordinate component of the cosmopolitan struggles. For precise purposes or in specific political contexts law may however be an important tool if not the most important tool of a given struggle. As it is characteristic of cosmopolitan legality in general, law here means not just state law but also cosmopolitan global law, subaltern community law, etc.

The initiatives under way are multiple and highly diverse. For instance, cooperatives of informal workers – from garbage pickers in India[51] and Colombia[52] to housewives in the *favelas* of São Paolo[53] – as well as co-operatives of industrial workers laid off during process of corporate 'downsizing'[54] have used imaginatively the tools of state law – and its cracks – to advance solidaristic forms of production and distribution of goods and services. In many other cases, the third and fourth abovementioned goals are pursued together as the two components of the same initiative. Alternative markets are often promoted for products and services produced by non-capitalist units of production. Concerning the third aim, the creation of alternative markets, the most salient cosmopolitan initiative is the fair trade movement. According to the Fair Trade Association: 'The word 'fair' can mean a lot of different things to different people. In alternative trade organizations, 'fair trade' means that trading partners are based on reciprocal benefits and mutual respect; that prices paid to producers reflect the work they do; that workers have the right to organize; that national health, safety, and wage laws are enforced; and that products are environmentally sustainable and conserve natural resources'.[55] Very much in the same vein, Mario Monroy, a Mexican fair trade activist and director of 'Comercio Justo Mexico, AC', affirms: 'What is characteristic of fair trade is the co-responsibility between the producer and the consumer. The small producer is responsible for the production of a product of excellent quality, ecologically responsible and produced without human exploitation. Thus, fair trade is the means, the end is the person and the organization. The consumer is responsible for paying a just price, which is not an alms, but rather a product of much quality, caring in nature and produced with love'.[56]

---

[51] Bhowmik, 2002.
[52] Rodríguez, 2002.
[53] Singer, 2002.
[54] Bhowmik, 2002; Singer, 2002.
[55] http://www.fairtradefederation.com/faq.html. Visited 2 July 2002.
[56] Mario Monroy, talk given at the University of Wisconsin-Madison in April, 2001. According to Transfair, a monitoring and certifying agency for fair trade, 'the world price (of coffee) is 60 cents a pound and after the dealers take their cut, the small producers end up getting between 20 and 30 cents a pound. Thus through fair trade there is a considerable benefit for the producers; after paying the co-operative's costs, they receive between $1 and $1.06 per pound'.

Fair trade is a promising tiny island in the unjust ocean of capitalist world trade. Of 3.6 trillion US dollars of all goods exchanged globally, fair trade accounts for only 0.01 per cent. But it is growing. Cosmopolitan legality may operate at two levels in the fair trade movement: through the legal challenge of global legality for violating national laws resorting for that to demo-liberal legal tools and through the struggle for cosmopolitan global law in this field by pressing the inclusion of fair trade clauses in international trade agreements. The first legal strategy is being used, for instance, by the United Steelworkers of America in their challenge of the constitutionality of NAFTA. The latter strategy is a constitutive component of the fair trade movement, as it fights for the principles upon which fair trade agreements should be based: multilateralism, democracy, transparency, representation, equity, subsidiarity, decentralization, diversity and accountability.

The legal component of these cosmopolitan struggles consists often in pressing for local and national laws that establish special legal regimes for popular economic organizations to allow them to compete in fair terms without giving away the local values and local culture embedded in their products. As the nation states are in general incapable or unwilling to resist against the neo-liberal global law in principle hostile to what it sees as barriers to trade or the infringement of market rules, the local or community governments are often more open to such alternative legislation. In this way, local/global linkages may be developed.

Another instance of law and alternative production systems are the new forms of counter-hegemonic legal plurality being advanced by movements and organizations of landless peasants or of small farmers in their struggle for access to land and land reform. This new form of cosmopolitan legality may in some cases involve the facilitative co-operation of the state – as was the case for sometime in South Africa – [57] but in most cases they confront the state and state legislation – as in India, Brazil[58] and Mexico. The fate of this type of cosmopolitan legality is strictly dependent on the political mobilization which the movement or organization can generate. Very often, subaltern legal enclaves are created in the occupied land – as the *assentamentos* (settlements) of the Movement of the Landless in Brazil – and they last as long as the occupation may be sustained. In some cases it is possible to develop alliances between this cosmopolitan legality and the demo-liberal state legality as, for instance, when the state is forced to 'regularize' the land occupation.

These types of alliances may also take place in urban areas. Such might be the case of informal housing in the cities along the US-Mexico border as studied by Jane Larson. According to her, poor households in the US have been increasingly turning to informal housing in order to survive the lack of basic social guarantees, in particular the squeeze between falling real wages and declining governmental support for either affordable

[57]   Klug, 2002.
[58]   See Navarro, 2002; Carvalho, 2002; Lopes, 2002.

"*regularize it*"

housing or income maintenance.[59] And indeed informal housing is already moving from the borderlands to the heartlands. Given the improbability that state housing policies will provide normal housing for the working poor, Larson calls for a positive engagement with informality. Rather than declaring it illegal, 'regularize' it. Regularization 'scales' back regulatory standards for some populations and 'legalizes' some illegal housing conditions, in a programme aimed at encouraging self-help investment in shelter.

As in the case of the landless peasants, the cosmopolitan potential of regularization lies in the space it opens for the political organization and mobilization of the working poor (residents' associations, community organizations, etc), and the pressure it can exert on the state to commit more resources to this area of social policy and gradually upgrade informal housing to the level of adequate housing. This is what Larson calls 'progressive realization', an alternative model of legality.[60] Progressive realization, combined with the political mobilization that makes it possible as something other than state populism, distinguishes itself both from the neo-conservative repression of informality without an alternative and the neo-conservative celebration of informality *à la* Hernando de Soto.[61]

7.4 *Law for non-citizens*

Citizenship as the sum total of rights effectively exercised by individuals or groups is a matter of degree in capitalist societies. There are the super-citizens – those that belong to the intimate civil society – and the rest. The rest is the strange civil society that includes multiple shades of citizenship. And then there are the non-citizens, those individuals and social groups belonging to the uncivil civil society and to borderlands between the strange and the uncivil civil society. The life experiences of the people in the latter category correspond to this absence of citizenship and indeed characterizes not only their relations with the state but also their interactions with other people, including at times those sharing the uncivil civil society. Such life experiences differ according to whether the non-citizen has been expelled from some kind of a social contract and therefore of the social inclusion it made possible (post-contractualism) or whether the non-citizen has never experienced any kind of contractual social inclusion (pre-contractualism). In the first case citizenship is lived as a ruin, or as a memory, while in the second it is either an unrealistic aspiration or an utterly unintelligible idea. Non-citizenship is the degree zero of social contract-based inclusion. Whatever social inclusion is achieved at this level is achieved on a non-citizenship basis, on paternalistic philanthropy or on genuine solidarity. It is, in other words, an inclusion that confirms if not fosters the system of social exclusion.

59   Larson, 2002, p 142.
60   Larson, 2002, p 144.
61   De Soto, 1989.

One may wonder what might be the role of law in situations of non-citizenship, let alone the role of cosmopolitan law. Non-citizenship is the intended or unintended result of demo-liberal legality. For demo-liberalism, non-citizenship is a marker of its impotence as a political practice, while for cosmopolitanism non-citizenship is the negative imperative that generates a task for social inclusion and emancipation. Indeed cosmopolitanism focuses specifically on non-citizenship, as illustrated by the instances of cosmopolitan legality analyzed above. After all, the indigenous peoples and the landless peasants are, in Latin America at least, the most cruel example of non-citizenship.

Under this heading I refer more generally to situations in which minimal dignifying inclusion is sought and thus in which it is hard to think of social emancipation, even in its thinnest or weakest conception, as a realistic prospect. Often what is at stake is sheer survival since the nearest and most realistic probability at hand is death. From a cosmopolitan perspective, law is an almost dilemmatic necessity of the struggles around non-citizenship. On one side, the political mobilization of the law is here particularly adequate since this is a social field in which alliances with demo-liberalism are likely to succeed. On the other side, the strength that the legal strategy may have in this field is a marker of the narrow limits of its being accomplished.

I distinguish three types of cosmopolitan legality in this area, covering different scales of legality. The first one is global law. It refers to the *political mobilization of international human rights* or of international conventions on humanitarian intervention in situations of extreme, life-threatening forms of social exclusion. The second one deals with state law whenever the state is pressed to *establish minimum standards of citizenship-based inclusion* – second-class or third-class citizenship. The most important instance of this kind of legal mobilization in the core countries is the issue of 'regularization' of undocumented migrant workers. In the US alone, the number of undocumented workers is estimated at 11 million. The struggle for general amnesty is today on the agenda of human rights organizations and of many labour unions. Indeed, the participation of labour unions in this struggle is quite recent and represents a radical change of perspective on the part of labour unions that before tended to see the undocumented workers as enemies taking away from them the jobs available. These cosmopolitan alliances involving labour unions and taking them beyond the confines of their conventional activism represent one of the most promising developments in the labour movement in the direction of what is being called 'social movement labor unionism' or 'citizen labor union'.

The third type of cosmopolitan law in this area is local law and refers to local communities which, having found themselves in a situation of non-citizenship vis-à-vis larger communities or the national society, establish local Constitutions whereby a political and legal pact is sealed among the members of the communities with the purposes of better defending themselves against outside exclusionary forces be they the state or non-state agencies, legal or illegal agents. The most remarkable example of this type of local subaltern cosmopolitan legality is the peace community of San José de Apartadó, Colombia. The population of this small village located in the region of Urabá, under the worst possible conditions, set out in the late 1990s to establish an autonomous peace community in the middle of crossfire. Facing an intensification and deterioration of the armed conflict in its territory, this village opted for peace, subscribing to a public pact according to which its inhabitants committed themselves to not becoming involved with armed parties – the paramilitary groups, the guerrillas or the army – and demanding respect from all of them, including the State, and to producing the village's own form of social organization. They thus sought to take a pacifist position and refused to abandon their plots of land and their homes. The public pact was written down and became the local Constitution binding all the villagers.[62]

7. 5 *The state as the newest social movement*

The heading of this section may be somewhat surprising and calls for justification. In my view, the current decline of the regulatory power renders obsolete the theories of the state that have prevailed up until now, both of liberal and Marxist origin. The depoliticization of the state and destatization of social regulation, resulting as stressed above from the erosion of the social contract, show that under the same name – the state – a new, larger form of political organization is emerging, articulated by the state itself, and composed of a hybrid set of flows, networks, and organizations, in which state and non-state, national and global elements combine and interpenetrate.

The relative miniaturization of the state inside this new political organization is usually conceived of as erosion of the state's sovereignty and of its regulatory capacities. As a matter of fact, what is occurring is a transformation of sovereignty and the emergence of a new mode of regulation, in which the public goods up until now produced by the state – legitimacy, social and economic welfare, security, and cultural identity – are the object of permanent contention and painstaking negotiation among different social actors under state co-ordination. This new political organization does not have a centre, and thus the co-ordination by the state functions in fact as imagination of the centre. In the new political constellation, the state is a partial and fragmented political relation, open to competition among agents of political sub-contracting and franchising carrying alternative conceptions of the public goods to be delivered.

Under these new terms, rather than a homogeneous set of institutions, the state is an unregulated political battlefield where the struggles bear little resemblance to conventional political struggles. The various forms of social fascism look for opportunities to expand and consolidate their own despotic regulations, thus turning the state into a component of their private sphere. The cosmopolitan forces, in turn, must focus on models of high-intensity democracy comprising both state and non-

[62]   Uribe, 2002.

state actions, thus transforming the state into a component of a variety of non-state public spheres. This state transformation is what I designate as *the state as the newest social movement*.

The major features of this transformation are as follows. In the emergent political organization it behooves the state to co-ordinate the different organizations, interests, and networks that have emerged from the destatization of social regulation. The democratic struggle is, thus, before anything else, a struggle for the democratization of the tasks of co-ordination. While before the struggle was about democratizing the state's regulatory monopoly, today the struggle must be about democratizing the loss of such a monopoly. This struggle has several aspects. The co-ordinating tasks concern mainly the co-ordination of divergent, even contradictory, interests. While the modern state assumed as its own a version of these interests, nowadays the state only assumes as its own the task of co-ordinating interests that can be both national and global. Having lost the monopoly of regulation, the state still keeps the monopoly of meta-regulation, that is to say, the monopoly of articulation and co-ordination among sub-contracted private regulators. This means that, today, notwithstanding appearances to the contrary, the state is more than ever involved in the politics of social redistribution – and hence in the criteria of inclusion and exclusion, as well. This is why the tension between democracy and capitalism, which needs to be reconstructed urgently, can only be reconstructed once democracy is conceived of as distributive democracy comprising both state and non-state action.

In a public sphere where the state incorporates non-state interests and organizations whose actions it co-ordinates, redistributive democracy can not be confined to representative democracy, since the latter was designed for conventional political action, that is, confined to the state realm. Actually, herein resides the mysterious disappearance of the tension between democracy and capitalism at the beginning of the twenty-first century. Indeed, representative democracy has lost the meagre redistributive capabilities that it once had. Under the new conditions, social redistribution is premised upon participatory democracy, engaging both the state actions and the actions of private agents, firms, NGOs, and social movements, whose interests and performances the state co-ordinates. In other words, it does not make sense to democratize the state if the non-state sphere is not democratized at the same time. Only the convergence of the two processes of democratization guarantees the reconstitution of the public sphere.

Today, there are many concrete political experiences around the world of democratic redistribution of resources obtained by means of participatory democracy or a combination of participatory and representative democracy. In Brazil, for example, mention must be made of experiences of *participatory budgeting* in cities ruled by the Workers' Party (PT), particularly and with special success Porto Alegre.[63] Although

---

[63]   On the experience of participatory budgeting in Porto Alegre, see, among many others, Santos, 1998b, 2002.

these experiences have been so far of a local scope, there is no reason why the application of the participatory budgeting could not be extended to regional or even national government.

The limit of experiences like the participatory budgeting is that they only concern the use of state resources, the process of collecting these resources. On the basis of the participatory democratic struggles and initiatives already taking place, I suggest that the participatory logic of redistributive democracy must concern itself also with obtaining state resources – thus, with fiscal policy. As concerns the tax system, redistributive democracy defines itself as fiscal solidarity. The fiscal solidarity of the modern state, to the extent that it exists (progressive taxation, etc.), is an abstract solidarity. Under the new political organization, and given the miniaturization of the state, such solidarity becomes even more abstract, and ends up being unintelligible to most citizens. Hence the various tax revolts we have witnessed for the past few years. Many such revolts are passive, rather than active, and have expression in massive tax evasion. A radical shift in the logic of taxation to adapt it to the new conditions of political domination is imperative. I speak, thus, of *participatory taxation*. Since the state's functions will concern more and more co-ordination rather than direct production of welfare, controlling the linkage between resource collection and resource allocation by means of the mechanisms of representative democracy becomes virtually impossible. Hence the need to resort to mechanisms of participatory democracy.

Participatory taxation is a possible means of recuperating the state's 'extractive capacity', linking it to the fulfillment of social objectives defined in a participatory way. Once both the general levels of taxation and the set of objectives susceptible of being financed by the state budget are established at the national level by mechanisms combining representative and participatory democracy, citizens and families must be given the option of deciding collectively where and in what proportion their taxes should be spent. Some citizens or social groups may prefer to have their taxes mainly spent in health, whereas others may prefer education or social security, and so on and so forth.

Both participatory budgeting and participatory taxation are crucial pieces of the new redistributive democracy. Its political logic is the creation of public, non-state spheres in which the state is the key agency of articulation and co-ordination. The creation of these public spheres is, in the present conditions, the only democratic alternative to the proliferation of fascist private spheres sanctioned by the state. The new democratic struggle, as a struggle for a redistributive democracy, is an anti-fascist struggle, even though it occurs in a political field that is formally democratic. This struggle will not assume the forms that the previous one, against state fascism, once assumed. But neither can it limit itself to the forms of democratic struggle legitimated by the democratic states that rose from the ruins of state fascism. We are, therefore, about to create new constellations of democratic struggles allowing for more and ampler democratic deliberations on greater and more differentiated aspects of sociability. My own definition of socialism as democracy without end goes in this direction.

Besides participatory budgeting, which is already in place in some parts of the world, and participatory taxation, which in the form advanced here is a mere cosmopolitan aspiration, there is a third initiative which is already under way in several European countries and is being tried out at a smaller scale in other countries such as Brazil and South Africa. I mean *universal basic income*. By guaranteeing a minimum income to all citizens regardless of their employment status that covers the necessities of life, this institutional innovation is a powerful mechanism of social inclusion and opens the way for the effective exercise of all the other rights of citizenship.[64] The struggles for guaranteed basic income are cosmopolitan struggles to the extent that their logic is to establish economic entitlements that are not dependent upon the upturns and downturns of the economy, and as such they are not mere responses to the accumulation needs of capital.

The emphasis on redistributive democracy is one precondition for the conversion of the state into the newest social movement. Another one is what I designate as the *experimental state*. In a phase of turbulent transformations concerning the role of the state in social regulation, the institutional matrix of the state, for all its rigidity, is bound to be subjected to strong vibrations that threaten its integrity and may produce perverse effects. Moreover, this institutional matrix is inscribed in a national state time-space that is undergoing the combined impact of local and global, instantaneous and glacial time-spaces. The conclusion must be drawn that the institutional design of the new emerging state form is still to be invented. It remains in fact to be seen whether the new institutional matrix will consist of formal organizations or of networks and flows, or even of hybrid forms, flexible devices, susceptible of being reprogrammed. It is, therefore, not difficult to predict that the democratic struggles of the coming years will be basically struggles for alternative institutional designs.

Since what characterizes periods of paradigmatic transition is the fact that in them old-paradigm and new-paradigm solutions coexist, and that the latter are often as contradictory among themselves as with the former, I think that this condition must be taken into account while designing new institutions. It would be unwise at this stage to adopt irreversible institutional options. Thus, the state must be transformed into a field of institutional experimentation, allowing for the coexistence of and competition among different institutional solutions, as pilot-experiences, subjected to the permanent scrutiny of citizen collectives charged with the comparative assessment of the performances. The rendition of public goods, specially in the realm of social policy, can thus occur in various forms, and the option amongst them, if it is to take place, must occur only after the alternatives have been scrutinized by the citizens for their democratic efficacy and quality.

Two principles should be borne in mind in embarking in institutional experimentation. First, the state is only genuinely experimental insofar as the different institutional

---

[64]   Van Parijs, 1992.

solutions are given equal conditions so that they can develop according to their own logic. That is to say, the experimental state is democratic to the extent that it confers equality of opportunities to the different proposals of democratic institutionalization. Only thus can the democratic struggle truly become a struggle for democratic alternatives. Only thus is it possible to fight democratically against democratic dogmatism. Institutional experimentation will necessarily cause some instability and incoherence in state action, which may eventually generate new unexpected exclusions. This is a serious risk, all the more so because, in the new political organization of which the state is part, it still behooves the democratic state to provide basic stability to the citizens' expectations and basic standards of security and inclusion.

Under these circumstances, the state must not only guarantee equality of opportunities to the various projects of democratic institutionalization, but also – and herein lies the second principle of political experimentation – basic standards of inclusion, in the absence of which the active citizenship required to observe, verify, and assess the performance of alternative projects will not be possible. The new welfare state is an experimental state, and the continuous experimentation through citizens' active participation is what guarantees the sustainability of welfare.

The state as the newest social movement carries with it a major transformation of state law as we know it under the current conditions of demo-liberalism. Cosmopolitan law is here the legal component of struggles for democratic participation and experimentation in state policies and regulations. The field of cosmopolitan struggles emerging is vast; as vast as the forms of fascism that threaten us. The cosmopolitan struggles cannot, however, as results from the above, confine themselves to the national time-space. Many of the struggles presented above presuppose international co-ordination, that is to say, collaboration among states and among social movements aimed at reducing international competition amongst them and at enhancing co-operation. Just as social fascism legitimizes or naturalizes itself internally as pre-contractualism and post-contractualism imposed by insurmountable global or international imperatives, so it is up to the cosmopolitan forces to transform the national state into an element of an international network aimed at reducing or neutralizing the destructive and excluding impact of those imperatives, in search of an egalitarian redistribution of the globally produced wealth. The Southern States – particularly large semi-peripheral states, like Brazil, India, South Africa, a future democratic China, or a Russia without mafias – have in this regard a decisive role to play. The increase of international competition among them will be disastrous for the large majority of their inhabitants and fatal for the population of the peripheral countries. The struggle for a new, more democratic and participatory international law is, thus, part and parcel of the national struggle for a redistributive democracy.

8   CONCLUSION

This chapter was written under the logic of the sociology of emergence. My aim was to unfold the signs of the reconstruction of the tension between social regulation and social emancipation, as well as the role of law in such a reconstruction. The credibility of the signs was built on excavation work upon the foundations of the paradigm of modernity – a work that confirmed the exhaustion of the paradigm, while revealing as well the wealth and vastness of the social experience it rendered possible at the beginning, and later went on to discredit, marginalize or simply suppress.

The reconstruction of the tension between social regulation and social emancipation forced the subjection of modern law – one of the large factors of the dissolution of the tension – to a radical critical analysis, indeed to an act of unthinking. This unthinking, however, had nothing to do with the deconstructive mode. On the contrary, its objective was to free pragmatism from itself, that is to say, from its own tendency to abide by dominant conceptions of reality. Once these dominant conceptions were put aside, a rich and broad legal landscape could be identified, a reality that is right under our noses but we often fail to see because we lack the adequate reading perspective or code.

As I tried to show in the first three chapters, this lack can be accounted for by the conventional disciplines for the study of law, from jurisprudence to philosophy of law, from sociology of law to anthropology of law. These disciplines are responsible for the construction of the modernist legal canon – a narrow and reductionist canon that arrogantly discredits, silences or negates the legal experiences of large bodies of population.

Once this socio-legal experience was recuperated, it was possible to grasp it fully in its internal diversity, its many scales, its many and contradictory political and cultural orientations. The analytical objective of Chapters Four, Five, and Six was precisely that. In Chapters Seven and Eight, I concentrated on presenting the prolegomena of a theory capable of accounting for that rich socio-legal experience in such a way that it might even enrich and strengthen it.

One further task, however, was still ahead: to assess the potential of that experience to reinvent social emancipation. The last chapter was dedicated to this issue. Once formulated – can law be emancipatory? – the question was subjected to critical analysis in order to clarify both its possibilities and its limits. The wealth of the legal landscape identified in the preceding chapters made possible the sociology of emergences. In other words, a wide variety of struggles, initiatives, movements, and organizations, both local and national and global, in which law is one of the resources used for emancipatory purposes, were rendered credible.

As I made clear, this use of law often goes beyond the modernist legal canon. Forms of law frequently not acknowledged as such (informal, non-official forms of law) are resorted to. Furthermore, when state, official law is resorted to, the use made of it is never conventional – rather, such law becomes part of a vaster set of political resources. Often law is present under the guise of illegal practices through which an alternative legality is fought for.

Finally, what is designated as legal, illegal or even a-legal consists of components of legal constellations that can be activated at the local, national, and global scale. I designated them as a whole as subaltern cosmopolitan legality. Once this trajectory has been completed it is possible to show that the question – can law be emancipatory? – turns out to be as profitable as inadequate. After all, law can be neither emancipatory nor non-emancipatory; emancipatory or non-emancipatory are the movements, the organizations of the subaltern cosmopolitan groups that resort to law to advance their struggles.

As I have stressed, under the logic of the sociology of emergence this subaltern cosmopolitan legality is as yet but in the bud; it is, above all, an aspiration and a project. But there are already enough signs to justify the adoption of broader conceptions of reality and realism. Such conceptions are to encompass not only what exists but also what is actively produced by society as non-existent, as well as what only exists as a sign or trace of what can easily be disregarded. The best way to capture this reality is by means of an open research agenda. Such was my purpose in this chapter.

Conventional theory and sociology will always find it easy to discredit the signs of subaltern cosmopolitan legality, as well as the research agenda that aims to unfold them. It is easy for them because all they have done historically is to discount the alternatives of a new future that go on happening nonetheless. They hold theoretical and political conceptions that are grounded in narrow notions of realism, resort to pragmatism to disguise their cynical reason, and present themselves as paladins of scientific scepticism to stigmatize as being idealist all that does not fit the narrowness of their views and analyses.

These views and analyses derive from a kind of rationality that in his preface to *Theodicy* [1710 (1985)] Leibniz called 'lazy reason'. It consists in the following: if the future is necessary and what must happen does happen regardless of what we do, it is preferable to do nothing, to care for nothing, and merely to enjoy the pleasure of the instant. This form of reason is lazy because it gives up thinking in the face of necessity and fatalism, of which Leibniz distinguishes three kinds: *Fatum Mahometanum*, *Fatum Stoicum*, and *Fatum Christianum*.

The most nefarious social and political consequence of lazy reason is the waste of experience. This book was written against lazy reason and the waste of experience it brings about.

Bibliography

Abel, Richard 1974 'A Comparative Theory of Dispute Institutions in Society' *Law and Society Review,* 8: 217–347

Abel, Richard (ed). 1982. *The Politics of Informal Justice.* 2 volumes. New York: Academic Press.

Ades, Alberto and Rafael di Tella 1997 'The New Economics of Corruption: A Survey and some New Results,' in Heywood (ed) 80–99

Adler, Max 1922 *Die Staatsauffassung des Marxismus* Vienna: Verlag der Wiener Volksbuchhandlung

    nd *Zuchthaus und Fabrik* Leipzig: Ernst Oldenburg Verlag

AFL-CIO 2000 'Building Understanding, Creating Change' *A Report on the AFL-CIO Forum on Immigrant Workers' Rights* Washington, DC: AFL-CIO

Aglietta, Michel 1979 *A Theory of Capitalist Regulation: The US Experience* London: NLB

    1986 *La fin des devises clés* Paris: La Découverte

Aguirre, Francisco B 1980 *Etnia y represión penal* Lima: CIPA

Al Faruqi, Isma'il R 1983 'Islam and Human Rights' *The Islamic Quarterly,* 27(1): 12–30

Albrow, Martin and Elizabeth King (eds) 1990 *Globalization, Knowledge and Society* London: Sage

Alger, Chadwick 1990 'Grass-Roots Perspectives on Global Policies for Development' *Journal of Peace Research,* 27: 155–168

Allott, Philip 1991 'The European Community Is Not the True European Community' *Yale Law Journal,* 100: 2485–2500

An-na'im, Abdullahi A 1990 *Toward an Islamic Reformation* Syracuse: Syracuse University Press

(ed) 1992 *Human Rights in Cross-Cultural Perspectives. A Quest for Consensus* Philadelphia: University of Pennsylvania Press

Ana Maria 1996 'Discurso inaugural de la mayor Ana María en el Encuentro Intercontinental 'Por la humanidad y contra el neoliberalismo'' *Chiapas,* 3: 102–103

Anaya, S James 1996 *Indigenous Peoples in International Law* New York: Oxford University Press

Anderson, J (ed). 1986. *The Rise of the Modern State.* Brighton: Harvester Press.

Anthony, Constance 1991 'Africa's Refugee Crisis: State Building in Historical Perspective' *International Migration Review, 25:* 574–591

Appadurai, Arjun 1990 'Disjuncture and Difference in the Global and Cultural Economy' *Public Culture,* 2: 1–24

1996 *Modernity at Large: Cultural Dimensions of Globalization* Minneapolis: University of Minnesota''Press

(ed) 2001 *Globalization* Durham: Duke University Press

Arenas, Luis C 1998 *La Justicia, el Sistema Político y los Derechos Humanos en Colombia* (unpublished manuscript)

2021 '*Poscriptum*: sobre el caso U'wa,' in Santos and García-Villegas II: 143–157

2002 'A luta dos U'wa contra a exploração petrolífera no seu território: um estudo de caso de uma luta local que se globalizou,' in Santos (ed) (2002c) (forthcoming)

Arminjon, Pierre, B Nolde and M Wolff 1950 *Traité de droit comparé* Paris: Librairie Generale de Droit et de Jurisprudence

Arrighi, Giovanni 1994 *The Long Twentieth Century. Money, Power, and the Origins of Our Times* London: Verso

Assies, WJ and AJ Hoekema (eds). 1994. *Indigenous Peoples' Experiences with Self-Government.* Proceedings of the Seminar on Arrangements for Self-Determination by Indigenous Peoples within National States, 10 and 11 February, 1994, Law Faculty, University of Amsterdam. Copenhagen: IWGIA, doc. 76.

Auerbach, Erich 1968 *Mimesis. The Representation of Reality in Western Literature* Princeton: Princeton University Press

Avci, Gamze and Christopher McDonald 2000 'Chipping Away at the Fortress: Unions, Immigration and the Transnational Labour Market' *International Migration,* 38(2): 191–214

Bach, Hanne 1991 'Miskito Indians in Nicaragua – The First Ethnic Group to Obtain Autonomy in Central America?' *Newsletter IWGIA,* 3, November–December: 38–42

Baker, Dean, G Epstein and R Pollin (eds). 1998. *Globalization and Progressive Economic Policy.* Cambridge: Cambridge University Press.

Ball, Terence, J Farr and R Hanson (eds). 1989. *Political Innovation and Conceptual Change.* Cambridge: Cambridge University Press.

Barrett, Michèle 1980 *Women's Oppression Today* London: Verso

Barrow, Nita 1985 'The Decade NGO Forum' *Africa Report,* 30: 9–12

Bartky, Sandra. 1990. *Femininity and Domination: Studies in the Phenomenology of Oppression.* New York: Routledge.

Baslar, Kemal 1998 *The Concept of the Common Heritage of Mankind in International Law* Dordrecht: Martinus Nijhoff

    1998. *The Concept of the Common Heritage of Humankind in International Law.* The Hague: Nijhoff Publishers.

Basok, Tanya 2000 'He Came, He Saw, He…Stayed Guest Worker Programmes and the Issue of Non-Return' *International Migration,* 38(2): 215–238

Bataillon, Claude, *et al* 1982 *Indianidad, etnocidio, indigenismo in America Latina* Mexico City: Institute Indigenista Interamericano

Baudrillard, Jean. 1981. *Simulacres et simulations.* Paris: Galilee.

Bauer, Otto 1924 *Die Nationalitätenfrage und die Sozialdemokratie* Vienna: Verlag der Wiener Volksbuchhandlung

Bauer, Joanne R and Daniel A Bell (eds) 1999 *The East Asian Challenge for Human Rights* Cambridge: Cambridge University Press

Bauman, Zygmunt 1992 *Intimations of Postmodernity* London: Routledge

Baxi, Upendra 1982 'Taking Suffering Seriously: Social Action Litigation in the Supreme Court of India' *International Commission of Jurists Review,* 29: 37–49

    2002a 'Operation "Enduring Freedom": Towards a New International Law and Order?' *Beyond Law,* 25:1–15

    2002b *The Future of Human Rights* Delhi: Oxford University Press

Beck, Ulrich, Anthony Giddens and Scott Lash 1994 *Reflexive Modernization: Politics, Tradition and Aesthetics in the Modern Social Order* Cambridge: Polity Press

Beck, Ulrich 1999 *World Risk Society* London: Blackwell

    2000 *The Brave New World of Work* London: Blackwell

Becker, David and Richard Sklar 1987 'Why Postimperialism?' in Becker *et al:* 1–18

　　et al 1987: *Postimperialism: International Capitalism and Development in the Late Twentieth Century* Boulder: Lynne Rienner Publishers

Beneria, Lourdes and G Sen 1981 'Accumulation, Reproduction and Women's Role in Economic Development: Boserup Revisited' *Signs,* 7(2): 279–298

Benda-Beckmann, Franz von 1988 'Comment on Merry' *Law and Society Review, 22:* 897–901

　　1991 'Unterwerfung oder Distanz: Rechtssoziologie, Rechtsanthropologie und Rechtspluralismus aus Rechtsanthropologischer Sicht' *Zettschrtft für Rechtssoziologie,* 12:97–119

Bercusson, Brian 1997 'Globalizing Labour Law: Transnational Private Regulation and Countervailing Actors in European Labour Law,' in Teubner (ed): 133–178

Berg, Robert 1987 *NGOs: New Force in Third World Development* Washington: Center for Advanced Study of International Development

Berger, Adolf 1953 *Encyclopedic Dictionary of Roman Law* Philadelphia: The American Philosophical Society

Bergesen, Albert (ed) 1980 *Studies of the Modern World-System* New York: Academic Press

　　1990 'Turning World-System Theory on its Head,' in Featherstone (ed): 67–81

Berlin, Isaiah. 1976. *Vico and Herder: Two Studies in the History of Ideas.* London: Hogarth.

Berman, Harold. 1983. *Law and Revolution. The Formation of Western Legal Tradition.* Cambridge, MA: Harvard University Press.

　　1988. 'The Law of International Commercial Transactions.' *Emory Journal of International Dispute Resolution, 2:* 235-310.

　　and Felix Dasser. 1990. 'The 'New' Law Merchant and the 'Old': Sources, Content and Legitimacy,' in Carbonneau (ed): 21-36

Berman, Marshall 1983 *All That Is Solid Melts Into Air* London: Verso

Berman, Nathaniel 1999 'In the Wake of Empire' *American University International Law Review,* 14: 1521–1554

Bernal, Martin 1987 *Black Athena: The Afroasiatic Roots of Classical Civilization* Volume 1: *The Fabrication of Ancient Greece, 1785–1885* London: Free Association Books

Bickel, Alexander 1962 *The Least Dangerous Branch: the Supreme Court at the Bar of Politics* Indianapolis: Bobbs-Merrill

Bilder, Richard et al 1989 *Legal Regimes for the Mining of Helium-3 from the Moon* Madison: Wisconsin Center for Space Automation and Robotics

Billet, L 1975 'Political Order and Economic Development: Reflections on Adam Smith's Wealth of Nations' *Political Studies*, 23(4): 430–441

Blakemore, M J and J B Harley 1980 *Cartographica* Special issue 17: 4,1–120

Blankenburg, Erhard 1984 'The Poverty of Evolutionism A Critique of Teubner's Case for "Reflexive Law"' *Law and Society Review*, 18: 273–289

Blaser, Arthur 1985 'Human Rights in the Third World and Development of International Nongovernmental Organizations,' in Shepherd, Jr and Nanda (eds): 273–285

1990 'The Common Heritage in Its Infinite Variety: Space Law and the Moon in the 1990's' *The Journal of Law and Technology*, 5: 79–99

Blomley, Nicholas (ed). 2001. *The Legal Geographies Reader: Law, Power, and Space.* Oxford: Blackwell.

Bloom, Harold 1973 *The Anxiety of Influence* Oxford: Oxford University Press

Bobbio, Norberto 1942 *La Consuetude Come Fatto Normativo* Padova: CEDAM

Boeles, P 1992 'Schengen and the Rule of Law,' in Meijers *et al,* 135–146

Boer, Gérard de 1992 'Trends in Refugee Policy and Cooperation in the European Community' *International Migration Review, 26:* 668–675

Boggs, S W 1947 'Cartohypnosis' *Scientific Monthly,* 64: 469

Bohannan, Paul 1957 *Justice and Judgment among the Tiv* London: Oxford University Press

Bolten, J J 1992 'From Schengen to Dublin: The New Frontiers of Refugee Law,' in Meijers *et al*: 8–36

Borges, Jorge Luis 1974 *Obras Completas* Buenos Aires: Emecé

Borocz, Jozsef 1996 *Leisure Migration: A Sociological Study on Tourism* Tarrytown: Elsevier Science

Boserup, Esther 1970 *Women's Role in Economic Development* London: Allen and Unwin

Bosniak, Linda 1991 'Human Rights, State Sovereignty and the Protection of Undocumented Migrants under the International Migrant Workers Convention' *International Migration Review,* 25: 737–770

Bottomore, Tom and P Goode (eds) 1978 *Austro-Marxism* Oxford: Clarendon Press

Boulding, Elise 1991 'The Old and New Transnationalism: An Evolutionary Perspective' *Human Relations,* 44: 789–805

Bourdieu, Pierre 1980 *Le sens pratique* Paris: Editions de Minuit

1982 *Ce que parler veut dire* Paris: Fayard

Bowen, Gordon 1985 'The Political Economy of State Terrorism: Barrier to Human Rights in Guatemala,' in Shepherd, Jr and Nanda (eds): 83–123

Boyer, Robert (ed) 1986 *Capitalismes fin de siècle* Paris: Maspero

1990 *The Regulation School: A Critical Introduction* New York: Columbia University Press

Boyer, Robert and Daniel Drache (eds). 1996. *States Against Markets*. London: Routledge.

Brandt, Hans-Jürgen 1986 *Justicia Popular: Nativos, Campesinos* Lima: Centro de Investigaciones Judiciales de la Corte Suprema de Justicia de la Republica

Braudel, Fernand 1979 *Civilization matérielle, économie et capitalisme XVe–XVIIIe siècle* Vol II Paris: Armand Colin

Braverman, H 1974 *Labor and Monopoly Capital* New York: Monthly Review Press

Bravo, María A Bel et al (eds). 1994. *Ecofeminismo: Un encuentro con la naturaleza.* Jaén: Universidad de Jaén.

Brecher, Jeremy, T Costello and B Smith. 2000. *Globalization from Below: The Power of Solidarity.* Cambridge, Mass: South End Press.

Breckenridge, Carol, Sheldon Pollock, Homi Bhabha and Dipesh Chakrabarty (eds). *Cosmopolitanism.* Durham: Duke University Press.

Brenkert, George 1992 'Can We Afford International Human Rights?' *Journal of Business Ethics,* 11:515–521

Brenner, R 1977 'The Origins of Capitalist Development: A Critique of Neo-Smithian Marxism' *New Left Review,* 104: 25–92

Breton, Raymond 1989 'The Vesting of Ethnic Interests in State Institutions,' in Frideres (ed): 35–55

Brockett, Charles 1985 'The Right to Food and International Obligations: the Impact of US Policy in Central America,' in Shepherd, Jr and Nanda (eds): 125–147

Brolmann, Catherine, R Lefeber and M Zieck (eds) 1993 *Peoples and Minorities in International Law* Dordrecht: Martinus Nijhoff Publishers

Browmik, Sharit, 2002 'As cooperativas e a emancipação dos marginalizados: estudos de caso de duas cidades na Índia,' in Santos (ed) (2002b): 369–400

Brown, Peter and Henry Shue (eds). 1981. *Boundaries: National Autonomy and its Limits.* Totowa, NJ: Rowman and Littlefield.

Brubaker, William R (ed) 1989 *Immigration and the Politics of Citizenship in Europe and North America* Lanhan, MD: University Press of America

1989 'Introduction,' in Brubaker (ed): 1–27

Brunkhorst, Hauke 1987 'Romanticism and Cultural Criticism' *Praxis International, 6:* 397–415

Brush, Stephen B, and Doreen Stablinsky (eds) 1996 *Valuing Local Knowledge: Indigenous Peoples and Intellectual Property Rights* Washington, DC: Island Press

Brysk, Allison 2000 *From Tribal Village to Global Village Indian Rights and International Relations in Latin America* Stanford: Stanford University Press

Buckle, Stephen 1991 *Natural Law and the Theory of Property: Grotius to Hume* Oxford: Clarendon Press

Buergenthal, Thomas 1991 'The CSCE Rights System' *George Washington Journal of International Law and Economics,* 25: 333–386

Bumiller, Kristin 1988 *The Civil Rights Society. The Social Construction of Victims* Baltimore: The Johns Hopkins University Press

Burawoy, Michael 1979 *Manufacturing Consent* Chicago: University of Chicago Press

Burger, Julian 1987 *Report from the Frontier: The State of the World's Indigenous People* London: Zed Books

Burnett, Alan 1985 'Propaganda Cartography,' in Pepper and Jenkins (eds): 60–89

Buttler, Judith and Joan Scott (eds) 1992 *Feminists Theorize the Political* New York: Routledge

Buvollen, Hans Peter 1989 'Regional Autonomy in Nicaragua. A New Approach to the Indigenous Question in Latin America' *Alternatives,* 14: 123–182

Bynum, Caroline, S Harrell and P Richman (eds) 1986 *Gender and Religion: on the Complexity of Symbols* Boston: Beacon Press

Caldeira, Teresa 2000 *City of Walls Crime, Segregation and Citizenship in São Paulo* Berkeley: University of California Press

Call, Charles .1998. 'Institutional Hearing within ICITAP' in Oakley et al (eds) pp.315-363

Carbonneau, Thomas (ed). 1990. *Lex Mercatoria and Arbitration. A Discussion of the New Law Merchant.* Dobbs Ferry, NY: Transnational Juris Publication, Inc.

Carbonnier, Jean 1979 *Sociologia Jurídica* Coimbra: Almedina

Cardoso, Fernando H and Enzo Faletto 1979 *Dependency and Development in Latin America* Berkeley: University of California Press

Caron, R 1980 'Les choix du cartographe,' in *Cartes et Figures de la Terre:* 9–15

Carroll, Lewis 1976 *Complete Works* New York: Vintage

Carothers, Thomas 1998 'The Rule of Law Revival' *Foreign Affairs*, 77(2): 95–106

Carson, WG 1979 'The Conventionalization of Early Factory Crime' *International Journal of the Sociology of Law, 7:* 37–60

Carvalho, Horácio Martins de 2002 'A emancipação do movimento no movimento de emancipação social continuada (resposta a Zander Navarro),' in Santos (ed) (2002b): 233–260

Cascio, Nina 1990 'Human Rights in South and Southeast Asia: A Selective Bibliography,' in Welch, Jr and Leary (eds): 235–298

Casscse, Antonio (ed) 1979 *UN Law Fundamental Rights: Two Topics in International Law* Alphen aan den Rijn, The Netherlands: Sijthoff and Noordhoff

   1979 'Political Self-Determination - Old Concepts and New Developments,' in Cassese (ed): 137–173

Cassirer, Ernst 1946 *The Myth of the State* New Haven: Yale University Press

Castells, Manuel 1996 *The Rise of the Network Society* London: Blackwell

Castles, S, *et al* 1984 *Here for Good: Western Europe's New Ethnic Minorities* London: Pluto Press

Ceceña, Ana Esther 1998 'De cómo se construye la esperanza' *Chiapas,* 6: 135–147

   1999 'La resistencia como espacio de construcción del nuevo mundo' *Chiapas,* 7: 93–114

   2001 'Por la humanidad y contra el neoliberalismo. Líneas centrales del discurso zapatista' *Observatorio Social de América Latina,* 3: 25–30

Charny, David 1991 'Competition among Jurisdictions in Formulating Corporate Law Rules: An American Perspective on the 'Race to the Bottom' in the European Communities' *Harvard International Law Journal,* 32: 423–456

Chase-Dunn, Christopher 1991 *Global Formation: Structures of the World-Economy* Cambridge: Polity Press

Chatterjee, Partha 1984 'Gandhi and the Critique of Civil Society,' in Guha (ed): 153–195

Chekki, Dan 1988 'Transnational Networks in Global Development: Canada and the Third World' *International Social Science Journal,* 40(3): 383–397

Cheng, Lucie 1998 'Global Interaction, Global Inequality, and Migration of the Highly Trained to the United States' *International Migration Review,* 32(3): 626–653

Chiba, Masaji 1989 *Legal Pluralism: Toward a General Theory through Japanese Legal Culture Tokyo*: Tokai University Press

Chomsky, Noam and Edward Herman 1979 *The Political Economy of Human Rights Vol 1: The Washington Connection and Third World Fascism*; Vol 2: *After the Cataclysm: Postwar Indochina and the Construction of Imperial Ideology* Boston: South End Press

Chossudovsky, Michel. 1997. *The Globalization of Poverty: Impacts of IMF and World Bank Reforms.* London: Zed Books.

Cifuentes, Jose Emilio 1993 'El Procedimiento Penal y los Derechos Humanos de los Pueblos Indios en los Umbrales del Siglo XXI' Paper presented at the Annual Conference of the ISA Research Committee on Sociology of Law Oñati, July 5–9

Clapham, Andrew 1991 *Human Rights and the European Community: A Critical Overview* Baden–Baden: Nomos Verlagsgesellschaft

Clapham, A and Weiler, J (eds) 1991a *Human Rights and the European Community: Methods of Protection* Baden-Baden: Nomos Verlagsgesellschaft

1991b *Human Rights and the European Community: The Substantive Law* Baden-Baden: Nomos Verlagsgesellschaft

Clark, John 1990 *Democratizing Development: the Role of Voluntary Associations* West Hartford: Kumarian Press

Clegg, S and D Dunkerley 1980 *Organization, Class and Control* London: Routledge and Kegan Paul

Cobban, Alfred 1964 *Rousseau and the Modern State* 2nd edition London: George Allen and Unwin

Cochrane, Allan and J Anderson 1986 'States and Systems of States,' in Anderson (ed): 211–229

Cocks, Joan 1989 *The Oppositional Imagination* London: Routledge

Coelho, João Paulo Borges 2002 'Estado, comunidades e calamidades naturais no Moçambique rural,' in Santos (ed) (2002d) (forthcoming)

Cohen, G A 1978 *Karl Marx's Theory of History: A Defense* Princeton: Princeton University Press

Cohen, Robin 1987 *The New Helots. Migrants in the International Division of Labour* Aldershot: Avebury

and Shirin M Rai (eds) 2000 *Global Social Movements* London: The Athlone Press

Colletti, Lucio 1974 *From Rousseau to Lenin Studies in Ideology and Society* New York: Monthly Review Press

Collier, George 1995 *Structural Adjustment and New Regional Movements: the Zapatista Rebellion in Chiapas Ethnic Conflict and Governance in Comparative Perspective* Latin American Program Washington, DC: The Woodrow Wilson Center Working Paper, 15

Comaroff, Jean and John L Comaroff (eds) 2001 *Millenial Capitalism and the Culture of Neoliberalism* Durham: Duke University Press

Compa, Lance and Stephen Diamond (eds) 1996 *Human Rights, Labor Rights, and International Trade* Philadelphia: University of Pennsylvania Press

Connell, RW 1987 *Gender and Power* Stanford: Stanford University Press

Copeland, Emily 1992 'Global Refugee Policy: An Agenda for the 1990s' *International Migration Review*, 26: 992–999

Correa, Carlos M 2000 *Intellectual Property Rights, The WTO and Developing Countries: the TRIPS Agreement and Policy Options* London: Zed Books

Cowhey, Peter. 1990. 'The International Telecommunications Regime: The Political Roots of High Technology Regimes' *International Organization,* 44(2): 169-199.

Crawford, James (ed) 1992 *The Rights of People* Oxford: Clarendon Press

Crotty, James, G Epstein and P Kelly. 1998. 'Multinational Corporations in the Neo-Liberal Regime' in Baker et al (eds): 117-143.

Cunha, Manuela C 1992 'Custom Is Not a Thing It is a Path: Reflections on the Brazilian Indian Case,' in An-na'im (ed): 276–294

d'Entreves, Passerin 1972 *Natural Law* London: Hutchinson

Dahl, T S and Snare, A 1978 'The Coercion of Privacy,' in Smart and Smart (eds): 8–26

Daoyu, Li 1992 'The Right to Development—An Inalienable Human Right' *Beijing Review*, 35(51): 8–9

Darian-Smith, Eve 1998 'Power in Paradise: The Political Implications of Santos's Utopia' *Law and Social Inquiry,* 23: 81–120

and Peter Fitzpatrick (eds) 1999 *Laws of the Postcolonial* Ann Harbor: University of Michigan Press

David, René 1950 *Traité elementaire de droit civil comparé* Paris: Libraire Générale de Droit et de Jurisprudence

and J Brierly 1978 *Major Legal Systems in the World Today* London: Stevens and Sons

Davis, Martha 1993 'Domestic Workers: out of the Shadows' *Human Rights,* 20(2): 14–15, 28–29

Debray, Regis 1967 *Strategy for Revolution* New York: Monthly Review Press

Del Vecchio, G 1957 *Persona, estado y derecho* Madrid: Revista Occidente

Delaney, David 1991 *On the Boundedness of Law in a 'Global' World* Paper presented at the Law and Society Association and ISA Research Committee on Sociology of Law Conference Amsterdam, June

Della Porta, Donatella and Meny, Yves 1997 *Democracy and Corruption in Europe* London: Printer

    and Vannucci, Alberto 1997 'The 'Peverse Effects' of Political Corruption,' in Heywood (ed): 100–122

Delgado, Gary 1983 'Organizing Undocumented Workers' *Social Policy,* 13: 6–29

Delmas-Marty, Mireille 2002 *Towards a Truly Common Law : Europe as a Laboratory for Legal Pluralism* New York: Cambridge University Press

Descartes, René 1984 *Discurso do Método e as Paixões da Alma* Lisbon: Sá da Costa

Desroche, Henri 1975 *La societé festive. Du fouriérisme écrit aux fouriérismes pratiqués* Paris: Seuil

Dewey, John 1949 'Common Science and Science,' in Dewey and Bentley: 270–286

    and Arthur Bentley 1949 *Knowing and the Known* Boston: Beacon Press

Deyo, Frederic (ed) 1987 *The Political Economy of the New Asian Industrialism* Ithaca: Cornell University Press

Dezalay, Yves 1990 'The *Big Bang* and the Law: The Internationalization and Restructuration of the Legal Field,' in Featherstone (ed): 279–293

    and Bryant Garth 1997 *Dealing in Virtue: International Commercial Arbitration and the Construction of a Transnational Legal Order* Chicago: University of Chicago Press

Diamond, Irene and G Orenstein (eds) 1990 *Reweaving the Wood: the Emergence of Ecofeminism* San Francisco: Sierra Club Books

Dicey, Albert Vern 1948 *Law and Public Opinion in England* London: Macmillan

Diemer, Alwin, *et al* 1986 *Philosophical Foundations of Human Rights* Paris: UNESCO

Dijk, Teun A van 1987 'Elite Discourse and Racism,' in Zavala, Dijk and Diaz-Diocaretz (eds): 81–122

Dingwall, R and P Lewis (eds). 1983. *The Sociology of Professions.* London: MacMillan.

Donaldson, T 1989 *The Ethics of International Business* New York: Oxford University Press

Donnelly, Jack 1984 'The "Right to Development": how not to Link Rights and Development,' in Welch, Jr and Meltzer (eds): 261–283

1989 *Universal Human Rights in Theory and Practice* Ithaca: Cornell University Press

1992 'Human Rights in the New World Order' *World Policy Journal,* 9: 249–277

Donzelot, J 1977 *La police des families* Paris: Editions de Minuit

Drabek, Anne G 1987 *Development Alternatives: The Challenge for NGOs* New York: Pergamon Press

Draetta, Ugo, R Lake and Ved Nanda 1992 *Breach and Adaptation of International Contracts An Introduction to Lex Mercatoria* Salem, NH: Butterworth Legal Publishers

Dubly, Alain and Alicia Granda 1995 'Los derechos indígenas en el Ecuador' *El Otro Derecho* 18, Vol 6(3), Bogotá: ILSA

Dunne, Tim and Nicholas Wheeler (eds). 1999. *Human rights in global politics.*: Cambridge: Cambridge University Press.

Dupuy, René-Jean 1974 *The Law of the Sea* Dobbs Ferry, NY: Oceana Publications Inc

1958 *The Rules of Sociological Method* Glencoe, IL: The Free Press

Durkheim, Emile 1964 *The Division of Labor in Society* New York: Free Press

Dwyer, Kevin 1991 *Arab Voices. The Human Rights Debate in the Middle East* Berkeley: University of California Press

Dworkin, Ronald 1986 *Law's Empire* Cambridge, MA: Harvard University Press

Edelman, Murray 1964 *The Symbolic Uses of Politics* Urbana: University of Illinois Press

Eder, Klaus 1986 'Prozedurale Rationalität Moderne Rechtsentwicklung jenseits von formaler Rationalisierung' *Zeitschrift für Rechtssoziologie*, 7(1): 1–30

1987 'Die Autoritat des Rechts Erne soziale Kritik prozeduraler Rationalität' *Zeitschrift für Rechtssoziologie,* 8(2): 193–230

Ehrlich, Eugen 1936 *Fundamental Principles of the Sociology of Law* Cambridge, MA: Harvard University Press

Eliassen, Kjell and M Sjovaag (eds). 1999. *European Telecommunications Liberalization.* London: Routledge.

Elkins, Paul 1992 *A New World Order: Grassroots Movements for Global Change* New York: Routledge

Ellul, Jacques 1965 *The Technological Society* London: Cape

Elster, Jon 1985 *Making Sense of Marx* Cambridge: Cambridge University Press

1998. 'Coming to Terms with the Past: A Framework for the Study of Justice in the Transition to Democracy' *Archives Europeennes de Sociologie,* XXXIX:7–48.

Emmanuel, A 1972 *Unequal Exchange: a Study of the Imperialism of Trade* New York: Monthly Review Press

Epstein, A L (ed). 1967. *The Craft of Social Anthropology.* London: Tavistock.

Epstein, Cynthia F 1988 *Deceptive Distinctions Sex Gender and the Social Order* New Haven: Yale University Press

Escobar, Arturo and Mauricio Pardo 2002 'Movimentos sociais e biodiversidade no Pacífico Colombiano,' in Santos (ed) (2002d) (forthcoming)

Evans, Peter 1979 *Dependent Development: the Alliance of Multinational, State and Local Capital in Brazil* Princeton: Princeton University Press

1986 'State, Capital and the Transformation of Dependence: The Brazilian Computer Case' *World Development,* 14: 791–808

1992 'The State as Problem and Solution: Predation, Embedded Autonomy and Structural Change,' in Haggard and Kaufman (eds): 139–181

Evans, Peter, D Rueschemeyer and T Skocpol (eds). 1985. *Bringing the State Back In.* Cambridge: Cambridge University Press.

Ewald, Francois 1986a *L'état providence* Paris: Grasset

1986b 'A Concept of Social Law,' in Teubner (ed): 40–75

Eze, Osita 1984 *Human Rights in Africa: Some Selected Problems* Lagos: Nigerian Institute of International Affairs

Fabian, Johannes 1983 *Time and the Other: How Anthropology Makes its Object* New York: Columbia University Press

Falk, Richard 1981 *Human Rights and State Sovereignty* New York: Holmes and Meier Publishers

1992a 'Cultural Foundations for the International Protection of Human Rights,' in An-na'im (ed): 44–64

1992b *Explorations at the Edge of Time: The Prospects for World Order* Philadelphia: Temple University Press

S Kirn and S Mendlowitz (eds) 1982 *Toward a Just World Order* Boulder: Westview Press

Fallers, Lloyd 1969 *Law without Precedent: Legal Ideas in Action in the Courts of Colonial Busoga* Chicago: University of Chicago Press

FAO 2001 *Food Insecurity: When People Live with Hunger and Starvation* http://wwwfaoorg/docrep/003/y1500e/y1500e00htm, accessed in June 2002

Farjat, G 1982 'Reflexions sur les codes de conduite privés,' in Fouchard (ed): 47–66

Featherstone, Mike (ed) 1990 *Global Culture: Nationalism, Globalization and Modernity* London: Sage

Febbrajo, Alberto 1986 'The Rules of the Game in the Welfare State,' in Teubner (ed): 128–150

Feuerbach, Paul J Anselm 1989 *Paul Johann Anselm Ritter von Feuerbachs Leben und Wirken* Published by Ludwig Feuerbach (1852) Berlin: Akademie Verlag

Fine, B, et al (eds). 1979. *Capitalism and the Rule of Law.* London: Hutchinson.

Fitzpatrick, Peter 1983 'Law, Plurality and Underdevelopment,' in Sugarman (ed): 159–182

  2001 *Modernism and the Grounds of Law* Cambridge: Cambridge University Press

Flórez Alonso, Margarita 2002 'Protecção do conhecimento tradicional?' in Santos (ed) (2002d) (forthcoming)

Fontenau, G 1992 'The Rights of Migrants, Refugees or Asylum Seekers under International Law' *International Migration,* 30 (special issue): 57–66

Foucault, Michel 1976 *La volonté de savoir* Paris: Gallimard

  1977 *Discipline and Punish: the Birth of the Prison* New York: Pantheon

  1980 *Power and Knowledge* New York: Pantheon

Fouchard, P (ed). 1982. *Le droit des relations économiques internationales.* Paris: LITEC.

Fourier, Charles 1967 *Théorie des quatre mouvements et des destinées générales* Paris: Jean-Jacques Pauvert, Editeur

Fraser, Nancy and Linda Nicholson 1990 'Social Criticism without Philosophy: an Encounter between Feminism and Postmodernism,' in Nicholson (ed): 19–38

Fraser, Nancy. 1999. *Adding Insult to Injury: Social Justice and the Politics of Recognition.* London: Verso.

Frideres, James (ed). 1989. *Multiculturalism and Intergroup Relations.* New York: Greenwood Press.

Frieden, Jeff 1987 'International Capital and National Development: Comments on Postimperialism,' in Becker *et al:* 179–191

Friedman, Lawrence 1975 *The Legal System: A Social Science Perspective* New York: Russell Sage Foundation

Friedman, Neil 1986 'A Human Rights Approach to the Labor Rights of Undocumented Workers' *California Law Review,* 74: 1715–1745

Fröbel, Folker, J Heinrichs and O Kreye 1980 *The New International Division of Labor* Cambridge: Cambridge University Press

Frühling, Hugo 1992 'Political Culture and Gross Human Rights Violations in Latin America,' in An-na'im (ed): 253–275

Fung, Archon, Dara O'Rourke and Charles Sabel 2001 *Can We Put an End to Sweatshops?* Boston: Beacon Press

Gaard, Greta. 1998. *Ecological Politics: Ecofeminists and the Greens.* Philadelphia: Temple University Press.

Galanter, Marc 1981 'Justice in Many Rooms: Courts, Private Ordering and Indigenous Law' *Journal of Legal Pluralism,* 19: 1–47

    1983 'Mega-law and Mega-lawyering in the Contemporary US,' in Dingwall and Lewis (eds): 152–176

    1991 *Competing Equalities Law and the Backward Classes in India* Delhi: Oxford University Press

    1992 'Law Abounding: Legalization around the North Atlantic' *The Modern Law Review,* 55(1): 1–24

Galilei, Galileo 1970 *Dialogue Concerning the Two Chief World Systems* Berkeley: University of California Press

Galtung, Johan 1981 'Western Civilization: Anatomy and Pathology' *Alternatives, 7:* 145–169

Gamble, A 1982 *An Introduction To Modern Social and Political Thought* London: MacMillan

García-Villegas, Mauricio 1993 *La Eficacia Simbólica del Derecho Examen de Situaciones Colombianas* Bogotá: Ediciones Uniandes

    and César A Rodríguez (2001) 'La Acción de Tutela en Colombia,' in Santos and García-Villegas (eds): 423–454

Gardner, James 1980 *Legal Imperialism American Lawyers and Foreign Aid in Latin America* Madison: The University of Wisconsin Press

Garst, Daniel 1985 'Wallerstein and His Critics' *Theory and Society*, 14: 469–495

Gedicks, Al 2001 *Resource Rebels Native Challenges to Mining and Oil Corporations* Cambridge: South End Press

Geertz, Clifford 1973 *The Interpretation of Cultures: Selected Essays* New York: Basic Books

    1983 *Local Knowledge: Further Essays in Interpretative Anthropology* New York: Basic Books

Gereffi, Gary and Miguel Korzeniewicz (eds) 1994 *Commodity Chains and Global Capitalism* Westport, Conn: Praeger

Gessner, Volkmar 1990 *Structure and Culture of Cross-Border Legal Relations* Zentrum für Europäische Rechtspolitik, University of Bremen

and A Schade 1990 'Conflicts of Culture in Cross-Border Legal Relations: The Conception of a Research Topic in the Sociology of Law,' in Featherstone (ed): 253–277

Ghai, Yash 1993a 'Asian Perspectives on Human Rights' Hong Kong: Law School, University of Hong Kong

1993b *The Rule of Law and Capitalism Reflections on the Basic Law* Paper presented at the Workshop on Globalization and the Future of Law in China Madison: Global Studies Research Program, October 1–2

1993c *Ethnicity and Governance in Asia: A Report to the Ford Foundation* Draft New York: Ford Foundation

1999 'Rights, Social Justice and Globalization in East Asia,' in Bauer and Bell (eds): 241–263

(ed). 2000a. *Autonomy and Ethnicity: Negotiating Claims in Multi-ethnic States.* Cambridge: Cambridge University Press.

2000b. 'Universalism and Relativism: Human Rights as a Framework for Negotiating Interethnic Differences' *Cardozo Law Review,* 21: 1095-1140.

2001. *Human Rights and Social Development: Toward Democratization and Social Justice.* Geneva: United Nations Research Institute for Social Development.

Giddens, Anthony 1979 *Central Problems in Social Theory* London: MacMillan

1981 *A Contemporary Critique of Historical Materialism* Berkeley: University of California Press

1984 *The Constitution of Society* Cambridge: Polity Press

1990 *Sociology* Oxford: Polity Press

1991a *The Consequences of Modernity* Oxford: Polity Press

1991b *Modernity and Self-Identity* Cambridge: Polity Press

1998 *The Third Way: the Renewal of Social Democracy* Cambridge: Polity Press

Gilroy, Paul 1993 *The Black Atlantic Modernity and Double Consciousness* Cambridge, MA: Harvard University Press

Glenn, H Patrick. 2000. *Legal Traditions of the World.* Oxford: Oxford University Press.

Gluckman, Max 1955 *The Judicial Process among the Barotse of Northern Rhodesia* Manchester: Manchester University Press

Goldman, Berthold 1964 'Frontières du droit et lex mercatoria,' *Archives de Philosophie du Droit,* 9: 177–192

Goldsmith, Edward 1988 'Gaia: Some Implications for Theoretical Ecology,' *The Ecologist,* 18(2–3): 64–74

Golub, Stephen 2000 'Battling Apartheid, Building a New South Africa,' in McClymont and Golub (eds): 19–54

Gómez, Magdalena (ed). 1997. *Derecho Indígena.* Mexico, DF: Instituto Nacional Indígena.

Goodwill-Gill, Guy 1989 'International Law and Human Rights: Trends Concerning International Migrants and Refugees' *International Migration Review,* 23: 526–546

Gordon, David M 1988 'The Global Economy: New Edifice or Crumbling Foundations?' *New Left Review,* 168: 24–64

Gordon, Linda 1990 *Woman's Body, Woman's Right Birth Control in America* Revised and updated New York: Penguin

(ed) 1991 *Women, the State and Welfare* Madison: The University of Wisconsin Press

Gordon, Michael E and Lowell Turner (eds) 2000 *Transnational Cooperation among Labor Unions* Ithaca: Cornell University Press

Gottman, J (ed). 1980. *Centre and Periphery: Spatial Variation in Politics.* Beverly Hills: Sage.

Gouldner, Alvin 1970 *The Coming Crisis of Western Sociology* New York: Avon

Gramsci, Antonio 1971 *Selections from the Prison Notebooks* London: Lawrence and Wishart

Gregory, Derek and John Urry (eds) 1985 *Social Relations and Spatial Structures* New York: St Martin's Press

Griffiths, John 1986 'What is Legal Pluralism?' *Journal of Legal Pluralism,* 24: 1–56

Grolin, Jesper 1987 'The Question of Antarctica and the Problem of Sovereignty' *International Relations,* 9: 39–55

Gros, Christian. 2000. *Políticas de Etnicidad: Identidad, Estado y Modernidad.* Bogotá: Instituto Colombiano de Antropología e Historia.

Grotius, Hugo 1964 *De Jure Belli ac Pacis Libri Tres* Volume II New York: Oceana Publications

Guevara-Gil, Armando 1992 *The Impact of Development Efforts on the Configuration and Enforcement of Fishing Rights in Lake Titicaca, Peru, 1930s–1990s* Madison: University of Wisconsin, Department of Anthropology

Guha, Ranajit (ed). 1984. *Subaltern Studies III: Writings on South Asian History and Society.* Delhi: Oxford University Press.

Guidieri, Remo and Francesco Pellizzi 1988 'Introduction: "Smoking Mirrors" – Modern Polity and Ethnicity,' in Guidieri, Pellizzi and Tambiah (eds): 7–38

Gulliver, Phillip 1969 'Introduction to Case Studies of Law in Non-Western Societies,' in Nader (ed): 11–23

Gurvitch, Georges 1942 *Sociology of Law* New York: Philosophical Library

Gutiérrez, Francisco and Aana Maria Jaramillo 2002 'Pactos paradoxais,' in Santos (ed) (2002c) (forthcoming)

Habermas, Jürgen 1978 *Zur Rekonstruktion des historischen Materialismus* Frankfurt: Suhrkamp

   1986 'Law as Medium and Law as Institution,' in Teubner (ed): 203–220

   1987 'Wie ist Legitimität durch Legalität Möglich?' *Kritische Justiz,* 20: 1–16

Haggard, Stephan and BA Simmons 1987 'Theories of International Regimes' *International Organization,* 41: 491–549

   and Robert Kaufman 1992 *The Political Economy of Democratic Transitions* Princeton: Princeton University Press

Haken, Hermann 1977 *Synergetics: An Introduction* Heidelberg: Springer

Hakovirta, Harto 1993 'The Global Refugee Problem: A Model and Its Application' *International Political Science Review,* 14: 35–57

Hall, Stuart and Bram Gleben (eds) 1992 *Formations of Modernity* London: Polity Press

Hall, Stuart 1996 'Who Needs Identity?' In Hall and du Gay (eds): 1–17

   and Paul du Gay (eds) 1996 *Questions of Cultural Identity* London: Sage

Hammer, Thomas 1989 'Comparing European and North American International Migration' *International Migration Review,* 23: 631–637

Hancher, Leigh and M Moran (eds). 1989. *Capitalism, Culture and Economic Regulation.* Oxford: Clarendon Press.

Handler, Joel F 1983 *The Discretionary Decision: Adversarial Advocacy – Reform or Reconstruction?* Conference on Reflexive Law and the Regulatory Crisis, Madison: Institute for Legal Studies

   1992 'A Reply' *Law and Society Review,* 26(4): 819–824

Hannerz, Ulf 1990 'Cosmopolitan and Local in World Culture,' in Featherstone (ed): 237–251

Harley, J B 1989 'Deconstructing the Map' *Cartographica,* 26(2): 1–20

1990 'Cartography, Ethics and Social Theory' *Cartographica,* 27(2): 1–23

Hart, Herbert 1961 *The Concept of Law* Oxford: Clarendon Press

Hartigan, Kevin 1992 'Matching Humanitarian Norms with Cold Hard Interests: the Making of Refugee Policies in Mexico and Honduras, 1980–1989' *International Organization,* 46: 709–730

Hassan, Riffat 1982 'On Human Rights and the Qur'anic Perspective' *Journal of Ecumenical Studies,* 19(3): 51–65

Hathaway, James 1991 *The Law of Refugee Status* Toronto: Butterworths

Haveman, Paul. 2000. 'Enmeshed in the Web? Indigenous Peoples' Rights in the Network Society' in Cohen and Rai (eds): 18-32.

Hay, Douglas, *et al* 1975 *Albion's Fatal Tree: Crime and Society in Eighteenth Century England* New York: Pantheon

Hayek, F 1979 *Law, Legislation and Liberty* Chicago: University of Chicago Press

Hegel, GWF 1981 *Grundlinien der Philosophie des Rechts oder Naturrecht und Staatswissenschaft im Grundrisse* Berlin: Akademie Verlag

Heintze, Hans-Joachim 1992 'International Law and Indigenous Peoples' *Law and State,* 45: 37–67

Heisler, Martin 1992 'Migration, International Relations and the New Europe: Theoretical Perspective from Institutional Political Sociology' *International Migration Review,* 26: 596–622

Held, David 1993 'Democracy: From City-States to a Cosmopolitan Order?' in Held (ed): 13–52

(ed). 1993. *Prospects for Democracy.* Stanford: Stanford University Press.

Heller, Agnès 1976 *The Theory of Need in Marx* London: Allison Busby

1993 'A Theory of Needs Revisited' *Thesis Eleven,* 35: 18–35

Heller, Thomas 1992 *A Retrospective on Law and Development* Paper presented at the Asia Foundation Asian Law Conference Chaing Mai, Thailand, August 31– September 4

Hendley, Kathryn 1995 'The Spillover Effects of Privatization on Russian Legal Culture' *Transnational Law and Contemporary Problems,* 5(39): 40–64

1996 ' Law and Development in Russia: A Misguided Enterprise?' *Proceedings of the American Society of International Law,* 90: 237–240

1997 'Legal Development in Post-Soviet Russia' *Post-Soviet Affairs*, 13: 231–256

1998 'Growing Pains: Balancing Justice and Efficiency in Russian Economic Courts', *Temple International and Comparative Law Journal,* 12:301–331

1999 'Rewriting the Rules of the Game in Russia: The Neglected Issue of Demand for Law', *East European Constitutional Review* 8: 88–95

2001 '"Demand" for Law in Russia – a Mixed Picture', *East European Constitutional Review,* 10:72–76

Henkin, Alice (ed) 1979 *Human Dignity The Internationalization of Human Rights* New York: Aspen Institute for Humanistic Studies

Henrikson, A 1975 'The Map as an 'Idea': The Role of Cartographic Imagery during the Second World War' *The American Cartographer*, 2: 19–53

1980 'America's Changing Place in the World: from "Periphery" to "Centre"?' in Gottmann (ed): 73–100

Henry, Stuart and D Milovanovic 1993 'Back to Basics: A Postmodern Redefinition of Crime' *The Critical Criminologist,* 5(2/3): 1–6

Heywood, Paul (ed) 1997 *Political Corruption* Oxford: Blackwell

Higgott, Richard A, Geoffrey RD Underhill and Andreas Bieler. 2000. *Non-State Actors and Authority in the Global System.* London: Routledge.

Hilferding, Rudolf 1981 *Finance Capital: a Study of the Latest Phase of Capitalist Development* London: Routledge and Kegan Paul

Hirsch, Marianne and EF Keller (eds) 1990 *Conflicts in Feminism* New York: Routledge

Hirschman, Albert 1977 *The Passions and the Interests* Princeton: Princeton University Press

Hobbes, Thomas 1946 *Leviathan* Edited with an Introduction by Michael Oakeshott Oxford: Basil Blackwell

Hobsbawm, Eric 1975 *The Age of Capital 1848–1875* London: Weidenfeld and Nicolson

Hodgkiss, AG 1981 *Understanding Maps. A Systematic History of Their Use and Development* Folkestone: Dawson

Holloway, John. 1998. 'Dignity's Revolt' in Holloway and Peláez (eds): 159-198.

and E. Peláez (eds). 1998. *Zapatista!: Reinventing Revolution in Mexico.* London: Pluto Press.

Hoogenboom, T 1992 'Free Movement of Non-EC Nationals, Schengen and Beyond,' in Meijers et al: 74–95

Hooker, M 1975 *Legal Pluralism: An Introduction to Colonial and Neo-Colonial Laws* Oxford: Clarendon Press

Hoon, Shim Jae 1993 'Judging the Judges' *Far Eastern Economic Review*, December 9: 28–30

Howard, Rhoda 1983 'The Full-Belly Thesis: Should Economic Rights Take Priority over Civil and Political Rights? Evidence from Sub-Saharan Africa' *Human Rights Quarterly*, 5: 467–490

    1984 'Evaluating Human Rights in Africa: some Problems of Implicit Comparisons' *Human Rights Quarterly,* 6: 160–179

Huet, Jérôme and Herbert Maisl 1989 *Droit de l'informatique et des télécommunications* Paris: Litec

Human Rights Watch 1996 *The Small Hands of Slavery. Bonded Child Labor in India* Human Rights Watch Children's Rights Project, Human Rights Watch/Asia Available at http://wwwhrworg/reports/1996/India3htm, accessed in June 2002

Humm, Maggie 1990 *The Dictionary of Feminist Theory* Columbus: Ohio State University Press

Hunt, Alan 1978 *The Sociological Movement in Law* Philadelphia: Temple University Press

    1993 *Explorations of Law and Society* New York: Routledge

Hunter, Allen 1992 *TANGO Bibliography* Madison: A E Havens Center for the Study of Social Structure and Social Change

    and Louise Trubek 1992 *NGO's and Democratization* Research proposal Madison: Global Studies Research Program

Hyndman, Patricia 1992 'Cultural Legitimacy in the Formulation and Implementation of Human Rights Law and Policy in Australia,' in An-na'im (ed): 295–338

Ignatieff, Michael 1978 *A Just Measure of Pain* London: MacMillan

Ihering, R 1915 *The Struggle for Law* 2nd edition Chicago: Callaghan

Inada, Kenneth K 1990 'A Buddhist Response to the Nature of Human Rights,' in Welch, Jr and Leary (eds): 91–101

Jahangir, Asma 1990 'Protection of Religious Minorities and Women: The Impact of Islamic Law in Pakistan,' in Welch, Jr and Leary (eds): 206–217

James, William 1969 *The Writings of William James. A Comprehensive Edition* New York: Modern Library

Jameson, Fredric 1984 'Postmodernism, or the Cultural Logic of Late Capitalism' *New Left Review,* 146: 53–92

Janis, Mark W 1988 *An Introduction to International Law* Boston: Little, Brown and Company

Jankovic, I 1977 'Labor Market and Imprisonment' *Crime and Social Justice*, Fall-Winter: 17

Jasentuliyana, N 1990 'Space Commerce on a Global Scale' *The Journal of Law and Technology*, 5: 1–8

Jelin, Elizabeth and Eric Hershberg. (eds). 1996. *Constructing Democracy: Human Rights, Citizenship, and Society in Latin America.* Boulder: Westview Press.

Jencks, Charles 1987 *Post-Modernism The New Classicism in Art and Architecture* London: Academy Editions

Jenkins, Rhys 1984 'Divisions over the International Division of Labor' *Capital and Class*, 22: 28–57

Jervis, WW 1936 *The World in Maps A Study of Map Evolution* London: George Philip

Jessop, Bob 1990a *State Theory. Putting Capitalist States in their Place* University Park, PA: The Pennsylvania State University Press

  1990b 'Regulation Theories in Retrospect and Prospect' *Economy and Society,* 19: 153–216

Joerges, Christian 1991 'Market without a State' Florence: European University Institute

Jonas, Hans 1985 *Das Prinzip der Verantwortung* 5th edition Frankfurt: Insel Verlag

Jones, Carol 1993 *The Globalization of Rule of Law? Some Questions from Asia* Paper presented at the Workshop on Globalization and the Future of Law in China Madison: Global Studies Research Program, October 1–2

Joshi, Barbara 1990 'Human Rights as Dynamic Process: The Case of India's Untouchables,' in Welch, Jr and Leary (eds): 162–185

Joyner, Christopher 1986 'Legal Implications of the Concept of the Common Heritage of Humankind' *International and Comparative Law Quarterly*, 35: 190–199

Junqueira, Eliane and Jose Rodrigues. 1992. 'Pasargada revisitada.' *Sociologia. Problemas e Práticas,* 12: 9-17.

Kahn, Philippe 1982 'Droit international économique, droit du développement, lex mercatoria; concept unique ou pluralisme des ordres juridiques?' in P Fouchard (ed): 97–123

Kahn, Paul 2000 T*he Cultural Study of Law: Reconstructing Legal Scholarship* Chicago: Chicago University Press

Kaldor, Mary 1999 'Transnational Civil Society,' in Dunne and Wheeler (eds): 195–213

Kantorowicz, Ernst 1957 *The King's Two Bodies* Princeton: Princeton University Press

Kantorowicz, Hermann 1958 *The Definition of Law* Cambridge: Cambridge University Press

Keane, John 1988a *Democracy and Civil Society* London: Verso

1988b *Civil Society and the State: New European Perspectives* London: Verso

Keates, J S 1982 *Understanding Maps* London: Longman

Keck, Margaret and Katherine Sikkink. 1998. *Activists Beyond Borders: Advocacy Networks in International Politics.* Ithaca: Cornell University Press.

Kelly, D R 1984 *History, Law and the Human Sciences: Medieval and Renaissance Perspectives* London: Variorum Reprints

Kelsen, Hans 1962 *Teoria pura do direito* 2nd edition Volume II Coimbra: Amado

1967 *The Pure Theory of Law* Los Angeles: University of California Press

Kendall, Laurel 1985 *Shamans, Housewives and Other Restless Spirits Women in Korean Ritual Life* Honolulu: University of Hawaii Press

Kennedy, David 1988 'A New Stream of International Law Scholarship' *Wisconsin International Law Journal*, 7: 1–49

1999 'Images of Religion in International Legal Theory,' in Janis and Evans (eds): 145–153

Kennedy, Duncan 1997 *A Critique of Adjudication* Cambridge, MA: Harvard University Press

Kennedy, Paul 1993 *Preparing for the Twenty-First Century* New York: Random House

Keohane, Robert 1985 *After Hegemony: Cooperation and Discord in the World Political Economy* Princeton: Princeton University Press

and Joseph Nye 1977 *Power and Interdependence* Boston: Little, Brown and Company

Kessler-Harris, Alice. 2001. *In Pursuit of Equity: Women, Men and the Quest for Economic Citizenship.* Oxford: Oxford University Press.

Kimball, Lee 1983 'The Law of the Sea – on the Shoals' *Environment,* 25(9): 14–20, 41–44

King, Anthony D 1986 *The Bungalow: the Production of a Global Culture* London: Routledge

Kiss, Alexandra 1985 'The Common Heritage of Mankind: Utopia or Reality?' *International Journal,* 40: 423–441

1989 *Droit international de l'environnement* Paris: Pedone

Kitchin, William 1995 'Legal Reform and the Expansion of Judicial Power in Russia,' in Tate and Vallinder (eds): 441–459

Klug, Heinz 1996 *Constitutionalism, Democratization and Constitution-making for a New South Africa* LLM dissertation University of Wisconsin – Madison Law School

> 2000a *Constituting Democracy: Law, Globalism and South Africa's Political Reconstruction* New York: Cambridge University Press

> 2000b 'Accidental Outcomes? The Contradictory Impact of Multiple Spheres of Politics on the Definition of Global Rules' Paper presented at the Law and Society Association 2000 Annual Meeting, Miami

> 2001a 'From Floor to Ceiling? South Africa, Brazil, and the Impact of the HIV/AIDS Crisis on the Interpretations of TRIPS' *Socio-Legal Newsletter*, 34: 4–5

> 2001b 'WTO Puts Public Health Before Patents – but …' *Socio-Legal Newsletter*, 35: 14

> Forthcoming 'Access to Health Care: Judging Implementation in the Context of AIDS' *South African Journal of Human Rights*

Konvitz, Josef 1980 'Remplir la carte,' in *Cartes et Figures de la Terre:* 304–314

Korten, David 1990 *Getting to the 21st Century: Voluntary Action and the Global Agenda* West Hartford: Kumarian Press

Koselleck, Reinhart 1985 *Futures Past: On the Semantics of Historical Time* Cambridge, MA: MIT Press

Koser, Khalid 2001 *The Return and Reintegration of Rejected Asylum Seekers and Irregular Migrants An Analysis of Government Assisted Return Programmes in Selected European Countries* London: International Organization for Migration

Kothari, Ashish (1999) 'Biodiversity and Intellectual Property Rights: Can the two Co-Exist?' *Linkages* 4(2) Available at http://wwwiisdca/linkages/journal/kotharihtml, accessed on 6 June 2002

Kotz, David 1990 'A Comparative Analysis of the Theory of Regulation and the Social Structure of Accumulation Theory' *Science and Society,* 54: 5–28

Krasner, Stephen (ed) 1983 *International Regimes* Ithaca: Cornell University Press

Kuletz, Valerie 1992 'Eco-Feminist Philosophy: Interview with Barbara Holland-Cunz' *Capitalism, Nature, Socialism,* 3(2): 63–78

Lacoste, Yves 1976 *La Géographie, ça sert d'abord a faire la guerre* Paris: Maspero

> 1980 'Les objets géographiques,' in *Cartes et Figures de la Terre:* 16–23

Lâm, Maivân 1985 'The Imposition of Anglo-American Land Tenure Law on Hawaiians' *Journal of Legal Pluralism,* 23: 103–128

1991 *Indigenous Claims and the Re-Configuring of Self-Determination in International Law* Madison: Institute for Legal Studies

2000. *At the Edges of the State: Indigenous Peoples and Self-Determination.* Ardsley, NY: Transnational Publishers.

Lanzerotti, Louis, *et al* 1993 *Science and Stewardship in the Antarctic* Washington, DC: National Academy Press

Larson, Jane E 2002 'Informality, Illegality, and Inequality' *Yale Law and Policy Review*, 20: 137–182

Lash, Scott and John Urry 1987 *The End of Organized Capitalism* Oxford: Polity Press

Layoun, Mary. 2001. *Wedded to the Land?: Gender, Boundaries and Nationalism in Crisis.* Durham: Duke University Press.

Leary, Virginia 1990 'The Asian Region and the International Human Rights Movement,' in Welch, Jr and Leary (eds): 13–27

Lecourt, Dominique 1976 *Lysenko: histoire réelle d'une science prolétarienne* Paris: Maspero

Leites, Justin 1991 'Modernist Jurisprudence as a Vehicle for Gender Role Reform in the Islamic World' *Columbia Human Rights Law Review,* 22: 251–330

Lennox, Malissia 1993 'Refugees, Racism, and Reparations: A Critique of the United States' Haitian Immigration Policy' *Stanford Law Review,* 45: 687–724

Lessnoff, Michael (ed) 1990 *Social Contract Theory* Oxford: Basil Blackwell

Lev, Daniel 1990 'Human Rights NGOs in Indonesia and Malaysia,' in Welch, Jr and Leary (eds): 142–161

Levi-Bruhl, Henri 1971 *Sociologie du droit* 4th edition Paris: Presses Universitaires de France

Levitsky, Sandra R 2001 *Narrow, But Not Straight: Professionalized Rights Strategies in the Chicago GLBT Movement* Thesis (MS) in Sociology, University of Wisconsin – Madison

Lewellen, Ted C 1985 'Structures of Terror: A System Analysis of Repression in El Salvador,' in Shepherd, Jr and Nanda (eds): 59–81

Lindholm, Tore 1992 'Prospects on the Cultural Legitimacy of Human Rights: The Cases of Liberalism and Marxism,' in An-na'im (ed): 387–426

Lipietz, Alain 1989 *Choisir l'audace. Une alternative pour le XXIᵉ siècle* Paris: La Découverte

Lippman, Matthew 1985 'Multinational Corporations and Human Rights,' in Shepherd, Jr and Nanda (eds): 249–272

Lipson, Charles 1985 *Standing Guard: Protecting Foreign Capital in the Nineteenth and Twentieth Centuries* Berkeley: University of California Press

Little, Cheryl 1993 'United States Haitian Policy: A History of Discrimination' *New York Law School Journal of Human Rights,* 10: 269–323

Locke, John 1952 *The Second Treatise of Government* New York: The Liberal Arts Press

    1956 *An Essay Concerning Human Understanding* Oxford: Clarendon

Lodge, Juliet 1989 *The European Community and the Challenge of the Future* New York: St Martin's Press

Lohrmann, Reinhard 2000 'Migrants, Refugees and Insecurity Current Threats to Peace?' *International Migration,* 38(4): 3–22

Lopes, João Marcos de Almeida 2002 ''O dorso da cidade': os sem-terra e a concepção de uma outra cidade,' in Santos (ed) (2002b): 288–326

Lorenz, FM 1995 'Democratic Reform and the Rule of Law in Cambodia' *Washington State Bar News,* February, 26–30

Lovelock, J E 1979 *Gaia: A New Look at Life on Earth* Oxford: Oxford University Press

Luhmann, Niklas 1972 *Rechtssoziologie* Reinbek: Rowohlt

    1979 *Trust and Power: Two Works* New York: Wiley

    1984 *Soziale Systeme: Grundriss einer allgemeiner Theorie* Frankfurt: Suhrkamp

    1986 'The Self-reproduction of Law and its Limits,' in Teubner, (ed): 111–127

    1988a 'The Unity of the Legal System,' in Teubner (ed): 12–35

    1988b 'Closure and Openness: On Reality in the World of Law,' in Teubner (ed): 335–348

Lukács, Georg 1972 *Studies in European Realism* London: Merlin Press

Lukes, Steven 1974 *Power: a Radical View* London: MacMillan

M'Baye, Keba 1991 'Droits de l'homme et pays en développement,' in *Humanité et droit international*: 211–222

Macaulay, Stewart 1963 'Non-Contractual Relations in Business: A Preliminary Study' *American Sociological Review,* 28: 55–66

    1983 *Private Government* University of Wisconsin-Madison, Disputes Processing Research Program Working Papers, 6

    1987 'Images of Law in Everyday Life: the Lessons of School, Entertainment and Spectator Sports' *Law and Society Review,* 21(2): 185–218

MacEachren, Alan. 1994. *Some Truth with Maps. A Primer on Simbolization and Design.* Washington, DC: Association of American Geographers.

Macpherson, C B 1962 *The Political Theory of Possessive Individualism: Hobbes to Locke* Oxford: Clarendon Press

Maduro, Luís Miguel 1992 *An Institutional Comparative Approach to the Regulatory Problems in the European Community* Florence: European University Institute

Maduro, Miguel 1998 *We The Court: The European Court of Justice and the European Economic Constitution.* Oxford: Hart Publishing.

Mahnkopf, B 1988 'Soziale Grenzen fordistischen Regulation,' in Mahnkopf (ed): 99–143

(ed). 1988. *Der gewendete Kapitalismus: kritische Beiträge zu einer Theorie der Regulation.* Muenster: Westfälischer Dampfboot.

Maizels, Alfred 1992 *Commodities in Crisis* Oxford: Oxford University Press

1999. *Economic Dependence on Commodities.* Geneva: UNCTAD.

Mancini, Frederico 1989 'The Making of a Constitution for Europe' *Common Market Law Review,* 26: 595–614

Manfrass, Klaus 1992 'Europe: South-North or East-West Migration?' *International Migration Review, 26:* 388–400

Marés, Carlos Frederico 2000 *O Renascer dos Povos Indígenas para o Direito* Curitiba: Juruá Editora

Marques, Maria Manuel L 1987 'A Empresa, o espaço e o Direito' *Revista Crítica de Ciências Sociais, 22:* 69–82

Marshall, TH 1950 *Citizenship and Social Class, and Other Essays* Cambridge: Cambridge University Press

Martin, David 1989 'Effects of International Law on Migration Policy and Practice: the Uses of Hypocricy' *International Migration Review,* 23: 547–578

Marx, Karl 1963 *The Poverty of Philosophy* New York: International Publishers

1970 Das *Kapital,* Volumes I, II, III New York: International Publishers

1973 *Grundrisse: Foundations of the Critique of Political Economy* Harmondsworth: Penguin

and Friedrich Engels 1967 *Communist Manifesto* Harmondsworth: Penguin Books

Massell, Gregory 1968 'Law as an Instrument of Revolutionary Change in a Traditional Milieu' *Law and Society Review,* 2(2): 179–228

Massey, Doreen 1984 *Spatial Divisions of Labour: Social Structures and the Geography of Production* London: MacMillan

Mayer, Ann Elizabeth 1991 *Islam and Human Rights: Tradition and Politics* Boulder: Westview Press

McChesney, Allan 1992 'Aboriginal Communities, Aboriginal Rights in the Human Rights System in Canada,' in An-na'im (ed): 221–252

McClymont, Mary and Stephen Golub (eds) 2000 *Many Roads to Justice The Law-Related Work of Ford Foundation Grantees around the World* New York: The Ford Foundation

McCormick, John. 1999. *Supranational Challenges to the Rule of Law: The Case of the European Union.* Oxford University Press.

McHaffie, Patrick, et al 1990 'Ethical Problems in Cartography' *Cartographica*, 7: 3–13

McMichael, Philip and D Myhre 1990 'Global Regulation vs the Nation-State: Agro-Food Systems and the New Politics of Capital' *Review of Radical Political Economy*, 22: 59–77

Medina, Vicente 1990 *Social Contract Theories: Political Obligation or Anarchy?* Savage, MD: Rowman and Littlefield

Meijers, H, et al 1992. *Schengen. Internationalization of Central Chapters of the Law on Aliens, Refugees, Privacy, Security and the Police.* 2nd edition. Leiden: Stichting NJCM-Boekerij.

Mellor, Mary 1992 'Eco-Feminism and Eco-Socialism: Dilemmas of Essentialism and Materialism' *Capitalism, Nature, Socialism,* 3(2): 43–62

Melossi, D 1978 'George Rusche and Otto Kirchheimer: Punishment and Social Justice' *Crime and Social Justice,* Spring-Summer: 73–85

and M Pavarini 1981 *The Prison and the Factory* Totowa: Barnes and Noble

Mendelson, Oliver and Upendra Baxi (eds). 1994. *The Rights of Subordinate Peoples.* Delhi: Oxford University Press.

Meneses, MPG 2002 '"Quando não há problemas, estamos de boa saúde, sem azar nem nada": para uma concepção emancipatória da saúde e das medicinas,' in Santos (ed) (2002d) (forthcoming)

Merry, Sally 1988 'Legal Pluralism' *Law and Society Review,* 22: 869–896

Merryman, John 1985 *The Civil Law Tradition: An Introduction to the Legal Systems of Western Europe and Latin America* 2nd edition Stanford: Stanford University Press

Merton, Robert 1968 *Social Theory and Social Structure* New York: Free Press

Messick, Richard 1999 'Judicial Reform and Economic Development: A Survey of Issues' The World Bank Research Observer, 14, 1: 117-136

Meyer, William 1987 'Testing Theories of Cultural Imperialism: International Media and Domestic Impact' *International Interactions*, 13: 353–374

Mies, Maria and Vandana Shiva. 1993. *Ecofeminism.* New Delhi: Kalhi for Women.

Mignolo, Walter. 2000. *Local Histories/Global Designs: Coloniality, Subaltern Knowledges and Border Thinking.* Princeton: Princeton University Press.

2002. 'The Many Faces of Cosmo-Polis: Border Thinking and Critical Cosmopolitanism', in Breckenridge, Pollock, Bhabha and Chakrabarty (eds): 157-187.

Mill, J S 1921 *Principles of Political Economy* London

Miller, G A, et al 1972 'Plans,' in Spradley (ed): 52–64

Miller, Mike 1992 'Citizen Groups: whom Do They Represent?' *Social Policy,* Spring: 54–59

Mitra, Kana 1982 'Human Rights in Hinduism' *Journal of Ecumenical Studies,* 19(3): 77–84

Monmonier, Mark 1981 *Maps Distortion and Meaning* Washington: Association of American Geographers

1991a *How to Lie with Maps* Chicago: University of Chicago Press

1991b 'Ethics and Map Design' *Cartographic Perspectives,* 10: 3–8

1993. *Mapping It Out: Expository Cartography for the Humanities and Social Sciences.* Chicago: Chicago University Press.

Montesquieu, Charles de Secondat, baron de 1989 *The Spirit of Laws* Cambridge: Cambridge University Press

Moody, Kim 1997 *Workers in a Lean World: Unions in the International Economy* New York: Verso

Moore, Sally F 1978 *Law as Process: An Anthropological Approach* London: Routledge and Kegan Paul

Moravcsik, Andrew 1991 'Negotiating the Single European Act: National Interests and Conventional Statecraft in the European Community' *International Organization,* 45:19–56

Moyo, Sam and Yemi Katerere 1991 *NGOs in Transition: An Assessment of Regional NGOs in the Development Process* Harare: The Zimbabwe Energy Research Organization

Muchlinski, Peter T 1997 ''Global Bukowina' Examined: Viewing the Multinational Enterprise as a Transnational Law-making Community,' in Teubner (ed): 79–108

Muehrcke, P C 1986 *Map Use* 2nd edition Madison: JP Publications

Munger, Frank 1998 'Mapping Law and Society,' in Sarat, Constable, Engel, Hans and Lawrence (eds): 21–80

Muracciole, D 1980 'Le rond et le plat,' in *Cartes et Figures de la Terre:* 235–239

Murphy, Craig and R Tooze (eds). 1991. *The New International Political Economy.* Boulder: Lynne Rienner Publishers.

Mustill, Lord Justice 1988 'The New *Lex Mercatoria:* The First Twenty-five Years' *Arbitration International, 4:* 86–119

Mutua, Makau 2001 'Savages, Victims, and Saviors: the Metaphor of Human Rights' *Harvard International Law Journal*, 42(1): 201–245

Muzaffar, Chandra 1990 'Ethnicity, Ethnic Conflict and Human Rights in Malaysia,' in Welch, Jr and Leary (eds): 107–141

Nader, Laura (ed) 1969 *Law in Culture and Society* Chicago: Aldine

Nafziger, James and Barry Bartel 1991 'The Migrant Workers Convention: its Place in Human Rights Law' *International Migration Review, 25:* 771–797

Nanda, Ved 1985 'Development and Human Rights: the Role of International Law and Organizations,' in Shepherd, Jr and Nanda (eds): 287–307

    J Scarritt and G Shepherd, Jr (eds) 1981 Global Human Rights: Public Policies, Comparative Measures and NGO Strategies Boulder: Westview Press

Nandy, Ashis 1987a 'Cultural Frames for Social Transformation: A Credo' *Alternatives* XII: 113–123

    1987b *Traditions, Tyranny and Utopias Essays in the Politics of Awareness* Oxford: Oxford University Press

    1988 'The Politics of Secularism and the Recovery of Religious Tolerance' *Alternatives*, XIII: 177–194

Navarro, Zander 2002 '"Mobilização sem emancipação" – as lutas sociais dos em-terra no Brasil,' in Santos (ed) (2002b): 189–232

Nelken, David 1996 'The Judges and Political Corruption in Italy' *Journal of Law and Society* 23(2): 95–112

Nett, Roger 1971 'The Civil Right We Are Not Ready For: the Right of Free Movement of People on the Face of the Earth' *Ethics,* 81: 212–227

Nicholson, Linda (ed). 1990. *Feminism/Postmodernism.* New York: Routledge.

Niessen, Jan 1992 'European Community Legislation and Intergovernmental Cooperation on Migration' *International Migration Review, 26:* 676–684

Nino, Carlos S 1993 'On the Exercise of Judicial Review in Argentina,' in Stotzky (ed): 309–335

Noel, A 1987 'Accumulation, Regulation and Social Change: An Essay on French Political Economy' *International Organization,* 41: 303–333

Nordahl, Richard 1992 'A Marxian Approach to Human Rights,' in An-na'im (ed): 162–187

Nutger, Adriana and Jan Smits 1989 'The Regulation of International Telecommunication Services: a New Approach' *North Carolina Journal of International Law and Commercial Regulation,* 14:191–218

Oakley, Robert, M. Dziedzic and E. Goldberg (eds) .1998 *Policing the New World Disorder: Peace Operations and Public Security.* Washington, DC: Institute for National Strategic Studies.

Obiora, L Amede 1997 'Bridges and Barricades: Rethinking Polemics and Intransigence in the Campaign against Female Circumcision' *Case Western Reserve Law Review,* 47: 275–378

O'Connor, James 1988 'Capitalism, Nature and Socialism: A Theoretical Introduction' *Capitalism, Nature, Socialism* 1(1): 3–14

   1991a 'Socialism and Ecology' *Capitalism, Nature, Socialism,* 8: 1–12

   1991b 'The Second Contradiction of Capitalism: Causes and Consequences' *CES/CNS Pamphlet,* 1

Offe, Claus 1985 *Disorganized Capitalism* Oxford: Polity Press

   1987 'The Utopia of the Zero-Option: Modernity and Modernization as Normative Political Criteria' *Praxis International,* 7: 1–24

Oladipo, Olusegun 1989 'Towards a Philosophical Study of African Culture: A Critique of Traditionalism' *Quest,* 3(2): 31–50

Olaeghulom, F Ugboaja 1992 'Human Rights and the Refugee Situation in Africa,' in An-na'im (ed): 197–229

Oliveira, Luciano 1989 'Derechos humanos y Marxismo. Breve ensayo para un nuevo paradigma' *El Otro Derecho,* 4: 7–39

Ominami, C 1986 *Le tiers monde dans le crise* Paris: la Découverte

Ong, Walter 1977 *Interfaces of the Word: Studies in the Evolution of Consciousness and Culture* Ithaca: Cornell University Press

Onselen, Charles van 1976 *Africa Mine Labour in Southern Rhodesia 1900–1933* London: Pluto Press

Oommen, T K 1993 *Race, Ethnicity and Class: An Analysis in Interrelations* Delhi: Center for the Study of Social Systems, Jawaharlal Nehru University

Ortiz, Roxanne D 1987 'Indigenous Rights and Regional Autonomy in Revolutionary Nicaragua' *Latin American Perspectives,* 52: 43–66

Oruka, H Odera 1990 'Cultural Fundamentals in Philosophy' Quest, 4(2): 21–37

Osiel, Mark J 1995 'Dialogue with Dictators: Judicial Resistance in Argentina and Brazil' *Law and Social Inquiry*, 20: 481–560

Pacem in Maribus XX 1992 Ocean Governance: A Model for Global Governance in the 21st Century Malta: International Ocean Institute

Panikkar, Raimundo 1984 'Is the Notion of Human Rights a Western Concept?' *Cahier*, 81: 28–47

Pantham, Thomas 1988 'On Modernity, Rationality and Morality: Habermas and Gandhi' *The Indian Journal of Social Science*, 1(2): 187–208

Pardo, Arvid 1968 'Whose Is The Bed of the Sea?' *American Society, International Law Proceedings*, 62: 216–229

Parsons, Talcott 1971 *The System of Modern Societies* Englewood Cliffs, NJ: Prentice-Hall

Payoyo, Peter 1997 *Cries of the Sea: World Inequality, Sustainable Development and the Common Heritage of Humanity* Dordrecht: Martinus Nijhoff

Peet, Richard and N Thrift (eds) 1989 *New Models in Geography: the Political-Economy Perspective* London: Unwin-Hyman

Peixoto, João 2001 'Migration and Policies in the European Union: Highly Skilled Mobility, Free Movement of Labour and Recognition of Diplomas' *International Migration*, 39(1): 33–61

Pepper, David and Alan Jenkins (eds). 1985. *The Geography of Peace and War.* Oxford: Blackwell.

Perelman, Chaim 1951 'Reflexions sur la justice' *Revue de l'Institut de Sociologie*, 24: 255–281

　　1965 'Justice and Justification' *Natural Law Forum*, 10: 1–20

　　1969 *The New Rhetoric: a Treatise on Argumentation* Notre Dame: University of Notre Dame Press

Peters, Antoine 1986 'Law as Critical Discussion,' in Teubner (ed): 250–279

Petras, Elizabeth 1980 'The Role of National Boundaries in a Cross-National Labour Market' *International Journal of Urban and Regional Research*, 4: 157–195

Picciotto, Sol 1989 'Slicing a Shadow: Business Taxation in an International Framework,' in Hancher and Moran (eds): 11–47

Pierson, Christopher 1991 *Beyond the Welfare State: The New Political Economy of Welfare* University Park, PA: Pennsylvania State University Press

Pieterse, Jan N 1989 *Empire and Emancipation. Power and Liberation on a World Scale* London: Pluto Press

Piore, M J 1986 'The Shifting Grounds for Immigration' *Annals of the American Academy of Political and Social Science,* 485: 23–33

and Charles Sabel 1984 *The Second Industrial Divide* New York: Perseus Books

Pogge, Thomas 1992 'Cosmopolitanism and Sovereignty' *Ethics,* 103: 48–75

Poggi, Gianfranco 1978 *The Development of the Modern State: A Sociological Introduction* Stanford: Stanford University Press

Polanyi, Karl 1944 *The Great Transformation* Boston: Beacon Press

Pollis, Adamantia 1982 'Liberal, Socialist and Third World Perspectives of Human Rights,' in Schwab and Pollis (eds): 1–26

and P Schwab (eds). 1979. *Human Rights. Cultural and Ideological Perspectives.* New York: Praeger.

and P Schwab. 1979. 'Human Rights: A Western Construct with Limited Applicability,' in Pollis and Schwab (eds): 1-18.

Pomeranz, William. 1996. 'Judicial Review and the Russian Constitutional Court: The Chechen Case'. Review of Central and East European Law, vol 23, no 1 (1997), pp 9-48.

Popkin, Margaret and Roht-Arriaza, Naomi 1995 'Truth as Justice: Investigatory Commission in Latin America' *Law and Social Inquiry*, 20: 79–115

Portes, Alejandro 1979 'Illegal Immigration and the International System' *Social Problems*, 26: 425–438

and J Walton 1981 *Labor, Class and the International System* New York: Academic Press

and Jozsef Böröcz 1989 'Contemporary Immigration: Theoretical Perspectives on its Determinants and Modes of Incorporation' *International Migration Review*, 23: 606–629

and Min Zhou 1992 'Gaining the Upper Hand: Economic Mobility among Immigrant and Domestic Minorities' *Ethnic and Racial Studies,* 15: 491–522

Pospisil, L 1971 *Anthropology of Law: A Comparative Theory* New York: Harper and Row

Potter, Michael A 1989 'Human Rights in the Space Age: An International and Legal Political Analysis' *The Journal of Law and Technology*, 4: 59–76

Potter, Pitman 1993 'Popular Attitudes Toward Civil Obligations: Responses to Modernization Among the Getihu in Shanghai' Paper presented at the Workshop on Globalization and the Future of Law in China Madison: Global Studies Research Program, October 1–2

Pound, Roscoe 1937 *The Future of Common Law* Cambridge, Mass: Harvard University Press

1950 *New Paths of the Law* Lincoln: University of Nebraska Press

1959 *Jurisprudence* St Paul: West Pub Co

Poulantzas, Nicos 1978a *Political Power and Social Classes* London: Verso

1978b *State Power and Socialism* London: NLB

Posey, Darrell Addison (ed) 1999 *Cultural and Spiritual Values of Biodiversity* London: Intermediate Technology

Pratt, Mary Louise 1992 *Imperial Eyes: Travel Writing and Transculturation* New York: Routledge

Preuss, Ulrich 1988 'Entwicklungsperspektiven der Rechtswissenschaft,' in *Kritische Justiz,* 21: 361–376

Prillaman, William 2000 *The Judiciary and Democratic Decay in Latin America* Westport, Conn: Praeger

Procee, Herik 1992 'Beyond Universalism and Relativism' *Quest,* 6(1): 45–55

Prothero, R Mansell 1990 'Labor Recruiting Organizations in the Developing World' *International Migration Review,* 24: 221–228

Pureza, José Manuel 1993 'Globalização e Direito internacional: da boa vizinhança ao Património Comum da Humanidade' *Revista Crítica de Ciências Sociais,* 36: 9–26

   1998a *O Património Comum da Humanidade. Rumo a um Direito Internacional da Solidariedade?* Porto: Afrontamento

   1998b 'Eternalizing Westphalia? International Law in a Period of Turbulence' *Nação e Defesa,* 87: 31–48

Quam, L 1943 'The Use of Maps in Propaganda' *Journal of Geography,* 42: 21–32

Randeria, Shalini 2002 'Pluralismo jurídico, soberania fracturada e direitos de cidadania diferenciais: instituições internacionais, movimentos sociais e o Estado pós-colonial na Índia,' in Santos (ed) (2002c) (forthcoming)

Racine, J B *et al* 1982 'Escala e Acção Contribuições para uma interpretação do mecanismo de escala na prática da geografia' *Revista Brasileira de Geografia,* 45

Ramose, Mogobe B 1992 'African Democratic Traditions: Oneness, Consensus and Openness' *Quest,* VI: 63–83

Rao, Brinda 1991 'Dominant Constructions of Women and Nature in Social Science Literature' *CES/CNS Pamphlet,* 2

Reich, Norbert 1992 'Competition Between Legal Orders: A New Paradigm of EC Law?' *Common Market Review,* 29: 861–896

Reitan, EA 1986 'Popular Cartography and British Imperialism: the Gentleman's Magazine, 1739–1763' *Journal of Newspaper and Periodical History* II: 3, 2–3

Renner, K 1976 *The Institutions of Private Law and their Social Functions* London: Routledge and Kegan Paul

Renou, L 1968 *Religions of Ancient India* New York: Schocken Books

Renteln, Alison D 1990 *International Human Rights. Universalism Versus Relativism* Newbury Park: Sage

Riess, Joachim 1991 'Das europäische Tele-Kommunications Recht: Recht zwischen Markt and Technik' *Computer und Recht,* 9: 559–561

Rivière, J-L 1980 'Cartes polémiques,' in *Cartes et Figures de la Terre:* 351

Robertson, Roland 1990 'Mapping the Global Condition: Globalization as the Central Concept,' in Featherstone (ed): 15–30

Robinson, A, and B Petchnik 1976 *The Nature of Maps: Essays toward Understanding Maps and Mapping* Chicago: University of Chicago Press

Rodríguez, César A 2001a 'Globalization, Judicial Reform and the Rule of Law in Latin America: The Return of Law and Development' *Beyond Law*, 7(23): 13–42

   2001b 'La Justicia Civil,' in Santos and García-Villegas Volume I: 547–614

   2001c 'La Justicia Laboral,' in Santos and García-Villegas Volume I: 615–682

   2002 'À procura de alternativas econômicas em tempos de globalização: o caso das cooperativas de recicladores de lixo na Colômbia,' in Santos (ed) (2002b): 329–367

   Forthcoming 'Globalization, Labor Law and Legal Pluralism: The Implementation of Codes of Conduct in the Global Factories of Mexico and Guatemala', *Beyond Law,* 26

Rogers, R 1992 'The Politics of Migration in the Contemporary World' *International Migration* Special issue, 30: 33–52

Rojas, Fernando 1986 'A Comparison of Change-Oriented Legal Services in Latin America with Legal Services in North America and Europe' *Institute for Legal Studies Working Papers* Series 1: 9

Romein, Jan 1978 *The Watershed of Two Eras: Europe in 1900* Middletown, CT: Wesleyan University Press

Rosanvallon, Pierre 1981 *La crise de l'état providence* Paris: Seuil

Rosenberg, Gerald 1991 *The Hollow Hope: Can Courts Bring about Social Change?* Chicago: University of Chicago Press

Ross, Andrew (ed) 1997 *No Sweat Fashion, Free Trade and the Rights of Garment Workers* New York: Verso

Rousseau, Jean-Jacques 1973 *The Social Contract and Discourses* London: JM Dent and Sons

Rowat, Malcom, Walled Malik and Maria Dakolias (eds) 1995 *Judicial Reform in Latin America and the Caribbean* Washington: The World Bank

    1995 'Judicial Reform in Latin America and the Caribbean: Operational Implications for the Bank,' in Rowat, Malik and Dakolias (eds): 16–18

Rubin, Barnett 1990 'Human Rights in Mass-Based Ethnic Conflict: South Asian Examples of Dilemmas of Definition, Monitoring and Protection,' in Welch, Jr and Leary (eds): 186–205

Rusche, G and O Kirchheimer 1968 *Punishment and Social Structure* New York: Russell and Russell

Sachs, Jeffrey 1998 *Globalization and the Rule of Law* New Haven: Yale Law School

Said, Edward 1985 *Orientalism* London: Penguin

    1993 'Nationalism, Human Rights and Interpretation' *Raritan,* 12(3): 26–51

Sajo, Andras 1990 'New Legalism in East Central Europe: Law as an Instrument of Social Transformation' *Journal of Law and Society,* 17: 329–344

Salt, John 1987 'Contemporary Trends in International Migration Study' *International Migration,* 25: 241–250

    1989 'A Comparative Overview of International Trends and Types, 1950–80' *International Migration Review,* 23: 431–456

Samuels, W 1979 'The State Law and Economic Organization,' in Spitzer (ed): 65–99

Sánchez, Beatriz E 2001 'El reto del multiculturalismo jurídico. La justicia de la sociedad mayor y la justicia indígena,' in Santos and García-Villegas Volume II: 5–142

Santos, Boaventura de Sousa 1971 'Law Against Law' Yale University, Program in Law and Modernization, *Working Papers,* 4

    1974 *Law Against Law: Legal Reasoning in Pasargada Law* Cuernavaca: Centro Intercultural de Documentacion

    1977 'The Law of the Oppressed: The Construction and Reproduction of Legality in Pasargada' *Law and Society Review,* 12: 5–125

    1979 'Popular Justice, Dual Power and Socialist Strategy,' in Fine *et al* (eds): 151–163

    1980a 'Law and Community: The Changing Nature of State Power in Late Capitalism' *International Journal of the Sociology of Law,* 8: 379–397

    1980b O *discurso e o poder. Ensaio sobre a sociologia da retórica jurídica* Coimbra: Boletim da Faculdade de Direito

1982a 'Law and Revolution in Portugal: The Experiences of Popular Justice after the 25th of April, 1974,' in Abel (ed), Vol 2, 251–280

1982b 'O Estado, o Direito e a questão urbana' *Revista Crítica de Ciências Sociais*, 9: 9–86

1983 'Os conflitos urbanos no Recife: O caso do Skylab' *Revista Crítica de Ciências Sociais*, 11: 9–59

1984 *A justiça popular em Cabo Verde* Coimbra: Centro de Estudos Sociais, Faculdade de Economia

1985a 'Estado e sociedade na semiperiferia do sistema mundial: o caso português' *Análise Social*, 87/88/89: 869–901

1985b 'A crise do estado e a aliança povo/MFA em 1974–75,' in *25 de Abril-10 Anos Depois* Lisbon: Associação 25 de Abril

1987 *Um discurso sobre as ciências* Porto: Afrontamento

1990a 'Review of Ball, 1985 and White, 1985' *History of the Human Sciences*, 3(3): 467–474

1990b *Introdução a uma ciência pós-moderna* 2nd edition Porto: Afrontamento

1990c *O estado e a sociedade em Portugal* (1974–1988) Porto: Afrontamento

(ed) 1993 *Portugal: um retrato singular* Porto: Afrontamento

1993 'O Estado, as relações salariais e o bem-estar social na semiperiferia: o caso português,' in Santos (ed): 15–56

1995 *Toward a New Common Sense Law, Science and Politics in the Paradigmatic Transition* New York: Routledge

1998a 'Oppositional Postmodernism and Globalizations' *Law and Social Inquiry*, 23: 121–39

1998b *Reinventar a democracia* Lisbon: Gradiva

1998c. 'The Fall of the *Angelus Novus*: Beyond the Modern Game of Roots and Options' *Current Sociology*, 46: 81-118.

2001a *A Critique of the Lazy Reason: against the Waste of Experience* Paper presented at The Modern World-System in the Longue Durée – Conference to Celebrate the 25th Anniversary of the Fernand Braudel Center Binghamton University, Nov 2–3

2001b. '*Nuestra América*: Reinventing a Subaltern Paradigm of Recognition and Redistribution' *Theory, Culture and Society*, 18: 185-217.

2001c. 'Toward an Epistemology of Blindness: Why the New Forms of 'Ceremonial Inadequacy' Neither Regulate nor Emancipate' *European Journal of Social Theory*, 4: 251-294.

(ed) 2002a *Democratizar a democracia Os caminhos da democracia participativa* Rio de Janeiro: Record

(ed) 2002b *Produzir para viver Os caminhos da produção não capitalista* Rio de Janeiro: Record

(ed) 2002c (forthcoming) *Reconhecer para libertar Os caminhos do cosmopolitismo multicultural* Rio de Janeiro: Record

(ed) 2002d (forthcoming) *Semear outras soluções Os caminhos da biodiversidade e dos conhecimentos rivais* Rio de Janeiro: Record

(ed) 2002e (forthcoming) *Trabalhar o mundo Os caminhos do novo internacionalismo operário* Rio de Janeiro: Record

2002 'Orçamento participativo em Porto Alegre: para uma democracia redistributiva,' in Santos (ed) (2002a): 455–597

and Maria Manuel L Marques, João Pedroso and Pedro Ferreira 1996 *Os tribunais nas sociedades contemporâneas: o caso português* Porto: Afrontamento

and Mauricio García-Villegas 2001 *El Caleidoscopio de las Justicias en Colombia* 2 volumes Bogotá: Colciencias-Uniandes-CES-Universidad Nacional-Siglo del Hombre

and Joao Carlos Trindade (2002) *Conflito e Transformação Social:Uma Paisagem das Justiças em Moçambique* 2 volumes Porto: Afrontamento

and César Rodríguez (2002) 'Introdução: para ampliar o cânone da produção,' in Santos (ed) (2002b): 23–77

Santos, Laymert Garcia dos 2002 'Predação high tech, biodiversidade e erosão cultural: o caso do Brasil,' in Santos (ed) (2002d) (forthcoming)

Sarat, Austin, Marianne Constable, David Engel, Valerie Hans and Susan Lawrence (eds) 1998 *Crossing Boundaries: Traditions and Transformations in Law and Society Research* Evanston: Northwestern University Press

Sartre, Jean Paul 1976 *Critique of Dialectical Reason* London: NLB

Satz, Debra 1999 'Equality of What among Whom? Thoughts on Cosmopolitanism, Statism, and Nationalism,' in Shapiro and Brilmayer (eds) pp 67–85

Sassen, Saskia 1991 *The Global City: New York, London, Tokyo* Princeton: Princeton University Press

1998 *Globalization and its Discontents: Essays on the New Mobility of People and Money* New York: The New Press

1999 *Guests and Aliens* New York: The New Press

Sbragia, Alberta M (ed) 1991 *Euro-Politics: Institution and Policymaking in the 'New' European Community* Washington, DC: Brookings Institution

Schiller, Friedrich 1967 *On the Aesthetic Education of Man* Edited and translated by E Wilkinson and L A Willoughby Oxford: Clarendon Press

Schlag, Pierre 1990 'Normative and Nowhere to Go' *Stanford Law Review*, 43: 167–191

  2002 'The Aesthetics of American Law' *Harvard Law Review*, 115: 1049–1118

Schmidhauser, John 1992 'Legal Imperialism: Its Enduring Impact on Colonial and Post-Colonial Judicial Systems' *International Political Science Review*, 13: 321–334

Schulte, B 1991 'Die Folgen der EC-Integration für die wohlfahrtsstaatlichen Regimes' *Zeitschrift für Sozialreform*, 37: 548–580

Schwab, Peter and A Pollis (eds) 1982 *Toward a Human Rights Framework* New York: Praeger

Selby, M 1989 'Human Rights and Undocumented Immigrant Workers in Japan' *Stanford Journal of International Law*, 26(1): 325–369

Selznick, P 1969 *Law, Society and Industrial Justice* New York: Russell Sage Foundation

Shalleh, Ariel. 1997. *Ecofeminism as Politics: Nature, Marx and the Postmodern.* London: Zed Books.

Shapiro, Martin 1993 'The Globalization of Law' *Global Legal Studies Journal*, 1(9): 37–64

Shapiro, Ian and Lea Brilmayer (eds) 1999 *Global Justice* New York: NYU Press

Sharabi, Hisham 1992 'Modernity and Islamic Revival: The Critical Tasks of Arab Intellectuals' *Contention*, 2(1): 127–147

Shariati, Ah 1982 'Reflection of a Concerned Muslim: On the Plight of Oppressed Peoples,' in Falk, Kirn and Mendlovitz (eds): 18–24

  1986 *What Is to Be Done: The Enlightened Thinkers and an Islamic Renaissance* Edited by Farhang Rajaee Houston: The Institute for Research and Islamic Studies

Sharkey, M 1984 'Cartography in Advertising' *The Cartographical Journal*, 22: 148–50

Shaw, T M 1990 'Popular Participation in Nongovernmental Structures in Africa: Implications for Democratic Development' *Africa Today*, 37(3): 5–22

Shepherd, Jr, George 1985 'The Power System and Basic Human Rights: From Tribute to Self-Reliance,' in Shepherd, Jr and Nanda (eds): 13–25

  and Ved Nanda (eds) 1985 *Human Rights and Third World Development* Westport, CT: Greenwood Press

Sheth, D L 1989 'Nation-Building in Multi-Ethnic Societies: The Experience of South Asia' *Alternatives*, 14: 379–388

Sheth, DL and G Mahajan (eds). 1999. *Minorities, Identities and the Nation State.* New Delhi: Oxford University Press.

Shihata, Ibrahim FJ 1995 'Legal Framework for Development: The World Bank's Role in Legal and Judicial Reform,' in Rowat, Malik and Dakolias (eds): 13–15

Shiva, Vandana 1997 *Biopiracy* Boston: South End Press

Shivji, Issa 1989 *The Concept of Human Rights in Africa* London: Codesria Book Series

Shutkin, William A 1991 'International Human Rights Law and the Earth: The Protection of Indigenous Peoples and the Environment' *Virginia Journal of International Law*, 31: 448–511

Sieder, Rachel (ed). 2002. *Multiculturalism in Latin America: Indigenous Rights, Diversity and Democracy.* London: Palgrave.

Sikkink, Kathryn 1992 'The International Dimensions of Human Rights Policies and Practices in Latin America' Paper presented at the SSRC workshop on Human Rights, Justice and Society in Latin America Buenos Aires, 22–24 September

1996 'The Emergence, Evolution, and Effectiveness of the Latin American Human Rights Network,' in Jelin and Hershberg (eds): 59–84

Simmel, Georg 1955 *Conflict* Glencoe, IL: The Free Press

Singer, Paul 2002 'A recente ressurreição da economia solidária no Brasil,' in Santos (ed) (2002b): 81–129

Singh, Ajit. 1993. 'The Lost Decade: The Economic Crisis of the Third World in the 1980s: How the North Caused the South's Crisis.' *Contention,* 3: 137-169.

Siu-Kai, Lau and Kuan Hsin-Chi 1988 *The Ethos of the Hong Kong Chinese* Hong Kong: The Chinese University of Hong Kong

Skinner, Quentin 1989 'The State,' in Ball, Farr and Hanson (eds): 90–131

Sklair, Leslie 1991 *Sociology of the Global System* London: Harvester Wheatsheaf

2001. *The Transnational Capitalist Class.* Oxford: Blackwell.

Skocpol, Theda 1977 'Wallerstein's World Capitalist System: A Theoretical and Historical Critique' *American Journal of Sociology,* 82: 1075–1090

1979 *States and Social Revolution* Cambridge: Cambridge University Press

1985 'Bringing the State Back in: Strategies of Analysis in Current Research,' in Evans, Rueschemeyer and Skocpol (eds): 3–37

Slater, David 1991 'New Social Movements and Old Political Questions: Rethinking State-Society Relations in Latin American Development' *International Journal of Political Economy,* 21: 32–65

Smart, Carol and Barry Smart (eds). 1978. *Women, Sexuality and Social Control.* London: Routledge and Kegan Paul.

Smith, Adam 1937 *An Inquiry into the Nature and Causes of the Wealth of Nations* New York: Modern Library

Smith, Anthony 1981 *The Ethnic Revival in the Modern World* Cambridge: Cambridge University Press

1988 *The Ethnic Origins of Nations* Oxford: Blackwell

1990 'Towards a Global Culture?' in Featherstone (ed), 171-191

Smith-Rosenberg, C 1985 *Disorderly Conduct: Visions of Gender in Victorian America* New York: Alfred Knopf

Snyder, Francis 1980 'Law and Development in the Light of Dependency Theory' *Law and Society Review*, 14: 723–804

1982 'The Failure of 'Law and Development'' *Wisconsin Law Review,* 3: 373–396

1990 *New Directions in European Community Law* London: Weidenfeld and Nicolson

(ed). 1996. *Constitutional Dimensions of European Economic Integration.* Cambridge: Kluwer.

Sohn, Louis and Thomas Buergenthal (eds) 1992 *The Movement of Persons Across Borders* Washington, DC: The American Society of International Law

Soto Hernando de 1989 *The Other Path. The Invisible Revolution in the Third World* New York: Harper and Row Publishers

Speier, H 1941 'Magic Geography' *Social Research,* 8: 310–330

Spitzer, S (ed). 1979. *Research in Law and Sociology: A Research Annual.* 2 volumes. Greenwich, CT: Jai Press.

Spradley, JP (ed). 1972. *Culture and Cognition: Rules, Maps and Plans.* San Francisco: Chandler.

Stallings, Barbara 1992a 'International Influence on Economic Policy: Debt, Stabilization and Structural Reform,' in Haggard and Kaufman (eds): 41–88

1992b, Sustainable Development with Equity in the 1990s Policies and Alternatives, Madison: Global Studies Research Program

Starr, June and Jane Collier (eds) 1989 *History and Power in the Study of Law* Ithaca: Cornell University Press

Stavenhagen, Rodolfo 1988 *Derecho indígena y derechos humanos en America Latina* Mexico City: El Colégio de Mexico

1990 *The Ethnic Question* Tokyo: United Nations University Press

and Diego Iturralde (eds) 1990 *Entre la ley y la costumbre* Mexico City: Instituto Indigenista Interamericano

2002. 'Indigenous Peoples and the State in Latin America' in Sieder (ed): 20-37.

Stefanic, Jean 1998 'Latino and Latina Critical Theory: An Annotated Bibliography' *La Raza Law Journal*, 10: 1509–1584

Stein, L von 1888 *Handbuch der Verwaltungslehre* Stuttgart: JC Cotta

Stephen, Lynn 1997 'Redefined Nationalism in Building a Movement for Indigenous Autonomy in Southern Mexico' *Journal of Latin American Anthropology*, 3(1): 72–101

Stiglitz, Joseph. 2002. *Globalization and its Discontents*. New York: Norton.

Stiles, Kendall 2000 'Grassroots Empowerment: States, Non-State Actors and Global Policy Formation,' in Higgot, Underhill and Bieler (eds) *Non-State Actors and Authority in the Global System* New York: Routledge: 32–48

Stoecker, Christoph 1990 'The *Lex Mercatoria:* To What Extent Does It Really Exist?' *Journal of International Arbitration, 7:* 101–125

Stotzky, Irwin P (ed) 1993 *Transition to Democracy in Latin America: The Role of the Judiciary Boulder*: Westview Press

and Carlos S Nino 1993 'The Difficulties of the Transition Process,' in Stotzky (ed): 3–20

Streeck, Wolfgang and Philippe Schmitter 1991 'From National Corporatism to Transnational Pluralism: Organized Interests in the Single European Market' *Politics and Society,* 19: 133–164

Sugarman, David (ed). 1983. *Legality, Ideology and the State*. London: Academic Press.

Sugarman, David and Gunther Teubner (eds) 1990 *Regulating Corporate Groups in Europe* Baden-Baden: Nomos Verldganstalt

Svensson, Tom 1992 'Right to Self-Determination: A Basic Human Right Concerning Cultural Survival. The Case of the Sami and the Scandinavian State,' in An-na'im (ed): 363–384

Swart, AHJ 1992 'Police and Security in the Schengen Agreement and Schengen Convention,' in Meijers *et al:* 96–109

Swart, K 1949 *Sale of Offices in the Seventeenth Century* The Hague: Nijhoff

Swingewood, Alan. 1975. *The Novel and Revolution*. London: MacMillan.

Tamanaha, Brian 1993 'The Folly of the 'Social Scientific' Concept of Legal Pluralism' *Journal of Law and Society*, 20: 192–217

2001. *A General Jurisprudence of Law and Society.* Oxford: Oxford University Press.

Tambiah, Stanley 1989 'Ethnic Conflict in the World Today' *American Ethnologist*, 16: 335–349

Tate, Neal and Torbjörn Vallinder (eds). 1995. *The Global Expansion of Judicial Power.* New York: New York University Press.

Taylor, A 1972 *Laissez Faire and State Intervention in Nineteenth Century Britain* London: MacMillan

Taylor, Prue 1998 *An Ecological Approach to International Law: Responding to Challenges of Climate Change.* London: Routledge.

Teague, Paul 1989 'Constitution or Regime? The Social Dimension to the 1992 Project' *British Journal of Industrial Relations*, 27: 310–329

Teubner, Gunther (ed) 1986 *Dilemmas of Law in the Welfare State* Berlin: de Gruyter

1986 'After Legal Instrumentalism? Strategic Models of Post-Regulatory Law,' in Teubner (ed): 299–325

(ed) 1987 *Juridification of Social Spheres: A Comparative Analysis in Areas of Labor, Corporate, Antitrust and Social Welfare Law* Berlin: de Gruyter

1987 'Juridification: Concepts, Aspects, Limits, Solutions,' in Teubner (ed): 3–48

(ed) 1988 *Autopoietic Law: A New Approach to Law and Society* Berlin: de Gruyter

1988 'Evolution of Autopoietic Law,' in Teubner (ed): 217–241

1989 'How the Law Thinks: toward a Constructivist Epistemology of Law' *Law and Society Review*, 23: 728–757

1991 'La théorie des systèmes autopoietiques' *M, Mensuel, Marxisme, Mouvement*, 44 (February): 36–40

1992 'The Two Faces of Janus: Rethinking Legal Pluralism' *Cardozo Law Review*, 13:1443–1462

1997 '"Global Bukowina": Legal Pluralism in the World Society,' in Teubner (ed): 3–27

(ed) 1997 *Global Law without a State* Aldershot: Darthmouth

Thakur, Ramesh and Hyam Gold 1983 'The Antarctic Treaty Regime: Exclusive Preserve or Common Heritage' *Foreign Affairs Reports XXXII*, 11–12: 169–186

Thapar, Romila 1966 'The Hindu and Buddhist Traditions' *International Social Science Journal*, 18(1): 31–40

The Crucible Group 1994 *People, Plants and Patents: the impact of property on trade, plant biodiversity, and rural society* Ottawa: IRDS

Therborn, Göran 1992 *Routes To/Through Modernity* Paper presented at the Theory, Culture and Society 10th Anniversary Conference Seven Springs Mountain Resort, Pa, August 16–19

Thomas, George, et al 1987 *Institutional Structure: Constituting State, Society and the Individual* Beverly Hills: Sage

Thomas, Cheryl A 1995 'The Attempt to Institute Judicial Review in the Former USSR,' in Tate and Vallinder (eds): 421–440

Thomas, Stephen 1985 'Chinese Economic Development and Human Rights in the Post-Mao Era,' in Shepherd, Jr and Nanda (eds): 149–163

Thompson, EP 1975 *Whigs and Hunters* New York: Pantheon

Thompson, Kenneth (ed) 1980 *The Moral Imperatives of Human Rights* Washington, DC: University Press of America

Tickner, J Ann 1991 'On the Fringes of the World Economy: A Feminist Perspective,' in Murphy and Tooze (eds): 191–206

Tie, Warwick 1999 *Legal Pluralism Toward a Multicultural Conception of Law* Dartmouth: Aldershot

Tigar, Michael and Madeleine Levy 1977 *Law and the Rise of Capitalism* New York: Monthly Review

Toulmin, Stephen 1990 *Cosmopolis The Hidden Agenda of Modernity* New York: Free Press

2001 *Return to Reason* Cambridge, MA: Harvard University Press

Townsend, Janet et al 1999. *Women and Power: Fighting Patriarchy and Poverty.* London: Zed Books.

Trakman, Leon 1983 *The Law Merchant: The Evolution of Commercial Law* Littleton, Co: Fred Rothman and Co

Trubek, David 1985 'Max Weber's Tragic Modernism and the Study of Law in Society' Madison: Institute for Legal Studies

and Marc Galanter 1974 'Scholars in Self-Estrangement: Some Reflections on the Crisis in Law and Development Studies in the United States' *Wisconsin Law Review:* 1062–1102

et al 1993 'Global Restructuring and the Law: the Internationahzation of Legal Fields and the Creation of Transnational Arenas' *Global Studies Research Program Working Papers Series,* 1

Tuck, Richard 1979 *Natural Rights Theories: Their Origin and Development* Cambridge: Cambridge University Press

Tushnet, Mark 1984. 'An Essay on Rights.' *Texas Law Review, 62:* 1363-1403.

1993. 'The Judiciary and Institutions of Judicial Review.' *American University Journal of International Law and Policy*, 8: 501-516.

Twining, William 2000 *Globalisation and Legal Theory* London: Butterworths

Unger, Roberto. 1987. *False Necessity*. Cambridge: Cambridge University Press.

1996 *What Should Legal Analysis Become?* London: Verso

1998 *Democracy Realized* London: Verso

Uprimny, Rodrigo 2001 'Las Transformaciones de la Administración de Justicia en Colombia,' in Santos and García-Villegas Volume I: 261–315

Uribe, Maria Teresa 2002 'Emancipação social em um contexto de guerra prolongada: o caso da Comunidade de Paz de San José de Apartadó, Colombia,' in Santos (ed) (2002a): 217–253

USAID 1994 *Weighing in on the Scales of Justice: Strategic Approaches for Donor-Supported Rule of Law Programs* Washington, DC: USAID Program and Operations Assessment Report no 7

1996 USAID's Strategies for Sustainable Development: Building Democracy Website release

van Cott, Donna Lee (ed). 1994. *Indigenous Peoples and Democracy in Latin America*. New York: St. Martin's Press and The Inter-American Dialogue.

2000. *The Friendly Liquidation of the Past: The Politics of Diversity in Latin America*. Pittsburgh: Pittsburgh University Press.

van den Bergh, GC 1984 'What Law for Whose Development? Some Theoretical Reflections on Law and Development' *Contributions in Honour of JG Sauveplanne:* 29–44

van der Velden, Frans 1984 'Uniform International Sales Law and the Battle of Forms,' in *Contributions in Honour of JG Sauveplanne:* 233–249

van Parijs, Philippe 1992 *Arguing for Basic Income: Ethical Foundations for a Radical Reform* London: Verso

van Velsen 1967 'The Extended-Case Method and Situational Analysis,' in Epstein (ed): 129–149

Varese, Stefano 1982 'Restoring Multiplicity: Indianities and the Civilizing Project in Latin America' *Latin American Perspectives,* 33: 29–41

Vico, Giambattista 1953 *Opere* Volume II: *Principi di scienza nuova* Milan: Riccardi

1961 *The New Science of Giambattista Vico* Edited by Bergin and Fisch Garden City, NY: Anchor Books

Viner, Jacob 1927 'Adam Smith and Laissez Faire' *The Journal of Political Economy,* XXXV: 198–232

Visvanathan, Shiv 1997 *A Carnival of Science: Essays on Science, Technology and Development* Oxford; Oxford University Press

Vogel, Lise 1983 *Marxism and the Oppression of Women: Toward a Unitary Theory* New Brunswick: Rutgers University Press

Von Mehren, Arthur and James Gordley 1977 *The Civil Law System: An Introduction to the Comparative Study of Law* 2nd edition Boston: Little Brown and Co

Vroey, Michel de 1984 'A Regulation Approach Interpretation of the Contemporary Crisis' *Capital and Class*, 23: 45–66

Wallerstein, Immanuel 1974 *The Modern World-System I: Capitalist Agriculture and the Origins of the European World-economy in the Sixteenth Century* New York: Academic Press

   1979 *The Capitalist World-Economy* Cambridge: Cambridge University Press

   1984 *The Politics of the World-Economy: the States, the Movements and the Civilizations* Cambridge: Cambridge University Press

   1991a *Unthinking Social Science* Cambridge: Polity Press

   1991b *Geopolitics and Geoculture* Cambridge: Cambridge University Press

Walton, John 1985 'The Third 'New' International Division of Labor,' in Walton (ed): 3–16

   (ed). 1985. *Capital and Labor in the Urbanized World.* London: Sage.

Walzer, Michael 1981 'The Distribution of Membership,' in Brown and Shue (eds): 1–35

Wamba dia Wamba, Ernest 1991a 'Some Remarks on Culture Development and Revolution in Africa' *Journal of Historical Sociology,* 4: 219–235

   1991b 'Beyond Elite Politics of Democracy in Africa' *Quest,* VI: 28–42

Warde, Alan 1997 *Consumption, food and taste: culinary antinomies and commodity culture* London: Sage

Warzazi, H 1986 *Exploitation of Labour through Illicit and Clandestine Trafficking* New York: United Nations

Weber, Max 1948 *From Max Weber. Essays in Sociology* London: Routledge and Kegan Paul

   1954 *Law in Economy and Society* Cambridge, MA: Harvard University Press

   1978 *Economy and Society* 2 volumes Berkeley: University of California Press

Weiler, Joseph 1981 'The Community System: the Dual Character of Supranationalism' *Yearbook of European Law,* 1: 267–306

1991a 'The Transformation of Europe' *Yale Law Journal,* 100: 2403–2483

1991b 'Problems of Legitimacy in Post-1992 Europe' *Aussenwirtschaft,* 46: 411–437

1992 'Thou Shalt Not Oppress Strangers: On the Judicial Protection of the Human Rights of Non-EC Nationals – A Critique' *European Journal of International Law,* 3: 65–91

Weinreb, Lloyd 1987 *Natural Law and Justice* Cambridge, MA: Harvard University Press

Welch, Jr, Claude. 1990. 'Global Change and Human Rights: Asian Perspectives in Comparative Context,' in Welch, Jr. and Leary (eds): 3-12.

and Ronald Meltzer (eds). 1984. *Human Rights and Development in Africa.* Albany: State University of New York Press.

and Virginia Leary (eds). 1990. *Asian Perspectives on Human Rights.* Boulder: Westview Press.

Westing, Arthur 1992 'Environmental Refugees: a Growing Category of Displaced Persons' *Environmental Conservation,* 19: 201–202

Westlund, Andrea. 1999. 'Pre-modern and Modern Power: Foucault and the Case of Domestic Violence' *Signs,* 24: 1045-1067.

White, Mary V 1982 'The Common Heritage of Mankind: an Assessment' *Case Western Reserve Journal of International Law,* 14: 509–542

Wieacker, Franz 1967 *Privatrechtsgeschichte der Neuzeit* Göttingen: Vandenhoeck and Ruprecht

Wiethölter, Rudolf 1986 'Materialization and Proceduralization in Modern Law,' in Teubner (ed): 221–249

Williams, Sylvia M 1981 'International Law Before and After the Moon Agreement' *International Relations,* 7: 1168–1193

Wilson, William J. 1987. *The Truly Disadvantaged. The Inner City, the Underclass, and Public Policy.* Chicago: University of Chicago Press.

Winckler, HA (ed) 1974 *Organizierter Kapitalismus: Voraussetzungen und Anfänge* Göttingen: Vandenhoeck and Ruprecht

Winn, Jane K 1993, Relational Practices and the Marginalization of Law: A Study of the Informal Financial Practices of Small Businesses in Taiwan, Paper presented at the Workshop on Globalization and the Future of Law in China Madison: Global Studies Research Program, October 1–2

Wöhleke, Manfred 1992 'Umweltflüchtlinge' *Aussen Politik,* 43: 287–296

Wong, Siu-lun 1985 'The Chinese Family Firm: A Model' *British Journal of Sociology,* 36: 58–72

Wood, Ellen Meiksins 1981 'The Separation of the Economic and the Political in Capitalism' *New Left Review,* 127: 66–95

　　1996. *Democracy Against Capitalism.* Cambridge: Cambridge University Press.

World Bank 1996 *The World Bank's Partnership with Non-Governmental Organizations* Washington: The World Bank

　　1997 *World Development Report 1997* New York: Oxford University Press

Wright, Erik O 1978 *Class, Crisis and the State* London: Verso

　　A Levine and E Sober 1992 *Reconstructing Marxism* London: Verso

Wright, Sanford 1985 'The Political Economy of South Africa: An Analysis of Selected Economic Factors on US Leverages,' in Shepherd, Jr and Nanda (eds): 231–245

Wuthnow, Robert 1985 'State Structures and Ideological Outcomes' *American Sociological Review,* 50: 799–821

　　1987 *The Meaning of Moral Order* Berkeley: University of California Press

Xaba, Thokozani 2002 'Prática médica marginalizada: a marginalização e transformação das medicinas indígenas na África do Sul,' in Santos (ed) (2002d) (forthcoming)

Young, Iris M 1990 *Justice and the Politics of Difference* Princeton: Princeton University Press

Zaffaroni, Eugenio R 1997, Globalización y Sistema Penal en America Latina: de la Seguridad Nacional a la Urbana, Paper presented at the Summer Course on Globalization and Legal Cultures Oñati: International Institute of Sociology of Law

Zavala, Iris, Tuen van Dijk and Myriam Diaz-Diocaretz (eds). 1987. *Approaches to Discourse, Poetics and Psychiatry.* Amsterdam: Benjamin's Publishing Company.

Zeidan, Shawky 1985 'A Human Rights Settlement: the West Bank and Gaza,' in Shepherd, Jr and Nanda (eds): 165–195

Zeitlin, Maurice 1988 *The Civil Wars in Chile* Princeton: Princeton University Press

Zifzak, Spencer 1996 'Hungary's Remarkable, Radical, Constitutional Court' *Journal of Constitutional Law in Eastern and Central Europe,* 3(1): 1–56

Zion, James 1992 'North American Indian Perspectives on Human Rights,' in An-na'im (ed): 191–220

Zolberg, Aristide 1981 'Origins of the Modern World System: A Missing Link' *World Politics,* 33: 253–281

1989 'The Next Waves: Migration Theory for a Changing World' *International Migration Review,* 23: 403–429

Zweigert, Konrad and Hein Kötz 1987 *Introduction to Comparative Law* 2 volumes 2nd edition Oxford: Clarendon Press

Index of Names

Index of Subjects